D0951947

THE LIFE AND TIMES OF
Mickey Rooney

THE LIFE AND TIMES OF

Mickey Rooney

WILLIAM BIRNES *and* RICHARD LERTZMAN

GALLERY BOOKS

NEW YORK LONDON TORONTO SYDNEY NEW DELHI

I was a fourteen-year-old boy for thirty years.
—Mickey Rooney

I don't want to hurt him, poor darling. He ain't got a fucking cent.
He's been raked over the coals for millions
by those goddamn wives he kept getting married to after me.
What is it they say? "The fucking you get for the fucking you got?"
—Ava Gardner

Contents

Foreword by Roger Kahn

Mickey Rooney was his own sort of enigma, reinventing himself as the situation demanded. I should know, because I was one of his first biographers. Now Bill Birnes and Rick Lertzman have taken on this task in the wake of Mickey's passing, in a thorough look at not only the life of Mickey Rooney, but at his times as well.

My introduction to Mickey was precipitated by a series of profiles I had written. One of them, a very popular article for *The Saturday Evening Post*, was based on a day with Robert Frost. My editors asked me, "What would you like to do next?" I said that I'd like to do one on Sean O'Casey, but they told me that they didn't believe too many people in Kansas City would care for an article on a left-wing Irish playwright. They asked, "How about Jackie Cooper?" So I went to Jackie Cooper, who said he would cooperate only if he were part of the byline; we gave it to him. The piece was called, "Unfortunately, I Was Rich." I didn't love it because his lawyer gutted anything that had to do with Jackie's issues with his biological father, which was sort of a key to his strange life, but other people liked it. It convinced the publisher that if I could work with Cooper, I could work with Mickey Rooney.

There was a pretty good pot of money involved—for the 1960s. It was seventy-five thousand dollars for Rooney and me to split. I thought this fellow had an interesting life; he started working when he was barely two years old. I guess his first couple of years he just lay around the house. I met Mickey in an office building at the corner of Hollywood and Vine, with his lawyer, Dermot Long. Mickey came bouncing into the office and announced that the book "will be about a loud little guy who doesn't want to be loud. It's a story of a guy who thinks well twice a month. If I had gone slower, if the drinks had been lighter, and if the girls had been gentler, this would have been a much nicer story."

I liked his idea, and it seemed like a pretty good opening. We went on a bit. The publisher said that if I thought I could do it, I needed to write a presentation for a forty-minute meeting. I did, and they approved it—but then Rooney disappeared. Our first meeting, we went to Santa Anita Park racetrack and he said, "I'll mark your card." I thought he knew a great deal about the horses, but as it turned out, he didn't. As soon as we got to the track, he'd asked, "Could you let me have six hundred dollars? I've got to settle with a guy in the next box." So I gave him six hundred dollars. And he said, "Dermot will give it back to you. Dermot handles the money." So I saw Dermot a couple of days later and asked for my six hundred dollars back. And he said, "I can't do that. I'm operating under the thumb of the IRS, and they had to approve every check I write. And they won't approve a check to pay off a debt at the racetrack." Dermot, who always tried to be decent, said he could get it from one of Mickey's performances in Vegas and write it off as an expense. So that was our beginning.

At the track, Mickey had an intricate system that didn't work very well. When he came to pick me up, he said he had a small car. I thought he meant it was a Corvette. He was actually driving a Corvair. A small car. From my place, he drove straight to a gas station to fill up. Immediately the attendant recognized him. He said, "Mickey Rooney, wow!" Mickey chuckled and he said, "A dollar's worth please." He turned to me and said, "It's all these little cars will hold," No. It was all he could afford. So we had a miscellaneous kind of a day.

WHEN WE STARTED THE interview, I asked, "Will a tape recorder bother you?" He said no. Actually, it was the whole project that bothered him. Once he had Dermot Long deposit the publisher's check, he disappeared. Every day, while he was physically in Encino, I would call Dermot who'd say, "He can't see you today; he has to visit his in-laws," or "He has to audition for a part," or "He can't see you today; he has a meeting at his church." After two or three weeks of this, I called my agent and said forget it. My agent said, "You can't. The publisher really wants the book. And if you back out now, you're looking at litigation, and you'll be in three-way litigation with the publisher and Rooney, and it will be a mess." And I figured out that it would be a mess, so I continued my efforts, got nowhere, stayed in Hollywood at the Chateau Marmont, and did some other pieces, like one on director Stanley Kramer, who was an interesting fellow, and it made for a good piece. I did one on Joan Baez, who was obnoxious, and it didn't make for a good piece. And then I said again we'd have to drop the Rooney book, but again I was warned of the litigation.

Then I got to see him for bits and pieces of time. But there was never any serious talk. If there had been, I could have wrapped it up in three or four weeks. Instead, I had little smidgens of things. I was writing this under the threat of litigation, and saying to myself, "How did I get into this?" and thinking I was going to have to fire my agent, and having all sorts of diffuse thoughts occupy my head. So I wrote a draft of the first chapter. *The Saturday Evening Post* liked it very much and offered twenty-five thousand dollars. At the time, Rooney was married to Barbara Thomason, his fifth wife. When I told Mickey about the fee, Barbara said, "I heard Cary Grant got a hundred and fifty thousand from *The Saturday Evening Post*." I didn't say, "Mickey isn't Cary Grant," but I tried to say, "Well, this is what the market is offering." Mickey got very angry then and said, "Fuck 'em. They can't have it."

It fell upon me to tell The *Saturday Evening Post* that he'd said no. They weren't happy and thought that the twenty-five grand was a good offer, as did I. I kept kind of slogging along, and the publisher kept waiting. After a bit, I finally pieced together something, which was at best mediocre, because I was getting no cooperation. So I turned it in and I thought, good, now I'm done. But the publisher wanted more.

So I went to a lawyer, a very good literary lawyer named Charles Rembar. He said, "From what you're telling me, you're going to have to sue these bastards." Rembar said that it didn't matter what you sued for; ultimately the judge decided what you'd get. Rembar said, "Do you want to sue for a million?" I said, "Sure." So we sued for a million, and it had the effect that Rembar wanted, which was to get the attention of Rooney's lawyer and Rooney. So then I went back to Rooney and got some more material, but I still didn't have enough. The publisher was still pressing. Rembar told Rooney's lawyer that I needed Rooney for two days, full time, with no distractions, no phones, no nothing. And if I had those two days, I could finish the research for the book. So I went out there, and Rooney asked, "Have you written anything?" and I said, "Yes." And he said, "Let me read it." So he started reading the draft aloud. I had used the word *façade*, and he read it as "fo-cade." It turned out that he couldn't really read very well. Everything was through the ear.

He would make cracks. I asked him what his honeymoon with Ava was like. He said, "I played golf. I was looking at the wrong hole." One-liners. Nothing substantial. I gathered that Ava had said that he was a pretty good lover. Mickey finally told me that he had been at the Hollywood Palladium with Ava when he went onstage and did a

Lionel Barrymore imitation, played the drums and the trumpet, but ignored Ava. She went back to their home, which was a modest house in Stone Canyon. Rooney came home several hours afterward and jumped on her, and she looked at him and said, "'If you ever knock me up, you little sonofabitch, I will kill you.' I said what did you say? So she got up and headed toward the bathroom. And my God, Ava was a beautiful nude and she went to the bathroom and locked it. I pounded on the door and went to my knees and said, 'Why Ava, Why?' and I learned. She did not like to be ignored."

With gems like these, I slogged along, and had my attorney call Rooney's again. And Rooney returned, but he spent his time reading drafts rather than giving me the information I needed. So at this point, my perspective was that nothing wonderful was going to come of it. I just wanted to finish it and get back to real writing. So I did a final draft and met the deadline of eighty thousand words, but it truly was not very deep and did not get to the core of the man. If there *was* a core of that man.

In between, I wrote magazine stories. One was the story of the heavyweight championship fight in Miami between Floyd Patterson and Ingemar Johansson. It was a very good fight. When I got back, I told Rooney about the fight. I said I knew how Johansson threw his right hand. Rooney said, "Show me," and I did a very slow-motion version of Ingemar throwing his left and bringing his right hand over it. So Rooney said, "Let's box." Well, he was a very little man with very short arms. I would say he was the worst boxer I've ever encountered. So we sparred. And, well, I wasn't going to hit him in the mouth. Then we sat down, and he said, "Let's spar again, but first let's have a martini." I replied, "It's ten thirty in the morning." He said, "I know, but martinis are great before lunch." That was how it went. Every time I said, "Let's go to work," he would find some excuse not to. He had to go somewhere, see someone. He was never willing or able to look at his life the way I wanted him to, and he never took the book seriously. So, finally, I got out of Los Angeles. I wrote the book the best I could with zero cooperation and moved on.

I resolved that I would never again collaborate. I almost kept true to that—until I was offered a ton of money to collaborate with Pete Rose. I was facing some unexpected family expenses, so I ended up taking the Rose deal. The first person I collaborated with, Mickey Rooney, went bankrupt. That was then. But now the documented story of Mickey Rooney is being told in full in this book by Bill Birnes and Rick Lertzman, probably the first book to tell the real truth about one of the greatest talents in film and one of the most complicated human beings I ever met.

Roger Kahn is the author of The Boys of Summer.

Introduction by Jeanine Basinger

Mickey Rooney had talent to burn, and he burned it. He lived a long and often messy life, going up and down the ladder of success as if it were a department store elevator. He did everything there was to do in show business: vaudeville, radio, nightclubs, theater, television, and of course movies, where he ranked at the top of the box office in 1939, 1940, and 1941. He could perform both comedy and drama equally well, and he did impressions of everyone from Franklin Delano Roosevelt to Carmen Miranda. He sang, he danced. He played the piano, the drums, and the banjo, and he composed music. He also wrote books, taught acting, spearheaded various business ventures, and served his country during World War II, earning the Bronze Star for performing in combat zones.

When he died at age ninety-three in April of 2014, Rooney had been working in some form of entertainment for nine decades. Along the way, he won an Emmy, two Golden Globes, and racked up countless nominations for others, including two Oscar bids for Best Actor and two more for Best Supporting Actor. He had also been awarded two honorary Oscars, the first in 1939, for "bringing to the screen the spirit and personification of youth," and another in 1983, "for his 60 years of versatility in a variety of memorable performances." The latter award seemed at the time to close the book on Rooney, acknowledging the man who had been performing for more than sixty years. Yet Rooney carried on for another three decades. He died with his boots on, leaving behind small roles in two unreleased movies: *Night at the Museum: Secret of the Tomb* (2014) and *Dr. Jekyll and Mr. Hyde* (2015).

Rooney's success is a unique American tale. He wasn't necessarily the type for box office stardom. Standing only a little more than five feet, two inches tall, with a boyish face, a shock of untamable hair, and a sort of "gosh, darn" demeanor, he might have been limited to a brief career or no career at all, but his prodigious talent transcended his limitations. He proved to be a performance Everyman who could play a wide variety of roles: a maniacal Puck in *A Midsummer Night's Dream* (1935); a heartbreaking Western Union messenger who delivers the World War II telegrams that announce the deaths of young soldiers in *The Human Comedy* (1943); the roustabout jockey who helps an adolescent Elizabeth Taylor ride to victory in *National Velvet* (1944); the down-on-his luck drummer in the underrated *The Strip* (1951); a doomed GI in *The Bold and the Brave* (1956); the psychopathic killer in *Baby Face Nelson* (1957), which won him the French César Award; a sympathetic boxing trainer in *Requiem for a Heavyweight* (1962); the elderly and sensitive horseman of *Black Stallion* (1979); and the mentally handicapped man in the TV movie *Bill* (1981). Even the horror of his now-politically incorrect Mr. Yonioshi in *Breakfast at Tiffany's* (1961) is somehow fascinating. Yet even without any of these standout roles, Mickey Rooney would be an important part of film history.

If he had made only musicals with Judy Garland or just his sixteen-movie series as Andy Hardy, he'd still be famous. Rooney and Garland were young and hopeful together, and the wow factor of the energetic talent they unleash in such movies as *Babes in Arms* (1939) and *Girl Crazy* (1943), among others, is unparalleled. Rooney said, "Judy and I were so close we could've come from the same womb," and this instinctive sympathy, rhythmic harmony, and mutual survival skills infuse all the numbers they perform. They sing it sweet and they sing it hot, but they are always amazing. And as to his embodiment of Andy Hardy, Rooney is immortal.

Despite the fact that he was chasing girls, gambling, drinking, and carousing off-screen while he made films, on-screen Rooney perfectly captures the spirit of an American teenager of the late 1930s and early 1940s. Andy Hardy is often called a fantasy figure, the imaginary kid MGM envisioned to goose up its box office receipts. The character is far more honest and believable than that, or else the low-budget series built around him would never have lasted. There may be hokeyness in the Hardy family stories, but there's also something audiences recognized as true, and that truth was in Mickey Rooney's performance.

With so many well-remembered film roles across so many decades, it makes one wonder why Mickey Rooney wasn't more respected in his elder years. For Rooney, there was no Kennedy Center Honors award, no American Film Institute Life Achievement Award, and certainly no luxurious retirement to a villa in Switzerland. (He left only eighteen thousand dollars in his estate.) The older Rooney was always just a little bit over the top, lacking what Hollywood thought was class. He went bankrupt, became addicted to sleeping pills, and ran up gambling debts. He incited lawsuits, quarreled with his family, and often gave crazy interviews that went way beyond what could be labeled as merely eccentric. Most spectacularly of all, he married a legendary (and tacky) eight times. ("Always get married in the morning," he was quoted as saying. "That way if it doesn't work out, you haven't wasted the whole day.") These very public peccadillos no doubt kept him off the A-list of Hollywood legends—except, of course, where it counted: in the history books and in the hearts and memories of his fans.

A book that tells Mickey Rooney's full story and puts his life and work in proper perspective has been long overdue, and Bill Birnes and Rick Lertzman have done the job. They don't ignore the embarrassing parts of Rooney or his tragedies and failures, but they emphasize the Mickey Rooney that counts: the one who was first, last, and always a performer who never let his audience down. Birnes and Lertzman understand Rooney, presenting him as a colorful American guy who had it all, lost it all, and regained it all, but no matter what, never gave up. It's the story of a true professional, and a great read by anyone's standards.

Jeanine Basinger is the Corwin-Fuller Professor of Film Studies, Wesleyan University, and trustee emerita at the American Film Institute.

The Last Movie

The Victorian home on Valerio Street in Van Nuys, California, sits heavy with memories that hang over the present, resonating across a near-century of motion picture history. You can see the home from a distance, standing in contrast to the stucco plaster Spanish-style homes, with big picture windows in front, that line the streets of this San Fernando Valley community. An artifact from a gilded age, today it is a movie set again. On the first floor, as the audio mixer snakes his cable to a mike boom and fiddles with the dials on his Cantar sound recorder, Margaret O'Brien adjusts herself nervously into the cushion of an upholstered love seat in the sitting room. You remember Margaret O'Brien, don't you, the MGM child star famous as "Tootie" Smith, smiling through tears as Judy Garland sings "Have Yourself a Merry Little Christmas" to her in Vincente Minnelli's 1944 classic, *Meet Me in St. Louis*?

Margaret O'Brien is in wardrobe, wearing a high-collar dress from the 1890s. She fidgets slightly as the set electrician adjusts one of the lights above her just before the Canon's digital camera lens in front of her chair comes into focus. Sitting right next to her, wearing a pull-over sweater and sweat pants, is her old friend from when they were stars together. His is an all-too-familiar face, albeit through sagging cheeks, heavy jowls, a balding head now ringed with snow-white hair, a face marked with lines of age, but smiling a puckish smile of youth, and his eyes still dancing with a delight belying his ninety-three years. It is Mickey Rooney. It is Andy Hardy.

From behind the camera the actors hear director Brian Barsuglia bark, "Roll sound."

"Rolling."

"Camera speed."

"Speeding."

"Slate it." A production assistant snaps the slate closed.

"Scene twenty-two, take one."

"Action!"

The scene begins.

O'Brien turns her head away from the two men, also in Victorian wardrobe, standing over her chair. One of the actors is Zan Alda, Alan Alda's nephew. The other is David Beatty. Then she looks at Mickey Rooney beside her on the chair. He is playing Mr. Louis to O'Brien's Mrs. Stevenson. Off camera, a script assistant feeds Mickey his line.

"It's okay, dear, tell them," Mickey's character says. "Tell them what you saw. What you told me." Mickey's Mr. Louis is the proprietor of a Victorian house of ill repute, an opium den, a place where gentlemen of means, no matter how acquired, can purchase the evening's delights they seek, no questions asked. Characters Mr. Louis and Mrs. Stevenson are talking about the mysterious Edward Hyde, the alter ego of Dr. Jekyll, who committed a murder the night before in that very house, in that very same room, bludgeoning an unfortunate man to death with his cane.

"It was horrible, Mr. Louis," Margaret O'Brien's character complains. "Awful. How many times must I relive this ordeal?"

Mrs. Stevenson witnessed the murder, and retelling the story of the bloody violence she saw is traumatic for her. She is reluctant to speak. But Mickey Rooney's character, her employer, cajoles, urges, and then commands her to relate the details of the crime. Mickey dominates the scene, improvising the lines he's fed because he wants his character to finish with a flourish. He argues with David Beatty's character, the detective interrogating him and pushing him to incriminate the villain, no doubt a return paying customer.

Beatty glares at Mickey and once again demands, "Did you see Mr. Hyde? What does he look like?"

"I don't know," Mickey's character says, now veering off script. "But I must go. Time [beat] is fleeting."

This is a small scene, perhaps no longer than seven minutes of camera time, but critical because it identifies the killer in this remake of Robert Louis Stevenson's *Dr. Jekyll and Mr. Hyde*. Mickey Rooney and Margaret O'Brien, bringing to the film a wisp of glory from the golden age of studio-produced motion pictures, underplay their roles just enough to show the rest of the cast what veterans can do when the camera comes on.

"Mickey was the only one at the studio that was ever allowed to call me Maggie," O'Brien said after the filming of the movie. "He was undoubtedly the most talented actor that ever lived. There was nothing he couldn't do. Singing, dancing, performing—all with great expertise. Mickey made it look so easy. He seemed fine through the filming and was as great as ever," she said, adding, "Mickey was in my first film [*Babes on Broadway*, 1941], and I was in Mickey's last film, *Dr. Jekyll and Mr. Hyde*." Her comments echoed what Spencer Tracy, who costarred with Rooney, once said about him: "Mickey Rooney was the most talented man in the history of movies . . . He was whatever he was portraying."

Tracy's comments echo those of Sir Laurence Olivier, who, when asked to name his favorite, said, "Mickey Rooney is the greatest actor America every produced."

In an interview later in his life, Mickey explained why he was able to portray the roles he played so effortlessly. He revealed his secret when he told his interviewer that he "never acted," but always played himself. He was the character, not the actor.

Dr. Jekyll and Mr. Hyde director Brian Barsuglia said that he first met Mickey on Valentine's Day 2014, at a dinner with Mickey's stepson Mark Aber Rooney and Mark's wife, Charlene. Margaret O'Brien was at that dinner. "During and after dinner Mickey was surrounded by fans. He was very gracious, posed for pictures and signed autographs. He was constantly bothered during dinner, but was very nice about it," Barsuglia said, although with his stepchildren he was far more contentious. Three weeks later, on March 8, Barsuglia filmed Mickey's scene with O'Brien on a set where Mickey was surrounded by both cast and crew asking for advice. "Asked to explain his long career and the secret of it, Mickey said, 'Work hard, persevere, do your work, and get a good attorney,'" Brian told us. Mickey revealed to the crew, "Everyone stole from me," remembering his dealings with managers, agents, studio heads, and their lawyers. The director remembered that Mickey was especially cordial. He stayed on set after his scene, to watch Margaret O'Brien film her scenes, and then stuck around for lunch to talk with everyone. For Mickey, this was not just a film shoot; it was an occasion to step back into a role he had played since the 1930s: being an actor on a film set.

"Mickey was a hundred percent lucid," said actor David Beatty, who played opposite Rooney and O'Brien in the scene. Rooney had difficulty physically, moving slowly and with great effort. But when the scene required him to stand, he stood, albeit shakily. There were set hands nearby to catch him if he fell or complained of dizziness, and a script assistant was there to feed him lines when he needed it. What dialogue he didn't like he made up, but it fit the scene. Beatty described him as completely aware and totally in the moment for the scene, a consummate professional. "Mickey had an instinctual feel of how lines should sound as they were read," he remembered, and

Rooney even talked to the film director about changing dialogue he thought could be improved.

After the crew wrapped for the day, Beatty said he pulled Mickey aside for ideas on improving his own craft, asking him, "What is your advice on being an actor?" Mickey replied, "Son, my best advice I can give you is that you better have a damn good lawyer."

"Mickey was not only in the moment; he had a charisma about him and an awareness of his character," Beatty said. When he started the scene with Rooney and O'Brien, Mickey said to him, "Welcome to history." He was that much aware not only of his moment in the scene and in the picture, but of the importance of his coming together with another great child star for a performance that would ultimately outshine the rest of the picture.

Mickey's performances on camera in *Dr. Jekyll and Mr. Hyde* and in *Night at the Museum: Secret of the Tomb* (2014), opposite Dick Van Dyke and Ben Stiller, are in sharp contrast to the Mickey Rooney who, his daughter Kerry Rooney Mack told us, suffered from bipolar disorder and was on the mood-stabilizing psychotropic lithium for many years, bouncing from hypergrandiosity to deep bouts of bitter depression.

In his later years, Mickey, because of his own situation, became an advocate for people experiencing elder abuse at the hands of their caregivers. His pleadings in court regarding this issue suggested that he had led (ironically enough, just like Dr. Jekyll) a double life. He was the consummate on-screen and on-stage performer, seeking to transform his teenage persona into a sought-after mature character actor. But as the years wore on, he was also the off-screen victim of those life vicissitudes that can beset a teenager who never grows up even as he grows old, stuck like an insect fossilized in amber. He constantly worried about his deteriorating finances, and claimed he was plundered by everyone around him, from shady business managers to agents to members of his own, very extended family.

As Ed Gjertsen II said in a commentary on CNBC, Mickey claimed that he was the victim of financial elder abuse. He died with only eighteen thousand dollars in the bank, a minuscule sum for an artist who, at the height of his on-screen glory as a teenager, earned for Louis B. Mayer's MGM more than a hundred million dollars by 1940. Just consider that sum in today's dollars. For his performances in the Broadway musical *Sugar Babies*, he earned tens of millions of dollars. But it was all gone.

By 1962, after he'd married his fifth wife, Rooney had filed his first bankruptcy petition. His business dealings; partnerships with those who, he claimed, scooped money right out of his accounts; and his multiple marriages and divorces, he said, were the cause of his financial undoing. However, there was much more to the story.

Decades later, when he was ninety, Mickey testified before the U.S. Senate Special Committee on Aging, according to Sherisse Pham writing in the *New York Times* (March 3, 2011), that he was financially exploited by those who managed his money and was kept from making the "most basic decisions" about his life and finances. When he complained about it, he testified, he was told that he didn't know what he was talking about. "I felt trapped, scared, used, and frustrated," Rooney told the senators. But he also said that he was afraid to tell friends about it.[1]

In September 2011, attorneys representing Rooney filed a lawsuit in Los Angeles Superior Court against his stepchildren. The pleadings, according to a statement from Rooney's lawyers Holland and Knight, alleged that Mickey's stepson Chris and his spouse financially and verbally abused him over a ten-year period, taking money from his accounts and leaving Rooney powerless over his assets and personal life. As a consequence of that filing, the parties, two years later in October 2013, settled for $2.8 million in a stipulated judgment. To date, this judgment has not been paid.

Scott Feinberg, writing for *The Hollywood Reporter* and in an interview with us, said that he had interviewed Mickey on several occasions, including at the *Vanity Fair* post-Oscar party in February 2014 and at a Paramount Studios memorial for the legendary producer and Paramount executive A. C. Lyles on September 30, 2013. (Lyles and Mickey had both been married to actress Martha Vickers.) Feinberg said that on July 3, 2013, he conducted his one-on-one in-depth interview with Mickey and his wife Jan, and his stepson Chris Aber. During that interview, held at the Thousand Oaks Grill in Thousand Oaks, California, and captured on video,[2] Feinberg remarked that he was struck that Mickey was literally in tears about his business affairs and finances being controlled by crooked business managers and representatives, who would not follow his wishes. Rooney burst into histrionics more than once during the interview and, in Feinberg's words, became "ballistic" and had to be calmed down. Mickey had become very bitter during his last years, angry about fans who approached him, angry with his family, and angry that, to put it bluntly, he was no longer Andy Hardy. He constantly complained to anyone who would listen about fans who came up to him in public, "It's rude. I can't stand it. It's like they have to have a piece of you. Fuck 'em. They never leave me alone. For eighty years it never stops."

"They love you," his stepson Chris said. But Mickey, extolling the value of his autographs, didn't stop: "Love me, my ass, they'll go and sell it and make money off me. If I had the money they make off me, BULLSHIT!" he screamed. After his family tried to explain that the fans were only expressing admiration, Mickey continued, even more exasperated, "Give me the money, fuck being admired." These were not the complaints of a teenage boy testing the bonds of Middle America small-town family life. These were the ravings of an old man struggling against the passage of time and trying to hang on to his memories. He said once, looking back on his Andy Hardy successes, "When I was nineteen, I was the number one star for two years. When I was forty, nobody wanted me. I couldn't get a job."

The years had indeed passed the character of Andy Hardy right by, as had American society itself after the Great Depression and World War II. By 1950 the Mickey Rooney of the MGM glory days was essentially an anachronism, a figure of the past haunting low-budget film noir, a thirty-year-old has-been, as he described himself. The publicity he received in newspapers and gossip columns was snarky and condescending. He had become a laughable figure, a dead man walking. Former child star and Mouseketeer Paul Petersen, who played Jeff on *The Donna Reed Show*, knew that feeling well, explaining to us that "At eighteen you are the center of the world. By the time you're thirty, fans approach you and say, 'I used to love you on television.'"

By the 1960s, Mickey was portrayed as a stodgy, cigar-chomping womanizer who hung out at racetracks and had a drinking problem, a tragic has-been. He was laughed at in almost every newspaper story, described as "pint-sized" and with other condescending terms. However, he was only in his mid-thirties. As actor George Clooney once said, talking about psychological stresses on young performers, he was happy that he didn't reach stardom until he was in his thirties, adding that if he had been a child star, he would have been dropping cocaine into his eyes by the time he was thirty-five. If he hadn't had such fame as a kid, Mickey would have been considered, at thirty, a youthful rising star displaying superior talent. However, even earlier, by 1955, Rooney was considered an archaic figure, a shadow of the past. His friend character actor Billy Barty watched his "brother" from the Mickey McGuire films being "deconstructed" and said in our interview, "They put him on a pedestal as an idol [and] then proceeded to find his flaws until he became a mortal like them."

Mickey suffered from the catastrophe of success. He had nearly ten strong years at the top of the world at an early age, and then spent the next sixty years trying to regain that fame and repeat former triumphs. Paul Petersen calls it the "Jurassic Park effect," in which you become the fossil of what you were.

Many of Mickey's problems, particularly how he would face his elder years, stemmed from his dysfunctional, although professionally successful, childhood, when he was the primary breadwinner for his family. One might even suggest that his parents didn't raise him; he raised them. Consequently, Mickey spent most of his adult life looking for a mother figure to take care of him the way his own mother, Nell, had tried but failed to do when he was a young performer. He attempted to earn a living as best he could, at the one thing he knew how to do best: entertain. He also continued to lose money even faster than he could earn it, by doing the one thing he could not do well: gamble. He'd try to pick a horse that could win at Santa Anita or draw to an inside straight at late-night poker games at the old Beverly Hills Friars Club. As Mickey often said about his horse racing addiction, "I lost two dollars at Santa Anita and spent three million trying to get it back."

Feinberg, navigating a byzantine route through a web of business managers and Mickey's autograph-signing representative and memorabilia expert, Nelson Deedle, explained that in order to secure the exclusive sit-down with Mickey, he was told he would have to pay five hundred dollars in cash under the table to Mickey's stepson Chris. Mickey, his representative said, couldn't be trusted with the money. They agreed on a two-hundred-dollar check to Mickey's stepson, a check that had to be hidden from Mickey's view so he would not take it and gamble it away.

Feinberg said that he was struck not only by what Mickey said during the interview, and his frequent outbursts and rants, but by the actual physical dynamics of the encounter. First, he said, was Mickey's need for approval from his wife Jan, pausing after many a phrase to look at her to see if he had made her angry. Scott said that Mickey displayed a palpable fear of his wife, who was much taller and decades younger than he, as well as physically intimidating to the frail Rooney. Feinberg videotaped the interview, but remarked that he had to stop the camera several times, especially when Mickey said something his wife considered inappropriate. At one point, Scott said, she kicked Mickey so hard under the table that his chair almost fell over. Mickey let out a blood-curdling shriek and then started crying and screaming. Although his wife pretended not to notice Mickey's reaction, it was clear, Feinberg said, that Mickey had been kicked, and hard. This happened several times during the interview, and Mickey would burst into tears more than once. Yet, throughout, Mickey would repeat to Scott Feinberg that his wife was "his everything," waiting for her to give him either a look of approval or an angry glare.

MICKEY SAID THAT HIS youthful stardom, frozen as he was into the Andy Hardy character, impinged on his personal life. The studio wanted him to remain the squeaky-clean teenager in public that he played on-screen, even as he, in his private life, sought to have relationships with every young starlet he could find. He needed sexual gratification. "I was a kid. I dated everyone . . . I dated Lana Turner before she hit it big . . . She wanted to marry me . . . I taught Ava Gardner how to fuck. Then she was the best fuck I ever had . . . She called me her 'sex midget.' . . . I wanted to marry her right away but Louis Mayer said, 'no.'" No matter what sexual escapades Mickey sought to enjoy, his relationships were tempered by the studio that had employed Eddie Mannix, Mayer's head of security at Metro, to watch over Mickey and keep him in line. "Step out of line," Mickey revealed, "and Eddie Mannix talked to you. He was a tough guy and he made sure you kept your nose clean." Rooney called Mannix Mayer's "whip."

With Mannix looking over Rooney's shoulder and studio head Louis Mayer looking at his studio's bottom line and renting Mickey out to other studios for huge profits as if he were a piece of real estate,

Mickey had only one job: to keep making pictures. "They made loads of cash with Andy Hardy and they did not want me to screw up that idea from the public . . . So they kept me working. I made probably over a billion of today's dollars for them. I was their cash cow . . . I think Lewis Stone [the actor who played Judge Hardy] was making more than me. Look at what stars make now . . . If I had had better people watching over me things would have been different . . . I blew through twelve million dollars."

Mickey believed, as he compared himself to entertainers today, that the people he had hired (attorneys, agents, and managers) were working for the studio's interests more than for his own. "MGM had everyone by the balls," he said, acknowledging that his life and career were both under Louis B. Mayer's control as long as he was a contract player at MGM. His public image was crafted, just like Judy Garland's and Lana Turner's, and he had to inhabit the role of Andy Hardy even in real life. He admitted that even during the late 1930s, when Americans were still suffering through the Depression and families were under the extreme financial pressure of finding enough food to put on the table, the Andy Hardy movies pointed to a time of family values, when basic American ideals were preserved in a small-town culture. Andy Hardy may have bounced off the envelope of acceptable behavior, but the wise old Judge Hardy always brought his son back. This, Mickey said, was the heart and soul of the appeal of Andy Hardy: Everything would turn out for the best in the end. "They were Americana. They had great values. Families wanted to be like the Hardys. Everybody wanted to be like Hardy," Mickey explained. These were his golden years, but they were destined to change after he came back from World War II and was physically too old to inhabit the teenage character that had propelled his career.

As the stardom of his teenage persona faded, Mickey sought to rebrand himself, recreating the Andy Hardy character in roles that enabled him to explore different aspects of his maturing talent. But according to business consultant and memorabilia marketeer Nelson Deedle, it was as if Mickey lived only for the moment and had no long-term financial resources to provide for his future. His plan was to keep on earning money, a good plan, but you have to keep the money you earn in order for it to work. Mickey didn't. As a result, when his gambling, drinking, tax penalties, and court-ordered support payments drained him completely, and after all his finances were depleted by his managers, Mickey had to resort to anything he could do to bring in money. He turned to memorabilia. "He never thought he'd live into his nineties, so he had financial difficulty. He hadn't planned financially," Deedle told RadarOnline.[3]

After completing his scene for *Dr. Jekyll and Mr. Hyde*, Mickey returned to his rented house just outside Studio City, where he was living with his stepson Mark Aber Rooney and Mark's wife, Charlene. It was near the end of his life, after his separation from eighth wife Jan, and he spent his last few days there signing autographs. According to Feinberg, the Abers had called the Academy of Motion Picture Arts and Sciences to see if they could sell his two awards. But the Academy said no.[4]

Recipients weren't allowed to do that, according to Nelson Deedle, who speculated that the Oscars would have fetched between fifty thousand and seventy-five thousand each. "He earned the awards and should have the right to sell them," Deedle told RadarOnline. The sale would have made a difference. Mickey was cash-strapped and desperate because he owed the IRS hundreds of thousands of dollars. He owed the California Franchise Tax Board back taxes, and he had outstanding medical bills. Mark Rooney and his wife were taking donations to help Mickey meet expenses, but the money went out as fast as it came in. As a result, Mickey and Deedle arranged to sell autographs to fans at a show in California that would bring in thirty-five bucks, cash, each.

Ray Courts, the godfather of the Hollywood autograph extravaganzas, featured Mickey in many autograph shows throughout the United States. Ray recalled in an interview with us, "It was quite sad. A man of his age should not have to resort to this after his fine and long career. He had the highest pension from SAG. However, he showed up once, on a Saturday, when he wasn't scheduled. He needed to buy a plane ticket to Mexico where he was going to shoot a movie. He had blown [the] money [they'd given him for it] the day before at Santa Anita. So he came to the show to get the money for his airfare."

One can only imagine that his future might have been different if, according to producer Norman Lear, Rooney had accepted the part offered him: Archie Bunker in Lear's *All in the Family*. Lear had called Rooney and offered him the plum role. After explaining the part to Rooney, the actor was taken aback. "Norm," he told Lear, "this character is so racist, I'd be worried that they would shoot you down in the street." This was in 1968, soon after the assassinations of Martin Luther King Jr. and Bobby Kennedy.

On April 6, just about a week after his scene in *Dr. Jekyll and Mr. Hyde* wrapped, Mickey, who had set up a marathon autographing session so he could send the photos to Nelson Deedle and other autograph dealers, sat down for lunch at the house he shared with Mark and Charlene. He told his stepson he wasn't feeling well; was tired, short of breath, weak—all warning symptoms of heart disease. Mickey said he was in need of a nap. Mark told his stepfather he had to run errands, but that he would see him when he got up. When Mark came back from the store, however, Mickey still wasn't up. Maybe he still wasn't feeling well, Mark and Charlene thought. Time to check on him. It was just shy of three in the afternoon when Mark knocked on Mickey's door. There was no response. Mark opened the door.

He found Mickey still in bed in his room, but he was struggling for air. He was unresponsive, barely conscious, and his breathing was shallow and heavily labored. He seemed to be in great distress and gasping for breath. He was literally drowning in his own body fluid.

Mark called 911, and paramedics responded within minutes. First, the EMTs tried to wake Mickey as they set up an oxygen flow. But he was still unresponsive, and the oxygen didn't improve his breathing; his lungs were already filled with fluid. Finally, at 4:00 p.m., his breathing stopped completely, at which time the EMTs pronounced him dead.

"AYE, BUT TIME IS short." Mickey's very prophetic and improvised line resonated in *Dr. Jekyll*. It would be his very last line in front of a camera in his very last movie.

In a commentary on his life from his autobiography,[5] Mickey writes, "Had I been brighter, the ladies been gentler, the liquor weaker, the gods kinder, the dice hotter—it might have all ended up in a one-sentence story."

Mickey had been a performer since the age of one and a half, when his father first dragged him onto a burlesque stage, where he wowed the audience. He had been minded by producers and studios throughout his teenage years, and then by a manager who used him as a cash cow until he was in his late thirties. He always played a version of the same character, whether as the telegram boy in *The Human Comedy*, the song-and-dance partner of Judy Garland in *Babes in Arms*, or Andy Hardy—until a cathartic moment when he portrayed the developmentally challenged Bill. He worked until a week before his death, no longer Andy Hardy but still a movie legend, eking out a living by playing any part offered to him by producers seeking a bit of film history. Mickey's story is the story of show business in America, from a live burlesque house at the beginning of the twentieth century, through motion pictures, to television and beyond. And it all began in the drawer of a wardrobe trunk in a tiny room on Willoughby Avenue in Brooklyn.

1

Born in a Trunk

Sonny Yule (at one and a half years old) with his father, Joe "Red" Yule.
PHOTO COURTESY OF KELLY ROONEY.

was born into a burlesque family," Mickey said in a Screen Actors Guild interview when he had turned eighty years old. "I was born into the theater."

In 1894 the Ewells immigrated to America from Scotland with their two-year-old son, Ninnian Joseph. Ewell, born in Glasgow in 1892, would later change the spelling of his surname to Yule and drop the Ninnian. The young family moved to one of the toughest sections of Brooklyn, just south of Greenpoint, where, after two years, Joe's mother, Alice, died of influenza. With his father working at whatever odd jobs he could find, Joe had to take care of his younger brother, Jimmy. The two learned quickly how to handle themselves on the streets and in their family's cramped apartment on Willoughby Avenue.

The Ewell brothers found easy money during amateur nights at the Alcazar Theatre and at Hyde and Behman's. Joe showed a definite flair as a rough-and-tumble comic on the stage. At the age of twelve, he was spotted by a traveling burlesque show called Perry's Dandies and was offered a job as part of the cast. He took along his brother, Jimmy, and the Yule Brothers, as they now called themselves, traveled in a similar circuit as the Keaton Family. Joe and Myra Keaton's act was billed as the "Roughest Act That Was Ever in the History of the Stage," and featured their young son, Buster, who was the same age as Joe Yule, and later became a good friend of his. Joe and Jimmy Yule tried to emulate the Keaton Family act, but their bookings were erratic; they simply hung on and scraped by. According to fellow burlesque comic and later television star Phil Silvers—he played Sergeant Ernie Bilko on *The Phil Silvers Show*—"Joe Yule played some burlesque houses with me. He was strictly second rate. Not a Rags Ragland [a popular burlesque comic and Broadway performer]. He was a schlep comic. He played all the second-rate joints. He was fucking drunk half the time . . . make it all the time."

Since Joe knew the routines as well as the bits of business that he'd seen in the other shows (standard skits such as "Crazy House" and "The Doctor Sketch"), he jumped at the chance to fill in wherever he could. And despite Phil Silvers's assessment, Yule must have done a creditable job, because theater impresario Pat White ultimately made him the company's "top banana," or the starring act.

The term *top banana* (and *second banana* for the comic sidekick) was coined by comedian Harry Steppe, whom many comics tried to emulate. His routines, including the famous "Slowly I Turned" sketch (. . . step by step, inch by inch . . .) and the "Lemon Bit"—both later used by Abbott and Costello and the Three Stooges, among others—were the gold standard for comics like Joe Yule. According to Mickey Rooney, his father stood in the wings as a prop man during several of Steppe's performances and then later, in the tradition of most performers, used elements of the other comic's act.

Unlike his friend Buster Keaton, who was drafted, Joe enlisted in the army, in 1917; he served as a doughboy on the battlefields in Belgium. When he returned after the war, he had a difficult time finding any work as a performer. His brother, Jimmy, who had also served in the army, went to work in New York City's Garment District, having left show business. But Joe felt at home in the theater and had no thoughts of leaving it. He had no responsibility other than to watch out for number one, so he quickly latched on as a property man, the stage hand in charge of managing props for the performers and the show, in Percy Williams's vaudeville theater in Brooklyn. There were always jobs for young men who were willing to work the long hours. He then landed a gig as a prop man for a touring vaudeville troupe called Jack Reid's Record Breakers, which was in Manhattan for a short stand. This job would involve travel, which Joe looked forward to. New places, new girls. And it was in this touring troupe that he would meet Nellie Carter, a young dancer.

Burlesque of the early 1920s consisted of bawdy variety shows featuring dancing girls and comedy sketches much like what Abbott and Costello later performed in their "Crazy House" and "Who's on First?" sketches, rather than the risqué strip shows it had morphed into by the mid-1930s. Mickey was defensive about the burlesque of the early twentieth century, and was known to point out that it was different from the later stripper-driven performances of Gypsy Rose Lee or Ann Corio, the faces of burlesque. He once wrote, "'Your mother was in burlesque? What didn't she wear?' Such lines have no basis in the true history of show business or in the show biz lives of the Yules."

Mickey Rooney's mother, Nellie Willa Carter, born in Joplin, Missouri, in 1893, was also a performer. The third child of Palestine E. "Palace" Carter, a coal miner, and Sarah "Sallie" E. Wait, Nellie had two older sisters, Maggie and Edna, and a younger brother, Harry. In 1899, when Nellie was just five, her mother passed away, and seven years later, her father died of lung disease. Nellie went to live with her older sister Edna, who by that time was married to a steamfitter for the local school, Wade Prewitt. Edna had just given birth to a young daughter, Margaret Elizabeth, and Nellie helped out with her young niece. Their older brother, Harry, had left to seek his fortunes elsewhere.

Without having received any formal education, Nellie was still ambitious, and at fourteen grew restless in her sister's home and started to resent being a nanny to Margaret. She wanted to travel, to visit the great towns in America and beyond. Nell heard from a friend about an opportunity for a dancer in a stage show called *Miller's Maidens*. Nell loved to dance, and saw this as an opportunity to escape what she regarded as an empty existence. She auditioned and got the job as a chorus girl at what was, to her, an astounding salary of fourteen dollars per week. (She had been earning two dollars weekly in an S.S. Kresge dime store, the parent of Kmart.) Nell's dream was to be like the great entertainer Lillie Langtry, who was earning a thousand dollars a week and appearing in first-class theaters.

The act that Nell joined featured a small-time comic named Bobby Barker and Barker's brother, Owen, as the piano player and the comic playing a "dope," along with six dancing girls. They performed skits and songs accompanied by a four-piece band.

Mickey recalled, "The band was not the Philharmonic and the company was not the Old Vic." [1]

For three years Nell scrambled around with the troupe, performing in small-town theaters throughout rural Oklahoma and Utah. After catching the eye of a fiddle player who was in a larger traveling burlesque company, he recommended her to his boss, Jack Reid, to replace one of the dancers who had left their revue.

Jack Reid's show, Jack Reid's Record Breakers, was a huge troupe touted in ads as the "Largest Cast in Burlesque—50—MOSTLY GIRLS—50." Their revue, which closely resembled the Ziegfeld Follies but was saltier, featured lots of dancing girls (also called "hoofers"), singers, jugglers, magicians, and suggestive acts, and had secured booking at the top theaters in the Midwest and East Coast on the Columbia Circuit, an association of theaters like today's television station affiliates, where performers would be booked to tour. They played the venues where, Mickey wrote in *Life Is Too Short*, there "were sidewalks instead of cow paths and Indian trails around the theaters."

Nell was hired for the chorus line. There were usually two rows in a chorus line: The twelve tallest girls would dance in the back row and the twelve shortest girls in the front row. The back-row dancers were called showgirls, and the front row, ponies; the dancers at either end of the front-row line were called end ponies. Nell, who was five-foot three, became an end pony. She also appeared in bits with some of the comics. She loved the life of a theater vagabond and considered the troupe her "family." [2]

Nell stood out as the end pony, and was noticed by many reviewers. The *Milwaukee Sentinel* on June 27, 1918, wrote, "[T]here is a little redheaded pony on the left end by the name of Nellie Carter, who is one of the hardest workers in the business. She is little now, but if she continues for the entire season as she was for the opening, she will be about four ounces lighter than a cork." Although many credit Rooney's stage talent to his father Joe Yule Sr., it may have been Nell who had that great energy and charisma that Mickey exhibited. [3]

FILM CRITIC ROGER EBERT first popularized the expression "meet cute" in his review and commentary for the DVD of *Beyond the Valley of the Dolls*, whose screenplay he cowrote. Ebert described the scene where law student Emerson Thorne bumps into the female character Petronella Danforth. Ebert admits that he, as the screenwriter, wrote into the script a "classic Hollywood meet cute." He explains the meet cute as a scene "in which somebody runs into somebody else, and then something falls, and the two people began to talk, and their eyes meet and they realize that they are attracted to one another." Think of James Stewart and Margaret Sullavan in the 1940 *The Shop Around the Corner* or Tom Hanks and Meg Ryan in the modern remake, *You've Got Mail*. It was essentially a meet cute for Nell and Joe.

In a story Nell Carter told author Arthur Marx, Joe Yule had just started as a prop man for the Jack Reid show when Nell first met him backstage. She had sought out the new prop guy as she was about to go onstage because she needed a costume. But all Yule managed to dig out of his trunk was an evening dress large enough to fit a much heftier woman. Nell shook her head. "That's no good," she said. "I need a costume I can dance in, not get buried in."

Yule shrugged and said rather indifferently, "Sorry, lady, that's all I can find. Take it or leave it."

She left it, and stomped off in a rage.[4]

Yule remarked to his coworker, "Imagine bringing that home to Mom."

Though that first interaction didn't seem to hold any romantic promise, Joe and Nell started to tease and rib each other playfully as the days passed. Joe was very intrigued with Nell, and repeatedly asked her out for dinner, but Nell always gave an unequivocal no. Joe brought small gifts, wrote notes, but Nell was not to be swayed. She earned more money than Joe, had a far higher stature in the company, and was not going to get stuck with a lowly prop man, one who was even shorter than she. Joe Yule was, however, nothing if not persistent. In the meet cute realm, it was like the motion picture teaming of Tracy and Hepburn, or Hudson and Day. They continued their good-natured teasing and ribbing, but Joe was not to be deterred.

At the Riviera Theatre, near Niagara Falls, New York, Joe put the pressure on Nell, and she finally acquiesced to a date with him. They went to the Falls, and with the heavy spray hitting him in the face, he popped the question. Surprised and pleased, Nell accepted, and the two were married by a judge in a courthouse in nearby Rochester a few days later.

There was a well-defined caste system in the world of theater, clearly established social strata in which stage hands did not marry the talent, and in particular a lowly property man did not marry the gorgeous end pony. When producer Jack Reid discovered the marriage, he became outraged.

"This can't be," Reid bellowed. "You can't marry this worker, Nell. It just is not done." But she and Joe Yule were already married. And she loved him. She stood her ground and told Reid it was none of his business, that he had no right to tell her whom she could marry. It was said by other performers in the show that Reid had his own infatuation with Nell and was planning to feature her as a main performer. Notwithstanding his affections for Nell, Reid, realizing that he was not getting anywhere with the pugnacious end pony, turned to the new groom, and reiterated his feelings that the two could not be together. "It's too late," Yule told him. "We're already married. What's the use of talking about it?"

"You're right," Reid snapped back. "You're both fired!"[5]

Luckily, Nell was in demand, and with her talent and versatility, she was quickly snatched up in New York by Pat White and His Gaiety Girls. She was now part of a package deal, which included Joe, who got the job as property man. Actually, Pat White liked Yule, and after watching Joe's comedic reaction after dropping a heavy prop on his own foot one night, he thought he had the ability to be a comic. Joe had carefully watched the original top banana—the term originated from a routine loaded with double-talk in which three comics try to share two bananas—Harry Steppe, the stage name for Abraham Stepner, "the Hebrew Gent." Steppe, whose characters and routines, similar to those of "Funny Girl" Fanny Brice, brought the Yiddish dialect to both burlesque and vaudeville and was the gold standard for aspiring comics such as Joe Yule. According to Rooney, his father stood in the wings as a prop man during several of Steppe's performances and, in the tradition of most performers, adapted, or stole, many elements of his act.

Soon after Pat White took notice of Joe Yule's comedic abilities, the top banana of the show died unexpectedly, and White asked Yule to step in for him. Since Yule knew the routines as well as the bits of stage business he'd seen in the other standard comedic skits such as "Crazy House" and "The Doctor," he jumped at the chance to fill in. Pat White must have liked his debut performance, because after that night, he made Yule the company's top banana.

The Yules toured happily with Pat White for the next few months. They were in wedded bliss, and Yule was enjoying his newfound success as the banana. However, the calm was interrupted with the discovery of Nell's pregnancy. The Yules were still scraping by, and now with a baby on the way, Nell was forced to take a break. She remained in the chorus line until about six weeks before the birth. Meanwhile, Yule refused to accept his impending fatherhood. He wanted nothing to do with the birth. When he felt the baby kick in Nell's belly, he celebrated by getting drunk.

Six weeks prior to the birth, Nell retired to the rooming house they lived in on Willoughby Avenue in Brooklyn. She wanted her son born in a hospital, which required a one-hundred-fifty-dollar deposit, which the couple scraped together. However, Nell panicked when she read that hospitals could keep babies until the full bill was paid, so she decided to use a midwife at the Willoughby boardinghouse. Joe was able to convince the hospital to return his deposit.

Now, with their income sliced in half, the couple struggled. Luckily, the show had extended its run in Brooklyn, so Joe would be close to home for the birth. His brother, Jimmy, who had just been discharged from the navy, gave them three large naval kerchiefs, which Nell stitched together into a maternity dress. Joe continued in his top banana role in the Gaieties, but was unhappy and drinking heavily.

Joseph Yule Jr., who would later be known as Mickey Rooney, was born on September 23, 1920, weighing five pounds, seven ounces, in a back room three flights up in the brownstone on Willoughby Avenue in Brooklyn, where his first cradle was the top drawer of Nell's wardrobe trunk. Nellie was thrilled with her new baby and thought Joe would be, too. But when the Yules' neighbors found Joe to bring him the news that he had a son, he was sitting amid a pile of clothing at the bottom of a laundry chute with a bottle of Scotch in his hand, warbling the song "Glasgow Belongs to Me."

The day after Joe Jr. was born, the Gaieties moved across the Hudson to Newark, New Jersey. Joe went off with the show, leaving Nell to fend for herself. Then, because the family desperately needed the money, Nell packed everything up and joined her husband in Newark two weeks later, where she resumed her place as the end pony in White's Gaiety Girls chorus line.

Nell was very aware that Joe was unhappy and drinking heavily. But she was not going to let him disappear when they now had a son to raise. They would stay together as a family, Nell, Joe, and Joe Jr., but despite the public appearance of unity, there was a great deal of tension. Close friends on the burlesque circuit with the Yules noticed the friction and, in interviews years later, talked about it. Frank Faylen, for example, whom most people remember from his role as the cab driver in Frank Capra's Christmas classic *It's a Wonderful Life* and his role as Dwayne Hickman's father in the television series *The Many Loves of Dobie Gillis*, remembered how disconsolate Joe Sr. became as he shouldered the responsibilities of fatherhood. He didn't want them, and he drank until he could barely remember what he was supposed to do. "He could drink you under the table," Faylen recalled. Faylen's wife, Carol Hughes, who played the plucky blonde reporter Dale Arden standing up bravely to the Emperor Ming the Merciless in the serial *Flash Gordon Conquers the Universe*, among many other roles, remembered that "Joe was never sober. When we started appearing on the Columbia Circuit in 1928, Frank and I had a song and dance and comedy act called 'Faylen and Hughes.' Joe was a comic on the circuit. He chased every girl on the line. He was never a headliner. His main goal was drink and girls."

Nell, for her part, took her responsibilities very seriously, traveling with her husband around the country on the grueling circuit while caring for Joe Jr., whom Joe Sr. had nicknamed Sonny. In Oklahoma, Nell bought a padded Indian basket that served as Junior's crib. She turned their dressing rooms into nurseries, cluttering them up with bottles, bottle warmers, diapers, and other apparatus for the baby. Toys, gifts from Sonny's "uncles and aunts" from their show family, were strewn about. Joe resented having their income go directly to pay for this kid, but as long as they stayed together, there was nothing he could do about it—other than complaining, "You and that kid are going to drive me crazy yet."

At about ten months, Sonny began to walk on his own, mostly backstage, but he seemed fascinated by the goings-on in front of the audience as he explored the boundaries of his new world. He was pampered by the other performers, who all took a parental interest in the infant. The burlesque house, with all its colorful costumes, scenery flats, funny props, baggy-pants comics like his father, and showgirls with their flashy and skimpy attire, was Sonny's nursery school. Who needed a sandbox or toys? Sonny had the stage and the sounds of raucous music. The props served as his amusement. Just as a baby learns the first language it hears, Sonny Yule learned the language of burlesque, its rhythms, its patterns, its music—all of which were imprinted on his brain, building a neural network that would drive his talent for the rest of his life.

By the time he was one year old, Sonny began to talk while exploring the theater, soaking up the environment. During one particular performance, just as comic Sid Gold began his monologue, pattering away in his Yiddish accented English, Sonny wandered over to the orchestra pit and, with the audience carefully watching him, crawled onto the kettledrum and began aping the motions of playing it. The audience began to snicker, which only encouraged Sonny to play more energetically. The louder the laughter, the more animated Sonny became. The orchestra leader had no other choice but to go along with the antics, because now no one was paying any attention to Gold's monologue. The comic admitted defeat and left the stage, and Sonny became the sole performer before the audience. But this wasn't the first time, according to Mickey.

One night when he was one and a half, he was standing in the wings watching his father's act. "My father was onstage doing the 'bootblack' scene. And because of the rosin on the stage from the dancers, I had to sneeze. I sneezed. My father went backstage and said, 'What are you doing back there, Sonny?' I said, 'I don't know, Papa.' He said, 'What's that on your neck?' 'It's my harmonica,' I said. 'Can you play it?' he asked. I said, 'Sure,' And I played *hoop, hoop, book*. And everybody laughed. I looked over into the wings on the side and my mother was waving her finger at me as if to say, 'What are you doing with your father?' She was afraid he was going to spank my rompers good. So I went offstage, and the manager said to Joe [my father], 'Why don't we put the kid in the show?' My father said, 'He's too young. Maybe a little later on.' So we waited and I got put in the show." [6]

But Joe, watching his son cavort on the kettledrum, began to panic. He figured that Pat White would fire Nell and him on the spot for not controlling Sonny. However, White, watching Sonny perform to the audience's delight, knew this was a showstopper and decided to make the boy a regular part of Joe's act, instead of an occasional walk-on. He even had a fifty-dollar custom-made tuxedo made for Sonny to wear while he was doing his stuff on the drum. Soon, perhaps as in indication of his future talent, Sonny quickly became tired of just sitting on the kettledrum and pantomiming drumming. One night, when the tenor started to sing a popular ballad called "Pal of My Cradle Days,"[7] Sonny decided to chime in.

The now-two-year-old Sonny stood up on the drum and yelled out to the conductor, "Pardon me, sir. I bet I can sing that song, too." That brought down the house. Thoroughly embarrassed, the tenor knew he was in a no-win situation. As comedian W. C. Fields once said, "Never let a kid into the act." The tenor offered to pay Sonny five dollars on the spot if he could sing the tune. With a shrug, Sonny turned to the conductor for help. Realizing that the audience was eating this up, he led the orchestra back into the song, and Sonny launched into the number with the confidence of a seasoned trouper. And why not? He'd heard the song every night for three months and knew all eighteen lines of music, lyrics, and even the tenor's hand gestures by heart. According to Nell, there wasn't a dry eye in the house after he delivered the tear-jerking lyrics on one knee, Al Jolson style. Sonny knew he stole the show and loved every minute of the applause and adulation.

It had become apparent that Joe "Sonny" Yule Jr. was a born performer. He had everything it took, even at two years old, to make it in show business: chutzpah, talent, and a great competitive instinct. In an interview with *The Hollywood Reporter* in 1941, Joe Yule Sr. said about his son, "He was a natural born pirate. He swiped laugh lines from everybody's act, and when he'd get down on one knee on the runway and sing about his gray-haired mother, you needed a bucket to collect all the tears."

Recognizing Sonny's talents, Pat White partnered the now-three-year-old boy with comic Sid Gold, who had a female partner at the time, Babe La Tour. Gold, in an interview with entertainment reporter George Frazier in the October 1948 issue of *Coronet* magazine recalled his first meeting with Sonny Yule, then two years old:

> I remember Mick held his nose after I sang a song and made a wry face . . . I played it for all it was worth and said to the kid, "I suppose you can sing it better . . . I'll bet you a dollar you can't." As I dropped the humorous challenge . . . the kid borrowed a dollar from the orchestra leader and made a big show of that and then I swear, he tore my dollar in half saying that he will get that dollar back when he was finished. We kept that piece of business in the show every night after that. He later added an impersonation of Moran and Mack's "Two Black Crows" where once he forgot his lines. I'll never forget this—the kid looked at the audience and said he was sorry, the record got stuck. That kid has been "on" ever since.[8]

Sid's act with La Tour was made up of songs, patter, and corny jokes, with Sid as the straight man feeding Sonny the pipe for the punch line. For their finale, Sonny would break into "Pal of My Cradle Days," which made even the toughest burlesque audience members reach for their handkerchiefs. Soon Sonny's act with Sid Gold became a feature of the show, finding much success. After a while, Babe La Tour, who had built a reputation as a bawdy female comic and singer and was billed as the "Human Live Wire," quit the act and went back on tour as a solo. Sid was now working solely with a three-year-old. Teaming with Sonny Yule (Junior's new stage name) had bolstered Gold to a featured player rather than the comic who came onstage between the featured acts. Previously, Gold had delivered the punch lines. Now, with Sonny, he became a standard straight man. Yet Sonny, for his part, wasn't your typical comic. Bored with the same routine night after night, he began to ad-lib, which was difficult because it broke Sid Gold's pace.

Sonny was making money, but his salary went straight to Joe, for "booze and broads." Nothing was saved. While Joe resented his son for earning nearly his entire salary at only three years of age, Nell was proud of him and hoped the extra money could let her retire from the chorus line and concentrate on raising her son. At thirty-one years old, she was tiring of the grind as an end pony. It was grueling work, and having performed for nearly seventeen years, it had taken a toll on her. Most of the other girls were in their teens.

At its core, burlesque was a gentleman's show, playing mainly to a male audience who sought to be titillated by the showgirls and raunchy comics. On certain days, however, burlesque producers offered a "Ladies' Matinee," when the show was toned down for the sensibilities of the small contingent of women who'd peeked in to see what their husbands found so fascinating. Most of the comic routines were the same as in the evening shows, minus the strippers and the risqué jokes. During one of these matinees, Sonny decided to liven things up before the audience of women. When Sid Gold asked him the standard line, "Why does a fireman wear red suspenders?" instead of delivering the usual answer, "To hold up his pants," Sonny responded, "To hold his jockstrap up!" Not a sound. Sonny was pleased with his ad lib and broke into a wide grin, but there were no smiles in the audience. The women's silence was deafening. Sonny was unfazed, but Sid Gold's jaw dropped and Pat White was fuming—and later took it out on Joe Sr., who then gave his son a strict lecture about straying from the lines (an admonition Mickey would receive from Neil Simon more than sixty years later).

Because of the incident, someone reported young Sonny Yule to the Children's Society, a watchdog organization formed to stop child labor law violators. At age three, Sonny was prohibited by law from performing onstage. The Children's Society opened an inquiry and asked the Yules if they were putting their child onstage. As Mickey explained in his 1980 SAG interview, at first Joe Sr. denied that his son *was* a child, claiming that Sonny was a midget. His parents responded to the organization with the question "What three-year-old would be wearing a fifty dollar tuxedo?" That satisfied no one, and Sonny's brief stage career was almost at an end. But Pat White had an ace up his sleeve. He contacted Governor Alfred E. Smith's office and received a special work permit for Sonny. Smith was always fond of people in show business and was very lenient toward them. This turn of events even worked out for Gold, who, now a straight man and more valued than a comic, was hired by another circuit to perform. Pat White decided to offer Sonny a featured spot on his own. Dressed in his tuxedo, he would sing a song and tell some childish jokes. The audiences adored every bit of it and called him back for encores. Mickey was now a featured performer on his own.

Burlesque as well as vaudeville had its share of minstrel show entertainers, white performers, like Al Jolson, who made themselves up in blackface either as comics doing standard stock character bits or as singers. Among the well-known acts on the circuit were Moran and Mack, who billed themselves as the Two Black Crows. George Moran and Charles Mack did a patter act, sometimes called "fly gab," where they portrayed African Americans bantering very corny jokes in a stage minstrel dialect. Yes, these acts, indeed racist, were the progenitors to Freeman Godsen's and Charles Correll's *Amos 'n' Andy* radio show and movies, which became a television series in the 1950s, this time with African American actors Tim Moore, Alvin Childress, and Spencer Williams.

Sonny loved watching Moran and Mack, and soon began doing

impressions of them onstage—which audiences loved. One evening, while doing such an impression, he forgot the punchline. He froze for a moment, then repeated the feed line. When he still couldn't think of the punch line, he twisted his little face into a wide grin and exclaimed, "I guess the record's stuck."

The theater audience exploded in laughter, and everyone was amazed at this four-year-old's ability to think on his feet. Sonny repeated this feigned error at every performance after that, with consistently successful results. Before long, he had every adult performer wishing the boy had not been given that special work permit by Governor Al Smith.

In the 1920s the Pat White troupe traveled throughout the East, Midwest, and even into southern Canada. The troupe stayed in cheap show business boardinghouses, cooked in their rooms, and lived an itinerant existence. And this became Sonny's preschool education.

THE BURLESQUE THEATERS THAT Joe, Nell, and Sonny Yule worked in were not at all like the later version of burlesque, performed by strippers such as Gypsy Rose Lee, Betty Page, and Tempest Storm, who reigned from the 1930s to the 1960s—the type of burlesque that many remember from the stage and screen version of the musical *Gypsy*. The burlesque the Yule family appeared in from around 1912 to 1928 was far tamer and far less risqué. Nell once told writer Arthur Marx, the son of Groucho Marx, her thoughts on the burlesque she appeared in: "Our burlesque was very different. In Jack Reid's Record Breakers, you had to be able to dance. You couldn't just go out and show your body."

At that time, it was a much cruder version of vaudeville. The sketches were far broader and the songs were louder. The ticket prices were also much lower than those for vaudeville or the legitimate stage.

Burlesque's appeal then was more to the masses of immigrants and the blue-collar folks, who loved its over-the-top humor.

The Yules and Pat White's Gaieties worked for shows on what was called the Columbia Wheel, also known as the Eastern Burlesque Wheel as well as the Columbia Circuit, an organization that booked burlesque shows in American theaters between 1902 and 1927. The burlesque companies would travel in succession around a circuit of theaters, which ensured steady employment for performers and a steady supply of new shows for the participating theaters. For much of its history, the Columbia Wheel advertised relatively "clean" variety shows featuring pretty girls. Eventually, though, the Wheel was forced out of business due to competition from cinemas and from the cruder stock burlesque companies.[9]

William Friedkin's 1968 *The Night They Raided Minsky's*, starring Jason Robards Jr., Forrest Tucker, a young Elliott Gould, and veteran Bert Lahr, depicts the era in burlesque in which the Yules worked. It gives a realistic view of burlesque in 1922, and is loosely based on the legendary Minsky brothers, who produced burlesque shows at the Little Apollo Theater on 125th Street. The film succinctly depicts end ponies like Nell and top bananas like Joe Yule. Many of the famous performers of the day, such as Bert Lahr, W. C. Fields, Red Skelton, Sophie Tucker, and Fanny Brice got their start in burlesque. At one time, the Wheel had more than 350 affiliated theaters. However, by the late 1920s, motion pictures had irreparably damaged burlesque. By 1927 the Wheel was down to 44 theaters. Yet in the early 1920s, musical revues such as Minsky's dominated the burlesque circuit, and Sonny Yule, at age four, was just beginning to flex his entertainment muscles.

Sonny was now a performer in his own right—and now often billed as "Red" Yule, reflecting his shock of red hair. With his fame eclipsing that of his father, he was becoming the star of the family, and

Joe Sr. was harboring deep resentment. Nell spoiled Sonny. If there was money for just one steak dinner in the dining car, Nell would insist that Sonny, not her husband, get it, while she and Joe dined on cheese sandwiches. If Sonny tore his suit, they'd splurge on a new one for him, even though their clothes were getting threadbare.

Joe began to despise his son and wife. His drinking and womanizing were severally curtailed because of his professional and family responsibilities. He missed several shows due to his drinking, but was kept employed by Pat White thanks to the popularity of his son, who had become a valuable member of the troupe. Pat White often used Sonny as a shill in front of the theater, hawking the show, along with his appearances. As Mickey remembered, his spiel was "You, sir! Have you seen our show? Twelve beautiful dolls, the notorious Red Yule, Sid Gold, and Sonny Yule, and the music of Harry Humphrey's orchestra. Yes sir, step right up! Only a few seats left . . . down front." [10]

Joe remained angry at the world. He and Nell constantly argued. According to Arthur Marx, who interviewed Nell extensively, Joe Sr. was also physically abusive. He would often wander off after the show and not return till morning, smelling of "cheap perfume and liquor," which would usually set off a row between the Yules. Sonny knew that his father was a drinker. Joe would say hurtful things to him when he came home drunk: "Everyone loved me, right?" Rooney remembered. "Except maybe my father when he was drinking." [11]

During one of the shows, Sonny, during a costume change, discovered his father with one of the showgirls performing fellatio on him. He let out a loud screech that brought Nell running to see if he was all right. "I had always thought that my dad had a problem with Punch, not with Judy," Mickey recalled. After Nell discovered the tryst, she and Sonny went to Kansas City to live with her sister, Edna, and Edna's husband, Wade Prewitt. They lived in a neat little house that had the amenities that Sonny was not used to after living in boardinghouses and hotels, such as a kitchen and a backyard. Nell and Sonny no longer had to worry about using the Sterno to cook in their boardinghouse bedroom. Sonny got to play games with the neighborhood children. Edna, who was fifteen years older than her sister, was almost like a grandmother to young Sonny. Her daughter, Margaret, at nearly twenty, was already grown.

Eventually, Nell missed Joe and attempted a reconciliation in Chicago. She left Sonny with Edna in Kansas City, and for a while Nell and Joe traveled together in Pat White's show, but Joe returned to his drinking and his women. He had enjoyed being single and carefree in Nell's absence. After several breakups, Nell brought Sonny back with her for one more try. Not that Joe had requested to see his son or had missed him. "He didn't give a rat's ass about me. I was always that 'goddamn kid' to him," Mickey recalled.

Finally, after another bender by Joe, Nell announced that she could not go on any further. At the Chicago train station, where they were heading off to do another show, she instead bought tickets for herself and Sonny back to Kansas City. She told her husband, "Joe, we can't go on. This isn't fair to Sonny." She reached into her crocheted boodle bag, counted out the family savings of forty dollars, gave Joe his half, gave him a last kiss, and left on the afternoon train. Joe gave her no argument. Sonny was not disappointed that Joe didn't come running after them. "I was tired of him growling at my mother and [my] spending half of my life crawling under beds or behind sofas and cupping my palms over my ears so not to hear the drunken brawls. My mother told me that I wouldn't blame her for not seeing my dad anymore. I said, 'Good.'" [12] Yule hooked up with another stock company that was based out of Chicago, and Nell filed for divorce in Kansas City on the grounds of desertion. Sonny would not see his father again for another eight years. But Mickey explained, off and on through his life, his father taught him a lot about show business, even though, he joked, "You never learn from your parents." For a while, Nell was comfortable being back home and living a domesticated life.

For the present, Sonny was simply the child, albeit a talented child, of a broken family.

Nell carefully put away Sonny's and her costumes, and Sonny went to kindergarten, a four-year-old has-been. His mother found work as a telephone operator, but that lasted only a few weeks. She then decided to open up a restaurant with her friend Myrtle Sutherland, whom she had known from childhood. The restaurant specialized in home-cooked meals and featured fried chicken and hot biscuits. The restaurant was a moderate success not because Nell was such a good cook, but because the price was right. At Nell's restaurant, you could get a whole chicken dinner, including a glass of beer, for twenty-five cents.

Kelly Rooney, Mickey's eldest daughter, remembers fondly her grandmother's fried chicken. "Nanny Nell was such a character. She used to play all kinds of tricks on us to make us laugh. But her fried chicken dinners were so incredible."

Rooney said he enjoyed his life in Kansas City in 1924. His Uncle Wade took him fishing for catfish while his Aunt Edna spoiled him with wonderful meals. "I loved the smell of catfish that Uncle Wade and I had caught, frying in Aunt Edna's big black skillet. She would cook me a wonderful bowl of Cream of Wheat in the mornings . . . going with them to the Circle theater and seeing the silent movies there . . . eating hot buttered popcorn and the ride back home on the streetcar. In the summer evenings, we'd sit in the living room and wait with the front door wide open for the tamale man to come by on his bicycle . . . it was very idyllic." [13]

Nell, however, was bored. She missed the excitement of show business. Reading the trade news in *Variety* religiously, she was convinced that her Sonny had the makings of a star in the movies. When she read that producer Hal Roach was casting for child actors for his new series called *Our Gang*, short films about a group of rowdy kids who keep getting in and out of trouble, she convinced her business partner,

Myrtle, to go with her to California. They could sell the restaurant, buy a car, and take their chances in Los Angeles. Myrtle, who was also single, "paused and looked around her and adjusted her apron, flecked with blood and stinking of chicken gizzards and livers. Then she said, 'When do we leave?'"[14]

It took four weeks for them to drive to Los Angeles from Kansas City. They wanted to preserve what little money they had, so they roughed it on their journey west: They slept in a pup tent, bought food and cooked it on an open fire along the road, and rented road-side cabins for only fifty cents per night. Sonny claimed that Nell even caught a rabbit, near El Paso, Texas, and cooked it over a mesquite fire.

The three eventually reached California and rented a cheap apartment, using up their meager savings. Nell took Sonny to the casting call at Hal Roach Studios that she had read about. The assistant director told her they would hire Sonny for five dollars per day as a background actor; the other kids were getting twenty to twenty-five dollars per day. Sure, this was the reason she'd brought Sonny to Los Angeles, but five bucks a day was not enough for them to live on, she thought. She turned the job down. By Christmas, they were flat broke. They had to move to where the work was. In Oakland, Nell took a job as a chorus girl, which paid only twenty-five dollars per week. Nell just couldn't make ends meet. She sold Myrtle her share of the Model T they'd bought together, and she and Sonny returned to Kansas City to live with Edna and Wade.

In Kansas City, Nell ran into one of her old friends, Dorothy Ferguson, who was also a chorus girl. Dorothy introduced her to George Christman, who managed a theater in Kansas City and was trying to put together a burlesque troupe to tour the West. He hired Nell as an end pony, and agreed to allow her to bring Sonny on the tour. As Mickey remembered it, "There were eleven of us in two cars. We slept out of doors, not in a tent this time, but right out under the stars . . . this time it only took us eleven days."[15]

The show failed quickly, and once again, Nell and Sonny were broke and living in Los Angeles, where the tour had ended. Nell knew she was getting too old to be an end pony and that the only future they had in the business was through Sonny's talents. However, there were thousands of kids auditioning to be the next Jackie Coogan, the child star in the Charlie Chaplin film *The Kid*. Casting directors didn't see Sonny as right for the parts he went up for, and he was rejected at every audition. Nell was desperate and ended up taking a job as a telephone operator once again. She also managed a bungalow court, which paid no money but gave them a place to live. While she worked days, Sonny kept occupied at the Daddy Mack Dance Studio on Melrose Avenue, where Nell had enrolled him. Daddy Mack was a short, overweight former dancer who taught the fundamentals of dance to kids hoping for a chance he advertised to "make millions like Coogan."

Another former vaudevillian, Will Morrissey, ran a school for hopeful child stars and was also casting a small musical revue at the Orange Grove Theater on Hope Square in downtown Los Angeles. Although there was no room for Nell in the chorus, she did meet lifelong friends actresses Joan Blondell and Glenda Farrell there, and Morrissey hired Sonny at the casting call when he performed his old favorite "Pal of My Cradle Days." Sonny was paid the whopping salary of fifty dollars per week, which was sorely needed.

Sonny was singing for the Morrissey revue when fate stepped in. Famed *Los Angeles Times* drama critic Edwin Schallert had seen the show and took notice of Sonny crooning his song. He singled him out with a special mention in his review. Schallert was the father of noted character actor William Schallert (*The Patty Duke Show*, *True Blood*, *Desperate Housewives*, *How I Met Your Mother*, and *Star Trek: Deep Space Nine*). In an interview with us, William Schallert, who was around Sonny's age, remembered his father being shocked at the talent of such a young child.

Nell thought that this was their big break. She quit her jobs as a telephone operator and managing the bungalows and moved them into a small cottage complex, called the Bugs Ears, on Burns Avenue, just above Hollywood Boulevard. However, the job with the Will Morrissey Revue lasted only five weeks. Unemployed again and with their funds dwindling to nothing, Nell and Sonny went on dead-end casting calls all over the city. They were desperate. "We'd been reduced to eating rutabagas for dinner. If I didn't land something soon, we'd be eating dandelions," Mickey recalled.

> It was about the same time that I lost my innocence. When the money stopped coming in, my mother got desperate. I wasn't even six years old, but I knew something had changed. Mother started to see a lot of different men, entertaining them in our little apartment. I'd wake up in the middle of the night and hear the tinkling of glasses in the front room. Next night I'd hear whispers and sometime squeals and moans. Once, I got up and peeked around a hallway corner into the dimly lit living room to see some money changing hands. Carefully, quietly, I tiptoed back to my room and threw myself on my bed and covered my head with my pillow. I know, my dear mother, you did it for me.[16]

This no doubt affected Sonny. There are countless studies of children who become aware of their mother performing as a prostitute. It destroys childhood trust, destroys loyalty, and engenders a feeling of insecurity in the child. Dr. Ana-Maria Mandiuca wrote in the study, "The Impact of a Prostitute Mother on the Child Life Circumstances" that in the long term, "mothers anticipate the risk of marginalization of their children as future adults if they would be informed of the mother's occupation. In addition, experts identify the risk of developing deviant behaviours in the sphere of their sexual life, as future adults." [17] One only has to look at the careers and family backgrounds of some of our country's most notorious serial killers, such as the Green River Killer, Gary Ridgway, as examples of Dr. Mandiuca's assessment.[18]

Ohio child psychologist Dr. Marcia Crowne told us about the effect of the mother being recognized by her child as "selling herself" for monetary gain: "In short, there are certainly risks for substance abuse of your own; certainly a lack of boundaries; higher risk of childhood sexual, physical, and emotional abuse; higher risk of a lack of education; higher risk of intimacy issues; higher risk of early sexual activity of your own; statistically no high school diploma; statistically a much lower chance of post high school or adult education. In Mickey's case, there is no question that it had a major effect on his relationship with women and his own children that may have manifested in his lack of responsibility or authority. With eight children and eight wives and countless other relationships, he certainly is a textbook example of this syndrome."

Fate stepped in again when, in response to Edwin Schallert's review in the *Los Angeles Times*, Fox Films sent a scout to watch young Sonny. He was hired on the spot after Nell convinced the casting director that Sonny already had a tuxedo from his days in burlesque and, thus, the studio cold save money on his wardrobe.

Sonny Yule's first film was a Fox two-reeler, *Not to Be Trusted*, released in 1926. Mickey played a con man and a midget. According to Mickey (but otherwise unconfirmed), his costar was the burly Bud Jamison, a veteran comic who had appeared with the likes of Chaplin, Harold Lloyd, and Stan Laurel, and who would later became part of the Columbia shorts stock company and a familiar face in countless Three Stooges films. Jamison took a liking to Sonny, and was an early influence on the boy. Mickey told us, "Bud knew my Pop and had worked with him. He taught me how to play to the camera."

Mickey recalled in an interview with film historian Alvin H. Marill, "I was a midget and a con man who worked with a crack burglar that was played by Bud Jamison. I pretended to be a kid and an orphan that was up for adoption by a rich couple, even though I was really only six." Nell was on the set with Mickey, of course, and it was there that she met actress June LaVere, who had a small part in the film as a maid. LaVere had a notorious reputation as the mistress of a very wealthy Los Angeles Cadillac dealer, Don Lee, who also owned a radio station. Nell and June became close friends, and June was a great source of news and juicy Hollywood gossip for Nell. She was also a great influencer in Hollywood, and recommended Sonny to her friend director Al Santell for a role in a big-budget film at the Vitaphone Studios, a subsidiary of Warner Bros. The film was *Orchids and Ermine* and starred Colleen Moore, a major star whose films were eagerly awaited by fans. Santell and his assistant, the future director Mervyn Leroy, both appreciated Sonny's talent and were pleased that he had his own wardrobe of suits. They hired him on the spot. Now, by his second film, Sonny was getting typecast as a midget.

Santell wanted Sonny's look to be as authentic as possible, so he brought in Warner Bros.' legendary makeup artist Perc Westmore to turn Sonny into an adult little person. (Perc was the head of the studio's makeup department for more than thirty years. He later performed his magic on Paul Muni in the original *Scarface*, Errol Flynn, Edward G. Robinson, Bette Davis, Jimmy Cagney, and many others.) Mickey recalled, "He did my face, pasted a small mustache on my upper lip, and then covered it with glue. I can still smell that glue. It must have had ether in it or something like that." [19]

Filming went smoothly, except when Mickey, as in the script, bit off the end of a cigar. As he bit it, his front baby tooth fell out. The director was upset, until Nell replaced the tooth with the piece of the gum she was chewing. Since this was a silent film that didn't require any dialogue, the problem was solved.

Assistant director LeRoy was quite impressed with young Sonny Yule. "I'm going to write a lot of gags for you, kid, you just wait and see," LeRoy remarked.[20] For his one day of work, Sonny was paid seven dollars.

This second film helped Sonny get noticed and signed by agent John Michaeljohn, who managed to place Sonny in some local vaudeville shows where he sang his standard "Pal of My Cradle Days," but he was ultimately unable to land Sonny any film roles, so he released him as a client. It turned out to be a huge break, because in came Harry Weber. Weber was a successful agent and manager for several actors, including the legendary comic Ben Turpin. His posh fourth-floor offices on Wilshire Boulevard impressed Nell and Sonny. Weber was convinced the young boy had the right talent to be successful in films. As Mickey described him to us, "Harry looked more like an ex-boxer than an agent. He was kinda stocky, bald, and had this long crooked nose." He went on to say, "We called him 'Hurry-up Harry.' He always called my mother and said, 'Hurry, Nell, and get the kid to Metro,' or 'Hurry, Nell, and grab the streetcar, hurry, hurry.' We actually moved to an apartment on Hoover Street so we could be closer to the bus and streetcar lines due to Harry."

With Weber, Nell made another attempt to get Sonny cast in Roach's *Our Gang* comedies. Weber set up a meeting with the then-director of the series, Robert McGowan. McGowan liked young Sonny but felt he just wasn't right for the part, and didn't hire him. Weber continued to send Sonny on countless auditions. In fact, Sonny and Nell were running around so much to make auditions that the boy didn't have time to go to school. He and his mother were struggling just to survive, and frankly, education was not considered a matter of importance.

In the meantime, Nell and Joe Sr.'s divorce had become official in 1925. Besides Nell's "special dates" to earn much-needed money, she was not seeking a new beau. However, around early 1927, her friend June set her up on a blind date with a car salesman who worked for her "benefactor," Cadillac dealer Don Lee. Nell's date, Wynn Brown, sold used cars for Lee at his downtown Los Angeles lot. Tall and good looking, he was about seven years younger than Nell and, more important, single, having been divorced. He had a son about Sonny's age who lived back in Indiana, where Wynn was born in 1900. Wynn was attracted to the vivacious Nell and instantly bonded with her young son.

Nell married Wynn in 1929, and they moved into a tourist bungalow facility, a motel with separate cabins, near the Los Feliz area, which they also managed. Mickey recalled, "He liked my mother and he liked me. He didn't seem to mind when Nell came down to see him with me in tow, and many a night. Before they closed the lot at ten p.m., I would fall asleep in the backseat of her car as they talked . . . Wynn Brown and I became good friends . . . Wynn and I palled around together. He took me fishing, to baseball and football games, prizefights and wrestling—just about what the doctor ordered . . . slowly, but surely, I came to love Wynn Brown and I asked him if I could call him Dad. He held me close and said, 'Your real Daddy wouldn't like that.' He paused. I said nothing. I hardly even thought about my real daddy. I didn't remember much about him. Then he said, 'But if you want to call me Dad, I don't think anyone will tell him.' So Wynn Brown became my dad."[21]

Then there was a break: Weber signed Sonny to a long-term contract with First National Pictures, a former association of theater owners that had formed its own film studio that merged with Warner Bros. in 1928. (Its banner was used by Warners in its promotion until 1938.) It seemed the deal would finally place Sonny on the cinematic map. On December 7, 1926, Hollywood insider Jimmy Starr wrote of Sonny Yule in his Cinematters column in the *Los Angeles Record*:

"Wonderful actress Colleen Moore said she discovered him as a new actor with her in *Orchids and Ermine* and the tyke gets a long term contract just for that."

Unfortunately the deal was short lived. Sonny was released from the contract without being placed in any roles, and it is not clear why the studio never used him. This attempt to break into film became yet another dead end.

Once again things looked bleak for Nell and Sonny, but then Weber saw an ad that intrigued him. Placed by film producer Larry Darmour, the ad called for child actors to play characters from cartoonist Fontaine Fox's *Toonerville Folks,* and it portended a fame that would ultimately change Sonny's life and provide the stability Nell was looking for.

Mickey McGuire

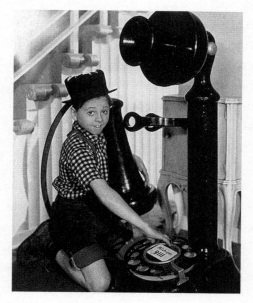

Mickey McGuire *promotional photo, 1929.*
PHOTO COURTESY OF G. D. HAMANN.

n 1908, illustrator and cartoonist Fontaine Fox had an inspiration. He described the moment an article that later appeared in *The Saturday Evening Post* on February 11, 1928: "After years of gestation, the idea for the Toonerville Trolley [initially called *Toonerville Folks*] was born one day up in Westchester County when my wife and I had left New York City to visit Charlie Voight, the cartoonist, in the Pelhams. At the station, we saw a rattletrap of a streetcar, which had as its crew and skipper a wistful old codger with an Airedale beard. He showed as much concern in the performance of his job as you might expect from Captain Hartley when docking the Leviathan."[1]

Toonerville Folks centered on a cast of characters in a sleepy suburban town and its trolley car, which met the trains coming up from New York City. There was Terrible-Tempered Mr. Bang, the Physically Powerful Katrinka, Little Woo-Woo Wortle, Aunt Eppie Hogg (the Fattest Lady in Three Counties), and Mickey McGuire, the town bully. The strip got its start in 1908 in the *Chicago Post* and was very popular from the beginning. In 1913 it was picked up for national syndication by the Wheeler Syndicate (and later, in the 1930s, by the McNaught Syndicate) and ran for nearly fifty years.

There were *Toonerville* silent film adaptations for Philadelphia's Betzwood Film Company. These starred Dan Mason as the Skipper, with Wilna Hervey as Katrinka. There were about seventeen made altogether, and the series ended in 1922.

Fox, wanting to keep his films coming, continued to shop his characters from the Toonerville Trollies to Hollywood. Around early 1927, Hollywood producer Larry Darmour approached Fox about creating a series based on the McGuire character that would resemble and contain elements of Hal Roach's immensely popular *Our Gang* shorts. Film critic Leonard Maltin commented, "During its heyday, the *Our Gang* series was imitated by numerous fast-buck producers of which the most successful was Larry Darmour. Darmour's Mickey McGuire comedies had almost every element of the *Our Gang* comedies from Roach. However, its popularity and longevity could be attributed to the presence of Mickey Rooney. There were other similar rip-offs of *Our Gang*, which had various degrees of success. One series, The McDougall Alley Kids, . . . patterned itself so closely after *Our Gang* that the black youngster was named 'Oatmeal' [*Our Gang* had Farina]."

Larry Darmour, born in Queens, New York, to James F. Darmour and Julia Ducey on January 8, 1895, was the filmmaker who started

Sonny Yule's career in motion pictures. He was an innovator who learned about the functionality of the motion picture camera, understood its importance and value, and built his own apparatus, one that was lighter and was more portable, to record events. In 1912, at age seventeen, he took his idea to Frank Reich, one of the production heads of the French Gaumont Film Company, which had started a division in New York City, and became their first American cameraman. Later he would secure a more lucrative job with Myron Selznick and his Selznick Newsreel.

Larry Darmour joined the army in 1917, where he gained a reputation as a daredevil cameraman and captured great footage during World War I. After the war, he was sought after by every newsreel company as the preeminent newsreel cameraman. He also met a California beauty, Alice Whitaker, who convinced him to move to Los Angeles, where he first worked for Paramount Pictures and Adolph Zukor. But the ambitious Darmour wanted more, and sought to create a film production company in the tradition of Hal Roach and Mack Sennett.

His production unit's first attempt at a series failed miserably. The films were copycats of popular comics such as Harold Lloyd and Fatty Arbuckle. For the Harold Lloyd knockoffs, he hired actor/writer/director Al Herman. Herman had been in films since the teens and had worked extensively with Western film actor Bronco Billy Anderson, where they were the only Jews cast in a Western.

Larry Darmour, one of early entrepreneurs of silent short films, made his movies on a tight budget and thus became one of the producers working in what was known as Poverty Row (what today would be called B movies), more a descriptor than a location—though many Poverty Row production companies were located along Gower Street in Hollywood. Although most of the Poverty Row studios were gone by the early 1950s, succumbing to the economic competition from television and the Hollywood antitrust case (*United States v.*

Paramount Pictures[2]), which barred studio ownership of exhibition theaters, studio owner Harry Cohn's Poverty Row studio ultimately morphed into Columbia Pictures.

Darmour had been a writer and cameraman for cowboy actor Fred Thomson, who was starring in films for the Film Booking Offices, run by Joseph P. Kennedy. Thomson introduced Darmour to Kennedy, who approached Darmour with an idea for kids' shorts similar to the *Our Gang* series, which was already becoming popular in the era of silent films. Darmour suggested using the character Mickey McGuire from *Toonerville Folks* as a basis for the shorts. Kennedy told him he would finance both the licensing of the rights to the cartoon characters and a separate production unit, run by Darmour, to shoot the films to be released through Pathé. And thus Darmour Studios was created, and Darmour sought a character-set license to exploit the Toonerville characters from Fontaine Fox.

Darmour—whom film critic and historian Leonard Maltin characterized as a "fast-buck" low-rent, low-budget, churn-out-as-much-as-you-can-in-the-shortest-amount-of-time studio head[3]—set up shop on Santa Monica Boulevard in Hollywood at what used to be Pacific Film Laboratories. With his studio facility in place, Darmour approached Fontaine Fox, who licensed, in the form of a lease, the character Mickey McGuire for the series at a thousand dollars per short. However, as a precondition for granting the license, Fox demanded and received final approval for the casting of McGuire.

MORE THAN TWO HUNDRED seventy-five child actors showed up for the audition. Sonny Yule was one of them. At that time, Sonny was unemployed. He had been working for five dollars a day for the Hal Roach Studios—until Nell demanded more money, and he was fired.

Nell and Sonny caught a break when a talent scout friend of Nell's tipped her off that a producer was casting for the part of the "tough kid" for a series based on Fox's *Toonerville Folks*. Although Weber had spotted the ad for the casting call, it was Nell's friend who brought it to her attention. The scout told Nell that Sonny was sufficiently tough and homely enough to qualify for the role.[4] Nell agreed to bring her son to the casting director, but when Sonny came home from school that day, he was more eager to play with his friends than audition for a part. Yet Nell was not about to give in. Money was tight, and she had just been fired from her job as a telephone operator, a job that was keeping the two of them fed and sheltered while she looked for parts for Sonny. To persuade her son, she laid out on a table several *Toonerville Folks* strips from newspapers and said, "We've got some studying to do." She showed him the Mickey McGuire bully for which he was to audition, slowly reading the strip dialogue to him, and made him study every detail of the character. By bedtime, Sonny knew Mickey McGuire as well as himself—because the character was much like the Sonny character he had played on the burlesque stage.

The next morning, Sonny and Nell arrived at the Darmour Studio only to find the outer office already jammed with other stage mothers and their sons, all eagerly waiting for their turn to audition. Nell looked around at the boys, many of whom looked like they could easily play McGuire. Every one of them had dark black hair, just like the McGuire character in the strips. Then she looked down at her son and decided that she could not have him test for the part with his blond hair. She didn't want the studio moguls to have to use their imaginations to visualize Sonny as a brunette. In a moment of great inspiration, she jumped up from her seat, grabbed Sonny's hand, and dragged him out of the office to the shoeshine stand on the studio lot, where she explained her plight to the bootblack. When Sonny returned to the audition, he was no longer blond.[5]

Back in the studio waiting room, a dark-haired Sonny and Nell now waited patiently for their turn to be tested. One by one, the other boys and their mothers were called into the office. Each time a new candidate was summoned, Nell said a silent prayer, putting the hex on the unsuspecting moppet. She watched as, one by one, each boy left the office head down, having failed to satisfy producer Larry Darmour and director Al Herman. (Al Herman had worked for Hal Roach Studios and had become good friends with one of Roach's most valuable assets, director/writer Robert McGowan of the *Our Gang* series.) The perfect Mickey McGuire was the key element to the success of the series, so a lot hinged on selecting the right young actor. Nell was heartsick, not out of compassion for the losers, but at the idea that Sonny might be rejected, too. She said another silent prayer.

Finally, late in the afternoon, Sonny was summoned. If Nell had entered that room with trepidation, Sonny was bursting with his usual confidence that shone like a bright light. First Al Herman, who was casting the talent for McGowan, interviewed Sonny. He then led the boy to a brightly lit stage with a barnyard set. He quickly explained to Sonny the action for the test scene. Herman wanted to closely monitor Sonny's ability to focus and concentrate, as McGowan had taught him.

When Herman yelled, "Camera!" Sonny sneaked around the corner of the make-believe barn, his tiny face emitting impish charm while wearing the rough, tough scowl Nell had coached him to wear in mimicking Mickey McGuire's aggressive character. Then he sat on a box and, crossing his short legs, pulled a rubber cigar out of his pocket and started to chew on it like an inveterate smoker. Al Herman was impressed. He called, "Cut," and then told Nell and Darmour, "Let's try him in costume tomorrow."

Early the next morning, when Nell brought Sonny back to the studio, he was outfitted in the derby, checkered shirt, and ragged trousers associated with the Mickey McGuire character. Now in wardrobe, he returned to the stage and repeated the scene from the previous day, strutting, swaggering, scowling, and chewing on his rubber stogie with a confidence and toughness that exuded McGuire, the camera laying down Sonny's every move on film. The following morning, when Darmour, Fox, and Herman viewed the screen test, they knew they had *the* Mickey McGuire they'd been looking for. Fox was certain that the millions of fans of the comic strip would instantly recognize and fall in love with this kid as McGuire. They were ecstatic, and phoned Nell to bring Sonny back to the studio for a third day. Out came the shoe polish again.[6]

What they did not realize, even though they might have interviewed Nell about her son's experience, as well as Sonny, was that by six years old, Sonny Yule was already a seasoned performer, with a repertoire of characters to draw from, while most of the other boys who had auditioned for the part didn't have any—and certainly couldn't compete with Sonny Yule, who at the time he auditioned for the role of McGuire, was working for a local vaudeville show.

"Your boy was great in the test," Al Herman told Nell.

Darmour told her, "We want to sign him to a five-year contract."

Because Nell had kicked around in the business since she was a teenager, she was not going to sell her son cheap. She saw the excitement in Darmour's eyes.

"How much does it pay?" she questioned.

"Fifty bucks a week," Darmour responded.

Nell decided that this was too important to handle herself and called Sonny's agent, Harry Weber, to come immediately to the Darmour Studios to help her negotiate. After some brief haggling, Darmour agreed with Weber to a salary of $250 per short film. And after the meetings were over, there was this exchange:

"Of course there's one thing, "Herman said. "Before we can actually finalize a deal."

Nell looked worried. "What's that?"

"Sonny'll have to have his hair dyed black," Herman grinned. "That shoe polish is not going to fool anyone."[7]

• • •

One reason for what would quickly become the success of the Mickey McGuire series was that McGowan was a natural with kids. He knew just how to explain scenes and comic business to his young actors to elicit convincing performances from them. Al Herman secured his job as the director of the McGuire shorts because of his friendship with McGowan. Darmour paid McGowan around five hundred dollars per short, under the table, to help Herman develop the early scripts and for suggestions in emulating and recreating the *Our Gang* essence in the McGuire shorts. It was this legendary McGowan touch passed along to Al Herman that helped make the McGuire series a huge hit.

With Sonny now cast in the title role of Mickey McGuire, Darmour put in place the financing for the series. Through Joseph Kennedy, Darmour secured both the distribution, through Kennedy's FBO Studios, and later through RKO, and the funds to produce the films. (He was already shooting a low-budget domestic series called *Toots and Casper*.) The goal was to shoot the series for less than $7,500 per short—cheap, even for 1927—and look for a quick return. Darmour, as he did throughout his career, sought to create a carbon copy of other popular film series and cash in on its similarity. Most of the series he created had a short shelf life, lasting less than a year.

The McGuire series began with the release, on September 4, 1927, of *Mickey's Circus*. This first McGuire film was written by creator Fontaine Fox himself and introduced the characters he had made famous in his syndicated strip. The cast of characters included the tough, cigar-smoking Irish kid Mickey McGuire, the title character, a streetwise leader of a gang called the Scorpion Club who got into trouble in each film and got out of it only by his wits.

Mickey had a younger brother, Billy McGuire, who followed him around everywhere. Billy was portrayed by three-year-old Billy Barty, who was later known for his short stature—as an adult he was three feet, nine inches tall—and who went on to a long career as a character actor in film and television. (Mickey and Billy began a close a friendship that lasted until Barty's death in December 2000.)

We interviewed Billy Barty in Studio City, California, in 1994, at which time he described his first encounter with Mickey: when he was hired to play Billy McGuire. Barty remembered that he first met Mickey on the set of the first McGuire short. Like Sonny, Barty had appeared onstage with his parents, starting at two years old. He joked, "Mick loved me. I've been his only costar who had to look up to him." He also told us, "I was with Mickey in many films and TV shows until recently [1994], when we were in the Western *The Legend of O. B. Taggart* that Mick wrote. He also had our school friend [from the Lawlor School for Professional Children] Gloria DeHaven in the film. Mick was always someone I looked up to. I literally was always bowled over by the awesome talent that was part of him . . . he just never stopped. We were kids together, and now we find ourselves as old men together. And even as old men we were kids." [8] Billy McGuire, though sometimes regarded by his older brother, Mickey, as a nuisance, was always loyal, and in films such as *Mickey's Race*, it was Billy McGuire who saved the day. [9]

Mickey McGuire's sidekick in the short films is an African American named Ham, actually Hambone Johnson, portrayed by Jimmy Robinson. His is a stock character out of the minstrel show tradition, an exaggerated stereotype. While Mickey McGuire often exploits Ham, making him do impossible chores, Ham is loyal, even though he often asks Mickey why he has to do the things Mickey tells him to do. When we look back on the Hambone-McGuire relationship, we should remember that this was the era of D. W. Griffith's *The Birth of a Nation*, Jim Crow laws across the South, and the Ku Klux Klan. It was a different America.

Every great hero has to have an antagonist: Hector to Achilles, Lex

Luther to Superman, the Joker to Batman, Megyn to Rachel, Reggie to Archie, Sharon Waxman to Nikki Finke. Mickey McGuire's antagonist is Stinky Davis, a wealthy, arrogant, snobbish son of the Toonerville mayor, Henry Davis. Stinky makes life miserable for Mickey and the members of his Scorpions, deriding them and challenging them at every opportunity. But time and again, in the tradition of the hero, Mickey manages to turn the tables on Stinky, pulling off the impossible without Stinky's even realizing how Mickey does it.

Actress Delia Bogard portrayed Tomboy Teri Taylor, the only girl in Mickey's gang who, though wearing a dress and bloomers, is treated exactly like the boys and holds up her end, particularly in a fight—and there are more than enough fights in the Mickey McGuire films.

The strongman of the group is a character named Katrink, whose remarkable strength belies his normal size. When there is a situation requiring someone to lift an impossibly heavy object in a moment of crisis, that job falls to Katrink.

Mickey's Circus boasts many firsts. It was the first starring film role for Sonny Yule. It was the first of seventy-eight Mickey McGuire films by Darmour, and the first for Al Herman, who directed or oversaw the production of many of those films. It was also the first entry to feature a four-year-old "midget," as little person Billy Barty was then known. It is also the first of many "lost" silent film comedies that will be restored, in this case through a partnership between the San Francisco–based National Film Preservation Foundation and the esteemed EYE Filmmuseum of Amsterdam, after a print of the film was discovered in the Netherlands.

Film professor and historian Lou Sabini commented, "The discovery of *Mickey's Circus* in the Netherlands has excited many serious collectors of silent film and was highly sought after. It is our first glimpse of an important film icon, Mickey Rooney. It gives the film scholar a peek at his skills in his first starring role at the age of six. In the film, Mickey and his gang create their own circus, with Rooney as the ringmaster. It is apparent that he has the charisma and energy to be the central character and to carry the spotlight. It really is an amazing debut. I am rather excited to view a restored print of the film, as it is considered to be a classic. Interestingly, Mickey was billed as Mickey Yule—for this film only. He became Mickey McGuire in all the following films." Sabini also said that Mickey's popularity launched Darmour into other short films.[10] The writers for the McGuire series were Joseph Levering, George Gray, E. V. Durling, and noted silent comedian Larry Semon. Al Herman continued to direct most of the shorts, even as he also started directing some full-length feature films for Darmour. His assistant, Jesse A. Duffy, replaced him for a few entries, along with Earl Montgomery. Sabini added, "The money from the McGuire films allowed Darmour to eventually start to move beyond the shorts and to create low-budget features that utilized his own studio space on Santa Monica Boulevard. This is an early indication of then–Sonny Yule's potential star power and his role as an earnings machine, which would ultimately help to sustain MGM through the Depression."

The McGuire shorts became one of the first licensed character sets from print cartoon to make it into a live-action film series. In so doing, it became one of the first of what would become a number of "Mickey Rooney firsts" over the ensuing eighty-five years of his career, firsts that would transform the entertainment industry.

According to Sonny's costar Delia Bogard in a 1989 interview, the McGuire films, most of which were filmed on location in what is now North Hollywood, were more like playing than working. "We played on camera," Bogard said. "And we played in between scenes, too. . . . It was fun." The Mickey McGuire clubhouse was in Studio City, right behind Republic Studios, and the cast named it the Scorpion Club. There were no stand-ins back then, Bogard remembered, "So Mickey, Billy Barty, and I did our own stunts." It was rigorous, she said, because the McGuire films were all about action, even after they began making talkies in the 1930s. They had plenty of stunt gags, physical stunts reminiscent of burlesque humor, such as pies in the face. "We had to stand there and take the pie right in the face with our eyes wide open," Bogard said. In films such as *Mickey's Circus*, and many others, the cast had to work with animals of all kinds. "We worked with chickens, goats, bears, alligators, and even a lion. But the lion was toothless, and that helped a lot." [11]

There was an incredible amount of energy on the set, Bogard remembered, primarily because Sonny Yule and Billy Barty played off one another so well, each infusing the other with energy. The films were packed with action, and that helped pump up the energy. Also both Sonny and Billy Barty had the ability to act the clown when a scene called for it. After a scene, Bogard said, "watching Sonny and Billy play off each other, the crew would be so entertained they would actually clap because they were so happy. These would be one-take scenes. If they had to do two, the second one wasn't so good." Mickey himself said years later, "I always played it for the laughs."

"I DID TWO HUNDRED twenty Mickey McGuire comedies"—only seventy-eight shorts, or two-reelers, each running for twelve to eighteen minutes, were produced—Mickey boasted in his 1980 SAG interview, "and we used to shoot them in two days per picture." Full-length features back then, he said, were shot in eight to ten days. [12]

"I remember the Larry Darmour studios well," Mickey told his SAG interviewer. "It was a rickety old building in Hollywood where the production offices were. I went for lunch there one day, and they had a bunch of broken-down offices. I could see a silhouette in one of the offices. I was dressed in wardrobe. I had my big shoes on, my derby hat, my checkered shirt. I was dressed as Mickey McGuire. The silhouette was moving and I called out, 'Hello.' I opened the door and said, "I'm Mickey McGuire, what is your name, sir?' He said, 'My name is Walt Disney.' I said, 'I don't know you, Mr. Disney.' He said, 'I want to show you something.' So he took me into his office and said, 'Sit on my knee. I want to show you this picture.' So I climbed up on his knee, and he showed me the picture of a mouse. I said, 'It's a wonderful picture, Mr. Disney, what do you call him?' He says, 'Mortimer Mouse.' And I said, 'That's wonderful.' And he said, 'Thanks, Mickey,' and he stopped and said to himself, 'Mickey.' Then he looked directly at me and said, 'How would you like it if I named this mouse after you, Mickey Mouse?' And I said, 'I'd like it, but right now I have to go and get a cheese sandwich.' That is a true story that happened when I was about seven." [13]

There was never confirmation from Walt Disney, Disney Studios, or any other source to verify this story. Walt Disney always claimed that his wife suggested the change of name from Mortimer to Mickey Mouse. The source of her inspiration was never identified.

For nearly six years, Sonny worked constantly, creating more than twelve shorts per year as Mickey McGuire. Darmour and Herman encouraged him to talk his very worst. "The tougher he gets to be in real life," Larry Darmour told the surprised Nell, "the easier it'll be for him to play Mickey McGuire." Over the course of the productions, Sonny Yule rarely had a minute to himself as he trudged from scene to scene.

His schooling before Darmour hired him was almost nonexistent. Back in Kansas City, Sonny had been homeschooled by Nell and her sister, Edna, although neither was well-schooled herself. Then, when he got the part of McGuire in 1927, Nell was forced to enroll him in public schools, in accordance with California law. Months after he entered the local public school, Nell finally had the funds to place him in the Lawlor School for Professional Children, which gave them the flexibility to work at the studio. Lawlor compensated for Sonny's missing kindergarten, first grade, and nearly most of second grade.

The Mickey McGuire shorts were a huge hit from the very moment audiences saw *Mickey's Circus*. But for young Sonny Yule, the shooting was a grueling experience, with Darmour and his directors driving the cast as hard as they could to churn out as much footage as they could in the amount of daylight they had. In essence, given the heavy physical nature of the McGuire films, the schedule amounted to flogging them to perform scene after scene.

The series made Larry Darmour very wealthy and put his studio on the map—albeit as a Poverty Row producer, but lucrative enough to allow Darmour and his wife to build a beautiful beach house and an estate in the Hollywood Hills. While it didn't make the Yules wealthy like Darmour, Nell and Sonny were enjoying more prosperity than they had ever experienced. With $250 per short and ten shorts per year, they earned about $2,500 annually. During the summer breaks, usually about ten to twelve weeks, they'd tour the country, with Sonny making personal appearances on the B. F. Keith–Orpheum vaudeville circuit as Mickey McGuire, performing some of the material he'd done on the burlesque stage and mimicking his McGuire bits, and thus merchandising himself and the McGuire name. Keith-Orpheum had just been acquired by Joe Kennedy and RCA chairman David Sarnoff. To allow Nell to tour with Sonny and to set up the Keith-Orpheum deal, Darmour demanded a fee of $1,500, a backdoor form of a license fee for use of the character's name and a kickback because Sonny was a Darmour contract player. Nell reluctantly paid up, even though Sonny's personal appearances proved to be far more lucrative than his weekly salary from Darmour. At one particular venue, Sonny and Nell were paid about $2,500 for a three-day stint. Nell usually demanded some cash under the table as well, cash she could pocket and not have to report to Darmour. As she told author Arthur Marx decades later, she did not have high hopes that this McGuire "gig would last very long, and we needed to make hay while we could." [14] This was only one of the reasons Nell resented the $1,500 she was forced to pay to Darmour to do the vaudeville tour, and she subsequently sought to raise the fee that Sonny would be paid for each McGuire picture.

In early 1931 the McGuire films made the changeover to talkies, and through Sonny's agent, Harry Weber, Nell demanded a raise to $500 per short. To make their point, Sonny, held back by his mother, did not show up for work on two of the shorts, which included the 1931 *Mickey's Helping Hand*, for which Darmour cast Katrink actor Marvin Stephens in the role of Mickey McGuire. Audiences came away unhappy, and after numerous complaints from the theater owners and from RKO, Darmour acquiesced and gave Sonny his raise. By this time, Sonny essentially ceased being Joe Yule Jr. As Mickey told us, "I was being called Mickey anyway by everyone after the first couple of pictures. Even my mother took to calling me Mickey, and so did my friends and teachers at school."

The new technology of sound posed a huge problem for Darmour: The cost of wiring the studio for sound was astronomical. Many of the Poverty Row studios were forced out of business. Yet heads were rolling at every studio, as the inevitable talkie revolution ended careers and devastated studios financially. Full-feature dramatic films were the first to see the change, in 1927, with the inaugural talkie, *The Jazz Singer*, starring Al Jolson, but the comedy shorts lagged behind. The Roach Studios, by this time the premiere studio producing comedy (with Laurel and Hardy, *Our Gang*, Will Rogers, and others) was still doing well in 1928 with silents. However, Hal Roach knew he needed to wire the place for sound, and made the changeover in mid-1929.

Larry Darmour knew he also had to make the change, to compete with Roach, so in late 1929 and early 1930 he had his studio converted to sound. It was easier and cheaper for Darmour than for other film production companies: RKO was far more technologically advanced than many of the studios, since it was partly owned by RCA, whose labs had created its own systems for sound on film. David Sarnoff, one of the founders of RCA and ultimately the National Broadcasting Company, had worked for the Marconi Company in radio and understood the technology of audio capture and distribution.

Sound offered another problem outside of cost: talent. Some actors could handle the changeover to speaking dialogue; others did not fare so well. *Our Gang* comedies, for instance, were completely recast in 1929 to accommodate child performers who were adept at reading lines. But the McGuire films made only one change: Delia Bogard, was replaced by Shirley Jean Rickert, who had previously been in the *Our Gang* films. Delia Bogard later reflected, "I completely understood when I was replaced. I no longer fit the part. I really had grown close to Mickey, Billy, Mavin, Jimmy, and the others. We were like a family. I knew I had outgrown the part and I knew it was just a matter of time for Mickey to be booted as well. Billy could go on playing his part forever." [15] (Delia went on to perform onstage as a dancer, and appeared in some supporting film roles.)

Actress Shirley Jean Rickert had gained some notoriety as the "blonde girl with the spit curl" in the early sound films of *Our Gang*. When Darmour offered her mother the astounding sum of $225 per short to join the McGuire films, she jumped at the chance. Rickert played Tomboy Teri for the last two years of the series. Lou Sabini talked to Shirley Jean Rickert in 2002 about her work with Mickey. She said, "It was a lot of fun working on those films. Mickey and Billy were also sweet, but Mickey was always pulling off pranks. He was always fun." [16]

As sound films impacted film production, Darmour was looking at ways to cut costs even though he had already acquired a reputation as a low-budget, shady producer. Actor Sidney Miller, who worked for him on the Mickey McGuire series called him "a real angle-shooter. He always was looking for how to connive. He paid my parents under the table for me to work for him when I was free even though I was under contract to Warner Bros." [17]

By 1930, Darmour was clearly getting tired of paying the thousand-dollar royalty to Fontaine Fox for use of the Mickey McGuire name. With Sonny Yule now being recognized, even in vaudeville, as Mickey McGuire, Darmour thought up a scheme to change Joseph Yule Jr.'s name legally to Mickey McGuire, thus demonstrating that he needed no copyright for the McGuire films, even though he had contractually agreed to pay Fontaine Fox a license fee for the characters. Darmour insisted that Nell change her son's name, saying he would pay her a seventy-five-dollar weekly salary if she agreed.

Thus, on November 16, 1931, Joseph Yule Jr. and his mother, Nell Carter Yule, through Darmour's attorney at Loeb and Loeb, petitioned the local Los Angeles County court to change their names from Joseph and Nell Yule to Mickey and Nell McGuire. Thus, Sonny briefly became Mickey McGuire. However, Fontaine Fox knew that Darmour was attempting to avoid paying him his per-picture royalty—and he was correct. After the name change, the checks stopped coming.

In a copyright lawsuit filed against the Yules, Darmour, Al Herman, and RKO Films, Fontaine Fox charged them with fraud. Darmour answered the claim with a countersuit, asserting that Mickey McGuire had the right to use his legal name as an actor. It took over two years for the court to decide the issue. In May 1934, the court found in favor of Fontaine Fox. The litigation settlement awarded damages to the owner of the cartoon character, and compelled the twelve-year-old actor to refrain from calling himself Mickey McGuire on- and off-screen.

THE MICKEY MCGUIRE SERIES had become a financial success, surviving the advent of sound, and maintained its popularity for seven years, often rivaling Hal Roach's *Our Gang* series. In fact, the McGuire films were distributed well into the 1940s, and RKO used the shorts as a bargaining chip when negotiating with some of its B movies, forcing theater owners to take lesser low-budget RKO films if they wanted the McGuire two-reeler. It was an early example of what would become known as block booking, a system perfected in the 1930s by Adolph Zukor at Paramount. The barter was popular with theater owners, who'd market the eighteen-minute short films in order to sell the low-budget RKO films that came with the "block" of films they'd received. Ultimately, the popularity of the *Our Gang* films, with their stronger television distribution, forced the McGuire series into obscurity. Today the McGuire films are remembered mainly by film historians or film buffs, eclipsed as they have been in people's minds by the *Our Gang* films.

By 1931, Mickey had established himself as a bankable child star. For him and Nell, the series provided a comfortable life and the security they'd lacked. The steady paycheck and other streams of income enabled them to live comfortably in a middle-class section of Hollywood without having to scramble overmuch to come up with the rent money the first of every month. Seven years of steady work is an eternity in the film business. Nevertheless, working for a Poverty Row studio like Darmour's did not provide the stability of working for the large film studios such as MGM, Paramount, or Universal.

By 1931, Mickey was appearing in films other than the McGuire series. While he was still legally able to bill himself as "Mickey McGuire," he appeared uncredited in *The Last Parade* in April 1931 (with Jack Holt and Constance Cummings). In November 1931 he did a film with Noah Beery Jr. (remembered later as James Garner's character's dad, Rocky, on *The Rockford Files*), *The Kindling*, for Columbia. In December of 1931 he was in a Buck Jones film, also at Columbia, called *High Speed*, which came out the following year. Harry Cohn was impressed with young Mickey McGuire and wanted to sign him to a contract. However, Mickey was still under an exclusive agreement with Darmour, according to columnist Jimmy Starr in the *Los Angeles Evening Herald Express*, on December 3, 1931.

For most of these non-McGuire films, Mickey received a relatively low salary. In the 1932 Tom Mix film *My Pal, the King*, Universal paid him $250 for a ten-day shoot, and gave him a rare second billing, even though his was actually the central role. In the film, Mickey plays the seven-year-old—he was really eleven—boy king of "Alvania," who takes an interest in Tom Reed's (Mix's) Wild West show and the two become friends. Palace intrigue ensues when Mickey's character takes Tom's sage advice instead of that of an evil count. Double-crossed, the count kidnaps the young king, but finds his plans thwarted when Tom learns that the king has been abducted and rides off with his troop of men, without any real bullets for their guns, to rescue him. The film features a notable cast member, Native American Jim Thorpe, an Olympic champion and professional football player for the New York Giants. (The town, Jim Thorpe, in Pennsylvania, is named after him.)

Mickey opened a lot of eyes with his role in *My Pal, the King*. He carries the acting load and pulls off a very flimsily plotted picture almost single-handedly. For his part, Tom Mix, who gained glory as a hero in silent Westerns, seems to have difficulty with the dialogue and gives a very wooden performance. Mix was not a gifted actor, rather more a personality. This was one of his last roles. After 276 films, he would finish his contract with Universal the next year and appear in only six more films before his death in an auto accident in 1940. He was fifty-two at the time of this film, and no longer the youthful performer of the past.

It was *My Pal, the King* that brought Mickey to the attention of Universal founder Carl Laemmle, when Mickey received some positive reviews. The *New York Times* wrote on October 4, 1932, "Little Mickey McGuire appears as Charles and he does quite well."

As he approached the age of twelve, when most children experience a growth spurt, Mickey started to get concerned about his height. He was not growing. Despite Nell's nourishing meals—she was an excellent cook—he was four inches shorter than an average boy of eight. Larry Darmour and Al Herman, though, were happy he was not growing. Ever concerned that he would outgrow his Mickey McGuire part as he got older, they were always on the lookout for a replacement. However, no one ever approached the energy and charisma of Mickey.

As he watched other children he knew shooting up in height, Mickey tried all sorts of stretching exercises to induce growth. He slept on a hard bed. He answered scores and scores of advertisements that guaranteed "at least an inch a month." However, the line on the measuring tape did not move. He could, and did, lick many boys who towered over him, but his pride was suffering. He also resented the cracks made to him at the studio, especially by Al Herman who constantly called him Shorty or Runt. He threatened to quit if Herman persisted in his insults.[18]

By 1932 the McGuire comedies had run out their string. Whereas in 1931 the box office was still strong for the films, in 1932 they dropped like a thud. Audiences were tiring of the redundant plots, the familiar chases, the same tricks and stunts. Exhibitors reported that men, women, and even children were growing weary of the tough boy in the derby hat who, though short for his age, was getting too large to be "cute" like the Mickey McGuire of old. The fickle public stopped coming to see him. The grosses of the comedies took a resounding dive, and the losses to the studio mounted. Theater owners squawked and refused to run any more of the comedies, the bankers shuddered, and Larry Darmour began looking for another property.[19]

On August 7, 1932, just after returning from their summer tour, the unsuspecting Nell and Mickey received a legal letter from Larry Darmour's attorneys Loeb and Loeb stating that the services of Mickey McGuire, "Esq." were no longer required. Second, it demanded that the name of Mickey McGuire be returned to its copyrighted owner Fontaine Fox. (Darmour had given up the battle to keep the name, since he was ending production on the series anyway.) Good-bye, good luck, and don't let the door hit you on the way out. Darmour had shot enough shorts to distribute well into 1934, and no longer needed the services of Mickey/Sonny/Joe.

Nell understood that there was an end to every gig. However, she exploded in anger at the demand that Mickey give up the name she had legally acquired for him. After hiring her own attorney, it was agreed that while he would have to relinquish the McGuire surname, no one had a legal right to force him to change his first name. For the time being, he would use the name Mickey Yule.

Nell thought there would be more gigs. But through Weber, she learned very quickly that Mickey was no longer a hot property. He had been stamped as the tough, dark-haired Mickey McGuire with whose character the public had grown exhausted. Other studios had very little interest in hiring the typecast actor. Weber suggested to Nell that they reinvent Mickey for a new generation of motion picture roles. Accordingly, Nell let her son's hair grow out to its natural blond, in the hope she might be able to reintroduce Mickey to casting directors. She and Mickey both hoped he would grow taller, so he could slide into teenage roles. Mickey auditioned all over Hollywood. Then Weber suggested they retry a vaudeville tour. After some legwork, he was able to talk veteran producer Will Morrissey into a spot for them in the Midwest tour of the Will Morrissey Revue.

Will Morrissey was a legendary name in vaudeville. He had a career as a song lyricist, performer, playwright, and theatrical producer. Based in New York City, Morrissey was also a frequent stage personality and producer on the West Coast and in Chicago. He had one of the early radio programs on the CBS network, and his vaudeville shows featured a mix of comics, singers, acrobats, and other performers—a typical early twentieth-century vaudeville revue.

Mickey and Nell were offered a weekly salary of $750 for an indefinite tour, an opportunity they grabbed. They played on the bill for Morrissey with the young comic Milton Berle and his straight man Robert Cummings, who would go on to become one of Alfred Hitchcock's favorite actors.

"Rooney was a very talented kid," remembered Berle in an interview with us in 1992. "He sang a few songs, told a few burlesque jokes that were real creakers, and did some imitations, like Tracy and Gable. I remembered he did a Mae West imitation of 'Come up and see me sometime' in a dress with pearls and a boa. It's hard to follow a kid like him."

Berle certainly liked Mickey, but the reviews of Mickey's act in the Morrissey Revue were not kind. The *Chicago Sun-Times* called his performance "tired" and "dated." The audiences had bought tickets to see Mickey play the character they were familiar with from the two-reelers, Mickey McGuire, not some tired burlesque act from the 1920s. But Nell feared legal action, and purposely didn't have Mickey use the McGuire character, instead relying on their old routines. But with the lukewarm reviews, both realized that if they wanted to continue on the tour, they'd have to make a drastic change. Thus, they decided to use a disclaimer to skirt the legalities while giving the audiences what they wanted

Each night, Mickey would step to the footlights and explain to his "friends" in the audience that "While I no longer have the legal right to call myself Mickey McGuire [the lawsuit was well publicized], still and all, I am Mickey McGuire." The audiences ate this up, and he was able to segue into his songs, dances, and imitations. No matter how corny, they laughed and applauded for more. Soon, Mickey started to draw big audiences in Chicago, Cleveland, Detroit, Pittsburgh, Milwaukee, St. Louis, and other stops in the midwestern tour.

• • •

WHEN FONTAINE FOX HEARD about Mickey's vaudeville act billing as McGuire, he called his lawyers, who sent cease and desist orders to Nell and Mickey, and to Will Morrissey. They were forced to stop the Mickey McGuire part of the act, and once again the audiences dried up. The country was also in the throes of the Great Depression, which had put a stake in the heart of vaudeville. The show closed, and Mickey and Nell were out of work.

Despite the cease and desist letter from Fontaine Fox, a desperate Nell tried to squeeze every bit of value out of the McGuire name. She took Mickey to grocery store openings, department stores, and restaurants across the country. They would get appearance fees of between one hundred and five hundred dollars for a couple of hours of singing, dancing, and signing.

"Mickey was like a trained monkey," recalled his friend Billy Barty in our interview. "I felt so bad for him. I know that Nell was just trying to earn a living, but he was dragged everywhere to make appearances in the McGuire getup."

In August 1932, feeling beaten and tired, Mickey and Nell returned to their modest home in Hollywood. Nell called Harry Weber and pleaded with him to find Mickey work at the studios. Former McGuire writer Gerald Beaumont recommended Mickey to Universal for a film he was writing called titled *Fast Companions*. While it wasn't a starring role, it did star box office attractions Tom Brown and Maureen O'Sullivan (Mia Farrow's mother and Tarzan's Jane).

In September, Universal founder "Uncle Carl" Laemmle was quite impressed with young Mickey at his audition for *Fast Companions*. He called Harry Weber and offered Mickey the pivotal role of Midge, and a six-year studio contract. Nell was thrilled that they had steady employment once again. Yet, after the injunction filed by Fontaine Fox, Laemmle was cautious regarding how to bill Mickey. Since Darmour had released him from his contract in August, this was the only obstacle to signing Mickey to a long-term agreement.

A hearing was held to decide if Mickey could retain the McGuire surname. Reporter Joe Crow of the *Hollywood Citizen-News* covered the hearing:

TWO MICKEYS OFFER PUZZLE TO HOLLYWOOD

(Los Angeles 2/11/33)—The McGuires, the Yules, the Stephenses, the Fontaine Foxes, the Darmours, the Laemmles and two or three judges—to say nothing of the poor newspaper people—were in a sorry muddle today over a matter of names.

It all centered around the question of which two Mickey (Himself) McGuires is really Mickey himself.

Also, it became known today through the w.k. Inside informant, a third Mickey—a Mickey Brown, whose name, with the qualifying statement that he is "professionally known as Mickey McGuire"—appears on a brand new six-year Universal contract now waiting court sanction.

One of the Mickey McGuires goes by the name Marvin Stephens in private life. It is this Mickey McGuire who is now playing Mickey for Larry Darmour Productions.

Baptized Joe Yule

The other Mickey McGuire was baptized Joe Yule Jr. who created the original Mickey roles, with Marvin Stephens in the featured part of Katrink. After his legal name change, he was known in private life as well as on screen as Mickey McGuire, being so called by his schoolmates and so billed in personal appearances.

Three weeks ago Fontaine Fox brought an injunction

against the 11-year-old lad restraining him from the use
of the name of the two-fisted cartoon character which Fox
made famous.

But Mrs. McGuire [still Mrs. Wynn Brown at that time]
came forward today to announce that the injunction had
been dissolved by Judge Walter Gates in Superior Court, and
that she intended to put the dispute to trial in order to clear
her son's asserted right to professional use of his legal name.

What Fontaine Fox and Larry Darmour will do about the
matter was still in the dark.

Meanwhile the Laemmles of Universal are going ahead, it
was reported, with plans to cast Mrs. McGuire's boy in *The
Jockey Kid*, probably in the title role. The McGuire's [sic]
and Laemmles have agreed to the stipulations of a six-year
contract, it was understood, although both parties have been
waiting for a definite outcome to the name dispute before
making the signing public.

Played with Colleen

The *Jockey Kid* role will be the most ambitious Mickey has
essayed since he came to California five years ago to play
with Colleen Moore in *Orchids and Ermine*, in which he
played the midget, being dubbed in the film "the big hog
man from Walla Walla."

Mickey made his first stage appearance when he was
15 months old, his mother says. As a wee he did a vaudeville
act with Sid Gold, a one-time partner of the legendary Babe
LaTour. When he was four, he had a special permit from
Governor Al Smith to play New York.

He played recently in *City Sentinel* at MGM, in *High
Speed* with Buck Jones, and in *Riffraff.*

A natural blonde, Mickey, or Joe Jr., was forced to dye his hair black for the Mickey roles. Now he plays "straight." [20]

When Universal discussed how Mickey was to be billed, Mickey and Nell had to make a decision. They certainly wanted to keep the first name of Mickey. However, "Mickey Yule" did not flow quite right. The Universal publicity man suggested something that ended with a *y* that would fit the first name. He suggested Maloney, Downey, even Looney. When he mentioned Looney—it was essentially as a joke—it reminded Nell of an old friend from vaudeville, Pat Rooney. Like McGuire, it gave him an Irish last name. After the PR guy ran it by the producer, they all agreed upon the last name of Rooney. According to Mickey, he was told, "Well, kid, that's your new name, 'Mickey Rooney.'"

"Making the transition [from McGuire] was not a problem for me," Mickey wrote in *Life Is Too Short*. "After all I was going to play kid parts for the next twenty years." [21]

3

Ma Lawlor and Universal Studios

Sonny Yule dons his first tuxedo at age two to perform in burlesque.
PHOTO COURTESY OF ROBERT EASTON.

The newly christened Mickey Rooney was a source of profit for Laemmle and Universal. He was a versatile child performer who had great energy and such diverse talents that he could be used in a multitude of films. Not only could he sing and dance, and exuded a great natural charisma, but he had the chops to perform comedy or drama. So Laemmle could both have him act in Universal films and loan him out to the other studios for a handsome profit: While his starting salary at Universal was $175 per week, he could command fees as high as $3,000 in loan-outs. So even though Mickey was making far less than he had with Darmour, his talent, Weber hoped, would eventually bring him a larger salary. Weber told Nell they could "pick up the difference" in the fast-fading but still relatively lucrative small theater vaudeville gigs.

While Mickey was working on his first official films for Universal, *Fast Companions* and *My Pal, the King,* the Mickey McGuire comedies continued to be released, because Darmour had stockpiled his films. By 1934, when Mickey was two years into his Universal agreement, Darmour was releasing the shorts through Columbia Pictures. However, any hopes of his continuing the series through Columbia were dashed with the arrival of a young Jules White, who became head of the new Columbia shorts department. White was determined to release only shorts produced at Columbia's Gower Studios. He had discovered a young comedy team called the Three Stooges, who would anchor the Columbia shorts for the next twenty-four years. Mickey knew the Stooges well. He had toured with Ted Healy and His Stooges throughout the Midwest in the summer of 1932.

Mickey Rooney settled into his new home at Universal, at least for the ensuing year and a half. At that time, Universal Studios had hit hard times along with most of the studios facing dwindling audiences due to the ongoing Great Depression. While Universal was doing well with its stable of horror films such as *Frankenstein* and *Dracula* and their respective sequels, and with B pictures and dramas such as *Imitation of Life* and *All Quiet on the Western Front*, it faced several financial challenges, which culminated in its 1936 financial collapse. Yet while the studio was teetering, Mickey was making progress.

His next feature at Universal, *Fast Companions*, was loaded with some wonderful performers: Maureen O'Sullivan was loaned from MGM, character actors James Gleason and Andy Devine added color, and Tom Brown was cast as the romantic lead. The film was quite successful, and the critics applauded Mickey's performance. Film critic Jack Townley of the *Hollywood Citizen-News* wrote, "A sure-fire heart interest angle is introduced in the jockey's [Tom Brown] befriending a hungry young urchin (Mickey Rooney) who thereafter refuses to leave his side. It is through the kid's idealistic hero worship that the jockey turns straight. Mickey Rooney, known in short comedies as Mickey McGuire, is splendid as the youngster." [1]

Laemmle took advantage of Mickey's critical acclaim and loaned him out to every studio that asked. He appeared in late December at Allied Studios with character actor Monte Blue in *Officer Thirteen*; in January 1932 with animal expert Clyde Beatty in *The Big Cage* at RKO; then to Warner Bros. for the James Cagney film *Reform School*. Columnist Harrison Carroll wrote in the *Los Angeles Evening Herald Express*, on January 13, 1933, that "while we know that Archie Mayo will direct the film, production head Darryl Zanuck selected little Mickey Rooney before he decided to cast Cagney."

Mickey had gained enough popularity by this point to become attractive to radio producers as entertainment radio was flexing its muscles at the outset of the Great Depression. He made his first radio performance on January 2, 1933, for the program *Hollywood on the Air*. Zumma Palmer in the *Hollywood Citizen-News* wrote on January 2, 1932, "[O]ne of the performers was Mickey Rooney, child actor. Before going on the air he took off his overcoat and hat, but left on his new pigskin gloves. One of the visitors pleased the youngster by noticing the gloves. Mickey held up his hands and said, 'Ain't them honeys?'"

Mickey still toured during his free time. In March of 1933 he was at the New Orleans Orpheum Theater in a vaudeville show along with the film *The Cohens and Kellys in Trouble*," a cross-religion marital triangle story loosely following a tradition established by the 1928 comedy *Abie's Irish Rose*. About Mickey's stage appearance, the New Orleans *Times-Picayune* wrote on March 24, 1932, "Three headliners will occupy the stage: Mickey Rooney, the screen counterpart of Mickey (Himself) McGuire of Toonerville comic strip fame; Tom Patricola, New Orleans dancer who is back home after a season in the movies at Hollywood and vaudeville on Broadway; and Lester Cole and his Singing Soldiers of fame. Imitations of movie stars including Maurice Chevalier and Roscoe Ates, will be specialized in by Mickey, who also sings and dances. He is an exciting young talent."

In 1933, but also in later years, Mickey spent his idle hours swimming, boxing, bowling, and playing tennis and table tennis Despite his height, he was good at all these sports and exceptional at tennis and Ping-Pong. When Mickey was just beginning his interest in tennis, he appeared in the annual Motion Picture Tennis Tournament, playing doubles with movie star Gilbert Roland, movie mogul Carl Laemmle Jr. (his boss at Universal), and producer Albert J. Cohen.[2]

There was hardly a free moment for Mickey, and his mother worried that he wasn't getting a proper education. Because of the large presence of the entertainment industry within its borders, California has some of the most explicit laws protecting child actors, laws that go back as far as 1928. A child actor, because he or she is a minor, must secure a state-authorized entertainment work permit before accepting any paid performing work. Compulsory education laws mandate that the education of the child actor not be disrupted while the child is working, whether the child actor is enrolled in public, private, or even a home school. While on set, the child does assigned schoolwork under the supervision of a studio teacher.

Thus, during and after Mickey's McGuire years, Mickey's education was divided between a public school and a studio classroom, which he attended whenever he was making a film. Mickey was not a scholar in either place. He was too restless to sit with his nose in a book for very long. He didn't mind geography or history, but arithmetic wasn't for him, which became glaringly obvious in his later years from the way he handled his finances.

It is likely, given his lifestyle and his family's nomadic existence during his early years, that Mickey was too distracted to be happy within the confines of the average public schoolroom. In addition, he might have had attention deficit disorder and even a language problem, even though he was able to master dialogue. He constantly spewed obscenities, not only in the company of other children, but also in front of the teachers. During his short career in public schools, he was warned repeatedly to curb his language or face expulsion.[3] This tendency was exacerbated by the attitude of Larry Darmour and Al Herman, who encouraged Mickey to speak in a rough, colloquial way. They felt that the tougher Mickey talked, the more it would en-hance the McGuire character. Thus, when it came to acceptable social skills, the demands of Mickey's career at a very early age impacted him negatively. Regardless of his classroom performance and deport-ment, though, California law still required him to attend school.

As early as 1928, while Mickey had established his career, and even while he was at Universal, Nell arranged for him to have the education she had not enjoyed when she was a child. She was encour-aged by McGuire director Al Herman to take Mickey out of public school and enroll him at the Lawlor School for Professional Children. The school was nicknamed "Ma Lawlor's" after the headmistress, Mrs. Viola Lawlor. Mrs. Lawlor, however, was far from the moth-erly type. She was tall, wore her hair in a severe bun, and was very much a no-nonsense, strictly conservative educator. Still, she was aware of the needs of working children and kept the curriculum light and manageable.[4] After all, her students were working professionals whose careers were important to their employers. Accordingly, the school ran its classes on a looser schedule than public schools. Classes were held only in the morning, leaving students free in the afternoon for auditions and rehearsals. Ma Lawlor never made a fuss when her students missed school to take an out-of-town job. Some of her students attended school in name only, because they were either on set or on location. Mickey was not far off as he explained to us, "Ma Lawlor's school was just a dodge, a way of pacifying the Los Angeles Board of Education." Mickey started at Ma Lawlor's in late 1928. The August 28, 1927, issue of the *Los Angeles Times* published the first glimpse into the Lawlor School for Professional Children: "Two years ago, Mrs. Viola Lawlor, considering the need for a school for professional children, started the Hollywood Professional Children's School. This year, additional space and more teachers have been added to accommodate the enrollment. The reasons for this success are said to be individual instruction, assuring rapid advancement, tuition fees within the reach of every one and half-day sessions. The school is being recommended by acting, music and dancing teachers because their pupils have the entire afternoon in which to do their practicing. Mrs. Lawlor is assisted by May Ely, who has full charge of the instruction. Enrollment will take place between September 6 and 10 . . . and personalized courses of instruction were promised for each student. All grades were taught, kindergarten through high school."

The Lawlor school had impressed the newspaper with the professional credentials of the faculty, which included violinist Lizette Kalova, actor Arthur Kachel, and pianists Philip Tronitz, Alexander Kosloff, and Frances Mae Martin.

While Mickey was never the great student, he fit in far better at Ma Lawlor's than at public school. The Lawlor faculty was more accepting of his personality as a performer than teachers in public schools had been, he was in his niche, his own element, at the school. He loved being around other child performers. They accepted his idiosyncrasies as he did theirs. He met many of his lifelong friends at the school. Deanna Durbin, film director Dick Quine, Jackie Cooper, his costar Judy Garland, and one of his closest friends, Sidney Miller.

Mickey had already known Miller, who had appeared in some

Mickey McGuire films. Mickey looked up to Sid, who was about four years older. Tall and thin, with a distinctive hawk nose, Sid was under contract to Warner Bros. He and Mickey became close friends over the years, and Sid often served as Mickey's personal assistant and became his confidant. "When I did the McGuire films, Mickey was of course the star. I had some *ferkakta* part," Miller told us in a 1996 interview. "My first impression of Mickey was that he was a 'tough,' like the character he was playing. You could see how talented he was. He knew his craft. He is one of the only actors I know who could cry, on cue, without any inducement. His focus in front of the camera was absolutely amazing. I knew right there that Mickey was going to be a big star someday." [5]

Of Nell, Miller told us, "I remember that his mother was always there on the set with him. Her presence was always felt. I mean, my mother was there as well, but I don't think she paid attention to what I was doing. Not Nell. She made sure that Mickey was up there, in front of the older actors. Her boy was the best. He was doing what he was supposed to be doing, stealing the scenes from the older actors. He really got that drive and ambition from Nell, not that he needed to be pushed. It was built in. It certainly wasn't from Joe." [6]

Another person Mickey met at Ma Lawlor's ultimately became very important to him, in both his life and his career. In fact, Mickey told interviewers many times, including the *Hollywood Reporter*'s Scott Feinberg, that she became his first love. This young girl was Frances Ethel Gumm. Born in Grand Rapids, Minnesota, in 1922, she was nicknamed Babe, since she was the youngest of three sisters. Her parents ran a movie theater that featured vaudeville acts, and much like Mickey, she began singing onstage early, at two and a half. Along with her two siblings, she appeared as one of the Gumm Sisters at their parents' theater. Following rumors that her father, Frank Gumm, had made sexual advances toward male ushers, the family relocated to California in June 1926. Frank purchased and operated another theater in Lancaster, and mother Ethel, acting as their manager, began working to get her daughters into motion pictures. By 1934, they had changed their name to the Garland Sisters, after being called the Glum Sisters by a Chicago critic. Frances changed her name to Judy after a famous Hoagy Carmichael song, "Judy," which he wrote with Sammy Lerner.

Mickey reminisced to us about seeing Babe, as Judy was referred to by her friends, for the first time at Ma Lawlor's: "She was very plain. You never would have noticed her. Then Mrs. Lawlor asked her to introduce herself to everyone with a song. I can remember it like it was yesterday. She sang 'Blue Moon,' and her voice just hit you. *Boom.* I mean when she hit that last note time stopped and everyone was cheering and clapping. It was amazing. I was in awe. We became such good friends. She had more bounce to the ounce than anyone." [7]

According to Gerald Clarke's biography of Judy, *Get Happy: The Life of Judy Garland*, it was a mutual admiration society between Judy and Mickey. She thought Mickey bounced high himself. "Well, I met Mickey Rooney," Babe said the day she first came home from Ma Lawlor's. "He's just the funniest . . . he clowns around every second!" [8] Later, Mickey, along with another Lawlor student, Frankie Darro, would drive out to Frank Gumm's Valley Theater to watch the Gumm Sisters perform. Sometimes, Darro and Mickey would jump on the stage and join in with the sisters. It was a good life for Mickey: a series of movies for Larry Darmour and classes at Ma Lawlor's with his new friends. But just as he'd settled into being comfortable at Ma Lawlor's, Fortune's Wheel took another spin in his favor when the films he'd made for Universal in loan-outs to other studios were released and accolades and recognition started pouring in.

Mickey promoted his films nonstop and appeared in countless benefit performances throughout Los Angeles with other celebrities. His youth and energy drew much attention, which he always enjoyed. The spotlight shone on Mickey, and he performed, as expected. Arthur Marx told us, "He was a young trained seal. An organ grinder's monkey. I can never remember him being off. He was always *on*." This work ethic, this countless round of appearances, never off camera and never offstage, would inform Mickey's life to the end of his days.

Meanwhile, Mickey continued his prolific output of films through loan-outs to almost every studio, large and small. In March 1933 he appeared in Warner Bros.' *The Life of Jimmy Dolan*, a film that costarred a youthful Loretta Young and Douglas Fairbanks Jr. In May 1933 he went to Eagle Pictures, located on Poverty Row, to appear in the cheapie B movie *The Big Chance*, with J. Carrol Naish and others. It reunited him with Al Herman, who directed the film. Then, in June, he went to MGM to make his first film there with his pal and fellow child star Jackie Cooper, *Broadway to Hollywood*. Cooper later said, "Mick and I had so much in common. We were quick friends."[9] That film was also the screen debut of singing star Nelson Eddy.

The nonstop work continued in 1933. Among Rooney's films were *The World Changes*, which featured Paul Muni and was directed by the legendary Mervyn LeRoy. Then it was *The Chief*, with radio comic and vaudevillian Ed Wynn. Mickey was being exposed to almost every type of film, from comedy, musical, melodrama, and mystery. His roles varied but were mostly minor. While he was still a background player, Mickey made the most of his screen time. "His performances always brought a burst of energy to each film," remarked film historian Lou Sabini.[10] Rooney appeared in six films through his Universal contract in 1933. He also performed in vaudeville, signed autographs, appeared on radio, did benefit performances, and attended school. It would be an exhausting schedule for an adult performer; however, he was only twelve and thirteen years old.

For Mickey, 1934 was a watershed year. He started the year back at his home studio of Universal in *Beloved*, a tearjerker with John Boles and Gloria Stuart (who sixty years later would star in the James Cameron–directed *Titanic*). He followed with another drama, *I Like It That Way*, also with Gloria Stuart. He quickly filmed the comedy *Love Birds*, which featured comic actors Zasu Pitts and Slim Summerville. In May he moved on to the romantic comedy *Half a Sinner*, which starred Joel McCrea and was based on a successful Broadway play.

Nell asked for a break for Mickey in early 1934, so he could appear in some summer vaudeville shows, as the $175 weekly salary at Universal was barely keeping them afloat. With the cost of Ma Lawlor's school and outside interests, they were not getting rich. Carl Laemmle Jr., who was now head of production at his father's company, refused, and instead sent Mickey to the Poverty Row studio Mascot to do a serial with famed animal trainer Clyde Beatty. Mickey was thrilled to work with the lion tamer, whom many kids had idolized through his pulp books. Nell, though, was less than thrilled with the frantic pace of putting Mickey in a Saturday afternoon serial, which was being released through March of 1934. She was "fed up," according to Mickey, that his career seemed to be stuck in one gear.[11] Mickey was working, receiving his weekly stipend, but the roles remained marginal, and Nell feared that although he was getting good work, he was not getting any real traction as a headline performer. She was ambitious for her son and saw in him a future as a major star.

It was at this time in January 1934 that Nell separated from Wynn Brown and sought a divorce. She and Brown had drifted apart, and she wanted him out of their way. Mickey was earning far more than Brown, who was still an auto salesman in the San Fernando Valley. Mickey was heartbroken. He and Wynn had established a good relationship.

"Mickey had grown very close to Wynn," recalled Sidney Miller.

"He cared about Mickey, who looked up to Wynn. He took us to ball games and was a pretty straight guy. It was kinda surprising when Nell dumped him. I mean she was a rather plain, sorta heavier woman. She was very tough and matter-of-fact." [12]

Mickey remembered, "I thought we had a good thing going in the family, but then, all of a sudden Wynn was leaving. He came to see me one day and said that he and mother were getting a divorce. 'You mean,' I said, 'that we're not going fishing anymore?' He smiled bravely and said he guessed not. "No more baseball and football games? No more fights or wrestling matches?' He turned away so I couldn't see him cry. But I cried. I cried like a baby. I had lost another dad." [13]

4

Selznick Rescues Mickey: The Start at MGM

Mickey and his longtime manager, "Hurry-up" Harry Weber, signing his contract at MGM. It was Weber who secured Mickey the Mickey McGuire *series, a contract with Universal, and his agreement with MGM.*
PHOTO COURTESY OF ROBERT EASTON.

Although Mickey was gaining some momentum in feature films, he still was featured in mostly minor roles at Universal and in the loanouts. His career seemed to be leading nowhere. His salary had not risen in the year and a half since he had started working in the studio. Nell, who wanted stardom for her son, complained to manager Harry Weber that Mickey's career was "stagnant." Weber attempted to renegotiate the agreement with Laemmle Jr., but the studio boss refused. So the manager asked to release Mickey from his agreement.

Junior acquiesced on the condition that Mickey work on one more film, a loan-out to Warner Bros. titled *Upper World*.[1] Weber agreed, convinced that Rooney had enough recognition to move on to more significant parts.

Weber turned out to be quite prescient: MGM came calling. While there is no definitive tale of how Mickey was hired by MGM—Mickey's accounts (he had several) seem mostly apocryphal—we have cobbled together the most logical version of how it occurred. We heard the same story retold by Jackie Cooper, Sidney Miller, Billy Barty, Carla Laemmle (niece of Universal Studios founder Carl Laemmle), and several others whom we interviewed, and the following version contains the most common threads reinforced by our research.

The dreamed-of "big break" was to come from the unlikeliest of sources, a game of table tennis one Sunday afternoon in March 1934 when Mickey was appearing in an exhibition match at the Ambassador Hotel. Seeing that he had an appreciative audience, the ham in Rooney kicked in and he began to show off. "I entertained them," he later wrote in *Life Is Too Short*, "with a line of picturesque speech and patter and some pantomime that had them in hysterics."[2] One of those most delighted by Rooney's antics was the game's referee, who turned out to be none other than David O. Selznick, an avid table tennis fan. The now-legendary moviemaker was then a bright, young producer at MGM, where he worked under his father-in-law, Louis B. Mayer. Following the match, Selznick reportedly tried to convince Mayer to sign his new discovery, but Mayer, already familiar with Mickey Rooney's work, told Selznick that Rooney, at fourteen, was a has-been.

Selznick, undaunted by his father-in-law's dismissal, wrote a sixteen-page memo to Mayer on why MGM should reconsider making an investment in the teen. He also cast Rooney in a small showcase one-off performance in his latest production, *Manhattan Melodrama* (1934), a Depression-era pre-noir film set to star Clark Gable, William Powell, and Myrna Loy. That there was no part for a boy in the gangster film did not faze Selznick, who called in writers Joseph L. Mankiewicz and Oliver H. P. Garrett to write one. This resulted in new scenes showing Clark Gable's character, Blackie, as a boy, played by Mickey Rooney of course.

Mickey received strong reviews for his small part. Harrison Carroll of the *Los Angeles Evening Herald Express* wrote on June 21, 1934, ". . . and little Mickey Rooney is rather impressive as a young Blackie." Mickey became an immediate sensation, and the Mickey Maguire typecast disappeared. The now-blond actor was now just Mickey Rooney.

Manhattan Melodrama, about two boys growing up in a tough Manhattan neighborhood who wind up on opposite sides of the law (Gable a hoodlum kingpin and Powell the district attorney who would send him to the electric chair) was what bank robber John Dillinger was watching in the "air-cooled" Biograph Theater to escape the summer heat in Chicago on July 22, 1934, when he was shot and killed. Audiences nationwide flocked to see the last film Dillinger watched.

Rooney's standout performance in *Manhattan Melodrama* forced Louis B. Mayer to reconsider his earlier dismissal, and on July 30, 1934, the studio head offered Mickey a much-coveted contract with MGM.[3]

While Mayer acquiesced to Selznick, he refused to offer anything more than $150 per week. Nell and Mickey had been hopeful that being at the Tiffany of the studios would lead to a more lucrative agreement, but this was less than Mickey had received as a Universal contract player and far less than he had received to play McGuire. The MGM agreement was also far more restrictive than the Universal contract. It curtailed any outside vaudeville work, which Nell had relied on for the bulk of their income. Still, Nell saw a bright future for Mickey at MGM, and was willing to settle even though it was a detrimental compromise. "Why be famous and not be able to cash in on it?" Mickey once remarked.[4]

Mickey found himself out on loan during those first couple of years as an L. B. Mayer contractee. "MGM didn't lend me, it rented me out at two or three times my MGM salary," Mickey recalled. "Of course I had no way of knowing this at the time."[5]

In fact, in 1934 it loaned him out three times more than the studio itself used him. Mickey remembered, "They not only got my services free, but they made money on me to boot . . . [I]t was something like slavery, except that slaves, at least can feel the whip."[6]

For instance, Mickey was loaned to Warner Bros. to play a jockey (a role he frequently played over the years) in the low-budget *Down the Stretch.* The film, which was shot in August 1934, was not released until 1936. MGM received $600 a week for four weeks of work, for a total $2,400 from Warners. Mickey received $600 in total, which made for a profit of $1,800 for MGM. Selznick had been right in his memo: Mickey was a great investment.

When looking back at this seventy years later, Mickey grew angry. "I appreciate everything Mr. Mayer did for me, but that wouldn't work today. But I was far better off than my father, who was scraping by in a cheap burlesque joint," he recalled in 2007.[7]

When Mickey left Universal in 1934, let out of his contract by Carl Laemmle Jr., his deal was that he still owed the studio two films. Therefore, he had two separate contractual obligations at the same time to different studios. By then, Mickey had appeared in a total of eleven films. It was an amazing output for one so young.

PRIOR TO SIGNING THE MGM agreement that restricted Mickey's vaudeville appearances, Nell cashed in one last time. Mickey made appearances on the West Coast as Mickey Rooney but dressed as Mickey McGuire. This benefited old cast mate Billy Barty, too, who recalled, "I was basically out of work after the *McGuire* shorts ended in 1932. I did some bit parts in a *Gold Diggers* film [*Gold Diggers of 1933*] and an *Alice in Wonderland* one, but it was a very dry period. Nell contacted my mother to appear with Mick in some live shows. This was right before Mickey signed with MGM. We were so happy to see each other again. It was like a reunion of sorts."[8] Barty also recalled receiving about a hundred dollars per week on the tour, although he was unaware of what Mickey was earning.

Mickey then appeared at MGM in August 1934's *Hide-Out*, by director W. S. "Woody" Van Dyke, who also directed the *Thin Man* films. The comedy starred Robert Montgomery as a racketeer hiding from the law and Mickey's former costar Maureen O'Sullivan as the unsuspecting farm girl whom he falls for. O'Sullivan remembered, "Woody loved that Mickey could improvise. They padded his part beyond the script. He was in a couple films before that with me and later played my kid brother in 'Hold That Kiss.' He is an amazing talent."[9]

Variety on October 31, 1935, raved about him: "Rooney well-nigh steals the picture." Right out of the gate, under his fresh new agreement with MGM, he hit a home run. Mayer was pleased, and Selznick pointedly reminded him of his "Mickey" memo. Mayer's son-in-law had been prophetic. Mickey was a bankable star as well as an amazing talent.

A Midsummer Night's Dream

Mickey as Puck in A Midsummer Night's Dream *in 1935.*
Poster courtesy of the Monte Klaus Collection.

Before Mickey signed his new contract at MGM, he was effectively a free agent and had started to draw attention with *Manhattan Melodrama* and *Hide-Out*. While his mother anxiously waited for Harry Weber to finalize the agreement with Mayer, Mick spent his summer playing tennis and enjoying the respite from work. Nell had rented them a recently constructed Spanish-style house designed by architect Vincent Treanor in 1929, in the neighborhood of Carthay Circle. Finally, they were in their own home and out of the many cramped rooming houses they'd been forced to live in. The four years Mickey Rooney would spend in that house on Schumacher Drive would be among the most important of his career.[1]

The ambitious Nell, who religiously scoured the Hollywood trade papers every morning, one day read with interest of the open casting call for the great Max Reinhardt's production of Shakespeare's *A Midsummer Night's Dream* at the Hollywood Bowl. While the stage was daunting to many film actors, Mickey at fourteen was a seasoned pro. As for this production, the trades were rampant with rumors of noted actors who were interested in snagging a role. While Nell had no knowledge of anything connected to Shakespeare, friends told her that Mickey would be perfect for the role of the sprite Robin Goodfellow, otherwise known as Puck. She also read that "America's Sweetheart" forty-one-year-old Mary Pickford had shown some interest in the role, as had eighteen-year-old Olivia de Havilland. But any opportunity to join that cast would depend upon the decision of famed director Max Reinhardt.

Max Reinhardt was an Austrian-born Jew who lived in both Berlin and Salzburg, Austria, and had a worldwide reputation as the founder of the prestigious Salzburg Festival, where he became legendary as the director of stage spectacles such as *Faust*, *Oedipus Rex*, *The Miracle*, and, in 1927, a highly acclaimed production of *A Midsummer Night's Dream*, which he later brought to Broadway. Reinhardt was presciently correct in fearing Hitler's eventual Anschluss of Austria in 1938, and had sought permanent asylum in the United States in the summer of 1934. He quickly accepted an invitation by the Southern California Chamber of Commerce to produce and direct a revival of his 1927 production of *A Midsummer Night's Dream* at the Hollywood Bowl. The costly $125,000 extravaganza would be underwritten by the mostly "Jewish moguls," as the *Los Angeles Times* referred to them, at the major studios, according to author David Wallace.

Times publisher Harry Chandler cajoled them to "unzip their pocket-books" and bring some culture to Southern California.[2]

For Reinhardt, this was an important opportunity. He was known as a great stage director and an impresario, but he had met only reluctance in his attempt to become a film director, with studio bosses not convinced he could make the crossover from stage to screen. Reinhardt felt that if he could produce a great success—and he was confident that he would—with *Midsummer*, one of the studios might give him the chance to direct films.

Reinhardt sent his son, future film director and producer Gottfried Reinhardt, to make advance arrangements for the play. Gottfried recalled that his father sent a telegram to him in Los Angeles to secure a cast of "All-Stars," one that included Charlie Chaplin for Bottom, Greta Garbo for Titania, Clark Gable for Demetrius, Gary Cooper for Lysander, John Barrymore for Oberon, W. C. Fields for Thisbe, Wallace Beery for Lion, Walter Houston for Theseus, Joan Crawford for Hermia, Myrna Loy for Helena, and Fred Astaire for Puck.[3]

Though Reinhardt was clearly ambitious, he was self-deluded in dealing with these mega stars. Certainly none of these box office actors would be interested in working for a tenth of their salaries, and had nothing to gain from being involved in the difficult production, Shakespeare or not. So Gottfried placed announcements in the Hollywood trade papers and contacted the talent agencies and casting offices to let the industry know that he was holding open auditions for all the parts in the play.

Harrison Carroll of the *Los Angeles Evening Herald Express* wrote on June 14, 1934, that "actors and actresses have dropped their tennis rackets, picked up their Shakespeare anthologies and started practicing their elocution."

With Mickey at his leisure for the summer, Nell asked Harry Weber to ask MGM if he could try out for the part. Although the contract was not signed yet, it was nearly formalized, and she did not want to rock the boat if the studio had plans for Mickey. Mayer recognized the importance the experience would have for Rooney, and for MGM if the play was successful, and allowed him to try out for the role. Fortune, again, smiled. This time through Louie Mayer.

In late June of 1934, Mickey and Nell went to the suite at the Hollywood Roosevelt Hotel where Reinhardt was holding the auditions. The director's associate, Felix Weissberger, held court as hundreds of noted performers auditioned for him. He was immediately smitten with Mickey's looks. Physically, the young actor was exactly what he envisioned as the perfect Puck:[4] his small stature, age (Mickey was a young teenager), and looks (he had an impish, in fact, puckish, face). The important test, of course, was whether Mickey could handle the Shakespearean dialogue, not the street cant he spouted in *Manhattan Melodrama*. When Weissberger handed Mickey a script and asked him to read some stanzas of Puck's dialogue, Mickey furrowed his forehead, took a deep breath, and stumbled through Puck's opening lines as best he could.

> *How now, spirit, whither wander you? . . .*
> *The King doth keep his revels here tonight*[5]

As Mickey recalled, "Weissberger said, in his heavily accented English, 'Not bad, not bad. Now I vant you should go home and memorize all zis und come beck for anozzer audition. Verstehen sie?' He then handed me a script with my lines marked in red."[6]

This was indeed a challenge for a young actor trained in vaudeville and burlesque. However, that experience may have held a key to his tremendous skill as an actor. Dr. Kevin Hagopian, a film historian and professor of film at Penn State University, offers an interesting perspective on Rooney's training: "I strongly believe that his early training in vaudeville and burlesque gave him the tenacity to undertake roles like Puck. In burlesque, you undertook any part you were given. If the producer asked if you could play the trumpet, whether you could actually play or not, you answered in the affirmative. Then you went out and learned how. You performed before crowds that had no tolerance. You either succeeded or flopped on stage. There was no in between. It was a rough and tumble world and you learned to adapt. It taught great versatility. It was an amazing training ground. It was why I believe what the great film critic of the 1930s, Otis Ferguson, wrote in *The New Republic*, that 'James Cagney and Mickey Rooney were among the finest actors of their generation.' Both Cagney and Rooney were from burlesque and vaudeville." [7]

Nell beamed with pride as her son passed the first test. However, Mickey was anxious, and had little of his usual confidence with this audition. He carped to Nell, "I can never learn these words and make them sound right!" Nell reassured him that all it took was familiarity with the lines. Mickey then started to memorize Puck's speeches, with Nell feeding him his cues. Gradually he began to understand the character of Puck and get a feel for the rhythm of Shakespeare's verse. [8]

At the second audition, Mickey was letter perfect. Although he did not understand all Shakespeare's nuances, and he was still befuddled by the phrasing and archaic language, he just gave a reading of the lines as they were printed on the page. He imagined, with Nell's encouragement, the merry impish spirit of Puck. Weissberger was astonished as Mickey embodied the character, from Puck's mocking of the donkey's braying to his maliciously playful child's giggle. "Yah, goot!" Weissberger told Rooney, and then reminded him that he had one more hurdle. He had to get the approval of Herr Doctor Reinhardt. [9]

The day of the meeting with Reinhardt, Mickey and Nell waited nervously for the director's arrival. Although they had been through countless auditions and cattle calls, this one was different. Hollywood was abuzz about Reinhardt's production, and many performers felt that this could be the spotlight they needed to establish themselves firmly as accomplished actors. This was not for money or nationwide recognition; this was for prestige and honor.

A short time later, the imposing figure of Max Reinhardt strode majestically into the room at the Hollywood Roosevelt Hotel, where he was holding the auditions. Reinhardt nodded curt greetings to Mickey and Nell, and then dropped into a chair. Reinhardt was a squarely built man with piercing black eyes, which he fixed on Mickey momentarily before, through Weissberger—Reinhardt spoke very little English—ordering Mickey to begin.[10]

One could easily have become intimidated by this powerful man at such an important audition. But Mick was ready. He had faced audiences in burlesque since he was a year and a half old. He knew his lines and understood the character. He now had Puck down pat, understood the childish playfulness of the role above and beyond any meaning it had for an Elizabethan audience. Puck was an ebullient prankster, and Mickey understood that. With the confidence of a veteran performer at the Old Vic, he rattled off the lines with remarkable ease. He even added a few facial expressions and comedic touches. Then he emitted Puck's famous laugh-cum-cackle, which he had carefully worked on with Nell the previous night. Enchanted, the great and powerful Reinhardt cracked a rare smile and hired Rooney on the spot. "Forget Pickford and the others," Reinhardt told Weissberger and his son, Gottfried, "*Das Lache* [that laugh] *ich mag ihn gern* [I like it]."[11]

Mickey and Nell were elated that he got the part of Puck, a potential watershed in his career. Even better, he was hired at three hundred dollars per week, double his MGM salary. Reinhardt filled out the rest of the cast with Walter Connolly as Bottom, and for Flute, Sterling Hayden (who would later become the voice of Pooh in Disney's *Winnie the Pooh*). Reinhardt cast the trained Shakespearean actor

Philip Arnold as Oberon, Evelyn Venable as Helena, and a teenage Olivia de Havilland as Hermia. Mendelssohn's score was adapted by Erich Wolfgang Korngold; and Bronislava Nijinska choreographed the ballet, which featured dancer Nini Theilade. Rehearsals were set to begin in early September.

With the MGM contract signed, and with Mickey's casting as Puck, Louis B. Mayer was finally impressed: "I think we have a raw diamond on our hands," Mayer told Selznick, and agreed that his son-in-law had been right to push to get Rooney under contract.

After four weeks of rehearsal, the troupe was ready for the premiere. The *Los Angeles Illustrated Daily News* of September 5, 1934, carried the headline "Eddie Cantor to Preside at Big Reinhardt Feast." The article gushed about Max Reinhardt and the production of *Midsummer*:

> More than 250 men and women who have given most of their lives to the cultural development of Los Angeles and to entertaining the world from stage or screen or concert rostrum will pay tribute to Max Reinhardt, Viennese theatrical genius, at a dinner and reception at the Biltmore. Sponsors of the Reinhardt presentations of "A Midsummer Night's Dream" at the Hollywood Bowl commencing September 17 as hosts of this evening's dinner at which Rupert Hughes will act as toastmaster and at which Eddie Cantor will serve as Master of Ceremonies introducing such entertainers as Rubinoff, celebrated radio maestro; Ethel Merman, Broadway musical star; Hazel Hayes, concert and film singing star; Mickey Rooney, who plays Puck in the Reinhardt-Bowl presentations; and other celebrities.[12]

Early praise for the production was giving Mickey a certain acclaim he had never experienced before. The legendary gossip colum-

nist Louella Parsons, in the *Los Angeles Examiner*, proclaimed on
September 8, 1934:

> Mickey Rooney, the freckle-faced thirteen-year-old young-
> ster, is the very "Puck" that Max Reinhardt has been look-
> ing for all of these years. "He has that elfin quality, that
> mischievous impishness," said Reinhardt, "that is so diffi-
> cult to find, and he is the best Puck I have ever had."
>
> I sat in at the rehearsal of "Midsummer Night's Dream"
> and heard Mickey read lines that astounded me. It took
> a Reinhardt to discover this little boy's talents. "Mickey,"
> said Reinhardt, "is fantastic." And now what about our
> film producers? Are they going to let Max Reinhardt return
> to Salzburg without producing a Shakespeare play?

Before the play ever premiered, the Los Angeles papers covered
almost every rehearsal as if it were an event in itself. W. E. Oliver in
the September 13, 1934, *Los Angeles Evening Herald Express* wrote
the front-page story "Stars Frolic in Bowl Under Reinhardt's Eye." In a
story about the "production of the biggest outdoor Shakespeare effort
on record," Oliver extolled Reinhardt's "genius" and explained how
he was "modifying the spirit of 'Midsummer Night's Dream' to catch
the spirit of the California setting." The article focused on Mickey as
Puck "screeching in practice under the scaffolding."

On September 17, 1934, the big night—and a beautiful evening at
that—finally arrived at the Hollywood Bowl. Mickey remembered,
"The play went off without a hitch, not even a hitch in my jockstrap.
In fact, it seemed over almost before we knew it had begun. All of a
sudden, I was into my closing lines."

> *Give me your hands, if we be friends,*
> *And Robin shall restore amends.*[13]

Mickey recalled, "I raced up the long, flowered ramp to what I remember as thundering applause, a roar that I thought everyone in Los Angeles could hear. My gosh, I said to myself, they're cheering for me." [14]

The play was a complete triumph. Critics from coast to coast raved about it, making it a national sensation. Elizabeth Yeaman for the *Hollywood Citizen-News* wrote:

> Long before the memory of man, Dame Nature fashioned the Hollywood Bowl, endowed with wooded beauty and astounding acoustic properties. Shakespeare, preceding the imaginative fantasy of Walt Disney by over 300 years wrote his immortal play of love, sprites and buffoonery and called it "A Midsummer Night's Dream." Max Reinhardt, German of colorful, dramatic spectacle, assumed the task of blending these two miracles—one man-made and one wrought by a higher-power. And last night the Weather Man conferred his blessing on the undertaking by providing a midsummer's night of incredible perfection—a sky flecked with clouds that even a Reinhardt could not have produced and lighted by a moon suspended low against the Bowl horizon. And yet, even with the aid of Dame Nature, the Weather Man, Shakespeare and Max Reinhardt, "A Midsummer Night's Dream" would have lacked its wondrous fulfillment last night without the presence of Mickey Rooney, 13-year old Irish genius who was known, a year or so ago, as Mickey McGuire of short comedy fame. The achievement of Master Rooney in the role of Puck ranks second to none along with Shakespeare and Reinhardt.

Quite heady stuff, the kind of praise usually reserved for the crowning achievement of a career in the theater for the likes of an

Olivier, Barrymore, or Gielgud. This was for a Rooney, who was only thirteen years old.

And the accolades kept on coming. On September 20, 1934, Louella Parsons, in the *Los Angeles Examiner*, wrote, "This suggestion comes from Edgar Allen Woolf and it sounds like a good idea. Edgar, who was one of the first to persuade MGM to put Mickey Rooney, the inspired Puck of the Reinhardt festival, under contract [everyone was now claiming credit for having discovered Rooney], sees the child as Peter Pan. Always a girl has played the part—Maud Adams and Betty Bronson—but Mickey could do it and be more like Barrie's delightful character than anyone I know."

Selznick must have appreciated this chorus of cheers for Rooney. Mayer was thrilled, too, not just because he had the hottest child star under contract, but because he had him under contract for only $150 per week.

After twenty-seven sold-out days at the Hollywood Bowl, a record at that time, Reinhardt took the show on the road, according to plan. There were two weeks at the University of California at Berkeley; then onto the nearby San Francisco opera house for four weeks, where the play was standing room only; and then to Chicago for four weeks at the Blackstone Theatre. Beyond the sudden acclaim and spotlight, Mickey and Nell were thrilled with the $300 a week for the play and their $150 stipend from MGM. This was a windfall for them.

Meanwhile, back in Hollywood, no studios were rushing to fulfill Reinhardt's dream to direct. A Shakespeare film, hardly a commercial endeavor, was not alluring, especially in the midst of a depression. No doubt great prestige would be attached to such a film, but it would also create a large financial loss that most studios could not afford. The Laemmles at Universal were swimming in debt. Mayer and Thalberg rarely attempted "arty" projects. Zukor and Paramount considered the project, but were having an awful year financially. One studio was above water, though, and that was Jack and Harry Warner's Warner

Bros. It was doing quite well that year, with its gangster epics. And Jack Warner was interested in taking *Midsummer* on.

This was so for a few reasons, according to Kevin Hagopian, who, in recounting the history of the making of *Midsummer*, writes:

> It was to be Warner Brothers' entry into prestige film-making, a bid for the carriage trade by a studio whose trademarks were the staccato burp of the gangster tommy gun and the clatter of the newsman's city room. But there was no denying the noisy hoi polloi that was Warner Brothers in 1935. What emerged from its sound stages was a Mulligan's Stew of performance styles that showed off the vitality of American immigrant and ethnic culture at its most.
>
> Jack Warner's decision to take a flyer in high art would prove financially disastrous; the film lost heavily at the box office. But that's not what "A Midsummer Night's Dream" was all about. The Warner family had fled Krasnashiltz, then in Czarist Russia, in 1883, to escape the murderous anti-Semitism of the Cossack pogroms. Jack and three of his brothers had clawed their way to the top of the fledgling motion picture industry by the late 1920s, and now, Jack was eager to cement his new status as an American aristocrat. Warner had seen Max Reinhardt's "epic theater" production of "A Midsummer Night's Dream" at the Hollywood Bowl, and though he'd understood little of it and enjoyed even less, the appeal of Shakespeare to a boy from a shtetl family was irresistible. The colonnaded Greek-revival house in Beverly Hills, the exclusive private schools for his kids, the polo matches, the charity soirees, even the Ronald Colman mustache—"A Midsummer Night's Dream" was to be the capstone in a campaign to signal high society that

Jack Warner had arrived. This 1.5 million dollar production would seal Jack Warner's miraculous transformation from the 12th son of a Russian Jewish refugee to English gentility, a make over possible only in Hollywood. Warner determined to make "A Midsummer Night's Dream" tonier than anything his lot had ever produced.[15]

Indeed, Jack Warner heeded *Los Angeles Times* publisher Harry Chandler's call and unzipped his wallet to produce something of culture, the sound of flutes and the choreography of dancing sprites, to replace, at least for an hour and a half, the sound of submachine-gun fire and the ballet of bullets.

On October 7, 1934, about two weeks after the debut of the play, it was announced that Warner Bros. would produce the film version.

The casting of the film was of great speculation throughout Hollywood. Jack Warner wanted to include many of Warner's contract players, to bring them prestige. He was insisting on their hottest star, James Cagney, and on dancing star Dick Powell. He also wanted to use an English actor with a Shakespearean background, Ian Hunter. Reinhardt had no problem with the fact that many of the actors Warner wanted to cast had no experience with Shakespeare; the director had faced this in past productions. However, he wanted to be the auteur of the film and make his imprint on it.

Throughout the process of preproduction and into filming, Reinhardt, whose huge artistic ego was on the line since this was his first major Hollywood film directorial venture, butted heads with Jack Warner, whose financial ego was on the line. They disagreed in several areas. Reinhardt kept escalating the cost of the film, which infuriated Warner, and Reinhardt was aggravated over Warner's using William Dieterle as the lead director, because Reinhardt spoke very poor English. Another major argument took place when Mickey broke his leg. Warner wanted to replace Mickey with George Breakston, Mickey's understudy, but Reinhardt loved Mickey and refused, saying he would shoot around him while the actor's leg healed.

Reinhardt's son, film director Gottfried Reinhardt, claimed that Jack Warner "derived pleasure" from humiliating subordinates. "Harry Cohn was a sonofabitch," he said, referring to the head of Columbia, "but he did it for business; he was not a sadist. [Louis B.] Mayer could be a monster, but he was not mean for the sake of meanness. Jack was." [16]

Reinhardt thought Warner an illiterate, uncouth bully, but he needed to do this project to prove he could direct American films, and he was determined to do it his way. Elizabeth Yeaman of the *Hollywood Citizen-News* reported on October 30, 1934, about Reinhardt's assembling a staff of his own choosing:

> Speaking of technical experts, Warner appears to be making an effort to corner the market for their production of "A Midsummer Night's Dream." Max Reinhardt is supervising every aspect of the picture as they now have Erich Wolfgang Korngold, famous German composer to orchestrate the Mendelssohn music for the score; Bronislava Nijinskaia, sister of the famous dancer, Nijinsky, has been engaged to direct the dances; Anton Grot will design the sets; Max Rée will design the costumes; William Dieterle will direct; and Charles Kenyon and Mary McCall, Jr. are working on the screen adaptation of Shakespeare's play! So far only Mickey Rooney is engaged for the role of Puck and is the only member of the cast definitely set."

While the Rooneys assumed that MGM would easily loan Mickey out to Warner for *Midsummer*, Louis B. Mayer wanted to play some hardball. MGM producer/writer Sam Marx recalled, "Mayer knew he had Warner over a barrel . . . that little Mickey was the cornerstone to any success of that picture and that they needed him. Mick was getting next to nothing in salary, to boot. In the end, [Mayer] got ten times his salary and some great return cheap loan-outs [to MGM] for some Warner players." [17] This was one of the profit streams Mayer enjoyed by lending Mickey out for films he never would have made at MGM.

The drama of casting Mickey played out in the newspapers. On November 5, 1934, the *Hollywood Citizen-News* reported, "Despite rumors to the contrary, I have the assurance that Mickey Rooney will be definitely contracted for the role of Puck in the Warner production of 'A Midsummer Night's Dream' . . . although they suggested they could substitute young George Breakston in the role of Puck . . . however after seeing Rooney as Puck it would be a Herculean task for any other child to fill his shoes." On November 7, the paper printed an update: "[T]here is some confusion over Mickey filling the role of Puck." It was hard to keep up.

Mickey appeared sporadically in the traveling play (the first three performances in Chicago and for part of the run in San Francisco and Berkeley) because he was also being loaned out to the Fox Film Corporation to costar with Will Rogers in *The County Chairman*. His replacement in the play during this period was his understudy and threatened replacement in the film, George Breakston (who later played Breezy in the Andy Hardy films).

After much deliberation and bickering among the Warner brothers, the film version of *Midsummer* was budgeted at the then-astounding cost of $1.5 million. Oldest Warner brother, Harry unleashed his fury on his youngest brother, Jack, when he saw the budget, screaming, "Are you trying to destroy us for the name of prestige?"

Reinhardt was hired to direct, of course. However, director William Dieterle was brought in both to assist Reinhardt and to interpret for him in much the same way Weissberger had done in the stage production of the play. Under Reinhardt's supervision, Dieterle would carefully oversee every detail. Mickey was the first actor to be cast, followed by Olivia de Havilland. They were the only two who made the transition from the stage version to the screen.

On November 27, 1934, the studio and Reinhardt announced the casting of the film. As Elizabeth Yeaman reported in the *Hollywood Citizen-News*:

> Joe E. Brown will definitely play the role of "Flute" . . . [W]ith him will be Jimmy Cagney as "Bottom," Dick Powell as "Lysander," Jean Muir as "Helena" Donald Woods as "Oberon," Ian Hunter as "Theseus," Frank McHugh as "Snout," Otis Harlan as "Starveling," Grant Mitchell as "Egeus," Anita Louise as "Titania," Hobart Cavanaugh as "Philostrate," Ross Alexander as "Demetrius," Eugene Pallette as "Snug," and Arthur Treacher as "Ninny Tomb." [18] Frank McHugh ended up playing Quince.

The cast was a mix of some Warner players who had Shakespearean backgrounds, such as English actors Ian Hunter and Hobart Cavanaugh, and great character actors such as Eugene Pallette and Frank McHugh. Included in the cast, but not mentioned in Yeaman's column, were Olivia de Havilland and Mickey Rooney. Also on hand, based on Mickey's suggestion, was Mickey's friend from the McGuire shorts, Billy Barty, who would play the elfin Mustard Seed. There was some other interested casting with vaudeville comic Hugh Herbert, actor Victor Jory (who, instead of Donald Woods, ended up playing Oberon, and would go to play the evil overseer in *Gone with the Wind*), and celebrated dancer Nini Theilade.

Comic Joe E. Brown later remembered, "Some of us were certainly not Shakespearean actors. Besides myself from the circus and burlesque, there was Jimmy Cagney from the chorus and Mickey Rooney and Hugh Herbert from burlesque. At the beginning we went into a huddle and decided to follow the classic traditions in which Herbert and I were brought up. I really believe Shakespeare would have liked the way we handled his low comedy and I'm sure the Minsky brothers did. The Bard's words have been spoken better but never bigger or louder." [19]

Jimmy Cagney recalled that the actors often stood around on the sidelines whispering to one another and that Reinhardt didn't realize that some of them didn't understand the lines they were speaking. "Somebody ought to tell him," Cagney said in the November 1935 issue of *Screenplay* magazine. The confusion [over the meaning of Shakespeare's verse] didn't bother Dick Powell, who said he never really understood his lines, anyway."

Right before the start of principal photography, Mickey was reunited with his father, Joe Yule Sr.—a rare treat, as Mickey had had only intermittent contact with his dad over the previous ten years—and the two went to the Big Pines Resort in California, near Lake Tahoe. It was here where Mickey broke his femur while tobogganing. He later claimed, in *Life Is Too Short*, that he himself reset the break, or "yanked it back into position," and that the medics later told him he would make a great doctor. They put his leg first in a splint and then later a hard cast.

There have been some discrepancies among reports over when Mickey had last seen his dad. In both his autobiographies, *i.e.*, and *Life Is Too Short*, Mickey claims he did not see his father until after he had filmed *Boys Town* in 1938, a separation of about thirteen years. In both those books, Mickey claims to have gone to Big Bear with his mother even though newspapers said he had gone with his father to Tahoe.

Yet in an article by Elizabeth Yeaman in the *Hollywood Citizen-News* on January 15, 1935, she wrote, "It was a sad blow to Warner and the entire cast of 'A Midsummer Night's Dream' when young Mickey suffered while on a tobogganing expedition Sunday near Big

Pines. Mickey's father, Joe Yule Sr., ruefully admitted that there were 10,000 people on vacation at Big Pines Sunday and Mickey was the only one to be injured." No matter who was with him, the tobogganing accident became a national news event and a disaster for Warner.

The *Hollywood Citizen-News* reported on January 15, 1935:

> [A]ll the [Warner] executives went into a huddle yesterday to seek a solution to the great problem, since Mickey has already appeared in several scenes and the production is too expensive to be held over and wait until his leg permits him to run again . . . George Breakston is a brilliant little actor and had some fine notices for his work on the road as "Puck" and he knows the part just as well as Mickey Rooney. For the present, at least, Georgie will do the running and elfin sprints for the long shots in the picture. Warner may be able to use Mickey Rooney for the remaining close-ups.

Jack Warner was reportedly apoplectic. As Mickey wrote, "Jack Warner didn't get angry. He went insane. The first thing he wanted to do was kill me. 'Then after I kill him,' he said, 'I'm going to break his other leg."[20]

Arthur Marx wrote in his Mickey Rooney biography, and told us in an interview, "There was a special clause in Mickey's contract specifically forbidding him to engage in any contact sports."[21] This story (told by others as well) was untrue because Rooney, although he did have an agreement with Warner Bros. for this particular film, was under contract with MGM, not Warner Brothers.

IN THE END, WARNERS could not cut out the scenes already shot with Mickey. The studio had spent almost a quarter of the budget.

As reported in the *Hollywood Citizen-News*, the studio revised the shooting schedule, shot the long shots with George Breakston as Puck, and waited for Mickey to return.

In the end, Mickey spent the next months recuperating in a hospital bed at Hollywood Presbyterian Hospital in a heavy cast. Eleanor Barnes, in the *Hollywood Illustrated Daily News*, wrote on February 9, 1935:

> Mickey, gifted boy actor, left Hollywood Hospital yesterday after spending several weeks there with a broken left leg, suffered while tobogganing at Big Pine Lake. Although his leg is in a cast, Mickey insisted upon being taken to Warner Brothers' Studio, where he reported to Max Reinhardt and said he was ready to resume work on "A Midsummer Night's Dream." Mickey was given a rousing reception by James Cagney, Joe E. Brown, Jean Muir, Veree Teasdale [*sic*], Anita Louise and other players in the cast, and all of them autographed his cast.

Despite all the hype, Reinhardt's film adaptation of *A Midsummer Night's Dream* did rather poorly at the box office, as expected. The movie was a spectacle, to be sure, and it had a powerful cast, but the story itself didn't resonate with theatergoers during the height of the Great Depression. Moreover, audiences seemed surprised, and perhaps disappointed, to see the likes of James Cagney running around in theatrical versions of Elizabethan costumes and mouthing sixteenth-century verse. The reviews were mixed. The film won only two Academy Awards, for Best Cinematography and Best Film Editing (and was nominated for Best Picture and Best Assistant Director). While the cinematography, use of Mendelssohn's music, and dance sequences were highly praised, the acting received much criticism, especially Dick Powell's. Early on, Powell, then a "Hollywood crooner," had realized he was completely wrong for the role of Lysander and asked to be taken off the film, only to have Warner demand that he play the part.

Negative reviews notwithstanding, the film transported Mickey Rooney from the ranks of second-rate kid actors and into the forefront of child stars. He was talked about in every column, appeared on countless radio shows, and was now in demand for the choice roles at his home studio.

Did the film transform Jack Warner, as he had probably wished, from the "12th son of a Russian Jewish refugee to cultured English gentility"? Not at all. (However, it did vindicate Harry Warner's outrage over the oversize budget.) Yet Jack Warner's decision to open his wallet for what was surely going to be a money-losing proposition, and Max Reinhardt's acquiescence to the demands of a studio production populated by song-and-dance men and a teenage ingénue, Olivia de Havilland, who barely understood their lines at first, became a great Hollywood moment. The film brought the breadth and egalitarian optimism of Shakespeare's sylvan vision of a topsy-turvy society to an audience of everyday folk struggling to make a buck under the grinding weight of the Great Depression. And the magic of Mickey Rooney's Puck was at its center as, laughing like a mischievous child, he spouted to an audience of modern-day groundlings, "Oh, Lord, what fools these mortals be."

6

The Gates of Hell

Mickey holding his special Academy Juvenile Award.
PHOTO COURTESY OF ROBERT EASTON.

n his memoir *i.e.,* **Mickey Rooney** writes, "MGM was this vast factory, the General Motors of the movie business, dedicated to Mr. Mayer's views of morality, and to mass entertainment. For along with his public view of virtue, Mayer believed, publicly, privately, profoundly, in profit."[1]

Indeed, MGM's studio head, Louis B. Mayer, was a moneyman first and foremost, and he would do almost anything for the stuff. In fact, Mayer was once quoted as saying, "There's only one way to succeed in this business, step on those guys. Gouge their eyes out. Trample on them. Kick them in the balls. You'll be a smash."[2] Helen Hayes characterized Mayer as "an untalented, mean, vicious, vindictive person."[3] And that, more than anything, was what it was like working with L. B. Mayer. His unpalatable character shaped not only his business model as a studio head, but also his social relationships, especially the way he handled the talent in the studio star system he helped create—and it would shape Mickey Rooney's perception of the man who would turn him into the highest-grossing actor at MGM in the 1930s.[4]

"We will take care of you like family," a dissembling Louis Mayer once said to Mickey Rooney, addressing him like a father to a son.[5]

On August 2, 1934, riding the wave of success from the stage version of *A Midsummer Night's Dream*, Mickey strode triumphantly through the Culver City gates on his first day on the lot as an MGM contract player, when he was scheduled to meet with the great and powerful Louis B. Mayer. He had casually met L.B at tennis matches and other events, and they had had some polite conversations. Nobody or nothing intimidated Mickey. At fourteen-plus years, he had seen pretty much everything, and had met every type of character, from his drunken and abusive father Joe, to the loud and surly burlesque performer Pat White, to his mother's late-night dates in their living room, to the obnoxious bottom-feeding schlepper Larry Darmour, to the great auteur Max Reinhardt. He had seen every type of megalomaniac and had suffered the humiliating derision of narcissistic burlesque comedians before he was even five years old. He had also worked under directors and producers who were demanding and crude, flogging him to perform athletically in scene after scene even when he was so weary from a day's shooting that he could barely stand upright. He had lived no childhood, had inhabited no bubble of innocent bliss.

Louis Burt Mayer, however—who was born Lazar Meir in 1884 in Dymer, in the Kiev Governate of the Russian Empire, now Ukraine— was a completely different beast. He had earned his stake as a scrap metal dealer in the Boston area after his family emigrated from Russia to St. John in New Brunswick, Canada, driven out by the czar's pogroms. Mayer worked his hands bloody from the time he was a child and invested his savings from his scrap metal business into a small burlesque house, where he began showing motion pictures. Even then, he kept to the mantra of buying low and selling high—and that's how he ran his studio.

Mickey, when he strode through the gates in Culver City, did not realize they were actually the gates of hell. Mayer was the Mephistopheles to whom Mickey had sold his soul. The studio head ran an amoral enterprise, one completely detached from any form of human decency and devoid of anything but the projection of his power and his (and his board's) obsession with the bottom line. Mayer's morality was money, and his money derived from his control over his assets (the talent), control that was near fanatical. If rejection of any other morality was an affirmative act, then the "kingdom" of Louis B. Mayer was absolute in its amorality. For example, his control over the lives of his contract players was complete, from getting Clark Gable out of hot water after he ran over a pedestrian with his car, to obtaining abortions for young women who had been impregnated by MGM actors and executives. No one at MGM made any decisions for him- or herself unless Mayer approved. As Mickey would see firsthand, Mayer did not run a studio; he ran a feudal state in which he controlled the lives of his contract players, and a brothel for his employees and guests. (He even made sure the unfortunate starlets who became pregnant out of wedlock would get safe medical abortions.)

Author Scott Eyman sets forth a different view of Mayer in his book *Lion of Hollywood, the Life and Legend of Louis B. Mayer*.[6] In an interview for our book, Eyman, who did extensive research on Mayer's life and tenure at MGM, disputes many of the allegations leveled by E. J. Fleming in his book *The Fixers: Eddie Mannix, Howard Strickling, and the MGM Publicity Machine*.[7] Eyman has said that claims such as those raised by Helen Hayes, Ava Gardner, and Mickey Rooney about the evil nature of Louis Mayer are baseless.

Eyman writes that it was only business. "Mayer was first and foremost a businessperson. He would do nothing to damage any actor who was making a profit for his company based on spite or vindictiveness. The claims against Mayer destroying John Gilbert or any of his contract players is simply not true. Mickey Rooney, Judy Garland, John Gilbert, and the others whose careers spiraled downward were the victims of their own self-destruction. It happened by their own hand and was really not to be blamed on Mayer. They created their own problems."

Mayer, Mannix, Strickling, and their executives were just seeking to run a profitable company, Eyman attests. "Mickey's downfall occurred after he left the employ of MGM," Eyman remarked. "Even his later films at MGM were turning a profit. He left while Mayer was still in control of the studio, not [Dore] Schary. Mickey was his own worst enemy."[8] However, some of Mayer's actions do speak for themselves: for example, the doping with uppers and downers of Mickey and Judy, as film historian E. J. Fleming documents and as Mickey and Judy attested to in interviews over the years.[9]

In 1932, Mayer and Mannix decided to open up a company brothel to accommodate visiting exhibitors, overseas representatives, sales reps, and assorted actors. It was placed in a Victorian-era former boardinghouse located north of the Sunset Strip. They installed silent film actress Billie Bennett, who had appeared in fifty-two films between 1913 and 1930 to act as the "madame." Fleming claims in his book that when she ceased making films at the end of the silent era, Bennett ran this high-class bordello in this exclusive part of Los Angeles. Her girls were made up to look like movie stars of the period, even undergoing surgical alterations to achieve the illusion.[10] Charles Higham, in *Merchant of Dreams*, wrote, "One MGM executive veteran recalls that when a Mexican executive arrived [he had already placed his order] he wanted to bed a blond movie-star actress—any actress. Since it was impossible to organize a guaranteed night of sex, Billie Bennett arranged for a very pretty girl, the dyed-blond double of Jean Harlow, to become her for the night. Billie told the MGM veteran, 'It's all set up. But remember when he goes down on her, he's going to end up with a mouthful of peroxide.'" [11]

Mickey would soon, through the courtesy of fatherly Mr. Mayer, visit this MGM-designed fun house. In our interview with Fleming, he stated, "It was actually Groucho Marx who introduced him to this studio-sponsored whorehouse." [12]

MAYER WAS AIDED AND abetted in his machinations by the person who became his director of security and wound up as studio vice president, Joseph Edgar Allen John "Eddie" Mannix. Eddie Mannix started as a maintenance worker and bouncer at the Palisades Amusement Park, in New Jersey, owned by Nicholas Schenck, who early on noticed Mannix's ability to resolve problems and his toughness in handling crises. Mannix was also brilliant financially. Schenck promoted him to treasurer within a short period and relied on his unique skills in settling differences and handling people. When Schenck and his Loews Inc. created Metro-Goldwyn-Mayer, he sent Mannix to watch over L. B. Mayer, whom he did not trust. However, Mayer and Mannix were simpatico. They were both street guys who did whatever it took to succeed. Mayer appreciated the skills Mannix had to fix issues. They were both amoral and Machiavellian in every sense. Much to Schenck's displeasure, Mannix worked hand in hand with Mayer to build a kingdom that set its own rules, on its own terms. Mannix became the general manager and executive vice president of MGM. As Peter Evans writes in *Ava Gardner: The Secret Conversations*—in what was supposed to be a memoir but wound up as a series of interviews with his coauthor, Ava Gardner—Gardner claims that "Mickey said [Mannix] did Mayer's dirty work for him and Frank [Sinatra] later told me that he had Irish Mafia connections in New Jersey."

Evans continues: "But in all likelihood, Sinatra was right." [13]

Actor Roddy McDowall once described Mayer as "a very tough, able, responsible, energetic, and sometimes demoniacal creature. The figure of such tremendous theatricality. All those scenes he put on to accomplish his ends. Weeping and wailing. That was his way . . . So, there Mr. Mayer was Daddy, and so on and so on. Mr. Mayer was a very shrewd guy." [14]

Esther Williams wrote about Mayer, "MGM, as far as L. B. Mayer was concerned, was one big happy family. Well, he used the word "happy." A lot of people weren't happy. He thought he was our father. First of all, he was the son of a pushcart junk dealer, and here he has all this power. What does he come up with so that he can get by with it and his lack of education and culture? Intimidation! That was his number one tool. He was such an actor; the biggest ham on the lot. Oh, he'd throw himself on the floor and foam at the mouth. I always wondered what he would put in his mouth so he could do that." [15]

"It was almost feudal in the way it was so self-contained," remembered actress Janet Leigh to author Scott Eyman.[16] "Everything was grown inside. It was a complete city. There were doctors and dentists, there were people to teach you acting and singing and dancing. There were people to help you with your finances. You could live there. And the people were like family, because everybody was under contract, not just the actors and producers, but the electricians. If I finished one picture, I might find a different crew on the next one, but the one after that would probably have the same crew from the first picture. You had a sense of being surrounded by friendly, familiar faces; you had great continuity.[17]

"MGM functioned like General Motors," remembered actor

Ricardo Montalban. "It was run with such efficiency that it was a marvel. It was done by teamwork. They could project the product, and the product was not any individual movie, it was the actor. They created a persona that they thought the public would like; they tailor-made the publicity to create a persona throughout the world. It was amazing." [18]

Ava Gardner remembered Mayer as "not an attractive-looking man, which wasn't his fault, but he made me uncomfortable the way he looked at me through his small, round, gold glasses."

Evans writes, "[H]e had a mottled-pink face, a thin, hard mouth, and a large head of thinning white hair. But neither his expensive suits nor the rose-colored polish on his manicured fingernails could detract from the power of his body."

"[H]e was very sure of himself," said Ava. [19]

When Mickey signed his agreement in August 1934, Irving Thalberg was still the head of production. Until Thalberg's untimely death in September 1937, Mayer bowed to Thalberg's choices of product. However, L.B. still oversaw every aspect of the studio and was very particular as to what talent would become part of the MGM family. He told producer Sam Marx that Mickey had the "perfect Goyim look." [20]

Mayer's vision for MGM's films was quite different from Thalberg's. Mayer believed that MGM should be the "ultimate creator of cinematic fantasies," writes blogger Chris Whiteley, "and the maker of many classic movies of all genres, which painted for world consumption Mayer's rosy, idealized picture of an innocent and wholesome America, which never, in fact, existed. With great energy, skill and determination he built MGM into the most financially successful motion picture studio in the world." [21]

Upon his first "official" meeting with young Rooney, Mayer wanted both to establish trust and to leave Mickey with the complete understanding that he, Mayer, was in control. He had heard tales of

Mickey's mischievousness and his tendancy to improvise in scenes, disregarding the written word, which Mayer might have regarded as simple adolescent behavior that had to squelched at the outset. Their meeting was scheduled for the early morning—the first on L.B.'s calendar that day. Nell wanted Harry Weber to attend it, but Mayer forbade that. He wanted to talk to Mickey one on one, father to son, if you will.

Mickey entered L.B.'s plush inner office, which was custom-designed with white leather walls, a wraparound desk, and an adjoining soundproof telephone room where Mayer could consult with New York a half dozen times a day. At the end of the room, Scott Eyman writes, "behind a white-leather-sided crescent-shaped desk, sat the five and a half feet and 175 pounds of Louis (always pronounced Louie) Burt Mayer, who made the decisions that helped shape the parameters of the American Dream for twenty-five years of the twentieth century. He looked rather like a very small, very charming white penguin, and he had soft, silken hands that disguised the fact that he had done manual labor for years." [22]

"Young man, we are all happy to have you join our family," Mayer proclaimed as he slid an arm around Mickey's shoulder, "You know I care deeply about each and every person here on the lot. We will watch after you," so Mickey told us, imitating Mayer.

Ava Gardner claimed that Mayer's speech pattern was carefully modulated. "I think he had voice lessons." [23] She also claimed that "Uncle L.B." gave both Mickey and her the identical speech when they first met him. "He was very sure of himself, and he could be funny, too. I don't know whether he meant to be, but he was. He said, 'My whole life is making movie stars,'" as she mimicked his liturgical cadence, and he continued, 'All the billboards in the world don't make a movie star. Only Louis B. Mayer can make a somebody outta a nobody.' Well, you couldn't argue with that," she laughed." [24]

Mickey was impressed. He had never felt this type of acceptance in his young career. He had worked for Larry Darmour for six years and had been treated like any other of the children who could easily have been replaced. The Laemmles hired him and promptly sold off his services to the highest bidder. He was always chattel on the auction block with a lot number around his neck. Not anymore, it appeared. He liked this warm, almost father-like man, and he was encouraged to do his very best work for him.

Yet Mayer was a businessman first. Mickey's contract with MGM is a strong example of this. While Mayer knew that, after the actor's performance in *A Midsummer Night's Dream*, Mickey would be of great value to the studio, even if only in loan-out fees, he never offered him fair compensation.

His agreement was the last contract negotiated by Mickey's long-time agent, Harry Weber. Weber was critically ill, and had not been at his best when he negotiated the deal. In fact, he retired shortly after getting Mickey set up at the studio, putting Mickey's career in the hands of his assistant, David Todd. Mickey's long-term agreement with MGM gave him a starting salary of $150 per week, guaranteed for forty weeks per year, with the right to loan him out to other studios without his consent. If his option was picked up at the end of six months, his salary would be raised to $200 per week. After that, the options would be on a yearly basis, beginning with $300 a week, all the way to $1,000 per week, if all the options were exercised. Although this was a nice salary for a fourteen-year-old boy during the Depression, it didn't take long for Harry Weber to realize that Mayer had gotten the better end of the deal by far.

Now that Mickey was employed full time at a studio, he was going to have to adhere to the State of California rules of education. In the summer of 1934 his mother enrolled him in the Pacific Military Academy, as it was in Culver City, near the MGM lot. She felt that maybe the school could teach him the discipline she couldn't seem to instill in him, and that it would get him out of the house following her divorce from Wynn Brown. Mickey had respected and loved Wynn, and Wynn's departure had left him quite hard to handle. Nell was bringing home dates, which angered Mickey. He was emphatic in his dislike of the men she was dating and got into rows with Nell about them. The academy, she felt, would give Nell time to find her next husband—which she did. As part of his enrollment contract, Mickey was ordered to live at the Academy. He'd work at nearby MGM in Culver City during the days and then return to Pacific Military, also in Culver City, at night.

However, the melding of Mickey Rooney and a military school was a bad fit, and it did not take. Mickey was quite unhappy at the academy. He didn't like being forced to wear uniforms that made the boys look like "Hollywood's notion of Russian Cossacks." He was constantly getting into fights, and at night he had to listen to the "kids who cried in their sleep at night or smell their urine from wetting the beds." [25] The military academy experiment lasted only four weeks before he forced Nell to pull him out.

In October he enlisted at Hollywood Fairfax High, but lasted less than a semester there. Since MGM was constantly keeping him at work, he was missing much of his school work. With four pictures already scheduled for him in 1935, it was decided that he would attend the "Little Red Schoolhouse" on the MGM lot, so Nell enrolled him with the MGM schoolmarm, Mary McDonald.

In Mickey's class were English actor Freddie Bartholomew; Deanna Durbin; Bonita Granville; Virginia Weidler; Gloria DeHaven, who later dated Rooney; and eventually Lana Turner. It was truly a one-room schoolhouse as if out of the *Huckleberry Finn* movie. It was one story, white, and had a porch in front with a couple of creaking rocking chairs on it. It even had a cobblestone walk leading to the front porch.

The State of California mandated that students attend classes for a minimum of five hours a day. However, that rarely happened. MGM child actors would usually attend for three hours in the morning (from 9:00 a.m. to noon) and then spend the other two hours with tutors on their respective sets. Mickey remembered, "Some of the tutorial sessions were a joke. Fifteen minutes of English, then back in front of the camera for an hour, then fifteen minutes in arithmetic then back in front of the cameras again. I guess it goes without saying that we did not discover good studying habits." [26]

Schoolmarm Miss McDonald looked like she was right out of Central Casting, thin, severe-looking, with her hair pulled up into a tight bun. She survived for years at MGM because she knew how to bend to the studio's needs, not the state's requirements. She understood that films had to be completed on time or it would cost the studio extra dollars. So she made it easy for the students to adapt their schoolwork to their filming schedule.

McDonald appreciated Mickey's quirks. When he daydreamed during class, she would snap him back to attention by loudly calling his name: "Mr. Rooney!" She once admonished him when she caught him gazing upon Lana Turner's ample bosom, again screaming, "Mr. Rooney!" Mickey feigned innocence and replied sweetly, "Yes, Miss McDonald?" She just smirked at him, and he knew what the smirk implied.

The studio's head of publicity, Howard Strickling, was under orders to create an image for young Mickey—not only for his MGM films but to increase his value as a loan-out performer to other studios. Strickling, along with studio vice president Eddie Mannix were known as the fixers. They would clean up nasty rumors, fix awkward situations, and create a wholesome image for their stars. Author E. J. Fleming told us—and wrote in his book *The Fixers*—"Eddie Mannix and Howard Strickling are virtually unknown outside of Hollywood and little remembered even there. But as general manager, VP, and head of publicity for MGM, they were lords of the star-studded universe of Hollywood's golden age from the 1920s through the 1940s. When MGM stars found themselves in trouble, it was Eddie and Howard who solved their problems, hid their crimes, and kept their secrets. That's why they were called 'the Fixers.'" Fleming told us that "through a complex web of contacts, Mannix and Strickling covered up some of the most notorious crimes and scandals in Hollywood history, keeping stars out of jail and their indiscretions out of the papers. They handled problems as diverse as the murder of Paul Bern, the husband of Jean Harlow; the studio drugging of both Mickey and of Judy Garland, addicting them both; the murder of Ted Healy, who created the Three Stooges, at the hands of Wallace Beery; and the adoption by an unmarried Loretta Young of her own child fathered by a married Clark Gable."[27] The two bought and paid for media coverage to suit their own needs, managed a brothel for stars and executives, secured abortions for starlets who got pregnant, and supplied drugs, especially methamphetamine, to underage contract performers.

They set up the illusion of Hollywood that was accepted outside the Culver City gates, the illusion that MGM was a nice family; that Mickey was overseen by the fatherly L. B. Mayer, publicized by his kindly "uncle" Howard Strickling, and controlled by his tough-guy "uncle" Eddie Mannix. Mickey learned that he had to keep his family happy.

Murray Lertzman, the author's cousin and a well-known Beverly Hills attorney who represented stars such as Lana Turner, Esther Williams, Jayne Mansfield, and Rock Hudson, knew Mannix and said that "while Mannix was clearly a bully and a thug, Strickling was far more nefarious. They could make life easier for you and, on the other hand, make your life a complete living hell. If they wanted to destroy you or void an agreement, Strickling could plant the right items in the media and let the studio come out smelling like a rose. This is what would happen to Mickey in the early 1950s, when they had no more use for him."[28]

Murray Lertzman also recalled the underworld connections of Eddie Mannix: "He undoubtedly had clear racket connections. Whenever any of our Metro clients had a problem in something Mafia connected, such as at a nightclub like Ciro's, we would call Mannix, who directly told us that he would make a call to a notorious racketeer, who helped found the Las Vegas gaming industry, Benjamin Siegel, or LA gangster Mickey Cohen, to clear up the mess." [29] Rich Cohen (no relation to Mickey Cohen), in his book, *Tough Jews*, said that Siegel, who would kill for fun and "was sent by the Mob to put the LA Underworld into the Syndicate," [30] would usually call his top lieutenant, Mickey Cohen, who was "Siegel's torpedo," to do the dirty work. According to Lertzman, there was a direct connection from Mannix to Siegel. "Mickey Cohen also had a bodyguard and hit man who did his bidding named Johnny Stompanato, who was Lana Turner's boyfriend. He later was stabbed to death by her daughter [Cheryl Crane]. At that time, we referred Lana to Jerry Geisler to represent her daughter based on Mannix's advice. Mannix had to clear everything with Mickey Cohen as well." [31] As the story goes, Stompanato was a vicious man who physically abused Turner to the point where Turner's daughter, Cheryl, took matters into her own hands and plunged a knife in him. This threatened to become a huge scandal that not only would have sent the teenage Cheryl Crane to jail, but would have tainted Turner's career. Worse, Johnny worked for the Mob, and his death had to be cleaned up. That job fell to Mannix and Strickland.

This is the culture that teenage Mickey Rooney entered on August 2, 1934. He remained under that watchful eye until July 30, 1948, when, at twenty-eight years old, he left the protective custody of his "family."

As restrictive as the studio was, though, it was the place where Mickey would perform in a series of movies as Andy Hardy, and with Judy Garland, that would ensure his stardom in the history of motion pictures.

Mickey and the Lion

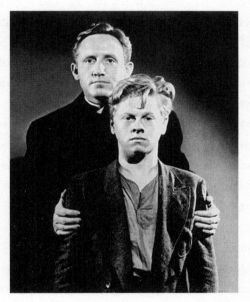

Spencer Tracy and Mickey in Boys Town *(1938).*
PHOTO COURTESY OF ROBERT EASTON.

After Mickey signed his agreement in August 1934, MGM wasted no time putting him right to work with a slate of motion pictures ready to shoot. Even though his roles were relatively minor at first, he soon started to shine, and garner recognition from critics and fans. His loan-out value had already been established with *A Midsummer Night's Dream*, and Mickey soon accumulated important experience working with A-list actors such as Clark Gable, Joan Crawford, Maureen O'Sullivan, Robert Montgomery, William Powell, Jean Harlow,

Lionel Barrymore. Spencer Tracy, and the beloved Will Rogers. He also followed the direction of such MGM veterans as Clarence Brown, Woody Van Dyke, Edward Sedgwick, and Victor Fleming.

Mickey hit the ground running with *Hide-Out*. Though in a sixth-billed part as Willie Miller, he received praise from *Variety*, which wrote, "Rooney well-nigh steals the picture." Next up was *Chained*, directed by Mayer favorite Clarence Brown and starring the hot re-teaming of Clark Gable and Joan Crawford. In it, Mickey was billed twenty-second, in a relatively small part, but the movie gave him the chance to appear with two of the top box office stars of the day.

Next for Mickey was a loan-out to the Poverty Row studio Columbia for a quickie called *Blind Date*. It starred a young Ann Sothern, later the star of the comedy *Panama Hattie*, and on the 1950s television sitcom *Private Secretary*; and former silent film star Neil Hamilton, later Commissioner Gordon in the TV series *Batman*. Mickey was fourth-billed as Freddy Taylor, Sothern's younger brother. Then he quickly returned to Culver City to film *Death on the Diamond*, directed by the prolific Eddie Sedgwick. The film starred Robert Young and Madge Evans. Mickey enjoyed doing the baseball-themed film in which he play Mickey, the batboy of the St. Louis Cardinals, a small part once again. "Anytime I got to do a film with sports," he recalled, "it was a big thrill. They had Ty Cobb on the set as a technical adviser, which was exciting." [1]

His next picture, completed in five months during 1934, was the loan-out to Fox *The County Chairman*, starring the immortal Will Rogers. Mickey is fifth-billed as Freckles, a part that received some good reviews. This would be one of the last films of Rogers's career before he was killed in an airplane crash with Wiley Post a few months later, in August 1935. Almost sixty years later, Mickey would play Rogers's father in the Broadway musical *The Will Rogers Follies*. Mickey recalled that Rogers was very complimentary to him on the first day of shooting, saying, "You handle yourself very well, son . . .

You know your lines. You don't interfere with mine. You know how to have fun with your script. Your performance makes mine better." [2]

After *A Midsummer Night's Dream*, Mickey went directly back to work in *Reckless*, directed by the macho Victor Fleming (best known for *Gone with the Wind* and *The Wizard of Oz*). *Reckless*, a musical with a score by Jerome Kern and Oscar Hammerstein, reunited Mickey (in the role of Eddie) with his benefactor, producer David Selznick. The film starred William Powell and Powell's real-life fiancée, Jean Harlow. It also had Ted Healy, with whom Mickey had appeared in vaudeville. Mickey was then sent on a loan-out to the ultra-low-rent studio Monogram, to take the third lead in *The Healer*, which starred Ralph Bellamy, one of the popular stars of the 1930s, but perhaps best known to modern audiences for his role in the Eddie Murphy film *Trading Places* and as Dr. Sapirstein, the Satan-worshipping obstetrician in Roman Polanski's *Rosemary's Baby*.

In *The Healer*, Mickey chews up the scenery as Jimmy, a boy who has polio and has lost the use of his legs. This was a convenient part for Mickey because he was still on crutches from his sledding accident. Ralph Bellamy plays the doctor who is committed to helping Jimmy walk again. Jimmy Starr, in the *Los Angeles Evening Herald-Express* on May 23, 1935, wrote, "When you see Mickey on crutches in "The Healer," it's the real thing . . . [L]uckily enough, the producer timed the finish of the film so that Mickey could walk for the final fade-out." Mickey received strong notices for the role in *Film Daily*, which on May 28, 1935, wrote, "Rooney plays a prominent role that grabs your heart." Mickey recalled that "Directors never had to pull any tricks to get me to cry; nobody had to tell me my dog had just died; I'd been crying on cue all my life." [3]

Throughout 1935, Mickey continued to move from movie set to movie set at Metro, churning out pictures as if he were an assembly line worker, as the Howard Strickling publicity machine worked overtime to expose him in the media. Along with stories about

Mickey's continued recovery from his broken leg—"No More Sledding for Mickey" (Jimmy Starr, *Los Angeles Evening-Herald*, February 7, 1935)—Rooney made appearances at several charity events. On April 26 of that year, Louella Parsons reported in the *Los Angeles Examiner* that "Mickey Rooney and other All-Stars will perform in special skits to benefit the Public School Protective League"; and Harrison Carroll in the *Los Angeles Evening Herald-Examiner* of May 24 wrote, "Groucho Marx's thirteen year old son, Arthur, is teamed with Mickey Rooney in a tennis tournament at Midwick Country Club." Arthur Marx recalled, "Mickey was actually quite a good athlete. He was rather untrained in tennis, but he was a real competitor."[4] Harrison Carroll also reported, on June 20, 1935, that "Clarence Brown will sponsor Mickey Rooney's football team, which will play at halftime at the professional games here."

Director Clarence Brown, in addition to sponsoring Mickey's football team, sought him out specifically for the role of Tommy Miller in his film adaptation of Eugene O'Neill's *Ah, Wilderness!*; Brown had managed to secure Wallace Beery and Lionel Barrymore for roles, too. The play depicts a young man's coming of age against the tapestry of his family dealing with issues that started well before the play begins, but that come to a head on a July 4 holiday in 1906. The film version was a success. This success, and the relationship between Mickey and Barrymore as his father and Spring Byington as his mother, would spur the development of the 1937 *A Family Affair*, which would be the first Andy Hardy movie. *Ah, Wilderness!* was the type of film that pleased Louis B. Mayer, who sought to produce his version of Americana, perhaps as a way for him, as a Jewish immigrant who fled persecution in Russia, to amalgamate himself deep into the American social fabric. As Mickey writes, "Creating this New England utopia was all part of L. B. Mayer's master plan to reinvent America."[5]

Mickey's final film of 1935 was *Riffraff*, his first film with Spencer Tracy, in which he plays Jean Harlow's kid brother. "Harlow was a hoot. She was really down to earth," Rooney recalled. "I don't think Spence cared for her that much. She was too blunt."[6]

Nineteen thirty-five turned out to be an eventful year for Rooney, with six films under his belt, including his memorable role as Puck in *A Midsummers Night's Dream*. Although he was still stuck in mainly secondary parts, he was starting to garner attention. He was also starting to feel comfortable working with some of the greatest actors and directors of the period. Directors such as Clarence Brown and Victor Fleming recognized his skilled professionalism, and sought him out for their upcoming films.

In 1936, David O. Selznick once again requested Rooney for a loan-out—by this time, Selznick had left his father-in-law's company to set up his own production company, Selznick International Pictures, which was distributed by United Artists. His adaptation of *Little Lord Fauntleroy* would be his first film. The star of the film was the twelve-year-old English actor Freddie Bartholomew. "He was making five times what I made [about a thousand dollars per week], and I was a bit intimidated," said Mickey in *Life Is Too Short*. Rooney played a bootblack named Dick who was a friend of Bartholomew and character actor Guy Kibbee. "I wasn't jealous, though. He was not stuck up at all. In fact, he was just a regular kid. I got to like Freddie very much. He was a bit younger, but he was always interested in everything I did." The film was an early success for the budding production company. "The film cost less than a half million to make and cleared Selznick International a profit of two million dollars," Rooney recalled.

With the success of this film, MGM rushed Rooney into another film in which he again appeared with Bartholomew: *The Devil Is a Sissy*, directed by Woody Van Dyke. The film costarred another famed child star, Jackie Cooper, already a friend of Mickey's. Mickey was third-billed, but again garnered strong notices for his work. The *New York Times* in its September 19, 1936, review of the film, noted, "His is, without question, one of the finest performances of the year."

The film was yet another success at the box office, and it made a triple return for MGM—it had cost less than four hundred thousand to produce and returned nearly $1.2 million. With all this success, Mickey was starting to feel a bit resentful of the way the studio was working him. "While I was turning big bucks for MGM and they were working me day and night, they were fucking paying me four hundred lousy dollars a week. Sixteen grand a year. Okay, I know gas cost ten cents a gallon then, but they really fucked me. They were squeezing me dry while they were raking in the dollars. I think they made about ten million dollars on the films I did that year, and they never even offered me a bonus or any taste,"[7] he recalled. However, Mickey was indeed getting noticed at the studio—and considered more and more important, his parts becoming more central to each succeeding film. A good example of this was his stature at the studio vis-à-vis that of Metro's Freddie Bartholomew.

Mickey and Freddie made four films together. In the first film, Mickey was in a minor supporting role and Bartholomew was at his peak. By the time they made their last film together, *A Yank at Eaton*, in 1942, their positions had drastically changed. Mickey was the number one box office attraction in the world, while Bartholomew was badly forgotten. Film historian Alvin Marill noted in his book *Mickey Rooney*, "Freddie's career suffered at the hands of Rooney. Perhaps the audiences found the English Bartholomew, initially, as described by Efraim Katz in *The Film Encyclopedia*, 'a curly-haired, dimpled, angelic boy star of Hollywood films,' rather sissified as opposed to rough-and-tumble, swaggering Rooney, but they were great friends as well as rivals on the MGM lot." Bartholomew later told Alvin Marill, "Mickey and I used to compete for roles. I was under the wing of David Selznick. L.B. apparently wasn't as enamored with David because of his bent for somewhat more highbrow pictures—taken from classics of British literature, Kipling, Dickens and such—rather than the family fare which Mayer aimed at middle America. I usually ended up playing the dandy, who was the lead, and eventually I kind of grew out of a movie career in my teens." [8] In actuality, the legal problems with his parents, demands for a higher salary by his agents, and his size—he grew to over six feet tall by the time he was sixteen—also played a strong part in Bartholomew's fall from stardom. By the mid-1940s, he was working at *Poverty Row* studios such as PRC while Rooney was still a top box office draw.

Mickey's next film was a low-budget B movie at Warner Bros., *Down the Stretch*, with Patricia Ellis, in which Mickey was second-billed as jockey Snapper Sinclair. He was then placed in a film that he remembered as one of his favorites, the classic *Captains Courageous*, which reunited him with director Victor Fleming and costarred Freddie Bartholomew, Spencer Tracy, and Lionel Barrymore. Although his part as Bartholomew's friend, Dan Troop, was sixth-billed, it was a pivotal role. Mickey recalled, "I learned a lot about playing to the cameras by watching all the great actors around me. I also learned that Spencer Tracy wasn't like the God-like figure I imagined him to be. He grumbled about having his hair permed every day and put into a hair-net so he would look more like a Portuguese fisherman, and off camera he drank quite a bit." [9] It was a hard shoot, with much of it done in Southern California's Catalina Channel, off Redondo Beach. "Fleming believed in action; he thought that's what movies were for. I overheard him telling someone, 'Hey Hamlet's "To be or not to be" is great literature but I couldn't film it to save my life,'" Rooney recalled. [10] When *Captains Courageous* came out, Mickey received strong reviews once again, the film was nominated for Best Picture, and Tracy won the Oscar for Best Actor.

Mickey was hitting his stride as he finished *Captains Courageous*. He was being sought after by the best directors, his films were proving to be big moneymakers for MGM, and he was being recognized as one of the leading juvenile male actors in Hollywood. The next film he was scheduled to shoot, was a "programmer" for director George

Seitz. A programmer is another name for a B movie, a low-budget film that is used as part of a double feature to fulfill a studio's distribution requirements to theater owners. B movies began when theater owners, who would book performers alongside films, asked studios for cheaper films to replace the more expensive live acts, the last vestiges of vaudeville.

This B film, the first in the Andy Hardy series, would reunite Mickey with his *Ah, Wilderness!* costars Lionel Barrymore and Spring Byington in a family "dramedy" based on the Broadway play *Skidding*, and renamed *A Family Affair*. In it, he would play a character who would forever change his life.

The Make-Believe World of Andy Hardy's America

Lewis Stone and Mickey in Judge Hardy and Son *(1939).*
PHOTO COURTESY OF THE MONTE KLAUS COLLECTION.

In the midst of these ominous times," President Bill Clinton said to his biographer, Janis F. Kearney, describing the lives in Arkansas of his mother and father during the late 1930s, "Americans found ways to forget their lots in life for moments, even hours, at a time. Some of the era's most memorable movies . . . such as . . . the Andy Hardy movies . . . drew record crowds. Actors such as Shirley Temple, Mickey Rooney, and the Three Stooges became symbols of make-believe lives during that period." [1]

Bill Clinton saw that, for his family in Hope, struggling as they did during the Great Depression before World War II and years before he was born, an idealized world of a family run by a respected judge who had to wrangle his children, especially his son, who was straining at the leash, was not just entertainment; it was the promise of a dream. The Andy Hardy movies were for America what they became for their star, Mickey Rooney: a cornerstone.

For seventeen films that spanned more than twenty years, Rooney was everybody's all-American teenager/young adult. Rooney's Andy was the standard, the ideal for every teenager not just in the United States, but worldwide. And that ideal would last intact right through the 1980s. Andy Hardy was the model child you wanted your child to emulate. He was the clean-cut all-American young man who was respectful to his elders, ambitious, patriotic, and pious. And for many children, Andy Hardy's life in small-town America was the ideal life. Yet this was not the real Mickey Rooney, only a character.

Although in real life Rooney had very few of Andy Hardy's traits, and certainly none of the character's background, he subconsciously became, at least in the public's perception, the real Andy Hardy. By an early age, Mickey had seen it all. By age fifteen, Andy Hardy, however, was a refreshingly naïve teenager from a privileged, upper-middle-class midwestern family whose father was a judge and who had mundane worries.

Actress Spring Byington (*December Bride*), who played Mickey's mother in *A Family Affair, Ah, Wilderness!,* and *The Big Wheel,* always spoke fondly of this part of Hollywood history and Rooney's role in it. She told author Alvin H. Marill, "His Andrew Hardy— that's how I like to refer to him—was the idealized small-town teenager of the day, respectful, honorable, eager to please his parents and to have those father-son chats with the judge that were part of every film. Mickey was the perfect son that every mother of the time would have loved. That's not to say that his public off-screen life, as laid out in the movie magazines of the '30s and '40s and the Hollywood columnists like news hens Hedda Hopper and Louella Parsons and later, Earl Wilson, Ed Sullivan and Sidney Skolsky mirrored that of the Judge's son." [2]

The first appearance of the fictional Hardy family was at the Pasadena Playhouse in November 1926, in a two-week showcase called *Skidding*. Written by Aurania Rouverol, who was born in Utah in 1886 into an apostate Mormon family, the play featured the prototype of Andy Hardy, a character who would create a mold for the all-American teenager for the next ninety years.

Aurania, according to her daughter, Jean Rouverol Butler, in an interview fifteen years ago, was an independent spirit who really "did not want a husband, just children, and was just looking for a sperm donor." [3] Aurania had married a bank teller in Utah in 1912, but left him after the birth of her son and daughter, to seek her fortunes in Los Angeles. "She just kidnapped us and left," recalled Jean. Aurania was an early feminist who believed in her abilities. She never sought the "bourgeois life of the middle class." [4] In Los Angeles, she worked first as an actress, appearing in various silent films. But her true love was writing. After her play was produced at the Pasadena Playhouse, she was determined to succeed as a writer and moved with her two children to New York City, where she would attempt to find investors to help get her play on Broadway. Once she relocated, she supported herself as a script reader for the Shubert Organization. Within a year, she found an interested producer for her intergenerational-family drawing-room comedy, *Skidding*, in Hyman Adler, who then hired Marion Gering, a highly regarded dramatic director, to stage and direct the play. The action would be centered on only one set, the living room of Judge Hardy in "a certain town in Idaho" (the fictional town of Carvel).

On May 21, 1928, Aurania Rouverol debuted *Skidding*, at the Bijou Theatre on Broadway, where her story of an Idaho judge, James K. Hardy, and his family captured a pre-Depression small-town family dealing gently and benevolently with the changing social values they had come to rely upon. It starred prolific character actor Walter Abel, who had played d'Artagnan in the film *The Three Musketeers*; Clara Blandick, later Aunt Em in *The Wizard of Oz*; and young Charles Eaton as Andy Hardy. (Eaton came from a famous acting family and was a top juvenile performer.) *Skidding* had an ignominious Broadway opening and was panned by every critic in New York City. Acerbic critic George Jean Nathan wrote in *The American Spectator* on May 22, 1928, "If this play runs longer than two weeks, I will resign my position." The play was highly successful, lasting 429 performances before closing on July 17, 1929. (Nathan did not resign.)

Jean Rouverol Butler recalled, "Although they papered the house for the first four weeks, inviting people to fill the audience seats, it caught on after that. Irving Thalberg bought the property and hired my mother to adapt screenplays in Los Angeles. It's quite interesting that by the time they adapted *Skidding*, Mickey had a featured role as the youngest son, Tommy, who meets the Hardy family. The ironic aspect here is that the all-American Hardy family was really adapted by her son-in-law, my husband [Hugo Butler]." [5]

Paradoxically, Hugo Butler, a highly regarded screenwriter for MGM, was later blacklisted by Senator Joe McCarthy in 1950, and exiled to Mexico with his wife for over ten years, along with Academy Award screenwriters Dalton Trumbo (*Spartacus*) and Ring Lardner Jr. (*M*A*S*H*). It was Butler, a strong proponent of the American Communist Party, who set the template for the seventeen Hardy films, beginning with the first, *A Family Affair*. He was also consulted on a majority of the later movies in the series. Thus, the Hardy series was created by a feminist who eschewed the traditional middle-class family values of small-town America, was adapted for the screen by a card-carrying Communist who despised the bourgeois values held by the Hardy family, and starred a rebellious juvenile from a dysfunctional family who was the very antithesis of his clean-cut on-screen character. Together they created the prototype for the American family that has resonated for generations, not only in motion pictures but in television situation comedies as well. Millions of families have striven mightily to model their lives on this fictional family who set the pattern for television families such as the Andersons of *Father Knows Best*, the Cleavers of *Leave It to Beaver*, the Stones of *The Donna Reed Show*, the Nelsons of *Ozzie and Harriet*, the Bradys of *The Brady Bunch*, the Keatons of *Family Ties*, and the Huxtables of *The Cosby Show*.

Hugo and Jean, an actress as well a noted writer along with her husband, shared their utopian radicalism and joined the American Communist Party in 1937. They were recruited by their friend, screenwriter Waldo Salt (*The Philadelphia Story*, *Midnight Cowboy*, *Coming Home*). Rouverol states in her autobiography, *Refugees from Hollywood: A Journal of the Blacklist Years*, "It wasn't a difficult decision. The political climate encouraged it . . . [W]e had hoped that perhaps revolution was not inevitable after all, that a peaceful transition to socialism might be possible. But perhaps the most telling reason was that most of our friends, who were screenwriters, were already members." [6]

Hugo Butler wrote the screenplay for other Metro film classics, such as *Young Tom Edison*, which starred Mickey Rooney; *The Adventures of Huckleberry Finn*, also starring Rooney; *Edison, the Man*, with Spencer Tracy; and *Lassie, Come Home*, with Elizabeth Taylor.

In 1935, Clarence Brown directed the screen version of Eugene O'Neill's stage hit *Ah, Wilderness!*. Adapted by the great MGM writing team of Frances Goodrich and Albert Hackett, this coming-of-age story has the dark Jungian undertones typical of O'Neill's exploration of the human psyche, in which he cantilevers the outward manifestations of his characters against their private and otherwise unseen (except to the audience) primal motivations. Yet it mostly captures the comings and goings of family life in small-town America on the Fourth of July in 1906. In 1935, America, as well as the boy at the center of the story, was coming of age, and even though it was not slated as a major film, *Ah, Wilderness!* would become a sleeper hit for MGM that year.

In September 1937, Louis B. Mayer secured full control of studio production. Now, after Irving Thalberg's death, Mayer would be able to shape the films at MGM to express his particular vision. Though Thalberg had produced MGM's most prestigious ventures, he had just nixed a proposal to produce a film based on Margaret Mitchell's soon-to-be-published book, *Gone with the Wind*. Although Thalberg said it would be a "sensational" role for Gable, and a "terrific picture," he decided not to do it, saying, "No more epics for me now. I'm tired. I'm just too tired." Thalberg famously told Mayer, "[N]o Civil War picture ever made a nickel." [7]

With Thalberg gone, Mayer was in control, and he wanted more profits, not break-even or money-losing prestigious artistic films. He maintained his control of studio production by sending hefty profits back to Nicholas Schenck, the chairman of Loews Inc. and owner of MGM Studios in New York—also a studio head for whom the bottom line was most important. Due to Schenck's stringent management, MGM was successful, becoming the only film company that continued to pay dividends to stockholders during the Depression. [8]

Mayer's instincts were correct: The combination of Americana and the idealized family sold tickets. He'd seen how the film *Ah, Wilderness!*, which was made for under two hundred thousand dollars, had turned a huge profit, and he wanted another vehicle in that vein. MGM began reviewing all the properties in its library. It was writer/producer Sam Marx, the executive story editor at MGM, who recommended a film version of *Skidding*. Sam Marx told writer Arthur Marx:

> In 1928, I saw a play in New York called "Skidding" by Aurania Rouverol. It was a play about a small town and judge and his family and very charming. I remembered it

when I moved to Metro in 1936 and decided I wanted it for the "B" unit at Metro, which was under the supervision of Lucien Hubbard. But I practically had to get him down on the floor with my knees on his neck to make him buy the play . . . Anyway . . . we picked up the property for something like five thousand dollars. Maybe less. But Hubbard had so little confidence in the project that he wound up letting me produce it under his supervision. And quite frankly, I had no feelings about it turning into a blockbuster either. I figured it was going to be a nice little picture.[9]

When Marx and Hubbard presented the project to Mayer, he loved it. According to Marx, Mayer was reminded of his own provincial and proper childhood in St. John, New Brunswick. His father, Jacob Mayer, was much like Judge Hardy in his strictness; and as in the Hardy family, his word was the law. Mrs. Hardy reminded Mayer of his mother, in a gentile version. The story reworked his memories of his nineteenth-century Jewish family into a twentieth-century WASP version. But here was the oddity. For Mayer, desperately assimilating himself into American culture through his films, the underlying story of his 1937 *A Family Affair* was still subversive: corruption in American small-town politics challenges the moral rigor of Judge Hardy. Whereas *Ah, Wilderness!* was about psychological corruption (Uncle Sid's drunkenness, Richard's night of carousing after his romantic importuning is summarily rejected, and Essie's seeming obliviousness to the metastasizing difficulties in her family), *Skidding* and its film adaptation, *A Family Affair*, had the undertones of financial corruption and how it tainted politics and even seeped into the heart of an otherwise upstanding American family.

Mayer overlooked all this because the Andy Hardy story was pure Americana and afforded him an opportunity to feature the studio's hot young juvenile, Mickey Rooney. It also had all the elements that had helped *Ah, Wilderness!* succeed. Mayer was, by this time, very impressed with Mickey. He noted to Sam Marx that Rooney had a bottomless well of energy and inventiveness to draw from. He felt the young actor had manic, cheerful dynamism.

Skidding was not completely to Mayer's taste. Mayer, governed as he was by traditional conservative values and by a longing, as most Jewish immigrants had in the early twentieth century, to assimilate into American society, albeit on their own terms, thoroughly disliked Aurania's feminist and socialist values. He also did not like the stage-bound set of the property—the play was centered on one set, the Hardy drawing room, in and out of which characters made their entrances and exits—and wanted to see it reconstructed as more cinematic. And the dialogue was more declamatory than dramatic. Mayer thought it simply lacked cinematic value and needed to be broadened. To do this, Sam Marx summoned Hugo Butler, who had just met Aurania's actress daughter, Jean. Thus, although he didn't know it yet, the second film Butler would work on was the stage play written by his future mother-in-law.

Most people at Metro were nonplussed by the *Skidding* project. The team in Howard Strickling's publicity department, for example, referred to the *Skidding* adaptation as "that potboiler with Lionel Barrymore that the B-picture guys are working on." [10] Also there were no plans beyond this one film for *Skidding*. Writer Kay Van Riper suggested to the film's producers, Sam Marx and Lucien Hubbard, that the title be changed from *Skidding* to *A Family Affair*, to reflect the Hardy family dominating the film. George Seitz, one of Mayer's favorite directors was assigned to the project, and the MGM "family" was included in the production, including sound director Douglas Shearer, art director Cedric Gibbons, and musical composer David Snell, who created most of the familiar themes of the Andy Hardy movies.

On February 3, 1937, Elizabeth Yeaman wrote in the *Hollywood Citizen-News* about the upcoming film:

MICKEY ROONEY JOINS CAST

Mickey Rooney today joined the cast of "Skidding" at MGM, thereby completing the quintet of players who were featured in "Ah, Wilderness!" If the producers just added Wallace Beery, they would have the cast almost complete for "Skidding." Furthermore, "Skidding" is planned as a human interest family comedy of the general type of "Ah, Wilderness!" It will have to be good to claim a corner in the same category with the Eugene O'Neill play. "Skidding" concerns a judge engaged in a political fight and his family. Lionel Barrymore will play the Judge, Spring Byington his wife, and the others are Eric Linden and Cecilia Parker.

Obviously, somewhere between February 3 and March 12, when the picture was shipped out, the name was changed to *A Family Affair*.

Mickey told writer Alvin Marill that "Barrymore didn't want to play the wise old Judge Hardy in a 'b' movie, but he, like everyone else, was under contract. One of the many actors MGM had on call. Since MGM had nothing else for Barrymore at the moment, he took the part." [11] Mickey also said that the studio had originally cast child actor Frankie Thomas—a character actor in the Saturday matinee serials *Tim Tyler's Luck* and *Nancy Drew . . . Reporter*, and a lead actor in the 1950s television series *Tom Corbett, Space Cadet*—as Andy, however, he was growing too fast, and he tested "too tall" for the part. [12] For Mickey, height was "on hold" because he had simply stopped growing. Despite this, and even though Mayer was already impressed with Mickey's talent, he was forced to screen-test for the part, to make sure he had the right look. Ann Rutherford, who later played Polly Benedict in the series, remembered, "They thought that having a short Andy Hardy would be a little more amusing and more touching." [13]

A Family Affair, like *Skidding*, starts with Judge Hardy facing political problems at work and family problems at home. Powerful men in town are upset with his judicial decisions, which run contrary to their interests, and want to see him impeached. His daughters, Joan and Marion, have romantic problems; and his son, Andy, discovers Polly Benedict in his first burst of adolescent love. As in the stage play, the world of Judge Hardy, both in the courthouse and in his drawing room, is skidding out from under him, caught in the riptide of a changing culture. Firm but benevolent, Judge Hardy envelops everyone in the family with his concern, even as he contends with political influences that seek to undermine his steadfast reliance upon the sanctity of justice. In the process of coming to terms with his reality, he lends wisdom and calmness to all.

This first film sets up the central relationship between Andy and his father (played by the crusty Lionel Barrymore), a man of absolute moral integrity with a stern demeanor but a droll sense of humor. Andy strains against the reins as he feels his oats, but his father reaffirms the boundaries. This film sets the pattern for the typical plot of the next sixteen Andy Hardy films, which would involve Andy getting into minor trouble with money or girls, usually because of a youthful lack of impulse control and a willingness to fudge the truth. This would invariably lead to a man-to-man talk with his father, an establishment of shared values amid an array of disruptive influencers, after which Andy would do the right thing.

This first film is different from the subsequent Andy Hardy films in tone and subject matter because of its political undertone. As Judge Hardy, Lionel Barrymore must fight off some higher-ranked city politicians who want to blackmail him into approving a plant coming to town. They plan on using a scandal involving his daughter Joan, played by Julie Haydon; while his other daughter, played by Cecilia

Parker, strikes up a relationship with a new man. How will Judge Hardy navigate the shoals of political Scylla and domestic Charybdis? It is via his come-to-Jesus interaction with Andy that the absolute necessity of honesty comes shining through. This is the intersection of *Skidding* and *A Family Affair*.

The film was shot in just seventeen days, February 3–20, 1937, at a cost of only $190,000 (coming in $7,000 under budget). It was released just twenty days later, on March 12, 1937, and was a profit windfall for Metro.

To Mickey, *A Family Affair* was just another film and seventeen days' worth of yeoman's work. He was not aware of the significance that this "programmer" would have on his career. At the time, he was looking forward to, according to Elizabeth Yeaman of the *Hollywood Citizens-News* "receiving his high school diploma from the MGM school, and he will enroll in UCLA. When Mickey starts to college the studio will have to start giving him grown-up roles . . ." This blurb, most likely created by Metro's Howard Strickling, paints the picture of a typical adolescent boy at seventeen, graduating from high school and hoping to start college. Mickey's life was far from that. He was followed around by Sylvester, his African American valet, who did his bidding; he drove an expensive car; and he supported his mother and her new husband, Fred Pankey. Mickey was now a breadwinner in his own right. If there was ever a moment of childhood bliss, the bubble of innocence that young children enjoy before the harshness of adult life presents them with Hobson's choices, Mickey never remembered it. He was a working actor whose roles defined his reality.

A Family Affair was not highly publicized because very little expense went into its promotion. A film had to cost in the high six figures before it received the big push from Strickling. MGM did not expect the film to gross more than three hundred thousand dollars. Such projections were based on the cast, who, except for a star like Barrymore, rated only a line on the marquee. However, this little "programmer" hit box office gold. Though it received just fair reviews, it grossed nearly half a million in its first few weeks and soared to over a million, in Depression-era dollars, by the end of the year.

The expectations were low. As Frank Nugent of the *New York Times* wrote on April 20, 1937:

> Lionel Barrymore wears the mantle of justice and a crown of thorns with his usual patience . . . as the dutiful Judge Hardy whose restraining order has checked the construction of the Carvel (Idaho) aqueduct, turned the town against him and even has begun to alienate the affections of his family . . . Mr. Barrymore knows how to handle those things, and so do the other members of the cast. Spring Byington invariably is a model of wifely and motherly understanding. Mickey Rooney is the epitome of all 14 year olds who hate girls until they see a pretty one in a party dress. Julie Haydon, who can do better things, weeps convincingly as the troubled married daughter. Cecilia Parker and Eric Linden are Young Love in its usual form. They have all taken their "Family Affair" rather seriously and although it was not that important, we rather enjoyed eavesdropping at Judge Hardy's home.

The *Daily Variety*, on April 21, 1937, thought so little of *A Family Affair* that it consigned its "favorable" criticism to its "Miniature Review" department, which made no mention of Mickey. The *Chicago Tribune* of April 22, 1937, disliked the film and called it "a boob trap" that failed to work. The *Film Daily* on April 22, 1937, wrote, "Swell domestic comedy-drama with glove-fitting cast that is a natural for the family trade . . . Mickey Rooney does a grand job as the adolescent and gets most of comedic business and handles it with a telling effect . . . George Seitz's direction is very good . . . the interest in the film is the fine sentiments and the homey touches centering around the home life of the Judge's family."

However, when the film opened, moviegoers spoke loud and clear at the box office. City after city, town after town, reported that the cash customers were going "wild over the Hardy picture." There were many repeat customers, which was a rare occurrence for a film that was basically a family drawing room comedy with no physical action sequences.

When the bottom-line-minded Mayer saw the box office figures for the film, he took notice. He was still preoccupied with Thalberg's death, and how the production departments of the studio would be managed. However, what may have gotten L.B. to sit up was a wire he received from a Rochester, New York, motion picture exhibitor:

> FOR GOD'S SAKE, LET'S HAVE MORE OF THAT ROONEY KID. STOP. HE REALLY WOWED THEM. STOP. THE WAY HE TRIPPED OVER THE DOORMAT AND LOOKED INTO THE EYES OF THAT POLLY BENEDICT GIRL. THAT WAS REALLY SOMETHING. STOP. THE KID'S A GOLDMINE. STOP. SO IS THE REST OF THE CAST. STOP. PLEASE MAKE ANOTHER HARDY PICTURE RIGHT AWAY.[14]

Mayer, it was speculated, didn't want to make another Hardy picture right away. Rooney wrote in *Life Is Too Short*, "During the spring of 1937, I am told, many a conference was held in Mr. Mayer's white carpeted office to figure out what to do about 'the Hardy problem.' If the fans were turned on by little Andy Hardy and his little-boy romance with Polly Benedict, then maybe they were tired of the romantic leads. Maybe this was a trend that would depreciate MGM's investment in its Gables and its Tracys and its Taylors. That could be a disaster."[15] Eddie Mannix told Mayer, "Let's make another Hardy family picture. If it flops we will be rid of the headache. And if it clicks, then we'll damn well know that the thing is a trend and that they want more of this Hardy family crap." [16]

Historically, sequels were not looked on as a good investment, but Mayer decided to hedge his bets with this follow-up film—actually a series of lower-budget pictures, with this second film set to launch the series. The script, developed by writer Kay Van Riper, was originally titled *A Family Vacation* or *Second Family Affair*, before the studio settled on *You're Only Young Once*.

When they decided to make a sequel, George Seitz, Kay Van Riper, and Hugo Butler were not available. Sam Marx had left temporarily to work with Sam Goldwyn; Lucien Hubbard had left to open a dude ranch in Palm Springs. Eventually, a story written by Kay Van Riper was used for the sequel's screenplay, which was written by veteran Carey Wilson. George Seitz's schedule was rearranged so he could direct again. *You're Only Young Once* was rushed into production so that the studio could preserve the momentum from the first Andy Hardy movie.

As for the on-screen talent, Mayer had wanted Barrymore to continue as Judge Hardy. Yet Barrymore, a member of theatrical royalty, was said to have bristled at the notion not only of doing a B picture at that point, but at getting stuck in a B series (even though he did later get stuck in the role of Dr. Gillespie, opposite Lew Ayres, in the Dr. Kildare series. He told Mayer that he would continue as the Judge in future entries if the studio tore up his current contract and, say, doubled his salary. Barrymore was also annoyed by the scene-stealing Mickey, to the point where he had told Sam Marx that he had "developed homicidal tendencies toward the kid [Rooney]" during filming. Mayer decided that he didn't really need Barrymore for the part. It was that young "whippersnapper" Rooney who sold the pictures. He was the star.[17]

Mayer selected his close friend veteran character actor Lewis Stone as the new Judge Hardy. Stone was a courtly New Englander who had the presence of a Judge. In another cost-cutting measure, Mayer also recast Fay Holden to replace Spring Byington as Mrs. Hardy. Byington wanted too much money, and L.B. wanted to keep his costs as low as possible on this sequel. Cecilia Parker would continue as Marian, Sara Haden as the spinster Aunt Milly; but Ann Rutherford, a young starlet from Canada, would become the new Polly Benedict. Rutherford knew Mickey all too well from Metro's Little Red Schoolhouse. He had been harassing her for the last couple of years—following her, pulling her hair, and even shooting spitballs in her face. "I actually was rather upset at being cast opposite Mickey, but I knew this could be an important role for me," Rutherford recalled.[18]

With the changes in cast and the replacement of Butler with Carey Wilson, the tone of the film changed. Barrymore had been a bit harsher than Lewis Stone, who inherited the role. The subject matter was also darker in the original, with the discussion of a scandal and even a brief mention of suicide. Also, the small-town flavor of Carvel, an America before the Fall, that we see in the later films just doesn't ring true, because the city is full of some harsh people who will sink to the bottom in terms of blackmail and nefariously ugly dealings. Also, the characters are not as well drawn when the series hits its stride in later films. The rest of the cast is clearly trying to find what they want to do with their characters.

Still, the template for the Andy Hardy sequels is set in *A Family Affair.* As author and film historian James Robert Parish points out in *The Great Movie Series* (and told us in our interview), "Despite the Metro screenwriters shipping the Hardys frequently outside of Carvel's town limits to other destinations, the folksy influence was always there. At the slightest infractions of social norms, Judge Hardy would be ready with his fatherly talks and Andy, gulping in silent confusion and realization of his errors, would be a reformed boy-man. The fact that Rooney was twenty plus in many of the films and was portraying a teenager bothered audiences little."

You're Only Young Once was another low-budget B movie: It came in under $190,000, had a quick shooting schedule of two and a half weeks, and was slated as the second half of a double bill. However, in some ways the film is more lavish than most studio pictures. Its simple tale of a small-town family trying to get through their summer vacation in one piece perfectly melded the elements of high-spirited youth and parental wisdom that would make the Hardy films so successful. The sets from *A Family Affair* had been left standing, since there was only a few weeks' break between the shooting of that film and that of its sequel.

A large portion of the story line here is with sister Marian, who falls in love with a lifeguard who turns out to be married, a situation exposed by her older and wiser parents. Such beloved series elements as Andy Hardy's foolishness and the Judge's wise counsel and ability to get his children out of sticky situations had already been established. As was the tendency to showcase the younger actresses cast opposite Rooney. This time out, Andy's love interest is Eleanor Lynn as a spoiled rich girl who tries to lead Andy into the fast life. (Unlike such later Rooney leading ladies as Judy Garland, Lana Turner, and Esther Williams, Lynn did not move on to stardom.)

Mayer now had a personal interest in the Hardy films. He watched the rushes with keen interest. His growing enthusiasm for the subsequent Hardy films almost became a personal crusade for him. He would sit through previews next to Carey Wilson, the veteran producer-writer, in order to transmit his criticisms directly. After a scene in which Andy Hardy refused to eat, to indicate how lovesick he was, Mayer went into a rage: "Don't you know a boy of sixteen is hungry all the time?" he screamed. "You tell me you were brought up in a good American home—in the kitchen! You lied to me! You've let Andy insult his mother! No boy would tell his mother he wasn't hungry!"[19] Then Mayer told Wilson exactly how to rewrite the scene.

Before production even began on this second film, Mayer and

Mannix had committed to turning out more pictures in the series. Van Riper started on the next film, *Judge Hardy's Children* (1938) as soon as location shooting for *You're Only Young Once* started on Catalina Island. The promise was sealed when at the end of the film, Lewis Stone, in a spoken epilogue, alludes to more Hardy films in the future. The studio's faith was well founded. The first true Hardy film grossed well over two million, and most of that was pure profit. For the next two years, MGM would turn out a new Hardy film roughly every three months. The production team (including producer J. J. Cohn, director George B. Seitz, and Van Riper) would remain mostly intact through the remaining thirteen films in the series, most of them more popular than the big-budget pictures they had been designed to support.

Unlike with *A Family Affair*, the reviews for *You're Only Young Once* were mostly positive. On November 22, 1937, the staid *New York Times*, which usually disliked family films, raved about *You're Only Young Once*, remarking, "The average American family (if, indeed there is such a thing) has been so frequently libeled by the average program film it is a surprising experience and occasion for a relief to come upon. 'You're Only Young Once' . . . Here, at least, is a 'series' family (for that is what MGM intends it to be) in which individual members react like human beings instead of like third-rate vaudevillians . . . best of all is Mickey Rooney the gosling son."

The reviews greatly pleased Mayer, who loved the films and Stone's portrayal of the perfect American father so much that he guaranteed the actor a position at the studio for the rest of his life. Mayer looked upon every aspect of this series as his crowning glory. The Academy agreed. In 1941, MGM even landed a special Oscar in recognition of the series' "achievement in representing the American way of life" according to the presentation speech. It was the only film series of Hollywood's golden age to be honored like that.

Mayer was pleased on several levels at the potential benefits of the series for the studio. First, he was sitting on a gold mine in which MGM would take very little risk for a huge return. The second film returned more than ten times its initial investment. The upside was unlimited. Second, he would be able to use these vehicles to show-case young talent and build his roster of actors from within. Third, and possibly the key element, was that the series would allow L.B. to promote his vision of the all-American family. It would garner him the respect he craved as the son of a Jewish junk peddler from Minsk, his ultimate assimilation into American life. He would influence how families raised their children, solved their problems, and pursued their aspirations.

Mayer was in a unique position in that he had the power to influence how people lived their lives. Motion pictures were at their peak then, and never in the history of civilization had there been a tool as powerful as the cinema. Mayer himself said, in the October 1937 issue of *Photoplay*, "Hollywood brings the world to the United States and the United States to the world. This interchange—of writing brains, talent, music, tradition—is important to world peace. It is equally important to good entertainment which knows no geography and has no international boundary lines." (Mayer's most salient quotes, including this one, also appear in his minibiography on the Internet Movie Database: http://www.imdb.com/name/nm0562454/bio#quotes.)

The studio moguls, Mayer included, had little respect for the intelligence of the audiences they wanted to reach. Adolph Zukor, head of Paramount, which was the largest producer, distributor, and exhibitor of films in the world, was once heard to remark that the average moviegoer intelligence is that of a fourteen-year-old child. Therefore, movies that appealed to that demographic succeeded mightily, particularly the Andy Hardy series.

Until Andy Hardy, there had never been films that appealed directly to adolescent and teen moviegoers. The Hardy films, however—though Mayer and his executives did not realize this at first—played to that fourteen-year-old child, opening up a huge new audience for cinema to target: teens. Initially, Mayer and Mannix panicked over how this new trend might affect their existing star system, which appealed to older audiences. They needn't have worried. MGM could now target both the adult and teen audiences with vehicles aimed directly at those segments. On one level, the adults who were attracted to the Hardy family values were the prototype for what followed in television, family comedies that adults liked as much as their children. Yet, decades before these television family comedies, teens flocked to movie houses to see Andy Hardy and his dating dilemmas, how he and his friends dressed, and what music they listened to. Mayer and Mannix were wrong: This was not a trend; it was an entirely new market to target.

In a *New York Times* column from April 9, 2000, titled, "The Triumph of Burbopolis," writer Michael Pollan comments on the Hardy phenomenon: the Hardy's effect, and that of their television progeny, on many families' lives. He called it "Cleaverism," an idealized projection of suburban life that became, in his words, "the sitcom image of suburbia." As in the Hardy series during the Great Depression, the idealistic image of family life in the suburbs in the decade after World War II was just that, an ideal—yet more for parents than for their children, whose rejection of that ideal helped define the baby boomer 1960s. Yet, back in the 1930s, as Bill Clinton said about his parents, audiences looked to the Hardys as their ideal.

For his part, Mickey said of the Hardy family, "Andy had a father who was a small-town judge as honest as Abe Lincoln, and a mother who was as sweet as my own. The Hardy family was so clean Andy only shook hands with her." [20]

However, one should not dismiss the series as Depression-era feel-good fluff from the Metro factory. It had one of the greatest impacts in movie history. Author and film historian James Robert Parish wrote in his book *The Great Movie Series* that the Hardy films were "geared to have strong but restrained humor, set in a sensible and warm atmosphere. Slapstick and wisecracks were carefully avoided in the homey series. Judge Hardy's success with his children was due to his ability to be a guide, philosopher, and friend. In his heart-to-heart, fireside talks with his son, he moralized without being intolerably sentimental or sententious. The teamwork of the repertory group among the Hardy clan was hard to beat." [21]

By the summer of 1937, it was clear that the Andy Hardy films were becoming a significant money grab for MGM. Mayer and the Loews shareholders were getting rich from this profit machine—MGM received a neat two million dollars in clear profit on *You're Only Young Once*—and the future seemed limitless. Everybody was doing well except Mickey, who was still stuck at his five-hundred-dollar weekly salary. No more, no less. Nell, who was aware of the huge earnings MGM was making, in part because of her son, made her move.

Since Harry Weber's illness, David Todd had been in charge of Mickey's career at the Weber Agency. Nell was advised by all their friends that Mickey was being shortchanged. She hired noted Hollywood attorney Martin Gang to help Todd renegotiate the seven-year pact Mickey was being held to with MGM. Gang, of the law firm of Gang, Kopp, and Brown, had a list of high-powered clients including George Burns, Bob Hope, Olivia de Havilland, Myrna Loy, Lucille Ball, and Frank Sinatra.

Kopp, Nell, and David Todd met with Nick Nayfack, the head of business affairs for Metro. Nayfack reminded Nell that MGM had taken a chance and hired Mickey when he was basically a "nobody." Gang got Nayfack to admit that Mickey was grossly underpaid. MGM finally agreed to a $250 raise above the base salary of $150 he was receiving. But Nell was still unhappy.

Enter the powerful head of the William Morris Agency, Abe Lastfogel. "Uncle Abe" came to visit Mickey and Nell and told them that the Weber Agency and David Todd were neither prepared nor able to provide the clout necessary for a star the caliber of young Rooney. Lastfogel sent gifts, took Nell and Mickey to lavish dinners, and even suggested that he could get Fred Pankey, Nell's new husband, a well-paying job. Eventually, after much wooing, Lastfogel won, and in January 1938, after more than ten years with Weber, Mickey switched to the William Morris Agency.

Immediately, Lastfogel launched a campaign to get Mickey a new deal at MGM worthy of his star power. He would constantly call Mannix, Nayfack, and even Mayer himself. One of Lastfogel's "lieutenants," Harry Friedman, on July 20, 1939, wrote an extensive memo to Lastfogel that contained a concise breakdown, picture by picture, of how MGM was ripping off Mickey. The actor was receiving a base $3,333.33 per film, plus the bonus that Martin Gang negotiated in 1938, for a total of $5,000 per picture. This amounted to $15,000 per year. It was the ammunition that Lastfogel needed to fight Mayer. He went directly to Mayer and told him how "unhappy" both Mickey and Nell were. With Mickey's contract nearing completion, Mayer was not going to take a chance on the actor leaving and going to one of his rivals. Thus, at the end of 1939, Mickey received a new three-year contract that was a definite improvement. Under the new pact, Rooney would receive $1,000 per week, guaranteed for forty weeks the first year; $1,250 per week the second year; and $1,500 per week for the third year. Moreover, MGM held the option for four additional years, beginning at $1,750 per week and raised incrementally to $3,000 per week by year four. Mickey would also receive a $25,000 per-picture bonus with MGM and a guarantee of no fewer than two bonuses per year.[22]

Mickey, only eighteen, was protected under the Coogan Law until he was twenty-one. This California law to protect child actors was written after child actor Jackie Coogan was left broke by his mother and stepfather. Thus, two-thirds of Rooney's money would be put into an irrevocable trust fund in the California Bank, not to be touched until he was sixty years old. The other third went into a separate trust for Rooney's mother. Nell was also allowed $800 per month for living expenses for herself, and Mickey was given $100 for his own use.[23]

From the bonuses, Mickey and Nell bought a rambling two-story Spanish-style house on Densmore Drive in Encino for $75,000. It was near Clark Gable and Carole Lombard's ranch. The house was on five landscaped acres with walnut, lemon, and orange trees throughout the property, and the customary swimming pool. Tour buses and sight-seers' cars provided a constant stream of traffic passing the house. According to Arthur Marx, "The way Nell decorated the house on her own with contemporary Barker Brothers furniture. It really was rather ordinary."[24]

Despite the new contract terms and the bonuses, it still was not enough financially. The agents, attorneys such as Martin Gang, and his associates took their substantial cuts; and then there was the com-mission to William Morris. A memo from Martin Gang to MGM requested that "all taxes on moneys paid into Mickey's trust fund and on Mickey's contract salary should be paid from the trust; also all commissions payable on the moneys payable into the trust should be deducted." Gang noted that this was necessary because it was "im-possible for Mickey and his mother to get along on his $40,000 per year salary under their present set-up, for under present existing con-ditions they are in the red approximately $6,500 after taking into consideration all their necessary expenditures." So, after starting at $150 per week at Metro and making about $7,800 in 1934, with all the new raises and bonuses, Mickey and Nell were now struggling on more than $100,000.[25] As Arthur Marx told us, "Who would have dreamed that there would come a time when being $6,500 in the red would look pretty good to Mickey?"[26]

The Andy Hardy character was indelible to Mickey Rooney, and he remained Andy Hardy to many fans worldwide almost sev-enty years later. Upon Mickey's death, reporter David Hinckley in the April 7, 2014, *New York Post* wrote, "Mickey Rooney was still Andy Hardy to Americans, despite a life of turmoil. Despite a life with more wreckage than Lindsay Lohan and Britney Spears combined, Mickey Rooney somehow never stopped being Andy Hardy." As Karen Kramer, the widow of producer Stanley Kramer, told us, she grew up watching Andy Hardy and had a schoolgirl crush on Rooney. When she saw him decades later at an anniversary celebration of *It's a Mad, Mad, Mad, Mad World*, he was Andy Hardy all over again.

Mickey and Judy and the MGM Backyard Musicals

Mickey and Judy in one of the backyard musicals.
PHOTO COURTESY OF ROBERT EASTON.

Judy turned to drugs because she was in pain and because drugs made her feel good. As one of the MGM kids, she'd been treated for most of her life to magical, instant, solutions to everything . . . She could never accept herself so she was always on the run.

MICKEY ROONEY

Sometimes movie history is made when the chemistry of two stars acting, singing, and dancing together explodes across the screen, and the totality of their joint performance exceeds what either one has done individually. Fred Astaire and Ginger Rogers both performed in solo roles, Ginger winning an Oscar for Best Actress for the 1940 *Kitty Foyle*, and creating a lasting character in *Roxie Hart*, but together in movies such as *Top Hat*, *Flying Down to Rio*, and *The Gay Divorcee*, Ginger and Fred were beyond magic. Studios look for such combinations. The protosexual friction between Spencer Tracy and Katharine Hepburn generated a flashing electricity as they played off each other for over thirty years, and the on-screen romantic interplay between Tom Hanks and Meg Ryan in *Joe Versus the Volcano*, *Sleepless in Seattle*, and *You've Got Mail* was an expression of pure happiness as the two conveyed to audiences the belief that love will always find a way. But one of the most exciting song-and-dance combinations in motion picture history was that of Mickey Rooney and Judy Garland, friends since they were students together at Ma Lawlor's Professional School in 1930 and continuing their friendship when both became contract players at Metro.

Mickey entered the MGM system a year earlier than Judy, and was almost immediately propelled to the edge of stardom by *A Midsummer Night's Dream*. His career quickly accelerated, while Judy was used only marginally. They both attended the studio school together, and remained schoolmates and friends. Mickey was two years older than Judy, which at that age was a wide chasm, and they were more like childhood siblings than a romantic couple.

Thanks to a deal Mayer struck with Judy's agent, a former bootlegger and pimp named Frank Orsatti, Garland was earning three hundred dollars a week. Mickey, at that time, was paid five hundred a week plus some minor bonuses. But the money they would soon earn for the studio when they began performing together would eclipse that of many of the other romantic pairings at the studio, because both entertainers possessed the ability to play off one another psychically, going beyond what the screenplay and the director called for.

The ten movies that Mickey and Judy appeared in together, which were all at MGM, under their studio agreements, were: *Thoroughbreds Don't Cry* (1937), *Love Finds Andy Hardy* (1938), *Babes in Arms* (1939), *Andy Hardy Meets Debutante* (1940), *Strike up the Band* (1940), *Life Begins for Andy Hardy* (1941), *Babes on Broadway* (1941), *Thousands Cheer* (1943), *Girl Crazy* (1943), and *Words and Music* (1948).

Rooney's and Garland's chemistry was obvious to Louis Mayer from their very first performance in the 1937 *Thoroughbreds Don't Cry*, which generated such a positive audience reaction that Mayer and his ad hoc board of advisers (referred to as the College of Cardinals) were convinced that they were looking at sheer magic, something that went beyond acting. The two were playful and innocent, a pair of friends joyfully cavorting together captured on-screen and framed so beautifully that it became abundantly clear to Mayer and his top execs that this combination should go on for as long as audiences wanted. Although Louis Mayer, when presented with a pitch for a new film, liked to pull out box office figures from similar features and look at the numbers to predict a bottom line, he sometimes allowed himself to be engulfed by the magic of a really good film. And that's what happened with *Thoroughbreds Don't Cry*.

In the film, for the first time in her career, Judy Garland (whose previous film was *Broadway Melody of 1938*, in which she sings "You Made Me Love You" to a Clark Gable photo) received top billing. *Thoroughbreds Don't Cry* was the first MGM film for Ronald Sinclair. A *Motion Picture Herald* news item on July 31, 1937, noted that, in the picture, Douglas Scott was to replace Freddie Bartholomew, Mickey's frequent costar and the leading male juvenile lead at MGM, who at the time was involved in a contract dispute and lawsuit with Metro. Also, much to Mickey's delight, parts of *Thoroughbreds Don't Cry* were shot on location at Santa Anita racetrack, Mickey's home away from home. Even though the film did not have a huge box office return, Mayer, to his credit, quickly recognized the magic and electricity created by Garland and Rooney in their scenes together. The *Hollywood Reporter*, on March 17, 1938, wrote that a sequel to this film was to be made entitled *Thoroughbreds Together*, which never occurred.

Louis Mayer knew what he was watching was pure gold, and upon his directive, Judy was rushed into the Andy Hardy film *Love Finds Andy Hardy*, to exploit her chemistry with Mickey. Judy was an instant romantic fit, playing Andy's platonic friend Betsy Booth, who desperately wants more than friendship with Andy. Then came Judy's monster hit *The Wizard of Oz*, after the filming of which she was rushed into *Babes in Arms*, along with her Oz costar Margaret Hamilton. Based on the 1937 Broadway play by Richard Rodgers and Lorenz Hart, *Babes in Arms* was adapted and tailored to both Rooney and Garland, with added songs by Oz composers Yip Harburg and Harold Arlen, and by MGM composers Arthur Freed and Nacio Herb Brown.

Produced by Arthur Freed, *Babes in Arms* was written by Jack McGowan, Kay Van Riper of the Hardy writing team, and Annalee Whitmore, and was directed by Busby Berkeley in his first film at Metro after gaining fame for his work at Warner Bros. Curiously, most of the Broadway songs written by Rodgers and Hart were cut, except for the title tune, "The Lady Is a Tramp" (later made famous by Frank Sinatra), which was used as background music during a dinner scene; and Garland's heart-stopping rendition of "Where or When." Freed and Brown wrote a new song for the film, "Good Morning," that later gained more notoriety in *Singin' in the Rain* as performed by Gene Kelly, Donald O'Connor, and Debbie Reynolds. *Babes in Arms*, which also featured one of the best tap dance numbers of Mickey Rooney's entire career, became a huge hit, one of the ten biggest of the year, earning almost four million dollars in the domestic gross and nearly two million in pure profits. At nineteen years old, Mickey was nominated for an Academy Award for Best Actor.

The film version of *Babes in Arms* showed audiences something vibrantly new and bursting with excitement. Just watch Mickey at the head of the throng of teenagers in *Babes*, leading an army of youth, marching in optimism and joy even during the throes of the Great Depression. While their parents might have scrounged for pennies to buy the next bottle of milk, here was an entire generation rising to the music. Sure, they did not know what lay before them: war, bodies piled on the beaches of Normandy and Iwo Jima, the incineration of entire cities, death camps. These were our parents who fought that war for us, and now they're gone. But on that screen, with that music, with that joy, captured on celluloid in majestic chiaroscuro, they are forever young.

Mayer's instincts about pairing Mickey and Judy had been correct. The film proved to be a triumph, and Mayer saw dollar signs for a Garland and Rooney team. He now had Judy with the Oz film, and Rooney with the Hardy films and a slew of other features, all returning large revenues for the studio as audiences showed no letup in their desire for more Rooney and more Garland. Accordingly, Mayer rushed into production *Strike up the Band*, with the same creative team, now supervised by Arthur Freed, whom Mayer believed was a genius. MGM empowered its recent steal from Warner Bros., flamboyant director/choreographer Busby Berkeley, to realize his vision by staging elaborate routines featuring Mickey and Judy and the band they sought to have perform on a national stage. The next two films, *Babes on Broadway* (1941) and *Girl Crazy* (1943), employed the same team. *Babes in Arms* (1939), those two, and *Strike up the Band* are often referred to as the "backyard musicals."

Berkeley and Garland had several blowout arguments during filming of the backyard musicals, after which the studio removed him as director. However, Rooney was amused by Busby. Mickey wrote, "He was hard on all of us . . . he could be quite charming with his flashing eyes and a smile that warmed everyone around him . . . [H]e had an alcoholic's perfection . . . [B]oth vaudeville kids, Judy and I were troupers enough not to complain. This is after all, what we lived for. If we weren't working, we'd have complained. But we did work." [1]

Film historian Lou Sabini remarked to us that "Those films, which have been called the 'backyard musicals,' were considered to be low-budget musicals for MGM, while it certainly would have been a major production for most other studios. These films were about teens putting on a show that spotlighted not just the leads but various other young performers who were part of the MGM studio system. The concept, which started strong, started to wear thin." [2]

Producer Arthur Freed clearly wanted to duplicate the first film, *Babes in Arms*, in its two sequels. Fred Finklehoffe, who had created the second outing, *Strike up the Band*, wrote a carbon copy for the final film of the backyard quartet, *Babes on Broadway*. Burton Lane wrote the music for the songs, with Arthur Freed's brother Ralph and E. Y. "Yip" Harburg as the lyricists for various numbers. Freed would write the score's biggest hit, "How About You," but Harburg would have the more lasting relationship with Lane, with whom he would later write the Broadway hit musical *Finian's Rainbow*. In order to introduce a wider variety of musical styles into the score, Freed assigned Roger Edens, Garland's longtime mentor at MGM, to arrange the score.

Berkeley kept things hopping in *Babes* with his elaborate staging of the production numbers. He spent days endlessly rehearsing before shooting, in marathon sessions that upset the front office by going over the projected budgets. At one point, Louis B. Mayer even sent his minions to the set to see why Berkeley was belaboring the shooting schedule. Berkeley got rid of them in his usual way: He climbed on the camera boom and had technicians raise him so high that the executives couldn't talk to him. After they left, he got the entire number on the first take, releasing the company early for the day and saving the studio thousands of dollars.

Toward the end of the musical series, the critics were beginning to notice that the stars were getting a bit old for this "gee whiz, let's put on a show" theme. Rooney was now involved with Ava Gardner, and Judy had her own love interest. Thus, by the last of the backyard musicals, *Babes on Broadway*, it was obvious that the child stars Garland and Rooney had clearly grown up off-screen. In fact, during the third week of filming *Babes on Broadway*, Garland eloped to Las Vegas with composer David Rose. She asked for a few days off for a honeymoon, but Mayer forced her back on set the next day, disappointed that she had deprived him of the chance to garner publicity with a lavish wedding. Meanwhile, Rooney's soon-to-be first wife, Ava Gardner, was watching him perform in Carmen Miranda drag, on her first day at the studio. This was Hollywood after all.

Babes on Broadway marked the film debut for Margaret O'Brien, who recalled to the authors, "It's rather remarkable that my first film was with Mickey and his last film was with me. A stunning coincidence. He was just such a great person and performer, right until the end." [3]

By the time *Babes on Broadway* was released, in late 1941, critics were complaining that both stars needed to take on more adult roles. Audiences loved them regardless, and though the film was a modest hit in comparison to *Babes in Arms*, it still wound up in the black for the studio. Even though it saw the box office decline for *Babes on Broadway*, the studio was undaunted in reuniting the *Babes* team for another go-round, casting Rooney and Garland, and attaching Berkeley as director, for *Girl Crazy* later that year.

During this period, Mickey and Judy were at the mercy of Louis B. Mayer. E. J. Fleming, in *The Fixers*, writes that the studio ruthlessly exploited Judy in *Babes on Broadway*, and he later told the authors,

"Judy, like Mickey, became a slave to MGM. They had them on a brutal work schedule. *Babes* [*on Broadway*] was completed in thirty-one days, along with publicity and personal appearance schedules that they undertook to maximize their value to the studio. Mayer, to keep Judy going and to keep her weight down, was given the drug Benzedrine, commonly known as speed, and to give her energy."

Judy was quoted by Paul Donnelley in his biography of her: "They had us [Mickey and Judy] working days and nights on end. They'd give us pills to keep us on our feet long after we were exhausted. Then they'd take us to the studio hospital and knock us out with sleeping pills—Mickey (Rooney) sprawled out on one bed and me on another. Then after four hours they'd wake us up and give us the pep pills again so we could work 72 hours in a row. Half of the time we were hanging from the ceiling but it was a way of life for us."[4] In an interview with the *Daily Mail Online* republished on September 3, 2014, by Caroline Howe, Judy said of the pills, "That's the way we got mixed up. And that's the way we lost contact." In this way, both Mickey and Judy were being stretched to the limits by the studio, and revealed it publicly only years afterward.

Just as the studio would later assign Les Peterson to watch over Mickey, and Eddie Mannix to supervise Peterson, Mannix assigned Betty Asher to watch over Judy. It was the studio's way to keep their teenage stars managed and, most important, working through their rigorous filming schedules as if they were on an assembly line. As William Asher, Betty Asher's brother, told us in March 2007, "Betty worked in publicity and was a handler for Garland. She loved Judy. Betty was like a sister to Judy. They may have been even closer, *really closer*, than that." According to William Asher, Mayer was aware that Betty was a lesbian and that she had seduced Judy when she was fifteen years old. Asher, whom we interviewed in connection with Dr. Feelgood, had a long history in Hollywood and was a noted director/producer of shows such as *I Love Lucy* and *Bewitched*. "Betty and Judy lived together for a while, but when Judy married Vincente Minnelli, the relationship ended. Betty was the maid of honor at Judy's wedding to Minnelli."

Mickey Rooney expressed his opinions about Judy's sexuality in *Life Is Too Short*, saying, "She always idolized her own charming father—only to learn, after she'd grown up, that he was a homosexual. She couldn't accept that in him. And then, she had an even harder time accepting a trace in herself. She had an affair with a female singer and, caught up in guilt, couldn't accept herself." [5]

Mickey and Judy's relationship remained strong throughout the years, until Judy's suicide in 1969. They were confidantes, intimates, and lifelong friends. Although there is no direct evidence of a physical relationship, Mickey's six-decades-long mistress, Ms. Smith (not her real name and whom we shall meet later), suggested that she was at parties in the early 1950s where Mickey and Judy escaped to the bedroom together and then returned to the party casually disheveled. Mickey's friend Sidney Miller, whom we interviewed extensively, also suggested a possible sexual relationship, stating, "Mickey and Judy were always close. I think, at times, they may have been closer than people think." [6]

The way Judy and Mickey were drugged at MGM turned out to be a tragedy. Judy came to rely on drugs because she was in pain and because drugs made her feel good. Actress and Andy Hardy costar Ann Rutherford said in an interview with us, "As one of the MGM kids, she'd been treated for most of her life to magical, instant, solutions to everything . . . She could never accept herself so she was always on the run."

During an interview for the 1992 documentary film *MGM: When the Lion Roars*, Rooney described his friendship with Garland: "Judy and I were so close we could've come from the same womb. We weren't like brothers or sisters but there was no love affair there. There was more than a love affair. It's very, very difficult to explain the depths of our love for each other. It was so special. It was a forever love. Judy, as we speak, has not passed away. She's always with me in every heartbeat of my body."

Mickey sometimes contradicted his take on Judy, saying variously, in a decades-old TV interview: "We were so close . . . [I]t transcended any love affair . . . She was my sister from the beginning—the sister I never had . . . She was the love I'd searched for."

London Sunday Express writer Clive Hirschhorn interviewed Judy in 1969, the last interview she gave before she died of a drug overdose on June 22, 1969. Hirschhorn wrote, "I met her backstage after the show, and she was in a good mood. She joked that my socks were too short. She talked about how MGM had hooked her and Mickey Rooney on drugs to keep them awake during filming, and she told me that Louis B. Mayer never let her forget that she didn't have movie-star looks. He called her 'my little hunchback.' But she didn't moan about it. There was no malice or sense of exploitation. She told me, '. . . If you want fame you have to pay for it—and brother, I have!' "

The families remained close. Liza Minnelli, Judy's daughter, released a public statement after Mickey's death, saying, "Mickey was somebody that everybody loved, but to me he was part of the family. He was one of a kind, and will be admired and respected always."

Mickey's oldest daughter, the talented Kelly Rooney, told us, "I clearly remember going to Judy's beach house with my dad and my sisters and brother on Sundays. While the kids were all out playing, you could hear him roaring with laughter at the stories that Judy was telling about the old days. They both were having a good ol' time enjoying drinks and old times. It was just magical watching them together laughing, singing, and reminiscing. I will never forget that image." [7]

The documentary *MGM: When the Lion Roars* was filmed after Judy had been gone for twenty-three years. It some instances, Mickey's recollections seem like the cloudy memories of an old man in winter mourning a long-lost colleague. However, it is almost a case of déjà-vu; Mickey used similar words when he was a guest on *The Judy Garland Show* thirty years earlier: "We've had a wonderful seven days together here," Mickey says at the close of the show, his arm around Judy's waist as she caresses the lapel of his tuxedo. "This is not only 'tradition,' this [woman] is the love of my life. My wife knows this— my wives know this. [She] always has been, because there never will be, there aren't adjectives enough to express, in the world, how the one and only Judy—is Judy." There is an awkward sweetness to his obviously ad-libbed words spoken with unfeigned sincerity.

Judy and Mickey struggled with many of the same issues after they were forced out of MGM. They had parallel challenges with pills, liquor, and bankruptcy; a roller-coaster ride in their careers; and several failed marriages. While Mickey survived the battle for ninety-three years, Judy made it only into her late forties before overdosing herself.

As Mickey eerily remarked to us in 2008, "Sometimes I wonder if Judy had the right idea . . . to exit all this bullshit."

10

Mickey Goes Wild

Andy Hardy's true love, Polly Benedict (played by Ann Rutherford).
POSTER CARD COURTESY OF ROBERT EASTON.

When I met him, I still didn't know he was the biggest wolf on the lot," Ava Gardner once recalled about Mickey. "He was catnip to the ladies. He knew it too. The little sod was not above admiring himself in the mirror. All five-foot-two of him! The complete Hollywood playboy, he went through ladies like a hot knife through fudge. He was incorrigible. He'd screw anything that moved. He had a lot of energy. He probably banged most of the starlets who appeared in his Andy Hardy films—Lana Turner among them. She called him *Andy Hard-on.*"[1]

Frank Sinatra once said, as Mickey's good friend and sometime business adviser Nick Sevano told us, "Mickey was the best lay in Hollywood. He was also the greatest talent in Hollywood."[2]

By early 1938, the Andy Hardy screen phenomenon had begun, and Mickey was the driving force behind it. MGM knew it had a gold mine in young Mickey Rooney. However, it was also aware that there was a great division between the real-life Mickey and his on-screen alter ego. Mickey was far more streetwise than the typical Depression-era teenager. He'd already seen too much. Raised in burlesque houses and with a father who still worked in strip-tease joints, growing up backstage and in dressing rooms with nearly naked women strutting their stuff, and with a mother turning tricks in their living room, he was no stranger to the seamier side of life. On the few occasions Joe Yule Sr. did visit his son after he split with Nell, he would invite Mickey to watch him perform at the Follies Burlesque in Los Angeles, and let his friends come along. Mickey's friend Sidney Miller told us and Arthur Marx, "It was a real treat for horny teenagers like us to see all the bare tits and ass at the burlesque. We were able to even go back and watch the girls get undressed. Mickey would even get a lap dance with some of the girls."[3] Even as he portrayed a naïve, innocent teen on celluloid, Mickey's hormones were roaring in real life.

It was also in 1938 that Mickey portrayed a character with a bad-boy image, in *Boys Town*, opposite Spencer Tracy. The cast included Mickey's lifelong friend Sidney Miller. *Boys Town* was a monster hit for MGM, held over in its run at theaters throughout the United States and Canada. The film was nominated for Best Picture, Best Screenplay, Best Director, and won Oscars for Spencer Tracy for Best Actor and for Eleanore Griffin and Dore Schary for Best Original Story. This film cemented Schary's position at MGM, and he would eventually succeed Mayer as studio head. Mickey won a special award at that year's Academy Awards: a five-inch-high Oscar for "significant contribution in bringing to the screen the spirit and personification of youth." (As a side note, that statuette was given to Jeri Greene, comic Shecky Greene's first wife, who was Mickey's girlfriend in the late 1960s. As Shecky told the authors, the statuette was handed down to his daughter.)

MGM mogul Louis B. Mayer called *Boys Town* his favorite film created during his tenure at MGM. The film grossed $4,133,000 in 1938 dollars. It's still generating profits on DVD sales and rentals for Turner Films, which bought the MGM film library in 1986. The film also signaled to the MGM marketing team and to Mayer the power of the youth market. In fact, it was so popular with young audiences that it forced the modification of a Canadian law that prohibited the admittance of children under sixteen to movie theaters. It also sparked a sequel, *Men of Boys Town*, released in 1941, though it was not as successful as the original.

At age eighteen, and upon his success in *Boys Town*, Mickey had become a worldwide motion picture star and was riding high. "Everything came at him nonstop," remembered his friend, director Dick Quine. "We just watched in awe. Here he was purchasing a palatial home in Encino, buying this knockout baby-blue Ford convertible and he was spending his nights chasing broads. He was knocking down south of one hundred thousand dollars a year. It was just fucking incredible." [4]

It was a situation similar to what occurs with young stars today when all of a sudden they become nationally recognized, when they are suddenly multimillionaires from whom every hanger-on looks to carve a piece. Such stars are faced with multiple challenges, which can cause a significant, almost traumatic, change in both their personal and professional lives, and they are usually not equipped to make the proper decisions. Mickey had had no guidance from his father, whose own life was never an example to follow. For her part,

Mickey's mother, had been too overwhelmed and destitute after Joe abandoned her, all alone and struggling to support their child. Thus, Mickey had had to confront a reality that no six-year-old should have had to confront. No wonder he regarded Louis B. Mayer as a kind of patriarchal figure, and studio fixer Eddie Mannix as a surrogate father, even as Mannix led him down paths that were contrary to his own best interests.

For MGM, where the bottom line was the most important thing, they needed to protect their asset, who was making millions for the company, keeping Nick Schenck and Louis Mayer very happy with the return on their investment. Accordingly, the public image of Mickey Rooney/Andy Hardy needed to be closely guarded.

At first, Louis Mayer was willing to overlook Mickey's teenage indiscretions. Peter Evans writes, "[The Hardy films] also more than satisfied Mayer's greed, and the old showman was always willing to overlook Mickey's extravagant whims. When his minders warned Mayer that on weekends Mickey drank insatiably, Mayer ignored them. 'He would say I was a good little fella and pat me on the head— he made about ten million dollars a pat at the box office,' Rooney said." [5]

Eddie Mannix and Howard Strickling so meticulously guarded MGM publicity that they controlled not only every aspect of their stars' lives but the Hollywood media as well. In fact, Louella Parsons didn't type a line about a Metro star unless she'd cleared it first with either Mannix or Strickling. No reporter would dare go rogue on a Metro personality if he or she wanted to be kept in Strickling's loop. The best example of the way Strickling controlled the media with an iron hand to protect his stars involved Lana Turner, her lover, and her daughter. When mobster Johnny Stompanato was murdered at Lana Turner's house in Beverly Hills, Turner called her mother. Did her mother call the police? Did she call an ambulance? No, she called two people. One was attorney Jerry "Get Me" Giesler, the Hollywood lawyer once dubbed "defender of the damned." The second was Howard Strickling. Even though Turner was no longer under contract to MGM, she sought out Strickling for his help. After all, it was Stricking who had covered up her abortions and a suicide attempt in the past. She had relied on him for over twenty years. He had shielded her from the journalists and the columnists just as he had shielded her affair with Mickey Rooney. She knew with his help that she was destined to be OK. Her image had been so carefully controlled no one dared print the real story. And once again, Strickling carefully orchestrated the media that went into damage control and in the end prevented any damage to her career.[6]

Katharine Brush, a popular author at the time, remarked on MGM's desire to project a wholesome image for Rooney in a story (essentially an insider's gossip column) she wrote titled *Andy Hardy's Private Secretary* for *Reader's Digest*. She recalled the incident in which Mayer, watching the rushes, objects to Andy telling his mother that the dinner she has cooked is no good: "Infinite pains are taken to keep the family precisely average," Brush wrote, "lest the parents protest that Andy is setting a bad example." The subsequent rewrite was ordered by Mayer himself, in the interest of family values.[7]

(The Hardy family values were not enjoyed by everyone. When MGM once offered Broadway playwright George Oppenheimer a job writing Hardy films at a substantial salary, he remarked, "Sure I'd love to write one, provided you let me have every member of the fucking family killed in a railroad accident in the last reel." [8])

MGM was very careful to preserve Rooney as if he were a specimen on a microscope slide fixed in the image created by Aurania Rouverol, Kay Van Riper, and Louis B. Mayer—even though the real-life Mickey was changing before their very eyes, morphing from the all-American teenager he played into a reckless young adult. Andy

Hardy had become his exoskeleton, while the real Mickey metastasized within. For example, when in 1938 the studio opened *Judge Hardy's Children*, the third film in the series, Mickey was forced to drive up to the premiere in the Model-A Ford with the torn roof from the films rather than in his new convertible. His date was gray-haired Nell, forever the stage mother and caregiver.

The studio's efforts notwithstanding, the flesh-and-blood Mickey had simply become vulgar. He would brag to anyone within earshot about his masculine prowess and the girls with whom he'd had sexual relations. He was on a tear, and the people he boasted to were shocked at the crude way he spoke. His close friends, however, were amused by Mickey's frankness and brand of braggadocio, too soon a man in the body of a child, now boozing, chasing women with fervor, and cursing like a stagehand in burlesque, as his hormones and lack of impulse control took over.

Sidney Miller recalled a get-together during the summer of 1938:

> We were once hanging out at Phil Silvers's apartment, shooting the breeze. Silvers was trying to get in film and was already a top banana in burlesque. We looked up to Phil, as he was older than we were and had been around the block. Silvers was telling us about the girls he had fucked in the burlesque show he was in, and we were very intrigued by his spiel. Mickey could[n't] care the less about his stories. He just wanted to find a girl to schtupp. Silvers said he knew this gorgeous hooker he could call. Mickey was drooling. He told Silvers to bring her to the apartment and we all agreed to split her cost. Phil called her and cut a deal. He got a group rate. Mickey started bragging that he could fuck her for the longest and made a bet that whoever lasted the longest with the girl gets paid the whole cost. I think it was like twenty or so bucks each.

I went first, then Jackie Cooper, then Silver, and Mickey took the last shot. None of us lasted long, probably three or four minutes. When Mickey went in, I mean he was in there for a good twenty, thirty minutes. We heard noises, squeals and loud noises. We were on the floor laughing. Then Mickey came out saying, "Did I tell you guys . . ." and he kept bragging. Then he thanked us for his free treat and left. When Silvers started paying the girl, he asked her, "Was he really that good? Did he really last thirty minutes?" She laughed and said, "Are you kidding? It was four minutes of fucking and twenty-six minutes of imitations."[9]

Even though outside the studio gates, Mickey was alluded to by Hollywood columnists, who spotted him cavorting at nightclubs and with different starlets, he remained totally professional on the set, his discipline impeccable. After all, he was a seasoned veteran with years in the business. It was only after closing time when the hormone-loaded Mickey was unleashed.

His behavior outside the studio was becoming legendary, in fact, news about him inevitably leaked. At eighteen, he was not yet of legal drinking age in California, but he certainly could skirt that issue when he wanted to. At a party at Chasen's, where they would not serve him a drink because he had no ID to show he was of age, he told his buddy Sig Frohlich, "Hey, meet me in the can, Sig, and bring along a straight shot."[10] Bartenders who knew Mickey's age would not serve him alcohol. And even if they did not know him, because of his small stature, they always asked for his driver's license. Girls were not a problem, though. Mickey remembered, "I could fuck any girl, anytime. Most wanted me because I was Mickey Rooney. They could not give a shit what we did in bed. They wanted to brag to their friends that they had fucked me."[11]

Mickey liked to have a good time, but he was not a great conversationalist or a wit. "It wasn't like going out with Groucho or Fred Allen," Sid Miller recalled.

> He was an actual bore one on one. But take him to Ciro's nightclub or the Mocambo and he'd be up on the band-stand playing the drums or dancing the rhumba with the singers. He always played to the crowds, and they loved it. He was the life of the party as long as he could perform. And he was a great dresser. Real loud clothes with checks and plaids. I mean he didn't shop at the May Company. He had these obscure stores he would take me to where they would find him what he liked and had to special-fit his clothes because of his size. And he just loved all the looks. He wanted to be the center of attention. I could see him coming into the room saying to everyone, "How's it going, toots?" He said it to everyone, even the real snooty ones like Claudette Colbert and her doctor husband, who tried to be very refined and pompous. He just slapped them on the back and did his "How ya, toots?" to them. It was such a hoot. When Mickey was invited to parties, he *was* the entertainment. He did his imitations. I played piano, and he sang songs and danced. The girls loved him. He always had a girl leave with him from the party. I was not always so lucky.[12]

Mickey was having the time of his life. However, back at the studio, Mayer was seething. While there was no damage at the box office yet, Mickey's girl-chasing image was nevertheless seeping into the columns and threatening Mayer's plans to keep his star's All-American brand squeaky clean. The stories of Mickey the party animal were spilling out to Hedda Hopper at the *Los Angeles Times,*

Louella Parsons for the Hearst syndicate, and the other columnists. As much as Mayer and Strickling tried to suppress the stories and protect the Rooney/Hardy image, the truth was becoming almost impossible to conceal. In 1938, there was an almost nonstop onslaught of stories about Mickey: Sidney Skolsky, on May 23, in the *Hollywood Citizen-News*: "Mickey has now his own apartment and a valet. He now can be seen out almost every night . . ."; Harrison Carroll, on June 9, in the *Los Angeles Evening Herald-Express*: "Who is that pretty girl on Mickey's arm late last night at the Hula Hut . . ."; and on June 14: "Mickey in his loud sportcoat has traded in his blue Ford convertible for a 12-cyllinder custom built car that is racing green much like Gable's . . ."; Ella Wickersham's column in the *Los Angeles Examiner* of June 28 noted: "Mickey Rooney was entertaining one and all with his antics . . . Mickey was seen dancing with many of the girls."

Mickey, who was playing youths on the screen in the backyard musicals and the Hardy films, was in danger of betraying that image. Mayer at first tried the fatherly soft sell on Mickey. He knew how to be smooth on the surface. But his breaking point may have come with the reported pregnancy, in 1940, of a teenage starlet under contract to MGM named Julia Turner—soon to become known as Lana. Mickey claimed to have met her when she was fifteen and he was sixteen, at Currie's Ice Cream (near Hollywood High), and started dating her soon after their meeting. He recalled, "I soon found out that she was as oversexed as I was, warm passionate, soft and moist in interesting places when she arrived at MGM in 1937. She had been discovered by my old friend Mervyn LeRoy [whom Mickey had known since he was six in the silent film *Orchids and Ermine*] and clearly he could help Lana's career more than I could. I had no more dates with Lana. I thought that Lana had just outgrown me, but I later learned from Lana that the real reason we stopped dating was this: Lana had become pregnant." [13] Mickey claimed that Lana told him many years later, at a fund-raiser, that she was in a "family way" from Mickey. "I was stunned and grateful at that moment that I hadn't known back then. I might have wanted her to have the baby." [14]

Mickey was summoned to studio chief's plush, white offices. It was like being called into the throne room before an angry monarch. "Mickey, you know you're like the son I never had," Mayer pleaded. "I care about you and worry. When I see your name always in the papers . . . Louella's talking about you at all the nightspots . . . you're with all the girls . . . they talk about you at the Cocoanut Grove, drinking and dancing that rhumba . . . You have got to remember the public expects different . . . you are Andy Hardy. You have to stop living like that, son."

Mickey replied, "But Mr. Mayer, I work like a dog when I work . . . real hard . . . I put everything into it . . . If I were just another kid and I was going on dates, nobody would say a word . . . Now I'm not supposed to do that because I'm Andy Hardy! What am I working for?"

Mayer remained calm and reminded Mickey, "Son, that is what I am paying you well for. You are supposed to work hard. Now, I know you're a normal young boy, full of piss and vinegar. And I don't care what you do behind closed doors. But you need to behave in public and don't get some jailbait [Lana Turner] knocked up. It could destroy everything. *Farshtey?*" [15]

Whether Mickey was the father or not, Lana Turner had become pregnant, and the studio had to make sure that the young starlet's inconvenient condition didn't make it into the news. For that, Eddie Mannix relied on studio doctor Edward Jones. Jones was, according to E. J. Fleming in his book *The Fixers*, "Strickling's ever-present Dr. Edward Jones, who prescribed Benzedrine, Phenobarbital and Seconal, among others, to keep [Judy] Garland working." [16] Fleming told us that Jones, under Strickling and Mannix's direction, was used to assist in such sensitive matters around the studio, including Jean Harlow's illness and her husband Paul Bern's earlier "suicide." It was Dr. Jones who, Mickey claimed, performed the abortion on Turner.

With Turner's possible pregnancy hanging in the air during Louis Mayer's lecture, Mickey said he understood and promised to be more cautious. Yet Mayer was still concerned. Mannix had told L.B. that Mickey was a "loaded gun ready to go off." Mayer needed, at all costs, to protect the Rooney image.

Enter Lester Peterson. Peterson was one of the rising young stars of Strickling's PR unit. Mayer liked the personable Les Peterson, who had helped him in various matters with his daughters. Les had the appearance of the all-American male. About thirty-five, he was particularly good-looking and tall, with a head full of blond hair. He was often seen at many of the nightclubs around Los Angeles, watching out for MGM's "family of stars." He dated, and married in 1944, the beautiful actress Eleanor Stewart. But now his job was watching over Mickey. When Arthur Marx once asked Peterson what he did at MGM, he replied, "I'm Mickey Rooney's keeper." [17]

Peterson was the perfect choice to become Mickey's keeper. An MGM company man through and through, "he ate, drank and slept Metro Goldwyn Mayer," recalled Arthur Marx. "If Mayer asked him to meet a visiting fireman at four-thirty in the morning, he would do it. If Mayer [had] asked him to jump into a lake with all his clothes on, he would probably have done that, too." Peterson accepted Mayer's command and took charge of the eighteen-year-old Rooney. His orders were to tag along with Mickey anywhere outside the gates of Culver City. Peterson told Arthur Marx, "I followed him everywhere, except to the john and his bedroom." [18]

Mickey was keenly aware of his importance to MGM. He recalled, "The studio, of course, was interested in counseling me. In fact, they had a man named Les Peterson, who was vice-president in charge of Mickey Rooney. But, in truth, Peterson was not in charge of me; he was in charge of my image. . . . For a time, Peterson was a confidant and friend. 'Don't do this, don't do that,' preserving the image and robbing me of fun, or sneak a drink, or a ticket on a winner or loser. It didn't strike me for a while that Les Peterson was not my friend at all. He was a friend of Metro Goldwyn Mayer, Incorporated. Personally I believe his constant surveillance had much to do with my youthful emotional rebellion.[19]

It was an interesting time for the gossip columns. Today we watch the antics of rebellious teen stars play out on social media and in the press. They are following a long line of young personalities acting out, but Mickey was the original. Before Mickey, gossip was focused almost exclusively on the adult stars. The stories were about Gable marrying Lombard, the death of Jean Harlow, or the Fatty Arbuckle rape and manslaughter scandal. But Mickey set a whole new trend, tapping into a rich new vein of fans interested in young stars and starlets: teenagers. *Photoplay* and *Hollywood* magazines noticed the trend and started creating stories about Rooney, Judy Garland, Deana Durbin, and others in their age group.

Howard Strickling and his PR machine noticed this uptick in the gossip skewing to the young. They carefully monitored the columnists and tried to drive a positive slant to the stories, chalking the teen stars' antics up to youthful exuberance. For example, the column from May Hobart in the *Hollywood Citizen-News* on November 3, 1937, "Wild party at the It Café—Buster Crabbe held a free for all at the 'It' Café with guests Mickey Rooney, John Carradine, Bela Lugosi . . ." was followed by a Strickling entry (by Robin Coons) the next day in the same newspaper, titled, "Love Life of Mickey Rooney Bared." Despite the scandalous headline, the story detailed Rooney's "$10 allowance," the height of his dates (never over five feet tall), and that

"Business Comes First." It was a clean-up job, to show that Rooney was a busy young man, and, frankly, that it was a wonder that he had any time for girls at all.

All his carousing and partying changed, however, if only for a little while, when Mickey crossed paths with Ava Gardner.

11

Ava

Mickey and Ava Gardner at their wedding on January 10, 1942.
PHOTO COURTESY OF THE MONTE KLAUS COLLECTION.

f America was distracted by the distant drumbeat of war across Europe
and Asia, Mickey was not. His own drumbeat was the constant
march of the films he was shooting on the Metro lot and the young
girls he was chasing around Hollywood. But all that would soon
change with a single glance.

It was a hot July day in 1941 on Metro's Stage 7, where Mickey
was filming *Babes on Broadway*, the sequel to the phenomenally
successful *Babes in Arms*, with Judy Garland. The director called,

"Cut!" and the scene ended. Mickey looked toward the camera—and his head snapped to a stop right there, jiggling the Carmen Miranda headpiece he was wearing. Who was that girl next to Milt Weiss, Howie Strickling's assistant in publicity? Where had she come from? Dark, smokey-eyed, and lanky, she was stunning—and Mickey could barely catch his breath. She was just standing there watching the scene alongside Weiss, seemingly rapt by the chaos taking place in front of her as the crew worked the set. Mickey couldn't take his eyes off her, and tried to catch her gaze with his—even though he was dressed in a Carmen Miranda costume: a long slit skirt, a bolero blouse with phony breasts, huge platform shoes, a fruit hat that was larger than he was, and full makeup. For Mickey, time suddenly stood still. Everything about the young woman by the camera was tantalizing, certainly more tantalizing than this tired sequel that didn't measure up to the original. But this movie would be of great significance to Mickey, because it was in that moment on that day, on that set during that scene, when he first laid eyes on Ava Gardner.

Ava would not forget the day, either. It was her first day at the studio, and Weiss was assigned to take her on a tour where she would lock eyes with the studio's most popular performer. She recalled the moment to Peter Evans:

> I can remember that first meeting with Mick very clearly—probably because he was wearing a bowl of fruit on his head. . . . He was playing the Carmen Miranda character . . . complete with false eyelashes, false boobs, his mouth smothered with lipstick.
>
> It was my first day in Hollywood [and] I was being hauled around the sets to be photographed with the stars. He came over to me and said, "Hi, I'm Mickey Rooney." He did a little soft-shoe shuffle kind of dance, and bowed to me. God, I was embarrassed. I don't think I said a word. I

might have said "Hello" or something, I was overwhelmed. His Andy Hardy films made the studio millions and cost peanuts. So did his Mickey and Judy pictures. I wanted to ask for his autograph but I could barely open my mouth.

The people on the set were laughing like mad at him. He loved an audience, of course. He was always at his best when he was in the spotlight. I just wanted the ground to open and swallow me up.

Ava said that she asked Mickey after they were married what he was thinking when he first saw her on that set that day. He said, as Ava told Peter Evans, "'Okay, when Milt Weiss said you were a new contract player, I figured you were a new piece of pussy for one of the executives. The pretty ones were usually spoken for before they even stepped off the train. I didn't give a damn, I wanted to fuck you the moment I saw you. . . .' Mick was always the romantic. I guess he meant it as a compliment but I was shocked. I was still capable of being shocked in those days." [1]

In *Life Is Too Short*, Mickey echoed what he'd told Ava:

She was a contract player. The studio was full of sexy young women who wanted to make it in Hollywood. Most often, Hollywood ended up making them because some of the women were there, first and foremost, as potential pussy for the executives at MGM. But when Ava said just "Hello" in the soft drawl of her native North Carolina, I was a goner. I had known many beautiful women in my lifetime, but this little lady topped them all. My technique in those days was a combination of early Neanderthal and late Freud. I'd approach a pretty girl with confidence and confess that, yes, I was the one, the only, the original Mickey Rooney. Then instead of waiting for her reaction,

I'd launch into a comedy routine that gave the girl only one option. She'd have to laugh. When I found a girl who liked my impersonations and was willing to accept me, I was elated. But I was young and my elation quickly turned into instant boredom. However Ava turned me down five times for a date. That only made me want her more, not just so I could go to bed with her. I wanted to make her the mother of my children.[2]

Ava recalled:

Mick called me that night and asked me out to dinner. I said no. I wasn't playing hard to get. I wasn't into that Southern Belle shit. I was just too shy. I said I was busy. That was a stupid thing to say. Who the hell was I busy with, fahchrissake? . . . I didn't know a goddamn soul in Hollywood, except my sister. And I'm *busy*? [He persisted in calling her.] Every conversation ended up with him asking me to have dinner with him. Finally, I just ran out of excuses.[3]

According to Mickey's buddy Sidney Miller, it was a conversation that he had with Ava that turned the tide. As Sid told us, "She was shooting some cheesecake stills, and I came in to relay Mickey's invitation to dinner . . . I did it as a favor to Mickey. He was going crazy over her and asked me to try to talk her into going out with him. I had lunch with her and her sister in the commissary a few times. I told her that, 'You don't know how good for your career it would be if you were seen with Mick.' She looked at me, and she was a knockout, and innocently asked me, 'You think it would get me lot of exposure if I went out with Mickey?' I assured her that it would. After that, she was more receptive to him.

"Mickey sent a chauffeur-driven limo to pick up Ava and her sister Bappie who was also invited on that first date. He was sitting in the back, dressed in a tux. Ava was surprised at how charismatic and good-looking Mickey was without the Carmen Miranda makeup," Sid told us.[4] And Ava said, "The only other time I'd seen him he was wearing that Carmen Miranda shit on his face. I'd seen him on the screen a hundred times but that was in black-and-white. His looks in the flesh, without the Carmen Miranda makeup, came as a shock. He still wasn't what I'd call a *handsome may-an*, and his shortness surprised me, but there was definitely something appealing about him. He had thick, red-blonde wavy hair, crinkly Irish-green eyes, and a grin that was . . . well it definitely wasn't innocent, honey, I can tell you that!"[5]

On that first date, they ate dinner at Chasen's, where he introduced her to Ronald Colman, Cary Grant, James Stewart, and W. C. Fields. They saw Jimmy Durante sing "Inka Dinka Doo" at the Cocoanut Grove nightclub in the Ambassador Hotel, where they also saw the Freddy Martin Band, and finished up at Ciro's nightclub.[6]

After that first night, Ava and Mickey were nearly inseparable. He picked her up every day and they drove together to the studio. Sidney Miller remembered, "He'd drive on the lot with his convertible and scream to everyone, 'Hey, look at my girlfriend,' or 'This is my new girl. Isn't she gorgeous?' He embarrassed the hell out of Ava, but I think she enjoyed all the attention. She was his arm candy, but I think he was totally crushed on her."[7]

Mickey was obsessed with Ava. He took her out to dinner nightly at Romanoff's, Ciro's, or the Brown Derby. He took her dancing at the Grove, Ciro's, the Mocambo, the Trocadero, or the Ambassador Hotel. He took her to the races at Santa Anita; to watch him play golf at the Lakeside Country Club; to auto races, baseball games, and more. Everywhere they went, there were fans, photographers, and welcoming headwaiters who announced his arrival. She observed the tremendous influence of his power and was aware that this would open doors for her. She may have been naïve, but she was not dumb. She enjoyed all this new attention, even if it was directed at Mickey.[8]

Ava recalled, "He acted, he sang, he danced. He told jokes, did impersonations—Cary Grant, Jimmy Cagney, Lionel Barrymore, he did them all. He'd have even turned somersaults if I'd asked him to." [9]

After every date, Mickey proposed marriage to Ava. In *Life Is Too Short,* he wrote: "After the first date, every day I proposed marriage. She didn't say yes, but her no began to sound less firm after a time. She went from 'You're crazy, Mickey, I hardly know you' to 'Marriage is a serious thing, Mick' to 'What'll our life be like?' It was clear to me that I was making some progress." Mickey told her that their life together would be as big stars, they'd go everywhere together; he'd buy her mansions, jewelry, and fancy cars. Life would be one big party.[10]

Ava told Peter Evans that marrying Mick was the dumbest thing she ever did. "[Y]ou have to remember," she told him, "I was eighteen! August 1941. I was still a virgin . . . [A] lot of booze has flowed under the bridgework since then." [11]

Ava feared that living with Mickey would be like living on a soundstage 24/7, and that Mickey would always be on. And he was, because he didn't know *how* to be off. He drove Ava around in his Lincoln, a personal gift from Henry Ford. Inside the car was a gold plaque that read, TO MY DEAR FRIEND, MICKEY ROONEY, WITH GRATITUDE, HENRY FORD. Mickey liked it when he drove Ava around in his Lincoln. He liked her company. He also disliked being alone. In fact, he absolutely hated the times when he was alone. Maybe it was all the social contact he'd experienced as a toddler, his exposure to a theater audience, but he thrived on being in the public eye, and quietly sulked when he was alone. Sidney Miller told us, "He just hated to drive alone in the car from Encino to Ava's Franklin Avenue apartment. So he had me pick up Ava in his car to bring her back to his house, so he wouldn't be alone." [12]

Wherever Mickey went, however, his shadow followed. Les Peterson was always within steps of Rooney. In press clippings, at studio events, the ever-present Peterson was there lurking in the background of a photograph. Ava Gardner remarked of Les, "I knew he was only doing what Mayer had told him to do." [13] But even beneath the watchful eyes of Les Peterson and his studio bosses, Mickey and Ava were becoming an item.

The news that Ava Gardner and Mickey Rooney were seeing each other soon spread around the studio. Starlets who had previously enjoyed Rooney's attention—many of whom had grown to count on it—took his neglect to heart. Eventually, Peterson decided that it was time to warn L. B. Mayer of the seriousness of his star's interest in Ava. Mayer, who had to have Ava pointed out to him, some five weeks after she joined MGM, asked how serious.

"He wants to marry her, Mr. Mayer," Peterson told him.

"Tell him he can't," said Mayer. "He belongs to MGM. Tell him a married Andy Hardy would break the hearts of all those little girlies out there who want him for themselves. Who knows what that would cost—him, me, the studio?"

"I've already told him, L.B. I've told him that at his age he should still be playing the field, and having fun. He won't listen," said Peterson.

"Is he slipping her the business?"

"He swears he's not, L.B."

"Why doesn't he fuck her? He fucks all the others."

"He says she's holding out like no dame he's ever known, L.B."

"She ain't the fucking Virgin Mary," Mayer said.

"He says it's giving him terrible headaches," Peterson said.

"He should just boff her and get her out of my fucking hair." [14]

Ava reminisced about Peterson to Peter Evans:

> I liked Les, and I think he liked me. He was devoted to
> Mickey, of course. But he knew which side his bread was

buttered. And who can blame him? Mayer was the boss of bosses. He was the king. They all owed their careers to him. Afterward, after Mick and I were hitched, I asked Les whether there was *anything* Mayer liked about me?

Les had to think about that. "Well, he once told me you obviously had cunt power," he said.

I said, "Am I supposed to be flattered by that, Les?"

He said, "Well, that's just about the highest compliment L.B. can pay a girl, honey." [15]

Meanwhile, the Hollywood gossip columnists were abuzz with stories about Mickey with this unknown starlet Ava Gardner. Almost every column included a Rooney/Gardner tidbit of information. Sally Moore in the *Los Angeles Evening Herald-Express*, on August 30, 1941, wrote, "Richard Quinne is the dinner host to Mickey Rooney and his mysterious lady, Ava Gardner at his home."

Louella Parsons for the Hearst syndicate, on October 2, 1941, wrote, "Is Mickey Rooney getting serious about Ava Gardner? He gave her a friendship ring with a large topaz setting."

Harrison Carroll wrote on October 29, 1941, "Ava Gardner was at the It Café with Bobby Stack and she certainly didn't look as if she was thinking of Mickey Rooney."

Hedda Hopper, on October 30, 1941, wrote, "Mickey was holding his sultry girl, Ava Gardner, close at the opening of 'They Can't Get You Down.'"

Elizabeth Yeaman in the *Hollywood Citizen-News*, on December 10, 1941, wrote, "Is there wedding bells [*sic*] for Mickey and Ava Gardner? Gardner is a native of Smithfield, North Carolina, and is still blessed with a soft Dixie accent. The 21 year old Rooney said that he had fallen in love 'at first sight.'"

Ava was beginning to enjoy the new respect she was now being given at the studio as the chosen girlfriend of Mickey Rooney. In a manner of weeks, she had gone from obscure starlet from North Carolina to a princess living in the fire pit of Mickey's world: nightclubs, openings, and parties at the homes of some of the biggest screen idols she had grown up admiring. If she broke up with Mickey, she knew she could go right back to being "just another" ingénue who had yet to appear in a film. She was enjoying life at the top of the heap and was starting to acquire a tremendous capacity for clubbing until early morning.

"The Beachcomber had become a favorite spot of mine," she recalled. "They served the best zombies in California. They tasted so good and seemed so innocuous. . . . Bacardi, dark rum, light rum, pineapple juice, lime juice, apricot brandy, orange juice, a sprig of mint, and a cherry. Only I always told them to hold the mint and cherry. . . . That's the secret of a good zombie. I swear I still hadn't tied one on in my life at that stage," the later notorious drinker recalled.[16]

It was in late November, five months after they met on the movie set, when, after a night of partying and drinking zombies at Don the Beachcomber, Mickey popped the question for the umpteenth time. Ava was prepared for an answer this time. Both Gardner's mother and her sister, Bappie, with whom she lived, were advising her to marry Mickey. So Ava said yes. She remembered,

"Okay, Mick," I said.

"I asked you to marry me," he said. He sounded stunned.

"I know you did, and I said okay—but not until I'm nineteen," I said.

I think I was a bit stunned myself. Maybe I'd heard what a rough time L.B. was giving him over me. Maybe I felt guilty about that. I really can't remember. I just remember thinking: why the hell not? . . .

So I said okay. But I sill had this thing about being a virgin on the day I was married—and nineteen years old.[17]

Two years younger than Mickey, Ava would turn nineteen on December 24, 1941.

Mickey and Ava spent hours discussing their future plans. It was all fun and games until they hit upon two possible roadblocks: "Uncle" L.B. and Mickey's mother. Ava had no familial worries; her mother and sisters were in favor of the marriage, and Bappie loved Mickey. The couple decided to flip a coin to determine whom they would tell first, and Nell was the winner. Ava and Mickey drove out to Encino break the news to "Ma" Rooney, who was now living in grand style in the twelve-room manor house Mickey had bought for her and Fred. Mickey's stepfather had closed his restaurant and was working in the bookkeeping department at Metro, a job Mickey had secured for him. Nell was going to the track during the days, and out drinking at night with Fred. It was a far cry from her days in burlesque, when she and Mickey weren't even sure where their next meal was coming from.

If Ava thought she would be embraced into the family by Nell, she was in for a surprise. Ava's story of her first meeting with her formidable future mother-in law was one of her favorite tales, which she recounted to her coauthor Peter Evans:

> I would replay it in my head whenever Mick did something so outrageous I wanted to kill him. I only had to think of that meeting to make me laugh, and all was forgiven. You had to forgive any boy who had a mother like Mick's Ma. . . .
>
> I was very nervous and very shy. Ma was sitting cross-legged on the sofa with the *Racing Form* across her lap, a bottle of bourbon by her side, and a big glassful in her hand. Did you ever see the comic strip Maggie and Jiggs? . . .
>
> Well Ma was a dead ringer for Maggie, even the tight, little curls were the same—like carroty Ping-Pong balls.

The scene was bizarre. It's something I'll never forget: Ma sitting in this big, beautiful house Mickey had bought her in the [San Fernando] Valley, sipping her whiskey, and studying the horses. She had divorced Joe Yule; she was married to Fred Pankey, a cashier at the studio.

Mick said, "Ma, I want you to meet Ava. We're going to get married."

She looked at me for a second or two, her expression didn't change. She was as calm as custard. "Well," she said, these were her first words to me: "I guess he hasn't been in your pants yet, has he?"[18]

It was a shocking first meeting, especially for a southern nineteen-year-old who was a newcomer to Hollywood and show business.

Ava recalled, "God Almighty, what a meeting that was. I have never been so embarrassed in my life. Today I would think it was one of the funniest opening remarks I'd ever heard, but then I just wanted to curl up and die.[19]

After they broke the news to Nell, Mickey was ready to shout the news to the world. He was floating on cloud nine. He told Sidney Miller, Dick Quine, Jackie Cooper, his sometime stand-in Dick Paxton, and his circle of friends.

Mickey then told Carey Wilson, who was the producer of the Andy Hardy films. "Oh, I know you think she's not the girl for me, but you're wrong. We're in love and she's going to be a great wife."[20] Then, Mickey personally called *Los Angeles Times* columnist Hedda Hopper and told her about Ava, the engagement, and how they were going to start a family. Hopper knew about the couple, because she had been reporting about their clubbing and appearances for the previous few months. However, true to form in the world of Mayer and Metro, she would not run the story without consulting studio publicity head Howard Strickling, who upon hearing the news from Hedda, went into an immediate denial. "Sure he's gaga for her," Strickling said. "But as far as an engagement—well, that's just wishful thinking. She's Charlie Feldman's girl." Feldman was Gardner's agent, and it was assumed he was having an affair with her. Strickling assured Hedda that if the couple became engaged, she would be the first to know. But Strickling was clearly concerned. This was not good news.[21]

"It was a slap in the face for Mayer," Ava said of Mickey's telling Hopper first.[22] Hedda was a powerful syndicated columnist, but according to author E. J. Fleming, she was also on the Metro payroll and would not dare cross the lion. She knew what she had to do and killed the story.

Strickling was furious. Mickey knew not to cross the line and talk directly to the media. Every MGM player knew the rules on how to talk to the press, especially to columnists such as Hedda Hopper, Louella Parsons, and Sidney Skolsky. Strickling hunted down Rooney and found him in his dressing room. Mickey was in bliss and confirmed his engagement news to Strickling. This only made Strickling more furious. Not only had Mickey popped the question without an okay from L.B, but he had had the audacity to break one of the golden rules for stars at Metro: You don't talk directly to the press unless publicity sets it up.

"Mr. Mayer is not going to like you marrying Ava," Strickling told Rooney.

"You're the biggest star in the business. You can't just throw your career away on anybody. Don't get me wrong. Ava's a very sweet girl, and she is certainly built. But you have an obligation to the public and to Mr. Mayer who believed in you enough to hand you the Hardy series on a silver platter." He continued: "L.B.'s protecting his investment in you, Mickey. Fans lose interest in stars who get married. They want them single and available. You see, in their fantasies, young girls see themselves married to you. Andy Hardy, in particular, ought to remain single and celibate. In the public's eye he is still a kid, and innocent. How can they think you're innocent when you're banging the hottest broad in town?"[23]

Mickey quickly responded that he wasn't "banging" Ava, that his relationship was pure, much like that between Polly Benedict and Andy Hardy. Strickling couldn't have cared less about the details. He feared the public perception of the marriage. Everyone in the business knew there was a vast divide between the real Mickey Rooney and the character Strickling and his boys painted to the press. Mickey was, for all intents and purposes, a feral child, the son of a mother who had turned tricks and a boozing father who took him to hookers as a youth. He was certainly not in any way Andrew Hardy, son of Judge Hardy. But this was Hollywood, and publicity was the stuff dreams were made of.

THE CONCEPT OF A public persona radically different from the true nature of the performer is a concept Budd Schulberg documents graphically in his screenplay for the 1957 movie *A Face in the Crowd*, which stars a young Andy Griffith as Lonesome Rhodes, whose sudden fame as a media persona overwhelms him. Schulberg's fictional character was reflected in a legion of real-life performers, a seemingly endless roster from Bob Hope to John Wayne to Rooney. Mickey, at this stage of his career, was a prime example of the strength of the MGM public relations team's transmogrifying an actor into his on-screen character. Before the marriages and scandals, parents wanted their sons to grow up to be Mickey Rooney. He was respectful to his elders and morally unblemished. How dare Rooney affect the carefully designed creature they had built by his scandalous behavior and ill-advised marriage? From the studio's perspective, this was not to be.

Strickling, fearful of the studio's reaction, but still eager to protect its star, swore Mickey to secrecy until he, Strickland, had met with L.B. to discuss the engagement. Mickey reluctantly agreed. Strickling had to quickly put a lid on the gossip and rumors until he had a plan for damage control.

Louis Mayer had been monitoring every aspect of this romance and was hardly in the dark about Mickey's love life. He was sent the daily clippings by Strickling and had heard the details from Les Peterson. He ordered Strickling and the marketing department to poll the effect that marriage would have on the Rooney image, and the results confirmed what Mayer already knew: it would damage that image, and possibly damage profits. In 1941, Rooney led the *Motion Picture Herald*'s list of top-ten moneymakers, followed by Clark Gable, Abbott and Costello, Gene Autry, Jimmy Cagney, Spencer Tracy, Bing Crosby, Bob Hope, Bette Davis, and Ginger Rogers. Of that list, only Rooney, Gable, and Tracy were MGM players.

Not only were the Andy Hardy films returning big revenue for Metro, but the Rooney-Garland backyard musicals such as *Babes in Arms* were also huge moneymakers. The formula L.B. devised for *Babes in Arms* had struck gold, and the film became one of the top box office draws in that amazing year for motion pictures, 1939. Far from the standard MGM musical, *Babes in Arms* may have been the first musical aimed directly at a far younger demographic than MGM's other pictures. This was clear starting with the title number, staged by Busby Berkley, which featured the most bizarre teenage riot in the background. While the large cast of youngsters is trying to start a bonfire and then dance around it, Douglas McPhail is singing a number on the top of a playground slide while Mickey gestures wildly behind him. *Babes in Arms* was clearly a new breed of film musical featuring young, fresh, cinematically innocent talent, which L.B. did not want to see changed.

Mayer called a meeting for the next day, with Rooney and Ava summoned to his throne room. The accounts of that meeting differ drastically depending on the source: Mickey, Ava, and even Benny Thau, who was part of the executive team under Mayer that included

Hunt Stromberg, Lawrence Weingarten, and the ever-present Eddie Mannix. This team was nicknamed "the College of Cardinals," because they closely counseled "Pope" Mayer. When Mickey walked into the meeting and saw both Thau and Strickling in attendance, he was aware of the importance of this meeting.

Rooney recalled that Mayer did not acknowledge Ava as they entered his office. "He just launched into a tirade," Mickey said, quoting L.B. as sputtering, "How dare you destroy the studio's best investment." Mickey claimed Mayer was near tears as he screamed, "That's all. I forbid it."

Mickey fought back, telling Mayer, "You've got no right to do that. This is my life."

Mayer yelled back, "It's not your life, not as long as you're working for me. MGM has made your life."

Mickey quickly responded, "Then maybe, I shouldn't be working for you. If you don't want to give us your blessings, Mr. Mayer, I'll be happy to go to another studio." Mickey characterized Mayer's proprietary ownership of his life as if he were Dr. Frankenstein.

Mayer quickly softened, "Mickey, it would break my heart to see you unhappy."

Mickey was later pleased by his "standing up" to Mayer and realized, for the first time, the power he exuded as the world's number one box office attraction.[24]

According to Arthur Marx, Mayer was far blunter at the meeting. "Ava was cowered in a corner, looking demure and awfully frightened. This was her first encounter with the tyrannical boss of the Culver City lot." Marx sums up L.B.'s charge as "How dare a nobody try to sabotage his hottest star! When his threatening failed, he tried to embarrass Mickey, saying. 'Why do you want to marry this girl? You know all you want to do is get into her pants.'"[25]

Benny Thau, no stranger to gruff talk as a former vaudeville booking agent, was nonetheless shocked to hear Mayer speak this way.

While researching a book on Elizabeth Taylor, author C. David Heymann interviewed Thau at the Motion Picture Home in early 1983, months before his death. Thau recalled to Heymann the meeting with Rooney and Gardner, saying, "Listen, I was no choirboy, but Louie went berserk in trying to intimidate the kid [Rooney]. He told him that 'You get all the free pussy you want; what do you need this broad?' I mean she was sitting right there as well. The kid stood up to him, he had some balls, and Louie backed down. I mean, here was our strongest asset and he wasn't going to risk antagonizing him. It just didn't work." [26]

According to Arthur Marx, Mayer switched to a paternalistic tack, saying, "He [Mayer] was the father figure again. Tears welled up in Mayer's ratlike pale eyes . . .'It would break my heart to see you unhappy. Please believe me, Mickey,' he pleaded, 'I've always been like a father to you. Believe me, this is not the girl for you.' Moreover, he continued, there was a war on. How could Mickey contemplate marriage knowing that he could be drafted any minute, leaving his wife pregnant and alone?" [27]

Mickey started feeling his own power, put his arms around Ava, and stood his ground. He told Mayer, "Mr. Mayer, I love this girl and she loves me. And if you don't want to give me your blessings, I'll be glad to go to another studio. I know a couple places that would love to have me." [28] Mickey had indeed reached Mayer's soft spot, his pocketbook, according to Arthur Marx, and Mayer knew he had lost this game of cat and mouse. He told Mickey, "Okay, congratulations, Mickey. Go get married. Just don't expect me to support her if you go off to war." [29]

It would be hard to imagine this meeting happening in today's studio environment. Any meeting between talent and management would be attended by the performer's management team. Can you imagine a Mike Ovitz, Sue Mengers, or Ari Emanuel sitting on the sidelines while their most important client was confronted by a studio head? Yet neither "Uncle" Abe Lastfogel nor any of Mickey's William Morris agents was anywhere to be seen. They were not about to cross swords with Mayer on this ticklish situation.

Ava Gardner had a totally different recollection of the meeting, saying that Mayer was less threatening, more fatherly, and sought to embrace rather than alienate them. According to Ava, she missed the first twenty minutes of the 8:00 a.m. meeting. She remembered that Mickey was called in first, while she sat in the outer office with Mayer's longtime secretary, Ida Koverman. For more than fifteen minutes, Koverman just looked at Ava, giving her the silent treatment. Her first words to her were "You know, young lady, a leopard doesn't change its spots."

Ava said to Peter Evans, "Between that and [Mickey's] Ma saying 'so he hasn't been in your pants yet,' I should have been warned. I should have walked out of there right then." [30] Ava was nervous. "I didn't want to go. Mick said Uncle L.B. wanted to give us his blessing. I doubted that. He wouldn't touch Mickey, of course, not right away, but men like that have long memories. I felt much more vulnerable. Old Uncle L.B. could make me disappear in the middle of the next scene if he wanted to!" [31]

She continued, saying that Mickey introduced her as:

"My future wife, Uncle L.B."

"I'm delighted to meet you, young lady," Mayer said.

He was perfectly polite. I could see why some people said he had plenty of charm when he wanted to use it, although he did remain seated behind his enormous desk. I don't think that was very polite. He was not an attractive-looking man, which wasn't his fault. But he made me uncomfortable the way he looked at me through his small, round, gold-glasses. I'm sure he wouldn't have objected if I'd genuflected to him. . . .

[H]e was very sure of himself, and could be very funny, too. . . . [He told us,] *"My whole life is making movie stars . . . [A]ll the billboards in the world don't make a movie star. Only Louis B. Mayer can make a somebody outta a nobody. . . ."*

Mick was so brave to stand up to him the way he did over me. I'm sitting here talking to you now because Mickey Rooney had the nerve to tell Louis B. Mayer he was going to marry me and if he didn't like it to go fuck himself . . .

[Mayer] gave us the whole business about marriage being sacred but Mickey stood up to him.[32]

The meeting that Ava found more intimidating took place the following day, when she was called to the office of Howard Strickling, who was waiting for her with Eddie Mannix. She recalled, "[Mannix] was about to piss on me, and that was only because Louis Mayer had ordered him to. It was nothing personal. That was his job, to carry out Mayer's orders."[33]

Mannix and Strickling had brought her in to discuss the wedding plans, which would be arranged around Mickey's shooting schedule. Mickey was shooting the latest Andy Hardy film, and they told her the best date would be January 10, 1942. According to Peter Evans, she told Mannix that she'd dreamed of a big wedding at the Beverly Hills Hotel with a star-studded guest list. She wanted MGM to create her bridal gown and all the accoutrements. "I was carried away. After all, Mick was MGM's biggest star. . . . Of course his own studio would want to put on a show for his fans! . . . I let my imagination run away with me. . . . [Mannix] was there to piss on my parade, honey."[34]

Mannix informed Ava that there would be no white wedding, no star-studded guest list, no hoopla, no Beverly Hills Hotel. The wedding would take place far from Hollywood, out of the spotlight. He said there would be no media circus. Mannix looked her square in the eye and said he would not let it turn "into a 'fucking donnybrook,' were his exact words. I've never forgotten them," recalled Ava.[35] She was aware of the reason behind this. MGM was not prepared to break the hearts of millions of adolescent girls and risk destroying the fan base of its most valuable franchise.

Mickey was so overjoyed that he could now marry Ava that he paid no attention to the fact that every aspect of the wedding was being planned by the studio without any of his or Ava's input. Every detail, from picking the wedding bands to the site of the ceremony to even finding the perfect home for the couple after the wedding, was being decided by Strickling and his "boys."

Strickling found the perfect person in Les Peterson to coordinate all the details. Peterson's stock had risen in the past four years by keeping Mickey's monkey business away from the press. Moreover, Peterson loved exploring California in his spare time, and knew many small towns or hamlets that would fit the bill for a wedding site.

Ava complained to Mickey that they were having no say in the details of their own wedding, but Mickey had always relied on the studio to arrange every aspect of his life. When he bought the house in Encino for his mother, the studio helped him select it. His clothes were selected by the Metro, his barber was on the lot, and he even picked up his laundry from the studio. To him this was no different.

First came the wedding rings. Peterson selected platinum wedding bands for them both, for which he got Mickey's approval. Then Peterson selected a small apartment in Westwood in a complex called the Wilshire Palms for the young couple to move into following the wedding. Ava still lived with her sister in their apartment, and Mickey was in the family home in Encino, nicknamed El Ranchita. Mayer, himself, had decided that Mickey and Ava could not live at El Ranchita because it was a regular stop for tourists and tour busses. Publicity had to be avoided at every turn. However, Mickey wanted to continue living with Nell and Fred. He had purchased the house for his mother, so he was not going to ask her and Fred to relocate. Accordingly, Mickey and Ava agreed to live in the apartment in Westwood. It was small, but more like a fancy hotel suite (with a living room and kitchen) rather than a retreat for the world's number one film star. It had white walls, white carpet, lots of mirrors, and beige leatherette furniture. It was indeed a step down from the Encino house, but the good news was that the studio was paying for it.

Meanwhile, Peterson was exploring California for the perfect wedding location. The last thing the studio wanted was a caravan of press following the wedding party to the chapel. He selected the small town of Ballard, about thirty miles north of Santa Barbara, in the Santa Ynez Valley. Peterson was diligent about every detail. First, to ensure that there would be no press, he swore the local media to secrecy—in return for which, he promised to supply them with exclusive official studio publicity pictures from the MGM photographer who would be at the ceremony. He arranged for the nuptials to take place at a little white Presbyterian church that was presided over by Rev. Glen Lutz, disregarding the fact that Ava was raised a Southern Baptist while Mickey was a Christian Scientist. Then he made sure the couple could secure a wedding license on the day of the wedding.

The studio also made nice. Mayer wanted Mickey to harbor no hard feelings after the rough treatment he'd received in L.B.'s office. He set out to make amends, gifting Mickey with a racehorse from his private stable as a wedding present. He then arranged a massive stag party for Mickey in his private dining room at Culver City the day before the wedding. The event was a star-studded affair attended by most of the MGM male stars. After the meal, each rose individually to offer ribald marital advice to the young groom, everything from how to prevent a bad back to how to explain lipstick marks on his fly when he came home from a busy day at the studio. (Mickey liked his oral sex.) They all laughed and kidded the future groom, who was serious when he told them that his life with Ava would be different.

Most of the stars looked at the coupling with a jaundiced eye; they had ridden the marriage-go-round and knew better. Mickey's parting comments were, according to Arthur Marx, "Thanks, you horny bastards. And the first guy I see looking hard at Mrs. Rooney gets a right hand to the teeth!"[36]

The day of the wedding was more like a caper film with a cloak-and-dagger feel to the process. The wedding party surreptitiously left Hollywood early in the morning of Saturday, January 10, 1942, hoping to avoid attention. They headed up the Pacific Coast Highway toward Santa Barbara in two cars. Ava, Mickey, and Les Peterson led the procession in Rooney's Lincoln. Bappie, Joe Yule Sr., Nell, Fred Pankey, and a studio photographer were crammed into the second car, a studio limousine. When they reached Carpenteria, just south of Santa Barbara, Mickey got out of the car to call the county clerk, J. E. Lewis, and asked him to prepare the wedding license for Ava and him. Then Peterson drove them to Lewis's house in Montecito, where they picked up the license. Peterson had arranged for Lewis to waive the three-day waiting period with a special contribution.

From Lewis's house, the wedding caravan snaked its way around the mountains to its destination in Ballard where the church was located. Waiting at the church was the Rev. Glen H. Lutz, a tall, heavy-set man with a buzz cut who resembled a U.S. Marine.[37]

Mickey wore a charcoal-gray double-breasted suit with a green polka-dot tie. He had selected the outfit at a Beverly Hills shop the week before, with Peterson's input. Ava had bought a navy-blue suit and had a corsage of orchids. She bought the suit with a special wedding bonus the studio had given her.

The only other person who drove there separately was Larry Tarr, sister Bappie's estranged husband. (They had been separated after he found out that Bappie had had an affair with the manager of the Plaza Hotel where Ava and her sister stayed when they first arrived in Hollywood.)

Mickey was quite nervous throughout the ceremony and became relieved as they neared the conclusion of the vows. The matching platinum wedding bands Peterson had bought bore the inscription LOVE FOREVER on the inside. (Mickey later made a crack to Jack Parr on the *Tonight* show that the inscription should have read, NUMBER ONE.) When the Reverend Lutz pronounced them husband and wife, it was time for the official wedding photo—which proved a challenge, as Ava, tall and lanky, would have to stand next to a five-foot-two Mickey Rooney. Luckily, Peterson had brought along a stool for just the occasion. It was the one they used at the studio for shots of Mickey in the Andy Hardy films to help him look at least as tall as his leading ladies. So, Mickey was as tall as Ava in the pictures that appeared in the next morning's newspapers.

Ava was radiant and beaming. She hid her disappointment at the small wedding and acted the good soldier for the studio.

"It was not a memorable occasion, honey," she recalled to Peter Evans.

After the wedding, the guests drove back in the studio limo to Nell's house in Encino for a reception. According to Ava, the reception was interrupted by "a tremendous drunken brawl at Ma's place." According to what Ava told Peter Evans, "Larry [Bappie's estranged husband] must have been at the wedding . . . and my sister said Larry was in the thick of it, as usual." [38]

Meanwhile, just moments after the photographs were taken, Peterson called Howard Strickling to set the Metro publicity machine in motion. As soon as Peterson confirmed that the wedding had taken place, Strickling sent out a press release. MGM had been deluged with countless hourly calls from the press corps. It was the hottest story in America, even with war looming. MGM had rushed into release the newest Andy Hardy film, *Life Begins for Andy Hardy*, to coincide with the announcement and to capitalize on the publicity bound to spread around the nation. Hedda Hopper, because Strickling and

Peterson had promised her the story, was already given the scoop in advance and had her piece prepared. All she needed were the photographs, which she received from Peterson. She released the story the next morning in the *Los Angeles Times* Sunday edition. "Mickey Rooney Weds Actress Ava Gardner . . . The Best Man Was Leslie Peterson, MGM Publicity Man and the Maid of Honor Was Beatrice Gardner, Sister of the Bride." Hedda's story took up almost half the *Times*'s front page, with the photographs accompanying the story. The article went into great detail about the wedding day, including the clandestine drive north to Ballard and the music played during the ceremony by the reverend's wife. Hopper received a substantial pay boost by *Times* publisher Norman Chandler, which syndicated its stories, for getting the Rooney wedding exclusive.

Louella Parsons followed right on her heels, with her column in the late edition of the Hearst newspapers on January 11, 1942: "[T]hey have become so accustomed to seeing him in juvenile roles that it will be difficult for a while for the fans of the nation's No. 1 box office attraction, Mickey Rooney, to realize he is a married man."

Front-page stories of the wedding dominated newspapers nationwide. It soon became clear that the MGM College of Cardinals' fear of damage to Rooney/Hardy had been unfounded. The interest in this young couple was unprecedented.

Ava would soon be drawing boatloads of attention nationwide as MGM's newest and sexiest star, now married to the king of the box office. Sidney Miller's advice to her that dating Mickey would help her career had been prescient. The marriage was probably the strongest stimulant in pushing Ava toward becoming a film legend. Her obvious talent notwithstanding, had it not been for her marriage to Mickey Rooney, she may well have languished along with the countless other hopefuls MGM was nurturing.

Along with the rings, Peterson had also selected the honeymoon venue: the Hotel Del Monte in Monterey. Peterson had picked the hotel because it would give Mickey an opportunity to play golf at nearby Pebble Beach, but he had an ulterior motive for selecting this location: he had arranged the promotional tour for the latest Andy Hardy film, *The Courtship of Andy Hardy*, to begin in nearby San Francisco four days after the start of the honeymoon.

As Mickey's minder, Peterson was ever-present even throughout the honeymoon. Whenever he met Ava throughout the ensuing years, long after she and Mickey had gotten divorced and Rooney had gone on to wives two, three, and four, he would remind her, "Remember me, Ava, three on a honeymoon?" How could she forget? She has said, "When we came down for breakfast, he was there. When you had dinner, he was there. And when you went to bed, he was damn near there."[39]

But Ava was fond of the guy, and remembered:

> It wasn't his fault he was tagging along on our honeymoon. But I was pleased he was there that first night. I invited him to our suite for a glass of Cristal. I still wasn't much of a drinker at that time but I had a glass of champagne, and another glass of champagne. Les kept trying to excuse himself and I kept hanging on to him. Oh, one more glass. Talk about first night nerves. We were going through the Roederer's Cristal like it was tap water. I was scared out of my fucking wits. I didn't want Les to leave us. I would have felt a whole lot more relaxed if Mick and I had got it on weeks before. But I was so determined to be a virgin on my wedding night, I'd barely let him give me a belly rub . . . [Bappie] bought me a sexy negligee. She sent me off with that—and a douche bag. "That's all a girl needs on her wedding night, honey," she said, and as usual she was right. . . . I caught on quickly. Very quickly. I enjoyed the whole thing thoroughly. Mickey was tender, actually

he was sweet. He couldn't have been a better first lover for a lady. He'd been around quite a bit, of course—and marriage didn't stop him for very long either.[40]

Mickey believed that this was a perfect honeymoon. He shot a 79 one day and was enjoying connubial bliss with Ava like a rabbit in his spare time. In his book *Life Is Too Short*, he added, "All night long she had my undivided attention. We ended up performing our own sexual symphonies. . . . We had a four day music festival, in between my rounds of golf . . . it was an ideal honeymoon: sex and golf and sex and golf. Ideal, that is, for me. It never occurred to me to ask Ava what she wanted." [41]

Golf had become a passion with Mickey, who had been shooting in the low 80s at the Lakeside Country Club. It was a sport where size did not matter, as long as you could swing a driver and lay down a putt. It was the great equalizer. Mickey did not care that his new wife didn't play the sport. She could follow him around this challenging course for eighteen holes, and he could show off his prowess. Ava recalled, "I had to learn to play golf quickly otherwise I'd never see the boy. He continued to be a fanatical golfer but whenever he got in a slump, he'd break our clubs. . . . He had a real Irish temper." [42]

When it came to being a husband, however, Mickey was clueless. He had no idea what his domestic duties were during their honeymoon with regard to companionship or anything other than sex. While Ava enjoyed spending the time just lazing around the hotel suite and enjoying the breathtaking views of the Monterey coast, Mickey was loaded with energy. He detested sitting around a hotel room. He liked constant motion. He would call his cronies and bookies back in Los Angeles, missing the action. He needed action. He needed to be involved and on the move. To be sure, Rooney had a thoroughly chauvinistic upbringing. He was raised to believe that a wife should look pretty, keep him company at dinner, not complain when he was out with the boys, and be ready to jump in the sack whenever the mood hit him.

Ava, meanwhile, was beginning to realize that she may have made a mistake and gotten herself into a mess. She was spending more time with Les Peterson than with her groom. During Mickey's long absences, Peterson kept Ava company by playing cards with her, entertaining her with stories about the studio, and treating her to ice cream and chocolate sodas, as she had no real money of her own. Ava remarked to Peter Evans, "He was pleasant enough company, but he was not a substitute for a real husband." [43]

Yet Ava was tired of being confined to her room and tired of Les. She was therefore relieved when Peterson announced to the couple, four days into the honeymoon, that they should pack their bags, as they were now embarking on a long promotional tour for the new Hardy picture, *The Courtship of Andy Hardy*.

"We drove to San Francisco," Peterson recalled, "and checked into the Palace Hotel, where we got the Presidential Suite—the same suite where President Harding died." [44] Peterson had been married for three years, to actress Eleanor Stewart, who became known as one of the queens of the Westerns, appearing in the William Boyd/Hopalong Cassidy films. Les understood what it was like to be married to an entertainer. Ava, too, would soon find out what it meant.

Out on the road for the promotional tour, Mickey was mobbed when he made his appearances at the premiere. *The Courtship of Andy Hardy* was the fourteenth Hardy film, with no sign of the series tiring or fear of saturation. The film, which costarred Donna Reed, cost only $329,000 to produce and turned a profit of over $2 million just domestically. Big-budget films that year, such as MGM's *Woman of the Year*, *Random Harvest*, or *Mrs. Miniver*, cost three times as much and turned a far smaller profit. The Rooney/Hardy films were in essence cheap programmers that kept MGM in the black.

While Mickey spent the day being interviewed, photographed, and fawned over, Ava sat in a corner looking pretty—and was totally bored. Since Peterson was a native of the area, he took Ava and Mickey on a sightseeing tour of the city, riding the cable cars, eating in Chinatown, cruising the bay in a boat, and being mobbed by fans everywhere they went. On their second day, it was reported that Carol Lombard had died in a plane crash while on a war bond tour, and the Andy Hardy appearances were temporarily put on hold for a day, out of respect for Lombard, but also for Clark Gable. That was the only respite to the newspaper exposure that followed Mickey and Ava's tour. The next day, Howard Strickling told Peterson to continue the tour, and the Mickey media frenzy resumed.

"My wife arrived by train, after Mickey finished his business in San Francisco," Peterson recalled, "and we proceeded to Chicago by Union Pacific. We spent the night at the Ambassador East and did some more promotion for the picture, then took the Twentieth Century for New York. We checked into the New Yorker Hotel, because Mickey and I were old friends of the proprietor." [45] Mack Kanner, who had built the forty-three-story hotel, had been rumored to be connected to organized crime in his development of the Garment District. He was also a close friend of Eddie Mannix.

As Ava recalled, Rooney took New York by storm, mobbed by fans as he plugged the new Hardy picture. He was the typical Mickey for the reporters: a little song, a little dance, a little seltzer down his pants.

Mickey appeared at a war bond rally, attended a couple of charity events, met with New York gossip columnists such as Walter Winchell and Ed Sullivan, and was greeted like a conquering hero, playing up each appearance as much as he could, with all his charm and charisma. Mickey was splashed across all the New York daily newspapers. He had a meeting with the executives at Loews, who owned MGM, including the chairman, Nicholas Schenck, Mayer's boss and arch enemy. Schenck was also one of the richest men in America. Mickey Rooney later said, "Nick Schenck was a very strange man."[46]

Bappie came to New York and joined the tour. Mickey was thrilled. Now Ava had a shopping companion. The studio gave Ava an expense account, and she and her sister went shopping in the elegant stores along Fifth Avenue. She was looking for an outfit to wear to President Roosevelt's birthday ball on January 30, to which Mickey and his traveling companions had been invited. Mickey, Ava, Les, and Bappie were to attend the party and have dinner with the president. Afterward, they were invited to stay and watch FDR deliver one of his Fireside Chats on the radio.

After New York, it was on to Boston, where Mickey was scheduled to entertain at a Red Feather Community Chest function, where Mickey and Ava hobnobbed with the Cabots and Lodges. Mickey was still the center of attention, yet this time not so favorably: Reporter E. J. Kahn of *The New Yorker* was less than impressed with the young actor, writing in the January 20, 1942, issue, "He tries to prove himself a man of intelligence and knowledge by talking rapidly and loudly on every subject under the sun and gesturing with his hands. . . . [I]f you asked him for the time, he'd end up telling you how a watch was made. . . . [H]e considers himself an authority on everything." It must have rankled Strickling that Mickey was out of his sphere of control in New York City, where the publicity head could not quash this type of negativity.

It was then on to Fort Bragg, North Carolina, where training was under way for World War II and where Mickey would do some photo opportunities with the soldiers. E. J. Kahn wrote about the visit in the same *New Yorker* article, mocking Mickey's indifference to the men. "He seemed only moderately interested in the activities of the enlisted men. His manager [most likely Les Peterson] spent most of his time looking at his watch." It's not clear if Mickey was fazed by the *New Yorker* article. But with the external pressure of the tour schedule, his desire to get back to California, his need to figure out how to meld himself into married life, or his narcissism—why should the issues of other people have had any impact on him?

As for Ava, she had mixed feelings about the tour. She believed her contribution was to be the eye candy while Mickey was honored at every stop. She recalled:

> [W]e took off on a whistle stop tour selling war bonds and Mickey's new movie. Chicago, Boston, Fort Bragg in North Carolina, Washington, God knows where else.
>
> But wherever we went, thousands of screaming bobby-soxers were there to mob him. I swear to you, they were every bit as wild as Frank's [Sinatra] fans when he was at the top. It was phenomenal . . . the enthusiasm, the hysteria of those kids made me understand why Mayer was so fucking desperate to keep our marriage off the front pages.
>
> Les Peterson, who was still with us, never introduced me as Mickey Rooney's wife, which pissed me off. I knew he was only doing what Mayer had told him to do—as Eddie Mannix was only doing what Mayer told him to do when he put the skids under my dreams of a white wedding. That was another thing that pissed me off: everybody obeyed Louis B. Mayer.
>
> Les said all I had to do was sit on the arm of Mick's chair at the press conferences and keep looking at him like a fan, like I was one of the bloody bobby-soxers—oh, and I had to make sure the reporters got a good look at my pins! He was incorrigible. "I'm only doing my job, honey," he'd say whenever I put up a squawk.
>
> But I was enjoying myself, so was Mickey. We were two kids having a whale of a time. We never for a minute forgot that it was our honeymoon! We were discovering

new things about each other all the time—as I said, there was plenty of scope for that! Like he was athletic in the sack, and I was plenty verbal, and we were *very, very* loud!

It was a hoot, and we made sure there was always time for a quickie. I was seeing and doing things I never thought I would do and see in my life.

In Boston we had dinner at the mayor's house. . . . From Fort Bragg we took a side trip to Raleigh to visit Mama. [Her mother was dying of cancer.] This was the first time she had met Mickey, and she'd gotten dressed up to the nines. He made such a fuss of her. My whole family turned out for him. . . . And Lord, when Mickey had an audience was he good. He did his impersonations, he sang, he danced. He clowned. He was the complete movie star and Mama loved her movie stars! He made her the center of attention. It was probably the last truly great day of her life. . . . I've never been able to express my gratitude for the things that touch me deeply and nothing had ever touched me as deeply as Mickey's performance for Mama that day. He treated her like a queen.

It went downhill so fucking fast from there. . . . If the sex hadn't been so good, it wouldn't have lasted as long as it lasted. It's a pity nobody believes in simple lust anymore.[47]

Mickey agreed—and years later, in *Life Is Too Short*, he said, "We were both athletic in bed, and pretty verbal, too. Once Ava lost her Southern reticence, she seemed to enjoy using the f-word. And I didn't mind a bit, when, for example, she would look me straight in the eye, raise a provocative eyebrow, and say, 'Let's fuck, Mickey. Now.' Some years later, Hedda Hopper would say of Ava, 'That girl was made to love and be loved.' I had to agree with that judgment."[48]

In Washington the couple went directly to the president's birthday ball, on January 30. Peterson recalled, "Ava, Bappie, Mickey and I all sat at one table. And there was the usual empty place for Roosevelt. After we were there for a while, Roosevelt wheeled over in his wheelchair and had one course with us. He had a hard time taking his eyes off Ava, then duty called and he said goodbye, thanked us for coming and wheeled over to another table." [49]

The next day, Mickey made a few war bond appearances. The war effort was fully under way, and the Hollywood Victory Committee went into a full court press with a war bond rally that started at this event in the nation's capital. They had recruited many of the leading actors and actresses, which included Mickey, Jimmy Stewart (now Lieutenant Stewart), William Holden, Betty Grable, Rosalind Russell, and Pat O'Brien, to push the effort. After the events, Mickey and Ava joined the group on the Sante Fe Chief's special train back to Los Angeles. War was just over the Pacific horizon, there were movies to make, war bonds to sell, and the Rooneys' honeymoon was officially over.

12

The First Divorce

Neither Mickey nor Martha Vickers appears happy as they sign their marriage application in Las Vegas on June 4, 1949.
PHOTO COURTESY OF PAM McCLENATHAN.

When Mickey and Ava returned to Los Angeles on the Santa Fe Special, which pulled into historic Union Station, it was back to reality. They settled into their new apartment at the Wilshire Palms, and Mickey started work immediately on the film *A Yank at Eton*.

But it was more than back to work; it was back to Mickey's old life. Whereas Ava wanted to settle into a life of domesticity, Mickey would have none of it. Growing up as he had, always on the road, with a dad who was hardly around, Mickey didn't know what a good marriage was. Thus, his marriage to Ava was troubled almost right from the start.

For Mickey it seemed that this marriage was just an episode to be quickly set aside as he resumed his daily life with work, calling his bookies from the studio, trying to escape work early to head to the track or the golf course, and clubbing at night. Ava, at this point, was still too shy for the fast lane Mickey sought. She wanted her new husband to come home to their apartment, where she could cook some Southern dishes, listen to records, or talk. Their concept of marriage was totally different. Ava was traditional, and looking to be domestic; while Mickey was still a twenty-one-year-old boy caught up in the Hollywood life. They came from different universes.

Mickey, however, was oblivious to this, and believed that their mutual sexual attraction was all they needed. He recalled:

> Oh, we told ourselves that we were very much in love, and our sex life helped us in that particular piece of self-deception. Once Ava got into the spirit of things, she wanted to do it all the time. And she quickly learned what it was that turned me on about her. Let me count the ways: a smoldering look, a laugh, a tear, kicking off her shoes as soon as she got in the house, getting all dolled up, not getting all dolled up, coming down to breakfast in a pair of shorts—and no top at all. In bed, let's just say that Ava was . . . well, she had this little rosebud down there at the center of her femininity that seemed to have a life of its own. I am not talking about muscles. One gal I knew had trained her muscles, so that she could snap carrots in her pussy, not hands. But Ava had something different. She had this little extra—it was almost like a little warm mouth—that would reach up and grab me and take me in and make my, uh, my heart swell. She also had big brown nipples, which, when she was aroused, stood out like some double-long golden

California raisins. And I sucked those warm breasts, I did taste her mother's milk.[1]

Sidney Miller told us that he was the first dinner guest of the Rooneys when they returned to Los Angeles. "It was like two different worlds. Ava was far more mature and respectful of marriage. She kept house, cooked, decorated, and really tried to make Mickey a home. Mickey had *schpilkas* and had to always be on the go. He couldn't just sit in that apartment while Ava was content to. I mean you could see they were in love, but they were miles apart."

Ava told Peter Evans:

> The idea of being married had always appealed to me, and I was hopelessly in love with him by this time. We lived in a tiny apartment on Wilshire and Palm Drive in Westwood that we'd rented from Red Skelton. One bedroom, living room, kitchen, and a tiny dining room. (There's a big high rise there now.) We were out all the time. . . . Oh God, Mickey and I were out practically every night of our lives together. We danced, he drank a fair amount—I was catching on pretty fast. But Mick was working every day, too. He was carrying the weight of the studio on his shoulders. I don't know how he did it. We had a damn good goose-feather mattress. I supposed that helped the boy!
>
> I wasn't working. . . . For a couple of months anyway I had no doubt that Mick was going to be my mate for eternity. We were seen everywhere together, Hollywood's most devoted couple. Well that's what I believed anyway. We were madly in love. We were screwing a lot.
>
> A week or so after we got back from our honeymoon, I . . . [had] an inflamed appendix. [After the surgery I]

stayed in the hospital for three weeks. So I came home and the first night I found evidence that Mick had been screwing someone in our bed. On the fucking goosefeather mattress! That ain't a very nice thing for a nineteen-year-old bride, quite pretty, too, to discover. I'd been away for three weeks and he'd already dragged somebody into our bed. I don't know who the hell it was but I knew that somebody had been keeping my side of the bed warm!

I remember it had something to do with a douche bag— somebody had been using my douche bag. I had what they called a tipped infantile uterus. . . . [O]ne time with Mickey I experimented with a rubber. I didn't like it one bit. No, no, no. But I never got pregnant, not until I was married to Frank anyway.

Anyway, I knew that somebody had been using my stuff. I called Bappie. She said don't you dare touch it! Get the little bastard to clean up his own fucking mess. He denied it, of course. He played the little innocent. Nobody could pile on the applesauce like Mickey. He was the best liar in the world—well Frank Sinatra can tell a good story, too. . . .

Mickey tried to make-up for the rotten douche bag business. . . . He bought us a small house in Bel Air, which I helped to choose and decorate. . . .

Mick also bought me the most beautiful diamond ring, a real iceberg—and asked for it back the following week to pay off his bookies. . . .

Actually I didn't mind the ring going back, well not too much, anyway—diamonds are an acquired taste and at nineteen I still hadn't acquired it. . . . His relationship with his bookies was built on eternal optimism. . . . He had a kind of cartoon resilience.

But once I knew he was fooling around, even though he continued to deny it, I should have checked out right there. Even though I knew the girls he was screwing didn't mean a thing to him. . . . He was just a lecherous sod who loved getting his rocks off. Everybody was fucking everybody in those days. Maybe it was the war! Lana Turner, who had become a good friend of mine, knew how distraught I was. She said a fuck meant nothing to men like Mickey. I should just brush it aside, she said.

"Well if you're not going to leave him, you must do something to let the little bastard know how you feel," Lana said.

That night we had dinner at Chasen's. Afterward, Mickey insisted on buying drinks for the whole bar. I knew that once he bought for the bar, he'd have to stay around until the bar bought drinks for him. It was a machismo thing. . . .

I knew the marriage was not going to last anyway. We were playing injury time with benefits—for both of us! We both liked screwing too much to give that up cold turkey. . . .

But I must say it's a lonely business fucking someone you no longer love. Especially a husband.[2]

As they pulled in different directions, and Mickey fell back into his old ways, Mickey and Ava's marriage was beginning to unravel. Mickey and Ava went out clubbing almost every night to the Hollywood hotspots: the Palladium, Ciro's, the Cocoanut Grove, the Mocambo. At the Cocoanut Grove, Mickey would often sit in with the Tommy Dorsey Band, on the drums, while Ava sat alone at their table as if she were an unescorted single girl. Now disconsolate at the life she had allowed herself to get into, Ava started drinking heavily, and not just zombies. She was still underage, but Mickey would arrange to have her served martinis in coffee cups.

Ava said she started to feel like one of the hookers (whom she called B girls) who sat at the bar looking for a pick-up to buy her a drink. And despite Mickey's protestations, she continued to catch him cheating on her. He was more incorrigible because he was simply wired differently. He couldn't stop. But he knew how to feign. Ava remembered that he was such a great actor; he would give her his "Andy Hardy, innocent look" when she accused him of fooling around on her. He was also gambling heavily, especially at the track, throwing money away as fast as it came in, as if he believed it would never stop. He had absolutely no impulse control—perfect for an actor, but a disaster for domestic life. When Mickey won at the track, he would bring her jewelry to placate her. However, he often took the gifts back when the bookies began chasing him to pay his debts. Even then, Mickey was skirting at the edge of trouble. But through it all, their sex life was the one saving grace for the couple.

"I was insatiable at that age," Ava recalled.[3]

Even in the most stable of marriages, spouses often evolve, and not always in the same direction. So it was with Ava: shy Ava was quickly being replaced by an Ava who was coming out of her shell, an Ava relying upon alcohol to ease the discomfort of her marriage. When she spent a night dancing with actor Tom Drake, while Mickey was off with friends at another part of the club, Mickey went into a rage, which resulted in a very public argument. Heads turned. Gossip columnists pricked up their ears. Rumors abounded. Strickling worked hard to suppress all the possible stories, with the help of Les Peterson, but the rumors reached Uncle L.B., who was quietly watching, and waiting.

Ava went on the attack, trying to hurt Mickey by telling him she was tired of "living with a midget." She knew that attacks on his height cut deep. She once slashed all their furniture with a knife. When

Peter Lawford told her about Mickey's black book, which contained the names of Gloria DeHaven, Lana Turner, Ann Rutherford, Donna Reed, and others, she went berserk. Lawford, who'd been shooting the film *A Yank at Eton* with Mickey, would carry tales between them, setting them up for battles.

Ava said that Lawford was ambitious. "He often sat with me at the Grove, keeping me amused, when Mick was sitting in with the Dorsey band. I liked him but he was a terrible gossip. It was a mistake to tell Peter Lawford anything. There was a lot of Iago in Peter." [4] This was indeed a prophetic statement, as Marilyn Monroe would experience, the hard way, twenty years later.

Four months into Mickey and Ava's marriage, it was Lawford who told her about Mickey's affair with a fifteen-year-old girl who was meeting him while he was at the Lakeside Country Club. That was the final straw. Ava confronted Mickey, who denied it. Later, while Mickey was at the studio, she tossed his clothes outside their Bel Air house and had the locks on the doors changed. She had reached her breaking point. Ava, in a fury, had grown tired of Mickey's dalliances, gambling, and absolute neglect, and wanted out of the marriage. Mickey moved back to Encino with Nell and Fred. However, he was upset. Ava would not take his calls. He was nearly arrested while trying to break down the front door late one evening. His unhappiness was the talk of the studio, and his name on a police blotter would have been anathema to his bosses at Metro.

"When Louis Mayer heard about that, all hell broke loose," Ava recalled. "Eddie Mannix was ordered to patch things up between us." [5]

The situation quickly became a crisis at Metro, a crisis that L.B. had tried to avoid by preventing the marriage; he already knew about Mickey's proclivities. For Mayer, there was a lot a stake if the story of Mickey and Ava's breakup, and Mickey's antics, became public. They had survived Mickey's wedding, and it had not affected the box office for the Hardy films or his other work. In fact, his box office take had grown since the wedding. Strickling and his boys had worked overtime to create the image of a happy couple. They had planted countless stories with Mickey as the respectable husband and Ava as his southern belle wife, cooking him wonderful down-home meals when he returned from his hard work at the studio. They had created the perfect scenario to complement the Mickey/Judy musicals and the Andy Hardy films. Rooney's grosses were through the roof. Even the relationship between Mayer and Schenck had calmed quite a bit as the box office revenue continued to flood in. Mayer had proven to Schenck and the board at Loews that with his family-oriented films, he could surpass what Thalberg had done as production chief.

Ava was quite aware that a lot of the studio's success rested on Mickey's twenty-one-year-old shoulders. He was, for all intents and purposes, the face of MGM in 1942. Many of the studio's megastars, such as Clark Gable, Robert Montgomery, and Jimmy Stewart, had enlisted or were preparing to. The clouds of war were gathering over the studio.

Mayer and Mannix had brought in Les Peterson to patch things up between the couple as relations between them deteriorated, and Peterson remained busy trying to help unruffle feathers. When Mickey said he wanted to get Ava a house, Peterson rented 1120 Stone Canyon Drive in Bel Air for them. He had helped Mickey pick out jewelry for Ava. Ava trusted Les, who often went over there to smooth out arguments. However, now that the couple had officially separated, the discord was clearly escalating.

When Mickey showed up for work on *The Courtship of Andy Hardy*, the fourteenth movie in the series, he was without his typical energy and spunk. Producer Carey Wilson alerted Mannix to Rooney's condition. Mannix ran to the screening room and watched the dailies. He quickly saw a more subdued Rooney, and noticed the dark rings under his eyes, which gave him a dissipated look.

"He's beginning to look as old as his father," remarked Mannix. "If we don't pull him out of this, we can change the title of the picture to 'Andy Hardy Goes to the Poor House!'" [6]

While very few outsiders were aware of the separation, Mannix, had started hearing whispers of it around the studio. He called in Peterson to make a game plan. Peterson suggested they both talk to Ava's sister, Bappie, whom Ava was now living with, having moved out of the Bel Air house. Bappie agreed to talk with them without her sister's knowledge, and she told them that Ava was unhappy sitting home all day and wanted a career. The studio machine swung into action.

A meeting was called at the studio between Ava and Mickey. Les Peterson was there, with Eddie Mannix doing all the talking. Mannix told the couple that marriage was sacred, that a lover's spat was expected in every marriage. (He never mentioned that he had recently divorced his first wife, Bernice. And unbeknownst to him at the time, his second wife, Toni, would have an affair with George "Superman" Reeves, which would end with Reeves's murder at the hands of his other mistress, Leonore Lemmon.) [7]

Ava feared Mannix. "Everybody was scared of Mannix. I wouldn't have liked to cross him. . . . He promised to try to get me some decent parts if I promised to behave," she recalled. [8]

Mannix kept his word, and secured a role for Ava in a loan-out to Monogram. In February 1943, Ava showed up for her first billed role, with the East Side Kids (some of whom were originally in a troupe called the Dead End Kids), in *Ghosts on the Loose*, which costarred Bela Lugosi, Leo Gorcey, and Huntz Hall. Huntz Hall once told the authors, "She was quite the looker. Leo [Gorcey] was just breaking up with his wife, Kay [who would later marry Groucho Marx] and tried to come on to her. She kinda laughed him off, and he was pissed." [9]

"It was . . . an awful little Poverty Row studio—I think the whole thing took about ten days to shoot, and no retakes, *ever*!" said Ava. "But I got my first billing on that picture, so it's still kind of special to me." [10]

The movie role was meant to placate Ava, and the couple reconciled. But it was short-lived. In fact, there were several breakups and reunions. At one point, Ava returned to their Wilshire Palms apartment and asked her close friend Leatrice Gilbert (the daughter of John Gilbert and silent film star Leatrice Joy), just two years younger than Ava, to move in with her. They lived together for almost five months.

Mickey called Ava faithfully every night. Leatrice kept him at bay, telling him Ava was out. In an interview with the authors, Leatrice recalled, "She had a real fear of Mickey. She said he had violent outbursts and she would wake up screaming at night thinking of them. I didn't doubt her one bit. He was messing around, and she wanted a stable life."

Ava was actually home most of the time. She had become close to actress Donna Reed and agent Minna Wallis, and they would take turns holding dinner parties and cooking for one another. Mickey, for his part, was in torment on the East Coast. He was both angry and jealous, imagining Ava partying at the Mocambo or the Cocoanut Grove with the likes of Tom Drake. As soon as he finished filming, he rushed back to Los Angeles and the Wilshire Palms. She was having a dinner party the night he returned, and when she refused to let him enter, he tried to break down the door. He started screaming outside the apartment, calling her a whore and other names. Ava threatened to call the police. Leatrice recalls the incident, "[H]e came to our door screaming. . . . He literally broke open the door and was shaking Ava. She truly wanted nothing to do with him. He really just wanted to have his cake and eat it, too. She was very shaken up. He had this real rage in his eyes. Luckily, his studio guy [Les Peterson] was there with him and got him out of there." [11]

When Peterson told the story to Strickland, who took it to Mayer and Mannix, MGM's fears only got worse. Ava had told Peterson that she would call up the columnists and spill the beans on their separation if they didn't keep Mickey away from her. Mayer's solution was "Keep them away from each other—and keep them both busy." [12] They promptly moved up the date for the on-location shooting scheduled in Connecticut for *A Yank at Eton*, and Mayer kept Ava busy in California by casting her in back-to-back films.

ALONG WITH HIS MARITAL woes, Mickey was facing another potential problem: military service. There was a war on. He believed that if he were drafted, there would be no chance for reconciliation with Ava, and that made him even more disconsolate.

Even more concerned at Mickey's impending induction was Louie Mayer. In the MGM archives at the Margaret Herrick Library of the Academy of Motion Picture Arts and Sciences is a huge file of correspondence between MGM and Local Draft Board 245, Mickey's draft board. Mayer had turned the problem over to his fixer Eddie Mannix, who, in a sworn affidavit to the draft board on behalf Loews Inc., submitted a formal request for "occupational deferment." The draft board was feeling the pressure from the world's largest film studio in its effort to keep Mickey Rooney out of uniform. It was financial pressure as well. As author E. J. Fleming explained, according to his research, Mayer, Mannix, and Strickling used financial gifts to influence newspaper reporters, sheriffs and police, judges, and officials to handle things in the best interests of the studio and of those whom L.B. favored, particularly when it came to squelching negative publicity. Thus, it can be conjectured that the Mayer team used any device it could to keep its most profitable asset out of harm's way.

The affidavit Mannix presented to the local draft board pulled out all stops, even using a scene from an upcoming Andy Hardy film, *Andy Hardy's Blonde Trouble*, to support the studio's request. The affidavit stated, "The 25 million Americans who will see this picture must gain a greater and fuller understanding of, and sympathy with, the American fundamentals. We plan that each succeeding Hardy picture will further the idea, carry Andy, as he grows older, closer to the war, and reveal through Andy and his parents, the actual experiences of the young American boy who has taken such a step. The morale of the Hardy family should, and will be the highest type of morale of the American family." [13]

Then Mannix really got to the heart of the studio's concern: "Moreover, Mickey is irreplaceable and it will cost the studio millions in other films planned and ready to go with him starring in them, if he is drafted." [14] Blunt and right to the point. Two more affidavits followed, with one stating, on August 28, 1942, that *The Human Comedy* was to begin shooting on August 31, and "it would be a real hardship on the studio to lose him."

The appeal was denied. However, Mickey was granted a three-month extension and temporarily reclassified as 2A. When the extension lapsed and he was reclassified 1A again, the studio brought in MGM's top attorney, Irving Prinzmetal, to appear before Local Draft Board 245 on December 30, 1942, to appeal that decision. Once again the request was denied. On January 6, 1943, Eddie Mannix dispatched another affidavit to appeal Mickey's status. In it, he wrote how important the motion picture business was to the nation's morale. Mannix even quoted Lt. Gen. Dwight Eisenhower's statement that "Motion picture entertainment is as important to the people on the home front as butter and meat." The affidavit was eight pages long. However, on February 3, 1943, the appeal was turned down yet again, in a vote of 5–0.

Mayer's worst nightmare, the loss of his top money-earning star to the war, was quietly becoming a reality. The studio had already seen some of its other stars drafted into service, but Mickey was probably its most important asset, because of the revenue his movies generated.

It had to keep him working. But it had to do it without any negative publicity as tens of thousands of other men Mickey's age were being drafted. Still, despite Strickling's best efforts, there were whispers of MGM's efforts to keep Mickey out of the service. The *Hollywood Citizen-News* wrote on March 3, 1943, about the appeal and the request for a deferment. MGM responded with "We're not unpatriotic. The government specially wants us to continue making pictures. But how can we make them without actors?"

Metro knew the sensitivity of Mickey being deferred while ordinary boys were being rushed to war and possibly their deaths. That kind of imagery could destroy an actor's career faster than a string of bad movies. Thus, Mickey, with Strickling's assistance, released a statement that appeared in the *Hollywood Citizen-News*, which commented:

> How does Mickey feel about the appeal? The customarily cocksure, flippant youngster said solemnly last night: "Whatever the Army wants that's good enough for me. I'll do whatever Uncle Sam says." Mickey's mother, Nell Pankey will have you know that it was the studio's idea for the appeal not Mickey's. She remarked, "He's just not that kind, he has never felt he was better than anyone else, or entitled to special consideration. It's true that he is only five feet tall, and has been bothered with heart flutter and high blood pressure, but that's nothing new, and Mickey wouldn't try to dodge his classification."

On March 15, when he reported to the army induction center for his physical, he was armed with medical records. It seemed that, out of the clear blue, studio physician Dr. Edward Jones recalled that he had discovered that Mickey suffered from a "heart flutter" and "high blood pressure" during the routine yearly physical examination required by the Los Angeles Board of Education for minors under contract to the studio. This was the same Dr. Jones who had loaded Judy Garland with tranquilizers and amphetamines since she was fifteen years old and had given Lana Turner her abortion. On March 16, Lt. Col. Edgar H. Bailey, the commanding officer of the Los Angeles army induction center, announced, "Mickey Rooney, the film actor, has been rejected for army service." Bailey added that the actor had been referred to the induction center by his draft board and had received a "thorough examination." Mickey was reclassified 4F. Les Peterson wrote a memo to L.B. reflecting this on March 18, 1943.

In a matter of days, Mickey had gone from an athlete with robust health at the age of twenty-two to a 4F classification for having serious health issues. Perhaps, in light of the standard operating procedure at MGM, there might have been some serious dollars changing hands in this process. It would not have been unusual for the studio to have bought Mickey out of a combat uniform.

The war would eventually sweep up Mickey, who in interviews throughout his life said he was proud of his later service to his country. After he was reclassified 1A, he was inducted into the service more than a year later, in June 1944, but never saw the invasion of Normandy or any combat, for that matter. Once in uniform, he proudly supported the troops, entertained the soldiers, and fondly recalled his time in the army. However, in 1942, raging against his marital breakup, he was able to avoid it.

Ava filed for a separation on January 15, 1943. This was followed by a summit meeting with Mickey and Mannix. After countless more separations and reconciliations, Ava finally filed for divorce on May 2, 1943. Immediately, Mannix called her to his office for a meeting.

Ava recalled in *The Secret Conversations*:

> Mickey wasn't happy—and neither was Louis Mayer, who
> set his attack dog, Eddie Mannix onto me. Eddie liked me

but I knew he had a job to do. He said, "You know, Ava, you'll be finished at this studio if you try to take Mickey to the cleaners. Mr. Mayer owns this town. If you do anything to hurt Mickey's career, you'll never work in Hollywood again."

I said, "I know that."

Eddie was sympathetic. He said, "It was never going to work out with Mick, you know. He is never going to be a one-woman kid."

I felt my temperature rising. "Why the fuck didn't you tell me that before?" I said.

"You didn't ask," he said mildly, but he was obviously startled by my language. So was I. Most people were afraid to say boo to him. "You got a mouth on you, kid. I give you that," he said, and started to laugh.

I was lucky he didn't fire me on the spot. When he stopped laughing, he said: "Now listen to me, young lady. I'm going to give you some good advice. Mr. Mayer isn't going to mind you telling it to the judge. He doesn't want you telling him more than you have to."

I didn't understand what he was talking about. I truly didn't. I was barely twenty years old. I could look smart and sophisticated as hell in those gallery pictures they took of me all the time. The truth was, I didn't know beans when the bag was open.

He obviously saw my confusion.

"Mr. Mayer doesn't want you to sue for adultery, kid," Eddie spelled it out for me. He handled me like a baby. "Mr. Mayer doesn't want Mickey's name dragged through the courts along with a bunch of dames you reckon he might have shafted. He doesn't want some shyster lawyer claiming Mickey beat you up, or did this, that, and the other," he said.

The penny dropped. "I'm not going to name anybody," I said. "I'll sue the little sod for incompatibility. . . ."

"Incompatibility, you'd settle for that? Mr. Mayer would really appreciate that," Eddie said. "I think the least said the soonest mended, don't you?"

It was such a childish thing to say, the kind of rubbish you say to kids. I wanted to laugh. But the way it was said was so chilling, I thought better of it.

"Incompatibility then? That's what you'll go for? Can I give Mr. Mayer your word on that?" he said.

"Sure," I said casually, but I really meant it. I knew that if I had sued Mick for adultery, and named some of the girls he'd been fucking, it would have blown his wholesome Andy Hardy image right out of the water. It could have destroyed his career stone dead. . . . I knew that citing "incompatibility" was the cleanest and fastest route out of the marriage.

Eddie said, "You're not as dumb as you look, kid."

He asked me what I was going to do after the divorce. The question surprised me. I knew the final decree would take at least six months or maybe even longer to come through and I hadn't planned that far ahead.

I said, "If the studio renews my contract, I'd like to try to make a go of acting."

"I think you should," he said.

A couple of weeks later, the studio renewed my contract and increased my salary.

It put my mind at rest.[15]

California is a community property state, which means that any income accruing to a married couple during the marriage, excluding gifts or bequests to one of the parties, is divided equally between the parties upon dissolution of the marriage. Therefore, when Ava filed for divorce, she made a claim, under California law, for half Mickey's property and earnings. The grounds for dissolution were grievous mental suffering and extreme mental cruelty, which was standard for most California divorces in those days before "no-fault" divorces. Mickey didn't contest her charges, and the case was heard in Los Angeles before superior court judge Thurmond Clarke on May 21. Ava wore the same blue suit in which she'd been married. Her demands, as a result of her meeting with Eddie Mannix, were dropped to twenty-five thousand dollars in cash, a car, her furs, and the jewelry Mickey had given her that had not been pawned. An interlocutory decree— literally a decree between the words of the pleadings and the words of the final judgment, establishing the status of the marriage prior to a final decree—was granted that day, and the couple would not be free to remarry until the divorce became final a year later. Mickey told Les Peterson that he would spend that year trying to win her back.[16] But in 1944 the war would intervene, Mickey still had many more movies to make, and like the Sirens' call, his premarital lifestyle was beckoning him toward the rocks, and the starter's trumpet was blaring at Santa Anita.

13

Mickey and the Pit Bull

Mickey in motion.
PHOTO COURTESY OF ROBERT EASTON.

Even before Mickey divorced Ava, he had gone back full speed to his vices of booze, women, and gambling. But the divorce put him into high gear. Gambling, especially, had become a serious addiction by this point. Mickey's quip that he lost his first two dollars at Santa Anita and spent millions trying to get it back is not far off the mark. He was clearly chasing something, even if he didn't know what it was. The thrill of gambling truly consumed his life right up until his death.

Did Mickey inherit an addiction gene from his mother, Nell? Ava

Gardner's characterization of Nell Pankey at their first meeting was more than revealing. She described "Ma" with the *Racing Form* spread across her lap as she was handicapping horses while holding a big glass of bourbon in the other hand. Similarly, Mickey's father, according to Sidney Miller, was "a hard drinking, whore chasing, compulsive gambler." Mickey Rooney, therefore, was a textbook example of someone with a genetic predisposition to addictive self-destructive behaviors. Given the stimuli he had from an early age, he was just like one of Francis Pottenger's epigenetically predetermined cats, manifesting the addictions of its parents, only worse.[1]

Typical of most addicts, Mickey loved both the highs and lows of gambling. The flow of the neurochemical dopamine, stimulating the brain's reward center, triggered for Mickey (as it likely did for his parents and hundreds of thousands of other biologically addicted people) an exhilarating thrill. In Mickey's case, the thrill of winning on a long shot and the low of losing both led to overextending himself financially, as he tried, vainly, to square himself with his bookies. Author Roger Kahn told us, "When I was assigned to write his 'autobiography,' it was nearly impossible as he was consumed by the ponies. He even still owes me money I lent him to bet on some races."

In a meeting with Mayer after the success of the second Andy Hardy film, *You're Only Young Once*, released in 1937, Mayer wanted to reward him for his contribution. Mickey requested a direct telephone line installed on the set so he could call his bookies at his whim. "Poor baby, Mick was hooked on the horses," recalled Ava. . . . "Installing that phone on the set for him was fatal. I'm surprised the studio would do it, but I guess they'd do anything for him as long as he was making money for them. . . . Those Andy Hardy pictures paid for MGM's great movies, *Ninotchka*, *Camille*, *Two-Faced Woman*, all those other Garbo movies that were a bust at the box office. Mickey's movies kept the studio running."[2]

Rooney admitted to us, "No matter what I did, Mayer would see me and pat me on the head and tell me I was a good little fella. He made about ten million dollars a pat at the box office." [3]

Meanwhile, Rooney and his gang of hangers-on, a dissolute entourage, were drinking insatiably, chasing every starlet on the Metro lot and elsewhere, and frequenting the racetrack on an almost daily basis. This was all under the watchful eye of Mickey's minder, Les Peterson. Mickey's buddies, including the ever-faithful Sig Frohlich, Sidney Miller, Dick Paxton, Dick Crockett, Andy McIntyre, and Dick Quine, were his constant companions as he immersed himself in whatever vices he could. Dick Paxton, a stand-in for Rooney on films such as *Huckleberry Finn* and *Babes in Arms*, even lived at his Encino house.

Of Paxton, Rooney recalled, "I was shooting Huck Finn and I was supposed to go in this stream. I mean it was fucking cold, so I said, 'Oh, Dick . . .' and Paxton did the shot. The director was not happy." [4]

Wherever Rooney went, his band of merry men followed his every step. Why wouldn't they have been merry? Mickey paid for everything, from the drinks to the girls, and made sure they were set up even when they made their visits to the MGM-funded brothel Mickey called the T&M Studios.

"[Milton] Berle first took me there. It was amazing. Every girl looked like a film star. Clara Bow, Jean Harlow, Greta Garbo, Norma Shearer. They were dead ringers," Mickey recalled of Billie Bennett's establishment, which had become notorious in Hollywood, a must-visit for not only Metro talent but also some of the politicians and city officials in Los Angeles. [5]

While Mickey played hard, he also worked hard. MGM suspected that Mickey might not be able to duck the war indefinitely. Thus, claiming that Mickey was a vital asset they couldn't afford to lose, they plunged him into one film after another. They didn't fear overexposure, because of his intense popularity and the revenue stream his films generated.

The years 1942 to 1944, war years in Europe and the South Pacific, saw Mickey starring in *The Courtship of Andy Hardy, Andy Hardy's Double Life, A Yank at Eton, The Human Comedy, Thousands Cheer, Girl Crazy, Andy Hardy's Blonde Trouble,* and *National Velvet.* He appeared in ten films, released in approximately eighteen months. And in these films Mickey stretched his talents from musicals, where he excelled at song and dance, to comedy, and even drama. It was an enormous achievement for a twenty-four-year-old.

"Today you're lucky if you see the top actor do a film every year or two. He was churning them out like McDonald's hamburgers," remarked film historian Lou Sabini. "There is no doubt that this type of saturation would erode his box office. He was truly a shooting star, but eventually the audiences tired of the repetitiveness of the films and his character." [6]

In most cases, Mickey was the Andy Hardy character whether the film was a Hardy movie, *Young Tom Edison,* or *Thousands Cheer.* There were a couple of exceptions, as he gave more restrained performances in William Saroyan's *The Human Comedy* and in *National Velvet,* which were both directed by Mayer and Rooney favorite Clarence Brown. *The Human Comedy,* Mayer later said, was his favorite film of all time. Meanwhile, even though Rooney was the titled star of *National Velvet,* it was the teenage and devastatingly beautiful starlet Elizabeth Taylor who shot to fame from that film. Mickey was not the teenage heartthrob he had been even five years earlier, and it was apparent both to MGM and to audiences that there had definitely been an erosion in his popularity, something that was becoming clear by the time he appeared in *National Velvet.* But that didn't stop the assembly line of films.

The studio was returning millions on his every film, but Mickey was still being paid his weekly salary of $2,500 and scheduled bonuses. Back then, an actor receiving a percentage of the box office grosses, nets, or "points" on a picture was unheard of. Today, under the auspices of the major agencies, first or second gross or even net has become a standard deal point in most artists' agreements. But Mickey was a contract player, and whether the film returned five hundred thousand or five million, his salary remained the same. Whether he was nominated for a Best Actor Oscar, as he was for *The Human Comedy* (though he lost to Paul Lukas for *Watch on the Rhine*) or won the *Motion Picture Herald*'s Top Money Making Film Actor award, there was absolutely no added bonus. Thus, given Mickey's exorbitant life style, his staggering expenses for gambling, and all his other forms of entertainment, he simply couldn't keep up.

To add to his growing financial woes, Mickey was also indebted to the studio for the expenses he incurred. With the per-film bonuses included, Mickey was being paid $125,000 per year as the number one box office attraction. After he paid his income taxes and his agents at William Morris, and after two-thirds of his income went into trust, he and Nell were left with $40,000 to spend. Yet every haircut, his clothing allowance, every visit to the T&M Studio, every dinner at the studio commissary, and any other studio ancillary expense he incurred was also charged to Mickey. When Les Peterson picked up the tab at nightclubs for Mickey or loaned him money for bookies, this was also deducted.

When his stepfather, Fred Pankey, sat Mickey down to discuss his future, he told Mickey that he had to take better care of his money, which wouldn't be rolling in forever. Mickey resented Fred, who both lived in the home Mickey had purchased and worked at a job Mickey had helped him acquire. Arthur Marx told us, "It put a real chink in their relationship. Mickey was furious at Fred and called him a spoilsport. He later realized that Fred was dead on the money."[7] The bottom line, as stepfather Fred explained, was that Mickey was quickly owing his soul to the company store, as Tennessee Ernie Ford would sing fifteen years later in "Sixteen Tons."

Whereas Mickey tended to reject Fred Pankey's advice (mainly regarding his financial concerns), he did seek advice on his problems and concerns from actor Lewis Stone, Judge Hardy in the Andy films. It was as if, because of Mickey's ability to immerse himself completely in the Andy role, the Hardy family had become his real-life family, at least during the life of the series. On the set, Lewis Stone would listen to Rooney's concerns and offer advice on matters ranging from financial problems to the young actor's self-image. Mickey had a deep respect for Stone, as did Louis Mayer, who was a close friend. When Rooney once told Stone that it depressed him when he was teased about his size, Stone told Mickey that some of the great men in the world stood less than five foot three, including Napoleon Bonaparte and New York City's mayor Fiorello La Guardia. Mickey later placed a portrait of Napoleon in his Encino home, to remind himself of that. When he became engaged to Ava, he immediately took her to the set and introduced her to Lewis Stone, as if Stone were his real father. Mickey would spend most of his life looking for a father figure.

SO DESPITE HIS LOFTY position as king of the box office, Mickey was sinking deep into the red. The loans he took from MGM to cover the shortfall were accruing interest, though he was probably unaware of the tab he was running up. He didn't have a team of business advisers or accountants, as many of today's performers do. As a show business financial manager once said, you put a third away for taxes, a third away for investment purposes, and a third for life's necessities. Mickey, though—who had very little education and came from a background of itinerant performers who lived from paycheck to paycheck—lived in the moment, for the moment. He saw no end in sight to his prosperity, even though that prosperity was only an illusion. If one compares Mickey's earning power to that of young stars today (who will never come close to the impact that Rooney had on his generation), the scales are tipped wildly in their favor.

Mickey, ultimately, was acutely aware of this inequity when he wrote:

> For all of our work on "Girl Crazy" . . . a film that grossed [in 1943] $5,866,000, we just got our salaries. . . . [N]either of us [he or Garland] got a dime's worth of royalties from all those great songs we recorded; MGM took all the profits through their records division. In reality, I think, "Girl Crazy" grossed more than $47 million worldwide. The thieves were still at work. You must remember that at this point in my life the peak of my earning pyramid, I had yet to earn my first million. This should lay to rest all the bullshit people write how Rooney has pissed away hundreds of millions. Oh, I've earned more than a billion bucks. But, I never saw very much of it.[8]

Rooney claimed to us that Jimmy Cagney told him he went on strike from Warner Bros. and Jack Warner for a payment of ten million dollars. Jack Warner had kept Cagney out of work for one year, refusing to pay him that fee and to teach him a lesson. Mickey said, "When Warner went to a board meeting in New York, he almost lost control of the company. The majority of the board was shocked to find out why Cagney hadn't made a picture in a year. 'You know how much money we've lost because of your fucking move? You're costing us hundreds of millions. Pay the son of a bitch the ten million.'" Mickey followed with: "[I]t's just too bad that I never made that kind of threat to Metro. Judy and I could have stood together against him. But we were no match for Mayer. We were vaudeville kids. How could we stand up to a man like L.B., who was the highest-paid executive in the land? Better for us to stick to what we knew best: singing and dancing."[9] Although we did not find any evidence to substantiate Mickey's story about Cagney, Cagney did go on a work stoppage from

Warners for a higher salary, which he received, and later formed his own production company.

Even when adjusting for 1943 dollars, there is just no comparison between today's media and the impact Mickey Rooney had on audiences in 1940–44. Yet his impact, great as it was, still left him living on the edge, hemorrhaging money as his popularity with audiences slowly, but perceptibly, began to erode.

Mickey's vulnerability was acute in September 1943. His divorce was pending, he was working nonstop at the MGM factory, and he was barely keeping his head above water due to his mounting debt. At just twenty-four years old he was shouldering the responsibility of being the key source of profits at MGM while becoming aware that he was accumulating debt. The $25,000 divorce payment and new car he'd bought for Ava came from a loan from Metro. He owed countless bookies thousands of dollars. Worse than that, future military service was looming.

In the late fall of 1943, he and Les Peterson prepared for a tour of the East Coast to promote the first Andy Hardy film in over a year, *Andy Hardy's Blonde Trouble.* The series was seemingly running out of gas. After all, how many films could Mickey make with the same character, same arc, and only minor plot twists? Worse, how could Andy Hardy, a throwback to the 1920s and '30s remain relevant in a world at war, especially when men of his age were being drafted into the service? This would become a quandary for MGM. Mickey was allowed to age slightly for this film—he was now going to college— but the critics, such as Harrison Carroll, writing in the *Los Angeles Evening Herald Express* on May 22, 1944, felt that "[H]is sex life remains at the gee-whiz-she-kissed-me stage." With a world war raging and with millions of deaths worldwide, the Pollyanna/Louis Mayer naïve world of Andy Hardy and small-town Carvel were becoming passé.

Mickey was aware of this shift. He'd started receiving negative reviews he'd never experienced before. *A Yank at Eton*, for instance, was savaged in a general review carrying no byline in the *New York Times* on October 16, 1942: "Draw a deep breath, ladies and gentlemen, and check your sensibilities at the door . . . Andy Hardy at Eton is a fearful thing to see . . ." The next year, for the musical *Thousands Cheer*, the *New York Times* wrote, "Mickey's stint is not exactly a show stopper." The film was a huge moneymaker, however. So it was full steam ahead.

Mickey remarked to us, "It didn't take a genius to realize that the studio wasn't going to let Andy Hardy grow up. . . . If the people at Metro had their way, I'd have remained a teenager for forty years." [10]

Peterson recalled, "I thought it was a good time to get Mickey out of town. He was still agonizing over Ava and spending his waking hours trying to devise ways to win her back." [11]

In 1943, Mickey had slipped from first to ninth position in the *Showmen's Trade Review* polling of the nation's exhibitors, behind Abbott and Costello and Bob Hope. Both Mayer and Strickling thought it would help Rooney's standing to do a media tour of the East Coast. The plan was to visit Cleveland, Philadelphia, Pittsburgh, Baltimore, New York City, and Detroit. While the turnout was still strong, it wasn't the major event he had experienced the prior year, when he toured with Ava. "There was certainly a slight diminishing of his drawing power. The luster was sort of wearing off," noted Sid Miller.[12]

At this point, Mickey was far more concerned about Ava than his career. She was doing films on her own, such as *Three Men in White*, which were bringing her some attention. She was now on the radar. Ava was rushed into the film *Masie Goes to Reno*, playing a rich divorcée, which many joked did not require much acting. Before Mickey left on tour, he was spotted with her by a *Los Angeles Examiner* reporter. Mickey talked with the reporter about a possible reconciliation, and Ava concurred.[13] However, the fact was, with each acting role, Ava was feeling far more independent.

Mickey was upset at being apart from her due to the tour, however Strickling said the tour was necessary to bolster his standing It was a seminal time in Mickey's life, for it was during the tour that he met a man who would significantly alter his career (not necessarily in a good way). That man was theater impresario Sam Stiefel.

Samuel H. Stiefel was an interesting character, described by *Time* magazine in his 1958 obituary as the "Father of Negro Show Business." Born in 1897 to a hardworking Jewish immigrant family in New Jersey, Stiefel, along with his brothers, built a chain of theaters known as the Chitlin' Circuit that catered to the black audiences. He owned three of the five theaters that showcased great African American performers such as legendary vocalist Billie Holiday, jazz great Duke Ellington, iconic band leader and cutting-edge performer Cab Calloway—who recorded the role of Sportin' Life in Gershwin's folk opera *Porgy and Bess*, but is probably best known for his unbelievable rendition of "Minnie the Moocher"—singer Billy Eckstine, and Moms Mabley—these and other black performers who were blocked from appearing in all-white theaters at the time. Show business in the 1930s and '40s, like baseball and even the armed services, was segregated. The Chitlin' Circuit included the Apollo Theater in New York City; the Uptown in Philadelphia; the Howard in Washington, DC; and the Royal Theatre in Baltimore. Stiefel owned the Roxy in Philadelphia and other theaters that featured both burlesque and movies. He also ran a talent management company with agent Eddie Sherman that managed Abbott and Costello, actor Peter Lorre, singer Andy Russell, and several others.

The last stop of the Metro-sponsored East Coast tour was in Pittsburgh. "I don't think Mickey will ever forget that stop," Les Peterson told Arthur Marx, "because that is where he met Sam Stiefel. If it hadn't been for his influence, Mickey might never have left MGM, which was one of the worst tactical errors of his life."

Peterson recalled to Arthur Marx, "We were at the theater one Saturday afternoon, when a man came to the stage door and asked the manager if he could meet Mickey Rooney. His name was Sam Stiefel, a name we were not familiar with, but it turned out he had money, owned a number of movie theaters in Baltimore and Philadelphia, and also had a string of racehorses on the West Coast. Anyway, we agreed to see him, so the stage manager sent him back to our dressing room. Stiefel was a short, squarely built man who wore suits with wide lapels and flashy silk ties and looked about as trustworthy as a pit boss in Las Vegas [in the 1940s]." [14]

Attorney Murray Lertzman recalled, "He certainly was part of the Jewish Mafia. He had this rough, gravely voice. He was right out of Central Casting. He had the mannerisms of a Eugene Pallette crossed with Sheldon Leonard. He carried a wad of bills that would have choked a horse. He was very flashy and quite persuasive. He knew every wise guy from Benny Siegel to Mickey Cohen. I think he even backed Cohen in a retail men's store. He lived in a beautiful house in Bel Air that was once owned by Jack Warner. He tried to set up production deals at every studio. Mickey Cohen was originally his calling card." He booked many of his clients at mob-related clubs. [15]

Stiefel told Mickey that he was his biggest fan and that he even had bought a pair of the drumsticks in an auction that Mickey had used to play with the Tommy Dorsey Band. He told Mickey about the theaters he owned, how he managed talent like Abbott and Costello and his racehorses. He had a limo pick-up Mickey and Les on Sunday, their day off.

"We were in Pittsburgh, where everything was closed on Sunday. So he took us to the Oasis Club, which was a mob joint in Cherry Hill, New Jersey, which was a long ways off [more than three hundred miles]," recalled Peterson. [16] On the way down to the club, Stiefel expressed sympathy for all the trouble Mickey had had with Ava. Then he pumped Mickey about his contract with Metro. When he found out Rooney, at this point, was still making only $1,750 a week for forty weeks and bonuses, he told Mickey that he was being stiffed. Peterson remembered:

> He told Mickey, "You should have your own production company and make your own pictures." When Mickey admitted that he was an actor and not much of a businessman, Stiefel offered to manage Mickey and run the company for him. What he didn't tell Mickey was that he wanted to get into movie production in the worst way and was using Mickey as a stepping-stone to that goal. You see, his former partner was a fellow named Eddie Sherman, who had gone to the West Coast and was managing Abbott and Costello, and Stiefel was jealous of him. He wanted to be in the more glamorous end of show business, too. Anyways, he spent the evening painting a glowing picture of what Mickey's career would be like if only he'd let Stiefel manage him. Mickey was intrigued, especially when Stiefel mentioned he owned racehorses. Before the evening was over he had Mickey thoroughly convinced they ought to go in business together and form their own production company." [17]

Basically, Stiefel was a nonentity in Hollywood, while his ex-partner Eddie Sherman had become an important manager. Lou Costello's youngest daughter, Chris Costello, told us she could not remember Stiefel's presence, "I clearly remember Eddie Sherman controlling the team, just not Stiefel." [18] Nephew Jay Robert Stiefel recalled, "He clearly had aspirations to be in the film business, and he bought a beautiful house in Bel Air to stake his claim. He told us about the parties he hosted and the stars who attended. He definitely wanted to make his mark there" [19]—but he could do that only through owning talent, and that talent was Mickey Rooney.

Stiefel told Rooney about his proposal and his plans for him unabashedly, in the presence of Peterson, who was an MGM company man through and through. You could be sure that Mayer and Mannix were fully aware of every detail of this meeting. Stiefel certainly was keenly aware that forming a partnership with one of the world's biggest film stars would be his entrée into the film business. Mickey, although he had grown up in the industry, was simply talent and not a savvy business guy. He'd never negotiated his own deals. He was twenty-four years old and no match for a streetwise, successful entrepreneur such as Stiefel. An astute businessman, Sam could sniff the desperation on Rooney.

Stiefel followed Mickey's trail, flying to the West Coast shortly after Mickey returned. He then began to work to win Rooney over, putting on a full-court press to gain his confidence in Stiefel's ability to manage him and make him financially independent from MGM. He loaned Mickey money and became friendly with Nell and Fred Pankey, taking them out to the "swankiest bistros," showering them with presents, and helping them out financially. Stiefel was a master manipulator, according to Les Peterson.[20] He saw that Mickey was struggling to live on a straight salary, a situation that Stiefel said could be rectified by having his own production company, which would help him shelter his income. Along the way, he massaged Rooney's ego, subsidized his losses at the racetrack, and even encouraged his gambling. He also helped out Mickey's troupe of hangers-on with gifts and cash. In the end, Mickey was convinced, especially after Fred advised him to move forward with Stiefel's proposal. Undue influence may have been attributed to Pankey's recommendation, as Stiefel was also financing Fred in opening a new bar.

Mickey recalled, "In the months that followed, Sam would become the kind of friend who would lend me money without question. At Santa Anita, if I was tapped out, he'd offer me money without my having to ask. 'Okay,' I'd say. 'Give me five hundred.' 'Here,' he'd say, flashing a big roll of hundred dollar bills, 'take a thousand.' I took his offerings, with thanks." [21]

When Stiefel relocated his family to Los Angeles, he bought a showcase home in Bel Air. "It was an amazing home that had the elegant screening room and this glassed-in room under the pool," recalled Stiefel's granddaughter Adrienne Callander.[22] "Being a theater impresario and being involved in show business, it was a common practice to work in the business with the underworld types who ran the booking agencies, such as MCA, or owned the clubs, like Frank Costello. Once, Al Capone called my grandfather from prison. He wanted his help in building a stage at the prison. My grandfather was amused that he called him," Callander recalled.[23]

She continued: "He had been running vaudeville in his theaters and discovered the niche of black entertainment. My father was always fascinated that their home was open to the legendary African American stars like Billie Holiday, and he got to know them. . . . And he became rather wealthy in the process."[24]

Les Peterson recalled, "Stiefel's pockets were always bulging with cash, which was available for a loan without collateral whenever Mickey ran into hard luck, but if there was one thing: Mickey was a schnook. It never occurred to him his new business partner might be keeping track of all the cash he laid out for Mickey."[25]

Stiefel set up a California corporation called Rooney Incorporated, and held lavish networking parties, to set up the kinds of deals that an independent production company could make without the involvement of a studio. The corporation's stockholders were Mickey Rooney, who was the president; Samuel E. Stiefel who was secretary/treasurer; and attorney Mort Briskin who was vice president. Once the corporation was certified as able to do business, Briskin sent a memo to MGM's accounting department, on March 21, 1944, demanding that all checks for Mickey Rooney be made payable to the order of Rooney Incorporated. Once Rooney Inc. had the capital to work with, Stiefel, through corporate counsel Briskin, began work on renegotiating Mickey's contract so he would have the right to make additional films outside MGM.

Briskin, who had been Johnny Carson's attorney, was a producer in his own right, of Stiefel-financed Mickey Rooney movies *The Big Wheel* and *Quicksand*. He recalled to Arthur Marx "Mayer agreed to give it to us, without much argument."

Rooney Inc.'s initial function was to book personal appearances; merchandise Mickey's likeness and name, particularly for a comic book line from Taffy comics; collect his salary; and invest his income. One of the investments was a stable of horses. Stiefel sweetened the pot by throwing in some of his own horses, which together with Mickey's money became part of the company's assets.

Meanwhile, Uncle Sam was beckoning Mickey to military service once again, and this time he wasn't in the mood to grant the actor any deferments. Mickey was reclassified 1A in March 1944. Eddie Mannix continued to write letters of appeal, but there was seemingly no other delay possible. On May 4 the draft board sent a very curt letter advising Mannix that Mickey Rooney "WILL be inducted sometime in May 1944."

Mannix sent in another plea, in response to which the draft board informed him that Mickey would be wearing army khaki in thirty days. Mannix instructed Pandro Berman, who was producing the film *National Velvet*, with the notoriously slow and deliberate director Clarence Brown, to "Shoot all remaining Rooney scenes first, no matter how it messes up the schedule."

Mickey, meanwhile, began to panic. He was informed by Mannix that his MGM salary would be suspended while he served in the army. His $2,500 weekly income would therefore be reduced to a fifty-dollar-a-month buck private's pay. His outlandish lifestyle would be interrupted, he would have to discontinue his pursuit of Ava, and his mother was going ballistic about her needs. Nell was worried about how she could keep El Ranchita, the house in Encino, and pay her expenses if Mickey went off salary at MGM. Fred Pankey seemed not to be capable of providing for her in the manner to which she had become accustomed, and any savings that Mickey had were tied up in an irrevocable trust.

It was Sam Stiefel to the rescue. Stiefel, after hearing from both Nell and Mickey about their plight, told them that there was nothing to worry about. If Nell ran short of cash, all she had to do was "holler," and Stiefel would be there to bankroll her until Mickey's return from the army.

In the midst of all this, Mickey was hearing rumors on the lot about the demise of the Hardy pictures. The bright light of his star was dimming. He was falling in the box office polls, and although his movies were still profitable, they had returned lower-than-expected grosses. Tastes were beginning to change with the impact of World War II. By 1944, MGM had produced fourteen Hardy films. Even successful series such as Sherlock Holmes, which starred Basil Rathbone, ended after fourteen films, mostly due to a repetitive plot and stagnant cast. In fact, only rarely did a movie series last beyond five years. A rare exception was the Blondie series, which starred Penny Singleton and Arthur Lake and ran for twenty-eight entries over twelve years (1938–50). The Andy Hardy films had lost their steam.

Bill Ludwig, an MGM screenwriter from 1938 to 1957 (the longest-serving), told us, "Those of us who wrote the Andy Hardy films were called the garbage man's dream. The initial films turned a huge profit, and Louis Mayer loved those movies. While I started at Metro for thirty-five dollars a week, we had huge salary increases, as Mayer loved how we constructed the films. I once received a five-thousand-dollar bonus from Mayer to rush a Hardy script for production. Of course I had to fight Eddie Mannix later to collect it. By the end of the war, [the films] had run their course, and Mayer had reluctantly come to that conclusion, as well." [26]

In addition to his job as an MGM screenwriter, Ludwig was a former attorney, and Rooney often went to him for advice. Ludwig found Mickey to be quite self-aware with an especially keen knowledge of his limitations due to his size and to audience perceptions. During this period in 1944, Mickey voiced his concerns to him. "What's going to become of me?" he asked Ludwig.

"You're a great talent. You'll keep right on going," Ludwig assured. [27]

"No, no. I'll end up playing bad jockeys like Frankie Darro. I'd love to direct, but they're never going to let me direct. They will never give a million-dollar film to a little Irish song-and-dance man," Mickey pouted.

"Come on, Mick. You know how good you are? Cary Grant told me the other day that he thinks you're the biggest talent in the business. You've got everything," said Ludwig.

"You know, Bill, I'd give ten years of my life if I were just six inches taller," Mickey said. [28]

As all this was unfolding, Mickey was still trying to reconcile with Ava. The newspapers carried countless stories of their attempts. The *Los Angeles Examiner* on June 16, 1944, wrote, "While the young couple were divorced in Las Vegas, Nevada, on September 15, 1943, they recently have been 'very friendly' and have been seen in each other's company at Hollywood night spots. 'I love Ava a great deal,' he said. 'We're young yet, and both of us are glad that we caught our domestic error in time to correct it for a long and happy life together.' Ava, whose hand Mickey held as the two talked, and her former husband's remarks were mutual. 'I couldn't get along without Mickey,' she said, 'and I guess he couldn't get along without me.'"

Sonny Yule at two years old in the burlesque days.
PHOTO COURTESY
OF ROBERT EASTON.

Sonny Yule with Tom Mix in My Pal, the King *in 1932.*
PHOTO COURTESY
OF MIKE COOGAN.

Sonny Yule and Coleen Moore in Orchids and Ermine *(1927).*
PHOTO COURTESY OF MONTE KLAUS.

Mickey McGuire's *broadcasting station. Mickey "Himself" McGuire with his "Gang" (1931).*
PHOTO COURTESY OF MONTE KLAUS.

Another Treat!

MICKEY ROONEY

Mickey (Himself) McGuire

Of the Toonerville Kids

Now at the

ORPHEUM THEATRE

Will Greet His Many Friends

WEDNESDAY AT 4:45 P. M.

In the Boys' Shop
(3rd Floor)

Labiche & Graff

NEXT DOOR TO N. O. PUBLIC SERVICE

BARONNE STREET

Advertisement for the Mickey McGuire films. PHOTO COURTESY OF G. D. HAMANN.

5¢ EACH OR 2 FOR 25¢

Mickey (right) *with McGuire costars Delia ("Tomboy Taylor") Bogard (center) and Marvin ("Katrink") Stephens (right).* PHOTO COURTESY OF MONTE KLAUS.

Babes in Arms *publicity photo with Mickey and Judy.*

This MGM artwork appeared in the New York Daily News *on October 29, 1939, to promote* Babes in Arms *(1939).*

PHOTO COURTESY
OF MONICA KLAUS.

Mickey with the great Will Rogers—months before Rogers's death—in The County Chairman *in 1935.* PHOTO COURTESY OF MONTE KLAUS.

Mickey and Carmen Miranda in Babes on Broadway.
PHOTO COURTESY OF ROBERT EASTON.

Mickey and Judy in the backyard musical Babes in Arms. PHOTO COURTESY OF ROBERT EASTON.

Mickey and Judy in politically incorrect blackface for the minstrel number in Babes on Broadway *(1941). Mickey also did a minstrel number in* Babes in Arms.

Mickey and Busby Berkeley.

A happier time on the set of Babes on Broadway. *Director Busby Berkeley, Louis B. Mayer, Mickey, and Judy Garland.*

Roger Imhof, Mickey, and Jean Harlow (a year before her death) in Riffraff *(1936).*

Mickey and Lana Turner during his Andy Hardy *days.*

Cartoon of Mickey and Judy.

Mickey and Elizabeth Taylor in National Velvet *(1944).* PHOTO COURTESY OF ROBERT EASTON.

Postcard of the Hardy family in Blonde Trouble. PHOTO COURTESY OF ROBERT EASTON.

Joe Yule and Mickey in Judge Hardy and Son *(1939).*

Christmas at Judy's *(1934).*

Mickey and Judy in 1963, at the time of her TV show.

Mickey and Judy in the early 1960s.

Friendship bracelet given by Judy to Mickey, inscribed "Mike" and "Jootes."

Back of friendship bracelet, with inscription from "Jootes" to "Mike."

Eleanor Roosevelt being greeted by Mickey Rooney, who entertained guests attending the inauguration gala in Constitution Hall in 1941. Next to Rooney is Charlie Chaplin. Behind the First Lady is her daughter, Anna Roosevelt. Behind Rooney is John Roosevelt.

Greer Garson, Eddie Cantor, and Mickey Rooney at the piano.

An amazing photograph at a historic event in Berlin on May 21, 1945, that honored Russian Marshal Konev. From left to right: legendary violinist Jascha Heifetz, Marshal Konev, General Omar Bradley, and Private Mickey Rooney. PHOTO COURTESY OF ROBERT EASTON.

Mickey in 1944 with Patton's Army, performing for the soldiers on the battlefield in Germany as part of the Jeep shows.

<small>PHOTO COURTESY OF ROBERT EASTON.</small>

Marilyn Monroe with Mickey along with Art Aragon (right) and Dale Robertson (left) at the Hollywood Entertainers Baseball Game in 1952.

<small>PHOTO COURTESY OF ROBERT FINKEL.</small>

Judy's and Mickey's Moms. From left to right: Ethel Marion Milne Gumm, Judy, Mickey, "Ma" Nell. PHOTO COURTESY OF G. D. HAMANN.

Mickey and Mickey Jr.

Timmy Rooney (left) *at age fifteen with stepbrother Dan Kessel, age eleven.*

The Fabulous Rooney Brothers at Columbia Recording Studios. From left to right: Timmy, Mickey Jr., and Teddy.

Timmy, Mickey, and Mickey Jr.

Meanwhile, Eddie Mannix continued to file appeals to keep Mickey out of the army. However, the appeals and medical records fell on deaf ears. In August 1942, Mickey was classified 1A, his number was called up, he got his "Greetings" letter, and was ordered to report to the army induction center in downtown Los Angeles for a physical. Andy Hardy was in the army now.

14

Greetings

*Mickey was PFC Rooney in Patton's Third Army in 1944. Here he is
part of the Jeep Shows at Tauberbischofsheim, entertaining the troops.*
PHOTO COURTESY OF ROBERT EASTON.

I was so fucking drunk, I would have married my drill sergeant.

MICKEY ROONEY ON HIS MARRIAGE TO BETTY JANE RASE

There was no avoiding it. The war was chewing up an entire generation of men, putting them in uniform, and sending them off to
Europe and the South Pacific, where Generals Bradley and MacArthur were now on the offensive. And Mickey was now part of that
war effort.

He was sent to Fort MacArthur, which overlooked the Los Angeles
Harbor, where he discovered, in a stunning realization, that he was
no longer at the dream factory. A tough drill sergeant reminded the

troops that they had a movie star in their ranks who shouldn't expect any favors. He received a fair amount of razzing from officers, non-coms, and fellow buck privates. But Mickey was an old pro at dealing with tough audiences. When he had to, he would give them a broad smile, fire back his own smart remark, dance away from trouble, and roll with the punches. What else could he do? He learned how to be accepted. After three days at Fort MacArthur, he was shipped off for basic training to the historic Fort Riley, Kansas, where General Custer's Seventh Cavalry was once mustered. This, too, was a far cry from the spoiled and pampered life he had become accustomed to as the world's top movie actor. There were no buddies to run his errands, no chauffeurs to drive him to locations, no young girls to enjoy.

Early in his period in the service, Mickey spent his spare time writing long love letters to Ava. She at first answered his letters and promised to wait for him until the end of the war. By the close of the summer, however, she no longer replied to his letters. Mickey then tried calling her. When he finally connected, she told him very bluntly that they were over as a couple and to please stop contacting her. As Mickey began sobbing to her that he still loved her, he asked her through tears if there was another person in her life. Click, she hung up the phone. Mickey was devastated. When one of his army buddies showed him a newspaper column carrying a story that Ava was now the steady girlfriend of millionaire movie producer and aviation pioneer Howard Hughes, he went ballistic. He went on a drinking binge and then went AWOL from Fort Riley.[1]

Not so, according to Mickey. He claimed in *Life Is Too Short,* in response to the accusation that he was AWOL, that he was in fact on a ten-day furlough to Los Angeles to take care of his mother after she received a death threat in the mail from an anonymous "kook." (He also claimed he got into a fistfight with Hughes in front of Ava's apartment, which she broke up. Hughes was nearly six foot three, insanely aggressive, and certainly no pushover. At the end of the fight,

Mickey claims, they all calmed down and drank Dom Perignon in the apartment. Mickey wrote that when he was leaving, he said, "I gotta go fight a war."

"Good luck," said Hughes, "and Mickey—don't get your ass shot off." [2] (Ava never mentioned this in *The Secret Conversations*.)

Yet authors Arthur Marx, Roland Flamini, and Jane Ellen Wayne put forth the AWOL claim. [3] Flamini writes, "MPs were waiting at Los Angeles Airport to take him back to Kansas, and Metro had to pull strings to prevent serious trouble. Strickling also succeeded in keeping it out of the papers." [4] In our research, we found several newspaper accounts of Mickey's being in Los Angeles. When rumors apparently began to spread, a story in a column by Louella Parsons in the *Los Angeles Express*, on August 5, 1944, said, "Reports that Mickey Rooney is out of the Army at this writing at least are apparently untrue. He is at Fort Riley and leaves soon to be in an Army show in Kansas City." However, on August, 23, 1944, Sidney Skolsky in the *Hollywood Citizen-News* wrote, "Mickey Rooney is in town on a furlough. Sidney Miller said, 'It's darned decent of Mickey to come back and entertain us civilians.' Rooney will go to Camp Siebert, and O.C.S. [Officer Candidate School]." [5] In talking with the authors, Sid Miller did not mention Mickey going AWOL. However, he did recall that both Eddie Mannix and Louie Mayer pulled strings and had Mickey shipped to Camp Siebert, Alabama, where he would be "out of harm's way, and would be assigned to Special Services to entertain the troops. Listen, Mick was the most talented, all-around performer, so why not put his skills to work to put a show on for our troops and lift their morale?" Sid also recalled, "Mickey was hitting the sauce pretty hard. He was out of his mind with Ava dating Howard Hughes and [his] being stuck in the army." [6]

It was at Camp Siebert that Mickey first met the person who would become his longtime friend legendary tenor sax player Jimmy Cook, who said to Arthur Marx, "I was in the day-room at the camp. Mickey was at the piano, playing the blues, probably for Ava, so I got out my horn and started playing with him. We sounded good together. I never suspected what a hell of a good musician Mickey is. I thought it was just publicity that he could play all those instruments, but he really can. Anyway, we had a lot in common, and we've been friends ever since."[7]

When he arrived at Camp Siebert, Mickey was drinking heavily and on the rebound from Ava, a dangerous combination. "Surprisingly, Mickey had a high threshold for alcohol. He could really pound 'em down. He was sort of a happy drunk. He told us the story of how drunk he was when he met B.J.," recalled Sid Miller, referring to Mickey's second wife, Betty Jane Rase.[8]

B.J., as she was known, was born on May 6, 1927, in Birmingham, Alabama, and was a trained musician, a pianist, by the time she was sixteen. Going by the professional name of Betty Jane Phillips, she was the 1944 Miss Alabama, and in September 1944 she was the fourth runner-up in the Miss America Pageant in Atlantic City, where she played the piano for the talent portion of the contest. Even at seventeen, B.J. was a very ambitious and driven woman, one seeking to get into show business. As a finalist in the pageant, she had attracted lots of attention, and in a whirlwind of activity after the pageant, she attended several parties and events in Alabama, meeting a lot of different people.

To honor Mickey's presence in Birmingham, a benefit showing of his film with Judy Garland *Girl Crazy*, at the Alabama Theater, was arranged on September 23, 1944, where officers from the camp were in attendance along with local media. Mickey was there with his army pal Jimmy Cook. The *Birmingham News*'s Lily Mae Caldwell, who'd worked as the arts and entertainment editor for forty-seven years, was a major force in the development of the Miss Alabama Pageant, and acted as its director for forty-six years until her death in 1980. (The pageant was sponsored by her employer, the *Birmingham News*.) That evening, Caldwell brought along Betty Jane Rase to the *Girl Crazy* party; she had become very close to B.J. and was very protective of her seventeen-year-old beauty queen prodigy.

In a *Birmingham News* story in 1975, Caldwell described the first meeting between Rooney and B.J., writing, "She was a very talented young woman. When I saw Mickey, I introduced myself as the News entertainment editor and his eyes went directly to B.J. I said, 'Mickey, I want you to meet my very good friend Betty Jane Rase. She's Miss Alabama.' He said, 'Well hello there Miss Alabama.' And she responded, in her very best elegant Southern greeting, 'Oh, Mr. Rooney! How Y'all?' I think it was love at first sight."

B.J. had several qualities that reminded Mickey of Ava. They both had a wonderful southern belle drawl and were long legged with a beautiful smile. The only difference was that B.J. was a blonde. Mickey told us, "I was so fucking drunk, I would have married my drill sergeant. I got stuck with a giant, goddamn hick from the sticks." [9]

Jimmy Cook recalled, "Mickey's eyes bugged out at the sight of Betty Jane's figure. She had more going on than a naïve little teenager who was impressed to be in the same room as a movie star. She had more on the ball than that. She was a very good musician. She played excellent piano and sang very well." [10]

In a recent interview with the authors, B.J.'s friend Pam McClenathan remembered, "She had a great sense of humor and was just an incredible musician." (Pam became B.J.'s friend when she was taking care of her and her son Tim Rooney, who was suffering from dermatomyositis, a fatal neuromuscular disease. Both have since died.) McClenathan remembered B.J. as "an accomplished singer and highly sought after as a back-up singer for Elvis, Bobby Darrin, Frank Sinatra, and countless others." She also sang in films, such as *The Flower Drum Song*, in which she laid down the vocal tracks for actress Pat Suzuki.

It had been a month since the blowup in front of Ava's apartment, and the divorced couple was no longer in contact. Mickey was lonely and isolated at the Alabama army base, way out of his comfort zone, and missing the life he had led for over ten years as a star at Metro. Wearing the uniform, he was looking at being shipped to Europe to join Allied troops still fighting pitched battles against the Wehrmacht, and as a consequence, he felt extremely vulnerable.

"I'm a little hazy about the courtship. In fact, I was a little hazy during the courtship. I'd been drinking," admitted Mickey.[11] "Hazy" was an understatement. "Obliterated" was probably more accurate. But there he was, staggering drunk and dazzled by B.J.'s beauty, and just as likely by her similarity to Ava. He wanted to nail her on the spot. Thus, almost three hours after meeting Betty Jane on that very same night, he proposed to her. Betty Jane immediately accepted. That night, Betty Jane took Mickey to meet her working-class parents, Edward and Lena Rase, who lived in a small house in Birmingham, to get their approval—which they gave immediately upon hearing the news. (It was indeed good news for Edward Rase, who was out of work at the time.)

Time was fleeting. Mickey was told that he would be shipped to the European Theater within ten days. Mickey no longer had Les Peterson to take care of every detail, so he arranged the wedding with his commanding officer, who invited the couple to hold the wedding at his home. And on September 30, 1944, Mickey Rooney and Betty Jane Rase were married. Jimmy Cook was Mickey's best man, and reporter Lily Mae Caldwell was Betty's maid of honor. Edward Rase gave the bride away. In a story that covered the event for the *Birmingham News*, Lily Mae wrote, "The Rases were as proud as if General Robert E. Lee had won the Battle of Appomattox."

Mickey, with a two-day pass, spent his wedding night at a hotel and returned on Monday morning for reveille. Two days later, his unit received its overseas orders for Europe, and Mickey was headed to the front as part of an entertainment unit. He received one more pass from his CO and spent the final weekend in Alabama with his bride of one week (and drank heavily). Then, on Monday, October 6, he found himself on a troop train bound for New York City. Two days later, Mickey was marching up the gangplank of the *Queen Mary* on his way to England, part of another generation of young men off to another war, many of whom would return to their families only in body bags, if they returned at all.

"It was a miserable voyage," Jimmy Cook said to Arthur Marx. "Four thousand GIs jam-packed aboard a ship built to accommodate a thousand. Not only that, we were billeted way down in the bowels of the ship. During the trip, the latrines above us broke and all that shit was coming down on our bunks and over everything. Then when we got to England some officers, who'd never been anything as civilians, suddenly decided to take it out on Mickey and the rest of us because he was a celebrity and we were an entertainment unit and not a fighting force. So they put us on twenty-one days straight of KP . . . Mickey, of course, hated it, as we all did, but he took it like a good sport, stuck it out, until we were eventually shipped over to Le Havre and then Paris,"[12] which had been liberated from German occupation six weeks earlier, at the end of August.

Once Mickey arrived in Paris, he was transported to the encampment in the outskirts of the city where Special Services had set up shop. There he met fellow entertainers such as comic Red Buttons, former child star Bobby Breen, and his pal Jimmy Cook. Broadway producer Josh Logan, who was in charge of the unit, told them they would have to improvise and create their own stages to entertain the troops. Mickey suggested they entertain off the flat bed of the jeeps they were set to travel in to reach the troops. Thus the "Jeep show" idea was born. Logan set up teams comprising a musician, a singer, and an emcee, who told the jokes.

Mickey embarked on his circuit with singer Bob Priester and accordion player Mario Pieroni, where he performed his old numbers from vaudeville along with his imitations. Priester sang to Pieroni's accordion accompaniment. The small troupe traveled to troops in Belgium, France, and parts of Allied-occupied Germany, all in all, according to Mickey, covering about a hundred and fifty thousand miles that first year. They roughed it, living mostly on C rations, individually canned, precooked wet rations that were issued when fresh food or packaged unprepared food from mess halls or field kitchens was impractical or unavailable. They worked in the rain, sleet, and snow, performing before audiences of GIs as bullets flew past them and bombs exploded nearby. They were truly in the thick of it. Mickey visited the troops in the field hospitals and visited the concentration camp at Dachau at the time U.S. forces liberated it. One can only wonder at the shock he must have experienced, if not the trauma (which many American GIs experienced) upon witnessing firsthand the absolute barbarity that could be inflicted upon human beings by other human beings.

Jimmy Cook recalled, "These shows were so mobile, we could drive anywhere with them. We'd go right up into the front lines, park, and do shows for guys who were in foxholes being shot at. Sometimes we were so close to the front that the Germans stopped their firing to listen to the music. Mickey did the emceeing, in addition to a lot of comedy bits and musical spots. We followed the troops all through the winter of 1944 and into the spring of 1945, as we slogged our way to Berlin through France and Belgium. Sometimes we slept on the ground, or if we were lucky, we were billeted with cooperative German families as we got closer to Berlin."[13] The travel was nonstop.

Despite being surrounded by people, Mickey was deeply lonely, as he wrote to Betty Jane on Christmas Eve 1944. Dated January 8, 1945, but referring to it being Christmas Eve, Mickey writes that he'd just returned from putting on a show for the troops. He'd had coffee and now was sitting down to be with his wife Betty Jane, if only in a letter. Though they are apart, he writes, just being apart means that he is closer to her "spiritually," and like the other troops thinking of their families back home on Christmas, Mickey is thinking of her. A soldier just walked into Mickey's billet and offered him candy and a "Merry Christmas," and, he says, he feels lucky having her as the girl he loves and cherishes. He feels the warmth of his family, his "sweet mother," and his life together with Betty Jane. These things are his, even in time of war. He may sound "a little blue," he writes, but he's not, and closes by saying that she is his "darling wife," he loves her, honestly he does, as her "loving husband." [14]

While Mickey was in France, he received a letter from Betty Jane informing him that she had given birth, on July 3, 1945, to a healthy baby boy. They had agreed he would be named Joseph Yule III, however, he was always known as Mickey Rooney Jr. (He lives a hermit-like existence in Hemet, California.) Mickey arranged for Betty Jane and the baby to live with Nell and Fred at El Ranchita. He flew them there by chartered plane with the help of Sam Stiefel, who was advancing him money (with accruing interest compounded almost every minute) to cover his expenses.

For his war efforts, Mickey was promoted to technical sergeant third class, and when the war ended on May 7, 1945, he continued to entertain the troops with the Army of Occupation in larger shows throughout Europe, as he waited to accumulate enough points for a discharge. Meanwhile, he performed shows such as *Up in Central Park* in Mannheim and *OK-USA* in Frankfurt, and he became a radio announcer on the Armed Forces Radio Network. Mickey once claimed he was offered the rank of lieutenant if he agreed to stay longer to entertain the troops, which he gently declined: "'Sir,' I said politely, 'you could offer me brigadier general and I would still say no. I want to go home.'" [15]

But it would take almost another year in the service before Mickey's discharge would come through, on March 6, 1946. In the end, he served one year, eight months, and twenty-one days. Then he was free to return to Metro, to his new partner Sam Stiefel, and to his new wife, Betty Jane Rase.

The war had a positive effect on Mickey. He had matured, and was feeling more confident about his future. His service, and the respite in his career, gave him time to reflect on his life and brought back the energy and optimism that had been flagging since the breakup with Ava. He now had the responsibility of a son and a wife. "When I left, I was older, wiser and still in one piece," he recalled.[16]

15

Rooney Inc.

From left to right: *Edsel Ford, Mickey, and Henry Ford. Mickey claimed that this was the only picture of Edsel and Henry Ford smiling together. This was taken at the premiere of* Young Tom Edison *in Detroit, Michigan, in March of 1940.*
PHOTO COURTESY OF THE MONTE KLAUS COLLECTION.

While Mickey was away in the army, Sam Stiefel remained hard at work for Rooney Inc. Mickey's MGM contract came up for renewal on November 4, 1944. While in peacetime MGM would have had to exercise its option for Rooney's services for another year, during wartime the studios adopted a type of force majeure rule: if an artist's option came up during his service in the military, rather than beginning immediately the renewed contract would begin only at the end of his military service (with the artist remaining unpaid during that service). Thus, Mickey, whose salary under a renewed option would normally have been increased to a minimum of $2,500 per week for forty weeks plus agreed bonuses, would continue receiving only his buck private's pay of $50 a week. However, Sam Stiefel and Rooney Inc. vice president and corporate counsel Mort Briskin decided to go against the grain and challenge MGM's force majeure clause. But Stiefel waited to spring this surprise on Mayer.

Two months before Mickey's option came up, Mort Briskin informed Metro by certified mail that there would be no automatic option of Mickey's agreement just because he was in the army. They placed a story on the front page of the *Hollywood Reporter* on August 28, 1945, which stated, "Morton Briskin, attorney for Rooney Inc., a corporation recently formed to handle Mickey Rooney's affairs, announced Saturday that his company will file suit in Federal court within the next two weeks, applying for a 'declaratory relief action,' and asking the court to uphold its contention that Rooney's entrance into the Army and not being paid his weekly salary by MGM automatically abrogates the star's contract with the studio."

This precipitated a blistering in-response commentary by the publisher of the *Hollywood Reporter*, the infamous Billy Wilkerson, a notorious gambler who co-owned nightclubs and the Flamingo hotel/casino in Las Vegas with mobsters Charles "Lucky" Luciano, Meyer Lansky, and Benjamin Siegel. In his August 28, 1945, "Tradeviews" column, Wilkerson wrote:

> We don't know what they have been feeding Mickey Rooney or who has been feeding him, but the announcement in a different column of your *Reporter* today is not the Mickey we have known or the boy you have admired so much. The whole thing looks to us as if the minority

of Mickey's new corporation is about to sink the major owner of that stock—Mickey himself . . . Mickey Rooney asking for a cancellation of his agreement with MGM, and the reasons for asking for such a cancellation, is a pretty weird piece of business. Pretty bad behavior . . . never in our looking over the affairs of this business have we ever seen such a protective hand on the shoulder of anyone as the one L.B. always extended to Mickey. He adored that kid, fought many studio battles to bring him up to where he is; watched his scripts, ordered them rewritten to care better for the advance of Rooney, counseled him at all times, giving him more attention than most fathers would give a son, and because of it Mickey has become one of the industry's great stars. Mayer . . . did EVERYTHING for the kid and in Mayer doing it, they get slapped in the face with a request for an abrogation his contract.

Was this written at the request of or as a favor to Mayer? Can we see the hands of Eddie Mannix and Howard Strickling at work here, Strickling pulling the strings of the Hollywood media and Mannix with his connections to mob figures in the entertainment industry? Probably. While Wilkerson was known to have a sometime contentious relationship with Mayer, Warner, Zukor, Cohn, and other studio bosses, he was at their mercy as well. So the *Reporter* in those years was, in essence, a company newsletter. While Wilkerson did draw some ire a few years later when he supported the Hollywood blacklist and attacked the studios, the studios were far stronger during this period.

An all-out attack on Rooney by the *Hollywood Reporter* was a major event. Was Rooney aware of this story when he was in Camp Siebert, Alabama? Was he told about this assault by Stiefel and Briskin? Apparently he was completely in the dark. Mickey wrote, "I soon learned that while I was away, my professional life had taken a wrong turn. Sam Stiefel had taken charge of Rooney Inc., and now he seemed to own me—and my family. He renegotiated my contract with MGM nearly a year before." [1]

Louis Mayer's College of Cardinals suddenly became panicked at this challenge to what had been standard studio procedure. The studio attorneys raised the possibility that "nobody can be quite sure how Briskin's claim will be interpreted by the Courts. We therefore advise that the studio ought to exercise its option and protect our interests and put him back on salary." Accordingly, Mayer, Thau, and Mannix decided to begin paying Mickey immediately. They had Floyd Hendrickson, who was vice president for business affairs for MGM, inform Briskin that they would exercise their option immediately and resume paying Mickey. They explained that this was without precedent, but they wanted no hard feelings from Mick.

The studio response signaled weakness to Stiefel, who, in creating his successful theater chain, had learned to play hardball. He told Briskin that Mayer was "running scared" and that he and Briskin had them exactly where he wanted. If Stiefel was a legitimate business manager and was representing Rooney as a client, he would be well worth his fee. However, as Mickey would ultimately discover, that was not the case. Briskin requested a meeting with Benny Thau to discuss a new contract. Thau immediately agreed. Briskin recalled, "Sam wanted the whole ball of wax. He knew that Mayer and his group wanted to hold on to Rooney, and [that] he could squeeze much more out of them. He had a rather keen awareness of both human nature and business. He was right on the target much of the time." [2]

The meeting was held on October 11, 1944. Benny Thau represented MGM, Sam Stiefel, Mort Briskin, and Abe Lastfogel of William Morris represented Mickey. They put their demands right on the table: Mickey gets the right to host his own radio show, the ability to make personal appearances, and a new weekly salary of $7,500 with a forty-week guarantee, or $300,000 a year flat. Thau said that while this was "preposterous," he might be able to negotiate a new pact they could all live with. The negotiations proceeded for the next few months. There were a lot of volleys back and forth, most of them on friendly terms. This was important to Stiefel, who was in this for himself, using the negotiations to raise his profile with the Hollywood power elite.

The new agreement was reached on February 4, 1945, while Mickey was slogging through the freezing mud in Belgium with Patton's Third Army. On February 5, 1945, it was announced in the *New York Times*, whose theatrical page reported:

> Mickey Rooney, now a private somewhere in Belgium or France, will resume his screen career for Metro-Goldwyn-Mayer after the war at a salary of $5000 per week. Under his new contract, the 24 year old star receives a number of unusual concessions in regard to radio and stage appearances, which conceivably could double his annual film earnings. In addition to the weekly salary, which runs forty weeks a year, the corporation receives a bonus of a hundred and forty-thousand for signing the deal; half of this amount has been paid; the remainder is payable in two years. The contract covers seven years with yearly options, and provides that MGM must exercise the first option (for the second year) thirteen days after Rooney is discharged from the Army. Among other concessions, the actor is allowed to do 39 weeks of radio a year plus four guest appearances. While MGM can limit these radio appearances to 26 weeks, if it is believed they are injuring his screen value. Rooney can resume broadcasting the following year, if MGM exercises its option for the succeeding forty weeks.

This was certainly not a Strickling news release, and most likely came directly from Stiefel and Briskin. While on the surface this looked like a win for Mickey, who now had strong representation, in actuality it would return even less money to him, because he was shouldering a 50 percent partner with massive corporate overhead and huge loans to pay back, including the $150,000 debt his mother and her husband had incurred during his tour of duty. Meanwhile, Stiefel was running stars such as Peter Lorre and singer Andy Russell, and his stable of racehorses, which did more eating than racing and would have made more money in a glue factory than on the track—and he was charging the whole thing to Rooney Inc., right off Mickey's new MGM salary.

By February 12, 1946, Mickey had amassed enough points to qualify for a discharge. On February 15, General Eisenhower awarded him the Bronze Star for "exceptional courage in the performance of his duties as a performer." His citation for the medal stated that "His superb personal contribution to the morale of the Armed Forces in the European Theater of Operations cannot be measured." Then, like his father before him, who had come on a troop ship from Europe after the World War I Armistice, Mickey returned to America.

In theory, he had a lot to look forward to. He had a newborn son, a young wife, and a brand-new contract guaranteeing him $6,250 per month while he was in the service. He was also planning a weekly radio program that would pay him more than his film contract. The *New York Times* on March 5, 1946, wrote, "Mickey Rooney said he has plans for a new radio program on NBC. He said that his partner, Sam Stiefel has signed an agreement with Campbell Soup to sponsor."

While Mickey was serving his last days in the service, his mother was watching after Betty Jane and little Mickey Jr. She was also entertaining with Fred, holding lavish parties at El Ranchita. Harrison Carroll, in the *Los Angeles Evening Herald Express*, as far back as

January 5, 1945, wrote, "Mickey Rooney's Ma, Nell Pankey is throwing a party at the ranch for 20 girls in the Coast Guard's 'Tars and Spars' show." On January 9 he wrote, "Mickey's bride, Betty Jane, watched a showing of 'National Velvet' at the studio with Mickey's mother, Nell Pankey. It will be followed by a reception at the ranch."

Meanwhile, Sam Stiefel was generating a stream of news releases about Mickey for the entire eighteen months he was in the army. Most extolled the virtues of Stiefel himself and how he had negotiated a big new contract for Mickey—such as the press release that appeared in a Louella Parsons syndicated column for Hearst on February 16, 1945, which stated, "If Mickey Rooney and MGM were ever seriously pouting about his contract, it's all over now. Through his partner, Sam Stiefel and the William Morris Agency a new big contract was signed between the Mick and Metro on Tuesday calling for a big increase in salary."

An interesting entry was released on March 15, 1945, by Harrison Carroll in the *Los Angeles Evening Express* about Stiefel: "Wait until Mickey Rooney comes back from the Army and sees the office that his business partner, Sam Stiefel is fixing up for him. It has everything that Mickey was crazy about—a grand piano, a recording machine, etc. On the door is the following sign: 'No admittance until Mickey Rooney returns.'"

News releases from Stiefel became routine, with Mickey as the hook in each one. On March 22, 1945, Harrison Carroll, of the *Los Angeles Evening Express*, wrote, "Mickey Rooney's partner, Sam Stiefel is signing a Mickey discovery . . . 19 year old vocalist, Marion Marett." On March 26, 1945, the *Hollywood Citizen-News* printed this: "Mick is 'sold on singer/composer Andy Russell, for Mickey's business partner, Sam Stiefel." On April 4, 1945, Harrison Carroll wrote, "Mickey Rooney ran into the nephew of his partner, Sam Stiefel, in Germany. Nephew's name is Irving Epstein and he managed two Stiefel theaters in Baltimore before the war."

Stiefel, meanwhile, was holding bashes at his new house in Bel Air. "My father, Bernie Stiefel, told me of the lavish parties my grandparents held at their home and the great stars that attended," recalled Stiefel's granddaughter Adrienne Callander.[3]

Ostensibly, the parties were held to "publicize" Mickey, but Stiefel invited other clients (such as Andy Russell, to sing). Nell and Fred Pankey were regular guests, too, as was Betty Jane Rooney. The parties, of course, were then charged to Rooney Inc., which Mickey would be required to pay back out of his own salary.

On March 6, 1946, Mickey walked down the gangplank of the USS *General G.O. Squier* transport ship in New York Harbor. He was first greeted by Sam Stiefel, who wanted him to stay in New York a few days to garner some publicity, and see some shows. "No, Sam. No shows," Mickey said he replied. "The only show I want to see is in my living room, where my wife and my son, Mickey Rooney Jr. are waiting for me."[4] He then jumped on the Super Chief to the West Coast. Nell and Fred were waiting at the station for the train to pull in, along with Betty Jane and the new baby, a child they'd conceived on the one night of their honeymoon during his two-day weekend pass. Mickey was still in his army uniform, his chest was covered with service ribbons and his Bronze Star. He had seen Betty Jane for only those few days, when they met and were married when she was only seventeen. Now, when he saw her, he was astounded by her size. "At seventeen, she had only been a couple inches taller than I. Now, more than a year and a half later, she seemed to tower over me by almost a foot," Mickey wrote.[5]

"Having survived the Nazis, I thought I'd have an easier time when I came back to Hollywood. I was mistaken," he wrote.[6] The very next day, Sam and Mort Briskin took Mickey to Hollywood Park to watch "their" horses and to bring Mickey up-to-date on the goings-on at Rooney Inc. Mickey had heard about the new MGM contract, the proposed radio show, and the appearances he would make. Then

Sam started to talk about the business, describing in great detail the new plush offices for Rooney Inc., at 8782 Sunset Boulevard. He told Mickey of the staff they had hired, and about his own personal office. "I soon learned that while I was away, my professional life had taken a wrong turn," Mickey recalled. "Sam Stiefel had taken charge of Rooney Inc." He realized that the decisions made around him and his career had put him in more debt than he had been in when he first went off to war.[7]

In the Rooney Inc. private box at the racetrack, Sam gently explained to Mickey that while he was serving his eighteen months, Nell had "borrowed" almost $160,000 for "living" expenses. She was unable to live on Fred Pankey's salary. (In 1946 dollars, that was an extraordinary amount, about $1.9 million in 2015 dollars.) "There are a few matters," Sam said. "First there is the money I lent you before the war—you remember—at the track, to pay off bookies, to buy Ava that car. Then we opened our offices. I took the money we received from Metro and reinvested in our stable here. Although they haven't returned any bucks, the upside is high."[8]

Mort Briskin laid out the great deals they'd pulled off in negotiations with Metro: the $5,000 per week for forty weeks, the $140,000 bonus, the right to do thirty-nine weeks of radio and personal appearances, the selling of his image for merchandising, a possible record deal, and the production of their own independent films. Rooney Inc. would be a thriving industry, they told Mickey; the future was indeed bright. Never mind that their entire stream of revenue would come from Mickey Rooney. All Mick had to do was keep making pictures, show up in theater venues, host his radio show, and produce his own movies. All would be well.

Sam was a master at warm chatter, the prototype for generations of multilevel marketing managers recruiting members for their "downlines," a process by which those recruited pay their recruiter's commission from their own work. In this instance, Mickey would do the work, pay back what Sam had advanced, cover Sam's overhead, and pay him a percentage on top of that. Stiefel, the ultimate confidence artist, completely overwhelmed Mickey, who, although streetwise from his upbringing on a burlesque stage, was completely ill equipped to deal with sharks like Sam Stiefel and Mort Briskin.

After the two raptors, converging on the just-repatriated army veteran in a pincer movement, painted a rosy, robust picture of the future, Stiefel lowered the boom. When Mickey asked about the money he owed Stiefel, Sam gently suggested, "Listen, why don't we just split everything fifty-fifty until we're even?"

Mickey later wrote, "What the hell, I thought. There was no limit now to the money I could earn on my own. And soon, I'd be on my own, an independent producer of my own movies and a star on network radio to boot. 'Sure Sam,' I said."[9] After all, Mickey had no reason to distrust this man who had just renegotiated his MGM contract and swung this great deal, who had watched after his mother while he was gone, and who'd given him money when he was short. No reason at all.

On the home front, Mickey moved back into El Ranchita with Betty Jane and baby Mickey Jr., yet, according to Sid Miller, "He really was still in love with Ava."[10] Ava, though, had become the fifth wife of bandleader Artie Shaw the year before. Mickey now had his own new wife and baby son. He had the responsibility of his own firm with several employees.

Mickey did not know Betty Jane at all, even after their marriage. They were the same strangers they had been upon their first meeting in Alabama, when he was drunk during their one-day courtship and wedding immediately after. She had spent the following year getting to know his mother and enjoying life in Hollywood, but when Mickey stepped off the train and joined her in Los Angeles, the two found they had nothing to talk about. He was excited, though, at having a young son who had many of his features, and he became determined to make the marriage work. When Betty suggested they move into a home of their own, Mickey acquiesced. He was reluctant to leave El Ranchita again, but he agreed that they needed their own space. He hired a realtor and they went house shopping.

Columnist Sheilah Graham wrote on June 22, 1946, in the *Hollywood Citizen-News*, "Mickey Rooney paid $90,000 for the Alan Hale home in the Valley. Pictures have certainly paid off for Rooney."

Sam Stiefel offered to "loan" Mickey the money for the down payment. He was more than happy to front the money for his "partner." Why not? As Harrison Carroll wrote on June 24, 1946, in the *Los Angeles Evening Herald Express*: "Look for Mickey Rooney to make a fortune on a personal appearance tour in the fall, according to his partner, Samuel Stiefel."

After Mickey and B.J. moved in and set up housekeeping in their beautiful new home, Betty Jane strove to become a part of Mickey's life. Yet when he brought over his old cronies Sid Miller, Sig Frohlich, Dick Paxton, Dick Quine, and new addition Jimmy Cook to drink, play poker, and swap war stories, they ignored Betty Jane as if she were a piece of furniture. Mickey started going out at nights as well.

"Betty didn't like my friends, not even my very oldest and best friends," Mickey wrote. "She knew nothing about my world and apparently she didn't care to know. . . . [W]hen Betty Jane conceived again, in May, about two months after I arrived home, I was surprised it took as long as two months, I thought all I had to do to get Betty Jane pregnant was hang up my pants. I kept Betty Jane home, barefoot and pregnant." [11] For her part, Betty Jane felt like a fish out of water. She had all the expectations of a nineteen-year-old girl from a humble working-class background, who wanted to become a performer in her own right, married to a movie star and living in Hollywood. But her existence had become mundane, and she had very few friends. Mickey would return from the studio moody and argumentative, much as he was with Ava during their marriage. If B.J. had expected to attend glamorous parties and premieres, the reality was these were few and far between.

Worse, Mickey was embarrassed by their size discrepancy. Columnist Sidney Skolsky wrote on May 18, 1946, in the *Hollywood Citizen-News*, "Mickey Rooney's wife is much taller than Mickey, and people wonder why, when they go out together, she generally wears a tall hat that makes her appear much taller." Skolsky wrote on June 22 of that same year, "Mickey Rooney at the ball game with his tall wife who is wearing a tall hat, and Mickey is telling the frau, 'I don't care that you're taller than I am, but don't wear such tall hats.'"

Mickey was now only twenty-six years old. He had a wife and son, mother and stepfather, and business and staff to support. He had a partner in Sam Stiefel, who was using the income Mickey was generating to run the business, while charging him interest on loans like a ticking taxi meter—with Mickey constantly borrowing money just to keep up. He also had his crew of friends, whom he kept afloat. And then there was his old life of gambling and drinking, which was again beckoning him no matter how hard he tried to resist its calls. The financial and social pressures were mounting.

> For a while my money worries kept me from thinking about my troubles at home. If I couldn't pick up where I left off before the war I wouldn't be able to afford a home in the Valley. Sure, I was making five thousand dollars a week during the sixty-seven days we took to shoot "Summer Holiday," but I didn't see much of that. Sam Stiefel took his 50 percent off the top. Then he paid the overhead and gave me what was left, generally close to nothing. Things weren't turning out the way I'd dreamed they would when I was bouncing around the war in Europe. The thought depressed me. I was even sadder when I realized that, up to this point in my life, I had never even had my own bank

account, never written a check, never had my own financial integrity.[12]

Although Mickey was paying Rooney Inc. overhead, for personnel expenses, most of Mickey's errands were not carried out by his "staff" or secretary. Les Peterson was still Mickey's shadow, his minder, making sure his needs were satisfied..

Peterson also knew Mickey's peccadillos, as did Ava. He was a serial cheater, and both were aware of his predilection for young girls. Rooney family friend since 1994, Pam McClenathan, who would become B.J.'s caregiver, told us a story recounted to her by Betty Jane:

> Betty Jane told me she went to visit Mickey at the studio in Culver City around June in 1946. She had Mickey Jr., in tow, and she was pregnant with Timmy. She was directed to Mickey's dressing room, while he was filming an Andy Hardy film [*Love Laughs at Andy Hardy*]. When she opened the door to the dressing room, Elizabeth Taylor was on her knees giving Mickey a blow job. Now, Betty Jane was just standing there with her baby and was shocked. I mean Elizabeth Taylor was just a kid herself. [She was fourteen.] After that, all hell broke loose. Betty got an attorney and met with Mr. Mayer and his team. That was the end for Betty and Mickey. She knew he was cheating, plus this was with a young girl. She got a top attorney and a big settlement, but Betty really was not happy after that. She wanted a faithful husband.

Sexually precocious and physically mature for her age, teenage starlet Elizabeth Taylor set her sights on older actors, according to authors Darwin Porter and Danforth Prince in their biography, *Elizabeth Taylor: There Is Nothing Like a Dame*.[13] Porter and Prince reveal that at age fifteen, Taylor went to thirty-six-year-old Ronald Reagan's apartment lobby for a film role. According to the book, the future California governor and U.S. president, who was married to actress Jane Wyman at the time, gave the five-foot-two Taylor a drink and treated her like an adult. "'I could tell he wanted to get it on but he seemed reluctant to make the first move,' Taylor later told friends. 'I became the aggressor. I wished they'd been casting Lolita around that time; I could have won an Oscar playing the nymphet. After a heavy make-out session on the sofa, we went into the bedroom,"[14] where, Taylor insinuated, she had sex with the Great Communicator-to-be.

Porter and Prince also claim that Taylor had a sexual encounter with future president John F. Kennedy, whom she first met as a seven-year-old in London. When she was reunited with the then-senator, who was fifteen years her senior, Kennedy persuaded her to go skinny-dipping in actor Robert Stack's pool. According to the book, Taylor told friends she ended up in a threesome with JFK and Stack. As a teenager whose sexual dalliances could have landed both future presidents in criminal proceedings for statutory rape, Liz Taylor was certainly not one of the "untouchables," but at least she was bipartisan in bestowing the pleasures of her amicability on both sides of the aisle. JFK's aberrant sexual proclivities (including his many affairs and his liaisons with prostitutes, his use of LSD obtained directly from Timothy Leary, and his long-term addiction to methamphetamine) are well known, but Reagan's are not.[15]

Mickey's dalliance with Taylor was par for the course. However, Betty Jane, having caught her husband in flagrante delicto with a teenager, was incensed enough to know that her marriage was over and shrewd enough to hire an attorney who would make him pay dearly for his sins: former Los Angeles municipal court judge (1927–30) Leonard Wilson, who was later convicted of accepting bribes in exchange for granting state liquor licenses. (In return for leniency, he named names, which included former state attorney general Fred

Howser. His law career was over, and he committed suicide on December 7, 1954.) Wilson was a Los Angeles insider and, according to columnist Hedda Hopper in a January 14, 1947, column, "a real barracuda."

Wilson arranged a meeting with Eddie Mannix to discuss Betty Jane's claims, in which he spelled out in minute detail what Betty Jane said she'd seen going on between Mickey and Taylor. He didn't have to explain that it meant a serious sex offense with a minor: the facts hung over them like the stench of sweat in a boiler room. Without doubt, it would have been the end of Mickey's career. Not only that, the studio would be involved as well as the corporation Rooney Inc. It would have been a blood bath all around, played out in the Hollywood gossip columns. However, this was California, it was the industry, and both Mannix and Wilson knew this could be solved with money. Lots and lots of money.

Mannix, whom Mickey had often referred to in interviews as "Mayer's whip," then met with Mickey's partners, Stiefel and Briskin. Neither was shocked at Mickey's behavior but both certainly worried about their fortunes. Stiefel approached his meeting with Mannix determined to protect Mickey, his breadwinner, at all costs. Since Mickey's option was picked up shortly after he had returned from the war in March, he would remain under salary. He would film one more film, *Summer Holiday*, a big-budget musical remake of *Ah, Wilderness!*, and then would embark on a long stage tour. Stiefel was pleased because Mickey would draw big dollars on a tour, dollars that would go directly to Stiefel to repay Rooney Inc.'s advances to Nell and Fred, to Mickey, and toward covering company overhead. Also, the agreement would give them time to negotiate a settlement with Wilson, who was well aware that under California law—especially if Mickey were prosecuted for a sexual offense with a minor—Betty Jane would get her hands on whatever assets came out of the partnership.

MGM was obviously very concerned about this brewing scandal

because of the revenue Mickey's movies were still bringing in and the publicity nightmare the studio would have to endure. As a result, it decided to play defense in advance of a settlement. Mickey had shot two numbers in April 1944 with Judy Garland that were to be included in *The Ziegfeld Follies of 1946*. Initially, the film was to be released in 1945, but the studio tinkered with the cut and released it for a roadshow in April 1946. A final version was ultimately released in June 1946 from which the studio had curiously cut both of the Rooney/Garland numbers they had filmed two years earlier, "Will You Love Me in Technicolor as You Do in Black and White?" and "As Long as I Have My Art." Both of those scenes and Mickey's entire part were excised, never to be seen again, according to film historian Alvin H. Marill. Was this the studio's way of preemptively playing defense in case Mickey wound up being prosecuted?

On June 17, around the time the Taylor affair was breaking, Mickey started work on *Summer Holiday*, marking his return to the musical films that had become an MGM staple. For the movie, Metro hired director Rouben Mamoulian, who had previously directed the original stage productions of *Oklahoma!*, *Carousel*, and *Porgy and Bess*. The studio gave Mamoulian complete control over the film, which was unusual for MGM. In the original film version *Ah, Wilderness!*, Mickey plays the younger brother, Tommy, who is setting off firecrackers on the Fourth of July. In this movie, he is the older brother, the philosophical Richard, who is coming of age, faces parental-inspired rejection from the girl of his dreams, and sneaks out on a night of drunken carousing with his friend.

Summer Holiday was budgeted at an astounding $2.3 million and was the type of nostalgic, schmaltzy film Mayer's vision had espoused after the death of Irving Thalberg left him in creative control of the studio. Mayer was clearly trying to repeat the surprise success of the original Eugene O'Neill property by turning it into a big-budget musical.

This is one of the most interesting aspects of the Mayer/Rooney relationship. Beneath their business relationship, the standard stuff of studio contracts in the old studio-owned player days, was something both men shared: Neither Mayer nor Rooney had enjoyed the type of all-American childhood depicted in the Hardy movies or *Summer Holiday* or *Ah, Wilderness!*, which were as foreign to them as if glimpsed through a telescope from *The Twilight Zone*. Mayer's family was the victim of lethal persecution from the Russian czar's Cossacks, and had had to flee for their lives to Canada. And Rooney never had a childhood in the first place. Did Mayer see in the Rooney character an American childhood that he'd never had? Did Rooney see in Mayer a father figure he'd never had, stability he'd never experienced? Whatever their dynamic, the films Mickey starred in at Metro defined the image of the American family and the joy of coming of age, a joy that neither Rooney nor Mayer had ever experienced. Maybe that's why these films were more than just business for the two men.

Although the shooting on *Summer Holiday* continued until October 14, Mickey completed his scenes by September 3, in order to embark on the tour that Stiefel had scheduled to get him out of town. This would earn Stiefel money, and allow him and Morty Briskin the time to negotiate with B.J.'s attorney, Leonard Wilson. The brief shooting time was just as well. Mamoulian was an absolute terror on the set, acting more like a theatrical stage director than a motion picture director. He fired the original cinematographer, Charles Rosher, replacing him with Charles Edgar Schoenbaum, even though Rosher had won two Academy Awards for his work and was adept at filming musicals.

The MGM top screenwriting team, husband and wife Albert Hackett and Frances Goodrich, wrote the original *Ah, Wilderness!* screenplay, but Irving Brecher wrote the adaptation for this musical remake. In an interview, Brecher, who went on to create the radio and television series *The Life of Riley* and the screenplay for the musical *Bye Bye Birdie*, recalled his experience on this film:

> I wrote the adaptation with Jean Holloway. I was under contract to Metro and Mamoulian sought me out to enhance the comic element. When he went to hire Jean, he asked her if she thought she could write as well as O'Neill, and she told him that if she could she certainly wouldn't be working for MGM. He was a very odd man and quite a taskmaster. Throughout the filming, I was there to punch up lines, if necessary. I had known Rooney at the studio and through Groucho. Mickey was rather subdued throughout the entire shoot. He didn't have his typical energy.[16]

What Brecher didn't know, because the lawyers kept mum and the studio wasn't about to release any information to the public, was that throughout the nearly three-month shooting of the film, Rooney's life was in turmoil. After the explosion in July with the Elizabeth Taylor incident, Rooney had returned to El Ranchita from his brand-new home with Betty Jane, now single and anchorless again. It had been less than one hundred days in which he had been discharged from the army and reunited with his wife and child, and already he had perpetrated a sexual act with a fourteen-year-old girl and been tossed out on the street.

Mickey breezes over the incident in his autobiography, offering an explanation of his incompatibility with Betty Jane and his boredom with the marriage; he never delves into any details from this period. Obviously, given the gravity of the criminal charges he might have faced, and the embarrassment and humiliation he did face when caught in flagrante delicto by his wife and child, he never talked about the incident openly for the rest of his life, not even to his best friends or to us. And of course the newspapers remained silent most of that summer regarding Betty and Mickey, except for a denial by Mickey that B.J. was pregnant.

Harrison Carroll wrote on July 16, 1946, in the *Evening Herald Express*, "Mickey Rooney, who ought to know, has been vigorously denying the stork but two of his friends insist he told them that the long-legged bird is due at his house in about five months." This story, which was accurate, was a rare personal mention of Mickey during this period. Except for a Sidney Skolsky column on July 24, 1946, about the filming of *Summer Holiday*, there was a virtual news blackout on anything Mickey. Not so much as a Stiefel press release appeared until the fall. A man who had been the center of press attention since his ascent in 1937 had virtually disappeared from public view.

This was an obvious move by Strickling, to put a lid on the volatile situation. Except for the Frank Borzage golf tournament in early July 1946, Mickey sightings were rare. But the Mickey craze in the media of the early 1940s had already run its course. His absence for nearly two years during the war had also cooled the jets of the entertainment columnists. Times and tastes were changing. Mickey was no longer the flavor of the youth market. After the war ended, an avalanche of new young talent came pouring out. The new breed of performer who attracted the youth audience in 1946 included Frank Sinatra, Perry Como, and Dinah Shore—all of whom were band singers. Fading, though still performing, were the big band leaders Harry James, Artie Shaw, and the Dorsey brothers, while film actors Van Johnson, Lana Turner (*The Postman Always Rings Twice*), and Rita Hayworth (*Gilda*) got lots of press. Ava Gardner (*The Killers*) was getting lots of press as well with her films and romances, and she was a box office draw. At twenty-six years old, Mickey was yesterday's news.

With no films released by the summer of 1946, Mickey was not on any box office list of stars. His proposed radio show hadn't yet happened, which was surprising: He was a natural for a variety show with his ability as an onstage performer. Before the war, Mickey had appeared more than 220 times on radio as a guest star, with Bob Hope, Bing Crosby, Jack Benny, and others. However, his original MGM agreement had precluded his having his own weekly series, which would have been very lucrative. When Stiefel renegotiated the MGM agreement in 1944 and 1945, he had that provision waived. Still, Mickey's first appearance on radio after his return was not until January 8, 1947, on *Philco Radio Time* with Bing Crosby, and then on January 12 on the *Lux Radio Theatre*, with none other than Elizabeth Taylor revisiting *National Velvet*. Mickey finally got his weekly radio program, called *Shorty Bell* and costarring his father, Joe Yule Sr., in March 1948, two years after his return.

Mickey was always career conscious, and panicked when he was not working. When he finished filming his scenes for *Summer Holiday* on September 3, he had no future films scheduled. This was a shock to his system: His entire being from the time he was one and a half had been performance oriented. Even his social interactions, especially with women, as Ava Gardner described, were based on his ability to entertain. Mickey had been in constant motion since he started shooting the Mickey McGuire shorts in 1927. Now, nearly twenty years later, he was idle.

Mickey was fading into a different category of performer. While he would eventually settle into life as a character actor, his days as a first-rank leading man were essentially ending. Mayer knew that both Rooney and Garland were no longer his top attractions. The eventual flops of *Summer Holiday* and *Words and Music* would make that quite clear.

For Stiefel, however, Mickey was still his breadwinner, and like Dracula, he was determined to squeeze every last drop from him until he found a new victim. In September, Mannix and Thau gave Stiefel approval for the twelve weeks they could take Mickey off payroll between October and January. This would be Mickey's longest period between films in twenty years: he would not shoot another film for almost one year, when he began to shoot the Mort Briskin–produced *Killer McCoy* in June 1947. Moreover, Mickey was no longer on the Culver lot on a daily basis. With the exception of his time in the army, he had been mostly on the Metro lot since 1934. He began to hang around the offices at Rooney Inc., on Sunset.

With no radio lined up, it was back to the stage for Mickey. When he signed with Universal in 1932, at the age of twelve, he thought his life in the rough-and-tumble world of vaudeville/burlesque was over. Now, however, Stiefel had lined up almost four straight months of a brutal forty-three-city vaudeville tour throughout the East Coast, starting in Boston.

Meanwhile, Betty Jane had returned to her parents in Birmingham. Her attorney, Judge Wilson, knew the high visibility that this divorce would garner. He started carefully looking at the books of Rooney Inc. and studying the agreements with Stiefel. He held the Elizabeth Taylor chit, which could be used if necessary to put the squeeze on Stiefel. Meanwhile, the newly allied combination of Mort Briskin and Metro legal had Betty, through Wilson, sign a confidentiality agreement to remain mum until the difficult divorce settlement could be worked out.

Hedda Hopper, in her column in the *Los Angeles Times* on August 6, 1946, wrote, "Betty Jane Rooney, who is expecting in January, is at present visiting her mother in Birmingham, Alabama, with Mickey Jr. and will return in two weeks." This was supported in Los Angeles Superior Court the next June (1947), when Betty Jane testified that Mickey "deserted me and sent me back home to Alabama to have my baby."

Mickey began his forty-three-city tour at the RKO-Boston on October 24, and by December 9, 1946, he had reached Cleveland and its Palace Theater. Mickey had last been to that theater on a vaudeville tour in August 1932, appearing with Ted Healey and his Stooges, Larry,

Moe, and Shemp. In the *Cleveland Plain Dealer* of December 9, 1946, W. Ward Marsh wrote about the tour and Rooney Inc., revealing:

> Mickey Rooney, MGM's fair-haired boy and the Palace's stage star this week has to stand on his tiptoes to even reach five-foot-four, but he stands on top of the world today and reaches almost as far into Big Business as do Crosby, Hope, et al. Maybe he reaches further. I have not examined his books. What I am getting at is Mickey Rooney, Inc. When I talked to him last Thursday after the first show, this business racket did not come out. Mickey was the stage star, sweating out a first performance and talking about his next pictures, "Love Comes to Andy Hardy" and the musical version of "Ah, Wilderness!" . . . While Mickey's manager, Sam Stiefel, is not in Cleveland this week, Al Holcraft, who travels as road manager for Mickey Rooney, Inc. is here. So too, is Dick Crockett, who has been Mickey's friend for 14 years and acts as personal representative, friend, guard, buffer, etc. Like the workers at Jack & Heintz [a large airplane parts plant], they are all called associates. Stiefel owns 50 percent of Mickey. But Mickey Rooney, Inc. founded three years ago, has more than Mickey on its staff to support. It pays regularly weekly salaries to such stars as Cleveland's own Ross Hunter, Peter Lorre, Andy Russell, Connie Haines (the song-bird on Mickey's show this week at the Palace), Abigail and Buddy, and George Jessel. Rooney is President of Mickey Rooney, Inc. Offices are in the Rooney Building, Sunset Boulevard, Hollywood . . . Mickey Rooney, Inc. has made some picture deals, but they do not know what the films will be. They also plan more radio appearances, but now they are sold on "live audiences" and stage appearances.[17]

Meanwhile, Judge Wilson was drilling down on Mickey's financial records. While Rooney had actually lived with Betty Jane for only about 120 days, he had been married to her for almost two years, albeit being at war and in Europe for almost 18 months; they also had one child, with one on the way. Because California is a community property state, by computing all the revenue that was flowing into Mickey's 50 percent of Rooney Inc., the money he was ostensibly making from MGM, and the money going into any trusts, Betty Jane would be entitled to one half of that, in addition to child support. Given Mickey's debt to Stiefel, including advances to Nell and Fred, and money's advanced to him by MGM, he would be even deeper in the hole than he already was.

Mickey's off-and-on business manager, Nick Sevano, who also managed Frank Sinatra, said, "He was never a good husband. He only married for the sex part of it. He never went home. I could tell you the minute he was bored with a wife. He'd say to me, 'What are you doing tonight, Nickeroo? I thought we'd have dinner . . .' You see," Sevano continued, "he was always on the make. A beautiful woman would drive him up the wall. Nutty lots of times, he couldn't lay the girl of his dreams unless he married her first. The man had deep insecurities because of his size. He was the Huckleberry Finn of America. Every kid wanted to be like him, but no dame wanted to be married to him. Because he wasn't handsome. To them, he was a crazy little kid. But a lot of dames used him as a stepping stone to movie careers. That's why he had to get married so many times."[18]

For Mickey, this tour had to have been a trip down memory lane. He played many of the same theaters he had played with his parents, and later as a solo. Though he dreaded putting on a smiling face while greeting fans, he was a performer and knew how much money was riding on his appearances. He said years later, "You are literally a slab of meat. They don't care about you. They just want a piece of you. You say the wrong thing or you don't smile right, they blast you in the papers. I can't enjoy a meal in a restaurant or even take a shit without being watched. You live in a fishbowl. I know it's a trade-off, but it gets tiring . . . sometimes I just grin and bear it." [19]

Countless people who have met Mickey have found his behavior reprehensible. He could be not only crude and vulgar, but also a quarrelsome drunk; a shameless womanizer, especially when he was chasing underage girls; and a reprobate who spent too much time on the phone with his bookies. Almost worse was a cruel streak in him, an insensitivity toward others that often broke the bounds of all social discourse. Author and television producer Geoffrey Mark Fidelman, who was at a 1999 *I Love Lucy* convention in Jamestown, New York, to sign copies of his book on Lucille Ball, recalled his meeting with Mickey, who also appeared at the convention: "Mickey was totally obnoxious. He was rude to fans, drinking, and a real prick. He was even cruel to a child from the Make-A-Wish Foundation who wanted to meet him."

Mickey was on the road throughout the Christmas season, living out of a suitcase. He earned over four hundred thousand dollars on his twenty-week tour. However, when he returned to Los Angeles in February, Stiefel informed him that he still was in the red. Stiefel had taken 50 percent off the top for his share and for "overhead," comprising office space, staff, road crew, hotels, food, drink, and the money Mickey borrowed for other expenses, such as gambling. Stiefel was still fronting money for Nell and Fred's upkeep and for the divorce: Judge Wilson's legal team was overwhelming Rooney's attorneys with a blizzard of discovery motions, all of which was led to mounting legal fees.

On January 4, 1947, while Mickey was still on the road, Betty gave birth to Timothy Hayes Yule in Birmingham, Alabama. Later, when in a deposition Betty Jane testified that Mickey deserted her, Mickey responded, "She left against my wishes and pleading for Birmingham [*sic*] to have her second baby. She has never returned or offered to return, although I admit such an offer would be meaningless. I naturally wished to be available when my baby was born. There exists [*sic*] insurmountable barriers between us which made our separation inevitable, and further marital relations, impossible."[20]

Strickling and Stiefel remained silent on the separation until it leaked out on January 27, 1947, in the *Los Angeles Evening Herald Express*:

> Long-rumored in Hollywood, the separation of Rooney and his Birmingham, Ala., wife was confirmed by the actor's business manager and associate, Sam Stiefel, and by Mrs. Rooney's mother. "There is serious trouble between Mickey and his wife," Stiefel said. "They are both very young and Mrs. Rooney knows nothing about the picture business. Hence they can't find a level of mutual interest." Mrs. Rooney's mother, Mrs. Rase said, "Nothing has been settled and no legal action has been taken. Property settlement discussions are underway."

This scoop blew the lid off the story, and the newspapers were ablaze with daily updates, mostly negative toward Mickey. Erskine Johnson, in *the Los Angeles Daily News*, wrote on February 1, 1947, "Explaining Mickey Rooney's separation from his wife, his business manager, Sam Stiefel said, 'They had no common interests.' Apparently two sons are not enough to interest the Mick."

Lloyd Sloan, in the *Hollywood Citizen-News*, wrote on February 11, "On top of all the adverse criticism about the way he handled the separation from his wife, Mickey Rooney will not meet with too many smiles at Metro for doing those Florida nightclub dates." Louella Parsons wrote for the Hearst syndicate on March 10, 1947, "You can make a good-size wager that Mickey Rooney is permanently out of the Andy Hardys. Mick has outgrown the adolescent role. The series is tottering . . . when Mickey returns from an appearance tour he needs a change of pace."

Mickey, meanwhile, returned to the road on February 27. He replaced Danny Kaye at the Copacabana in Miami, at a weekly salary of fifteen thousand dollars. The newspapers were still hot on his trail, with Harrison Carroll writing on February 6, 1947, "With Mickey in Florida, do you suppose he will see his new son for the first time? Alabama isn't far away."

In January, a basic agreement was drawn up for Mickey to pay Betty Jane alimony of fifteen thousand dollars per year for ten years, give her the house in Encino, and provide her with twelve thousand dollars to cover medical and attorney costs. Leonard Wilson flew down to Birmingham to get Betty Jane's signature. Her parents signed as witnesses. Once again, Mickey moved back to El Ranchita with Nell and Fred. However, by the May 28 court date for the divorce, Betty Jane decided to rescind the agreement because her attorney said that he had "discovered" that Mickey was "fraudulently hiding his real income and assets behind a phony firm." Wilson also accused Mickey of "playing around with other women." That, too, made the gossip headlines.

The *Hollywood Citizen-News* of June 6, 1947, under the headline "Mickey Rooney Denies Fraud in Settlement with Wife," read, "Mickey Rooney denied today that he used fraud in reaching a $15,000-a-year property settlement with his estranged wife, 'Miss Birmingham of 1944'. . . . He said he owned only 20% of 'Rooney Inc' and denied that the corporation was formed to keep his assets from his wife." Accordingly, Mickey, through Sam Stiefel, had to come up with twenty-five thousand dollars in cash to settle that dispute and an additional five thousand for B.J.'s attorney, Leonard Wilson. Also, B.J. would get full custody of the two boys.

Despite all the bad blood between them, Mickey attempted a reconciliation with Betty Jane, according to the Hearst syndicate's

Louella Parsons, who wrote on July 28, 1947, "Mrs. Rooney arrived in Hollywood a few days ago and has been the houseguest of her lawyer, former Judge Leonard Wilson and Mrs. Wilson . . . Judge Wilson, in an answer to my questions said, 'Yes it is true, Mickey and Betty Jane have decided to try it again.' Sam Stiefel, the fabulous Hollywood character who represents Mickey, said that Mrs. Rooney 'didn't understand Hollywood and the requirements of being a famous actor's wife.'" The *Hollywood Citizen-News*, on September 9, 1947, under the headline "Mickey Rooney Reconciliation Becomes Official," wrote, "Judge Wilson said the couple is looking for a home in Benedict Canyon."

Mickey, meanwhile, maintained a separate bachelor pad with his army buddy Jimmy Cook at the Argyle Apartments in West Hollywood. Cook recalled, "He said he'd never marry again. He never got over Ava, I don't think. I think that's why he got married so many times. He was always looking for another Ava . . . [W]e had the same in common—we liked girls, booze and carousing." [21]

IN THE SPRING OF 1947 Mickey was back at work at the studio, on a noir-type film called *Killer McCoy*, which was about as different from the all-American Andy Hardy as a movie could be. It was a new genre for Mickey, one that would take him through the late 1940s and into the early '50s. *Summer Holiday*, which he filmed the previous year, sat on the shelves awaiting a distribution date. The next year would prove to be a watershed year for him: he would begin his descent into the background.

Poet Emily Dickinson wrote, "Fame is a fickle food, / Upon a shifting plate." In 1948, Mickey would live these very lines.

16

The Lion Strikes Back

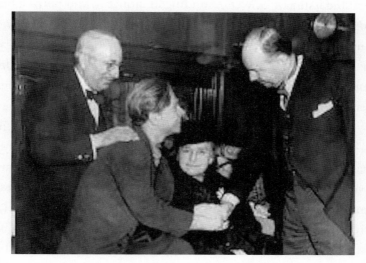

LB, Mickey, Mrs. Thomas Edison, and Harvey Firestone after Mickey's performance in Young Tom Edison.
<small>PHOTO COURTESY OF THE MONTE KLAUS COLLECTION.</small>

Mickey had a long love-hate relationship with Uncle L.B. On the one hand, he had a deep respect for L.B. It was Mayer who, once convinced of Mickey's box office appeal, had turned him into one of the biggest attractions in Hollywood. But it was also Mayer who leased him out like a car, earning huge returns on his investment— and fighting Mickey's representatives tooth and nail every time they asked for more money, even as Mayer recouped expenses incurred by Mickey for his extravagant lifestyle. By the end of their relationship, Mickey owed Metro a lot of money.

Mickey resented that MGM was making a fortune from his films while he was struggling just to stay afloat, and he complained about it to his dying day. He was a horrid businessman, clueless in basic financial matters. Still, almost instinctively, he was aware of the inequity between the hundreds of millions of dollars the studio had grossed from his work and the pittance of a salary he received in return. In one ear, he had Sam Stiefel reminding him of this, and putting out the carrot for independent production. (His stepfather, Fred Pankey, who was now the unofficial bookkeeper for Rooney Inc., reinforced Sam's vision.) In his other ear were Mayer and his College of Cardinals, advancing him money and shepherding what was left of his "teenage" career.

Typical of most addicts, whether alcoholics, sex addicts, or inveterate gamblers, Mickey lacked not only impulse control, but any skill at managing his finances; he also suffered from poor judgment and had very little common sense, primarily because he was never taught to develop it, by either parent. Given that his parents split early on, depriving him of a father figure, and that his mother engaged in the oldest profession other than show business, Mickey had been raised in a de facto no-parent household. He spent the rest of his life burning through eight marriages looking for a mother figure, and went through a succession of surrogate father figures, looking for what he'd never had: parents to take care of him. This made him easy pickings for anyone with a good sales pitch.

Mickey was a pure, genetically programmed performer whose near-perfect skills were reinforced by experience. As remarkably talented as he was, though, he paid a price for it. Every attempt Mickey made to create an enterprise was met with complete and utter failure. The eternal optimist, Mickey lacked an important skill set that successful entrepreneurs have: a healthy paranoia, along with a jaundiced eye for perceiving the downside of business deals. Also his ego, and his need to protect it, blinded him to the pitfalls of life.

It's one thing to be optimistic in the face of opportunities that seem promising, but quite another to be able to see beyond the glow of future benefits to the pitfalls of a deal. And at that, Mickey was sorely challenged. He trusted his friends completely, living in a cloud of oblivion when it came to believing the promises they made. Like a rock off a cliff, he fell for Stiefel's brand of confidence, as he would with others who followed. Typically, savvy businesspeople are a rarity among entertainers. For every Bob Hope, Bing Crosby, Art Linkletter, Fred MacMurray, Steven Spielberg, Oprah Winfrey, Joan Rivers, and George Lucas—who became entrepreneurs through building businesses in real estate, orange juice, television networks and studios, or lines of cosmetics or jewelry—there are far more celebrities who have experienced bankruptcy and financial ruin despite the millions they've earned. Even in today's heavily managed entertainment industry, many talented artists are inept when it comes to handling their finances. And with his utter lack of financial prudence, Mickey was the poster child for this disease.

Sam Stiefel, the first in line of those who exploited Mickey's vulnerability, embarked on a campaign to extricate Mickey from MGM's control, ultimately for his own benefit and to Mickey's detriment. When Mickey returned from his personal appearances, he was put back on the MGM payroll (at $5,000 per week). He was also in line to begin drawing from his MGM pension fund, which would have paid him $49,000 per year, guaranteed by Loews Inc., for the rest of his life. Even if his star power dimmed, he would undoubtedly still have continued in films, and therefore would have been in a secure position.

In leaving MGM, Mickey was easy to convince, because he believed (falsely) that the studio and Mayer sought to sabotage him and not only extricate themselves from his contract, but also torpedo his career once they saw his box office revenues on a downward trend. He believed that he was never given, nor would he ever be given the roles that could challenge him and showcase his talent. He believed that Stiefel's renegotiation of his contract and disrespectful attitude toward Mayer in their meeting had soured L.B. on Mickey. He wrote, "I thought I might be on my way to a second career as a character actor, but MGM disagreed. In retrospect, I think 'Killer McCoy' gave me a major clue about MGM's plans for Mickey Rooney: the studio seemed to want me out. All they needed was an excuse, and I think that the director of 'Killer McCoy,' Roy Rowland, had been told to set me up."[1]

"That is absolute bullshit," Scott Eyman told us. Eyman, who studied MGM for his book about Mayer, *The Lion of Hollywood*, absolutely disagreed with Rooney's assessment. "In the first place, they were still making money with Rooney. *Killer McCoy* turned a profit, and it certainly did signal that he could do more character roles. His size didn't hold him back or Alan Ladd or others. He had the talent. Rooney's biggest enemy was Rooney. Mayer was a businessperson who looked at the bottom line. Rooney sabotaged Rooney."[2]

Mickey, in an animated interview with Robert Osborne for TCM's *Private Screenings* on April 1, 1997, repeated the accusations: "They wanted to ruin my career, I was shooting 'Killer McCoy' and the director Roy Rowland tried to humiliate me on several occasions. Finally, I grabbed Rowland and told him to stop embarrassing me and went home. Eddie Mannix called me and told me to apologize to Rowland, which I did the next day. After the film, they started spreading the rumors that I was 'too hard to handle' and difficult to work with. I have known all my life that it isn't easy living with Mickey Rooney. However I have always been a professional, and they tried to destroy me."[3] Bob Osborne gave us his reaction to the interview: "Mickey became so agitated while recounting a battle he had with one of his directors, I thought he was gonna hit me!"[4]

It is true that moves that MGM was making behind the scenes fed Mickey's suspicions that the studio was seeking to cut him free of his contract. However, much of what Mickey was seeing derived from Stiefel's maneuvering rather than from Mayer's. First, MGM was unsure what to do with Mickey. It felt that he had outgrown the juvenile parts they had placed him in after the war, such as those in *Love Laughs at Andy Hardy*, *Summer Holiday*, and *Words and Music*. He was now in his late twenties. Maturity had overtaken his features. Frankly, he was grosser than he was cute. If he was maturing into a character actor, as he believed, of course he would have been less of an asset to MGM, and certainly would not have justified the huge contract Stiefel had negotiated with the studio. The MGM marketing department did a careful study of Rooney and was blunt in its assessment to Mayer that Rooney was on the downside as a leading man. The most recent Hardy film was a dud; *Summer Holiday* was a major flop; and the programmer *Killer McCoy* had turned only a minor profit.

Mickey was now failing on all fronts. In the summer of 1947, Stiefel made a deal with CBS for Mickey to do a radio show later that year. The network took a while to find a concept for him, until it scheduled a show slated for January 1948, called *Shorty Bell*. CBS hired playwright Samuel Taylor (later an Academy Award–nominated screenwriter with Billy Wilder for *Sabrina* and with Alfred Hitchcock for *Vertigo*) to create the program, in which Mickey would play Shorty Bell, a truck driver for a newspaper and a wannabe reporter. The cast included William Conrad (later the star of TV's *Cannon*), character actor Parley Baer, and actress Cara Williams. It also featured Mickey's father, Joe Yule Sr., in various roles. Stiefel struck a deal in which Mickey was paid three thousand dollars per installment. With the initially far larger cast of name performers, Cy Feuer's music direction and orchestra, and a high per-installment production cost, the budget for the subsequently revamped format (though pared down a bit later with staff actors and music direction) remained an expensive sustaining production for CBS. Soon, both formats for *Shorty Bell* had failed. By the tenth week, in one last major tweak, the network discarded the cub reporter format in favor of a totally reorganized variety format series called *Hollywood Showcase*, with Mickey as the emcee. *Hollywood Showcase* did indeed showcase up-and-coming talent, with Rooney providing the interstitial snappy patter, songs, and instrumentals. Yet on June 27, after thirteen weeks and a nose-dive in ratings, it was canceled.

Mickey and Stiefel were upset that Mickey was off salary for more weeks than he could afford—in late 1947, early 1948, Rooney Inc. was still spending, but not earning. After the failure of *Shorty Bell*, CBS made a suggestion for an Andy Hardy radio series. This precipitated the disastrous events that would follow: Stiefel proposed that they approach Metro to get approval of a radio version of the Hardy family, with the film actors recreating their roles. He arranged a meeting with Mayer with himself, Mickey, and Mort Briskin. Before they went off to the meeting, client George Jessel joked about Mayer's office, "There is so much white in that office, you could go snow blind." [5]

When Mayer saw that Briskin was with Rooney and Stiefel, his shields went up, and he was immediately on the offensive. Stiefel detailed to Mayer the proposal for an Andy Hardy radio show that would fully credit the studio and pay an agreed-upon royalty. Shooting Stiefel a hostile glance, Mayer turned to Mickey with his paternalistic manner and a touch of anger. "You know, Mickey," he said. "You've been one of my favorite people. I look upon you as I would my own son. And you're a great actor, and I'd like to help you out. But you have to understand, an Andy Hardy radio show would detract from the value of the pictures."

"But you already announced to the trades you're not going to make any more Hardy flicks," Stiefel reminded him.

"Suppose I change my mind?" Mayer tossed back.

"In that case," Mickey said, "You can get Butch Jenkins to play Andy Hardy." [6]

At that point the meeting became very contentious. Mayer was livid with Rooney, who he felt was treating him with disrespect. He threatened to throw Rooney and friends out of his office. Mickey jumped up and started screaming at Mayer. Mayer held back his anger, remarking, "You know what I've done for you, my son." Mickey replied, "No, but I know what I've done for you, I've made you, millions." And at that point Rooney, Stiefel, and Briskin left Mayer's office.

Mayer struck back immediately, ordering Mannix to place Mickey on immediate suspension. This was not like the incident with Ava in 1941. He was no longer the number one box office star. He no longer had the clout or the star power to confront Mayer as he had seven years earlier. Probably sensing this, Mickey's first inclination, and probably his best, was to return to the studio and apologize to Mayer. It would probably have smoothed over L.B.'s ruffled feathers. However, Stiefel used the incident to move forward with his own plan: he wanted Mickey to break his MGM agreement and forge ahead in producing independent films.

"Mickey this is our opening. We could be earning $100 to $150,000 thousand per film on our own," Mickey said Stiefel told him.[7]

But Mickey became emotional. He felt hurt at what he saw as Mayer's disrespect toward him. While Stiefel and Briskin were advising Mickey to let them break it off with MGM, he was torn. Sinatra's business manager and buddy, Nick Sevano, who had a gut feeling about the downside of Stiefel's proposed deal, told him he would be "insane" to leave Metro. Even his stepfather, Fred Pankey, who worked for Rooney Inc. urged him to make peace with Mayer.[8]

Sevano told us, "I called Sam and chewed him out. I said, 'Sam, you know what you're making this kid do? He'd be giving up the five grand a week and the pension.' But Stiefel had his own agenda. He had two pictures lined up at United Artists [*Quicksand* and *The Big Wheel*] that would bring the back $150 thousand per film . . . and he had a couple of other independent movies for Mickey . . . [H]e said

Mickey could be looking at a half million in future films. . . . I told Mick not to listen to Sam. Mickey told me, 'Nick, Sam's got a good deal. I couldn't make that in 10 years at Metro.' So he told Sam to go ahead and break his contract with the studio."[9]

When Briskin went to MGM to get Mickey's release, the studio flatly refused. He was contractually tied to MGM for five more years, and it would hold him to that. MGM brass told Briskin that they would create a new image for Mickey, and parts that were age appropriate. They said he still attracted audiences to films, and they had an investment in him. They told Briskin that if Rooney wanted to break the agreement, he would have to buy his way out.

Sevano recommended that Mickey hire Greg Bautzer and his office to deal with Mayer. Bautzer was a high-powered lawyer with clients such as Joan Crawford, Ingrid Bergman, Ginger Rogers, Howard Hughes, Billy Wilkerson, and Edward G. Robinson. A noted bachelor, he had been engaged to Lana Turner, Dorothy Lamour, and Barbara Payton. He was later married to actress Dana Wynter (of *Invasion of the Body Snatchers* fame). Bautzer's law partner, Murray Lertzman, recalled the Rooney negotiations. "Greg simply did not have the juice to extricate Rooney. Mayer had a hard-on for Mickey and wanted his pound of flesh. Rooney would have been far better off to have stayed at Metro. Greg told him that. However, he and his partner were adamant. The studio controlled him lock, stock, and barrel, and it was an inequitable situation. We were at their [MGM's] mercy."[10]

After negotiating the entire summer, on July 30, 1948, MGM attorney Floyd Hendrickson sent a memo to Benny Thau, the main points being:

- Mickey had to forgo his $5,000-per-week salary for forty weeks and had to work for $2,500 for twenty weeks.
- Mickey would have to give Metro a note for $500,000, "which indebtedness would be reduced by $100,000 for each

picture he completed under the new picture agreement," which would call for six-month options rather than the yearly options they now held.

- Mickey would receive $125,000 for each picture he made under the new agreement, but $100,000 of that would go to pay off the $500,000 bond he'd posted. In other words, he would be paid just $25,000 per film.
- In the event that Mickey defaulted under the new agreement, Metro would have the right to keep him from appearing in any other film with anyone else during his failure to perform services at Metro.
- Moreover, if Metro exercised its right to terminate the five-picture agreement by reason of Mickey's failure or refusal to work, the unpaid balance of the $500,000 was to be paid in cash to the studio upon demand. Also, Mickey still had to pay Stiefel 50 percent of the $25,000 per film and 10 percent to William Morris. If Mickey made all five films in one year, he would be returned $50,000, before taxes.

It was an absurd, insane deal that Stiefel pressured Mickey into signing.

On August 3, 1948, Mickey signed the agreement. One week later, unbeknownst to him, Herman C. Biegel, the administrator of the Loews pension plan, sent a memo to Eugene Leake, the treasurer of the fund, that stated, "After going over Rooney's new contract, it is my opinion that he is no longer a full-time employee of Loews. Therefore his membership in the plan has been terminated as of June 25, 1948." [11] The $49,000-per-year-for-life pension plan was now gone as well, and along with it the lifeline that would have saved Mickey as he got older.

Mayer was still angry. He scheduled no films, under the agreement, for Mickey to work in. MGM was in no hurry to put Mickey back to work. He would now have to rely solely on Stiefel. According to Mort Briskin, it was just an illusion that Stiefel would invest his own millions to finance the independent films as he had boasted. "Stiefel didn't want to take any risks with his own money. So I had to go out and get independent financing for our projects. For example, I was the one who found Harry Popkin. He put up most of the money for 'The Big Wheel.' Once we had the money, United Artists agreed to release it. So, in reality, Stiefel was in on a free ride. He got other people to put up the money, and he took forty percent of the profits"[12]—and this was in addition to getting the company overhead paid back. This was an early example of securing independent deficit financing for pictures outside the studio system so that a studio could act as a distribution company. Independent deficit financing is one of the mechanisms financing independent films today. An investor pool puts up money to develop a script that, if sold, might generate another round of financing. The distribution studio buys the film, paying back the investors, some of whom will leave their initial investment in the fund for another picture.

It later surfaced that the main reason Mayer so abruptly turned down Stiefel's proposal for a Hardy series on CBS Radio was that Loews and MGM had grander plans for its properties. They had been quietly purchasing radio properties, including WHN in New York in 1946. (In September 1948, they changed the call letters to WMGM.) The plan was to create their own radio network, using actors already under contract and film properties in their possession. They initially planned to syndicate the *M-G-M Theatre of the Air* with "At Home with Lionel Barrymore," "Hollywood, U.S.A.," "The Story of Dr. Kildare," "Good News from Hollywood," "Crime Does Not Pay," "Maisie," and their centerpiece, "The Hardy Family," which would reunite Rooney with Lewis Stone and Fay Holden. The series appeared on Wednesdays at 7:30 p.m. and ran from November 11, 1949, to May 8, 1951. It was syndicated to two hundred stations on the Mutual Radio Network. There were seventy-eight episodes created—twenty-six episodes to run per year that repeated once with the rest in the can. William Morris created this deal for Mickey by going around Stiefel to have MGM work directly with Rooney as a contracted-for-radio performer. The MGM network ended with the popularity of television, which dealt a deathblow to live entertainment programming on the radio and, by the 1950s, helped transform the medium into an arm of the recording industry. Top 40 stations arrived with the advent of rock 'n' roll, and then became talk radio and open-mike call-in radio, which itself is morphing into Internet on-demand radio as opposed to "appointment" radio.

Richard Crenna, a prolific actor on radio known for playing high school student Walter Denton on *Our Miss Brooks*—he portrayed Walter in the television series, and later appeared in *The Real McCoys*, television movies of the week, and the first *Rambo* film with Sylvester Stallone—played Andy Hardy's best friend, Beasley. Crenna recalled of the series, "Mickey was a hoot to work with. Great energy. It was a dream cast and it was a joy to work with Lewis Stone." Crenna was among a handful of actors, including Jack Benny, George Burns, and Dick Van Patten, who successfully made the transition from radio to early television to popular personality. Mickey, along with Robert Blake and Jackie Cooper, made the transition from silent movies to modern series television.

Amid the turmoil in his career, Mickey's home life was always active. He was dividing his time between El Ranchita and a house he rented in Laurel Canyon with Jimmy Cook. The divorce settlement from Betty Jane was approved by the court in June of 1948, with Judge Wilson extracting maximum dollars from Mickey, and would become final in June 1949. Mickey visited his boys on an irregular basis. "Betty Jane was a wonderful mother. Mickey was a father whenever he felt the whim," remarked her friend Pam McClenathan. Despite his troubles at the studio and in his career, he was back partying every night at clubs such as Ciro's, the Cocoanut Grove, and Slapsie Maxie's. Columnists spotted Mickey all over the town with a variety of starlets, including sultry Joi Lansing, Barbara Lawrence, Resa Alcott, Melisa McClure, Mavis Russell, Donna Reynolds, and Julie Wilson.

In January 1949, at Ciro's, Nick Sevano introduced him to a twenty-four-year-old actress named Martha Vickers. Vickers was a noted actress who'd played the second lead in *The Big Sleep* with Humphrey Bogart and Lauren Bacall. She had dated James Stewart after he returned from the war, and was now in the middle of a divorce from Paramount executive, Andrew C. ("A.C.") Lyles Jr. Their marriage had lasted only a few months (March–July 1948), before Martha filed for a divorce. A.C. recalled Vickers fondly when he spoke of her to us, saying, "She was an absolutely beautiful girl. She was discovered by David Selznick." [13]

"Mickey went crazy when I first introduced him to Martha," Savano told us. "He wanted to marry her right away." Mickey believed Martha was everything that Betty Jane was not. She was sophisticated, not the "hick" that he considered B.J. to be. She was only five foot three, and therefore didn't tower over him. She stroked his ego and was a good listener, in particular to Mickey's stories of sorrow about his career. She told him that he was a great star and would soon be back on top. He was smitten. Martha took him the very next night to have dinner with her parents, the MacVicars, in the home she shared with them in the Valley. Two days later, Mickey invited Martha and her parents to his small house in Laurel Canyon for a duck dinner prepared by his flat mate, Jimmy Cook. The next night, Martha had dinner with Mickey and his indomitable mother, Nell.

Columnists and newspapers were all carrying stories about Mickey and Martha. Louella Parsons wrote for the *Los Angeles Evening Herald Express* and Hearst on January 1, 1949, "Mickey's new heartbeat is Martha Vickers. They have an every night date, and on Thursday were at a table for two at The Kings."

As he did in his first two marriages, Mickey impulsively forged ahead with an instant marriage to Martha, who had told her friend actress Frances Lane that "Mickey was rather modest and not all over the place as he was supposed to be. He is intelligent and quiet, unless his mood is for fun." [14]

Martha's mother, Frances; and father, James, a sales representative for a Japanese steel manufacturer, were both impressed by Mickey, and the feeling was mutual. Mickey liked the very homey atmosphere of the MacVickar home. Frances was an excellent cook, and James a rugged outdoorsman. It was the type of family life he had always lacked. In a curious way, it might have reminded him of the all-American family he belonged to in the Andy Hardy series. It made him feel good. Accordingly, he decided to pursue Martha and settle down. He sold his bachelor pad home in Laurel Canyon and moved back to El Ranchita with his mother and stepfather.

Mickey's close friends at the time were actor Wally Cassell and his wife, RKO star Marcy McGuire. Wally, who was born Oswaldo Castellano, had been renamed Wally Cassell by Mickey, who told him it was a "better name for the films." Wally had a long career in both feature films and television, which included several pictures with Mickey, including the Sam Stiefel/Mort Briskin–produced *Quicksand*. Marcy was the star of several films, including 1943's *Higher and Higher*, co-starring Frank Sinatra. Both Marcy and Wally had known Mickey for over sixty years and were good friends with Martha Vickers.

Marcy told us:

Mickey included us in dinners with Martha, and we had them over for dinner. Martha was very sweet. She wanted nothing more but to please Mickey. They both were actually about the same in height, however, Martha wore heels and would tower over him. She felt it would embarrass him, so she started wearing flats. Mickey told her, "Honey, you look great in heels. You don't have to wear flats for me." He was pretty confident in himself. Martha was clearly in love with him and told Wally and I [*sic*], "I just know in my heart that there would never be another boy like him."

In around April of 1949, Mickey had really fallen head over heels for her. Just gaga. Wally and I had been married about two years by then. Wally took Mickey to the famous Joseff jewelers and ordered a large emerald-cut diamond engagement ring. He literally called Martha from the store and proposed. She accepted, but cautioned Mickey that they could not marry until her divorce from A. C. Lyles was final, which could be several months. Mickey did not want to wait. Wally arranged for Martha to get a Vegas divorce. In those days, to get a quickie divorce in Vegas, you had to have residency of six weeks. Mickey asked Wally to help them out. So Wally and I drove then to Vegas, and Wally arranged for them to be at an exclusive guest ranch owned by friends of Wally. It was a big spread, about four hundred fifty acres, but there was no gambling there. Martha stayed there, with us, and Mickey was doing a film, so he commuted back and forth. It wasn't a great place for Mickey to be near the casinos.[15]

Wally recalled, "Right when he got to Vegas, Mickey blew about five grand and he couldn't cover his markers he asked for. Well, these weren't the type of guys he could screw with. Mickey was flat broke. So I got the markers back for him after I talked to the boys. They knew who he was and it would be bad business for them to go out and put Andy Hardy in a cement block."[16] Still, Mickey would not stop the gambling in Vegas. He loved the atmosphere and playing craps, and he was addicted to the thrill of tossing the dice across the green felt and off the table cushion.

Marcy recalled:

> We once were having dinner at the nightclub and casino El Rancho with Mickey and Martha. Wally and I wanted to dance, so we gave our half to Mickey to pay the check. When we came back from dancing and went to leave the club, the maître d' grabbed Wally's arm and said to him, "Hey buddy, you're not planning to leave without paying your check, are you?" Wally explained that we gave Mickey the money to pay the check. He said Mickey skipped off, so we were stuck with the whole bill. When we went to the casino, Mickey was at the craps table playing with our money. Luckily, it only took six weeks to get a divorce. It was dangerous to leave him in Vegas. It was quite an interesting six weeks. Martha liked to have a good time, as well. She could match Mickey drink for drink.[17]

Martha's divorce from A. C. Lyles came through near the end of May, and five days later, Mickey's divorce from Betty Jane became final.

"Mickey wanted a simple wedding in Vegas, probably because he couldn't afford anything fancy. Martha wanted an elegant church wedding in front of her parents. Mickey had no choice but to give in to what Martha wanted," recalled Marcy.[18]

Mickey had to work hard to find a minister who would marry both a divorcee and the twice-divorced Rooney. He was turned down by several churches. However, the Christ Memorial Unity Church in North Hollywood agreed. The Rev. Herbert J. Schneider married Martha and Mickey on June 3, 1949, at 5:00 p.m. Mickey had just picked up his final divorce papers at 11:00 a.m. that same day.

His close friend Sidney Miller was not invited to the wedding but was present at Betty Jane's marriage to Buddy Baker, which took place five days after Mickey's wedding to Martha. Miller recalled, "I never got along with Martha, and she tried to cut me out of their circle of friends. Mickey and I still hung out at the track." [19]

Mickey, now with his third wife, was twenty-nine. He said at the wedding, "I've got me a wonderful girl this time. If I don't make this one last, there's something wrong with me." [20] He partied until late with friends, family, and Sam Stiefel. This was unusual, since Mickey had begun a very public dispute with Stiefel three months prior to the wedding.

"Why not?" Mort Briskin said with an amused grin when asked why he and Sam were at the wedding reception while Mickey was having a dispute with Sam over money. "Sam and I paid for the wedding." [21]

Mickey's feud with his partner Sam Stiefel began when Johnny Hyde, vice president at William Morris Agency West Coast and Mickey's former agent, was courting Mickey to return to the agency. Hyde was a legendary agent in Hollywood, known for being the Svengali and lover to Marilyn Monroe until his death in 1950. Hyde reminded Mickey that his career was going nowhere.

"Hyde was a real character," recalled Nick Sevano. "He was a little short Russian Jew. I think Budd Schulberg based Sammy Glick on him," Sevano said, referring to the take-no-prisoners ladder-climbing character in Schulberg's famous Hollywood novel *What Makes Sammy Run?* "He did everything to try to get Mickey to come back to Morris." [22]

In a story (undoubtedly planted by Hyde) headlined "Rooney Cuts away from Sam Stiefel," the *Daily Variety* on February 1, 1949, wrote, "Rooney was dissatisfied with the financial returns he had been getting out of the Rooney-Stiefel Corp. The actor was set in a deal Stiefel made with United Artists for release of *Quicksand*. However, he is now negotiating with King Brothers to make a picture with Lou Rantz repping the Kings to put together a package and also negotiating with RKO for a releasing deal with King and Rooney. . . . Since William Morris is now repping him, naturally Rooney will try to by-pass the Stiefel Quicksand deal."

Months later, other rumors surfaced in the papers about the split between Rooney and Stiefel, the first of which appeared in the *Hollywood Reporter* on April 9, 1949, which spoke of a project Hyde had set up at Twentieth Century–Fox for him: "Mickey Rooney attempted to withdraw from this production in order to star in 'A Ticket to Tomahawk,' but producer Samuel H. Stiefel, Rooney's partner in the independent production company, held the actor to his contract. Fritz Lang was considered for director and Ava Gardner and Jean Wallace are being considered for the film."

As William Morris attempted to negotiate the breakup of their partnership, Mickey learned that Stiefel was not to be trifled with. According to Stiefel, Mickey had accumulated a huge debt to the corporation, and to Stiefel personally. All the loans Mickey had taken for his debts and gambling, the money lent to Nell and Fred, the money fronted for Mickey's divorce from Ava and Betty Jane, the homes, the offices, the staff—Stiefel basically owned Mickey. Eventually, a deal was ironed out to extricate Mickey from this mess. Essentially, Stiefel kept all the proceeds from Mickey's earnings from Metro, from his personal appearances and radio show (*Shorty Bell*), and from Rooney's appearing in the three properties Stiefel and Briskin had sold to investors. Only two of those films were produced; these became the films noir *Quicksand* and *The Big Wheel*.

The third, unfortunately for Rooney, was never produced. It was a property Rooney Inc. had owned called *Francis, the Talking Mule*, based on a novel by David Stern called *Francis* that Mort Briskin had optioned. Briskin recalled, "Stiefel didn't have any faith in it and refused to put up his own money. Eventually, I dropped the option and

Universal bought it immediately." [23] It became one of the most profitable film series, made Donald O'Connor a star, and kept Universal afloat for most of the 1950s. Ultimately, the story turned up on television as a series about a talking horse, *Mr. Ed*, starring Alan Young. "The money that Mickey could have made from owning those movies would have cushioned him for life," recalled Billy Barty. [24]

Quicksand, an attempt to change the Rooney image, was the type of film noir that had become popular with audiences in the late 1940s and early '50s. It put Rooney alongside his old friend James Cagney's sister Jeanne and Rooney Inc. client Peter Lorre. Harrison Carroll wrote on March 15, 1949, "From now on, Mickey Rooney says he'll play only Jimmy Cagney type of roles on the screen. He started in that direction with the start of filming *Quicksand*."

For the second film under the Stiefel agreement, *The Big Wheel*, Stiefel and Briskin had secured some of the financing from former heavyweight boxing champion Jack Dempsey. The movie marked the final appearance in films for Hattie McDaniel, the first African American actress to win an Academy Award. According to Nick Sevano, Mickey was asked a favor by his off-and-on William Morris agent, Johnny Hyde, to create a small role his girlfriend, Norma Jean Baker, who appears as an extra in the film, one of her earliest performances before she became Marilyn Monroe.

Norma Jean was a stunner. She would go on to have a spectacular career and become friends with Sinatra and the Rat Pack and with President John F. Kennedy. Mickey was fascinated with Norma Jean and told us that he invented the name Marilyn Monroe, a story that doesn't have any credence, but a fun anecdote nonetheless.

He said, "I met her. She was Norma Jean Baker and she was at singer Vaughn Monroe's house. She needed a ride home and I drove her to her apartment. She blew me and then I suggested that Norma Jean was not a good name for movies. She said, 'Mickey, what do you think?' So I thought, Marilyn, from Marilyn Miller, who was a vaudeville star, and then give her Vaughn's last name, Monroe. She loved it." [25] The true story, however, is that Twentieth Century–Fox executive Ben Lyons helped her combine her mother's maiden name, Monroe, with the first name of his late fiancée, Ziegfeld Follies star Marilyn Miller.

Meanwhile, the stories about the Rooney-Stiefel breakup continued to appear in the press. Harrison Carroll wrote on March 8, 1949, "I hear Mickey Rooney and Sam Stiefel were rowing for hours yesterday at the General Service studio."

Another signal that Mickey's finances were running low came when he was forced to sell the beloved El Ranchita, which he'd given to his mother. Harrison Carroll wrote on March 8, 1949:

> When the lawyers come out of the huddles, Mickey will probably be free of his long-term contract to the corporation under which he and his partner, Sam Stiefel, have been operating, but of course there will be concessions . . . [A]s I get it Mickey will do the picture, Quicksand . . . and will make two other films at a special bargain rate on salary for these productions. Otherwise he'll be free of his seven year deal. Mickey is now living in the three-bedroom home of his mother and step-father, the Fred Pankeys. The five-acre ranch that Mickey gave to his mother was sold to director Roy Del Ruth. The smaller house was taken in trade.

The Sam Stiefel story is almost emblematic of how show business personalities with no business sense can easily be manipulated by managers and agents. By the time of the dissolution of Rooney Inc., Sam Stiefel had achieved his goal. The corporation had returned a hefty profit for him, and he became an independent film producer. After his years in Hollywood, Stiefel returned triumphantly to Philadelphia, now a legitimate successful film producer.

While Stiefel and Mort Briskin had achieved their objectives—they set up a company marketing the services of Rooney, used revenue generated by Rooney to cover the company expenses, advanced Mickey money then charged it back to Mickey out of his percentage, and topped it off by wrenching Mickey away from the one contract he had that promised a future—Mickey was left high and dry. Under the influence of Stiefel, he went from the world's number one box office star, with the security of a long-term agreement of the premiere movie studio, to an underemployed actor merely scraping by.

The Stiefels, the Annenbergs, and the Kennedys all rose to become patriarchs of empires and great philanthropists by adhering to the "three gets" of American society: Get rich any way you can; once you're rich, get legitimate as quickly as you can; and once you're legitimate, get philanthropic so nobody can touch you. And poor Mickey Rooney wound up involved with all three of these figures: financed by Joe Kennedy into Larry Darmour's Poverty Row studio, addicted to horse racing via Moe Annenberg's *Daily Racing Form*, and bled dry by Sam Stiefel.

The Stiefel-Rooney relationship was skewed from the start, for both men had divergent agendas, even though they seemed to be walking down the same path. Sam saw Rooney as the ripe talent he needed to break into the motion picture industry. Mickey saw Sam as a father figure. The partnership of Rooney Inc. was thus off on the wrong foot from day one.

In the end, Mickey felt no hard feelings toward Stiefel, despite the damage he had done to Rooney's career. On March 22, 1950, Rooney told Hedda Hopper, "I went down the sewer with Stiefel. Sam Stiefel and I made some lousy pictures. He's back in Philadelphia now, but there are no hard feelings between us. When trouble arises between the two people, I've learned its best to shake hands and go to a neutral corner." [26]

Rooney had been very susceptible to Sam Stiefel's charm. Neuropsychiatrist and author Dr. John Liebert (*Wounded Minds, Hearts of Darkness*) told us that given Mickey's lack of parenting as a growing child and his exposure to the theater and performance at such a tender age, he developed a "situational character," one that allowed him to become the consummate entertainer, but it was more an exoskeleton than a personality.[27] He was, therefore, psychologically a "hollow man," underdeveloped. Thus, for the rest of his life he would search for a core personality, which he would find only very late in life, when he met and empathized with Bill Sackler for his performance in the television movie *Bill*. But more on that later.

Bob Dylan wrote, "The times they are a-changin'," which aptly describes Mickey in 1949. Good-bye MGM, Betty Jane, Sam Stiefel, and *adios mi casa*, El Ranchita. Hello Martha, hello to a new mistress, and hello to a new decade. After his years at Metro and his disastrous partnership with Sam Stiefel, Mickey was peeking over the next hill, hoping for a fresh start. In reality, he was only staring into a red sky at morning.

The Mick, the Duke, and the Deuce in the Coconut

Mickey and his mother Nell dancing at the housewarming party for El Ranchita, their new home in Encino, California, in 1939.
PHOTO COURTESY OF ROBERT EASTON.

B y 1949, Mickey had become a vastly different person than the Andy Hardy of the 1930s. No longer a teenager, and now a war veteran and twice divorced, having severed contracts with Metro and Sam Stiefel, he found himself marching in place at the crossroads of his career and his life. He still owed Metro three pictures and had an obligation to complete three independent films with Stiefel, which would satisfy his agreement with the now-defunct Rooney Inc. (He ended up doing only one film for MGM, *The Strip*.) Also he would receive only a pittance of a salary as part of his negotiated departures. On top of that, as the new decade stared back at him, his new marriage was also quickly foundering on the rocks. As his marital adventures fed the daily tip sheets of the gossip columnists, he was repeating the same script: married but bored and looking around. And while the Rooney name still offered some box office attraction, it was driven mostly by audiences' ghoulish desire to watch in slo-mo the train wreck that he had become, inhabiting character roles that were no longer the leads he had played fifteen years earlier.

Mickey was a walking time bomb. He was drinking heavily, addicted to Benzedrine to keep up his energy, gambling at accelerated levels, over his head in debt, and according to his personal manager, Nick Sevano, "still fucking anything with a skirt."[1] And he was only twenty-nine years old.

Mickey's emotional decompensation, one must realize, went far beyond that of today's young performers acting badly. None of today's scandal-ridden entertainers command the box office power or garner the public attention that followed Mickey from the late 1940s through 1950. He was the original *enfant terrible* of the entertainment world. Through the end of his agreement with MGM in 1949, his every want or desire was indulged. Everyone, from Les Peterson to Sam Stiefel to Mort Briskin to his personal entourage of Sid Miller, Sig Frohlich, and Dick Paxton, was there to scratch his every itch. His bad behavior was whitewashed by Howard Strickling and his PR team at Metro. He was horribly irresponsible to his wives and children. He now had two ex-wives and a third divorce inexorably heading toward him like a mudslide along the canyon walls of the Hollywood Hills. He had two sons from his previous marriage whom he would barely acknowledge, but who were desperate for their father's attention.

While Mickey failed on almost every personal front, there is no disputing his talent as a performer. Even as he began his free fall into minor low-budget films throughout the 1950s, his performances were still right on target. As an evolving character actor, he lent each role the immediately identifiable Rooney energy and credibility that had become his trademark even as his star faded. Throughout our many interviews with directors, writers, actors, and crew, his colleagues revealed to us many of their memorable negative personal encounters with Rooney. But not one ever disputed Rooney's innate talent or the performances he could deliver regardless of the demands of the role. From the madcap farce comedies (such as 1957's *Operation Mad Ball*, with Jack Lemmon and Ernie Kovacs, in which he plays a wily army sergeant in the days after World War II) to the tragic dramas (such as the 1954 James Michener film *The Bridges at Toko-Ri*, a very early antiwar movie, in which he plays a navy helicopter rescue pilot shot down over North Korea while trying to retrieve a navy fighter pilot played by William Holden), there is no disputing that Mickey's performances were flawless. He never missed a beat.

While his output was nearly the same in the 1940s and '50s, when he made twenty-two films in each decade, the quality of the films themselves was markedly different. He had appeared in mostly A-level films in the 1940s, in which he was usually top-billed. But in the ensuing decade, despite some exceptions such as *The Bridges at Toko-Ri*, he was reduced to performing in low-budget, mediocre programmers, playing secondary or character roles. Yet he inhabited those roles with a gusto that went beyond professionalism. He also starred in a hardly noticed television comedy series and made personal appearances in any venue that would have him, just to pay the bills, the alimony, child support, and bookies—even as he was struggling against the current to stay financially afloat, yet slowly sinking beneath the waves. He was no longer, in most instances, an independent producer, as Sam Stiefel had envisioned for him, but a job-seeking actor who, in some cases, hat in hand, had to audition for a part. By the mid-1950s he was appearing in the series that his company, Rooney Inc., had optioned and jettisoned, *Francis the Talking Mule*, which by that time had become creaky and burned out. He performed in the sequel *Francis in the Haunted House*, replacing his friend Donald O'Connor, who had leapfrogged him in films. While O'Connor had received profit points when he did the series, Mickey was being paid far less, and had had to audition to beat out a then-unknown comic and future television producer, James Komack, for the part.

On the personal front, in 1949 Mickey and Martha Vickers, now Martha Rooney, bought Spencer Tracy's former home, a small bungalow at 4723 White Oak Avenue in Encino, near his mother. He chose the location so he could go home to Mama Nell when Martha became fed up with his antics and locked him out of the house, which she was wont to do whenever she felt Mickey needed reining in.

Director Dick Quine, who was a lifelong friend of Rooney, recalled to Arthur Marx, "How could they not be aware with his track record? The problem was always the same. His frenetic existence. It was impossible for a wife to keep up with him. But as I say, how could they have not known when they married him? I feel he's taken a bum rap about being a lousy husband. I think a lot of the women used him to get somewhere. After all, he was a tremendous star. He had clout in the business or at least they thought he did . . ." [2] Dick Quine himself was no slouch, having been married four times and having had a long engagement, but no marriage, to Kim Novak before his suicide in 1989.

Actress Marcy McGuire Cassell and her husband, Wally, close friends of both Mickey and Martha, told us:

> Mickey was just impulsive and spontaneous, and had little regard for his wife. He would toss around outlandish ideas. Once we were having dinner with Mickey and they were

talking about financing a movie. Martha was pregnant with
Teddy. Mickey had the cockamamie idea that he could get
a friend of his in New York City to put up the money. He
just called up the airline for reservations for he and Wally
[sic] to fly to New York for a week. I knew he had more
than financing on his mind. I just told Mickey that Wally
and I traveled only together and that he was not about to
leave Martha by herself. She was pregnant for Chrissakes.
She just sat there quietly, but he was out of control and very
inconsiderate.

Regarding Martha, Wally added, "When she was pregnant,
Mickey was out the door chasing other broads." Wally also told us,
"Mickey was a free spirit. He had a carefree attitude and did as he
pleased. I mean, most of the women he married knew how Mickey
lived. They knew he was never going to change."[3] As if to echo this
comment, Mickey's stepson Chris Aber, from his marriage to his last
wife, Jan, told us that even in his eighties, girls would throw themselves at Mickey, and he enjoyed every minute of it.

Writer Roger Kahn told us, "Mickey claimed that Vickers was
frigid. Cold as ice. She also was a big drinker. [But] you just couldn't
believe half the shit Mickey shoveled at you."[4] However, interviews
with her friends confirmed that she had become depressed that her
once-red-hot film career was sputtering and she realized that it was
not helped by her pregnancy. She subsequently started drinking. Her
problems were compounded by Mickey's boozing and gambling, which
ultimately spelled disaster for the couple. Martha found out quickly
that Mickey was not about to change. By the end of the decade, the
two were in constant battles. "It was almost like the fighting Bicker-
sons," recalled Marcy Cassell. "We would go over their house and
they would be in the middle of a huge fight that was usually fueled
by both of them drinking." She also told us, "Martha was drinking

very heavily. Beulah, their maid, used to call me all the time and ask for help. She was worried about her drinking at all hours. She would tell me that Martha would just lie in bed and was terribly depressed. Mickey would come home drunk, and started blaming everyone for his problems. He would threaten to quit the business. Martha would counter him by saying, 'Maybe that's a good idea, Mick. Why don't you just quit. You could become a milkman or something.'" [5]

Meanwhile, Joe Yule Sr. suffered a heart attack on March 30, 1950, and passed away at Santa Monica Hospital. He was buried at Forest Lawn, next to Mickey's famous costar Wallace Beery. While Mickey had seen his father infrequently over the years, Joe Sr.'s death affected him deeply; he became "really devastated," according to his friend director Dick Quine, who told us about how his father's death affected Mick.

Joe had married a stripper, Leota Hullinger, in 1940 and lived in a small bungalow in the Valley that Mickey had helped finance. Although the agreement that Mickey had set up for Joe with MGM had ended in 1946, he remained active, still in movies, playing the character Jiggs of the *Jiggs and Maggie* newspaper cartoon strip, and still drinking heavily.

As the decade progressed, everything was piling up on top of Mickey. His marriage was unraveling, his father had passed away, he had another child on the way, he was out of steady work and he was already behind on the alimony and child support payments for Betty Jane and the boys. His debts were eating him up. Mickey responded, according to Arthur Marx, with "booze, broads, and horses."

Under the direction of Martin Gang, Mickey crawled back to MGM to beg their forgiveness. Times had changed, however, at Culver City. By 1950, Mayer had been ordered to hire a new "Thalberg," and Loews had put Dore Schary in charge of production at Metro. With the backing of Nick Schenck, Schary wielded immense power at the studio, and Mayer was more an honorary than a hands-on executive.

Schary did not believe in the "star system." Slowly, quietly, he was not renewing agreements with many of the legendary contract players such as Garland or for the musical stars from the Arthur Freed unit such as Esther Williams. Mickey certainly did not fit into the future Schary envisioned.

Nonetheless, Mickey set up a meeting with Schary in January 1950. He told Schary that he had made a big "boo-boo" breaking his agreement and would like to be placed back under contract. Schary and Rooney had known each other for years and had worked together since *Boys Town*, for which Schary had won his Oscar for Best Screenplay. But Schary was dismissive. According to Mickey, Schary told him, "We'll see what we can do for you, kid," and then showed him the door. There was no great reprieve coming. Even though he had a short-lived return to MGM for *The Strip*, in 1951, and *A Slight Case of Larceny*, in 1952—features that were part of the agreement that Mort Briskin and Greg Bautzer had negotiated in 1948—it did not last. In the end, Mickey was on his own.[6]

Mickey then tried to set up his own independent production team. He hired attorney Martin Gang and Nick Sevano to act as his managers. He'd retained Johnny Hyde at William Morris as his agent; Hyde believed he could get Mickey to open a picture. Mickey's name still held some value at the box office, albeit in more budget-conscious low-rent productions; he was no longer a leading man. True to his word, Hyde found Mickey work in a low-budget drama at Twentieth Century–Fox about the roller derby, called *The Fireball*. Trying to recapture some of his *Boys Town* appeal, in it Mickey plays an orphan boy who becomes a roller derby champ with the aid of the orphanage priest, played by perennial clergyman Pat O'Brien. The movie was filmed from December 1949 through January 1950. Once again, Hyde's girlfriend, Marilyn Monroe, was given a bit part. The movie returned a small profit and garnered some positive notices for Mickey. James Barstow Jr. wrote in the *New York Herald Tribune*, "Rooney does a fine job in a part that appears to fit his proportions inside and out . . . his half-pint who hates the world until he finds his niche on a roller rink and then becomes overbearingly egotistical comes through with pungent conviction." His diminutive size, which in the past was part of his charm, now had become more glaring as he aged.

Next, Columbia studio head Harry Cohn, who hoped to catch a resurgent interest in an Andy Hardy type of film, signed Mickey to star in *He's a Cockeyed Wonder*, which began shooting in early April, shortly after Rooney's father's death. Mickey's face had weathered by now, and he looked paunchy and much older than his twenty-nine years. His costar was Terry Moore, who starred in the 1949 quasi-cult *King Kong* knockoff *Mighty Joe Young*, opposite the ape, whose mechanical eyes lasciviously oogled her throughout the film—as did the eyes of her reputed longtime companion Howard Hughes, Mickey's former antagonist/nemesis with Ava. Just watching the trailer for *He's a Cockeyed Wonder*,[7] viewers can sense the wear and tear of Mickey's hard living on his performance. On October 21, 1950, the *New York Herald Tribune* wrote, "The Hardy series died a natural death several years ago, with the generally accepted epitaph that enough is enough. It is painfully surprising, therefore, to see Mickey Rooney back at the same old stand in 'He's a Cockeyed Wonder.' The name has changed, this time it's Freddie Frisby, and there's no Hardy clan. But all of Andy's mannerisms are on tap including the exuberant mugging and Hardy's facility for getting in and out of contrived troubles." Mickey's innocent young lad act had clearly worn thin.

Meanwhile, Theodore "Teddy" Michael Rooney was born on April 13, 1950, at Valley Hospital in LA. Mickey, who was not living with Martha after the death of his father, was, like his father at his own birth, nowhere to be found. As Marcy Cassell explained to us, the couple had been fighting, arguments driven by alcohol, and Mickey tried to be away from her as much as he could. "Martha called Mickey the day before . . . and told him that the baby's birth would be very soon. She was already three weeks late. He told her that he was very busy and had to go to a party. While Teddy was born early in the morning [4:00 a.m.], Mickey sauntered in around 5:00 p.m." [8]

After Teddy's birth, Martha and Mickey attempted a reconciliation. As Martha told her friend Pam McClenathan, "She didn't want Teddy to be the victim of a broken home so early in his life." [9] That was Mickey's life script, and Vickers wanted none of it for her son. But Teddy's fate, because the chromosomal deck had been stacked against him at the moment of his conception, was sealed. Alcoholism and substance abuse would dog him his entire life.

THE MONTHS THAT FOLLOWED Teddy's birth were turbulent for the Rooneys. There was a series of breakups and reconciliations. The pattern was typical of Mickey, and would be repeated in future marriages and relationships. He simply was not interested in being trapped in domestic life. After a few days of being with his wife and kids, boredom would set in.

"Mickey was a ball of energy that always needed attention and action," said Nick Sevano.[10] Wally Cassell echoed Nick, telling us, "He had a frenetic existence and it was impossible for a wife to keep up with him. But with his wives he felt he could do anything that he pleased. He felt that he had the right to go anywhere or do anything as long as it pleased him. Mickey lived as many husbands had fantasized about living, which was to support his family but screw around as he pleased." [11] It was a lifestyle, though, that was fated to catch up with him.

Mickey's and Martha's alcohol-fueled arguments led to many knock-down, drag-out fights that ended with Mickey back at Nell's or with another woman. Marcy Cassell described them to us as "The Battling Rooneys."

Just as 1950 had begun to be an extremely difficult year for Mickey, things went from bad to worse. The year started out with the death of his father and the birth of another child, he continued his rocky relationship with Martha, his drinking and gambling intensified, his career had hit the rocks, and he faced financial disaster when the failure of Rooney Inc. cleaned out all his assets and left him flat broke. Lawsuits inevitably followed the shutdown of the company, for tax liabilities it had incurred. Not just the IRS, but the state of California was pursuing him. And while his prior obligations were siphoning off any dribble of income there was, he was being forgotten by Hollywood. Many industry executives, the folks who could green-light a film on their signatures alone, avoided him like the plague if they saw him at an event or function—assuming he was invited. As if by a gentlemen's agreement, and with nary a sound, the door to an industry that had embraced him with open arms since 1934 was suddenly shut in his face. When he did get an invitation to an event, gone were the crowds of photographers and fans who had previously mobbed him for an autograph or a photo op. He was becoming the textbook definition of a Hollywood has-been. And for a guy used to the bright lights, the sudden popping of hundreds of flashbulbs going off in his face, the whirr of rolling cameras, the roar of fast cars, and the cooing of willing starlets, the silence was deafening.

Mickey himself described what he went through during this period in an interview in the January 1958 issue of *McCall's* magazine. He had been invited by his old MGM shadow, Les Peterson, to be an Oscar presenter at the March 23, 1950, Academy Awards ceremony hosted by actor Paul Douglas. Mickey was thrilled to be included in the event, and hoped that this meant he was being accepted again by the industry. As Mickey recounted to *McCall's*:

> My pride was hurt during this period. I wanted to be wanted and needed, but I didn't know how. . . . I had an old tuxedo that didn't fit so good anymore, but there was

nothing I could do about that. On the night of the Oscars, I was finishing dinner with Martha, who was my wife at the time, when I got a call from Johnny Green, the Academy musical conductor. It was twenty minutes before I was due to leave for the theater. Green said he didn't know how to say this, but the Academy had changed their minds about me taking part in their show, and had elected him to break it to me. It seems that I'd been married so often that I was a bad representative of the picture industry. When I realized what he was telling me, I blew. Boy, how I blew! I told him where the whole Academy could go, and I resigned then and there at the top of my lungs. Then after I hung up, I cried.[12]

The quickly unraveling marriage with Martha, his topsy-turvy life headed for another divorce, had become the only story about Mickey the press was covering. Mickey claimed that this marriage to "Mart" ended the very night he was rejected by the Academy, during an argument fueled by booze. He said Vickers viciously attacked him as a has-been. "I think that was the night our marriage died. Martha never felt the same way about me again, and I didn't feel worthy of her. Soon, we were living apart," Mickey wrote in *Life Is Too Short*.[13]

Mickey began dating a bevy of starlets, including Diane Garrett, Kay Brown, Erin O'Brien, and Elaine Curtis. Mickey claimed that while on a break from filming *The Bridges at Toko-Ri*, he was on an aircraft carrier near Japan with his friend, actor Don "Red" Barry, and "they booked sixteen Japanese gals into our hotel room for an Asian style orgy. If there is one thing that Californians can learn from the Asians among us it is their acceptance, without guilt, of the erotic."[14] Mickey also claimed he had an affair with a divorced, rich San Francisco socialite who wanted to marry him and retire to a life of leisure, living off her inheritance—a proposition, he said, he declined.

Now broke, Mickey was forced to resort, again, to appearing in live stage productions to pay alimony and back child support, come up with cash for Nell, and provide for Martha and Teddy, not to mention himself. Nick Sevano picked up a lucrative gig for Mickey in June 1950 as the emcee of the *Hadacol Caravan*, in essence, an old-time medicine show that sold Hadacol, a tonic that was 26 percent alcohol and that seemed to be a universal remedy: Drink enough of it, and you forgot you were sick in the first place. It was the "cure-all" for every ailment, but was later banned by the Food and Drug Administration. Manufactured by a Louisiana state senator named Dudley LeBlanc, the alcohol-laced elixir was marketed throughout the South to "down-home folks," as LeBlanc called them, in commercials using famous country music stars such as Minnie Pearl, Roy Acuff and His Smoky Mountain Boys, and the Chez Paree Girls. The price of admission to *Hadacol Caravan* was a bottle top of Hadacol. According to the August 30, 1950, review in *Variety*, Mickey was earning $7,500 a week for fifteen weeks shilling for the drug. More than $110,000 for a summer of work was impressive money for 1950, but even before it came in, it was gone.

In December 1950, Mickey, now separated from "Mart," moved into Nell and Fred's new house on Dickens Street in Sherman Oaks. Martha was still living with Teddy in the house they'd bought on White Oak. The couple attempted a Christmas reconciliation, according to Hedda Hopper's column on December 16, 1950, in which she quoted Martha as saying, "We thought it was a shame to spoil the baby's first Christmas. We are going to see if we can't be a little more sensible and hang onto our tempers." However, on January 4, 1951, Martha told Hopper that she would seek a divorce, stating, "Mickey doesn't like the restrictions of a marriage." Then, in the *Los Angeles Times* on March 8, 1951, it was announced that "Mickey Rooney and his estranged wife, Martha Vickers, will leave on a second honeymoon in a few weeks. The Rooneys kissed and made up and decided to put their San Fernando home up for sale, so they can start fresh in new surroundings." The true reason behind selling their home was that Mickey again was flat broke, couldn't afford to live there, and simply needed the dough.

At that time, Mickey was just completing his last film for Metro, *The Strip*, as part of his negotiated release, for which he earned only $25,000. While on set, he was served with a writ of execution that demanded he pay $3,541.14 to Betty Jane for back alimony and child support or show up in court to face a charge of nonsupport. With the threat of a prison sentence hanging over him, he begged his friends to help him scrape together a payment, and it was Sam Stiefel who came to the rescue, loaning Mickey money to pay off the debt.

Mickey's star may have faded, but there was still an instant box office draw for any film with his name attached. Harry Cohn, the chairman of Columbia who had given Mickey a contract for *Cock-eyed Wonder*, recognized this and, with Nick Sevano, negotiated a three-picture deal for seventy-five thousand dollars per film in March 1951. Cohn put producer Jonie Taps in charge of creating projects for Mickey. Mickey suggested hiring his old friend Dick Quine to direct, and a young scribe named Blake Edwards to write a script. Based on Taps's idea of an Abbott and Costello service-type comedy, they created *Sound Off* as Mickey's first Columbia film.

On June 11, 1951, during the filming of *Sound Off*, Martha filed for divorce, charging Mickey with "extreme mental cruelty" and asking for custody of fourteen-month-old Teddy. Mickey's divorce attorney, James Needleman, began negotiating a settlement, and Mickey, once again homeless, and nearly penniless at age thirty-one, was back to living with Nell and Fred.

Dick Quine recalled to Arthur Marx:

> Mickey was in a state of depression all during the filming
> of "Sound Off," because he felt there was something wrong

with him that he couldn't make a marriage work. One day, when I was on the set and waiting to make our first shot, Mickey called in sick and said, "I can't make it, Dick. I can't make it, I'm sick." I said, "Come on, Mick. You can handle it. You were all right last night . . ." Mickey eventually showed up. He was having trouble sleeping. When Blake and I would go out to dinner with him after a day's shooting . . . we'd slip him a couple of phenobarbitals into his drink. That way he'd be sleepy after dinner and go home to bed instead of roaming around the city half the night getting into trouble.[15]

The wrap on the two-year-old Vickers-Rooney marriage came on September 25, 1951. Martha claimed Mickey was "extremely abusive and sometimes was drinking." The court awarded her a monthly alimony of $2,000 for 1951, $1,875 for 1952, $1,750 until July 1955, $950 for the rest of 1955, $750 in 1956, $600 in 1958, $450 in 1959, and $300 after that until she died or remarried. She also received $150 monthly child support for Teddy until he turned eighteen. Mickey would keep the house on White Oak, but not the furniture.

In October 1951, Mickey's income was also garnished by the IRS to repay $35,000 in back taxes. According to his friend Sig Frohlich, Mickey was suicidal. "I have to get out of town and you're coming with me," he told Frohlich.[16] They flew off to Houston. He chose Houston because he wanted to be away from the glare of Hollywood, out of the spotlight. They checked into an upscale hotel, the Shamrock, and hunkered down.

"Mickey just disappeared from the world for a few weeks," recalled his mistress of six decades, "Mrs. Smith" (not her real name because she asked us to keep her identity confidential). "He just knocked himself out with sleeping pills and booze. Sig helped him pull out of his depression. He was very suicidal for a bit, but he bounced back quickly. I flew up to see him, and he barely recognized me. I reminded him what he had to live for. He also dreaded the albatross he created with alimony and child support for two wives and child support for three sons, along with Nell. It was touch-and-go for a while." [17]

When Mickey returned to LA, he rented a small apartment with his buddy, cowboy actor Don "Red" Barry, himself a notorious drinker and womanizer. Barry became Mickey's constant companion as they gambled, partied, and drank until the early hours.

Mickey recalled, "Red fucked every broad that wore a skirt. He had banged Susan Hayward, Linda Darnell, and Joan Crawford. Crawford got hot when she was fucked in public and could get caught. She once fucked Barry in a limo while the chauffeur watched. That turned her on." [18]

Red Barry was the worst possible influence for Mickey at this point in his life. Barry, who had gained fame as "Red Ryder" in a series of B Westerns featuring Robert Blake, had a history of drinking and fighting on movie sets.

Sid Miller told us, "This guy was a real piece of work. He had a chip on his shoulder and was quick tempered. He was short and built much like Mickey. He was down on his luck and sponged off Mick. He was nothing but fucking trouble."

In October 1951, Mickey shot a quickie Western, *My Outlaw Brother*, at Poverty Row's Eagle-Lion Films. It was the last production for Eagle-Lion, whose president, Arthur Krim, left to take over United Artists; the studio was sold to Ziv Television. The film co-starred Robert Stack and Robert Preston. Mickey found a minor part for Barry.

In the 1950s Mickey was still working in roles that couldn't provide enough income to pay all his obligations, even as he sought to reignite his career. After a rather dismal showing for *The Strip*, MGM decided to pursue only one more film with Mickey, even though he owed them two more (one of which was canceled), and the studio cut ties with him on January 8, 1952, at which time Mickey would be released from any future obligations. But he still had two films owed to Columbia. *Sound Off* had fared decently enough to induce Harry Cohn to order another picture in that vein. He had producer Jonie Taps reassemble the same team, with Dick Quine as director and Blake Edwards as writer, for *All Ashore*, a naval farce that would be shot on Catalina Island, with singer Dick Haymes as the costar.

While Cohn sent Taps to ensure that Rooney stayed out of trouble, Mickey remembered in an interview with Arthur Marx, "I went to Catalina with them and the first guy to get drunk was, of all people, Jonie Taps." Taps said, "Mickey Rooney had to put me to bed. And when he did, he said, '[T]his is the last time you're going to get drunk ahead of me, Jonie.'" [19]

Rooney followed this film with another naval comedy at Paramount, *Off Limits*, which starred Bob Hope, with Mickey second-billed as brash boxer Herbert Tuttle. The film also costarred Hope's mistress, Marilyn Maxwell. "Hope would disappear with Maxwell during afternoon shoots. He'd be behind the flats with that broad [Maxwell] blowing him," Rooney recalled. [20]

No angel himself, Mickey, like his father, had always been attracted to strippers. In mid-1952 he started dating legendary statuesque stripper Tempest Storm, born Anne Banks, who was known as the "Fabulous 4D Girl." Mickey claimed to Arthur Marx that he bought her a ten-thousand-dollar full-length mink to win her over. Storm was also an off-again, on-again girlfriend of mobster Mickey Cohen, not someone upon whose girl you wanted to put the moves— not if you didn't want to end up like mob boss Benny Siegel, whom Cohen had his gunsels riddle with bullets as he sat in his living room. But Mickey recalled, "I fucked Storm for nine straight hours when we met. Such great tits." [21]

Marx told us, "Mickey was dating Storm when two thugs came to his apartment and pushed him around. They were Mickey Cohen's boys. Mick was scared shitless. They made it clear for him to stay away from Cohen's 'goil.' I don't think Storm ever heard a peep from Mickey ever again." [22]

Despite Nick Sevano's having secured him his three-picture deal at Columbia, Mickey was growing unhappy with the lack of work. He felt Sevano was paying too much attention to his childhood friend Frank Sinatra. He also was angered by Sinatra's romance and marriage to Ava Gardner. Sevano recalled, "He was out of control. He was frantic and demanded I get him a job as a director. He would have made a lousy director because he had no discipline. So we parted." [23] Mickey released Sevano as his manager in October 1952.

In December of that year, he began shooting his final film for Metro, *A Slight Case of Larceny.* This cheap B comedy teamed him with Eddie Bracken and was directed by television director Don Weis and written by Jerry Davis, who later became a prolific television writer/producer for shows such as *Bewitched* and *The Odd Couple.* Davis had married Hope's girlfriend, Marilyn Maxwell, after Hope dumped her.

Hearing that Mickey was now without a manager, the manager, producer, and theatrical impresario Maurice Duke decided to pursue Mickey as a client. Native New Yorker Duke, who had changed his name from Maurice Duschinsky, had knocked around the business in vaudeville as a harmonica player before becoming an agent/manager, writer, and a film executive for Sam Katzman at Monogram Studios. Duke was a Hollywood original, a member of the tribe from the old country (Brooklyn), a Damon Runyon type of character who held court at the Beverly Hills Friars Club. Until the mid-1990s he was also, with a group of friends, a daily fixture at the deli Nate 'n Al, on Beverly Drive in Beverly Hills. Duke, who had an outsize personality, was the self-proclaimed "King of the B Pictures," and was fond of telling everyone, "I produced one hundred and four pictures, all bad." [24] He would proudly proclaim that he had produced the worst film ever made, *Bela Lugosi Meets a Brooklyn Gorilla*, in 1952, a real cult stinker set in the jungle of a Pacific island. In it, Lugosi, playing the the evil evolutionist/biologist Dr. Zabor, turns a visitor to the island who is making lascivious eyes at his daughter into an oversize monkey. (How bad was the movie? It was so bad that not only could *Mystery Science Theater 3000*'s Cambot not find the words to describe it, but the film made Ed Wood's *Plan Nine from Outer Space* look like *Gone with the Wind*.) Shot for twelve thousand dollars in six days, it was directed, after a fashion, by the infamous William "One-Shot" Beaudine, who had helmed many of the Bowery Boys comedies at Monogram and had directed the *Jiggs and Maggie* series that starred Joe Yule Sr.

On an early morning in March 1953, the Duke, as he was called, went to Rooney's Woodland Hills house, having decided to cold-call Mickey. Duke, a five-foot tall, cigar-chomping, fast-talking, gravel-voiced hondler, was stricken with polio as a baby—well before, he always said, "it was popular." His leprechaun personality was a compensation for his disability. Part of Duke's charm was his zest for life, despite the Forest Gump leg braces he wore and the two canes that kept him ambulatory—and which once caused comedian Joe E. Lewis to describe him from the stage as "the only man who walks around with his own Erector set." [25]

In *Life Is Too Short*, Mickey recalled, "Maurice Duke, a lean, keen guy who knocked on my door one day, then limped into my living room . . . wanted to help me. I dared him to try. For five years, he did a helluva job for me." [26]

The Duke was a Hollywood legend, boasting connections with the likes of Frank Sinatra. His story was recently told in a nostalgic documentary made by his daughter, Fredrica Duke, appropriately titled, *Fuck 'Em*. Fredde Duke told us, "My dad always loved Mickey, but he was also realistic about him. He always said, 'Mickey is a real prick, but a talented prick.' My dad would always believe in Rooney and called him one of the five great actors of all time." [27]

Duke also represented the film comedian Huntz Hall, one of the original Dead End Kids before he became forever known as Sach in the Bowery Boys films at Monogram. Hall was a longtime drinking buddy with Mickey. An example of the Duke's escapades, and why Mickey liked him, comes out of a great story the Duke told in *Fuck 'Em* about how he tried to get Milton Berle to hire Hall to guest-star on his television show, *The Texaco Star Theater.* "Miltie didn't want to hire Hall because he reputedly had a bigger cock, and he was jealous," the Duke tells his interviewer in the documentary *Fuck 'Em.*

> You see, Milt was proud of having the biggest schlong in the business. He blamed not hiring Hall since he couldn't remember his lines, which wasn't true. He did many films, but bottom line, he was jealous of him. When I saw Milt having dinner with Sinatra at Danny's Hideaway in New York, I told the story to Frank and told him that Berle wouldn't put Huntz on the show because he's jealous . . . Sinatra said, "Why would Miltie be jealous of Hall?" And I explained it to him . . . Frank then put it to Milton, "If Hall's cock is bigger, will you put him on the show?" and he agreed. Frank was in stitches. So Sinatra set up a black-tie affair at his apartment at the Essex House and invited all of the hoi polloi in New York City. At the party, Frank had Milton and Huntz drop their shorts, and I measured their dicks with my cane with a marker. Milt was fuming when I declared that Huntz won the cock face-off. He screamed that I measured wrong and cheated by measuring Hall from his asshole and him from his balls. However, in the end, Milt honored the bet and hired Hall for his show."

Duke's daughter, Fredde, spoke extensively about her father's relationship to Rooney. "My father and Mickey chased broads together. They fucked the most gorgeous girls in Hollywood despite their both being extremely short and my father walked with two canes from polio. Mickey truly lived like a rock star. Mickey tried to even come on to my mother, even though my father was his manager. He just did not care." 28

Duke and Mickey's longtime friend June Wilkinson remembered a practical joke Duke played on Mickey:

> Mickey and Duke were in New York to promote *Hey Mulligan* [also known as *The Mickey Rooney Show*], and Rooney was driving Duke crazy. So he told Mickey that Ava was also in New York and was desperate to meet him. I think she had just had one of her breakups with Frank [Sinatra]. Duke found out where she was staying and told Mickey he should go see her and that she wanted him badly, which was not true. When Mickey knocked on Ava's hotel room and she opened the door and saw it was him, she freaked out. She went berserk. He ran for his life and was rather embarrassed.29

The third and final film for Columbia, *Drive a Crooked Road*, again reunited the Rooney team of director Dick Quine, writer Blake Edwards, and Jonie Taps as producer. Mickey received the same $75,000 he was paid for his first two Columbia efforts. Unlike *Sound Off* and *All Ashore*, however, *Drive a Crooked Road* was an action film about auto racing.

> Writer Austin "Rocky" Kalish told us, "Mickey never failed to impress me and he was always a thinking actor. I did a scene with him and he's crying in the scene, which the

script called for. And I was sitting there behind the camera crying along with him because he was so convincing. In the scene he was working with a girl named Diane Foster. And he was doing the crying bit. Mickey took Diane by the arm and gently moved her to a slightly different spot on the set. The tears continued to flow, however. And there was never a stop in the dialogue. I thought to myself, "Gee, he hasn't done that before—why did he move her?" And then I realized what had happened. She had gotten out of her "key" light, and he was putting her back in it. The facility of the guy is staggering." [30]

Blake Edwards, who went on to become a legendary director of such film classics as the *Pink Panther* movies, Truman Capote's *Breakfast at Tiffany's*, *Days of Wine and Roses*, *10*, directed the second unit for the first time in this film that turned out to be a modest success and again showcased Mickey's talents as a dramatic actor.

With a strong personal manager in place, Mickey felt recharged and ready for a return to the limelight. Duke was an early master at packaging projects. (Others, such as Lee Rich, Aaron Spelling, Joel Silver, and today's Scott Rudin followed the blueprint Duke created.) His plan was to get Mickey back in the limelight, and what better vehicle than the burgeoning television industry? It had worked for fading film stars such as Lucille Ball, Fred MacMurray, Robert Young, and Donna Reed. Duke felt that Mickey was a natural for a situation comedy. Nick Sevano had earlier structured a deal with CBS for Mickey, creating two pilots that never sold. The first was based on the life of Daniel Boone, with Mickey playing the legendary frontiersman, which is hard to fathom when you think of flintlock-toting tall-in-the-saddle Fess Parker in the role. The second failed pilot was based on the files of the Tokyo police, called *Dateline Tokyo*, with Mickey as a police detective. CBS put up thirty thousand dollars to produce each pilot, but was unable to find a sponsor.

This time, however, rather than turn Mickey into something he was not, Duke smartly decided to tailor a vehicle that utilized Mickey's comedic talents. He called his Columbia team of Richard Quine and Blake Edwards, and along with Mickey they tossed around ideas for a series concept in the same realm as *I Love Lucy*. They cast Mickey as a show business wannabe who works as a page at the fictional TV network "IBC" while waiting for his big break. Originally titled *For the Love of Mike*—the show was retitled *Hey, Mulligan* when it was discovered that announcer Mike Wallace had already registered that title—the story had the thirty-four-year-old Rooney playing Mickey Mulligan, a twenty-three-year-old. Duke worked with William Morris to put the package together and seek out a sponsor, which they found through the Leo Burnett ad agency, which signed on Pillsbury Flour and Jolly Green Giant. NBC quickly bought the project, and it debuted on September 4, 1954. However, it received a terrible slot, on Saturday nights at 8:00 p.m., opposite the popular *The Jackie Gleason Show* featuring "The Honeymooners," "Joe the Bartender," "The Poor Soul," and "Reginald Van Gleason III," sketches that were some of the most popular pieces of comedy in the 1950s. NBC and the Leo Burnett agency were hopeful that Mickey's strong name might put a dent in the Gleason juggernaut's ratings and give it a chance to survive.

The terms were good for Mickey and Duke. Mickey would be guaranteed thirty-three weeks at $3,500 per week, with options and ownership of the show. The exposure would be wonderful for his career, and Mickey was very optimistic because he had strong writers such as Edwards and Quine, veteran Leslie Martinson as the director, a powerful character and story foundation, and a seasoned supporting cast that included old character actors Regis Toomey and Alan Mowbray, comic Joey Forman, and even a young Angie Dickinson.

The show was critically acclaimed. The reviewers loved the writing, Mickey, and the plot's premise. Mickey was in his milieu, physical comedy, and Edwards and Quine knew his rhythms and could write dialogue directly to them. But while the ratings started strong from viewers wanting to see Mickey in a television role, in the face of the Great One's domination, they rapidly started to sink. Duke recalled, "By the tenth episode, Gleason was getting a forty-nine share, we were getting a seven. I think only Mickey's mother was the only one watching." [31]

Arthur Marx told us, Gleason himself was a fan of the show. After he watched it, he would phone Mickey, whom he called Spider, and say, "I want you to know, Spider, that one loyal American watched your show," and then he'd laugh and hang up. Despite guest stars such as Milton Berle, *Hey, Mulligan* remained in the ratings basement. Yet it's also the case that Mickey put very little interest in the program, concentrating on his horse racing. He left its direction up to Duke, Quine, and Edwards. He'd show up, read his lines, and then skip out. He once snubbed Leo Burnett and the Pillsbury executives when they visited the set. Yet they still loved him.

Here's why the show failed in spite of its support from the sponsors: An element of success in television, especially in the 1950s and '60s, when the sponsors controlled programming, was to appease the ad agencies and their clients. Desi Arnaz was brilliant at this, in creating Desilu and working with, acquiring, and keeping sponsors for the production company's programs. He was a master at schmoozing sponsors and at giving legendary parties. Danny Thomas's business partner, Sheldon Leonard, was a world-class salesman, too, once saving the *The Dick Van Dyke Show* from extinction by charming Procter and Gamble. Television was an advertising business, as network television is today, and stroking the egos of the sponsors was an integral part of the game. As depicted in the AMC series *Mad Men*, it was the ad agencies and sponsors who decided which programs would survive. A program could be very successful, such as *The Bob Cummings Show* (also known as *Love That Bob*), produced by George Burns's McCadden Productions, yet still be axed if the sponsor disliked the star (or, in the case of Cummings, the star's wife).

This was where Maurice Duke could shine. He had the ability to schmooze and sell. In his daughter's documentary, Duke says that above all, he loved making deals. Deals made him feel alive. However, Mickey had zero tact, lacked the ability to schmooze, and refused to stroke others' ego because his own overinflated ego got in the way. Thus, he was poison when it came to dealing with sponsors or studio heads or producers or the power brokers themselves.

Perhaps one of the best examples of Mickey's complete lack of interpersonal skills and social sensitivity comes from his good friend and off-and-on business adviser Donald Trump, who invested in Mickey's musical *The Will Rogers Follies*. Donald Trump told us about his being on a very exclusive golf course with Mickey and two very wealthy friends, both of whom had the ability to back Mickey in a Broadway play. When the two wealthy friends began whispering to each other, Mickey became irate and read them the riot act for disrespecting the legendary golf club. Both wanted to leave, until Trump convinced them that it was just Mickey being Mickey. Rooney lacked any filter, and spent a lifetime burning important bridges with his lack of tact. "I greatly respect Mickey's great talent. However, his anger issues sometime got the better of him," recalled Trump in our interview.

While the ratings for *Hey, Mulligan* were sagging because the Great One ruled Saturday nights, the sponsors liked the show and were willing to relocate it for the next season to a more favorable slot on NBC. Peter Jurow, the president of Pillsbury, key sponsor of the program, was a huge Rooney fan. Yet Mickey's inability to play the television sponsor game ultimately led to the show's demise.

In April 1955, Pillsbury told the Burnett ad agency and NBC that it wanted to renew *Hey, Mulligan* for another season. To discuss the renewal, Pillsbury invited Mickey and Duke to attend the anniversary celebration of the company at its headquarters in Le Seur, Minnesota. They would also participate in a celebrity golf tournament in the area. The tournament would include the foursome of Peter Jurow; Leo Burnett, who'd created the Pillsbury Dough Boy and the Jolly Green Giant; Gen. Lucius Clay, commander of the U.S. forces in Europe; and Mickey. (Duke would tag along in the golf cart, but could not play because of his physical handicap.) The event turned into an epic disaster.

Maurice Duke recalled how Mickey treated one of his sponsors, a huge fan:

> Before the tournament, the president of Pillsbury, Peter Jurow, wanted to meet with Mickey and I [*sic*]. He had this elegant office that had a map of the country with colored pins on it. He told us the colors showed where Pillsbury's sales were strong and the others were areas where sales needed to be picked up. He said—and I swear this to be the fucking truth—"You can stay with us forever, Mick, if you can pick up the places where we're weaker." Mickey got real agitated when he said this and said, "I'm not supposed to sell your product, Jurow. You hired me to be an actor!" I swear, the color drained from Jurow's face. I knew that we had blown the show right at that minute. I hit Mickey with my cane under the table. I tried everything to play it as Mickey just joking around. But he really pissed off this guy and there was no going back. I was hoping that we could save ourselves at the golf tournament. There was a huge crowd cheering Mickey. Mickey again seemed annoyed. He was unhappy with the slow play and he was cursing up a storm. He was pissed at his poor play, as well. Now he's

playing with this powerful group and he is treating these guys like they were sacks of shit. On the fourth hole, he takes me aside and says, "Let's get out of here, Duke. This is boring. I can't stand these guys." So I make an excuse that Mickey is having problems with an ulcer and he just threw his clubs down and left.[32]

So that night there is a huge celebration that was held at the Pillsbury mansion, where Mickey is the honored guest. I mean there was a huge orchestra, great food; the booze is flowing. Everyone is there, all their executives, the press, the Pillsbury family—everyone. Mrs. Pillsbury, this elegant older broad—I mean she had the jewels, the dress; she looked the part—like Margaret Dumont. She just loves Mickey. She tells him how much she loved Andy Hardy, his Judy Garland movies, and he just looks annoyed. She still likes him. I pulled him aside and told him to be nice to everyone and save the show. Mickey just was agitated and drinking a bit . . . so Walter Pillsbury, the son who ran the company, is talking to Mickey and calling him Charlie . . . sort of a slang. Now Mickey is really pissed off and tells me loudly, "Let's get the fuck out of here." I tell him that we need to charm them and we could save the show . . . But Mickey is ready to blow . . . So after dinner, Walter Pillsbury grabs Mickey by his lapel and pulls him toward the piano. He tells Mickey, "It's time to do your act, Charlie." Mickey gives him a look, and Pillsbury says, "We want you to sing and dance for us." Mickey looks at him and said, "Sorry, I don't feel up to it." Pillsbury looks at Mickey and says, "What do you mean you don't feel up to it? You're talking to Walter Pillsbury. We own you, Charlie." That was the last straw, and Mickey just exploded. The place got very quiet; all eyes were on us. Mickey screamed and said,

"No one owns me. Let's go Duke. I can't stand these bunch of crows another minute." We left and, of course, the show was canceled the next week.[33]

The show finished its run on June 7, 1955.

But the Duke had work lined up for Mickey: he set him up with his friend Herbert Yates and Yates's studio, Republic, for a feature, *The Twinkle in God's Eye*, with Mickey in a change-of-pace role as a reverend bringing religion to the west. Mickey was toned down and far more low-key opposite Hugh O'Brian and his pal Red Barry. Along with a small salary, Duke negotiated some profit-sharing points. In fact, from the start of his tenure with Rooney, he'd been hard at work to further Mickey's career. In 1946, he formed Mickey Rooney Productions Inc., to create properties for Mickey to star in and produce. They quickly made a deal with Yates to film *Jaguar* (1956), which starred Sabu, the Elephant Boy, for which they received both a producing fee and a profit-sharing deal. Duke had also previously set up a ten-week deal for Mickey to headline at the Flamingo hotel for the summer of 1953. It was a successful gig. Mickey was paid ten thousand dollars weekly, and the show was held over for an extra two weeks. Propitiously, he and his entourage ended up on the same plane with writer James Michener, the novelist who wrote *Tales of the South Pacific*, *Hawaii*, and *Centennial*, who had just sold the theatrical rights to his book *The Bridges at Toko-Ri* for a feature film.

"Michener took a liking to Mickey and said he would see to it that a part was written into the script for him," recalled Duke. "It was a small part, and Mickey had to take short money for it, but he wanted to be in a major movie again."

The Bridges at Toko-Ri, in the tradition of *All Quiet on the Western Front*, exposes the futility of war. Both William Holden and Fredric March give outstanding performances; Grace Kelly, underplaying her role as Holden's wife and then widow, is as beautiful as she ever was; and Mickey Rooney is strong as cocky Mike Forney, a Korean War helicopter jockey whose talent is rescuing downed navy pilots. Mickey received the strongest reviews in years. Bosley Crowther, on January 2, 1955, in the *New York Times*, called him a "pint-sized tornado." The film placed Mickey in a new light: as the character actor in a part written especially for him, a tragic hero who sacrifices his life to save the downed navy pilot played by Holden, himself sacrificed by bureaucratic war planners on a futile bombing mission. After the skein of low-budget films noir that Mickey had performed in, James Michener's *The Bridges at Toko-Ri* showcased just how Mickey could underplay a role to great effect. *Bridges* was a standout film during a time when Mickey was struggling to find the roles that would allow him to stretch his talents, to depict serious dramatic characters instead of middle-aged guys bumbling through life.

In the 1950s, Mickey was also on the lookout for his next mate. By now, he had moved on from Martha, Tempest Storm, and others, but remained on the lookout for wife number four—and he found her on a golf course. One of Mickey's passions in the 1950s had become golf. He could often be seen at the nearby driving range in Woodland Hills with a bucket of balls, mindlessly stroking them into the net. When he met his next spouse, he had just returned from a twenty-one-day USO tour of Korea and was looking for action. That was when he spied, in the next stall at Woodland Hills, a tall, striking redhead who closely resembled Ava, practicing her swing.

The beautiful redhead was twenty-three-year-old Elaine Mahnken, born Thelma Elaine Mahnken on January 10, 1930, a Southern California native who had been homecoming queen at Compton Community College. She had just returned from Montana, where she'd moved with her now-ex-husband, her high school sweetheart, Dan Ducich, a former college basketball player at Compton and Utah State. After

Ducich was sent to prison for armed robbery, Elaine divorced him and returned to live with her mother in Woodland Hills, right near Mickey's home, where she hoped to create a new life for herself.

She had started modeling when she was fifteen, including posing nude for some calendars for Theda and Emerson Hall, a husband-and-wife team of photographers known for crisp, vibrant color photographs at a time when the technique was difficult and rare; the Halls were used by almost all the film studios in Hollywood for many years.

Watching the redhead in the next stall take her swing, Mickey was immediately entranced by her, and later wrote, "I flipped for her—her body, her backswing, even her little dog, a Maltese terrier named Pepy." [34] Elaine had grown up watching the Andy Hardy films and, when she and Mickey met, she realized that despite his small stature and now-paunchy appearance, he was still the same Mickey Rooney she'd admired as a child.

"When he was doing the Andy Hardy series—I was just a kid then—my whole family adored Mickey," Elaine told Arthur Marx. "I felt I already knew Mickey when I met him. Also I was quite in awe of his musical talent. While we were dating he used to sit down and play the piano at his house and he'd make up lyrics, and they were beautiful. And I thought, 'This man must have a beautiful soul.' I fell in love with that talent. I felt [that] together we could be good, though I was not in love with him. But that didn't seem to bother him and he kept saying, 'You can learn to love me.' I was never madly in love with him, but I loved him in a particular way." [35]

Since her return home, Elaine, who had been under contract by Warner Bros. for a couple of years as a teen and had trained under acting coach Sylvia Rosenstein, was working nights as a carhop at the Dolores Drive-In, in the Valley, and auditioning during the day. Although Mickey later claimed in his 1965 autobiography that he was unaware of Elaine's "past"—her former husband had Mafia connections and was heavily in debt to the mob—she denied this to Arthur Marx.

"Mickey knew more about me than I knew about him . . . I certainly did not know he was in any financial trouble. When we were dating he used to drive me down Ventura Boulevard and say to me as he pointed out the car window, 'I own this side of the street.' It sounded like he owned all of the San Fernando Valley, he did act the big shot for my benefit," said Elaine.[36]

For thirty days, Mickey proposed to Elaine every night (reminiscent of his courtship of Ava). For thirty days, Elaine politely told Mickey that she wasn't in love with him. Eventually he wore her down, and on their thirtieth date, on November 15, 1952, at Don the Beachcomber, Elaine said yes. Mickey chartered a plane and flew that night to Las Vegas, along with his friends Gene and Sylvia Kahan, and married her at the Wee Kirk o'the Heather wedding chapel, which still exists. The wedding license was for Joseph Yule Jr. and Elaine Ducich, because Mickey had still not changed his name legally, even though he'd been using Rooney since his days at Universal. Elaine, who was still using her name from her previous marriage, gave her occupation as "model." They registered at the El Rancho casino/hotel as Mr. and Mrs. Joseph Yule. Mickey was thirty-two and she was twenty-three. It was a little over one year since his divorce from Martha.

The marriage was revealed on November 20, 1952, when a photograph appeared in the *Los Angeles Examiner* of Mickey carrying Elaine off the chartered plane at the Burbank airport, and was accompanied by the quip "I think they knew me there. Maybe they recognized the rice marks on my face."

The couple moved into Mickey's Woodland Hills home. "It was a small house—not the kind of place you'd expect to find Mickey living in—but a nice house in a typical Valley neighborhood," Elaine recalled. "Nice living room, nice master bedroom, a servant's room, a nice yard with a swimming pool."[37]

She stated that although Mickey loved to live high, buying Jaguars, having an extensive wardrobe, a "man-servant" named Arthur Baker and other extravagances, he owed money to countless creditors. She claimed that she helped straighten out his finances. "I handled the finances for about two and a half years. Finally, the government was paid, all our bills were paid. And I took the envelope that contained all of our unpaid bills. And said, 'Look Mickey, no more debts.' And what was the thanks I got? Two weeks later Mickey went up to Vegas to play a nightclub date. He went to the tables and lost fifty grand, just like that. We were back in the hole again. When I heard that I threw up my hands and said, 'No more. From now on he could take care of his own finances.'"[38]

Elaine brought her own baggage to the marriage, according to what she revealed to Arthur Marx. Her father, Fred Mahnken, needed a place to live, so she had him move into the guest bedroom and go on payroll doing "errands" for the Rooneys. Also, Mickey found out that Elaine was "meeting" her ex-husband. She claimed he owed money to the mob in Vegas and needed cash to repay them, and he needed it right away because they were putting the heat on him. She pleaded with Mickey to lend him the money, "as one human being to another," which he refused. Ducich also put the arm on Mickey for a life-saving loan, but Mickey turned him down. Ducich, though trying to stay out of sight until he could scrape up the dough, was eventually visited in Butte, Montana, on June 25, 1954, by a couple of button men working for Mickey Cohen, who put two rounds in the back of his head, charging off the debt family style. It wasn't the first time the mob had shouldered in on Mickey's life, and it wouldn't be the last time fatal gunshots whizzed by him, too close for comfort.

The pseudonymous Mrs. Smith told us, "She [Elaine] didn't give a shit about Mick. She saw him as a sugar daddy who might be able to get her in the movies . . . Mickey tried to keep her happy . . . [H]e bought her a vacation home in Lake Arrowhead, a new house in Studio City, and all kind of toys, like a speedboat, clothes, servants. She lived like a queen. But Mickey gets bored easily," his longtime mistress admitted. "They lived separate lives, and Mickey was on to new girls, gambling and living . . . well, living like Mickey. She was living in Lake Arrowhead and partying . . . I'm also pretty sure she was fucking her ex-husband, who was a hood and ex-con, and [she] was giving him money before he was killed. Mickey was constantly whining to me about her. He just dreaded another divorce." [39]

Elaine told *Parade* magazine in January 1967, "I gave the marriage everything I had. I tried everything Mickey suggested. After years and years I'd had enough. Living with Mickey is no bed of roses. Six wives can't all be wrong." Confronted with Rooney's version of the settlement, claiming she got a $125,000 mansion, a summer home, all their furniture, a motorboat, a Chrysler, assorted jewelry, and $21,000 a year in alimony for ten years, Elaine says:

> Mickey's always in hot water, and I'm not going to downgrade him with a recitation of what marriage to him was really like. But I'll tell you this: After being married to him for eight years, I'm marriage-shy. I've had half a dozen proposals in the past few years, but I turn chicken, especially when the proposals come from actors. I'm sure some actors make good husbands, but after Mickey, I'm afraid to take the chance. As for my divorce settlement, Mickey let his imagination run riot on that. I got a $75,000 house in Studio City, with a $45,000 mortgage. The reason I have to work now, doing bits here, feature parts there, is that I still have to pay that mortgage off. I don't live in that house. I rent it to meet the payments. The summer home at Lake Arrowhead—the same thing. Mickey's business manager used to give each of us an allowance. I put mine into a piece of mountain property. He put his into horses. The Chrysler I got was eight years old. All the jewelry consisted of my wedding ring, my engagement ring, and a watch. The

$21,000 a year for ten years—that's a joke, too. I got it for one year. Then it was cut back to $500 a month. It's been more than a year now since I've gotten a single payment.

With four marriages under his belt and still looking around, Mickey became the constant butt of comedians' monologues. To deflect the damage, he laughed with them, and once quipped to Johnny Carson on *The Tonight Show*, "Always get married early in the morning. That way, if it doesn't work out, you haven't wasted a whole day."

His critically acclaimed role in *The Bridges at Toko-Ri* unfortunately did not open up new opportunities, even though the *New York Times*'s Bosley Crowther, writing on January 21, 1955, was very impressed with the power of Mickey's performance. In his quest to obtain quality film roles in higher-budget movies, the offers for Mickey were few and far between. With the failure of *Hey, Mulligan*, and because Mickey had burned bridges in television when he snubbed Pillsbury and legendary ad man Leo Burnett, he was considered toxic to sponsors, and the ad agencies wanted none of him.

"Mickey was essentially blacklisted by Leo Burnett for many years from television," recalled Norman Brokaw, former chairman of William Morris. "Those guys ran the game, and if they hated you, you became a pariah. It was impossible for us to package anything with Mickey attached to it." [40] Brokaw also noted that Mickey tested poorly in his Q score, the measurement of the familiarity and appeal of a celebrity. The higher the Q score, the more highly regarded the item or person is among the group familiar with him or her. Due to the broken marriages and negative publicity, sponsors were reluctant to attach Rooney to any program. While he made guest appearances on television shows, an ongoing series with him was not considered again for nearly ten years.

"Mickey just fucked himself with the crap he pulled at the Pillsbury event," recalled Maurice Duke. "No matter how hard I tried to sell him, it was always a dead end. We picked up decent money in Vegas, but he blew most of it at the tables or the track. There was always an audience that wanted to see Mickey live, so we could always line up gigs." [41] Elaine recalled, "There was not one year I could remember [between 1952 and 1958] that Mickey made less than $150,000." [42]

Thus, Mickey relied upon personal appearances and cheap B movies for the remainder of the 1950s. Starting in 1955, with a couple of exceptions, he worked mainly for the Poverty Row studios Republic and Allied Artists (formerly Monogram), for indie producer Albert Zugsmith, and for RKO. The next few years were loaded with films, among them: *The Twinkle in God's Eye* (1955), at Republic; *Francis in the Haunted House* (1956), at Universal; *The Bold and the Brave* (1956), at RKO; *Magnificent Roughnecks* (1956), at Allied Artists; *Baby Face Nelson* (1957), with Albert Zugsmith; *A Nice Little Bank That Should Be Robbed* (1958), with Rank; *The Big Operator* (1959), with Zugsmith; *The Last Mile* (1959), at United Artists; and *Platinum High School* (1960), with Zugsmith.

Legendary writer Austin "Rocky" Kalish, who later wrote for *All in the Family*, *My Three Sons*, and *Family Affair*, among other television series, recalled, "Albert Zugsmith was a cheap, quickie producer that made Roger Corman look like David Selznick. He had movies such as *The Girl in the Kremlin*, *Female on the Beach*, and *High School Confidential*. I wrote one movie for him called *The Private Lives of Adam and Eve*, with Mamie Van Doren and Mickey, who played the devil. Zugsmith told me he decided to make the film when his thirteen-year-old son liked and approved the story. A real schmuck." [43]

The couple of notable exceptions came as a result of a reprieve from Mickey's old pal Dick Quine: to appear in the Jack Lemmon comedy *Operation Mad Ball* in 1957 and an attempt to resurrect Andy Hardy for MGM in *Andy Hardy Comes Home* in 1958. A popular comedy, *Operation Mad Ball* in particular showcased Mickey's ability to interact with younger comedians, such as Jack Lemon, who did not come out of burlesque.

By 1958, Mickey's sons Mickey Jr. and Timmy, from wife number two, Betty Jane, were now in their teens. In 1955 they were appearing with Paul Petersen, Annette Funicello, and other child performers on *The Mickey Mouse Club*. Their stepfather, Betty Jane's second husband, Buddy Baker, was the musical director at Disney, and had a close friendship with Walt.

Mickey Jr. bore little resemblance to his father, unlike younger brother Timmy. As a child, he wasn't button cute like Tim; he was taller and more somber. Like his father and mother, he was gifted in music. According to the website the Original Mickey Mouse Club Show:

> It's hard to gauge Mickey [Jr.]'s qualities as a young performer, because he appeared in so few skits. He was in the roll call for the Mouseketeers' debut at Disneyland. The only sequence with him readily available today is "Circus Day," where he and fellow short-timer Paul Petersen take part in acrobatics. This sort of action rough-and-tumble seemed to suit both Paul and Mickey better than musical variety. If there had been more of it to keep them involved, they might have lasted longer on the show. As it was, Paul was dismissed sometime after July 17, 1955, to be replaced by Tim Rooney. Timmy was the second-youngest Mouseketeer. Mickey Jr. and brother Tim were themselves dismissed a few weeks later, after they went into the paint department and mixed a lot of different colors together. This, combined with the fact that neither boy was proficient at dancing and that Mickey was a serious lad who did not readily smile, may have contributed to their dismissal.

The brothers were replaced in early August 1955 by Ronnie
Steiner, a professional tap dancer, and Dickie Dodd.[44]

Paul Petersen told the authors, "Both Mickey and Timmy were
talented musicians. Their father was never around, and he hardly saw
them. He was certainly an absentee father."[45]

After leaving *The Mickey Mouse Club*, Tim was set to move on to
other jobs, but at ten years old, in 1957, he was stricken with polio.
He was paralyzed for two years, and spent some time in rehabilitative
therapy afterward, so it was 1961 before he was able to resume his
acting career. He bore an amazing resemblance to his father in his
teenage years, less so in later life.

When MGM fell on hard times in the late 1950s, it decided to try
to recapture its glory days by reissuing new versions of its classic films
of the 1930s and '40s. However, the times had changed. Lewis Stone,
who had played Judge Hardy, had passed away in 1953, and his absence would make the cast seem incomplete. Mickey tried to persuade
Ann Rutherford to return as Polly Benedict, but she refused.

Ann Rutherford told Arthur Marx, "I said, 'Mickey, in the first
place, very few people grow up to marry their childhood sweethearts.
So that gets rid of me right away. And in the second place, you should
not come back as Judge Hardy [as the proposed script called for]. You
should come back as Andy Hardy. Andy would not grow up to be a
judge. Andy would grow up to be Bob Hope or Red Skelton or a great
radio performer.'"[46]

When MGM came to producer Aaron "Red" Doff about attempt-
ing to resurrect the Hardy series, Mickey jumped at the chance. Benny
Thau, one of Mayer's former cardinals, had taken over the studio from
Dore Schary. He wanted his girlfriend, actress Patricia Breslin, to play
Andy Hardy's wife, Jane. Breslin, who had starred in *The People's
Choice* TV series, with Rooney's old pal Jackie Cooper, and opposite

William Shatner in the classic *Twilight Zone* episode "Nick of Time," later became the wife of Cleveland Browns owner, Art Modell. Breslin told the authors, "Mickey was always in control of everything. He was hoping that we could start a new Hardy family series, but it was old hat by then. It was a real rush job, but Mickey was in great spirits to visit with his old friends from the past. His old pal Sig Frohlich was always at his side." [47]

Director Howard Koch told Arthur Marx, "On the sound stage next door, Paul Newman and Elizabeth Taylor were shooting *Cat on a Hot Tin Roof*, and here's Mickey, who'd been one of the world's biggest stars, and the fellow responsible for keeping Metro in the black all those years, when he was a kid, and no one even knew he was alive. Nobody came on the stage to wish us any luck. Nobody sent flowers. Nothing." [48]

Teddy Rooney recalled, "My dad desperately wanted to direct the movie, but they didn't trust him. Eventually, they got Howard Koch to direct." [49] Teddy costarred with his father in this Andy Hardy sequel and called getting to appear on-screen with his father one of the high points of his life.

Andy Hardy Comes Home had a budget of $313,000, which was low even by late 1950s standards for a major studio release. It also had only an eleven-day shooting schedule. While Mickey had high hopes for it, when it was released the film ended up being the lower half of a double bill. In it, Mickey Rooney returns in the starring role of Andy Hardy, while Fay Holden, Cecilia Parker, and Sara Haden reprise their original roles as mother Emily Hardy, sister Marian Hardy, and Aunt Milly. A portrait of actor Lewis Stone (1879–1953) as Judge Hardy is featured prominently in the film. *Andy Hardy Comes Home* also contains brief clips from some of the original Hardy family films. In MGM publicity materials, *Andy Hardy Comes Home*, which was released eleven years after the last Hardy family film, was described as "a continuation" rather than another in the series. However, in the closing credits, a title card reads: "To Be Continued." The *Variety* review states that MGM intended to re-embark on the Hardy series. According to MGM records, the movie earned $400,000 U.S. and Canadian box office and $210,000 elsewhere, delivering a loss to the studio of $5,000.

As the 1950s wound down, change was once again in the air for Rooney. By 1957, Maurice Duke, despite Rooney's self-destructive behavior in television and onstage, had continued to find Mickey well-paying gigs. But now he was tired of Mickey's antics. Unlike Sam Stiefel, Duke turned out to be of great help to Mickey throughout this rough period, keeping him afloat. Although most of the projects he found for him were second rate, Duke also scored Rooney particularly lucrative appearances in Las Vegas. In 1955, he teamed Mickey with his *Hey, Mulligan* sidekick, comic Joey Forman, to create a perfect vehicle to showcase Mickey's talents. Yet things did not turn out as Duke hoped:

> I booked Mickey into the Riviera when it first opened. I nego-tiated a pretty good fucking salary for him, around twenty grand per week [actually $17,500]. They were desperate, as they had used Hildegarde and actor Jeff Chandler, and they bombed. I hired comic Ben Lessy, who wrote great mate-rial for him and mounted a first-rate show. Mickey was a smash. I mean they had fucking lines to get into his show. They held him there for four weeks and wanted more. My old pal, Gus Greenbaum, ran the hotel and loved Mickey. Gus was one of Bugsy Siegel's childhood friends. So Gus calls me up and he is fuming. He is screaming and told me to get down to Vegas. Mickey had blown over fifty grand at the craps table and was going berserk. It seems Mickey during his show is fucking stoned and announced he was retiring. He makes a speech onstage and says, "I'm going to

retire to a farm and just take care of the cows and chickens and the horses. And all of you can go fuck yourselves." Now every newspaper picks this up and the headlines were "Mickey Rooney Retires." Now, he has this lucrative gig and he is really pissing off the wrong guys. I mean he's lucky he's not in a body cast or buried in the desert. I come down and make a deal with the bosses to get some of the money back for Mick. But Mickey is nowhere to be found. He flew back to Los Angeles. So these wiseguys are fucking pissed. They had wanted him back, as they were moving him to Moe Dalitz's Dunes to replace Wally Cox, who had bombed. Now he's being paid twenty Gs per week. He tells me, "I'm fucking fed up." I said, "How can you be fed up for twenty grand?" I had to beg Mickey to return to do the shows with Elaine [Rooney]'s help. I told him that I just manage you, but I have a big house in Beverly Hills, money in the bank, and you are flat busted—and you're retiring? I reminded him that he was making more for one week in Vegas than he did on some of those *ferkakta* films.[50]

As a postscript, one year later, during Thanksgiving 1958, the Riviera's boss, Gus Greenbaum, the man Mickey spurned and the one who took the blame for Mickey's actions, went to Scottsdale with his wife to get away from his hotel/casino for a few days. On December 3, 1958, the Greenbaums' housekeeper, Pearl, showed up for work at their house and found what was left of Gus and his wife, Bess. Both their heads had been hacked off and left neatly in plastic bags right next to their bodies. As he skirted on the edge, Mickey was leaving bodies, as well as wives and children, in his wake—a fact not lost on Duke.

Mickey had a long history of interaction with the underworld. His degenerate gambling habits initially put him in direct contact with figures such as Mickey Cohen and Benny Siegel. As early as the start of the 1940s, he owed debts that had resulted from his gaming losses to various bookies and loan sharks. MGM knew about this, and one of the duties of his MGM shadow and handler Les Peterson was paying off his markers with advances, actually loans, from MGM. Friends such as Sidney Miller and Billy Barty recounted tales of his legendary gambling and his owing money to racketeers. His friends Marcy and Wally Cassell recalled his skipping out on losses at the Las Vegas gaming tables, leaving legendary hoods such as Moe Dalitz and Gus Greenbaum angered, and considering consequences for Mick. Greenbaum, who ran the Flamingo for Bugsy Siegel and Meyer Lansky, was particularly on the hook for Mickey's debts. These were not street corner candy store bookies Rooney was trifling with.

Mickey's managers and partners throughout the years constantly tried to keep him out of harm's way. First, Sam Stiefel, who through his theatrical business, had worked with mobsters such as Al Capone, paid off Rooney's debts for almost ten years—which Mickey repaid with interest, leaving him nearly broke. Then Maurice Duke, who booked him in Vegas and elsewhere in lucrative gigs, received death threats from Gus Greenbaum and Moe Dalitz when Mickey skipped out on dates and money owed them. Duke eventually left Mickey, after Greenbaum's murder, believing that Mick's antics threatened his family's safety. Red Doff, likewise, was put in a compromising position, and questioned whether the drowning death of his young daughter in a swimming pool was accidental or otherwise. His other daughter, Melody Doff, confirmed to us that her father had had extra duties as Mickey's second with the mob.

By the 1960s, Mickey and his friend actor Dick Wesson, who was also a degenerate gambler, were forced to be both bagmen (debt collectors) for men such as Mickey Cohen in order to reduce the markers they owed. Wesson's daughter, actress Eileen Wesson, recalled tagging along with Rooney and her father on their excursions as debt collectors or to the track. Dan Kessel's memory of Rooney's trip to Vegas to see Howard Hughes suggested that Mick was in fear that the trip was a result of his gaming debt to the mob.

While it was inevitable that an entertainer such as Rooney would be exposed to mobsters, since he worked their clubs in Las Vegas and elsewhere, he exacerbated his involvement with them by being a compulsive gambler. Without a doubt, Mickey for many years was at their mercy. He needed the money from his appearances to support his addiction. Although Mickey was never associated in the public's mind with these racketeers—unlike many entertainers such as Frank Sinatra, Dean Martin, George Raft, and Louis Prima, who were all rumored to have mob connections—his involvement with the Cosa Nostra was a central part of his life for several decades, one that had a strong influence on both his personal and professional life.

And this came to a head onstage in Vegas. For Duke, Mickey's public announcement of retirement was the last straw. Mickey had insulted not only his audience, but also Duke's friend and Moe Dalitz associate Gus Greenbaum. Duke now feared for his own life and the lives of his family. Even though he remained friends with Rooney until his death, he formally removed himself from Mickey's management so he would no longer be blamed for the actor's escapades, especially those involving the mob, to whom Mickey was skating too close, too fast, and on very thin ice. Shortly after that announcement, and the subsequent death of Greenbaum and his wife, the Duke "retired" as Mickey's manager. He told Arthur Marx:

> I just walked up to him one day and I told him I quit . . . There was no particular incident. I just got fed up with him because he does stupid things. He's the greatest actor in the world—or one of the ten best, anyway—but he won't listen to you and he thinks everybody steals from him and blames all of his problems on them. Mickey steals from

himself. Mickey's his own worst enemy. He has a fantasy about making two hundred million a month. He's always going into these crazy enterprises, and losing his money, like "Mickey Rooney Macaroni" and "Soda Pop for Dogs." He goes into anything a promoter gives him a pitch on, but they all flop, and he winds up getting mad at his manager who advised him to stay out of them in the first place.[51]

Stepson Chris Aber recalled, "Mickey listened to every con artist who was going to get him rich quick. Lots of bullshit. I can't tell you how many crazy schemes he put money in. The Mickey Rooney acting schools, restaurants—every crazy idea. And he put his own money in it. I tried to talk him away from these leeches, but sometimes he didn't give a shit what you said. He always did what he wanted. He was a horrible businessperson."[52]

With Duke remaining a friend until his passing in 1996, Mickey now turned to his longtime publicist, Aaron "Red" Doff, to act as his new manager. He had met Doff in the army, where he was a captain and had received both the Purple Heart and Bronze Star. Doff had become a close friend of Mickey, and became his press agent in 1952. Doff, like Mickey, was a former child actor and radio performer.

Melody Doff told us about the forty-plus-year relationship between Mickey and her father: "I think my dad filled every role for Mickey. He was his confidant, manager, press agent, nursemaid . . . He was with him through several wives and tragedies. They had their arguments, but [they'd] always end up back together . . . My dad was with him when his wife was murdered, when he went bankrupt. They had a bond."[53]

By the time he became Rooney's manager, Doff was already a well-known press agent for several singers and musicians, representing Frankie Laine, Liberace, Ray Anthony, Margaret Whiting, Billy Eckstein, the Ames Brothers, Les Paul and Mary Ford, and Doris

Day. He was also the personal manager for Bob Hope sidekick Jerry Colonna. Doff followed in the tradition of Duke in packaging projects that would feature Mickey. For Rooney, he would produce the films *Andy Hardy Comes Home*, *Baby Face Nelson*, *The Big Operator*, *Platinum High School*, *The Private Lives of Adam and Eve*, and *Everything's Ducky*.

"Doff kept everything balanced when I did *The Private Lives of Adam and Eve*," recalled writer Rocky Kalish. "Zugsmith was a prick, and Rooney had his problems. Red kept the peace and kept Rooney under control." [54]

Life was not any easier for Doff than it had been for Duke. Mickey skipped out on shows he'd already been paid for at the Moulin Rouge Theatre in Hollywood. The theater's owner, Frank Sennes, who later ran several Las Vegas showrooms for the mobsters at the Desert Inn, Stardust, and Frontier, sued Rooney and Doff for breach of contract, a suit that was later settled for six thousand dollars. "Sennes never forgot, and [he] blacklisted Mick in Vegas," remembered Sid Miller. [55]

Things went from bad to worse for Mickey at the end of the 1950s. While he did a few TV appearances in the 1950s after the demise of *Hey, Mulligan*, he was still focusing on films and nightclubs. His fall at this time was well illustrated by a disastrously embarrassing appearance on the *Tonight* show that also demonstrated his love-hate relationship with television. In November 1960, Mickey had Doff schedule him for an appearance on *Tonight*, then hosted by Jack Paar. Paar was far different from the hosts who followed him behind the desk at NBC. Unlike Johnny Carson or Jay Leno or even early *Tonight* show host Steve Allen, Paar was confrontational with some of his guests. More a storyteller than a comic, Parr loved the conversation even more than he loved the humor, and he sought out conflict and controversy. He held long-running feuds with television icon Ed Sullivan and columnist Walter Winchell. His guests ranged from the brilliant but controversial conservative commentator and writer William F. Buckley to performers Peter Ustinov, Elsa Maxwell, and the caustic pianist Oscar Levant. Paar became an entertainment juggernaut, generating an almost obsessive fascination and curiosity in the press, public, and among critics about his on-screen comments, feuds, and antics, more than anyone who had ever hosted the show. Paar strove for compelling conversation, and his humor was acerbic, almost a precursor to that of Dave Letterman or Bill Maher on *Real Time*. Under Parr, *Tonight*'s ratings were off the charts, with Paar holding, at times, an unbelievable 80 percent share. What happened on Paar's *Tonight* was the fodder for conversations around breakfast tables and office water coolers for weeks across the country.

Twice a year, Paar went on location in Los Angeles. When he scheduled appearances in Los Angeles in December 1959, Mickey called and booked himself on the show.

Paar recalled to Arthur Marx, "I had never met Mickey Rooney . . . He was a legend to me, of course . . . Several times on the 'Tonight Show' when we asked a guest who [*sic*] they considered to be the best motion picture actor who had ever lived, it would usually be Mickey Rooney or James Mason. When James Mason was on the show and asked that question of the best actor ever, he replied, 'Mickey Rooney.'" [56]

Dick Cavett (at the time, one of Jack's writers for the show) explained that in the lead-up to Mickey's *Tonight* appearance, Paar was lying in wait for Mickey, as he did with many of his guests. In order to position Mickey for the verbal kill shot, Paar had asked Cavett to script responses, quips, that Paar could fire back once he got into it with Mickey. Paar, Cavett said, was more of a radio interviewer than he was a comedian, and he liked to have scripted material ready that would allow him to set up a guest with a pointed question and then knock the guest off balance or push him out of his comfort zone. If the guest came back with any hostility, Paar was ready with his own comeback—again, lines Cavett had written for him. And that's exactly the trap Paar set for Mickey.[57]

On the night he was to appear with Paar, Rooney had a few drinks before the show with his then wife Barbara Ann Thomason (stage name Carolyn Mitchell). He wasn't drunk, though: Mickey's having a few drinks was like most folks' having a couple of glasses of water. Although Paar had wanted to have lunch with Mickey, Mickey said he preferred meeting Paar on the show. Rooney even refused to schmooze with Paar in the green room, protocol for celebrity guests and their hosts, an opportunity for them to touch antennae before a show begins. When Rooney came out onstage, therefore, many believed that Paar, who'd been snubbed by his guest before the show, was especially aggressive, as if he were hunting bear. Cavett told us that Paar was looking for a fight. The writer explained that when facing off against Paar, it was futile to get into a quip contest with him. Paar was too fast on his feet and experienced in verbal fencing. Mickey was not. Immediately, the conversation became hostile and combative. When Paar asked Mickey what kind of woman Ava Gardner was, with Barbara sitting right there in the audience, Mickey was miffed. He felt stung, and took Paar's bait. "Ava's more of a woman than you'll ever know," he replied. And the war was on. Mickey went on to tell Paar that he liked a local talk show host, Tom Duggan, more than Paar. He and Paar became locked into an antagonistic confrontation. The audience felt the tension. Paar seemed to like it. Finally, he asked Rooney, "Are you enjoying my show tonight?" Bristling with hostility, Mickey replied, "Not necessarily." Then Paar remarked, "Then would you care to leave?" The audience began to applaud for Paar. Mickey stood up, shook hands with Paar, and left, while the audience cheered.

Paar remarked to the audience, "That's the only time I got a hangover just from listening . . . It's a shame. He was such a great talent."

The next day, Mickey took a beating in the press. There were claims that he was drunk during the appearance. Paar feasted on the media circus, and remarked, "I'm sorry he was drunk." Meanwhile, manager and press agent Red Doff went into spin control. He also sent a wire to the president of NBC seeking an apology from Paar and the network for alleged slanderous remarks, including Paar's sarcastic "He was such a great talent." Although Rooney later met with Paar, he never appeared on his program again. When Paar was asked if he had exploited the situation, he replied, "I really think Mickey should understand that I didn't need the publicity. I am rather successful." [58]

The fifties was a tough decade for Mickey despite making movies that still resonate today. But tough as it was, he worked and he had survived, clawing his way through more marriages and another decade in the business. His film output was still steady, though they were mostly low-budget programmers. He subsisted, paid his child support and alimony with revenues from his stage appearances. His fourth marriage was crumbling, major scandals were on the horizon, and bankruptcy would soon follow. While it was a bumpy ride for most of the fifties, the turbulence would be far rougher in the dawning decade, and danger would, yet again, rear its ugly head.

Bigamy and Barbara Ann

Mickey, Barbara Ann, Kerry (left), Kelly (right), and Michael in Barbara's arms.
Photo courtesy of Kelly Rooney.

By officially resigning from Rooney's management, Maurice Duke, as he later told his daughter, had "escaped the lunacy of Mick"—and after the murder of his friend Gus Greenbaum by mob associates of casino operator Moe Dalitz, the Duke believed he had also escaped with his life. He was quickly replaced by the competent Red Doff as Mickey's manager and press agent. But all was not rosy for Mickey, who, yet again, stepped into the spotlight of the gossip columns with his pending divorce from Elaine, his newest marriage to Barbara Ann Thomason, and his erratic behavior on *Tonight*. Mickey was certainly not fading away as many had predicted; though he did seem to be decomposing before a national audience.

One of the most important and well-known Hollywood screen-writers, Larry Gelbart (*M*A*S*H*, *A Funny Thing Happened on the Way to the Forum*, *Oh, God!*, and *Tootsie*), told us, "Sadly, the talent was always there. It was his real life that distracted him and made him the butt of many punch lines. I worked with him on a tour of *A Funny Thing* [Mickey played Pseudolus]. He had such great timing and knew the natural rhythms of his character." [1]

As Mickey was severing his business relationship from Duke, his marriage to Elaine was imploding. After he discovered her betrayal with her ex-husband—Elaine spent much of her time at their house in Lake Arrowhead with her male "friends"—Mickey set out on the prowl looking for his next conquest. His friend, car salesman Bill Gardner introduced him to his friend Barbara Ann Thomason, another tall and lanky beauty in the mold of Ava Gardner, only this time a blonde. Born in Phoenix, Arizona, in 1937, Barbara came from a military family. Her father was an officer in the air force, and the family moved around for the early part of her life, including a stint in England.

While attending Emerson Elementary School in Phoenix, she became known as the prettiest girl in town. Her family then moved to Inglewood, California, in 1951, where, while a student at Inglewood's Morningside High School, she began entering beauty pageants. By October 1953 her dreams of success started to come true when she won several local contests. In 1954 she was crowned Queen of the Championships of Southern California. Later that year, she won the Miss Muscle Beach and Miss Surf Festival titles. After graduating from high school, she became a dance instructor for Arthur Murray and then, as Tara Thomas, she became a model, appearing in *Modern Man* magazine in December 1957.

She was seventeen years younger than Rooney when they were introduced, but for Mickey, that made no difference. A beautiful girl was a beautiful girl regardless of height or age. An aspiring actress, Barbara lived with a roommate, nightclub singer Pat Landers, in a small apartment at 1436 Laurel Avenue, off the Sunset Strip. Using the stage name of Carolyn Mitchell, she did bit parts on television shows such as *Crossroads*. When she met Mickey, she had just finished her largest role, in Roger Corman's *Drag Strip Riot*, as Betty and was working on his film *The Cry Baby Killer*, as Carole Fields, which starred Jack Nicholson in one of his first leading roles.

"My mother was a real Southern California beach beauty," recalled Mickey and Barbara Ann's eldest daughter, Kelly. "She just fell head over heels in love with my father. Although her career was just taking off, she was more interested in a family life and children. I don't think she was starstruck with my dad, as she was already appearing in films."[2]

Mickey, who had returned to his typical pattern of wooing beautiful young women, was focused on Barbara immediately. In fact, right after they began to date, he bought her a $4,500 fur coat, a gift that was reported in Harrison Carroll's column on February 12. Elaine naturally noticed the story and exploded.

She told Arthur Marx, "I told Mickey that I had a boyfriend and I wanted to leave Mickey. But Mickey begged me not to. Mickey was still under the care of a psychiatrist. I felt sorry for him again, so I said okay, I would stay but I would not give up my young man. Mickey knew that right up front, and he didn't care. After he bought her a fur coat for $4,500, he felt so guilty, he even bought me one, a more expensive one at that. I figured what was the difference? If it was the end of a marriage, it was the end of a marriage."[3]

As Mickey began his relationship with Barbara Ann, he was blind to her emotional instability. He was head over heels in love with her. Barbara, too, was smitten, but when Mickey told her that he would not go through a divorce from Elaine to marry right her then and there, it led Barbara to three suicide attempts, one of which made national headlines and every show-biz gossip column.

Mickey had rented a new house, which belonged to longtime (and very controversial) Los Angeles mayor Sam Yorty, the perennial butt of many Johnny Carson jokes, at 12979 Blairwood Road in Sherman Oaks, where Barbara Ann took up residence shortly after Mickey moved in. The new house was always filled with Barbara's friends and acquaintances, including her former roommate Pat Landers and longtime friend actress Kim Chance from Albert Zugsmith's *High School Confidential*. Guests at the house also included famous baseball player Milwaukee Braves first baseman Frank Torre, former Yankee manager Joe Torre's brother; along with Braves pitcher Lew Burdette, Red Schoendienst, and Gene Conley. Reportedly, Barbara Ann passed out by Mickey's pool. When she was discovered, by Landers and Chance, to revive her they tossed her into the pool. When she didn't wake up, Landers fished her out and called for an ambulance to resuscitate her and transport her to North Hollywood Hospital, where she was admitted for one night. The girls blamed the incident on Mickey, who they said had tossed Barbara in the pool. But Barbara Ann, perhaps disconsolate over Mickey's refusal to marry her—he was still married to Elaine—had written and posted suicide notes with tape throughout the house. The papers the next day, August 13, carried sordid tales of the suicide attempt, Barbara Ann's nude body floating in the pool, and the currently married Mickey's involvement.

Red Doff, now in a difficult position as Mickey's manager and publicist, carefully responded by telling the *Los Angeles Daily Times*, a month later on September 13, 1958:

> Barbara was unconscious when Landers and Chance arrived, so they decided to wake her up by undressing her and putting her in the swimming pool. Just for good mea-

sure, Landers took off her clothes so she could get into the pool and dunk Barbara in the water. When that didn't work, Landers called her doctor, who told her to contact the police. The Fire Department also responded and took Barbara to North Hollywood Hospital, which released her the next day. When Mickey got home, he found notes all over the house and visited the hospital to check on Barbara and went home after he found out she was fine.[4]

The newspaper story continued:

> Barbara, who claimed she merely took the wrong pills by mistake, said of Rooney, "I'm madly in love with him and he with me." But Doff insisted to The Times that there was no romance. He said, "Mr. Rooney had left for an engagement at Harrah's Club in Lake Tahoe. It's all a publicity stunt cooked up by these three girls," Doff told The Times. "Sure Mickey knows Barbara and has taken her out a few times. But Mickey likes all girls. After all, he's not even divorced yet and here someone is trying to get him married already. I'm Mickey's closest friend and you can quote me as saying that he enjoyed Miss Thomason's company just as he did the many other girls he has been out with since separating from his wife. But that's as far as it went!"[5]

Elaine, who was not to be trifled with, knew early on that Mickey was always on the lookout for a pretty woman, and though she herself was cheating on him, she refused to put up with it. Once she caught him trying to get his office phone number to a beautiful girl serving hors d'ouevres at a party they were throwing, and she got so mad she walloped Mickey hard across his mouth, drawing blood. Although she claimed that Mickey had begged her several times to reconcile, she was fed up and embarrassed.

Now that a divorce was in the offing, she was determined to get the highest possible settlement. She hired divorce attorney Max Gilford, who was also an actor and producer and the husband of actress Anne Gwynne, to get her piece of the pie. Gilford played hardball and threatened to expose Mickey's lifestyle to the media. While Mickey and Elaine had officially separated in early 1958, the settlement negotiations dragged on for months. Elaine had requested a temporary alimony of $2,350 per month until a settlement was reached. Mickey was unhappy and did not feel she deserved that much. He hired divorce attorney Dermot Long and tried to play his own game of hardball.

Even after she had agreed on terms and the interlocutory degree was granted, on May 18, 1959, neither would be able to marry until June 7, 1960. But by the time of the interlocutory decree, Barbara was already five months pregnant with Kelly Ann, who would be born on September 13, 1959. According to Pam McClenathan, Elaine tried to extort Mickey for extra money in return for not reporting the pregnancy and overlooking the fact that Mickey had actually married Barbara, on December 1, 1958, in Mexico, while he was still legally married to Elaine.[6] Hence, already a pedophile because of Liz Taylor and Lana Turner, he was now also a bigamist, and was about to have an illegitimate child. Mickey refused to pay Elaine any hush money, and she promptly sought to sell the story to the gossip magazines. However, it was the *Los Angeles Times*, on June 3, 1959, before the final divorce decree that reported that Barbara was "four months pregnant."

"Mickey fucking dragged me and all the records into his divorce. I thought I was finished with him . . . apparently not," recalled Maurice Duke.[7]

Mickey's divorce from Elaine—public, ugly, tainted with the smudge of bigamy, and wrapped around her love for her first husband, who intruded himself into Mickey's life and then wound up getting killed by the very mobsters to whom Mickey was heavily in debt and for whom he even occasionally made collections—would probably have psychologically crippled most people. But not Mickey, who persevered into his next marriage and into another murder.

The Mickey Jinx and the Murder In Brentwood

The scene of Barbara Ann's murder, outside the Brentwood home.
PHOTO COURTESY OF MELODY DOFF.

While Mickey Rooney faced countless hurdles during his life, along with a multitude of bizarre and twisted experiences, none was more devastating, or threatening to him and his children, than the murder of his wife Barbara Ann, a tragedy that impacted his life until the day he died, and the lives of four of his children right up to today. Although the facts in the death of Barbara Ann and the suicide of her alleged lover and killer, Serbian actor Milos Milosevic, on January 30, 1966, appear to be clear cut in that the LAPD closed the case, forty years later many questions linger. Was it a murder-suicide, as claimed almost immediately by Los Angeles County deputy coroner Thomas Noguchi, or were Milosevic's underworld connections, stretching all the way back to Yugoslavia, contributory factors in the double murder? Several people, including the children of Mickey and Barbara, claim this was not simply a murder-suicide perpetrated by a jealous lover.

Conspiracy theories abound on the Internet, including some that conjecture that the official inquiry was a cover-up and that the two were actually both murdered in revenge for their affair. Two Serbian books were written about the tragedy, *Zagrljaj Pariza* (*The Embrace of Paris*), by Dusan Savkovic,[1] and *Ubij Bliznjeg Svog*, by Marko Lopusina; about the "real" story behind the murders; and one website deifies Milosevic as a victim of a gangland murder, possibly related to an international sex ring.

Barbara Ann and Mickey's friend Milos Milosevic was born on July 1, 1941, in the kingdom of Yugoslavia, three months after the Nazi invasion and partition in April of that year. As a teen after the war, he worked alongside his childhood friend Stevan Markovic for gangster Nikola Milinkovich. Milos had ambitions as an actor and sought out French actor Alain Delon when he was filming a movie in Belgrade. Delon liked the audacity of Milos and his friend Stevan, good-looking young men whose skills in procuring women for an evening's entertainment impressed the French actor. Delon took the two wannabe actors into his entourage, hiring them to be his "bodyguards," in which capacity they traveled with him everywhere.

In April 1964, while visiting the film set in Yugoslavia for Roger Corman's low-budget (six hundred thousand dollars) picture *The Secret Invasion*, an early version of *The Dirty Dozen*, Delon met Mickey and Barbara Ann, who was on set with her husband, and introduced them to his two burly bodyguards. The couple was already having problems, and in an attempt to reconcile with Barbara Ann,

Mickey had brought her, now pregnant with Kimmy, on location in Yugoslavia for the six-week shoot. In the film, Mickey plays a pivotal role as an underground fighter for the Irish Republican Army. (Barbara Ann and Corman knew each other from her earlier acting work on his 1958 picture *The Cry Baby Killer*.)

Mickey and Barbara went through a turbulent period after that trip to Yugoslavia. He had been having an affair with a stripper while rehearsing the road version of Larry Gelbart's *A Funny Thing Happened on the Way to the Forum* in Atlantic City. In late August, his new girlfriend created a row when Barbara Ann accompanied Mickey to the set for the filming of his television series *Mickey*. After the incident, Barbara had a massive fight with Mickey that resulted, in September 1964, in both parties contacting their respective divorce attorneys. However, they didn't divorce, but instead sold their Beverly Hills home and moved into a Brentwood house they'd bought relatively cheap, at only sixty-five thousand dollars, a property in which both the previous two occupants had died in freak accidents. The house turned out to be equally unlucky for Barbara.

Meanwhile, Delon came to Hollywood to try his hand at American films, and he brought Milosevic and Markovic with him. At a party at the house Delon had rented, Milos sought out Rooney, asking for his help in learning how to become an actor. Mickey called some friends and found the young man work as a stunt double. Milos auditioned and was eventually cast in the ambitious Esperanto-language horror film being directed by Leslie Stevens of the television series *The Outer Limits*, called *Incubus* (1966), starring *Star Trek*'s William Shatner. Milos played the title monster, Incubus.

In conspiracy-bound Hollywood, theorists still talk about *Incubus*, and how it seemed to be cursed, as many of those who worked on the film met unfortunate fates, including Milosevic. Actress Ann Atmar committed suicide weeks after the film wrapped. The daughter of actress Eloise Hardt (Amael in the film) was kidnapped and murdered, a case that remains unsolved. Director Leslie Stevens and actress Allyson Ames divorced, and Stevens's production company, Daystar, went bankrupt. William Shatner suffered personal tragedy in the death of his wife. And most chilling of all, Milos killed Barbara Ann Rooney and himself in a murder-suicide in 1966.

Rumors of a curse, and Milosevic's gangland connections, throw a strange light on the story of Milos's suicidal rampage. A handsome twenty-four-year-old who had no trouble ingratiating himself with the Hollywood set, Milos was gaining recognition as an actor. A gigolo in Europe who never lacked for female companionship, he was divorced and was leading the life he had always dreamed of in Hollywood. According to people who remember him, it made no obvious sense for him to kill himself over a woman with four children.

The murder-suicide of Barbara Rooney and Milos Milocevic spurred international headlines and was truly shocking for its time. It was the OJ Simpson case of the 1960s, a murder in Brentwood. Associated Press entertainment reporter Bob Thomas wrote a straightforward account of the events of January 30, 1966, explaining that the planned reconciliation between Mickey and Barbara Ann might have been the catalyst for her murder at the hands of the Yugoslav actor Milos, whom Mickey accused of being his wife's lover. Police found the bodies of Barbara Thomason Rooney and Milos in the bathroom of Mickey's Brentwood home. Thomas cited the police theory that this was likely a murder-suicide in which Milos, who had begun a relationship with Barbara while Mickey was filming in the Philippines, shot Barbara Ann and then turned the gun on himself. He wrote that police theorized that Milos committed the crime because Barbara and Mickey had decided to resume their marriage: in a meeting at Mickey's hospital, which private detective Herm Schlieske had taped, Mickey and Barbara reconciled, and Barbara returned to Brentwood where she and Shlieske and her attorney Harold Abeles broke the news to Milos who had appeared to accept her decision. But later that evening, the two retired to her bedroom. When they did not respond to the maid the next morning or to her friend Wilma Catania's knocking on the door, Wilma and the maid broke into the bedroom, found the bathroom door locked. When they opened it, they found the bodies of Milos and Barbara in the bathtub with Mickey's .38 revolver beside them. The Rooney children were in the house at the time of the murder-suicide. Mickey remained in the hospital under sedation after learning of the news of his wife's murder.

Mickey's eldest daughter by Barbara Ann, Kelly, was present in the house at the time of the murder. She recalled:

> My mother was wrongly presented in a terrible light and almost as a whore. Red Doff had planted stories that blamed her for seducing this Milos, which angered him and may have precipitated the murder of my mother. I am not certain of what happened, but we have always been upset at how my mother has been presented. Also, strange and violent events happened to everyone who was involved. Red Doff's four-year-old daughter, Carol, who was an excellent swimmer, drowned only three months later [May 3, 1966] in Hal March's pool; Cynthia Bouron, Milos's wife, was years later found bludgeoned to death and stuffed in a trunk [October 30, 1973]; his business partner, Stevan Markovic, was found murdered [1967]; the private detective my mother had hired [Herm Schlieske] was mysteriously murdered [he was only thirty-seven] the next year; and my grandmother Nell died on March 3, 1966, only a month after my mother's death—officially from a heart attack, but we still question that as well. And there were other strange incidents. I feel that my mother's murder was never properly investigated and she never received the respect she deserved.[2]

In his autobiography, *Life Is Too Short*, Rooney gives his version of events, stating that he preferred working on the stage:

> [B]ut [agent] Bullets Durgom kept getting me work in pictures. So the next job was "Ambush Bay," to be shot in the Philippines, the one trip in my life I wish I'd never taken. Barbara herself wanted to drive me to the airport the day I left LA for Manila. Milos was at the house. He came up to wish me luck. I shook his hand and said, "Take good care of my wife while I'm gone." He smiled and assured me he would. Well, Milos did take care of Barbara. He spent most of his nights with Barbara, and, by the time I returned at the end of November, they were in the middle of a very torrid love affair. I had hated my time in the Philippines. The plot of 'Ambush Bay' had us hacking our way through the worst kind of jungles on the island, fighting mosquitoes and drinking the local water. [Mickey said he returned quite ill.][3]

Mickey had made what would turn out to be the fatal mistake of asking his new friend Milosevic to look after his his wife. With the cat away, the mice did play. Barbara reportedly took Milosevic as a lover to get back at Mickey for his philandering. While Mickey was away, she accompanied Milosevic to Northern California, to the location shoot of *The Russians Are Coming, The Russians Are Coming*, in which he had a bit part. According to the official standard story, they were still having an affair when Mickey returned and moved out of the Brentwood house after finding out they were lovers. The couple filed for an official separation in December 1965, and it was reported that Milosevic moved into the Brentwood house to live with Barbara and her four children by Mickey, a story Kelly Rooney disputes: "This is absolutely not true. I lived in the house, and I would know this.

While he did visit the house, he never moved in, lived there, or even stayed overnight. This was an absolute lie."[4]

When Mickey learned that Barbara was planning to file a lawsuit for separate maintenance, seeking a judgment that would grant her payments from Mickey until the divorce settlement was approved by the court, Mickey struck first and filed for divorce on January 19, 1966, citing mental cruelty. In his suit, he asked the court for a restraining order to keep Milosevic out of the Brentwood house. Barbara began to panic when she learned she might lose her children in a custody battle due to her adultery, which Mickey would charge in his court pleadings. For his part, the story goes, Milosevic became jealous when he realized Barbara Ann was considering returning to Mickey. He was even more incensed when he heard a tape recording of a conversation between Barbara and Mickey discussing the divorce suit. The tape was made by LA private eye Herm Schlieske, who had wired Barbara for the purposes of getting Mickey to talk about his philandering.

On the tape, recorded inside Mickey's hospital room, Mickey pleads for reconciliation. If Milos Milosevic thought Mickey would argue for a divorce, he was trumped, because in response to Mickey's proffer of loyalty and his love for the children, Barbara agrees to keep the marriage alive. She tells Mickey that she will not see Milosevic again, even as a friend. Afterward, Red Doff concocted a story that Mickey had checked into the hospital for treatment of an exotic blood illness he had picked up on location. The hospitalization actually occurred due to an overdose of pills by Mickey during this period of turmoil (most likely an aborted suicide attempt).

On the night of her death, Barbara went out with Milosevic and her friend Margie Lane for dinner at the Daisy on Rodeo Drive. They returned to Brentwood and bid her friend a good night at 8:30 p.m. Three of the children were at home, while Kimmy Sue was visiting her maternal grandparents in Inglewood. The following day, Barbara's friend Wilma Catania, worried that the children were alone and Barbara was still locked in her bedroom, got the maid to bang on the door. When that didn't get a response, Wilma asked for the key, which the maid retrieved from the kitchen. They opened the door, but found the bed still made and the bathroom door locked. Wilma and the maid found a screwdriver and hammer, which they used to pop the bathroom door off its hinges. They were shocked at what they found inside.

In the bathtub were the bodies of Barbara and Milosevic. She was lying on her back, shot with a single round through the jaw. Milosevic, lying on top of her, facedown, had a bullet hole in his temple. According to the medical examiner and the LAPD, Milosevic had shot Barbara with Mickey's chrome-plated .38-caliber revolver and then turned the weapon on himself. Odd, though, that none of the three children who were in the house heard the shots. Officially, the police ruled it a murder-suicide perpetrated by a jealous lover. When Mickey learned about the crime, he went into shock and was forced to stay another day in the hospital.

In Emma Brockes's (London) *Guardian* interview on October 17, 2005, with Mickey's son with Barbara Ann (conducted backstage at the Albery Theatre, where the young Rooney was choreographing a new musical, *Ducktastic!*), the then-forty-three-year-old Michael Rooney recalled the murder-suicide, saying that he didn't remember anything that happened that night but that he knew his parents were going through a divorce. "My mum was kind of seeing somebody on the side," he said. "But then my father and my mother decided to get back together, and the guy my mum was dating wasn't having it. So he took the very gun that my father gave my mother for protection and killed her in our house. Then [he] killed himself. It was a murder suicide." [5]

Michael said that although he and his sisters were in the house when the murder-suicide took place, they were "scurried out" of the house and told they were going to see the movie *Mary Poppins*. They were never told at the time that their mother was dead. They were subsequently adopted by their maternal grandparents because, according to Michael, "My father was going through a tough time in the 1960s."

Michael, who had been trained as a dancer, got his first job as an extra on the TV series *Fame*. He said that he never knew what had happened to his mother (who simply disappeared from his life) until he was thirteen or fourteen. For years, he told his interviewer, he believed that his grandmother was his mother. Then one day "my grandmother sat us down and told us why our mother was no longer around. She started showing us pictures of my mother. The way they did it was really good."

Michael explained that he didn't have much contact with his father, who always seemed as if he were staring into a camera, even when they were alone together. For example, Michael said show business was the only thing the two of them talked about, even when the conversation wandered off into other subjects. But Michael said he realized that show business was the only thing his father knew. That was his only life, and there was nothing else for the two of them to talk about. It does make sense, he explained to his interviewer, because "my father was shooting two to three musicals at the same time when he was a kid. They were cranking 'em out back then. They used to put stuff in the soup to keep 'em going—everybody says it was cocaine—anyway, it was some kind of upper. But he's a survivor, unlike poor Judy [Garland]."

Years later, after the Thomason grandparents told the children that their mother had been murdered, Mickey told his son that Barbara Ann had been a good mother, "caring" and wonderful with the children, whom she deeply loved. Of all the women he had known,

Mickey said, Barbara Ann, to whom he'd been married for eight years, was the best wife he'd had. Michael said that after all the years had gone by, what Mickey said about his mother was something he had wanted to hear.

As of this writing, Michael's sister Kelly told us, the Rooney children have never fully investigated the police and coroner reports of their mother's death, even though that death is still shrouded in mystery despite the official explanations.

While the official determination of coroner Dr. Thomas Noguchi was that the death of Barbara Rooney and Milos Milosevic resulted from a murder-suicide, facts abound, nearly fifty years after this event, that question the veracity of the findings of the Los Angeles Police. The coroner's report was unclear. The website Murderpedia has: "The official inquiry provoked rumors and doubts that they were actually both murdered in revenge for having an affair." A website was even created to dispute the death of Milosevic, stating that his death was a murder: "Milos allegedly committed murder and suicide but this page is created to oppose artificial facts and dismiss public belief and disinformation. Milos was brutally murdered with Barbara Ann Thompson, and the proof for such an extensive claim is now ready to be published, including mortuary photos, death-scene report [sic], letters of threats and other significant evidence of what really happened. Teams of directors and producers are working together to develop a specific film project in creative collaboration."[6] Of course, this is purely speculative.

The mysterious circumstances and the events following the tragedy could be coincidence or could perhaps lend credibility to questions regarding the deaths of Milos and Barbara and others connected with the motion picture *Incubus*. In the movie-fantasy life of Mickey Rooney, the horrid event plays out like classic film noir, a curse that follows him through his life, impacting everyone around him.

Of her mother's death, Kelly Rooney has said:

My mother may have used [Milos] as a shoulder to cry on, but I do not believe there was a passionate affair. She was first a wife and mother. I remember Milos just sitting by the pool and bringing his German shepherd with him. He was a friend of both my parents. He had a very sinister aura about him. He always frightened me, as if he was the devil. Also, my mother was not well at the time. She was still recovering from a rough pregnancy and birth with Kimmy, and an invasive C-section. She was not out partying. My father, at that time, was loaded up with barbiturates and sleeping pills. When he went to the hospital, Doff made up a story of why he was in the hospital. He was really there because he was taking too many sleeping pills and other drugs.

One theory concerning Mickey's stay in the hospital was that he was so distraught over the relationship between his wife and Milos that he attempted suicide by taking an overdose of barbiturates. Kelly confided to us, "My father always regretted not being there for my mother. He told me in front of Jan, just three years before he passed, that 'Your mother was the love of my life.' I think he was being completely sincere."[7]

In an emotional retelling, sobbing over the phone as she dredged up memories of the traumatic event, Kelly said to the authors:

I was very close to my dad. I was his oldest daughter and I guess a daddy's girl. My mother was a hands-on mom. Milos was here illegally from Yugoslavia, with a very mysterious background. Milos was not a lover of my mother; that is not true at all. He may have been infatuated with my mom, but they were not involved. He feared he was going to be deported and wanted to use my mom to stay in the U.S. He feared returning to Yugoslavia. The gun used in the killing was a house gun my dad kept for protection. They were shot in my parents' bathroom . . . the door was locked to the bedroom. My mom usually got us up and ready for school, and that morning she did not. Her best friend came over to the house and was upset to see Milos's car there. She said, "What's his car doing there?" I am serious that he never spent the night at our house. Her friend was panicked, and we could not find the keys to the master bedroom. We looked all over the house for the keys and we got in and all started to go into the bedroom. Thank God my mom's best friend had the presence of mind to notice that the bathroom door was locked and knew something was wrong and moved the kids out of the bedroom, which I'm so grateful to this day that she did. She asked our maid to go into the bathroom, which she did. When the maid went in there, we heard her let out a blood-curdling scream. After that, the police came and we went to my dad's manager's [Red Doff's] house and stayed there for two weeks. We were not told anything. I mean we knew something was wrong. I was there when the police were spraying for fingerprints, and we went into the back of a police car. Red never told us. He waited for my dad to sit us down and tell us. It devastated the family. They made my mom out to be a whore in the newspaper, [but] it was my dad who was doing the cheating—not my mom. My dad was no saint. My grandparents—my mom's parents—kept us shielded. The media created this whole fabricated story about my mom and rode with it. There was more to the story, and the police just did not follow through. I want the true story to be told. It was and remains suspicious and untold. I mean the death of Red Doff's daughter Carol—

we stayed with him—just a couple months after this; my grandmother Nell died one month later; Milos's wife was later bludgeoned and stuffed in a trunk; the investigator, Herm Schlieske, who worked with my mom on her last day was killed months later at thirty-seven; Milos's business partner was murdered the next year. It does not add up.[8]

Speculating on what might have happened on the night of the murder and the events leading up to it, we suggest the following scenario of the *corpus delicti*: Milosevic, possibly because of prior criminal connections and a belief that he would be imprisoned or killed, was deathly afraid of being deported back to Tito's Yugoslavia. Staying in America, where had already enjoyed a starring film role and had befriended Barbara Ann, was his only chance at survival. But to stay in America, he needed a spouse. He was a manipulator who saw in Barbara Ann the possibility of a spouse if she divorced Mickey, which she was already in the process of doing. All he needed to do was nudge the process forward, get a good divorce settlement from Mickey, and marry her so as to establish a cause for his permanent residence in the United States. However, when Barbara and Milos conspired to get Mickey on tape, the plan quickly fell apart when Mickey, instead of providing evidence of his philandering and his desire for a divorce, begged Barbara to stay in the marriage. Barbara ultimately relented, shut the tape recorder off, and agreed to reconcile, promising that she would tell Milos to move out. She and her lawyer broke the news to Milos, who, according to witnesses, seemed to take it calmly. But, as Kelly Rooney has attested to, Milos had a dark and sinister side. This was also evidenced by claims made by Milos's former wife that he had beaten her, which is why she wanted a divorce. Thus, we can assume, for the sake of argument and based on the claims of his former wife and Kelly's own perceptions, that Milosevic had a violent side, especially when crossed.

Milos was also a very jealous and possessive man, one who could not brook breaches into his territory. And Barbara Ann, while Mickey was away on location shooting *Ambush Bay*, had become his territory. By his own admission, to Barbara's friend Michele Lamour, Milos had grown romantically attached to Barbara and was exhibiting some extremely powerful possessive sentiments. He told Lamour on the Thursday prior to the shooting, "If Barbara even looks at another man, I'll shoot her and myself. It'll be like a film. We'll be found sleeping like two lovers together." [9]

On the night of Barbara's death, Milos parked his blue VW Beetle outside the house. After Barbara's friend left, but while the three eldest children were in their rooms, Milos, behind the locked door of the master bedroom, made one final and desperate attempt to convince Barbara to save him from deportation by divorcing Mickey, according to the plan they'd hatched, and marrying him. He might have pleaded with her, claiming that it would be his doom if he were forced back to Yugoslavia. Maybe if she brought Mickey in on the plot, Mickey would agree. Milos possibly said he had it all worked out. But his pleading was to no avail. Barbara was adamant. She wanted to stay in the marriage, and Milos would have to leave. Perhaps Milos began to threaten her, maybe even tried to assault her, but Barbara had the loaded .38 that Mickey had bought her for protection. She got it out of a bedroom drawer and pointed it at Milos. Her finger might already have been on the trigger of the cocked revolver. It could have gone off with a simple squeeze. Milos grabbed the barrel as they struggled over the gun, twisting her wrist as he forced the barrel away from his head and tried to wrest the weapon from her tight grip. Suddenly, the gun went off, firing a single round through Barbara's jaw and into her brain. She collapsed in Milos's arms, dead. Now Milos is truly in the throes of panic. He has killed Mickey Rooney's wife. He would most certainly be prosecuted for it and face the gas chamber. He carried her into the bathroom and laid her in the tub. He locked the bathroom door. There was no escape now, only death. In a state of fear and hopelessness, he climbed on top of Barbara's body, possibly in a final embrace, and put Mickey's .38 to his temple. He fired the fatal shot.

If this scenario is correct, at Milosevic's autopsy, Los Angeles medical examiner Dr. Thomas Noguchi would have discovered powder burns on Barbara's and Milos's hands, and on Barbara's face, and blood spatter on both their hands. He would have noted that both the bedroom and bathroom doors were locked from the inside, seemingly precluding the theory that this was a mob hit. And an examination of the weapon would have revealed both Barbara's and Milos's fingerprints on the handle and trigger, left there by their struggle. Was this Mickey's curse on both their lives? Was it the curse of the *Incubus* that had struck? If so, would it strike again?

According to Barbara's friend Marge Lane (Mickey's sixth wife, whom he married shortly after Barbara's death and who heard the news of Barbara's death over the radio), Milos had a couple of other reasons for not wanting to live. Marge told Arthur Marx, "There was a warrant out for Milos in Florida for a gun carrying charge. The FBI were after him and so were a couple of members of the Mafia. So he must have figured what was the point of waiting around for them to get him? Now that he couldn't have Barbara, he'd save everybody the trouble." [10]

Rev. Douglas Smith, the minister who had married her and Mickey in 1959 presided at Barbara's funeral. Her services and interment were held at Forest Lawn Cemetery in Glendale. Fewer than one hundred mourners attended, including Red Doff and his wife, Bill Gardner, Jonathan Winters, Red Barry, Bobby Van, and Joey Forman. In Dr. Smith's eulogy, he said, "This beautiful girl was like a spray of roses, now only the fragrance remains." [11] Milos's body was shipped back to Belgrade, Yugoslavia, where his mother told the press there that Mickey "plotted to have my son killed." The story, which was carried throughout the United States, forced Red Doff into more spin control; he responded with vehement denials, and later told Arthur Marx that Mickey was in a state of utter shock during the rest of 1966 and hardly knew what he was doing or even where he was living.

A few years after the murder, Barbara's parents legally adopted the four children, Kelly, Kerry, Michael Kyle, and Kimmy. At that time, they took their grandparents' name, Thomason. The judge ruled that the children's best interests were served by "the regularity, reliability and stability of living with the grandparents at Mr. and Mrs. Don Thomason of Rolling Hills Estates."

In his autobiography, *Life Is Too Short*, Mickey said of Barbara's killing, "I died when she did. I am furious at what happened to her." [12] Of Kelly, he said, "She had blue eyes just like her Mom, and she was beautiful. Who was I to get such a gift? In my heart of hearts, I knew Kelly Ann came from God."

20

Career Swings

How to Stuff a Wild Bikini *with* (front row, left to right) *Dwayne Hickman,*
Annette Funicello, Beverly Adams, and Mickey Rooney.
PHOTO COURTESY OF WILLIAM ASHER.

Mickey's fifth marriage had ended in an explosion of gunfire, and
manager and press agent Red Doff immediately began the spin
on it, putting Mickey in the right and blaming Barbara for her dalliance with the dark and conniving Serbian. Mickey was the victim,
confined as he was to a hospital bed suffering from the ill effects of
his exposure to some foreign virus he had picked up on location in
the Phillippines. Even the scandal-mongering gossip columnists in the
Hollywood press corps couldn't blame Mickey for this one. He would
trudge on, Doff assured the press, despite his ill fortune.

Mickey was nothing if not dogged. Even in the midst of failed marriages and divorces he couldn't afford, threats from mobsters whose bullets buzzed past his friends and associates, tax liens and lawsuits, bankruptcy, womanizing, drinking and drug addiction, and a murder-suicide that, but for a locked door and a lucky turn of fate, spared the lives of his children, Mickey kept on ticking. He continued his professional roller coaster ride across the media. Amazingly, despite the terrible negative publicity and tragic events that surrounded him during this period, his talent continued to shine through. He was comfortable in any venue, blending in like a Zelig wherever he performed. By his own admission, he was only the character he played and nothing more. Where many of today's performers tend to be one-dimensional, Mickey's hard-knock life, stage education, lack of a core personality, and general cork-like resilience allowed him to wow audiences whether he was onstage in Vegas, playing the role of the wily Plautine character Pseudolus in the road company of *A Funny Thing Happened on the Way to the Forum*, doing on a television variety show, or appearing in a motion picture. When film or television stars are dependent on their physical features to appeal to audiences, they faced limited outlets as they age. Mickey experienced this when he tried to recreate Andy Hardy as he grew older, but then he morphed, becoming a chameleon who could adapt to whatever role he was offered. He gave producers, bookers, and casting agents a vast array of talents to utilize.

Mickey never stopped working. In the 1960s he appeared in sixteen motion pictures, had his own television program, did twenty-nine guest appearances on various television shows, did four extended tours with stage shows, "coauthored" an autobiography, and recorded an album. In short, it was another typical decade for Mickey Rooney.

"I learned early on, if you're knocked down, you've got to keep getting up. However, as you get older, you get up a hell of a lot slower and you keep thinking that you don't have the strength to get up again," Mickey told the authors in 2008, his voice barely rising above the screaming fans at Santa Anita.

Mickey's motion pictures in the 1960s included both showcases for his talent and utter schlock. From his now-reviled role as Mr. Yunioshi in the Blake Edwards production of Truman Capote's *Breakfast at Tiffany's*, to his acclaimed turns in the cult favorite *It's a Mad Mad Mad World* to Rod Serling's poignant *Requiem for a Heavyweight* to the comedic but awkwardly condescending attempt to embrace the post-Mouseketeer beach bum generation with *How to Stuff a Wild Bikini*, Mickey was both brilliant and unabashedly shameless.

The great actor George Raft once told us, "I learned the hard way. You need to keep working. Get your face in front of the audiences, whether you're starring or in a small part. Once they forget who you are, it's over." [1] Mickey certainly followed this advice.

The decade started painfully slow with two Albert Zugsmith low-budget films, *Platinum High School* followed by *The Private Lives of Adam and Eve*. Red Doff was a producer on both films, and as Mickey's manager, he set the actor up with profit-sharing participation.

Platinum High School allowed Rooney to return to his old stomping grounds at MGM, where the film was being shot. While Mickey was top billed, the focus was on the younger actors. This film was a remake of the Spencer Tracy film *Bad Day at Black Rock*. The May 14, 1960, *New York Times* review by Eugene Archer was fairly positive, stating, "Mickey Rooney, twenty-four years after his peak period as Andy Hardy, MGM's conception of the all-American boy, is still laboring for the studio with indefatigable professionalism. Unfortunately, he has done more for the studio than MGM has done for him. For Mr. Rooney's vigorous playing is the only merit in this shoddy and obviously inexpensive exploitation melodrama."

The Private Lives of Adam and Eve was shot at Universal as a risqué comedy, featuring Mickey in a dual role as a conniving gambler and a puckish Devil in the Garden of Eden via a dream sequence with Martin Milner and Mamie Van Doren. "Mickey was wonderful to work with. He was a real pro. He directed the sequences as well," recalled Milner (*Life with Father, Route 66, Adam-12*).[2] And our friend screenwriter Austin "Rocky" Kalish (*Maude, Good Times, Gilligan's Island*) told us, "Mickey was actually a talented director. I'm not certain why he didn't pursue that. He had a great vision of placement . . . and was incredible with the actors and crew. I know that Zugsmith was credited as well as the director, but I only remember Mickey in the chair."[3]

The *New York Daily News* review on December 1, 1960, hated the film but mostly enjoyed Mickey: "Aside from Mickey Rooney, who sometimes overplays, there is little evidence of talent."

HIS NEXT FILM WAS a major blockbuster, one that has been revered for over fifty years. However, Mickey's small role as *Breakfast at Tiffany's* Japanese photographer, Mr. Yunioshi, became emblematic of racism in films and has been credited with perpetuating a broad cultural and ethnic stereotype. While his role as Mr. I. Y. Yunioshi was minor, it has struck a nerve in many observers as demeaning to the Japanese. Upon Mickey's death, Jeff Yang of the *Wall Street Journal* (April 8, 2014) wrote a piece called, "The Mickey Rooney Role Nobody Wants to Talk Much About," that details the controversy that stemmed from Rooney's portrayal of Yunioshi:

At the age of 93, actor Mickey Rooney has passed away. As his many lengthy eulogies have made abundantly clear, his was a life of stratospheric highs and humiliating lows. He was one of the biggest stars in the world as a teen; he fell into bankruptcy and irrelevancy as an adult. He reinvented himself and rebounded. He crashed and burned. Few lives have had as many epic twists and turns, making his obituaries obsessively engrossing reading.

But there's one thing the newspapers have generally danced past, and it happens to be the role that has cast the longest shadow out of a career of thousands: His performance as Mr. I. Y. Yunioshi in the classic 1961 film "Breakfast at Tiffany's."

In the decades since the film was released, Rooney's portrayal of Yunioshi—taped eyelids, buckteeth, sibilant accent, and all—has become one of the persistent icons of ethnic stereotype, brought up whenever conversation turns to the topic of Hollywood racism. The depiction has prompted widespread protests whenever the film is screened. Paramount, the studio behind *Breakfast*, has now acknowledged Yunioshi as such a toxic caricature that its canonical Centennial Collection DVD release of the film includes a companion documentary, *Mr. Yunioshi: An Asian Perspective*, which features Asian American performers and advocates in conversation about the role's lasting cultural impact and the broader context of Asian and other racial stereotypes in entertainment.

Six years ago, after four decades of stolidly defending the role, even Rooney himself finally expressed some regrets, stating in an interview that if he'd known so many people would be offended, "I wouldn't have done it."

But he also added in a September 2008 interview in the *Sacramento Bee*, "Blake Edwards . . . wanted me to do it because he was a comedy director. They hired me to do this overboard, and we had fun doing it. Never in all the more than 40 years after we made it—not one complaint. Every place I've gone in the world people say, 'God, you were so funny.' Asians and Chinese come up to me and say,

'Mickey, you were out of this world.'"[4] In later years, Mickey apologized repeatedly for the portrayal, and in *Life Is Too Short*, he wrote, "I am downright ashamed of my role in 'Breakfast at Tiffany's' and I don't think the director, Blake Edwards was very proud of it either."[5]

The specter of Yunioshi continues to haunt Hollywood and Asian Americans today. Rooney's broadly comic performance, repurposed from his early vaudeville days into the brave new world of cinema, is the godfather of the stereotype that continues to rear its head. A recent flap over a *Colbert Report* tweet underscores this. In March 2014, @ColbertReport tweeted: "I am willing to show #Asian community I care by introducing the Ching-Chong Ding-Dong Foundation for Sensitivity to Orientals or Whatever." Although the tweet was not from Colbert himself, a campaign emerged demanding the cancelation of *The Colbert Report* for the remark. The point made by the activists behind the subsequent #CancelColbert campaign is a valid one: racially stereotypical images are problematic even when presented as progressive satire, because many who see them won't understand the context and will laugh for the "wrong reasons."[6]

In the documentary *The Making of Breakfast at Tiffany's*, director Blake Edwards remarked, "Looking back on the casting of Mickey— well, it's not my favorite part. At the time I cast Mickey, nobody complained and thought it was perfectly okay. Looking back, I wish I had never done that. I would do anything to be able to recast it. But it's there and onward and upward." Producer Richard Shepherd said, "I would rather have cast a Japanese actor to play the character. At one point, I wanted to replace Mickey."

It would be easy, and politically correct, to leave this discussion about the 1958 Truman Capote creation of an obviously broad-stroke satirical character right there, exactly where Mickey's *apologia pro vita sua* for his portrayal left it. But in the aftermath of the *Charlie Hebdo* attacks in Paris and the ISIS-inspired terrorist attacks in Garland, Texas—and the resulting counter-tide of unqualified tolerance for satire and comedy, no matter who's offended—the discussion is incomplete. We have to ask ourselves: What are the limits of racial satire inasmuch as words and images have the power to hurt? What is the moral and political balance along the spectrum of satire, racial stock humor, and unqualified support for free speech no matter what? Mickey Rooney found out where he stood with respect to satire versus racial offensiveness, and found it out the hard way.

IN THE WAKE OF *Breakfast*, Red Doff continued to pick up projects for Mickey. He did another low-budget film, *King of the Roaring '20s: The Story of Arnold Rothstein*, at Allied Artists, the former Monogram Studio. Cashing in on the popular gangster craze created by Desilu's popular television series *The Untouchables*, *King of the Roaring '20s* starred an old friend of Mickey's, David Janssen, as racketeer and gambler Arnold "the Brain" Rothstein, who preceded Meyer Lansky as head of New York City's Jewish mob. Rothstein is best known, among other exploits, for fixing the 1919 World Series and forever tarnishing the reputation of Chicago White Sox outfielder Shoeless Joe "Say it isn't so, Joe" Jackson. Mickey is third-billed as Rothstein's childhood friend Johnny Burke. His second son, Tim Rooney, had a small part in the film.

"Timmy just loved working with his father, as it was about the only time he got to spend time with him," recalled the boy's later caretaker, Pam McClenathan, who went on to say that, over the years, Timmy sought out any opportunity to be with his father, on-screen and off-, but Mickey simply wasn't interested.[7]

Mickey's next film, *Everything's Ducky* (1961), teamed him with his pal Buddy Hackett, the wildman comic with whom Mickey became friends while they were both playing Vegas clubs. "My father just adored Mickey," recalled Buddy's son, comedian Sandy Hackett. "They meshed so well together. While this film really was not highly regarded, it set them up as a team when Stanley Kramer hired them for 'It's a Mad Mad Mad World.' Their rhythms were in synch." [8]

The *New York Times* reviewer, on April 27, 1962, dismissed *Everything's Ducky*, writing, "It is an ostensible farce in which Mickey Rooney is required to play straight man to the comic Buddy Hackett and a talking duck. The alarming title is 'Everything's Ducky,' and that should be warning enough for anyone."

Following an established pattern in his career, Rooney went from a farce (*Everything's Ducky*) to a drama: Rod Serling's remarkable *Requiem for a Heavyweight*. Based on Serling's absolutely brilliant *Playhouse 90* television production, Mickey portrayed the trainer of a washed-up boxer named Mountain Rivera, masterfully portrayed by Anthony Quinn in the role that Jack Palance played in the television version. Jackie Gleason, playing Quinn's manager, who exploits his client for the money, demonstrated his dramatic abilities, too, a talent that would shine years later in the poignant *Soldier in the Rain* and *The Hustler*. The *New York Daily News*, on November 17, 1962, was complimentary toward Rooney in its review, writing, "Mickey Rooney is solid as the trainer who, unlike the manager, actually cares what happens to the man who was the source of his income for many years."

Following *Requiem for a Heavyweight*, Mickey did the now-classic comedy *It's a Mad, Mad, Mad, Mad World*, directed by Stanley Kramer. Shooting took nearly eight months, beginning on April 26, 1962, and wrapping on December 6. The film was jam-packed with nearly every comic actor in the business, including core stars Sid Caesar, Edie Adams, Ethel Merman, Dorothy Provine, Jonathan Winters, Milton Berle, Spencer Tracy, and (paired together) Mickey and Buddy. It was made on a huge budget (for the time) of nearly ten million dollars.

Stanley Kramer's widow, Karen Kramer, told us in 2015 that Stanley's rationale for making the film was his desire to show that he could make a comedy. Kramer is most recognized for socially provocative films such as *Home of the Brave* and *High Noon*—the latter film helped break the infamous Hollywood blacklist. As Karen Kramer explained, "Stanley was challenged by his friends [who thought] he was incapable of directing a first-rate comedy. Whenever someone remarked that he could not accomplish something, it fueled his inner fires to prove them wrong and he set out to create the ultimate comedy film." [9] Thus, he sought some of the most legendary comedians of his time, built them into a caper story, finding a treasure, and let them at it. The result, she said, was a classic, with Mickey Rooney at the top of his comedic game.

"Mickey was lots of fun. Although much of my footage was shot separately, we spent a lot of time together. Buddy was wonderful, as well," recalled Jonathan Winters to us shortly before his death in April 2013.

"My father loved working with Mickey," Sandy Hackett told us. "They had such an amazing time together. I'm surprised they didn't make any other films together. However, my father made so much more money in Vegas, it was hard to get away for eight months on location. He would just lose so much money."

"You'd think that with all these comics, it would be this wild, funny set," Mickey later said. "It was really boring. All these guys had their own shticks. I mean, I like Milton, but he always had to top you. Johnny Winters was funny; he was always doing bits that were crazy. [But] he was having some mental health issues on the set." [10]

Winters's psychological condition during filming was confirmed in the 1991 documentary *Something a Little Less Serious: A Tribute to It's a Mad, Mad, Mad, Mad World*, which states that Winters was mentally unstable throughout the shoot, channeling weird personalities (such as the Tuesday Bear, who came out only on Tuesdays). At the climax of the film, Winters and Dick Shawn are in a money pit together, wielding, respectively, a pickax and a shovel. The documentary shows Shawn unwilling to stand in the pit alongside Winters while Winters is brandishing the pickax, due to Winters's erratic behavior.

At a tribute to the film in 2013, Karen Kramer recalled to actor-producer Jeff Garlin (*Curb Your Enthusiasm*, in which he plays Larry David's agent, and *The Goldbergs*), "When Stanley called Jonathan Winters to be in the film, he told Kramer, '. . . I have to be honest with you Mr. Kramer, I just came out of a mental institution and they declared me certifiably insane,' where Stanley said, 'Mr. Winters, I have to be honest with you and tell you that almost every actor I've worked with is certifiably insane. I think you'll do just fine.'" [11]

As for Mickey, Sid Caesar recalled, "Stanley had us stick closely to the dialogue. Both Milton and I had toned down lots of extra business. However, Mickey added bits of business that upset Stanley. He threw Buddy off, too, when he did that." [12]

Actor Marvin Kaplan confirmed what Sid recalled, telling Jeff Garlin, "Nobody in the film was allowed to ad-lib in the picture. The only one Mr. Kramer allowe to ad-lib was Phil Silvers. He was the only one he trusted." [13]

Mickey, who said he was "proud of this film," had a different memory regarding his ad-libbing. In the famous airplane scene with Buddy Hackett and Jim Backus (best known as Thurston Howell III on *Gilligan's Island*), Mickey recalled, "I was told by Mr. Kramer that the script was just a map; he said put your own words and bits . . . have fun. I ad-libbed every scene in the picture. It was the fifth film I [had] made with Spencer Tracy, and even he ad-libbed." [14]

RED DOFF HOPED THAT these two highly acclaimed films would help revitalize Mickey's career and bring offers for more big-budget features. However, Mickey spent the rest of the 1960s in mostly low-budget, "drive-in" program fillers. His next four films after *It's a*

Mad, Mad, Mad, Mad World were cheap "foreign" films shot around the world.

The first was the Roger Corman film *The Secret Invasion* (1964), shot in Yugoslavia; followed by *24 Hours to Kill* (1965), an action film with with Lex Barker that was shot in the Middle East; *L'Arcidiavolo* (1966), shot in Italy with Vitorio Gassman; and finally *Ambush Bay* (1966), with Hugh O'Brian, shot in the Philippines. These films made almost no impact when released, and were quickly forgotten. Back in the States, Rooney did a quickie appearance in an American-international beach party movie, *How to Stuff a Wild Bikini* (1965), with former Mouseketeer Annette Funicello, *Dobie Gillis*'s Dwayne Hickman, and (in a brief appearance) director Bill Asher's wife, Elizabeth Montgomery (*Bewitched*). While it's easy to dismiss *Wild Bikini* as an exploitive and tired attempt to gather up as many names as possible in a weak and completely implausible plot, with lots of young bikini-clad women and buff, all-American surfer dudes cavorting on a beach, there's actually a bit of social commentary in the film. With older actors Brian Donlevy and Mickey Rooney (as ad agency shills for their corporate clients), surfer movie veterans Annette and Frankie, and even vaudevillian and silent film star Buster Keaton all inhabiting parts well beneath their talents, the film illustrates how a 1940s generation sought to capitalize on its vision of 1960s American youth, especially in Southern California. The movie failed, but to watch it is to look through a prism of misunderstanding and misinterpretation (all to cash in on what the American establishment *believed* its youth were up to).

When Sam Arkoff offered Mickey an easy five thousand dollars for a week's work on the movie, Mickey did not tell his personal manager, Bullets Durgom, about the part, thus circumventing his management. Durgom was blindsided, learning about the offer only while reading the notice in *Variety*—by which time Mickey had already begun shooting on the film.

Durgom recalled, "I said, 'Mick, I'd rather loan you the money. I can't keep your price up if you keep doing these cheap beach pictures.' Mick said, 'I need the money.' So I told him it was over and I quit." [15] Thus, for the third time, Mickey returned to use the services of Red Doff, a pattern that would repeat itself for the next thirty years.

When Doff first heard about the *Bikini* gig, he told Mickey to turn it down. He was trying to get Mickey back into more serious roles, and he said that this role, and the salary, would damage the actor, and Doff, in future negotiations. But Rooney had already taken the low-paying bit.

On the set, there was friction. Dwayne Hickman told us that, "Mickey was constantly trying to give me acting lessons. I had been in films for over twenty years, had been the star of a television series, and had worked with some of the greatest actors. It was insulting in his trying to teach me how to act." [16] Rooney's unsolicited acting lessons caused tension between the two, culminating in Hickman's complaining to director Bill Asher, and an insulted Rooney giving Hickman the silent treatment for the duration of the shoot. "Mickey, at times, could be a real pain in the ass," Asher told us in 2007.

The remainder of the decade was filled with some more unforgettable films, including *The Extraordinary Seaman* (1969), for MGM and director John Frankenheimer, with David Niven and Faye Dunaway, a movie widely panned by the critics and which achieved barely any commercial release because it was exhibited in so few theaters. Director John Frankenheimer said in an interview that of all the films he directed, this was his least favorite. It was, he said, the only movie he ever made that he considered "an absolute disaster from beginning to end." [17]

Another disaster was *Skidoo* (1968), a weird take on the 1960s drug culture through the eyes of director Otto Preminger. What made it even weirder was that it starred Mickey, Jackie Gleason, and

Groucho Marx. Given the cast and its director, the film should have performed much better—and might have, had it not been so over-burdened with personalities locked in their own respective shticks. Another forgotten Rooney film was *80 Steps to Jonah* (1969), with Wayne Newton.

An exception to these films was an ambitious motion picture written and directed by Carl Reiner, and starring Dick Van Dyke, called *The Comic* (1969). The film was Reiner's look at the sad downfall of a silent film clown whom both he and Van Dyke had idolized, a character modeled on the lives of screen legends Buster Keaton, Stan Laurel, and Harry Landon. In it, Mickey plays a character similar to silent film actor Ben Turpin, called Cockeye. Roger Greenspun in the *New York Times* praised Mickey: "It isn't a good movie but it is often an interesting one and it is full of lovely people. The loveliest is Mickey Rooney, as a cockeyed comedian, who plays old age as a quality as well as a time of life."

Carl Reiner told film and television historian Stuart Shostak in 2014, "'The problem I had with Mickey was that he couldn't cross his eyes for the Cockeye part, so we had to put a fake eyeball in, and that caused a major rash and infection. That forced us to only put it on him for the close-up shots, which we filmed as quickly as we could. All of the other shots composed were sans the fake eye, and they were far enough back away from him that it wasn't noticeable. It was the only way we could get through the picture on time. I was very pleased with his performance.'" [18] Shostak told us, "Dick Van Dyke and Carl [Reiner] . . . both thought that Mickey gave a great depth to his role. It was a period he knew well, and he['d] actually worked with many of the great silent comics." [19]

He may have known the silent film stars, but Mickey had little recall for his films from the 1960s: "I have to consult a film index to remember the films I did in the late 1960s and early 1970s," he wrote in his autobiography. . . . "I wasn't happy with my film work. No actor, now matter how good he is, transcends crap, and that's what I was reduced to accepting." [20]

During the lull in picture offers, Mickey performed live in Las Vegas and other cities, and appeared in tours of Broadway plays. Throughout the 1960s, Doff secured him a particularly lucrative salary of about seventeen thousand dollars per week in Vegas and other nightclub venues, such as the Latin Quarter. His act for much of the decade included dancer-singer Bobby Van, who had his early break as Dobie Gillis in the movie *The Affairs of Dobie Gillis*, opposite Debbie Reynolds and Bob Fosse, and later hosted TV's *Make Me Laugh*.

Sidney Miller recalled, "They had a real crowd-pleasing act. Van was the opening act; then he did bits with Mickey during his act. They did this 'Look in the moose' piece that was a take-off on *Candid Camera* that the audiences loved." [21]

Some of the performances were at regional theaters such as with the Kenley Players in Warren, Ohio, produced by the colorful John Kenley, who lured stage and screen stars to small towns by giving them top billing in the company's productions. In 1963 Mickey appeared with his nightclub partner Bobby Van in *The Tunnel of Love* at Kenley, theaters such as the Weschester County Playhouse in New York, and assorted Midwest venues.

In the summer of 1965 Mickey starred as wily slave Pseudolus in the road show of Larry Gelbart's modern interpretation of a Plautine comedy, *A Funny Thing Happened on the Way to the Forum*, a role created by Zero Mostel. Also in the show were Cliff Norton and Willard Waterman. One of the stops for the show was in Los Angeles, where Mickey received rave notices. The iconic theater critic Charles Champlin wrote in the *Los Angeles Times*, on June 20, 1979, "Rooney leers, chortles, giggles, struts, runs, dances, sings like a laryngical foghorn, and ad-libs all manner of regional and topical asides. The evening remains a largely personal triumph for Rooney."

In 1967, Mickey appeared at Caesar's Palace in Vegas as Oscar Madison in *The Odd Couple*, with Tony Randall in his first attempt at the role of Felix Unger. In a famous "what could have been" moment, Randall felt so comfortable playing against Mickey that, two years later, when he was selected to play Unger in a proposed television version of the play and motion picture, he recommended Rooney for the part of Oscar. Paramount Pictures thought highly of the casting, but producer Garry Marshall wanted Jack Klugman in the part, as it was Klugman who had replaced Walter Matthau in the Broadway production.

In a National Public Radio interview on February 26, 2006, Jack Klugman told Susan Stamberg, "Tony Randall wanted Mickey Rooney to play Oscar. When Garry Marshall brought me in for the first rehearsal, it was no love fest. Something I did in one scene bothered Randall. 'You mustn't yell,' he said. I said to the guy, 'Marshall, look, it hasn't cost anybody any money except the plane fare, which I'll give you back. But I can't work with this guy.' And Tony said, 'Why not?' I said, 'Well, I wouldn't have the chutzpah to tell you how to act. How are you telling me how to act?' He said, 'Well, I'm only trying to help.'"

In 1969 and 1970, Mickey performed in summer tours of the Broadway play *George M!*, as George M. Cohan, reenacting Jimmy Cagney's portrayal of Cohan in the 1942 film *Yankee Doodle Dandy*. Once again, Mickey received strong reviews during the tour. He had previously played Cohan in a television production in 1957 called *Mr. Broadway*, and recorded an album for RCA/Victor in 1957 in conjunction with that production.

Flash-forward to 1963, when Mickey made a big splash reuniting with Judy Garland on her weekly television series at CBS. Mickey was the first show's guest, although the broadcast was held back for a December air date. Although decades had separated their motion picture performances, Mickey and Judy still had their movie magic and slipped easily back into the on-screen relationship they had had. It was obvious to the star-studded audience that the two show biz pros, now shining together in a new medium, were in a love fest, displaying the respect they felt for each other as the best of friends. Even during rehearsals, Judy knew "the Mick" would keep her relaxed and happy for the June 24, 1963, videotaping of show number one. The packed studio audience, which included Lucille Ball, Clint Eastwood, Jack Benny, and Natalie Wood, cheered the team's reunion, and by the time Judy closed the show with the "Born in a Trunk" sequence's "Old Man River"—one of the defining moments of both her career and of television history—everyone felt the series could be Garland's greatest triumph yet. The *Los Angeles Times* so agreed with this assessment that it didn't wait for the series premiere and reviewed the videotaping: "Judy seemed so assured, so self-possessed, so happy in her work, that it sounds good for the shows." The episode with Rooney finally aired months later, on December 8, 1963, and was a success.

Mickey's appearance with Judy sparked interest by ABC producer Selig Seligman for a Rooney television show. It had been nearly ten years since the *Hey, Mulligan* disaster, and Mickey was still a tough sale on Madison Avenue, especially after his behavior with the sponsors on that show. Yet Seligman believed that Mickey, in the right vehicle could be sold. Through Mickey's assistant/secretary Bill Gardner, who had worked for Mickey for more than six years—until Barbara's death—Seligman set up a meeting with Mickey; his manager, Bullets Durgom; and writers Arthur Marx and Bob Fisher.

Marx and Fisher's concept was reminiscent of *The Danny Thomas Show*, with Mickey as an entertainer with a family. They thought that this format would allow Rooney to capitalize on his ability as an entertainer.

Mickey didn't love the concept initially: "I don't like the 'Danny

Thomas Show.' It was nothing," he told the group.[22] (*The Danny Thomas Show*, which debuted in 1953, became a hit and stayed on the air for ten seasons.)

Instead, Mickey pitched the idea of a character who ran a talent school like Ma Lawlor's, and that concept was explored first. However, ABC hated it and ordered a new script and format. The second concept had Mickey play a midwestern family man who inherits a motel in Marina Del Rey, California, a fish-out-of-water story. Durgom set up the contract for five thousand dollars per show for a guaranteed twenty-three shows. Mickey had two requests. He wanted a part for his nightclub partner, Bobby Van, and one for his second son, Timmy. They hired successful TV director Richard Whorf (*Beverly Hillbillies*) for the pilot. ABC loved the pilot and scheduled the show for Monday nights at 8:00 p.m. in September.

Unfortunately, Mickey was still poison to the 1960s Madison Avenue crowd, due to his five marriages, the Jack Paar incident, the bankruptcy, his headline-making antics, and the way he'd treated his Pillsbury sponsors. There were also headlines at the time placing his name in the "black book" of infamous call girl Pat Ward, which came up in the trial of a young playboy millionaire, Minot Jelke, who was being investigated for "procuring." ABC could not secure a main sponsor, but the network would owe Rooney the contractual one-hundred-thousand-dollar guarantee if it didn't produce the show. Thus, they ordered eighteen shows and put it in on Friday nights at 9:00 p.m. It was later moved to Wednesday nights at 9:00 against the popular *Dick Van Dyke Show*.

The TV series came at a propitious time in Mickey's life. His finances were even more precarious than they had been a decade earlier. He owed back taxes to the IRS, back alimony and child support, and had a load of debts, some to individuals you wouldn't want knocking on your door. He was forced to declare bankruptcy in May 1962.

With total assets of $500 and debts of $464,914, he had no choice. His attorney Dermot Long filed the bankruptcy, which resulted in more headlines. The AP story read, "Rooney Broke . . . Rooney is unable to explain where it all went. He blew twelve million dollars . . . the financial questions stump Rooney . . . Rooney claims that 'the ladies have cost me 5 million dollars to date.''

Mickey also owed over $100,000 to the IRS, which made a deal with Long. Mickey's father-in law, Don Thomason (Barbara Ann's father), who had a successful furniture store in Woodland Hills, was made co-signer of Mickey's checks, along with Long. Mickey was denied his own checking account. He later paid the IRS using money from the trust fund set up by Martin Gang when he was a child star at MGM. There was $126,000 in the irrevocable trust, which Superior Court judge Ben Koenig allowed him to break. He paid the IRS $100,371. With the money left over, despite the bankruptcy, he bought a beautiful Mediterranean-style villa at 1100 Tower Road in Beverly Hills.

Meanwhile, author Roger Kahn was hired by Putnam Books to collaborate on Mickey's autobiography, under terms that would split the $55,000 advance with Mickey. Kahn told us:

> I flew out to Los Angeles to interview Mickey for the book. I came out to the Coast for three weeks and Mickey was never available . . . [I]t was costing me money so I flew back to New York. I had to sue Mickey to work with me, as the publishers were demanding the manuscript. Finally, Red Doff apologized for Mickey and begged me to fly back, which I did. I was staying at the Chateau Marmont. When he finally met with me, he couldn't remember his life. I know the publishers wanted some salacious info on Ava, but all he could remember was that she was a virgin and that Martha Vickers was frigid. When we would start in

the morning at ten, Mickey was already mixing martinis. Then he hated working in the house and we'd drive around. Once we went to the track where I lent him $600 . . . [H]is attorney Dermot Long went crazy when I told him that. He said "He'll never pay you back." [He did.] I got much of the info from his mother Nell when she wasn't going to the races. She hated all of his wives . . . [S]he showed me a check of Mickey's that he wrote to Vickers with her lipstick on it. Nell said, "See the minute she married Mickey, she's kissing his checks. That's all she loved about him." Nell was a tough old lady. Mickey was impossible to talk to about his life. Lots of made up stories. Lots of pure bullshit. I wrote the book with all this bullshit for material.[23]

In the end, Kahn had a nightmare with the book. He had to turn down a lucrative offer of $25,000 from *The Saturday Evening Post* for an excerpt when, as he told us, Barbara Rooney screamed at Mickey, "Don't you dare take it—Cary Grant got $100,000 for his story." Eventually they sold excerpts to *Look* magazine for a three-part story, for less money. Then Mickey called Kahn and said that he was "too young to write my story." Kahn sued Mickey for $75,000 for breach of contract. Mickey settled the suit by having Kahn read him the manuscript, for which Kahn was paid $1,500 per day, all expenses, and first-class airline tickets. Mickey hated the manuscript and made drastic changes to it. Kahn wisely had his name taken off the project when (as he foresaw), the book, titled *i.e., An Autobiography*, with Mickey as the sole author, was savaged by critics. *Los Angeles Times* book editor Robert Kirsch wrote, "Mickey Rooney's biography is written unfortunately from a hundred Rooney scripts and interviews . . . Rooney should never have written it. This thing is soggy with sentiment, gritty with one-liners . . . I think the material deserved a better writer."

Kahn told us, "It was then I promised myself never to write another biography of a celebrity."

Mickey's new television series at ABC, now called *Mickey*, went into production in July 1964. Mickey was happy that it was being shot on the MGM backlot. Nevertheless, it had a rocky start. Mickey gave the producers countless problems. He argued with Marx and Fisher over the scripts. The network wanted him to wear a toupee, to make him look younger, which he refused. He wore a yacht cap instead.

"He was unhappy. He wanted to do a film called 'The Great Race' for his friend Blake Edwards that starred Jack Lemmon. The show prevented him from doing it," recalled Arthur Marx. "And we learned that if he wanted any script conferences, we had to schedule them before the first race at Santa Anita." [24]

Director Dick Whorf remembered, "He just treated the show as a sideline. One day he just talked about building a theater in the round in the Valley where he and Judy would play 'Girl Crazy.' He even had me draw up plans. He would sit on the set reading a *Racing Form* and ignored any rehearsal. The trouble with Mickey Rooney, I decided, was that Mickey couldn't keep his mind on the main job at hand." [25]

Marx wrote that Mickey was often very moody. He wrote, "Once Mickey showed up in an ugly mood. He said, 'I can't stand my wife and she can't stand me.' Later Bobby Van explained that Mickey had spent the weekend in Palm Springs with Peter Lawford, another fellow, and three high-priced young ladies at a friend's house—and that Barbara had found out about it." [26]

The series *Mickey* started with strong ratings, but eventually suffered a precipitous drop against *The Dick Van Dyke Show*. He hated the selection of the shows and complained, "ABC is fucking me. They've fucked me about our music, our titles. They fucked me on the time slot. And now that we had a chance to get an audience, they throw in the wrong show and fuck me again." [27]

Despite the ratings decline, ABC was happy with the program and expected strong competition against Van Dyke. One of the show's attractions was actor Sammee Tong, whom audiences had loved since his *Bachelor Father* performance with John Forsythe. The byplay between Mickey and Sammee worked well. However, Mickey's dire prediction at the mid-season wrap party that the show would get the axe affected Sammee Tong, who was a desperate gambler and owed substantial money to the Las Vegas and Reno mobs. Hearing Mickey's words, Tong saw no possibility of ever paying back his debts and, in a fit of depression, took his own life.

"It was unfortunate," Arthur Marx recalled to us, "as Mickey was wrong. ABC told Seligman that they liked the Rooney/Tong matchup and would have picked up our option. However, with Sammee gone, they did cancel the series in November. They said with Sammee gone, what was the use?"

Mickey, along with his television series, did a number of guest appearances on television throughout the decade. On January 1, 1960, he starred in *The Mickey Rooney Show* as part of the *Revlon Revue* on CBS, directed by Abe Burrows, creator of *Guy and Dolls* and father of famed television director James Burrows (*Fraser*). Later that year, on CBS, he did another special, *The Many Sides of Mickey Rooney*, with Gloria DeHaven, that drew strong reviews. Later that year, he appeared on the TV Western *Wagon Train*, with Ward Bond; and on *General Electric Theater*, in a piece costarring his third son, Teddy. In 1961 he appeared in the series *Checkmate*, with Sebastian Cabot and William Schallert.

"I was excited to act with Mickey. He always had advice, but he was wonderful to work with," recalled the great character actor William Schallert (*The Patty Duke Show*, *Star Trek*), whose father, *Los Angeles Times* critic Edwin Schallert, had praised Mickey in a review of his stage act that helped him get the part of Mickey McGuire back in 1927.[28]

Mickey stayed busy on television in 1961, appearing in *Hennesey* with his old friend Jackie Cooper; in an episode of *The Dick Powell Show* that became the pilot for the later *Burke's Law*, starring Gene Barry; on *The Investigators*, starring James Franciscus; in another *Dick Powell* episode, this one with Warren Oates and directed by future film director Arthur Hiller (*Love Story*); and on *Naked City*, with Maureen Stapleton and Paul Burke, in an episode also directed by Arthur Hiller. At a lunch with other writers, directors, and performers at Factor's Famous Deli in Los Angeles, Hiller said, "Mickey always had ideas—many of his ideas were actually fairly good and constructive."

Red Doff kept Mickey busy in a variety of television roles in the next several years. For a week of work, Mickey was able to command a high-end salary for each appearance, from five thousand to ten thousand dollars or more. In 1962 he appeared in *Frontier Circus*, with Chill Wills and John Derek; *Pete and Gladys*, with Harry Morgan and Cara Williams; and another couple of *Dick Powell Show*s, one with Barbara Stanwyck and Powell's wife, June Allyson, and another with Frank Sinatra as a guest host stepping in after Powell's death. Mickey remained busy in 1963 with the *Alcoa Premiere* with John Forsythe and Fred Astaire as host; Rod Serling's *The Twilight Zone*, in the episode "The Last Night of a Jockey," a one-man morality play and psychodrama written especially for Mick by Serling; and in the *Kraft Suspense Theatre*, in an episode directed by future film director Robert Altman and costarring James Caan and Bruce Dern. Mickey did not slow down in 1964, either, with appearances in *Arrest and Trial*, with Ben Gazzara and Chuck Connors; reprising Bob Hope's film role in *The Seven Little Foys* on *Bob Hope Presents the Chrysler Theatre*, with Eddie Foy Jr. and Mickey as George M. Cohan; on *Rawhide*, with Clint Eastwood; and on *Combat!*, with Ramon Navarro. After his series in 1964, he made only one appearance in 1965, on another *Bob Hope Presents the Chrysler Theatre*, with Jack Weston. In 1966 he made only three appearances, all with old friends:

the first was with David Janssen in *The Fugitive*; then with Lucille Ball on *The Lucy Show*, where he reprised his Mickey McGuire role; and finally with director Dick Quine, for *The Jean Arthur Show*.

The last show he did in the 1960s was a pilot called *Return of the Original Yellow Tornado*, with Eddie Mayehoff, in which he plays a retired superhero. The program, a precursor to superhero shows such as *Mr. Terrific*, *Captain Nice*, and *The Greatest American Hero*, was shot at Universal. The producers later brought Mickey, Mayehoff, and costar Eileen Wesson back to shoot extra footage, to expand the show into a feature film created by Dick Wesson (Eileen's father) and Mel Tolkin. Wesson was a creator of *The Bob Cummings Show*; produced and wrote the *The Beverly Hillbillies*, *Green Acres*, and *Petticoat Junction*; and played Rollo on *The People's Choice*, with Mickey's old pal Jackie Cooper. Wesson was an old golfing and racetrack buddy of Mickey's for many years. His daughter Eileen, a prominent character actress and Universal contract player, was known as "Queen of the Pilots" because she'd appeared in seventeen pilots for proposed television programs and later played Judy Barton in *Airport*. Of *Original Yellow Tornado*, Eileen said:

> My dad and Mickey played cards and golfed together. I grew up around all these comedians. I drove the golf cart for my dad and his buds, who included Bob Hope, Jackie Gleason, Rooney—and the list goes on. I knew them all very well. I do remember going back to shoot more scenes on *The Tornado*, to develop a love interest for my character and make me more of the one who was *always* getting Mickey and Eddie out of trouble. It was very fun . . . [N]ever a dull moment, and no one stuck to the script. Eddie and Mickey were so funny no one could stop them. I costarred as Eddie Mayehoff's niece. I do remember laughing so hard [off camera] while watching Eddie and Mickey

play off each other that I ripped my super hero outfit, a lot! . . .[29]

I went countless times with my father and Mickey to the racetrack. The racetrack was their kingdom. They were the court jesters and had the attention of everyone in the clubhouse with their antics. They were in their element where they could let loose, do shtick, drink, pick up "broads," and gamble. Their pattern was that they would get to the racetrack and announce they were going backstage. To them that meant they would go back to the paddocks, commiserate with the trainers, the jockeys, the stable boys, and get the inside information or even "fixes" to bet on. Then they'd go back to the clubhouse, bet big dollars on the tip they discovered, and almost certainly end up losing the bet. Then the pattern would repeat itself over and over. They were the life of the party, the center of attention, and they loved it. . . .

My father was always loyal to his buddies. My father was a performer, director, producer, writer, and show runner for programs such as *The Beverly Hillbillies* and *Petticoat Junction*, with Paul Henning. When he was lured to Universal to be a show runner and script doctor, he created the *Original Tornado*, which allowed him to cast his pals, Mickey, and another old friend, Eddie Mayehoff. It was such a hoot to work on. My dad gave them full rein and just let the cameras run, to catch all of their bits of business. We couldn't stop laughing at Eddie and Mickey playing off of each other. They were absolutely hysterical with each other. I had to play straight woman to both of them. And with my father there, it was this big party. . . .

Guys like my father and Mickey were truly educated on the stage. They were two street smart guys who were always on. They loved attention. They were wired differently. I once taped them at home. When my dad watched this, he was outraged. Mickey and my father never saw themselves as they were. They lived by this code of old vaudevillians. It was an old boys' fraternity. They thought they knew everything about women, and it was always the next conquest. It was always booze, girls, money, and gambling. They loved the constant action. It was from their upbringing in burlesque. Mickey and my dad loved each other for years and would each try to make each other laugh and outdo each other. My dad and Mickey would work on routines at the track or playing golf. They did an act onstage as well. However, with both of them, while they were very on and up for everyone around them, they also crashed. Mickey had breakdowns. My father had five nervous breakdowns and eventual shock treatments that would sap his energy, creativity, and his mind. They were products of being children from burlesque. They were performers and only performers. That was their life.[30]

Ellen also revealed to us that, like Mickey, her father never got out of hock to the mob. As a result, he worked for them until he was too old to make the rounds.

Throughout the taping of *Original Yellow Tornado*, Mickey's on-again, off-again relationship with Red Doff continued. Mickey had returned to Doff from a short stint with manager Bullets Durgom, whom Gleason had recommended. As ever, he sought more roles, anything to keep income rolling in to pay off former wives, back taxes, and bookies. Doff himself had faced his own demons, and the codependent relationship between the pair, with each enabling the other, may have strengthened their bond.

As the sixties drew to a close, Mickey was at yet another crossroads. The decade had been hard on him, harder than the fifties, even though he had enjoyed critical success. He was turning fifty; was balding, with a paunch; and was forced to wear glasses. Also, he no longer could shed his public persona as a temperamental womanizer with a penchant for gambling, drinking, and pills. All this had exacted a physical toll on him. He now looked his age and was not going gently into what critics thought would be his long good night. However, despite his name losing some of its luster, there was still recognition and respect for his talent.

MICKEY'S SECOND WIFE, B. J. Rase, herself a remarkable personality—her career as a backup singer for some of the biggest recording talents in the 1950s spanned decades, and some say she had an affair with Elvis Presley after her divorce from Mickey—left her stamp on Mickey's life, giving him children who went on to pursue their own careers in the entertainment and recording industries. They crossed paths with some of the top rock bands of the 1960s, including the Rolling Stones, and with the reclusive Howard Hughes, and orbited the periphery of Charles Manson's world. It's a heretofore unknown story that B.J.'s stepson (and friend of the Rooney brothers), Dan Kessel, was one of the most important music producers in America, alongside his friend Phil Spector.

"Timmy really resembled Mickey most of all," recalled Pam McClenathan, who watched after Timmy for almost eight years at her home near Hemet, California. "He was a talented musician and toured with his brothers as the Rooney Brothers. Mickey rarely saw him throughout the years. Betty Jane was a wonderful mother, [but Timmy] battled his demons."

Tim also battled disease. For five years before his death, he fought dermatomyositis, a condition that most often strikes adults between forty and sixty and results in progressive muscle weakness, making it difficult to move, swallow, or even breathe. For Tim it must have been a frightening reminder of the paralysis that affected him as a child, when he contracted polio. According to Pam, he bore this affliction in good spirits before his death on September 23, 2006.

Teddy Rooney, Mickey's son number three, with third wife Martha Vickers, also wanted to follow in his father's footsteps. Teddy was a blond-haired, precocious, ambitious youth—but fated to a life of addiction. In one of the last interviews he was able to give, speaking to us from underneath his respirator in his hospice bed, he told us in an interview:

> I was hoping for a chance to do something with my father. He was rarely around. But I idolized him. The short times we had together I worshiped him even though my father certainly never set a good example. When I was thirteen years old, my dad's birthday gift was taking me to a hooker that he knew. . . . When my mother heard about the part of Andy Hardy Jr., she suggested using me for the part. Mickey and Timmy were already too old for an eight-year-old. I loved acting. Red Doff got me a good role in a Doris Day/ Jack Lemmon film *It Happened to Jane*. By the time I did Andy Hardy with my dad, I'd done a *Playhouse 90* on television with my mother, did some other shows, and the film with Doris Day. She was such a great lady and was very sweet to me. We stayed in contact for years.

In 1966, Teddy and his brothers Mickey Jr. and Timmy formed the band the Rooney Brothers, establishing their own independent career in the recording industry and in films and television. Their story has become part of rock 'n' roll cult legend. Their interest in music was not surprising. Apart from having a song-and-dance man as a father, the three had expert training as musicians from their stepfathers, B.J.'s two husbands after Mickey, Buddy Baker and Barney Kessel.

Baker had a long career as the director of music at Disney; he was also a composer for countless Disney films. B.J.'s third husband, legendary jazz guitarist Barney Kessel, was extolled by musicians from John Lennon and George Harrison to Eric Clapton. *Esquire* magazine once called him the number one guitarist in the country. Kessel was a member of the group of session musicians informally known as "the Wrecking Crew," who played on countless albums for iconic musicians such as Charlie Parker, Billie Holiday, Oscar Peterson, and the Beach Boys. (Barney Kessel's sons from an earlier marriage, Dan and David Kessel, grew up as brothers to the Rooney boys. The Kessel brothers themselves became noted musicians and music producers with rock 'n' roll icon Phil Spector.)

Teddy Rooney remembered a great story about Kessel: "Timmy was playing pool with George Harrison. When Harrison found out that Timmy's stepfather was Barney Kessel, he went berserk. He begged Timmy to call Barney and let George jam with him. Timmy called Barney and Barney said, 'Sorry, son. I don't jam with amateurs and hung up.'"

Throughout the 1960s, the Rooney Brothers toured the country, gaining a strong following. While the Rooney name opened doors for them, making the most of those opportunities didn't always come easy. The brothers discovered that because of their famous name, they had to work twice as hard to prove themselves.

Mickey Jr. was a member also of the surfing music group the Sunrays, which had a hit with "I Live for the Sun." Junior also played bass in Willie Nelson's band, and has recorded an album called *The Song Album*. Like his height, his musical talent was inherited from his mother, a gifted vocalist. His maternal grandmother taught him how to play the ukulele by showing him the chords, which he then taught himself to play on an acoustic guitar. In addition to bass and guitar, Mickey Jr. played drums, harmonica, and keyboards, and wrote music.

According to Dan Kessel in our interview:

> My stepbrothers, Mickey Rooney Jr. and Tim Rooney and
> Ted Rooney, had already been independently active on the
> music scene. Mickey recorded for Liberty Records, toured
> on the road, performed musically on TV shows like *Shindig*
> and in films like *Hot Rods to Hell*, with Dana Andrews and
> Jeanne Crain. Tim, who had been under contract to Warner
> Bros. as a young actor, did lots of dramatic stage work and
> was in the regular cast of the family sitcom *Room for One
> More*, as well as guest shots in episodic TV like *Hawaiian
> Eye*, *Dragnet*, and *Bewitched*. He also appeared in the teen
> films *Village of the Giants* and *Riot on Sunset Strip*. In
> fact, we were all there outside Pandora's Box the night of
> the real riot, when the cops started arresting everyone.

In 1966, Columbia Records signed the Rooney Brothers and took
them to producer Jerry Fuller, who, Kessel said, "was charting with
hit records like 'Young Girl,' by Gary Puckett and the Union Gap, and
'Little Green Apples,' by O. C. Smith." The name Rooney was important of course, and even by the mid-1960s it could open any door in the
industry. But the Rooney Brothers were talented in their own right,
playing and singing well, and composing their own music. Mickey Jr.,
the eldest, was the singer and songwriter, and led his younger step-
brothers into making some excellent records that reminded listeners
of harmonies they'd heard from the Beatles and the Byrds.

"The guys sounded great and looked great, and did their fair share
of TV performances," said Kessel, who accompanied them to studios
for some of their TV appearances, such as on *The Woody Woodbury
Show* and *Mike Douglas*. Although they gave strong performances,
Kessel remembers, "Columbia just didn't promote the records, and
thus they didn't chart." As a result, the group soon disbanded. How-

ever, Tim was selected to take the place of Davy Jones on *The Monkees* when the Colpix/Screen Gems division of Columbia feared that Jones, then classified 1A, would be drafted and shipped off to Vietnam.

Dan described what he called the "Sunset Strip lifestyle" in Mickey Jr.'s apartment in Los Angeles, where Tim and Ted would stay over. (Although he was younger, Kessel tried to spend whatever time he could with them.) These guys, he said, belonged to the in crowd, and "ran with people like Candice Bergen, Don Johnson, Scott Walker, Liza Minnelli, Terry Melcher, [singer-songwriter] Bobby Jameson, Sharon Tate, Johnny Crawford, [character actor] Paul Petersen, and Brian, Dennis, and Carl Wilson of the Beach Boys." Yes, these were the sixties, and yes, it was *that* Terry Melcher, Doris Day's son, who spurned Charles Manson's attempts to produce his music or take his music to his mother.

Timmy Rooney had his own circle of friends, including promising actress Farrah Fawcett, who had just arrived from Texas and whom Tim hooked up with songwriter Jimmy George; and actor Tommy Rettig, Jeff on *Lassie*, who also appeared in *River of No Return*, with Marilyn Monroe and Robert Mitchum. Tim met, fell in love with, and became engaged to Art Linkletter's daughter Diane, who lived across the street, but the engagement was cut short when she fell to her death from her sixth-floor apartment. Her father claimed the death was an LSD suicide, but Tim and his brothers, and Diane's friends, disagreed—and were supported in this by the county's toxicology report, which found no traces of LSD (or any drug) in her system. Tim was devastated by the loss, and believed, as did Diane's friends, that she was murdered by a man named Ed Durston, a drug dealer who lived in her building and was believed to be associated with Charles Manson and Sharon Tate, and might have been involved in other murders. Dan Kessel remembers Durston as a menacing figure.

The Rooneys and Dan were habitués of the LA club scene, where some of the hottest bands of the sixties performed, especially along the Strip and in Venice Beach, the center of LA's drug culture. Dan said:

> One night, we took their dad, Mickey, to one of the clubs to see Jimmy Reed and John Lee Hooker perform. They were blues artists, who along with Muddy Waters and a couple of others inspired the early Rolling Stones. Mickey [Jr.] and Tim and I had their records and knew all their lyrics by heart. We kept telling Mickey [Sr.] how great they were and how much he would love them. Of course, that night, when Jimmy Reed hit the stage with his band, he was bombed out of his head and spent the first twenty minutes trying to tune his guitar, which never did get in tune, and the band kind of all fell apart when they started playing. We followed after Mickey when he finally stormed out of the club screaming, 'I refuse to be a witness to this form of musical embarrassment.' It was a bad night for Jimmy, and we felt bad for him. But we also felt bad that we put Mickey through that when he'd been such a good sport to go there with us. After that, when we invited Mickey to go with us to the Monterey Pop Festival or other musical happenings, he always declined. He was totally burned out from the Jimmy Reed gig.

Kessel remembers another, more troubling story about the elder Mickey: "One evening in 1968, when Tim and I were visiting Mickey at his home in Beverly Hills, there was a knock on the door, which Tim answered. A serious-looking man, who seemed like an attorney, asked if Mickey was home. . . . The man said, 'Tell Mickey this is Mr. Maheu, and Howard wants to see him.'" Was this payback for the fistfight Ava Gardner said Mickey and Hughes got into when Mickey found Howard Hughes in her apartment? Or was it worse? Had Hughes bought up Mickey's debts to casino owner Moe Dalitz and the Vegas mob, and was he now trying to collect? Mickey would soon find out.

When Tim told Mickey who was at the door, Kessel remembers:

> Mickey turned off the shower and started yelling, "Why didn't you say so, son? Go let him in and bring me my suit off the hanger. Hurry, son. Let Mr. Maheu inside. Tell him I'll be right there in just a minute." Mickey splashed on some 40 Love cologne, jumped into a suit, tied his tie, and combed his hair with lightning speed." When the man told Mickey he was taking him to Vegas, Kessel recalls, Mickey said to his sons and Dan, "'How'd you like to go roll some dice in Vegas with your little daddy?' Tim and I looked at each other. Mickey [Sr.] looked at me. Then he answered himself, loudly proclaiming, "Sure you would!" Then, looking back and forth at both of us, he screamed, "Of course you would! You'd like it just fine! Come on, boys. We're gonna go see Howie." Tim and I . . . liked the idea of Vegas, but when Tim began to ask his dad who the hell was Howie, Mickey cocked his head to one side, looking him directly in the eye, and slowly whispered, "He's a man who needs to see your daddy, son. Come on, boys. You're going with me. They're going with me, Bob," he said [to the man], walking out the front door.
>
> In the car on the way to Vegas, Mickey explained that Howie was in fact Howard Hughes . . . and made several unsuccessful attempts to find out from Mr. Maheu why it was that Hughes wanted to see him. Mr. Maheu's only reply was for Mickey to relax and to be patient until they

arrived there, which of course was like asking lava to stop flowing down a volcano.

During the next four hours, the whole way there, Mickey was his usual nonstop self, running the gamut from lengthy and extremely animated episodes to moments of contemplative, existential meanderings, all of which encompassed general observations regarding the state of the world, vivid reenactments of recollections from decades gone by, assorted homespun bromides, and outlandish, creative business ideas. Tim and I actively conversed with him. Mr. Maheu was polite, but was disengaged and mostly silent.

When we got to the Vegas Strip, we pulled into the Desert Inn and drove into a special parking area. Three men in black suits suddenly appeared from the shadows . . . [and] stayed with us as we followed Mr. Maheu into a special utility elevator, not for public use. We all went up together, nonstop, to the top floor. We then exited the elevator, proceeding down a dimly lit hallway [and] around a corner to an unmarked door.

"Wh-where are we? Where's Howie?" Mickey wanted to know.

There was no answer given. It was disconcerting when Mr. Mahue abruptly bid us a curt farewell and disappeared around a corner, as the men in the black suits opened the door and instructed us to enter the room. Then one of them walked through another door on the far side of the room. Two men stayed with us.

Mickey told us, "I bet Howard is going to offer to sign me to a million-dollar contract!" Then, a minute later: "Maybe he wants to invest in Mickey Rooney Macaroni. It's a great idea, you know."

The longer we were sitting there, the darker Mickey became.

"Oh God, maybe he's going to have me thrown out of the window. I do have gambling debts with some of his friends. Maybe Howard's not really here. I do owe some gambling debts to some of his friends. Maybe they're gonna throw me out of the window. He's mad at me. That's it. I probably said some really bad things about him once, but that was so long ago! I think I'd like to leave. Yes, we'd like to leave now!" he said to the two men in suits. . . . "Just stay put, Mr. Rooney. It won't be long, now," one of them replied.

But Mickey was getting more nervous. "Wha-what's going on here? Why does Howard want to see me now? It's been so many years. Why am I being kept waiting like this? I'm Mickey Rooney. Why am I being kept in the dark?" he cried out in anguish.

Tim and I recognized that Mickey was having one of the anxiety attacks that had started plaguing him sporadically since the tragic loss of his wife Barbara a couple of years before. [Finally] the first man who had left us what seemed like hours ago but in reality was more like twenty minutes ago . . . came back.

"Follow me, Mr. Rooney," he said.

Mickey was starting to become borderline hysterical. Tim tried to calm him down . . . "Don't worry, Dad," Tim said. "Dan and I will go in there with you."

Suddenly the door flew open.

"Finally!" Mickey exclaimed, jumping up. Pointing to us and motioning through the open door, he told the man in the suit, "They go with me everywhere I go." . . . [But] the man shook his head and said, "That's not possible." . . .

Later, when we were alone in our room, Mickey explained it to us like this. Hughes was in bed. . . . He told Mickey that he wasn't in the best of health and didn't know how much time he had left. Mickey asked what he'd been doing. Hughes said he'd been buying lights. Mickey asked him what he meant by 'buying lights.' From his bed, Hughes pointed toward the window, out to the night sky and the twinkling lights. He said he couldn't buy any more time for himself but that he could buy lots of lights.

'You're buying stars? Will the government let you do that?'

'Lights,' Hughes said.

He explained to Mickey how he was buying up hotels. But that's not what he wanted to talk to Mickey about. He wanted to apologize to Mickey because he said he always liked him and he felt guilty about Ava Gardner. Hughes said he had been pursuing Ava while she was still married to Mickey and that he might have been the cause of their divorce and that he felt bad about it for years. Mickey told Hughes it was all water under the bridge and, he told us, that in the end, when they said their good-byes, they both felt better about everything.

That was it in a nutshell. At dinner that night, Tim and I clinked glasses with Mickey as he proposed a toast to Howard Hughes.

And that was the story Dan Kessel told us about Mickey Rooney's seeing Howard Hughes before his death, hearing Hughes's final confession about what he believed was his role in Mickey's divorce from Ava Gardner. But most of all, this was about B.J.'s legacy and the glory days of the Rooney Brothers.[31]

The Seventies:
Aftermath of Tragedy

Mickey and Dick Cavett.
PHOTO COURTESY OF ROBERT FINKEL.

After Barbara Ann's death, Mickey was reeling. It was one thing to endure a publicly embarrassing and financially devastating divorce, but quite another to have violence and death spread through your life like an unstoppable virus.

Red Doff was the next victim.

Doff was both his personal manager and closest confidant. He had been with Mickey, first as a publicist and then as his personal manager, since the early 1950s. Their relationship had endured longer than his marriages and many of his friendships. Mickey trusted Red's judgment and often relied on his advice. Thus, when Red's four-year-old daughter, Carol, drowned only two months after Barbara's death, Mickey was deeply affected.

"Nobody could have been a better friend at a time like that," Doff recalled. "He stayed by our sides night and day, helping with the funeral arrangements and even paying for the catering after the funeral." [1]

"Mickey and my father had a bond," Melody Doff said in our interview. "I can remember my father giving him advice and really taking great concern of his well being."

Mickey suffered another startling and painful loss when his "sister," as he referred to his childhood friend and costar Judy Garland, died at age forty-seven. Garland had faced a roller-coaster ride when she departed MGM. After her divorce from director Vincente Minnelli, she had married the rough-and-tumble Jewish promoter Sid Luft. They had a rocky marriage, and Luft disliked Mickey.

"For many years, when she was married to Luft, we were not in contact much," Mickey told us in 2008. "He didn't like me, and it was vice versa. When she separated from him in the early sixties, Judy and I would get together. I saw her at the Palace perform, did her TV show, and we talked."

Kelly Rooney reminisced to us: "I remember all the kids going with Dad to Judy's beach house. We saw [her kids] Lorna, Liza, and Joey there, and we all hung out. I can remember Judy cleaning, wearing her 'cleaning clothes' and humming 'Somewhere Over the Rainbow.' While the kids got together, my dad and Judy would talk and reminisce and kick back a few. Judy was a hoot and so much fun. My dad and her would just have a blast together. It was wonderful to watch."

Mickey told radio and television host Larry King that he talked to Judy during her serious hospitalization in New York City during the mid-1960s, when she had overdosed and suffered another nervous breakdown. She had been in and out of hospitals over the years, fighting battles with drugs and alcohol. (It was actually in 1959 when Judy was in the hospital for weeks, due to hepatitis C and cirrhosis of the liver.)

King asked, "Did you talk to her, Mickey, during those days?"

Rooney said, "Yes, and I tried—I sent a football player to New York. She was in the hospital, and I wanted to get her out of there and take care of her . . . Ray Pearson, played for UCLA. He's a friend of mine.

King asked, "What, to pep her up, or to get her out?"

Mickey replied, "No, to help get her out. And so I called her on the phone and I said—I said, 'Judy,' I said, 'I've sent Ray Pearson to talk to you, see if you want to come home.' Anyway, she—she said, 'Do you think I can make it?' He said she answered him in that "little voice." [2]

A completely different version of Mickey's conversation with Judy than that recounted on the air with Larry King appears in his autobiography, in which he claims that he continued to try to help Judy throughout her tragic last years. In the autobiography, his version is that Judy was in Boston, not in a hospital, while he was preparing to appear in *George M!*, and that just before her death, she called him at three in the morning sounding desperate. Rooney writes, "She said, 'I can't get arrested.' I made a snap judgement. If she was calling me at 3 am, she was in real trouble. 'Judy,' I said, 'I want you to stop singing for a couple of years. You need money? I'll get you money . . . we'll make it together. I just want you to get off whatever you're on, Judy. I just want you to be well, my angel. I know you can make it.' She said, 'Mick, do-you-really-think-I can-make it?'" [3] Like many of the stories Mickey wrote about in both his autobiographies or that he told in countless interviews, the facts and events change or were ad-libbed. Mickey reinvented history for every conversation, every interview, contradicting himself even on basic facts that his readers and listeners already knew. He did this because, for him, truth was only what he needed at the moment. It was the essence of what made him a great performer: there was no reality underlying how he projected himself.

The facts regarding Judy's downward spiral and death are these: By the mid-1960s, Judy had moved to New York City. She had divorced Luft and married a bisexual con artist named Mark Herron, who physically abused her. She also had a relationship with a songwriter named Johnny Meyer, before her last marriage, to musician/mobster/drug dealer/con artist Mickey Deans, since deceased.

Author Rick Lertzman got to know Deans during the 1990s, and he gave his own version of Garland's last days: "Judy was on any drug she could get her hands on. She always wanted me to get her 'ludes [Quaaludes]. I remember Rooney was trying to get involved in some fucking acting school, the Mickey and Judy School or some fucking idiotic idea. He was just all lip service. He never helped Judy out. I don't think he had a pot to piss in. He was doing his own drugs."

After Garland's death, Deans cowrote the 1972 biography *Weep No More, My Lady: The Story of Judy Garland*.[4] He was also later suspected in the murder of his boss, Roy Radin, the producer of Francis Ford Coppola's *Cotton Club*. Deans passed away in 2003, ending his life as a promoter/mob character in Cleveland, Ohio.

When Mickey was told Judy had died, he claimed he was heartbroken. He wrote that when he heard of her death he was on a golf course, and he "felt a sudden deep chill in my bones. Then I walked over to the green, dropped to my knees and pounded the ground with my fist. 'Why, Judy? Why?' I hit the ground as hard as I could, maybe thirty or forty times. My heart was broken."[5]

With Barbara's death, Mickey now had the responsibility of being a father to their four children all under nine years old, even though they had been put in the custody of Barbara's parents. (Mickey Jr. and Timmy were living with Betty Jane, and Teddy with Martha Vickers.) His housekeeper, Mrs. Hogan, he discovered, had a drinking problem, so he relied on the aid of Barbara's close friend and his soon-to-be next wife, Margaret "Marge" Lane. Marge, who worked as a Realtor, helped keep the Rooney house running smoothly. Marge was not the type of woman Rooney often chased: She was older (forty-five, born in 1921), educated in accounting (rather than an aspiring entertainer), a member of the Church of Religious Science (and very religious), and more matronly and mature than Rooney's usual female companions. Other than having been Barbara's best friend, she had no connection to show business.

In 1966, Nell died of a heart attack, but Mickey was so overcome with the murder of Barbara Ann that he was numb to the death of his mother. He was a mess, taking countless drugs, prescription and otherwise, and drinking heavily. His in-laws were suing him for permanent custody of the kids. Also, Nell's passing did not come as a huge shock because she had long suffered from cardiac ailments. She had continued to drink heavily with her husband. Kelly Rooney remembered "Nanny Nell's" drinking, as did Sidney Miller, who said she was an alcoholic like her husbands, Joe Sr. and Fred Pankey. Miller said she was a heavy smoker as well.

Marge Lane told Arthur Marx, "About a month after Barbara's death, I started going over to Mickey's house to see if I could help with the children, particularly the babies. It was a lot for the housekeeper to take care of, and Mickey was most receptive. I'd sometimes do the grocery shopping, I'd take the children to church or pick them up at their grandparent's house in Inglewood and take them back to Mickey's when it was his turn to have them, and take them back again."[6]

When Mickey left for a three-month shooting of *The Devil in Love* on location in Malta, his assistant, Bill Gardner, was unable to take care of the kids, and the drunk housekeeper asked Barbara's parents to take them. When Mickey returned from Malta and saw how well his in-laws had taken care of the kids, he reluctantly made an arrangement of co-guardianship with them. He paid them one thousand dollars a month for their support and retained visitation rights. He arranged for the kids to sleep over on weekends, when it was convenient. He also moved to a smaller home in Benedict Canyon.

While Mickey could hardly afford another marriage, he liked the stability that Marge Lane brought to his life. She was almost like Andy Hardy's movie mother, Emily. Mickey was an utter disaster both emotionally and physically, and he began to count on her, and she made herself available to him. When he got down on one knee and proposed marriage, she readily accepted.

On September 10, 1966—only seven months after Barbara's murder—as was his pattern, he chartered a plane to Las Vegas and they were married with sons Mickey Jr. and Timmy as witnesses. Marge Lane became Mickey's sixth wife. He was now tied with Henry VIII—and paying for it.

"It was a strange marriage. Mickey was in such a state he would have married an orangutang," said Bob Finkel, who had hired Mickey for several variety shows he'd produced. "With the tall Marge and the diminutive Mickey it was an odd sight. The homunculus and the gazelle." [7]

Immediately after the wedding, Mickey embarked on a lucrative performance tour of Australia with Marge and his stage partner Bobby Van. Red Doff felt that Marge was disappointed that touring wasn't more glamorous. Mickey avoided autograph hunters, rarely ventured outside his hotel room after each show, and knocked himself out with sleeping pills. When they returned to the United States, a curious press took notice of the "new" Mickey and how he had seemingly settled down with a churchgoing woman only one year younger than he, who was known to his kids as Aunt Margie.

Marge told Arthur Marx, "Our whole marriage was planned by Mickey and his managers in order to change his public image. He needed work and had to show the world he was dependable and respectable again, not running after young girls, and not on pills. I didn't know anything about the pills, at the time. I was pretty innocent and just played right in their hands. I thought the world of Mickey, I really did, up until I discovered what was going on." [8]

"Aunt Margie" discovered a very different Mickey from the man she believed she knew. She recalled, "He had pills hidden in different places in the house, like Ray Milland and his liquor bottles in 'The Lost Weekend.' If he took them, he couldn't go to work in the morning. So I had to stay awake all night to try to keep him off them. I finally wound up with nervous exhaustion from keeping an eye on him . . ." And he was cheating on her. "Even on my birthday, one month after we were married, he was up in Tahoe with someone else," Marge said. He was also suggesting they engage in sexual activity that the religious Marge could not tolerate. She revealed, "Barbara told me of some of the sexual things she had to put up with. When he suggested, well you know, the imaginative things he wanted to do . . . well, I believe he has an aversion to women, quite a complex about proving his manliness. I think he got this from his early years backstage at the burlesque house. Anyway, I finally told him, 'Look Mickey, I'd have to lose my soul to do what you want to do. You can have another girlfriend if you want, but I can't do these things.'" [9]

In early December 1966, Marge caught the flu and went to her girlfriend's home to recover, to avoid infecting Mickey or the kids. During her recovery, Red Doff called her girlfriend and told her to tell Marge not to return to their house and that Mickey was filing for divorce. They had been married for only about one hundred days. Marge was hurt but relieved. On December 23, 1966, Marge, herself, filed for divorce. Thus, in less than a year, Mickey lost a wife to murder and another through divorce. Marge left the house and never spoke to Mickey again. It took about a year for their attorneys to negotiate a settlement. On December 14, 1967, the divorce was granted. Compared to the other divorces, this one came cheap. The alimony was $350 per month for one year and payment of community debts of $5,348, and Marge was allowed to keep her car. Despite the minimal alimony, Mickey lacked the funds to pay even that, and a bench warrant was issued for his arrest in September 1968 for nonpayment. He eventually paid up. In our interview with Rooney, when mentioning his marriage to Lane, he said—jokingly, because at that point his eight marriages had become the stuff of satire—"I think that was her name, anyway."

The 1970s started out extremely slowly for Mickey but picked up by mid-decade, and he wound up making a steady stream of movies. After a prolific mid-1960s on television, he was completely absent from the set from mid-1967 to October 1970. However, he did four films in three years: *The Extraordinary Seaman*, *Skidoo*, *The Comic*, and *80 Steps to Jonah*. His only theater appearance was a summer tour of *George M!* in 1969 and a few stints at the Flamingo in Vegas and the Cal-Neva Lodge in Tahoe, in 1968 and 1969 with Bobby Van, which paid some of the bills. To an objective observer, it did seem that Mickey was being forgotten.

In the aftermath of his failed series, he was a complete pariah on television, an untouchable to sponsors. No matter how hard Doff worked to get Mickey a part, he was always vetoed by the network. The actor was effectively blacklisted, not for his political affiliations (like writer Dalton Trumbo and others called before the House Un-American Activities Committee during the late 1940s and early 1950s), but, like movie and television star Bob Cummings, who a decade earlier became addicted to Dr. Feelgood's methamphetamine shots,[10] for his prescription drug problem. His drug use had become widely known, which frightened the film producers, who in addition to having to put up with Mickey on set fighting with directors, refusing to read the lines he was given, or insulting his sponsors and their ad agencies, had to prove to insurance companies that the actor was still insurable despite his drug problem. So, to pay the bills, Mickey set out on the dinner theater circuit, appearing in *Luv, See How They Run, Show Boat,* and *Good Night Ladies.* He returned to a similar circuit of his youth, performing at the Municipal Auditorium in Kansas City, Busch Palace in St. Louis, and the Packard Music Hall in Warren, Ohio. He was back onstage in the venue where he was raised and where he'd been understood. He had the moves, the rhythm, and the patter all down, which allowed him great freedom to expand and even ad-lib the parts he played.

In another strange business venture, Rooney also lent his name, and an investment, to a moderately priced resort in Downingtown, Pennsylvania, outside Philadelphia, called Mickey Rooney's Tabas Hotel. Mickey was given a part interest, along with Red Doff, and starred in their advertising campaign and as nightclub host. He continued to appear in the hotel's "Mickey Rooney Room" for nearly the next thirty years, along with performers such as Frankie Valli, Frank Sinatra Jr., and Bobby Rydell. The hotel closed in 1998, but many readers of New York and Philadelphia newspapers might remember the Sunday edition ads featuring Mickey's invitation to join him in Downingtown.

Doff had started a company to create investments for Mickey called Productions Eleven, Inc., but after a dispute with Rooney, he took leave of Mickey again. Their co-investor, Florida promoter Alexander O. Curtis, took over as Mickey's manager in 1969. Doff sued Mickey for back fees of $8,800 for bookings into the Fremont Hotel in Las Vegas and some television appearances, a suit they later settled amicably.

Curtis, who produced shows on the dinner theater circuit, stayed by Mickey's side for the next three years as the actor became known as the King of the Dinner Theater. Earning between $2,500 and $5,000 per week, Rooney and Curtis traveled through Illinois, Wisconsin, Missouri, Ohio, North Carolina, Louisiana, Florida, appearing at countless venues . He was a regular at Howard Douglass Wolfe's Barn

Dinner Theatre, who, along with his business partner Conley Jones, had a chain of twenty-seven such theaters in New York, Virginia, North Carolina, Tennessee, Texas, Louisiana, and Georgia that kept actors such as Rooney, Bob Cummings, Donald O'Connor, Jane Russell, Van Johnson, Lana Turner, and Joey Bishop busy for many years. (In the summer of 1966, Robert De Niro reportedly was canned midshow during a production at the Barn in Greensboro, North Carolina.) By 1975 there were 147 dinner theaters throughout the United States. The circuit became the source of income for Mickey for the next ten years along with his appearances at Downingtown.

Surprisingly, Mickey's output of films remained constant during the 1970s, picking up after a slow start, with twenty films spread across the decade. While most of the films were low-budget releases until later in the decade, he remained before the camera nonetheless.

The decade began with a fun piece of fluff called *Cockeyed Cowboys of Calico County*, in 1970, from Universal, starring *Bonanaza*'s Dan Blocker (Hoss Cartwright), with Mickey in a small role as Indian Tom, another politically questionable character. The next film has to be the low point in Mickey's nearly ninety-year film career: *Hollywood Blue* (1970), an embarrassing pornographic film, intersperses hard-core porn shots with a clothed Mickey and June Wilkinson, Mickey's and Maurice Duke's on-again, off-again shared romantic interest, talking about the Hollywood sex life. Mickey, who prided himself on doing family films, rarely mentioned this movie, which he had agreed to do because he was desperate for money.

The next year, he made only one, a picture called *The Manipulator*, or *B.J. Lang Presents*, which stars Mickey as a film-industry makeup man who goes crazy by kidnapping an actress and holding her hostage on a back lot. The film was R-rated for violence and nudity.

The next year, 1972, Mickey appeared in what has become a cult comedy classic, *Evil Roy Slade*. A precursor to *Blazing Saddles*, it was a made-for-television movie that spoofed Westerns and starred John

Astin (*The Addams Family*). Mickey received top billing as a railroad tycoon.

He followed this with another offbeat film, one that lampooned President Richard Nixon, called *Richard* (1972), in which he plays Nixon's guardian angel. His third film, *Pulp* (1972), starred Michael Caine. In it, Mickey plays Preston Gilbert, a washed-up 1930s movie star, a role close to home. He earned several great notices for it, including one in *Time* magazine, on May 22, 1972, that said, "The performance, like the movie itself, deserves to become some crazy kind of minor classic."

In 1973, Mickey did one only one picture, a slapstick spoof called *The Godmothers*, in which he is credited for the screenplay and the music. Mickey plays part of the film in drag, with comic Jerry Lester, à la *Some Like It Hot*. The story of the "witless wonders of the underworld," the film was shot in Mickey's new hometown of Fort Lauderdale, Florida.

He filled in the gaps with some television appearances, including *The Name of the Game*, with Gene Barry, Robert Culp, Tom Skeritt, and Susan Saint James in 1970. He then did the voice of Santa Claus in what has become a yearly holiday classic, *Santa Claus Is Coming to Town*, an animated special by Rankin/Bass that featured Fred Astaire as the narrator. (Interestingly, he did the porn film *Hollywood Blue* the same year.) He appeared in *Dan August*, with Burt Reynolds, the next year. In 1972, Mickey appeared in *Fol-de-Rol*, the Sid and Marty Krofft musical special that costarred Rick Nelson, Howard Cosell, Totie Fields, Ann Sothern, and Cyd Charisse. His final project in 1972 was an episode of Rod Serling's *Night Gallery*, with Mickey as a vicious crime boss. After his move to Florida, though, there was a two-year lull until his next television appearance, in 1974.

His dinner theater work continued in 1970 with *George M!* and *Hide and Seek*, and in 1971, *Three Goats and a Blanket*, with Mickey playing a part that hit close to home: a man with alimony troubles.

He portrayed the great film comedian W. C. Fields in a musical called W.C., that costarred the talented Bernadette Peters. Although the play was well received in the pre-Broadway tour in Baltimore, Detroit, and at the Westbury Music Fair in New York, it folded before hitting Broadway. The reviews were positive, however, with *Newsday* writing on July 10, 1974, "With Mickey Rooney playing W. C. Fields, the musical has a measure of charm, some bright tunes and solid lyrics by Al Carmines, a fairly interesting book by Milton Sperling and Sam Locke, and an engaging Fields impersonation by Rooney." Mickey had his heart set on a Broadway debut and continued to work toward it—a goal he would finally achieve with *Sugar Babies* later that decade.

After divorce number six from Marge, Mickey took his longest romantic hiatus since he married Ava at twenty-one. He was nearing fifty and after six marriages and seven children; the death of his mother, whom he once called a sponge and whose funeral he declined to attend; the murder of his wife; bankruptcy; his career skidding; and his public humiliation on national television; he had not had time to step back and evaluate his life. Was Mickey truly reflective about the direction his career had taken? Did he contemplate why he had failed in personal relationships with both men and women? He did not maintain any friendships with his ex-wives after their divorces. He never was a particularly hands-on father. He would see his kids as needed, when it suited him. He left the responsibility of child rearing to Betty Jane, Martha, and the Thomasons. His friendships were rooted more in who could assist him in promoting his career and earning him money. He was also always on the lookout for his new flavor of the moment. He changed management at a whim or when managers who tried to work for him found him unmanageable. Now, by the early 1970s, it was Alexander O. Curtis, whose work for Mickey focused on dinner theater productions. Amid the glare of lights from one venue to the next, even as audiences flocked to see him onstage recreating hits from favorite Broadway shows, even moving from one casual flirtation to another, wherever he went, Mickey Rooney was alone.

Even friends since childhood, such as Sidney Miller, Sig Frohlich, Dick Paxton, Dick Quine, and Jackie Cooper never really got close to Rooney, except when drinking and carousing. He had no extended family beyond his late mother and father. If Buddha is right that there is an island in each of us, and when we go home to ourselves we are on that safe island, then Mickey lived solely on that island. The one constant through the countless interviews we conducted for this book was that although many of the subjects claimed to have *known* Rooney, none ever truly knew him. They knew the persona Mickey had portrayed since he was a child—but that was really all there was to know. When we delved into what made Mickey run, no one could quite answer the question. Whether it was stepson Christopher Aber, who was with him almost daily for more than thirty years; his children Teddy, Kelly, or Kerry; his friends of more than seventy years such as Sidney Miller; or his wife of more than thirty-five years, Jan Chamberlin—no one truly knew what drove Mickey and who the real Mickey Rooney was. Was it possible no real Joseph Yule Jr. ever existed? That the person named Mickey Rooney was only a situational construct? Was the only real Mickey Rooney the guy who was on for the audience, on for the camera, or on for each of his wives and friends—until he was off? Was their no real person inside the created character that was Mickey Rooney? Simply put, was the secret of Mickey Rooney that there was no Mickey Rooney?

All of Mickey's remaining resilience would be tested as he approached two mileposts on his last attempt to resurrect his career. And they were coming up fast.

Escape from Los Angeles

Mickey directs actress Helen Walker in
My True Story *in 1951, his directorial debut.*
PHOTO COURTESY OF ROBERT EASTON.

As **Mickey's divorce from Marge Lane** moved from an interlocutory judgment to a final decree, Mickey was back on the chase, at least while he was legally barred from getting married again. In the late 1960s he entered a skein of relationships. One was with the ex-wife of comedian Shecky Greene, who told us that Mickey and Jeri, a former cocktail waitress, lived together for a while. Greene told us, "Mickey Rooney's another Elizabeth Taylor, only without the tits."

(Clearly Shecky did not know what had happened between Mickey and Liz.) Harrison Carroll wrote in the *Los Angeles Herald Examiner* on April 17, 1968, "Mickey was getting serious" with Jeri Greene. When he asked Mickey if he was making another trip to the altar, Mickey replied with his usual self-deprecating humor: "No, we're still very much in love . . . Marge Lane hasn't picked up her divorce decree yet. So I haven't married today. But give me time. It's only eleven o'clock in the morning."

Yet Mickey's holiday from marriage did not last long, and his first step in that direction began with a move to Florida. After the job in the quasi-porn flick *Hollywood Blue*, he claimed he felt humiliated and embarrassed. "I was so ashamed of my little part that I got the hell out of town, for good. I moved to Florida, determined that I would have nothing more to do with Hollywood."[1]

Packing up and leaving LA was not without its problems, though, particularly for his seven children, four of whom were under twelve. He also had obligations to two ex-wives and owed considerable money to attorneys, advisers, former managers, and others. His earning power was at its lowest in decades. For many years, even in what he had considered times of drought, he was earning between $200,000 and $300,000 per year. By 1970, however, many of the lucrative Las Vegas gigs (for which he was making around $20,000 per week) had dried up. He was relying on dinner theater, for which he got between $2,500 and $5,000 per week, which would have kept him barely abovewater, but there was a lot of downtime when the money pipe ran dry.

While he was in Miami in 1969 and playing a couple of nightclub dates, he was invited to a celebrity golf tournament at the famous Doral Country Club, where his friend Jackie Gleason often held court. (Gleason had relocated to Miami and was producing his weekly television variety show from Miami Beach.) While Mickey was there, a *Miami Herald* sportswriter introduced him to a pretty, young customer relations representative from the *Herald* named Carolyn Hockett. Twenty-five, divorced, with a three-year-old son named Jimmy, she bore an eerie resemblance to Barbara Ann. Born Carolyn Zack on August 19, 1943, in Columbus, Ohio, she was the eldest of six children. After an unsuccessful marriage to Jerry Hockett that produced a son in 1966, Carolyn moved to Miami. She was a strict Catholic and very outgoing. Mickey, twenty-three years her senior, was smitten and flew her and Jimmy to Los Angeles to meet his kids.

On May 27, 1969, after another short courtship, Mickey, following his by-now-established custom, chartered a plane to Las Vegas and got married. Red Doff had booked him into the Fremont Hotel to do a week of shows with Bobby Van. Mickey and Carolyn's daughter, Jonelle, was born seven months later, on January 11, 1970.

The press jumped on the news of Mickey's seventh marriage, and he was ready with the witticisms. He'd tell them: "I'm going to march in the Rose Bowl Parade in Pasadena some New Year's with Mickey Rooney and His All-Wife Marching Band"; or "When I said to the minister at the wedding chapel, 'I do, I do,' he said, 'I know, I know'"; or "I keep a wedding license with me at all times. It's made out to 'To Whom it May Concern.'"

The harsh reality was that his pockets were empty. He was flat broke. The dinner theater income paid the child support and alimony, keeping him out of jail, but he was drowning in debt. Carolyn talked him into moving to her adopted hometown in south Florida, where, through a friend, they found a small house on Forty-Fifth Street in Fort Lauderdale, near the Coral Ridge Country Club. The move worked out well when Mickey's old friend actor Eddie Bracken, with whom he had appeared in the 1953 film *A Slight Case of Larceny*, became part owner of Miami's Coconut Grove Playhouse about an hour's drive away. Thus, Mickey could live in Fort Lauderdale and find work at a local theater.

Bracken hired Mickey to appear in a new play called *Three Goats and a Blanket*, about a television producer with alimony troubles, a part to which Mickey could easily relate, especially as he played off Bracken, who costarred. Audiences loved the play, and they toured in this vehicle for nearly ten years. *Variety* wrote, "Putting Mickey Rooney into a farce about a man with alimony troubles must have seemed a likely gimmick. The acting is worthy of the vehicle. Rooney enters all over the place." *Three Goats and a Blanket* (*Stop Thief Stop* or *Alimony*), written by Woody Kling, would become a staple of dinner theater, a phenomenon over the next decade, and a high-grossing play.

While Mickey was back onstage, feeling alive again, his four children with Barbara were now living comfortably with their grandparents, the Thomasons, in a beautiful gated community in Rolling Hills, near Palos Verdes, California. The grandparents provided a stable life for Kelly, Kimmy, Kerry, and Michael Kyle, supported financially by Mickey, who paid a thousand dollars a month, whenever he could, in child support. On vacations and some holidays, he flew them in for a visit to Fort Lauderdale. In 1972, Mickey decided that having full custody of the kids would be cheaper than the thousand per month in child support and air fare, and he hired Beverly Hills attorney Robert Neeb to file a motion in Los Angeles County for sole custody.

Child custody cases are bitter and ugly, as anyone who has litigated one will sadly attest. So it was with *Rooney v. Thomason*, a particularly messy court case that came to trial on August 24, 1972, in Los Angeles Superior Court. The Thomasons displayed their serious intention to retain custody by appearing with their high-priced attorney, the celebrated Marvin Mitchelson (later known for winning the landmark *Lee Marvin v. Michelle Triola* case, in which Mitchelson argued the legal precedent for "palimony," still applicable law today in California). Mickey's former mother-in-law, Helen Thomason, testified that she did not dislike Mickey, only his actions. She testified that he traveled often and would leave without even acknowledging the children. She also said he had missed countless meetings, appointments, and arrangements with the kids. His former secretary, Bill Gardner, testified that the children were better off with their grandparents. In summary, the defendants argued, Mickey was an irresponsible, self-absorbed, unfit parent.

Arguing on behalf of Mickey, his pastor testified that Mickey had found God and had married a good Christian woman, who would help with the children. Then of course, on the stand, playing for the moment, Rooney gave a brilliant performance, stating how he had found God and needed his children to live with him to make his life complete. The court disagreed. Despite the Rooney performance, the pastor's testimony, and compelling testimony from Carolyn on her maternal skills, the judge held for the Thomasons, though it was unusual in California for a biological father, who had a wife to assist with child rearing, to lose custodial rights. However, the judge cited the stability the children had had with the Thomasons since 1966, and the lower court's initial action of placing the children with their grandparents after their daughter died and while their son-in-law was committed to work on movie locations out of the state. In a fifteen-page decision, Judge Mario Clinco stated that the children's life with the Thomasons had been one of "regularity, stability, love, strong emotional ties and dependence and companionship. To award Mr. Rooney sole custody would be detrimental to the children." He also said that in a meeting with them in his chambers, the children had expressed a preference for remaining with their grandparents.[2] Under the court's custody ruling, Mickey remained a co-guardian, with full visitation rights, and of course was ordered to make continued child support payments.

• • •

ENTER RUTH WEBB. WEBB is now known for her representation of supermarket checkout line tabloid headline makers such as the penile-challenged John Wayne Bobbitt; America's most famous guesthouse resident nonwitness Kato Kalin; and a celebrated auto mechanic whose tryst with the teenage "Long Island Lolita" propelled him into the national consciousness, and into jail, and thence into reality television. But for Mickey Rooney, who'd outlived many of his managers and agents and was desperate to find someone who would plug away to get him parts wherever they appeared, she was one of the few old-time talent agents still standing.

While kicking around the dinner theater circuit, Mickey was being represented by Milton Deutsch. When Deutsch suddenly passed away in 1970, the actor was left with no agent for the first time since Harry Weber took him on in 1926. Good fortune rained on Mickey, though, when pal Eddie Bracken recommended him to small-time Hollywood agent Ruth Webb. Mickey, who was accustomed to strong-minded male managers and agents such as Sam Stiefel, Johnny Hyde, Bullets Durgom, and Maurice Duke, liked the spunk of this former actress whose most notable client at the time was television actor Gene Barry (*War of the Worlds*, *Bat Masterson*, *Burke's Law*). She had previously represented major stars from the 1940s studio glory days.

Ruth didn't have an office. Instead, she operated out of her home, actually, as the *New York Times* described it in her obituary (December 17, 2006), her "unusually appointed bedroom." A postmodern interpretation of *The Addams Family* meets Castle Dracula, the room featured a clutch of stuffed and live raccoons, whom she lovingly fed by hand, and lace cobwebs that hung so deep from the stachybotrys-covered beams that they looked like curtains; you had to part them just to walk through. Her office-bedroom was hidden in the back of a house nestled hard against the collapsing walls of Nichols Canyon in the Hollywood Hills, where it was darker than the land of Mordor. Visiting clients would be forced to move the raccoon installations in order to sit near her bed, which, by the way, looked like it was covered in a thin layer of soil from the country of her birth. But it was the raccoons, the raccoons! Those eyes, red in the soft light, were unwavering; they would stare at you as she fed them. You would never forget them.

Webb, to her credit, was the major influence in the resurrection of Mickey's career in the 1970s. It was her strong belief in Mickey's talent that brought him back from obscurity to his great triumph on Broadway in *Sugar Babies*. A desperate Mickey more than appreciated her perseverance on his behalf, writing, "Agents should all take a lesson from Ruth Webb. She always gave more than I ever expected. Ruth Webb was a real striver. She was something of a dynamo, an energy source that pumped away day and night on my behalf . . . She made it impossible for people to forget me."[3] Comedienne Phyllis Diller, one of Webb's clients, told us, "Ruth was eccentric and quirky, but she was very loyal. She really was the 'unsinkable' Ruth Webb," Diller said, referring to the *New York Times* obituary for Webb. "She was a mix of Zsa Zsa Gabor and Auntie Mame." The *Times* also mentioned that Webb also represented screen stars such as Kathryn Grayson, Rhonda Fleming, Dorothy Lamour, Donald O'Connor, Gloria Swanson, Gig Young, Ann Sothern, Chuck Connors, Tiny Tim, Bert Parks, and Rose Marie. The *Times* also said that Webb was "a successful Hollywood agent who was a master of the art of professional rehabilitation, reviving dormant careers and representing clients few other agencies would touch." Indeed.

And Mickey stiffed her out of her final commission.

As Webb took over Mickey's career, she started finding him work in dinner theaters, small film roles, and some television. She worked hard, cared deeply for her client, helped him through his personal difficulties, and found him bookings anywhere someone would pay him.

As Mickey slogged through city after city in the tour of *Three Goats and a Blanket*, new wife Carolyn was spending his earnings freely. Timmy Rooney told Pam McClenathan, who later repeated it to us, that Carolyn's spending was the source of many arguments between the Rooneys. Their constant fighting over who could spend the money Mickey was bringing in created a rift between them, and the marriage started cracking within the first couple of years. "The constant touring, being away from home, the money troubles, and Mickey's wandering eye never helped," Sidney Miller told us.

Ever the optimist, and despite his complete lack of financial acumen, Mickey also tried his hand at business—and fell for countless schemes, lured by people he would meet on the road or at the racetrack, in which he would invest with blind confidence that he would strike it rich. There were innumerable (potential and realized) businesses and products, including:

- Mickey Rooney's Two-Ball Golf-a-Chair, for indoor golf facilities.
- Lovely Lady Cosmetics, with a woman's cologne called Me, and others called Trapeze, Taming the Shrew, and Twelfth Night. (It was even more surprising that he didn't develop a men's cologne called Kiss Me Kate.)
- Complete, an aerosol spray that painted on hair for men (a product that, surprisingly, actually exists, although it is not the one Mickey sought to develop).
- A pharmaceutical company called Elim, with products such as an analgesic, Elim-Ache; a laxative, Elim-n-Ate; a diet aid, Elim-a-Weight; and a foot powder, Elim-a-Itch. "Elim," get it? Nobody else did.
- Rip-Offs, disposable shorts for men and women in a hurry, either in the bathroom or in the bedroom. No need to fuss

with those pesky buttons or zippers. Just put your hands together and pull.

- Tip Offs. Yes, it was a disposable bra. Why? Nobody knows, but Fruit of the Loom rejected the idea faster than you could dispose of the bra.
- Puppy Pop, to give your dog a bubbly personality. This idea for a dog drink Ralston Purina turned down flat—flatter than yesterday's half-empty glass of Pepsi.
- Coins with movie star images, which the Franklin Mint turned down. Too bad Mickey didn't approach the U.S. Post Office, which, years later, issued stamps featuring movie star images.
- Mickey Rooney's Weenie World, a fast-food chain with a round hot dog on a hamburger bun, to be called the Weenie Whirl. Also to be included were the Mickey Yankee Doodle (mac-n-cheese), a relish called Micklish, Eric Von Weenie sauerkraut, and Mickey's Pancho Weenie.
- Mickey Melon, a melon-flavored soft drink marketed by Canfield Beverage, but not the one Mickey proposed.
- Thirs-T, a carbonated iced tea, a product which is available today not from Mickey, but from whole earth soft drink companies. Clearly, Mickey's idea was ahead of its time.

Every one of Mickey's get-rich-quick schemes met with failure, and ended up costing him money. His friend actor/director/producer Jackie Cooper explained to us that "Mickey had zero business sense. Even if they succeeded he had no organizational skills, never understood money management and surrounded himself with the cast of *Guys and Dolls* as advisers. He was in a no-win situation. It was a lose-lose proposition."

Donald Trump agreed: "He once asked me about an investment in a hotel near Philadelphia. I advised him against it, but he didn't listen and went ahead with the investment, which failed." [4]

One of Mickey's ideas, however, was reasonable. In 1972 he called Liza Minnelli's then-husband, Jack Haley Jr., whose father had been a star at MGM with Mickey (not to mention the Tin Man opposite Liza's mother, Judy, in *The Wizard of Oz*). Haley Jr. was then the head of MGM and in a position to discuss Mickey's idea, this time for a business Rooney understood: motion pictures. Mickey asked Haley for footage from his films to use in a documentary Mickey wanted to produce about his career. He told Haley he intended to intersperse clips with "wrap-around" on-screen introductions from Rooney. Haley said no, but the idea had traction. Four months later, he called Mickey back with a similar idea, a project called *That's Entertainment*, a retrospective of MGM musicals, which would include Mickey, Frank Sinatra, Gene Kelly, Fred Astaire, Peter Lawford, Donald O'Connor, Debbie Reynolds, Bing Crosby, James Stewart, Elizabeth Taylor, and Liza Minnelli (representing her mother, Judy Garland) doing the wrap-arounds. Haley promised that if Mickey participated, "we'll pay you well. And I'll give you some of your films, too. You can do whatever you want with the films." Mickey was paid scale ($385) in toto and was never allowed to use any clips. The film grossed nearly $40 million for MGM. The studio had essentially managed to trick Mickey one last time.

The traveling, the womanizing, the crazy investments, and the financial insecurity eventually got to Carolyn. As Ruth Webb recalled, "We started with the dinner theaters, and we were doing very well with them, until one day, Mickey went home to Florida. There wasn't any home, there weren't any children, there wasn't any marriage, there wasn't anything." [5] This was totally out of the blue. When he returned to Florida, Mickey discovered that Carolyn had filed under Florida's "no-fault" divorce law. She had to state only that the marriage was "irretrievably broken."

To say that Mickey was in shock would be an understatement. He was now essentially homeless, a wandering minstrel going from dinner theater to dinner theater. He was lost, dejected, and addicted to an array of tranquilizers, staggering through life, when the emotional damage caught up with him onstage in Houston in October 1974. Appearing for the umpteenth time in *Three Goats and a Blanket*, at the Windmill Dinner Theater in Houston, he collapsed onstage during the performance.

"Mickey was pretty much down to his last dollar," said Webb. ". . . I was told he collapsed on stage. I stayed with [him] for ten days. I took care of him. I read the Bible to him. Then I had to go back to my office on the coast. So I said, 'Mickey, anytime you can come to California, my home is yours.'"[6]

In *Life Is Too Short*, Mickey explained, "Rather than run toward life, I ran away. I tried to escape, again, into drugs. This time it was Quaaludes, fashionable new little pills that could put you on a mountain peak then drop you as quickly to the desert floor."[7]

Mickey Jr. and Timmy flew to Houston during Mickey's hospitalization and drug rehabilitation and lent him support. Ruth stayed in a bed next to his while he suffered from the DTs and struggled to get clean.

When Mickey was released, two weeks later, he was essentially homeless. With nowhere else to turn, he took Webb up on her offer and showed up on her doorstep, telling her, "I'm here, I'm cured."

Ruth's house was already crowded, and not just with the raccoons. There was Jamie, her live-in lover; her son, Mike; her ninety-six-year-old mother, who painted; an actor named Dean Dittman; and the raccoons, a cat, a dog, and a macaw named Sidney, who answered the phone.

Mickey was on the road to recovery, and Webb let it be known throughout the community. He went back on the dinner theater circuit and started receiving excellent notices. Late in October 1974, the

Los Angeles Times reviewed *Three Goats and a Blanket*, which was playing at Sebastian's West Dinner Playhouse in San Clemente, writing, "[T]he hair around Rooney's bald pate is white and he's developed a pretty good-sized pot. Otherwise, age is an entirely negligible condition. The wind-up doll moves are as abrupt as ever and the delivery is still crackling. He effectively uses every trick in the book to get laughs. He's the old-time boffo comic, faintly salacious (he claps his hands over his mistress's cheeks and declares, 'The Andy Hardy days are over'), with a positively ruthless desire to please." Mickey, now purportedly clean and sober, was on his way back.

Mickey continued to live in Ruth Webb's house of oddballs, where, from time to time, she'd have parties that threw together an eclectic mix of celebrities, musicians, poets, writers, and other assorted offbeat characters—a real-life Holly Golightly bash right out of *Breakfast at Tiffany's*. Mickey enjoyed meeting her guests, and Ruth even held a cocktail party to honor him. One of her guests was Mickey's oldest son, musician Mickey Jr., whom Ruth had gotten to know during his father's frightening Houston hospitalization. The now-twenty-eight-year-old Mick had befriended a thirty-five-year-old divorcee and country-western singer named Jan Chamberlin, with whom he had put together an act they performed in small clubs.

ACCORDING TO JAN ROONEY, she met Mickey Jr. on the music club scene in Los Angeles. She claims she didn't date him, had no romantic interest in him, and was just his stage partner. Jan said:

> Mickey Jr. is a very talented musician. We had known each other and had appeared in clubs, doing a variety of music. Mickey Jr. told me that his dad was back in town and they were throwing a party. I had heard from [him] of his dad's problems in Houston. Mickey Jr. said I should meet

his dad and that I would get a kick out of him. So I went with [him] to . . . Ruth Webb's home and this party. The house was like nothing I've ever seen . . . It was there I met Mickey and we started talking. Mickey was so talented, I remember him playing the piano that night. I sat down next to him as he was playing and I sang "I Can't Last a Day without You." I felt like Judy Garland next to him. Mickey was wonderful, very sensitive and very energetic. And with Mickey, you never know who you're going to get whether it's Whitey Marsh [the juvenile punk from *Boys Town*] or Andrew Hardy.[8]

For forty years a rumor has persisted that Jan was romantically involved with Mickey Jr., but that his father wooed her away. Jan, we believe, was honest when she said she and Mickey Jr. were only stage partners, not romantic partners, and that she met Mickey Sr. at his son's suggestion. However, in interviews with close family members we heard over and over, and emphatically, that Jan was engaged to Mickey Jr. and dumped him for his father, that her goal was to attach herself to Mickey Sr. and, in a Machiavellian move, she used Junior to achieve that goal. Even Mickey Sr. addressed the rumor, stating for the record in *Life Is Too Short*, "Jan had not been dating Mickey Rooney, Jr. (as some believe). My son just liked her singing, and he wanted me to meet her."[9]

Several of Mickey's children, including Mickey Jr. himself, speaking through family friend Pam McClenathan, tell a different story. McClenathan, relaying a statement from Mickey Jr., told us, "I'm sorry, but the truth was that Mickey Jr. was engaged to Jan and she did leave him for his father."

The combined support of Ruth Webb and Jan was the magic elixir needed to get Mickey back on the road to recovery. He and Jan had started dating, and Mickey soon found that Jan was the rock he had been looking for. Jan, for her part, gave up her career as a singer to travel and live with Mickey. Ruth Webb worked the phones, championed Mickey to every producer and casting director, and booked him into endless dinner theater dates. She painted a picture of a healthy Rooney who was packing in audiences in theaters nationwide.

Slowly, producers began to trust Rooney again. After his short but memorable appearance in *That's Entertainment* in 1974, he appeared in a series of low-budget films that offered him some interesting character roles. In the Spanish-Italian production of *As de Corazon* (*Ace of Hearts*) he appeared, albeit in a cameo, alongside Chris Robinson, who later became a soap opera actor (Rick Weber on *General Hospital*) and a close friend of Mickey's. The next film, directed by Robinson, *Convict Women* (aka *Thunder County*), costarred Mickey with Robinson and included Ted Cassidy (later Lurch on *The Addams Family*). Mickey then lent his voice as the Scarecrow in the animated *Journey Back to Oz*, which also featured Liza Minnelli as Dorothy (her mother's role) and Margaret Hamilton, the Witch of the West in the original motion picture, this time as Aunt Em.

In 1975, Mickey shot two international films: the first was a French James Bond spoof called *Bon Baisers de Hong Kong* (or "Good Kisses from Hong Kong," but translated as *From Hong Kong with Love*); and the second, *Rachel's Man*, an Israeli biblical epic.

Jan traveled with Mickey to different locations and sets, and took on an active, almost managerial interest in helping Mickey get his career back on track. He would go on location and shoot the films and then immediately return to the States, where he kept himself constantly busy with dinner theater dates. He was working furiously and enjoying it.

The next film he shot was an interesting Canadian comedy called *Find the Lady* (1976), which teamed John Candy with another Canadian actor, Lawrence Dane, in Abbott-and-Costello-type roles. Mickey played a gun-happy hood named Trigger.

With the support team of Ruth Webb and Jan, Mickey's career started to regain traction. He was in the Hollywood trades again as a working actor. "Slowly but surely, we were getting Mickey back on track," Jan recalled. "Ruth was tireless in her promoting Mickey. She was invaluable in getting him back on the map. It was a slow climb back, but she kept Mickey working steady."

Mickey and Jan found an apartment together in Hollywood, then a home in Sherman Oaks. They were constantly on the road—Jan's sister Ronna took care of her sons, Chris and Mark Aber, while they traveled—on film locations or working the dinner theater circuit, which was now at its peak. This was mainly because of Mickey's growing the market. He had brought the glory of Hollywood's golden age to local venues.

He and Jan eventually found a beautiful home in the planned community of Westlake Village, in a development on an island called Red Sail. "I had lived most of my life in the Valley," Jan recalled. "I grew up in Van Nuys. I felt most comfortable there, as did Mickey, who had lived there much of his life. We fell in love with Westlake Village."

Mickey was much more cautious about his relationship with Jan. Possibly he had finally learned from his past mistakes. Their romance was not highly publicized, remaining mostly under the radar. "Our families knew about our relationship," said Jan. "I was not eager to just jump into another marriage. We took it very slowly. We did not officially get married until five years after we met." When informed that this was the longest hiatus between marriages for Mickey, she remarked, "[T]hat may possibly be a reason that we had a long and successful marriage. We were together over forty years. Maybe it is due to the fact that we had time to get to know each other. It was not the same impulsive act he carried out with his previous seven wives." [10]

Although Mickey once joked to a reporter that he had married Jan while on location in Hong Kong, the fact was they took out a marriage license in July 1978 in Thousand Oaks. Mickey's eighth marriage took place on July 28, 1978, at the Conejo Valley Church of Religious Science. Mickey was fifty-seven, and Jan was thirty-nine. Sig Frohlich was Mickey's best man, and Chris Aber, Jan's oldest son, gave the bride away. This broke the pattern of Mickey's last five marriages, conducted in a Las Vegas wedding chapel. This time was different. This time, Mickey would tell Jan, it would work. "Mickey was determined to make our marriage work—as was I," Jan said.

Stanley Kramer's It's A Mad, Mad, Mad, Mad World *with* (from left to right) *Dorothy Provine, Sid Caesar, Jonathan Winters, Ethel Merman, Milton Berle, Mickey Rooney, and Buddy Hackett.* PHOTO COURTESY OF KAREN KRAMER.

Teddy sitting on Mickey's lap, from Andy Hardy Comes Home *(1958).*
PHOTO COURTESY OF PAM MCCLENATHAN.

Mamie Van Doren and Mickey as the Devil in The Private Lives of Adam and Eve *(1960).*

Mickey and Margaret O'Brien in the last scene of his film career in Dr. Jekyll and Mr.
Hyde *directed by Brian Barsuglia, released October 2015. Ms. O'Brien noted that she
appeared in her first film with Mickey and she was in his last.*

Ann Miller and Mickey in Sugar Babies *(1981).* COURTESY OF JAMES CARDILLO.

Mickey backstage in Sugar Babies *with costar Ann Miller and Michael Jackson.*

PHOTO COURTESY OF JAMES CARDILLO.

Mickey in a poster from Sugar Babies *in 1980.* POSTER COURTESY OF MONTE KLAUS.

Mickey in drag with Ann Miller in Sugar Babies.

PHOTO COURTESY OF MONTE KLAUS.

Mickey greets the first family backstage at Sugar Babies. *From left to right:*
Ann Miller, First Lady Nancy Reagan, President Reagan, and Mickey.

PHOTO COURTESY OF JAMES TEWKSBURY .

Mickey in the 1940s.

PHOTO COURTESY OF
ROBERT EASTON.

Rare PR photo of the guest stars of Four Star Productions' The Dick Powell Show *for the episode "Who Killed Julie Greer?" Standing, from left: Ronald Reagan, Nick Adams, Lloyd Bridges, Mickey Rooney, Edgar Bergen, Jack Carson, Ralph Bellamy, Kay Thompson, and Dean Jones. Seated: Carolyn Jones and Dick Powell.*

One of the Boys *with Dana Carvey* (left), *Nathan Lane* (center), *and Mickey.*
PHOTO COURTESY OF BERNIE ORENSTEIN.

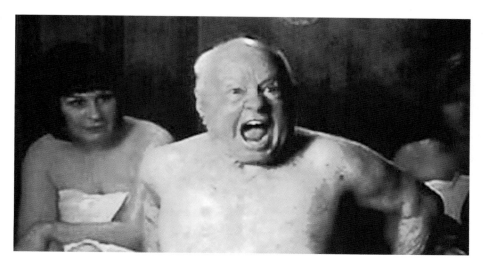

Mickey, at age eighty-four, in a 2005 Super Bowl ad for Airborne cold remedy that was banned by Fox when Mickey bared his behind in the commercial.
PHOTO COURTESY OF CODY KLEIN.

Mickey and Jan greet Queen Elizabeth II. PHOTO COURTESY OF RONNA RILEY.

Mickey's ninetieth birthday party at Feinstein's in New York with Tony Bennett (left), *Donald Trump* (rear), *Jan and Mickey* (center), *and Regis and Joy Philbin* (right).
PHOTO COURTESY OF ELLEN EASTON.

Ava Gardner. PHOTO COURTESY OF ROBERT EASTON.

THE EIGHT WIVES OF MICKEY ROONEY

Ava Gardner.

Betty Jane Rase.

Martha Vickers.

Elaine Mahnken.

Barbara Ann Thomason.

PHOTO COURTESY OF MONTE KLAUS.

Marge Lane.

PHOTO COURTESY OF MELODY DOFF.

Jan Chamberlin and Mickey.

PHOTO COURTESY OF CHRIS ABER.

Carolyn Hockett.

PHOTO COURTESY OF EDDIE BRACKEN.

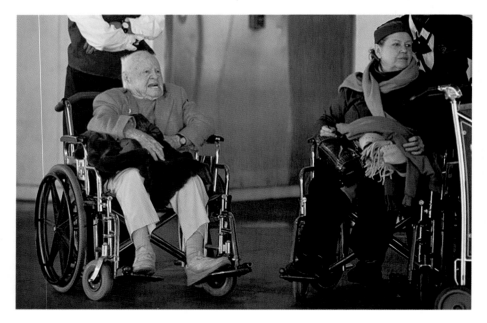

Last photo of Mickey and Jan. Photo courtesy of Chris Aber.

Betty Jane and the children (Mickey Jr. and Timmy).

Photo courtesy of the Dan Kessel Collection, © Dan Kessel Productions, all rights reserved.

Mickey, "Ma" Nell, and Ava Gardner at their wedding on January 10, 1942.

PHOTO COURTESY OF
MONTE KLAUS.

Mickey and Betty Jane's wedding.

PHOTO COURTESY OF
ROBERT EASTON.

Kerry Mack (left),
*Mickey, and Kelly
Rooney* (right)

PHOTO COURTESY
OF KELLY ROONEY.

*Kelly, Kerry, and
Michael Rooney are
escorted by manager
Aaron "Red" Doff
away from their
home where their
mother, Barbara
Ann Rooney, was
murdered on
January 30, 1966.*

PHOTO COURTESY
OF MELODY DOFF.

Mickey is supported by his manager Red Doff (left), *sons* Timmy (behind Doff), *Teddy* (obscured), *and* Mickey Jr. (behind Mickey) *at his wife Barbara Ann's funeral.*

Mickey with Kerry and Kelly as adults. The last photo taken of Kelly and Kerry with their father.

Mickey and Dan Beatty on set of Dr. Jekyll and Mr. Hyde, *one of the last photos of Mickey.*

PHOTO COURTESY OF BRIAN BARSUGLIA.

The Rooney family at the dedication of Mickey's second star on the Hollywood Walk of Fame on April 26, 2004. This star reads "Mickey and Jan Rooney."

PHOTO COURTESY OF KELLY ROONEY.

23

Sugar Babies

Mickey in Sugar Babies.
Unpublished photo.

The item in the morning paper one day in 1974 caught Norman Abbott's eye. It was buried deep in the *Los Angeles Times*, a notice Norm found while thumbing through the pages and drinking his coffee. It was a story that sparked a very old memory. They were tearing down the old Burbank Theatre on Sixth and Main Streets, in downtown LA, one of the city's oldest burlesque houses. What memories still lingered there! Abbott thought.

The Burbank Burlesque, as it was known, opened as a legitimate theater in 1893, and for many years it was Morosco's Burbank Theatre, before becoming a burlesque house—and the base, for many years, for its top banana, Joe Yule Sr., Mickey Rooney's father. The Burbank Burlesque in its later years had also become the West Coast home for noted strippers such as Gypsy Rose Lee and Tempest Storm, one of gangster Mickey Cohen's girls (whom Mickey Rooney dated and then ditched after he was slapped around by a couple of Cohen's *musculeros*).

When Norm Abbott read that the theater was to be razed, it touched a deep memory. Burlesque and the sights and sounds of performers on the Burbank stage were embedded in his blood. Norm and his wife, Ann, were aficionados of burlesque and collectors of its memorabilia. When Abbott read that someone was selling off (or giving away) memorabilia from the old house's glory days before knocking the place down, he knew he had to go. This opportunity was a collector's dream, especially for someone whose heart and soul was burlesque, whose very ancestry was spawned in the footlights.

Norm's family *was* burlesque. He had grown up around it, the son of burlesque/vaudeville performer Olive Abbott, the sister of Bud Abbot, Lou Costello's straight man. Abbott and Costello's act evolved from burlesque, through film, and into television. Bud Abbott, the greatest straight man who ever lived, was a piece of American history, and so was Norm. As a youth, he worked at the renowned Gaiety delicatessen in New York City, which abutted the legendary Minsky's Burlesque.

"The Gaiety was the first deli to serve overstuffed sandwiches," Norm told us. "And you could even order a half sandwich if you were short of cash. If things were really rough, you'd eat salami—'a nickel a shtikle'—or a hot dog, the real kind, rolled on a grill, but if you were flush, you'd have pastrami or corned beef. The Gaiety backed onto a burlesque theater on Forty-Fourth Street, and you'd always be elbow to elbow with actors. If they were really broke, that one overstuffed sandwich would be their only meal of the day." [1] Abbott recalled meeting the great burlesque legends, such as Gypsy Rose Lee, Rags

Ragland, Phil Silvers, Harry Steppe, and Sid Fields. Burlesque flowed through Norman Abbott's blood like a river, deep and full of life.

Norman Abbott eventually became a prolific motion picture and television director. He started out working for his uncle Bud on Abbott and Costello films such as *Abbott and Costello Meet Frankenstein*, *Hit the Ice*, and *Africa Screams*. He eventually directed hundreds of episodes of television classics, including *Leave It to Beaver*; *The Munsters*; *The Jack Benny Program*; *Welcome Back, Kotter*; *Sanford and Son*; *McHale's Navy*; and perhaps one of the best examples of vaudeville fly-gab, fast-talking back-and-forth patter (that is, after *Burns and Kaye*), *Burns and Allen*.

At the Burbank Theatre closing sale, Norm rummaged through suitcases of old promotional material, placards, scripts, posters, postcards, and photos, discovering a treasure trove of star memorabilia from some of the marquee burlesque performers. And then he came to Joe Yule. Looking at the original jokes, gags, and stage business, Norm told us, it was if he were hit by a thunderbolt. He'd discovered the mother lode of burlesque memorabilia, and it gave him an idea. "I suddenly had an inspiration, I told to my wife, Ann. I thought it would be wonderful to do an old-fashioned burlesque show on Broadway. Do all the old routines, music, and create the world of burlesque for both the new and older generations. We kicked around names, and the most obvious choice would be Mickey Rooney." He said that while the older performers were gone, Mickey was still rather young, and knew every nuance and rhythm of burlesque.[2]

Abbott heard that Broadway producer Harry Rigby was in Los Angeles trying to recruit Debbie Reynolds to star in a revival of *Hello, Dolly!* and happened to be staying at the house of Norm's friend. Norman called Rigby and told him about what he had found at the Burbank. When he later showed him his collection of memorabilia, Rigby was interested. But Abbott had one caveat: he wanted to direct the show. Rigby said, "You've got a deal." Abbott also told Rigby that it was imperative that they have Mickey Rooney as the top banana. "Mickey knows all the bits, and there is an innocence in his face that will keep the show from getting dirty," Abbott recalled saying to Rigby.

This was important to Abbott. Early burlesque was risqué but not outright pornographic. There was a flash of this, a hint of that, lots of brassy music, songs with a ragtime beat, lots of pratfalls, and skits and jokes (many that have stood the test of time)—and it was only Mickey Rooney, the last living and healthy performer from a bygone era of live onstage, raucous slapstick comedy who knew all the routines, patter, and timing to pull this off. Rigby agreed. Only Mickey. But how to sell Rooney on the idea? Norm said he would pitch to Mickey that this was the innocent kind of burlesque, the one that existed in the 1920s, before the strippers came along and changed it from "family" entertainment to salacious porn.

From that meeting in 1975, Rigby kept kicking around Abbott's idea. Then, in 1977, he attended the Conference of American Pop Arts at Lincoln Center, where several respected professors of the arts from several universities were giving lectures on different incarnations of popular American entertainment, including burlesque, minstrel shows, and carnivals. Rigby attended a presentation by Professor Ralph Gilmore Allen from the University of Tennessee, whose historical research on burlesque comedy had made him an aficionado of the art form. Rigby went to his seminar and, as he later told Arthur Marx, listened to Allen give a lecture on burlesque that had "the audience rolling in the aisles. I thought if he could get that type of reaction from that audience, then a burlesque show could do well." [3]

When Abbott initially called Mickey to talk about the concept, he said, Rooney "was very rude. I talked to his wife and she was very nice. When Mickey came to the phone and I told Mickey my idea, he said, 'Fucking Burlesque is dead.' And then he hung up. I had known Mickey for years. I directed him on several television shows and even directed him in a pilot [*Tempo*, 1963], so it wasn't as if I didn't know him. We later talked again about the idea, and he still wasn't very interested. When Rigby called him later, he told him that 'the idea is bullshit.' But Rooney also said that he would keep an open mind. He was still touring in dinner theaters and thought it might afford him to take a break from *Three Goats and a Blanket*."

Eventually, in 1977, Rigby signed Professor Allen to write the book for the proposed project, and create a musical book after the play book was complete. Taking a look at the tapes and interviews that Allen had compiled and Norm Abbott's memorabilia from the Burlesque, they selected the material that they believed would best engage modern audiences. After the first draft of the book was completed, Rigby sent it to Rooney. Then, when Mickey was in Louisville performing, Professor Allen went backstage to introduce himself—where, he claimed, he talked the actor into doing the show.

On October 14, 1978, *Variety* announced, "Ruth Webb pacted Mickey Rooney with Harry Rigby for B'Way-bound Sugar Baby [*sic*], a look at burlesque from 1898–1935. Rooney would play a Joe Yule, Sr.–like performer, Rehearsals are skedded to start in March."

"Rigby called me and was thrilled that he signed Rooney, as was I," Abbott told us. "He then told me we would sign an agreement to direct the project as we had agreed. However, no agreement was ever signed. I trusted Rigby's word that we had a deal."

Rigby then set out to find a composer. He wanted music you could hum leaving the theater. He first tried to use some Irving Berlin songs, but Berlin turned him down; he didn't want his music associated with burlesque. Sheldon Harnick (*Fiddler on the Roof*) also passed. But it was Mickey's costar who would help them find their music.

Like Mickey, Ann Miller was an MGM veteran. She was born in 1923, and by the time she joined Metro in 1947, she was a sound stage veteran, having done twelve musicals while under contract at Columbia. At MGM she appeared in such classics as *Easter Parade* (1948, replacing Cyd Charrise, who had broken her leg), with Judy Garland; *On the Town* (1949); and *Kiss Me Kate* (1953). After she left MGM in 1957, she appeared in nightclubs, on the dinner theater circuit, and on Broadway in *Mame* (1969), succeeding Angela Lansbury in the title role. In her book *Miller's High Life* Miller writes that she had romances with Louis Mayer, Conrad Hilton, and Howard Hughes, and in *Tapping into the Force* (1990) she claims she is the direct reincarnation of an Egyptian queen, Hathshepsut.[4] Theater producer Terry Allen Kramer said, "Annie was tough as nails. Mickey was overpowering and could get his way with most everybody. With Annie, he watched his step. He was more frightened of her." [5]

When signed to costar in the play, Miller suggested the music of the late Jimmy McHugh, whom she used to date. When Rigby bought McHugh songs such as "I'm in the Mood for Love," "I Can't Give You Anything but Love, Baby," and "On the Sunny Side of the Street," he discovered that McHugh had left a trunk of seventy tunes that had never been published and had no lyrics. Upon a recommendation from the choreographer he hired for the play, Ernest Flatt (*The Carol Burnett Show*), he hired Arthur Malvin to write the lyrics for those lost songs.

The show was originally titled *The New Majestic Follies and Lyceum Gardens Review*—really too long for a marquee. They needed something shorter, punchier, more to the point; something that communicated what drew audiences to burlesque in the first place. They then alighted upon the nickname Stage Door Johnnies, which describes the wannabe "sugar daddies," guys who waited outside the side entrances to theaters for the chorus girls they were picking up after the show, the "sugar babies." The title *Sugar Babies* might have also been inspired by Arthur Malvin's song "Let Me Be Your Sugar Baby." And then there was the name for the Sugar Babies candy developed in the 1930s.

The show was budgeted for $1.3 million, higher than some others of that time, but Rigby wanted to take the musical on a five-week pre-Broadway tour, which upped the cost of the production. He partnered with Terry Allen Kramer, whose husband, Irving Kramer, was a board member of Columbia Pictures. Along with Kramer's participation, Columbia also invested five hundred thousand dollars.

Rigby scheduled six weeks of rehearsals at the Michael Bennett studios in downtown Manhattan. (Jan and Mickey decided to stay in Fort Lee, New Jersey, instead of New York City because it was closer to golf courses Mickey wanted to play.) The first couple of weeks were devoted to the dance numbers choreographed by Ernest Flatt. Norman Abbott oversaw the dialogue. Problems started to creep up right away, though, when Mickey felt uncomfortable with the straight men (comedians in the mold of George Burns and Jack Benny) they had hired. A straight man's job is to set up the punch line for his partner. It's called "laying pipe." George Burns demonstrated it in the first episode of the *The Burns and Allen Show* when he described how a straight man asks the question, for example (to Gracie), "How's your brother, Freddie?" Then he pauses, looking casually around at the audience, his gaze maybe lingering on a prop. This pause is called a "beat." Gracie answers, "Oh, he just came back from Philadelphia." George stares at his cigar. He repeats Gracie's last line as a question—this is very important to lay the pipe for the next line: "Your brother Freddie just came back from Philadelphia?" "Yes," Gracie answers, and says nothing else. The straight man looks perplexed, scans the audience again, purses his lips, and finally takes the bait, asking, "Why was he in Philadelphia?" Gracie answers, "They were sitting at breakfast and his wife said, 'I'd love some Philadelphia Cream Cheese.'" Now take this same type of interchange and replace it with "Who's on first?" Now imagine Jerry Seinfeld talking to Kramer, and you get the picture. That's what a straight man does.

By the end of the second week, at Mickey's insistence, they had fired three different actors. Mickey was complaining about the material, the delivery, and the show's structure and timing. If he seemed obsessive, it was because he realized what this play could mean to his career. He was stuck in dinner theater and in low-level movies playing minor character roles. He was no longer a top-grossing motion picture leading man. Far from it. But this was Broadway. This was the burlesque in which he'd grown up and learned all his stagecraft. This was his home. If he failed at this, his last chance at a major Broadway show, it was back to $2,500 a week at the dinner theaters in small cities where blue-haired ladies and their retired husbands looked up from gumming their string beans and poached salmon to watch the Andy Hardy of their youth try to recapture what he was fifty years earlier. *Sugar Babies* had to work. The weight of the production was on his shoulders.

When no acceptable straight man was found by the third week, director Norman Abbott read the lines to Mickey. After all, wasn't Abbott the nephew of arguably one of the greatest burlesque straight men who ever lived? There was George Burns, there was Jack Benny, and there was Bud Abbott. Nobody else was even close. But Abbott was a director not a seasoned performer, and thus he kept throwing Rooney's timing off.

Fortunately, Mickey then remembered his friend and well-known character actor Peter Leeds, with whom he'd done shows, and they hired him. Leeds worked in seamlessly with Mickey, and the straight man/gag man patter started to click.

Mickey was also unhappy with Abbott as a theater director, even though it was Abbott who'd created the play and pushed to get Mickey back on a Broadway stage.

First, Abbott was a television director. He didn't understand, as his uncle and Mickey did, the cadences of burlesque before a live stage audience, where you have to leave it to your performers to play off one another and off the audience. A good stage comic can actually hear the audience breathe. He can feel the response of the audience to a line, knows when to pause, knows how to lay the pipe for the next joke, knows where and how to look—and, as straight man, knows how to bring the audience into the joke so as to get them to laugh at his consternation. Look at how Bud Abbott plays the flummoxed interviewer, gasping in frustration, opposite Lou Costello in "Who's on First?," or Jack Benny playing off Mel Blanc in the railroad station skit, or off Eddie "Rochester" Anderson when he's asked to spend a dime. And picture Carl Reiner and Sid Caesar or Mel Brooks as Reiner on the old *Your Show of Shows* lays out the setup and pauses before the next joke to the Two Thousand Year Old Man or the man who fell out of the plane, television staples in the 1950s. This timing, this sense of what his audience was thinking and expecting, was what Mickey learned from the time he was one year old standing in the wings as his father performed, and by watching the greatest burlesque comics cavort on stage. This became his language as his neurological pathways developed, as the syntax and rhythm of language became hardwired within the language center of his brain. Just as a child learns the language spoken to him by those who nurture him, so Mickey learned the patter and rhythm of stage comedy. In his opinion, Norm Abbott did not know it.

Second, Mickey felt that Norm was not authoritative enough with the actors. Also, he believed, probably correctly, that Abbott was unable to get the skits on their feet. While Abbott knew burlesque from his family background, Mickey had performed these routines since he was two years old. He was still doing the skits in his Vegas act.

Finally, Mickey approached Abbott and said to him, "I love you, baby, but this isn't going to work out. You can't control the actors." Then he turned to Rigby and demanded that he fire Abbott, which Rigby reluctantly did. But the whole project had been based on Abbott's conception. Abbott trusted Rigby and had not signed a contract, which left him vulnerable. He deserved at least a partial share in a project based on his ideas.

Abbott packed up and returned to Los Angeles to direct episodic television, which was his forte and expertise. Several months later, after the initial shock of being fired from a project that he had worked on for five years, he filed a lawsuit for breach of contract for nine hundred thousand dollars in Los Angeles Superior Court. Though he had no signed paper, he had enough extrinsic evidence to assert "promissory estoppel" if Rigby were to claim there was no contract. Abbott had performed his job as if he had signed a contract hence he could stop the producer from claiming there was no contract. Besides, no defense attorney in his or her right mind wants an LA County judge compelling the production of box office receipts to establish the value of a claim. Abbott and Rigby settled the suit about a year later, Norm told us, for an amount in the high six figures.

Meanwhile, Mickey suggested that Rigby call the colorful impresario John Kenley, who had employed Mickey for nearly twenty years for his theaters in Ohio. Kenley had been a huge help to Rooney when he couldn't find work, hiring him for starring roles in several productions and gaining him notice. In fact, Rigby knew Rooney's stage work *because* of John Kenley. Also, Kenley knew the art form in question, having assembled shows such as *This Was Burlesque* with Ann Corio. Mickey trusted his judgment. Merv Griffin wrote about Kenley in his book *Merv: An Autobiography*, revealing what had been gossiped about by many and known as fact by few that Kenley (who has since died) spent many a theatrical off-season traipsing around South Florida as a woman named Joan, wearing getups that would make Liberace look like Don Draper.[6] Kenley once said, "People have often wondered if I am gay. Sometimes I wished I was. Life would have been simpler. Androgyny is overrated."[7]

Kenley recommended his friend Rudy Tronto as director. Tronto had directed *The Best of Burlesque*, with Ann Corio, for Kennely, and Mickey had worked with him in *W.C.*, and trusted him. He was the perfect fit.

When Tronto arrived, Rooney grabbed him and said, complaining about some of the skits, stage business, and other material, "Rudy, we've got to get rid of all this shit. The stuff is terrible," recalled Tronto about some of the skits in the show, to Arthur Marx and thence to us.[8]

The show toured for six months. "Harry Rigby wanted this long pre-Broadway tour, which I thought, and still think, was far too long. It kept our costs higher," said producer and financial backer Terry Allen Kramer. The first stop was San Francisco, at the Curran Theatre. Mickey, for maybe one of the only times in his career, was walking a tightrope of nerves before opening curtain. He didn't have to worry. He brought down the house. The audience delighted in his every movement, joke, pratfall, and dance step. He didn't just keep in step with Ann Miller; he floated across the stage with her, and harmonized with her in songs that made the audience hum. Many experts of the theater believe that the first preview is a good indicator of the show's future. If that is the rule, then the eight curtain calls for Mickey were an excellent barometer. While the first preview was not sold out, by the next morning the word of mouth was so strong that there was a line around the block for tickets. *Sugar Babies* was sold out for the rest of the four-week run. The reviewers raved about Rooney and Miller.

Stage veteran Ann Miller kept Mickey in line right from the start. "Annie knew Mickey, and she kept him in place," recalled Terry Allen Kramer to us. "If he got too broad, she could tone him down. They made a great balance, and she would not take any of Mickey's stuff. She could definitely stand up to him."

As they assessed each road performance, Kramer, Rigby, Tronto, Flatt, and Malvin revised, tightened, and fine-tuned the show throughout the tryouts. They next played the Pantages Theatre in Hollywood, a historic venue and Mickey's old stomping ground. Again, the show sold out. Except for one negative review from Sylvia Drake of the *Los*

Angeles Times, in which she said the show was "for the Magic Mountain crowd," every other outlet praised Mickey and the show.

The show continued its gypsy existence for long runs in Chicago, Detroit, and Philadelphia, where it met with the similar accolades. "I've never had so much fun," said Kramer. "And I learned every step of the way. In today's theater world, I can't be so hands-on. It just can't be done today." She explained that in today's Broadway musical theater, she couldn't have had the level of intimate, day-to-day involvement that she had with *Sugar Babies*; nor could the play have toured for that long.

On Friday, October 9, 1979, at the Nederlander Organization's Mark Hellinger Theater, *Sugar Babies* finally made its Broadway debut. The word of mouth from the six-month tour was so strong that there was already over a million dollars in advance tickets sales.

"It was such a triumph for Mickey . . . all the anger for being forgotten and relegated to the bin, melted away," Jan Rooney told us. "Everyone recognized his tremendous talent."

On November 16, 1979, Mickey told the *New York Times,* "To sum it up, living with Mickey Rooney hasn't been easy. There have been crevices, fissures, pits and I've fallen into a lot of them. But the crux of it is, you can't quit on life, you've got to keep going." He also claimed that he had found God though the Church of Religious Science.

The triumph of the opening night of *Sugar Babies* would have made a great film arc in itself: from Mickey's rise to the top of stardom in films, through his long fall and successive tragedies, to his rise again to become the favorite son of Broadway. Here he was on opening night playing to an audience live onstage in the town where he was born, performing the very material he had grown up with, and playing a role his own father had played—and all of it to cheering audiences and rave notices. It doesn't get any better than that.

New York reviews, which could be brutal and rarely were sentimental, especially for this kind of play, one with so much shtick, created tributes to Mickey Rooney. Newspapers, television, radio, and every magazine sang his praises. Mickey's face appeared everywhere. He was on the cover of the March 1980 issue of *Life* magazine. He was featured in covers stories in *Time*, *Newsweek*, and even the *National Enquirer*. *Time* on October 29 featured a piece on him that read, "These days the sun is shining almost constantly at the Mark Hellinger Theater. At 59, Mickey once again has the approval he needs and demands. 'The audience and I are friends,' he says. 'We're family. They grew up with me. They allowed me to grow up with them. I've let them down several times. They've let me down several times. But we're all family, and it's time for a reunion. What warmth comes over you when they laugh! It's as if they're saying It's all been worth it, thank you.'" And that's what a stage performer not only understands, but absorbs.

Kramer, the producer alongside Rigby and also the main investor along with Columbia, was involved in every aspect of the production. This was the first time she was an active producer for a Broadway show. After *Sugar Babies*, she went on to become one of the most prolific modern Broadway producers ever. Her most recent plays include *The Elephant Man* with Bradley Cooper, Cyndi Lauper's *Kinky Boots*, and the musical version of Sylvester Stallone's *Rocky*. Speaking to us from her New York office, she said:

> Oh, I just adored Mickey. However, he was so extraordi-
> narily difficult . . . Right from the beginning, when we were
> on the road. We had a tremendous Rollerblading number
> that cashed in on that craze and was wonderful. It was a
> showcase piece, and Mickey was just great in it. In San
> Francisco, he said, "Terry, I don't want to do this number
> any longer." I told him that it was a showstopper. He said,
> "No, my leg hurts, and I can't do it any longer." And he

just lay down on the stage, flat on his back, and wouldn't move. Needless to say, we removed that segment. . . . While we were still on the pre-Broadway tryouts, I was paying Mickey fifty thousand dollars a week. He came to me and demanded seventy thousand per week. I told him we were barely breaking even on the road, and I couldn't do that. He then went on a tirade: how he can replace Ann Miller and take her part and her salary. He then did her dance steps in part to prove to me how he could do her part as well.[9]

According to Kramer, Mickey also received 10 percent of the gross box office. The play grossed more than $300,000 per week for three years, for 1,208 performances. Mickey also toured in the play for two more years and more than 600 performances. His return, by the finish of the last road show in 1985—according to Mickey's manager of nearly thirty years, Robert Malcolm, CEO of the Artists Group, who would later become his agent as well—was just south of $40 million. He was outearning his yearly return from MGM in three weeks of work. At sixty years old, after all the years of scuffling since being booted from MGM, Mickey had hit a grand slam, emerging from earning $2,500 a week in dinner theater to a weekly salary of $70,000 per week.[10]

From $70,000 a week for a total of $40 million, to filing for bankruptcy, to an estate worth less than $20,000 at his death—what happened? This question plagues family, friends, acquaintances, and observers of Mickey Rooney, as well as the court that oversaw his conservatorship. How did he go from the astounding income from *Sugar Babies*, performed in his sixties, and remain a constant earner in movies thereafter, to near poverty at the time of his death in 2014? We asked his agents, managers, business managers, publicists, family, friends, and acquaintances this simple question: How could he have plowed through tens of millions of dollars in just those years alone?

The stock answer was: gambling. His manager Robert Malcolm told us that Mickey was always at the track or on the phone to his bookie. Malcolm said, "Even when he was doing the 'panto' plays in London, I'd call there and his assistant would always tell me he was at the track. He went through much of his money in gambling and horse racing." Mickey's gambling addiction, notorious during his days at MGM and thereafter, continued throughout the rest of his life unabated until all his money was gone and he ended up in a conservatorship.

Terry Allen Kramer, who confirmed that Mickey earned millions from *Sugar Babies*, seconded this: "Besides his crazy ideas and products, he was a gambler, pure and simple. He'd always be at the track in the afternoons or on the phone with his bookies. He gambled his money away along with his families' hands that were always in his pockets," she recalled, reminding us that Mickey had fathered many children over the years through his eight marriages.[11]

His stepson Chris Aber, his assistant for over thirty years, confirmed this as well, telling us, "Mickey lived at the track. He blew countless dollars there. He also owned horses and always lost money on that. Until he just stopped, about ten years ago, he lived and breathed horse racing."

His sister-in-law of forty years, Ronna Riley, Jan's younger sister, said, "Mickey was a degenerate gambler. He would beg me to go with him to the races, as Jan refused to go. Once, while at Santa Anita, we saw the very elegant and dapper Cary Grant. Cary loves Mickey and once said that he considered Mickey to be the greatest living actor. Grant had this beautiful white Rolls-Royce he was getting into, and said to Mickey—who was rather sloppy, and [was] busy with his forms—'Mickey, Mickey . . . do you ever change your clothes?'"[12]

His longtime friend Sidney Miller recalled that Mickey could not get ahead of his losses at the track, even when he won early. Mickey's oft-quoted remark, "I lost two dollars at Santa Anita and I've spent three million trying to get it back," is not far off. In a visit to Santa Anita with the author, he lost quite a few dollars. (In fact, he still owes this author fifty dollars.)

Even with his well-documented gambling problem, it is still astounding that he could go through over forty million dollars. But it was more than gambling, we discovered. It was also his terrible business sense. When it came to business, he was the supreme ultracrepidarian, pitching ideas so far beyond his area of expertise that people who worked with him were astounded. "Mickey had absolutely zero business sense," Kramer explained to us in our interview.

> My father [Charles Robert Allen Jr.] was a world-famous venture capitalist [and founder of the investment bank Allen and Company]. . . . He had Mickey set up a trust for investment, where he could collect his dividends but never, ever touch the principal. He was emphatic to Mickey that you can never, *ever* touch the principal, and he'll have that forever. Eventually, he goes behind my father['s back] and tries to take out the principal. My father read him the riot act, but Mickey would not listen. Eventually, my father just threw up his hands and gave up trying to help Mickey.
>
> During the run of the play, Mickey would blow his money on ridiculous investments. Oh, he had all these hangers-on around him. He paid a fortune and bought this restaurant in Fort Lee, where he lived. He asked me for my advice before he bought it. I . . . pointed to the empty parking lot and said, "Mickey, don't you dare buy this. The shopping center is dead." Regardless, he bought it and it went bust. Later on, he decided to start a chain, in Los

Angeles, called Rooney's Weenie World of Hot Dogs. I invested ten thousand dollars in it. I remember I went to the opening and it must have been a hundred ten degrees and the air-conditioning wasn't working. They sold square hot dogs in a bun. Square hot dogs. I think that says it all. Obviously, I lost my investment.

Donald Trump, Mickey's friend for years, remarked to us, "Over the years I tried to help him, but he did as he pleased. He was a brilliant and talented artist. He just had no sense of business." Robert Malcolm said, "You could not talk him out of these crazy ideas. He always thought his next idea would be the big winner. That never happened."

His sister-in-law Ronna Riley said, "Mickey was the Midas touch in reverse."

Regardless of advice from some of the great financial gurus of our times—Donald Trump; Charles Robert Allen Jr.; Terry Allen Kramer and her husband, financier Irwin Kramer—Mickey was tone-deaf to their advice. He'd rather invest in Rooney's Weenie World than safe dividend-bearing investments recommended by Charles Robert Allen Jr. or Trump. With his crazy investments, his gambling addiction, and a lifestyle in which he spent without restraint, paying for things he couldn't afford while going shy on the IRS and the State of California, one can see how the scores of millions he earned could be gone at the end of the day.

Gambling wasn't the only vice Mickey continued to indulge in during his later years. Though he had now entered into his eighth marriage, and had claimed to have rediscovered God, according to Terry Allen Kramer, his womanizing ways continued. "Mickey constantly had girls up in his dressing room, and it wasn't just to visit," she said. "On one occasion, I needed to talk with Mickey and went into his dressing room where he was in the middle of a tryst with this girl. When I walked in, he stopped and in his boxers he held out his hand to me and said, 'Let us pray.' He said he had found God. I said to him, 'Mickey, you're so little in this world, how did God find you? Did he come through the window?' Mickey was not the least bit embarrassed to be caught." [13]

His stepson Chris told us that a steady stream of ladies made themselves available to Mickey, up until his late eighties. Although it may seem shocking that this went on while Chris's mother was Mickey's wife, Chris was not bothered, saying to us, "No, I think she realized that is part of the business. The girls were always available, and Mickey would be available."

Terry Allen Kramer believes that *Sugar Babies* struck gold largely due to Mickey Rooney. She recalled, "He was impossible to replace. I really have attempted to revisit *Sugar Babies* on Broadway, but I don't think it would succeed. First, I don't think that I could find anyone who could take Mickey's place today. Name me someone who could do what he did in a burlesque way? Secondly, I think the material is too clean for today's audiences." [14]

To Kramer's point: during Mickey's breaks, when he was shooting a film or when the show was on the road, his understudies for *Sugar Babies* were ineffective because they couldn't inhabit the role that Mickey had created playing his own father. After all, who could play Joe Yule Sr. better than Joe Yule Jr.? During the three-year run on Broadway, Mickey took three vacations, and his replacements included comic Rip Taylor, Joey Bishop, understudy and choreographer Rudy Tronto, Eddie Bracken, Phil Ford, and Robert Morse from *How to Succeed in Business Without Really Trying*. None of them could draw the audience that Mickey did. For example, when Joey Bishop substituted for Mickey for four weeks in February 1981, "the grosses dipped to practically nothing. It was a disaster," Kramer said.

And Bishop was not without his burlesque bona fides: "The funny thing was that when I was just starting out in Philadelphia in the late 1930s," he said, "I was part of a vaudeville act called the Bishop Boys, which is where I got my name. We were booked into the old Trocadero, which was a burlesque house, and I had a chance to see the world of striptease and baggy-pants comics at close range." [15]

When director Harry Rigby attempted an ill-fated road production of *Babies* during the original Broadway run, which starred Carol Channing and Robert Morse, and ran from August through November 1980, the show folded in Boston—and Kramer and Rigby took a million-dollar bath. "Channing did not fill Ann Miller's shoes, and Bobby Morse was not Mickey Rooney," Kramer recalled.

As Mickey and Ann Miller embarked on a national road show of *Sugar Babies* in 1984, Rooney was still enjoying himself as top banana. He loved coming up with new ad libs, pieces of business, and sometimes a jab from something he saw in the news. In effect, he was updating the dialogue in small ways as he went along. Thus, the show always seemed fresh, even though it was ostensibly the same script every night.

Mickey's former manager Bullets Durgom recalled that "when *Sugar Babies* was playing at the Pantages, I went to see him. Knowing I was in the audience, he started calling the people in the show not by their character names, but by the names of people we used to know and deal with when I was managing him: Sam Stiefel, Maurice Duke, Red Doff. That night he kept referring to Ann as Sam Stiefel. 'Hey, Sam,' he'd say to her. 'Come over here, Sam.' The audience was completely confused. But he was getting a kick out of it for my sake." [16]

Even Ava Gardner came to watch the show, and stopped backstage to visit Mickey in his dressing room and congratulate him. She told her coauthor Peter Evans, "He is still the same beautiful clown. I'm very proud of him." Their crossing paths again was a very poignant moment: Mickey's career was on an upswing while Ava was on her long, painful slide into alcohol-laced oblivion.[17]

It was much the same with his longtime childhood friend Richard Quine, who directed Mickey in his films after MGM and in his television show, and later gave him parts when nobody else would. Quine had once been one of Hollywood's hottest talents, but in 1984 he was living in obscurity. He visited Mickey's dressing room in Los Angeles, which may have been their last meeting. Quine remarked, "Mickey has the uncanny ability to always bounce back from whatever was thrown at him." [18] Quine, however, couldn't seem to bounce back, and he sadly took his own life in 1989.

By 1985, *Sugar Babies* had become a classic, having been on the stage for many years. It played at the Westbury Music Fair on Long Island rather than Broadway, and the Music Fair Theater in Valley Forge, Pennsylvania, outside Philladelphia. Ann Miller was replaced by Jane Summerhays; and Mickey Deems, Jay Stuart, Rudy Tronto, and Lucianne Buchanan took the place of Peter Leeds, Ann Jillian, and others. Juliet Prowse replaced Ann Miller, and in road shows, Eddie Bracken and Anita Morris took Mickey's and Ann's places. A national tour had Carol Channing and Robert Morse taking Ann's and Mickey's places in August to November of 1980, and Eddie Bracken and Jaye P. Morgan stepping in in 1982. Yet, as Terry Allen Kramer told us, none of the replacements was as powerful in his or her role as the original cast, particularly Mickey Rooney. And on July 7, 1985, the *New York Times* wrote, "Most importantly, 'Sugar Babies' has a national treasure in Mickey Rooney, who is truly, as a banner over the stage proclaims at the end, 'The Ambassador of Good Will.'"

Mickey's Back: The Oscars, and the Emmys, and *Bill*

Mickey and Bill Sackter, subject of the film Bill.
PHOTO COURTESY OF BARRY MORROW.

Even throughout the run of *Sugar Babies,* Mickey continued to work in both film and television. Two of them were *The Black Stallion* (1979), which some film historians believe is the finest performance of his career, and the television movie *Bill* (1981). These films garnered Mickey his greatest notices in over thirty years, including the recognition of an Academy Award nomination and an Emmy Award.

"An absolutely breathtaking performance. Flawless," recalled film professor Lou Sabini, describing Mickey in *The Black Stallion*.[1]

The Black Stallion is based on the classic children's tale written in 1941 by Walter Farley. Despite the book's wide popularity and that of its sixteen sequels, it wasn't adapted for the screen until Francis Ford Coppola purchased the rights. He planned to release the film as the first in a series of children's films. Coppola called on his former UCLA classmate Carroll Ballard to direct the first installment, making *The Black Stallion* Ballard's dramatic feature film debut. (His first movie is a documentary entitled *Harvest*, in 1967, which was nominated for an Academy Award.)

Mickey had just married Jan when he got a call from Coppola telling him that he "had a part in it for me, a former jockey called out of retirement by a little boy with a beautiful black Arabian horse and a dream about winning a race. Did I think I could play a former jockey? 'Gee,' I said, 'I don't know. I never played a jockey before.'" [2] Rooney was cheekily referring to his roles as a jockey in *Down the Stretch* (1936), *Thoroughbreds Don't Cry* (1937), and of course *National Velvet* (1944).

In the tradition of *National Velvet*, *The Black Stallion*, an exotic and often magical tale of a young boy and his horse, is a blend of fascination and childhood innocence. When the film opens, a boy and his father are traveling by ship when a fire breaks out, and the boy finds himself adrift in the rough seas with an Arabian horse he saw on board. Both the boy and the stallion are washed ashore on a deserted island, where they overcome an initial mistrust to form a strong bond. Soon the two are rescued and return to the United States, but the horse runs away. The boy eventually traces the animal to a farm owned by an ex-jockey, played by a now-aging Mickey Rooney. In time, the boy learns from the former pro how to be a first-rate rider and trains the stallion for a championship race.

In our interview with director Carroll Ballard, he recalled:

The studio [MGM] did not want Rooney. They thought he would distract and that the part was just an old man and was rather insignificant. What they didn't recognize was that this character was central to the story. I personally thought he was typecast, but I quickly recognized that he had far more dimension and skills in that he really could undertake any part. He was one of the greatest talents I have ever worked with. He has incredible artistry. When I cast Rooney, I was told by the studio that it was suicide. They told me, "He will eat you alive." As it turned out, Mickey is one of the most professional and hardworking actors. A real trouper. A great example is when we were shooting a scene at four in the morning in a horrible rainstorm. The cast and the crew wanted to go home. Mickey realized that the scene was perfect to capture in these conditions. He talked them into staying by telling them how important this was. They trusted him and they stayed and persevered.

Mickey was a huge asset to me and the film. He helped Kelly Reno [the young star of the film] with tricks on riding the horse and tricks of the camera. He carefully taught him how to turn to the camera. Mickey was absolutely amazing and has great improvisational skills. While I allowed him to improvise, he got in the moment and the character. He inhabits his character. I could not write what Mickey brought to his character. He knew his character and what and how he would say it. Without a doubt, he deserved the Academy Award. It was a shame what happened to him. I believe his talents were underutilized and he was typecast in thankless roles playing old guys. He was denigrated those last years.

We were so lucky. The studio suits were far more concerned with Francis's *Apocalypse Now* and did not pay attention to us. We were able to create the film without them breathing down our necks and analyzing daily rushes. They left us alone and we were able to create our vision without interference. There is no way to make a film like that today.[3]

Clarence Brown, who directed Mickey in several films, including *National Velvet* and his Oscar-nominated performance in Saroyan's *The Human Comedy*, told us in our interview, "Mickey Rooney, to me, is the closest thing to a genius I have ever worked with," echoing the praise of many directors who worked with Rooney over the years.

Mickey's Midas touch may never have worked in business ventures, but in movies it was pure gold, and it rubbed off on *The Black Stallion* in both the glorious reviews it received and the $40 million it garnered in its run (which more than made up for its $4.5 million budget), turning a handsome profit for Ballard and for Coppola's at-the-time financially struggling American Zoetrope studio. With the onset of home video, the movie turned into a bonanza for United Artists/MGM and Coppola, and for Ballard, who owned a piece.

The Black Stallion brought Mickey the professional recognition he had sought both at MGM and during his nomadic travels from studio to studio. For thirty years he had harbored resentment against the Academy of Motion Picture Arts and Sciences for embarrassing him by withdrawing their offer to have him as presenter in 1950. Now, thirty years later, he received the nomination for Best Supporting Actor for his role as Henry Dailey.

"Timmy called Mickey with the news that he was nominated. Mickey, for a rare occasion, was speechless. He was in tears. This was vindication for him," recalled Jan, who flew from New York with Mickey to attend the April 14, 1980, Academy Awards ceremony, held at the Dorothy Chandler Pavilion (with Johnny Carson as host).[4] In the Best Actor in a Supporting Role category, Mickey faced Robert Duvall (*Apocalypse Now*), Justin Henry (*Kramer vs. Kramer*), Fred-eric Forrest (*The Rose*), and Melvyn Douglas (*Being There*). While Mickey was certainly the sentimental favorite, Douglas won, honored for his long career. Mickey said that despite the 1950 snub, he attended the ceremony to "heal the deep wounds in my soul."[5] He had also reached the point of looking at his potential legacy. What would his history be?

After the *Black Stallion* triumph, Rooney received a flood of offers—which he was financially constrained from accepting. With the great success of *Sugar Babies*, he could not afford to do a film that required a long on-location shooting schedule. And now that he was in demand again, he was also looking to get out of doing some of the junk he had had to struggle through for over twenty-four years. He was being offered more "family-friendly" pictures, which he accepted (where the schedule allowed), as they were consistent with his newly professed Christian beliefs, and he liked to take breaks from *Sugar Babies* for film projects. He'd filmed Disney's *Donovan's Kid*, with Darren McGavin, just before the start of *Sugar Babies*. He followed this up in 1980 with *Arabian Adventure*, which starred Christopher Lee on loan from Columbia Pictures. He then filmed a television movie, *My Kidnapper, My Love*, directed by Sam Wanamaker and costarring James Stacy and Glynnis O'Connor. His next film, in 1981, was another TV movie, called *Leave 'Em Laughing*, directed by his childhood buddy Jackie Cooper. It was another dramatic part that allowed Mickey (as a failed clown who becomes a surrogate parent to thirty-seven orphaned children) to display his gift of pathos—and to chew the hell out of the scenery. He acts so well and uses the camera frame so completely that he seems to be the only person in the scene. Later that year he participated in the popular Disney animated film *The Fox and the Hound*, doing the voice for Tod, the fox. That same year, he flew to Toronto almost daily to film *The Emperor of Peru*, flying back at night to appear in *Sugar Babies*.

It was a grueling schedule, but he needed to work wherever he could. Mickey knew that he had to reap his harvest before the sun set, and he aggressively did that very thing. He did the voice of Santa Claus once again for Rankin/Bass, for the Christmas special *Rudolph and Frosty*, which followed his earlier work on the classic specials *Santa Claus Is Coming to Town* and *The Year without a Santa Claus*. All three specials continue to charm children today.

Just prior to his turn in *Sugar Babies*, Mickey had filmed a pilot for the same Norman Lear who in 1969 had offered him the part of Archie Bunker in *All in the Family*. This project, called *A Year at the Top*, in 1977, starred Mickey's old friend, Dead End Kid Gabe Dell, David Letterman's future bandleader Paul Shaffer, and Greg Evigan. Mickey played their uncle on the pilot but was written out of the short-lived series. Still, this role led him to another TV opportunity: In 1982 he was offered his own series on NBC, by Fred Silverman, called *One of the Boys*. It would be Mickey's last attempt at a situation comedy, and the network accommodated by agreeing to film the show in New York. The series' backstory has "Grandfather" Mickey leaving his nursing home and moving into his grandson's college dorm room. The series was created by the veteran team of Saul Turteltaub and Bernie Orenstein, who were hot commodities from their recent work as the showrunners for *Sanford and Son* (starring the sometimes difficult-to-direct Redd Foxx.). They had a long history of successful work on *That Girl*, *Love American Style*, and later *Kate and Allie*. The series signed up three very young stars, Dana Carvey, Nathan Lane, and Meg Ryan, along with Scatman Crothers—a dream cast.

"We had to uproot ourselves to shoot the program in New York City," executive producer/creator/writer Saul Turteltaub told us from his Idaho home. "However, we were looking forward to the challenge. We were thrilled to be working with Mickey. We were warned that he could be difficult to work with, but we did produce a show with Redd Foxx. They were wrong. He was terrific. He did not disappoint us. He is a pro's pro, offered some solid advice. I think it was Bernie and I that maybe didn't quite grab the situation. What a cast, with Dana, Nathan, Meg, and Scatman. We really had great hopes for the show." [6]

Executive producer/writer Bernie Orenstein said, "He has such great talent, he gives the writers such versatility that you can go in several directions. Mickey was still working nights doing *Sugar Babies*. It took great energy to undertake both projects." [7]

Costar Nathan Lane enjoyed working with Mickey, too. "Mickey is one of the greatest legends we have," he said at a ninetieth birthday celebration for Rooney. "I was honored to work with him and to have him as a friend. [8]

However, Dana Carvey disliked working with Mickey, and has since parodied him mercilessly, including in a 2002 appearance on *Late Night with David Letterman*, where he told Letterman that he did "some of the worst TV you've ever seen." When he mentioned *One of the Boys*, Letterman asked, "Could it really have been that bad?" Carvey replied, "It sucked!" He then went on to describe Mickey Rooney as "eccentric," and carefully added, "I don't want to meet his lawyers." Letterman offered the description "high-strung" as an alternative, and Carvey went on to imitate Rooney, saying, "I was the *number one* star in the world." Carvey also said, "He was one of those guys who would talk till he ran out of breath [imitating Mickey], 'I'm going to create Mickey Rooney Macaroni . . .'"

Turteltaub told us, "Mickey's and Dana's acting styles clashed." He explained that this might have been the reason Mickey—just as he did with Dwayne Hickman in *How to Stuff a Wild Bikini*—sought to be Carvey's de facto director. At this stage in his career, Mickey was seeing himself as a mentor, even to those who didn't want his mentoring.

Television audiences shunned *One of the Boys*, and the show barely lasted a season in early 1982. In 2002, *TV Guide* ranked the series number twenty-four on its list of "The 50 Worst Shows of All

Time." Mickey was not worried. He was still basking in the glow of *Sugar Babies* and his Academy Award nomination.

That glow helped him land his next TV role, and it was a role that would transform him personally as well as professionally. The made-for-television movie *Bill* was about the real-life Bill Sackter, a developmentally challenged person who had to find his way outside the institution where he had lived for most of his life. The way Mickey rose to embrace the role of Bill showed that, as with his work in *Sugar Babies* and *The Black Stallion*, he had made his mark in the industry that rose above even his days at MGM.

"I GAVE ONE OF the best performances of my life," Mickey wrote about *Bill*, the television movie that forced him to think and perform in an entirely new light.[9]

The story was born around an unlikely friendship between a mentally challenged man, Bill Sackter, and a young screenwriter. The developmentally challenged Bill had been institutionalized by his parents since he was seven. When he was released at sixty years old, he had to find a life for himself, make his way in a world he did not know. Screenwriter Barry Morrow met Bill at a staff Christmas party at the Minikahda Club in Minneapolis, where Bill had been employed as a dishwasher since his release. A friendship grew, and Barry began shooting videotape and Super 8 film footage of Bill, finding him to be a great subject for a documentary. After being offered a job in Iowa City, Barry moved away and had to leave Bill on his own. Shortly thereafter, Bill was hospitalized, and it was Barry's job to tell him that he needed to have his leg amputated and be sent back to the institution. In an unprecedented move, Barry instead petitioned the court to grant him legal guardianship over Bill, whom he then brought with him to Iowa City.

With Barry's help, Bill made a full recovery, and with the support of Barry and others in the community, Bill soon became a local celebrity. Morrow originally intended to memorialize Bill's entrance into society in a documentary, but CBS approached him about dramatizing the story of Bill's life as a scripted movie made for television. Further, the network, having taken notice of Mickey Rooney's resurgence in the entertainment industry, cast him as Bill and Dennis Quaid as Barry Morrow.

Morrow took this film very seriously. He wanted to send a message that would translate into creating advocacy groups for people with disabilities and their families and caretakers. Essentially, in the wake of federal and state policies mainstreaming developmentally challenged and mentally ill people, there was a need for such advocacy, lest the criminal justice system reinstitutionalize those released into society.[10]

Of course Morrow was very sensitive about the portrayal of Bill, and was a little surprised at Mickey's first attempt at the character. He recalled, "When Mickey began the film, his translation of Bill was not at all what I envisioned. He portrayed Bill as if he had a severe palsy or muscular disease. It was quite exaggerated . . . Mickey had adamantly refused to meet Bill or even watch the tapes of him. He had no real basis to understand what Bill Sackter was really like. He just tried to ape mannerisms that were quite exaggerated." [11]

Mickey had decided that he would play what he thought a developmentally challenged person should be, without regard to the real person. The result was a hollow characterization: demeaning, nearly comic, and absolutely devoid of verisimilitude.

"I was very upset at the initial footage," Morrow told us. "My contract, thank God, with CBS was ironclad, wherein I had veto power. The director that they assigned, Anthony Page, although he had done fine work in his career, was very weak with Mickey. Anthony let Mickey overrun him. Although Mickey was only five two, he has a very powerful presence and could be rather intimidating. Do not be fooled by his size." Morrow wasn't. He had invested more than a script in the story of Bill Sackter and was not about to see Mickey mug and stumble his way through a performance, intimidating his director and making a mockery of the real-life Bill. With his contract in hand and waving his veto power like a flag,

> I went to CBS at Black Rock in New York and met with their top executives, and I vetoed how Bill was being presented. I told them that the character needed to be toned down. There was a delay of several months, and I thought [the movie] might never be made. Luckily, CBS wanted to really make this film. Finally, they actually had their executives sort of sit on Mickey to have him tone down his outrageous, broad portrayal of Bill. They eventually scrapped all initial footage except for one scene where he is fighting with drunks in the dark and goes to jail. Mickey actually found his center and toned down the character. It was an amazing metamorphosis. Mickey found the heart of Bill.[12]

What was it that transformed Mickey's performance, that enabled him to inhabit the character of Bill Sackter? Morrow explained that after the execs from the network showed up to read him the riot act, Mickey had a blazing Saul-on-the-way-to-Damascus moment and realized that his success in *Sugar Babies* could be completely obliterated by a failure in a television production. He agreed to meet with the person he had been hired to portray, and the result was nothing less than an epiphany.

Morrow explained that the upshot of Mickey's meeting with Sackter, and his resulting performance, "was that the film, I believed, became a watershed of Mickey's later career. The next year, he won an honorary Oscar. I believe that *Bill* certainly played a big part in

THE LIFE AND TIMES OF MICKEY ROONEY **459**

making that happen. It brought him new respect by the industry. He also won an Emmy and a Golden [Globe] for this role."

Mickey had been able to navigate through roles his entire life, pulling from his actor's tool kit all the skills necessary to inhabit parts ranging from precocious teenagers to gangsters to prizefighters. But when it came to Bill, the usual tools wouldn't work. In the empty pit where Mickey's personality should have been, there was only a hollow echo of narcissism. Bill Sackter, walking through life as a stranger in a strange land, gave Mickey empathy, something that he might not have felt before, despite his desperate situations and tragedies. Perhaps for the first time in his life, Mickey saw the struggle of a real human being overcoming his personal disability, attempting to make two and two equal four so he could live on his own. For Mickey, carried onstage into a brave new world of bright lights, seminaked hoofers, brassy warblers, clowns in baggy pants flopping around the stage like fresh-caught fish on a ship's deck even before he was one year old, there was no personality to develop, only the skills to inhabit that specific world—and inhabit it he did, filling the emptiness of his being with every form of self-gratification. Then he met Bill Sackter, watched him as he moved, listened as he framed sentences, and realized that real human beings live not just to gratify themselves, but to inhabit the lives they live as human beings, not avatars. And in that moment, Mickey did an amazing thing: He amalgamated what he perceived in Bill Sacker and morphed it into a character. In that process, Mickey experienced true catharsis and was translated from a tired old irritable artifact, an anachronism, into a legend. He didn't just act the role, he understood it, he lived it, and the result on-screen was pure mimesis.

And, as Morrow told us, Mickey didn't just walk away from Bill after filming. Because he felt empathy, probably for the first time in his life, he committed himself to groups such as the Arc (for people with intellectual and developmental disabilities). His portrayal of Bill was the genesis, in Mickey, of better awareness and compassion for people with disabilities—and his impact will be felt far after his passing. (For his part, Morrow won an Emmy for writing *Bill*. He later won an Academy Award for writing *Rain Man*.) Life had now changed: He had peeked over the edge of his private reality and seen the universe.

ASIDE FROM SHOWING HIS ability to play an aged and impaired person, a role he inhabited so perfectly, *Bill* was pivotal in Mickey's career also for launching him into the label of "old guy" that would define him for the next thirty years. Whereas in the 1950s he might have been the middle-aged guy acting out the role of a superannuated teenager; and in the 1960s he was the awkward, behaving-badly artifact miscommunicating with bubbly Gidget wannabes and amply muscled young surfer dudes; by the 1970s, not even that worked. He now inhabited "old" and would venture through the rest of his professional life as the "old guy."

In 1983 his vindication from the Academy of Motion Picture Arts and Sciences came full circle. On Oscar night on April 11, 1983, at the *Fifty-Fifth Annual Academy Awards*, Mickey was bestowed with a Special Award for Lifelong Career Achievement. In a list of Oscar speeches, Mickey's acceptance speech is listed as the eighteenth best. The website Oscar, Oscar! wrote that it was a "humbling acceptance speech" and "one of the most profoundly sad and true acceptance speeches in Oscar history. . . . [H]e talked about back when he was a kid in the '30s, he was the number one star in the world. A few years later, he was broke, and nobody offered him work (nobody wanted me). He relayed the sad truth of Hollywood sometimes, that fame can be so fleeting and so temporary, and he ended on a positive note, thanking the people who helped get him work again."[13]

Going Ungently into That Good Night

Mickey played Oscar to Tony Randall's Felix in a 1968 production of
The Odd Couple *at Caesar's Palace and other locations. Rooney was*
Randall's first choice to play Oscar when casting the TV version.
PHOTO COURTESY OF TOM POSTON.

How does one become the professional old guy? When the bright red expiration light starts flashing in your palm, do you slouch grudgingly but obligingly into the vaporization beam or do you run for your life? Would Mickey continue the wild ways of his youth while inhabiting the body of the old guy, blinded by lechery as he chased after women more than half his age? Or would he gracefully shoulder the burden of a patriarch to his many children and grandchildren while professionally making the role of the old guy nonsuperfluous? Which direction could Mickey take?

There was indeed a path for Mickey for the ensuing decades, a path that began with an actor who represented, for producers and directors, a lucky charm. With his performance in *Bill*, Mickey had taken on the mantle not only of the old guy, but of a character hobbled by physical and developmental disability. Remember how Antigone schlepped her father Oedipus around town because his blood-scarred eye sockets represented his supreme act of contrition and a washing away of public sin? Playing Bill was an expiation of the compensatory sins of pride and narcissism that had marked every aspect of Mickey's life as he sought to justify acts of self-gratification that, like bags of potato chips, leave you hungry no matter how much you eat. In Bill Sackter, Mickey had seen that truth was the beauty of art.

Mickey would quickly learn, however, that where once he was the target of prejudice against his height (size-ism), he was now discriminated against because he was old. Ageism is rampant in Hollywood, where the folks who can green-light films are so young they're barely legal to drive. And where do people sixty-five and older fall? Into a pit of rusted Tin Men was the fate of Mickey Rooney as he turned sixty-five in 1985 after *Sugar Babies* ended its long run and he showed the world what he could do in *Bill*. After these back-to-back successes, Mickey was quietly relegated to the role of aging eccentric by what seems to have been a sub rosa gentlemen's agreement among Hollywood producers so young that aging was anathema.

Mickey's new struggle for professional credibility began because in the world he inhabited, the world of those who cut him the checks he then turned over to his bookies, even the most talented artists of a certain age were looked upon as disposable antiques—even though, according to Karen Kramer, the wife of *Mad, Mad World* producer and iconic filmmaker Stanley Kramer, they might have reached the peak of their artistic prowess.

Many of Mickey's friends told us they were befuddled at the transition in his career after *Bill*. Where Mickey saw his arc as a respectable avuncular character (a Lionel Barrymore or a Lewis Stone), instead he was relegated to thankless, throwaway roles as cantankerous old men or laughable sidekicks (a Gabby Hayes or a J. Pat O'Malley).

"It is pure and simple ageism," remarked Carroll Ballard, the auteur who helmed *The Black Stallion*. "I was completely in awe of Mickey's huge talent. I was pained to watch as his talents were underutilized and he was typecast in thankless roles playing old coots, whereas he had so much more finesse, depth, dimension, layers and skills." [1]

The nonagenerian Norman Abbott, who has been recognized over the years as one of the great television comedy directors, echoed these sentiments, not only about Mickey, but about older show business professionals in general, saying, "While your work is repeated and copied, you are considered old hat and stale. Mickey got even stronger as he aged. He had talent that was seasoned by generations of experience." [2]

Another nonagenarian, Rocky Kalish, who co-created *Gilligan's Island* and wrote and produced such programs as *My Three Sons*, *Family Affair*, and *Good Times*, said, "I can draw upon classic ideas and learned from brilliant men like Sheldon Leonard to Hal Kanter. Your talent ages like fine wine. Mickey maintained his talent as long as he lived." [3]

MICKEY, THOUGH NOW TYPECAST as elderly, continued to lead a diverse career, with constant appearances in theater, clubs, television, and as a published author. Despite his Emmy and Golden Globe, his film career was still a succession of mostly thankless roles, the only parts offered him. The sequel to *Bill* in 1983 was an exception. *Bill: On His Own*, again a television movie scripted by Barry Morrow, featured Dennis Quaid, Helen Hunt, and Teresa Wright. Although Morrow felt the story was weaker, the film was well received, and Mickey was again nominated for an Emmy. He followed this with another television movie, *It Came Upon a Midnight Clear,* a sentimental film costarring Scott Grimes, Lloyd Nolan, and as Mickey's spouse, his own wife, Jan. In it, Mickey portrays a retired cop who passes away and returns as an angel. He also did the voice-over for the animated *Care Bear Movie* in 1985, and had a small part in a television flick, *The Return of Mickey Spillane's Mike Hammer* in 1986, with Stacy Keach. That same year, he did another television film, for Disney, called *Little Spies,* with another small, eccentric role as Jimmy the Hermit.

This trend continued almost unabated for the next nearly thirty years. He never again, in films or television movies, was given the opportunity to stretch out or do anything more than create a very small role playing an eccentric. There would be nearly forty more films, but he was now a curiosity. For older viewers, he offered a glimpse at a faded superstar who wanted to continue working. For younger ones, he was just a crotchety old character actor.

There were bits and pieces, in various roles, where viewers saw glimpses of the old Mighty Mite. But he needed money, and the parts he took were mostly simply getting him a paycheck.

What became the saving grace for Mickey was that he still had the chops for being onstage, where he was allowed to spread his wings. Mickey was always a live audience draw, especially after *Sugar Babies.* He did the occasional dinner/regional theater for old friends such as John Kenley, for whom he appeared in a revised version of his old standby, *Three Goats and a Blanket,* now retitled *Go Ahead and Laff.* He performed it in the summer of 1986 with Jane Kean, who played Trixie on *The Honeymooners.* The next year, he did a four-month national tour of *A Funny Thing Happened on the Way to the Forum,* again as Pseudolus.

For two months in the 1970s, when starring in *Forum*, playwright Larry Gelbart was unhappy with Mickey's ad-libbing. He said, "We take great pains creating the dialogue and rhythm of the piece. Mickey took it upon himself to do extra throwaways, which both threw the other performers off and also distracted from the piece. This is not *The Carol Burnett Show*. I truly detest an actor breaking character."

Mickey Rooney told the *New Haven Register* on March 2, 1987, "Playwright Larry Gelbart hasn't been happy with the liberties I have taken with his script, [but] we've thrown caution to the winds, without degrading anything."

Where *Sugar Babies* had the flexibility for asides and ad libs, simply because Mickey was playing himself as his father in burlesque, *Forum* was not created for burlesque bits, and it was necessary that Mickey read his character's lines, not improvise. *Forum* was a nuanced piece that had been carefully constructed, and Gelbart was right in his judgment that the dialogue needed to be strictly adhered to. When Mickey followed the dialogue and played the character as the play demanded, he was a riot.

In 1988, Mickey finally produced the type of live show he had been proposing since the mid-1970s when he tried to borrow clips from Jack Haley Jr. and MGM. Called *Mickey Rooney in Mickey Rooney*, the show started with thirty minutes of clips from Mickey's classic films, including *Bill*, then some song and dance, followed by audience questions. The show played throughout the United States in stops such as San Francisco, Chicago, and Cleveland. They repeated the tour in 1994 in Australia and New Zealand.

"We were like conquering heroes in Australia," Chris Aber told us. "They just rolled out a red carpet for us. Mickey was like a national hero, and [he] just loved it. However, he ran right back to his hotel room after the show. He did not want to face the autograph seekers as soon as the show ended." According to Aber, Mickey had grown increasingly bitter at having to smile for the fans when he wasn't onstage or in front of a camera. With growing anger, Mickey was pulling a curtain around himself even as he kept on performing.

By this time, something was not right with Rooney. It turned out that the pills he was taking were catching up with him. He could no longer move with his old grace. He was hesitating in delivering his lines. And he seemed tentative and not full of the confidence that marked his former days. The *San Francisco Chronicle*, in its review of the live show on May 14, 1979, was vastly underwhelmed. While the paper heaped praise on him for *Sugar Babies*, it went to town on him in a story titled, "Mickey Takes His Ego for a Stroll": "After being trapped in the Theatre on the Square for two-and-one-half hours without intermission, I think we need a law against yelling 'Mickey Rooney' in a crowded theater. At the very start of this most peculiar, almost endless, one-man show, modestly called 'Mickey Rooney in Mickey Rooney,' the star says he hopes he fits the part. In fact, he's been badly miscast, playing the role of a windy, old showbiz bore, the one thing Mickey Rooney has never been."

Mickey was crashing and burning in front of audiences. He was having a public breakdown. The stop in Cleveland proved disastrous, according to Chris, who said, "Mickey was taking lithium and diazepam [Valium]. He was taking the lithium as he was diagnosed as being bipolar. He stopped taking the lithium as he thought it sapped his energy on the stage. What happened was that Mickey suffered a complete breakdown, a nervous breakdown. It was very frightening. I was there with him in Cleveland. He was put in the hospital. The play producers were panicking. The insurance claim was that Mickey was suffering from a bleeding ulcer. But it might have resulted from his medications. Mickey is his own worst enemy."[4] (Mickey's breakdown was confirmed to us by his manager Robert Malcolm and by *Cleveland Plain Dealer* television critic Mark Dawidziak.) Mickey spent nearly one month in Cleveland detoxing and rehabilitating from his addiction to painkillers and Valium, and adjusting his dosage of lithium.

Medical issues notwithstanding, Mickey needed to continue as the breadwinner for the Rooney family, a job that had not stopped since 1926, when he was the main breadwinner, at six years old, for his mother, Nell. At seventy years old, when many senior citizens are starting to enjoy their retirement, Mickey had to go back to work. He enjoyed performing—it was his life, his only life, though he had no choice. There was no nest egg, no great savings, even though he had earned tens of millions of dollars over the past seven decades and had ostensibly built up his guild pension.

Mickey's next show had him teaming with his old friend Donald O'Connor. He had met O'Connor in 1933 at a Talent Night at the Orpheum Theatre in Los Angeles. O'Connor, who, like Mickey, came from a family of vaudeville performers, told us, "Mickey was a dream to work with. We had similar sensibilities. We had worked together in the past, on *The Sunshine Boys* onstage. Mickey was always Mickey." [5]

Mickey seemed to have recovered from his breakdown as the two debuted a musical revue called *Two for the Show*, which played in venues throughout the country in 1989 and 1990. One of their appearances was at the Riviera Hotel in Las Vegas, on August 23, 1989, about which *Variety* wrote, "The 90-minute razzle-dazzle of the two showbiz vets heralds a new nitery team sorely needed in these times in Las Vegas. The matching of talent was exemplary, exhibiting both entertainers in song, dance, comedy, and plenty of theatrics."

The next year, Rooney and O'Connor returned in a fourteen-week tour of *The Sunshine Boys*. It was warmly received and garnered strong, positive reviews. However, the Rooney and O'Connor team was derailed by Donald's heart attack in 1990, followed by quadruple bypass surgery later that year.

In 1993, Mickey joined the touring group of Ken Ludwig's *Lend Me a Tenor* for nearly nine months. As he had as a youth, he toured the Midwest circuit of Chicago and other Rust Belt cities. After his triumph in *Sugar Babies*, audiences greeted the return of Mickey warmly. Richard Christiansen, chief critic of the *Chicago Tribune* wrote on May 13, 1993:

> "Lend Me A Tenor" Gets Rooney as Bonus. Mickey Rooney saves his best bits for his second entrance in "Lend Me a Tenor." The latest star to be imported here for the amazingly long Chicago run of Ken Ludwig's farce at the Apollo Theater, Rooney can't help but bring some of his inimitable personality to the show. He breaks character to shake hands with the customers, hurl mock insults at the audience and laugh at his own jokes. Inevitably, he works in funny lines about his size (short) and his wives (many). But he has to be a team player, too, if the slam-bang gags and the timing complexities of the farce are to work, and Rooney, while not neglecting his slapstick, speaks his lines and makes his moves more or less in synchronization with the rest of the cast. They're in fine form screaming, slamming doors and stripping off their clothes. And whenever the action threatens to sag, there's always Mickey Rooney, spitting out wax fruit or snoozing off during a long stretch of plot explanation. He's one of the last, and the greatest, of the big-time buffoons.

Mickey followed this in his return to Broadway in *The Will Rogers Follies*, which starred Larry Gatlin. Mickey joined the play during its 1993 run as Roger's father Clem, replacing Dick Latessa in the role at the Palace Theatre. Mickey took a minor role and expanded it in what many began to call *The Mickey Rooney Follies*. The producers were happy because it revitalized a dying show.

Donald Trump, whose then-wife, Marla Maples, was in the show, recalled to us, "Mickey was just amazing . . . [H]e just ad-libbed his way through the part. The audiences just loved him." [6]

Clive Barnes in the *New York Post* wrote, "This happily shuffling performance by one of the last, indeed perhaps *the* last, of the glorious old vaudevillians, is restrained, touching, rhythmic, and brilliant. Quite marvelous!"

Mickey then returned for one last hurrah in *Sugar Babies*, with Ann Miller, in London at the Savoy Theatre. In this West End version of the show, Mickey was still receiving forty thousand per week, plus three thousand weekly in expenses. At the end of the run, he made an important change in management. Ruth Webb, who had nurtured him through his drug breakdown in Houston and put his career back on track, including negotiating his deal for *Sugar Babies*, was unceremoniously fired, something she complained bitterly about for the ensuing decade. In fact, she eventually had to sue Mickey to recover her 10 percent agency commission for this last run in *Sugar Babies*. Webb was replaced by Robert Malcolm, who remained Mickey's manager and agent through 2014.

Meanwhile, Mickey went to work on the only successful television program of his career, *The Adventures of the Black Stallion*, in which he reprised his Oscar-nominated role as horse trainer Henry Dailey. The series, which lasted three seasons from 1990 to 1993, was shown on what is now the ABC Family Network, and was a huge hit; it is still in reruns worldwide. Rooney was nominated for a Gemini Award, Canada's version of the Emmys, in the category "Best Performance by an Actor in a Continuing Leading Dramatic Role." Mickey also promoted the show to press and potential sponsors. Cleveland television critic Mark Dawidziak attended a press conference in Los

Angeles at which Mickey was ostensibly promoting the show and re-called:

> I was sitting next to the Dallas critic Ed Bark, and I think it took us days to recover. It was summer 1990 at the Century Plaza Hotel, and it was for the cable channel then called the Family Channel. The press conference was for a series based on *The Black Stallion*. Rooney stunned the channel executives and the critics by *not* talking about *The Adventures of the Black Stallion*, but launching into a nonstop pitch session for a bunch of series ideas he had. In one, he would play Thomas Edison. In another, he would play the evangelist Billy Sunday. He pitched an animated show called *Lucky the Leprechaun*. He talked about an inter-racial comedy. We were on the other side of the Looking Glass, to be sure. Then he hit the topper of all time. He pitched a comedy about a man married to a woman wres-tler, who would periodically get mad and throw him out the window. We were fairly helpless at this point, but then he told us the proposed title for his series: *Wait Till the Swelling Goes Down.*[7]

The funny thing is that all these politically incorrect series not only made sense, but also were imaginative and would have taken advantage of Mickey's comedic talent. You could theoretically come across versions of these series on cable today or on Amazon, Netflix, or iTunes. (Before you dismiss this notion amid apoplectic peals of laughter, just remember the little-person-tossing scene in Scorsese's *Wall Street*. Not so far-fetched now, is it?) Yet, at the time, over twenty-five years ago, and pitched by a seventy-year-old looking for a starring gig, any gig, they sounded way "out there."

Despite the sometime frivolity in Mickey's appearances, his bipolar symptoms were getting out of hand, and he sometimes erupted into explosive rage during public appearances, even though his wife, Jan, tried to control his mood swings. Doug McDuff, a longtime radio host in the Chicagoland market and now at WBEL AM, recalled an interesting experience with Mickey when he appeared on McDuff's program in 2008. "We had Mickey as a guest with his wife, who were promoting their *Let's Put on a Show!* in Rockford [Illinois]. While on the air, Mickey was absolutely fascinating, recalling his heyday in Hollywood. He was just wonderful. Then, at the break, he was like another person. His poor wife. He was screaming at her: He was hungry, why didn't she have food for him? He was like a horrid spoiled child. Then, when he went back on the air, he was back to being wonderful."[8]

Geoffrey Mark Fidelman, author of *The Lucy Book*, was a guest at the May 2001 Lucy Festival in Ball's hometown of Jamestown, New York. Mickey was paid to attend the festival and talk about his work and his friendship with Lucy.[9] Mark recalled:

> I was there with my Lucy book. At the occasion was a young girl who was attending thanks to the "Make-A-Wish" foundation. She wanted to meet me because of the book and to talk with Mickey. Mickey's speech was about twenty seconds about Lucy and twenty minutes about Mickey. After the speech, he headed straight to the bar and was mixing his own drinks. Part of Mickey's "job" was to meet this dying young girl. I went up to Mickey to introduce this young girl and he just told me not to bother him. I said that she was from "Make A Wish," and again he told me to basically "Fuck off." I told him he had two choices: one, I would break his leg or, two, he would meet the girl. Reluctantly he talked to the girl, actually harshly, for a few seconds. As a recovering alcoholic, I knew the

signs. Mickey was his own worst enemy, and he certainly had an addiction problem.[10]

This anecdote seemed to be representative of how Mickey was with his fans, at least in his later years. While many fans were eager to meet him, he was not always eager to meet them. The majority of recollections, by fans and even friends, of meeting Mickey almost always reflect his rudeness and antagonistic attitude. Get Mickey in the right mood and he was ebullient with ideas and bubbling with enthusiasm, as attested to by Karen Kramer, who described Mickey's demeanor at a *Mad, Mad World* retrospective. He was just like the Andy Hardy she fell in love with on the big screen, she said. Yet catch him in a down mood or when he was off his meds, and Mickey would be hostile to the point of ugliness.

Said stepson Chris Aber, "Mickey wants always to appear to be a tough guy. He wants everyone to think that of him. I couldn't even count the confrontations and problems that Mickey had with his fans, friends, and everyone over the nearly thirty-five years I was with him."[11] Aber became Mickey's personal assistant after road manager Jack Krieg left in early 1983. He was replaced in 2012 by Kevin Pawley, who stayed with Mickey until the end, in 2014.

"When we were doing the first *Night at the Museum* films," Aber said, "the director was Shawn Levy, who is one of the top directors. When Shawn's mother, an elderly lady, came toward Mickey to talk with him, he pushed her away. When we found out it was Shawn's mother, then he was apologetic. Once, the owner of the New York Giants, Wellington Mara, came up to talk to Mickey and he told him, 'Why don't you go fuck yourself.' This story was constantly repeated."

Jan told us, "When he woke up in the morning, you never knew which Mickey you'd get, the angelic Andrew Hardy or *Boys Town*'s Whitey Marsh."

Jan's sister Ronna Riley told us, "Mickey was absolutely brutal to many fans. It was frightening. Thank God he was nice to the Queen of England and Prince Phillip when he met them."

Donald Trump echoed Ronna's statement, saying that Mickey didn't care whom he was talking to. He simply spoke his mind whenever he felt like it.

One of the many psychological issues Mickey was facing at this point in his life was a perception (which was true) that he had lost relevance, not only in his career, but also in his life. His frustration over that loss of relevance might have been what was driving the dark side of his personality off-camera. *Tea Travels* writer Ellen Easton, a friend of Jan's, revealed, "He could be outright rude, and I think sometimes even bigoted. He could be very, very nice and sometimes very, very crude." [12]

Hollywood Reporter journalist Scott Feinberg, who conducted one of the last interviews with Mickey (with Jan and Chris there), which he videotaped, recalled that Mickey displayed bizarre fits of explosive anger during their interview. "At times he was almost totally out of control. He would have an actual tantrum and crying fits if he didn't get what he wanted." [13]

When Fredde Duke, Maurice Duke's daughter, asked Mickey to participate in *Fuck 'Em*, the documentary she was making about her father, "he said, 'If you're not going to pay me,' to go fuck myself. He was horrible." Maurice Duke, Mickey's longtime manager, had rescued him from near oblivion and remained personal friends with him even after Mickey's antics had put the Duke and his family in jeopardy. But not even a project on Duke could elicit warm behavior from Rooney. [14]

Ray Courts, the founder of the Hollywood Show, a celebrity autograph convention, echoed stories about how Mickey dealt with fans:

I did nearly twenty years of autograph shows with Mickey.
I can tell so many countless stories of Mickey mistreat-

ing his fans, it would take hours. Once, an elderly lady, who had paid for his autograph and was clearly devoted to him, asked if he could personalize an autograph, and he replied, 'Listen, lady, I'm not writing a fucking book here.' He called people leeches. Sometimes it took both Jan and Chris to calm him down. He was always angry. Believe me, I felt for Jan. Anybody who could put up with Mickey's crap should go to heaven. Mickey traveled with us to autograph shows all over the country, like Chicago and Houston. He once skipped out on a hotel bill in Chicago, where he was staying for the show. I once was with him at a hotel gift shop, where Mickey just grabbed a bottle of aftershave, opened it, and poured a fistful in his hands, then put it back. He just did not care. . . . Mickey made a ton of cash at the autograph shows. Once, when he needed money for a plane ticket to Mexico to shoot a movie, he just showed up, unannounced, to the autograph show in Hollywood to make some cash. He literally begged [me] to set up a table, [to] which I acquiesced. Then he was mean and nasty to the fans. He just hated fans trying to come behind his table to take pictures with him. The great publicist Marvin Paige once told me . . . sadly, "You know, even if Mickey is rude, he shouldn't have to do this at his age. He should be able to enjoy the fruits of his labor, by this age." [15]

Comedian Rip Taylor, who filled in for Rooney in *Sugar Babies*, told us, "I kind of knew him, but his personality changed every half hour. You know I 'replaced' him in *Sugar Babies*. He gave me a lot of help and helped with my career. A real pro. Crazy and funny, but who isn't?" [16]

Author and television historian Steve Cox recalled joining Billy Barty and Mickey at Barty's tournament to sponsor the Billy Barty

Foundation, which covered medical bills for complications resulting from dwarfism. When the crowd tried to surround Mickey for autographs, he spurned the attention so they could focus on Barty, and said, "This is Billy's day." Despite his heavy mood swings, Mickey still had a sense of loyalty, especially to Barty, who had been his on-screen sidekick for decades.

Publicist Roger Neal, who hosted Mickey at his annual Oscar party in Beverly Hills, told us that "Mickey was very cordial to everyone and was accommodating to those who sought to meet him." In other words, when he was on, he was on, but when he wasn't, when he was on the downside in his bipolar depression, he became bitter to the point of cruelty.

Leatrice Gilbert, the daughter of screen legend John Gilbert and silent film star Leatrice Joy, told us in our interview with her, "When he was younger, Mickey was very cordial to his fans. He loved being the center of attention. When I was with Ava and Mickey, they loved being the focus of what was going on. When I met him years later he had changed. He was far more bitter and gruff."

Legendary television producer Robert Finkel said to us, "Although he was loaded with talent, I was always reluctant to use him . . . I was producing the Academy Awards in 1972 and we thought of using Mickey as a presenter. Sammy Davis Jr. was the cohost and said that Mickey was not reliable . . . and I thought they were friends. Sammy said that Mickey was always angry and could be a problem."

UNDETERRED BY HIS TYPECASTING, Mickey forged ahead working in films to the point where, amazingly, his output in the 1990s and 2000s was similar to that of the past seven decades. He appeared in twenty-one films between 1990 and the end of the millennium, and another twenty-one in the first decade of the new century. He was on his way to the same number of films in the 2010s, appearing in ten films from 2010 to 2015, including *Night at the Museum: Secret of the Tomb.* If we include the seventy-eight shorts he appeared in as Mickey McGuire, Mickey Rooney had appeared in more than four hundred movies in eighty-nine years. By any measure, this is an astounding feat.

Woody Allen once quipped, "Show business is not so much dog eats dog as dog doesn't return other dog's phone calls." Mickey followed Woody's other piece of sage advice: success also means just showing up. Mickey kept showing up.

Motivational speaker Michael Simkins wrote, "Acting isn't all about feeling the character and being in the moment. If you can't get a job, it's not about much at all. Acting is only possible if somebody's prepared to sit and watch you do it. To survive emotionally and professionally, you've got to both earn a living and nourish your beleaguered self-esteem." [17]

An old joke goes: Picture a circus parade moving through town. At the back is an old guy whose job is to shovel the manure from all the circus animals into a big bag slung over his shoulder. A passerby asks him how long he's been doing the job and how much he gets paid, to which he replies fifty years and fifty dollars a week.

"Well, why on earth don't you stop doing it and find a better job instead?" asks the passerby.

The old guy says, "What, and give up show business?"

So it was with Mickey Rooney, who had gone from the head of the parade to following the elephants.

26

Time May Lie Heavy Between

The Atomic Kid *(1954)*.

We were both at a party, a little tipsy and . . . well, it happened."
So begins the story of a former actress we call Mrs. Smith, to conceal her real identity—her long-term spouse is still unaware of her unconventional sixty-five-year love affair with Mickey Rooney, which lasted from the 1940s until his death. She was also his confidante, pen pal, friend, and possibly the only person to whom Mickey unlocked his deepest secrets, desires, and fears.

Throughout Mickey's different marriages (from his second wife, B.J., through Jan), Mickey had one constant thread, his relationship with Mrs. Smith, who is still alive today and, until we spoke to her, had lived under a self-imposed vow of silence concerning her decades-long affair with Mickey. In return for our promise of anonymity, she has provided us the intimate details of her unconventional love affair.

Mrs. Smith told us:

> I had known Mickey during the 1940s, even prior to my marriage. He was not my physical type. However, he was terrific fun to be with. I became sexually involved with Mickey between his divorce of B.J. and his marriage to Mart. Mickey is a very caring and passionate lover. While we never considered a relationship beyond clandestine meetings and correspondence, it also was a friendship like no other. We were able to tell each other our deepest secrets and confidences, which we have done for over sixty years. We never had a scheduled time or meeting setup; it just happened . . . well, when it happened. Whenever we could sneak away. While the sexual aspect eventually was not the focus, we remained almost soul mates. I heard about the travails with his flavor of the year, and I was able to unload my problems. We both listened and commented. It was actually better than being in psychoanalysis. Mickey was not his usual manic self, he listened and cared. We sometimes talked on the phone, and many times we corresponded. We never sent any letters to our homes; we were very careful. We were in contact until shortly before his death, when his daughter-in-law, [whom] he was living with, cut us off.[1] (That would have been Charlene Aber, who might have believed she was protecting Mickey.)

Mrs. Smith and Mickey led their own separate lives, burying their relationship deep beneath the social conventions as their paths crossed in the comings and goings of the movie industry. "I was around

Mickey in many social occasions as well," Mrs. Smith said. "I was at a party at Judy Garland's home, where we were all drinking. Mickey and Judy headed off to the bedroom and returned very disheveled. We knew they had slept together. Mickey was incredible at parties—he was everything, playing the piano, singing. He always left with a girl, sometimes even if he was with his current flavor."

Mrs. Smith was friends with Martha Vickers, and told us, "She was a notorious drinker and would humiliate him. He was on the downward spiral, and she simply looked at him like a loser. He knew that, and it hurt him."

Regarding his wife Elaine, who took money from him to help her first husband pay off his gambling debts, Smith said, "She loved her first husband. Mickey could provide for her, and that is what she was after. They never had kids as she was into herself. She squeezed him dry."

Barbara Ann Thomason was different, Mrs. Smith believed. Mickey tried to commit himself to her, had children with her, and was traumatized at her murder. "He truly loved her," Mrs. Smith said. "I thought they had a happy family for a while. For a while, he seemed content. I never met her killer, but I know he betrayed Mickey. [Mickey] was a literal mess when she was killed. It was a bad period for him."

Of Marge, Barbara's best friend, whom Mickey married shortly after the double murder, Smith told us, "Mickey was like a lost boy," a widower as well as a divorced man with children and a career he was hanging onto in desperation because it defined him. Marge was Mickey's nearest port in a storm, Smith said, possibly because "she looked like his mother. I think he wanted a mother then." At the very least, Mickey was seeking a mother for his four children with Barbara.

Carolyn was different, said Smith. She was not Hollywood, not in the business, and his marriage to her, short as it was, had become almost like a respite—until he was bored and his old demons resurfaced. "He met her in Florida. She wanted him to live there. He was just trying to run away from Hollywood and wanted to hide. I never met her, and he just hated to be alone."

By the time he met Jan at Ruth Webb's, Rooney was looking at the promise of stability. Of Jan, Mrs. Smith said, "I have met her and found her to be very possessive. However, you have got to hand it to her. He certainly settled down with her. We had dinner with her several times. They were like any couple and had their disagreements, but that's natural."

Mickey was very open in his letters to Smith, who read us some passages from his correspondence with her. Not love letters per se, they were filled with recollections and sometimes anger, but always Mickey in his own, heretofore unpublished words:

> March 1950: "[S]he [Martha Vickers] could hardly stand up when I came home. After I'm at the studio all day, and the kid is there, I don't need to be a nanny."
>
> June 1958, referring to Barbara Ann and specifically to her attempted suicide by an overdose of pills: "[T]hanks for your concern. She is all right. I just don't want to get trapped again. They use my house as if it's their house to party."
>
> February 1966: "I appreciate both of your calls and help. I appreciate 'Mr. Smith's' kind assistance. . . . [T]his has been the biggest nightmare and it never seems to end. . . . I'd like to meet sometime soon. . . . [P]lease call me . . . I miss being close to you—I can still smell your scent."

"I think I saw a side of Mickey that he revealed to no one else," Smith said. "He was very romantic, kind; he had a very nostalgic sense; and I was able to experiment sexually with him that I couldn't with my husband. He was very athletic. Very. He was quite inventive . . . and yes, he was very well endowed. I don't know if it was proportionate, but he could choke you with that . . ."

She continued: "Also, we lent him money over the years, and much of it was never repaid. We just chalked it up to Mickey. He did give Mr. Smith his start."

The years wore on, but Mickey continued to regard Mrs. Smith as his close confidante, revealing to her his disappointment that the life he had enjoyed when they first met in the 1940s was gone and that age had caught up with him. They stopped seeing each other when he was in his nineties, even though they were still writing. She told us that she attempted to contact Mickey just before his death.

"While we were in some communication, I was virtually locked out of his life after all the problems," she said. "It was as if the family crying for him had put a wall up between Mickey and the outside world. I tried several times but was thwarted each time. Just before his death, I attempted to send a car for him to bring him back to our house. I believe it was his daughter-in-law that said that he was not interested. I cannot believe that for one minute. At no time had Mick ever told me about abuse or anything like that. I learned about that on the news. He always told me how content he was."

In one letter to Smith, Mickey wrote, "As always, I miss you my dear. As we get older, I begin to forget this or that. But don't think for a minute that I ever forget about us. Sometimes I look around, as I think I become aware of your scent."

"As with everyone else," she told us, "I heard about his death on the news. I was crestfallen. My heart broke. I remember all of our good times, our closeness, our being intimate for over sixty years. I felt I lost a piece of myself with his death."

27

The Last Years

Timmy and Mickey at the Academy Awards,
where Mickey received his Honorary Award for lifetime achievement.

Shortly after Mickey turned eighty, his cardiologist discovered two artery blockages. They were revealed with a new CAT scan device called InsideTrac, which allows early-stage disease detection. The machine scans the body, much as an X-ray would, then produces a three-dimensional computerized view of the internal organs to determine if there are artery blockages or cancers. (Rooney later became the national spokesman for InsideTrac, promoting the device as a potential life saver.) Further hospital tests confirmed his ailment, and he was operated on December 20, 2000.[1]

Rooney underwent the three-and-a-half-hour double bypass surgery at Los Robles Hospital and Medical Center in Thousand Oaks, California. Recovering over Christmas, he spent his time revising his cabaret act with Jan. When a reporter asked him if he thought he might retire, he responded, "My motto is 'Never retire but inspire.'"[2]

During his last three decades, Mickey could rely upon stable support group, a team that included Kevin Pawley, his manager for his last twenty-five years. (Mr. Pawley, who is suffering from a very serious illness, was too ill to be interviewed for this book.) Also on the team were Jan's son Christopher Aber and Mickey's manager and agent for the last three decades, Robert Malcolm.

Attorney Michael Augustine, who handled Mickey's estate and conservatorship, provided us in our interview with an intriguing perspective on the latter third of Mickey's career, telling us that a web of conflicting family members actually worked to Mickey's detriment, even though they were, ostensibly, working for him. Augustine said that, over the years he worked for Mickey, he found that his client's life was "populated with some of the most colorful and persistent prevaricators I've ever seen in my life." Bolstering his claims of chicanery in Mickey's management circle, he told us, are "court documents, agreements, documentary evidence." He also said that the conflict between Chris and Mark Aber, Jan's sons, whom Augustine referred to as "like Cain and Abel" because of their hostility toward each other, also worked to Mickey's disadvantage. Jan Rooney also told us that the conflict between Chris and Mark went back years, forcing her to take sides even when it broke her heart. She said she was unclear over what started the conflict, but it metastasized over the years and got worse when Mickey's conservator moved him out of her house, they agreed to a separation, and Mickey took up residence with her son Mark.

Augustine told us that with the management of Mickey basically divided between Chris and Mark, he held a meeting with Jan, asking her to choose between Mickey and her son Chris. He told her, "There are two ways this dance can go." Jan should go to the Mickey camp and stand by his side. Instead, he said, she sided with Chris, over Mark and Mickey. Mickey accused Chris and Jan of pilfering money from him and abusing him in the process. That came to an end, Augustine said, when the court granted custody of Mickey to Mark Aber and his wife. "As soon as he moved in with Charlene and Mark, all that stopped," Augustine said, referring to what he believed was the physical, psychological, and financial abuse of Rooney.

Mickey sorely needed the advice of a top-notch business manager. While his wealthy friends Donald Trump and Terry Allen Kramer made attempts to advise him on investments, he needed someone solely looking out for the interests of him and his estate, rather than making risky investments to maximize profit.

Mickey's second bankruptcy occurred in 1996, when it turned out that he owed about $1.75 million to the IRS and the State of California. Where his accountants were in this mess is unclear. However, Mickey and Jan feared losing their Westlake Village home, were it to be seized by the tax authorities to pay off their obligations. While bankruptcy would not erase the IRS debt—federal taxes are generally exempt from bankruptcy protection—the Rooneys' declaration was more of a restructuring of their finances. This raises the same perplexing question: Since the debut of *Sugar Babies* in 1979, Mickey had been earning a huge yearly income from salary and residuals (seventy thousand dollars a week at its height). He had a television series, *The Adventures of the Black Stallion*, which ran for three years and was an international hit. His stage appearances after *Sugar Babies* were earning him a hefty salary (around fifty thousand dollars per week). He no longer had alimony; his previous wives were either remarried or deceased. Nor did he have child support; his biological children were now grown. Nor did he have a mother's lifestyle to maintain; Nell had passed away. It was theoretically just Mickey and Jan. Their lifestyle was not like that of Sinatra, who had a jet and flew all over the world. One would have expected he could live comfortably on his savings and continuing earned income. But Mickey had lived way beyond his means, invested in wild business schemes that always failed, gambled, and spent without regard to his earnings until there was simply nothing left and what was coming in went to pay past obligations.

Despite our efforts, we couldn't find any records that could definitively show the ways Mickey blew through tens of millions of dollars. No one could show us the money, not even the people who were paying him. Sure, he made some bad investments, particularly in race horses. However, his poor business decisions were never substantial enough to bleed him dry. And several of those decisions involved him lending his name rather than dollars. In fact, he even used other people's money on some schemes, such as his Weenie World, in which Terry Allen Kramer admitted investing ten thousand dollars, money that evaporated with the business's failure.

When asked where the money went, many people, such as Donald Trump, Terry Allen Kramer, Robert Malcolm, Ray Courts, Sidney Miller just shrugged their shoulders and look perplexed. Even *Night at the Museum* director Shawn Levy, who directed Rooney only one month before his death and paid him "in the low six figures," wondered how the star could have ended up in what his conservator described as poverty. Rooney's daughter Kelly told us that when she talked to him in 2011, he told her that he had no money for food or clothing and he was even gluing his shoes together.

Chris Aber told us, "Mickey could just not be controlled. It was his money, and he eschewed any advice. He made the final decision. The problem was, despite rarely making money, he listened to shady guys, con men and leeches who gave him ideas to make money. He forgot to pay taxes; he would spend without any controls and freely, as fast as he made it."

However, according to court documents filed by attorney Michael Augustine, Chris had managed Mickey's financial affairs since 1998, after Mickey's bankruptcy. In other words, Augustine said, the financial records showed that Mickey's finances were handled only by Chris Aber.

While Mickey continued his film work, he also made appearances on a mix of TV shows, such as *The Love Boat*; *Mike Hammer*; *The Golden Girls*; *Norm*; *Full House*; *The Simpsons*; *ER*; and *Murder, She Wrote*. He remained a hot commodity, and television networks brainstormed to create a vehicle for him, such as the series ten years earlier called *O'Malley*, in which Mickey was to be a tough New York private detective.

In 1999, Gail Radley's novel *The First of May*—a poignant story of a foster child who finally finds a friend in an elderly woman in a nursing home, and the two of them go off to join the circus—provided the backdrop for a meeting of two icons, Mickey and baseball legend Joe DiMaggio. The novel was adopted for a small low-budget motion picture by director Paul Sirmons, who filmed it in Orlando, Florida, in December of that year, assembling an eclectic cast of older actors, including Julie Harris, television's Charles Nelson Reilly, and Mickey Rooney as the circus owner who takes in the unlikely couple. This memorable film, now a favorite of Rooney and Julie Harris fans, won several honors, but it is also notable because it features the final appearance of Yankee baseball Hall-of-Famer Joe DiMaggio, as a mysterious stranger who encourages the young foster boy to chase his dreams. The film was completed just a few months before DiMaggio's death in March 1999 and was released at the time of his passing.

In Mickey's life, this film might have been just another footnote, another line on the Internet Movie Database—but for a conversation between Mickey and the Yankee Clipper on the set as the film was wrapping. Imagine two icons of a bygone age, each of whom looked up to the other, sitting down together to talk about the one thing they both had in common: Marilyn Monroe.

Mickey had claimed that he gave Marilyn her name, telling talk show host Larry King that he took her last name from singer Vaughn Monroe, at whose house he first met Norma Jean Baker, and that he chose the name Marilyn. Mickey later claimed that he and Marilyn had a very brief romantic relationship, but remained friends. The socially awkward Joe DiMaggio, who had the reputation of being publicity shy, had married Marilyn and also stayed friends with her, even after they divorced and she married playwright Arthur Miller. They were still friends when she began her affair with President John Kennedy. Joe also knew that Marilyn was a patient of Max "Dr. Feelgood" Jacobson, who had been giving her methamphetamine injections since the 1950s. Later, from 1961 to 1962, she received the injections from Dr. Thomas Jacobson, Max's son, who would get the drug from his father. Joe also knew that Marilyn had become pregnant and had an abortion. Tony Curtis once claimed that he got her pregnant when they had a romantic evening while shooting *Some Like It Hot*.

In a 2007 conversation with us, Mickey explained what it was like on the set of *The First of May* when the two heroes of their respective generations talked about the death of Marilyn Monroe. Mickey said he had written in a private diary—in reality, only random notes—as well as telling anyone who would listen, that he believed Marilyn had been murdered. He knew that she had complained about the way she was being treated by the Kennedy brothers, that she had called Attorney General Robert Kennedy to threaten him with public disclosure of her relationship with his brother and the secrets the president had shared with her about the CIA and Castro—dangerous pillow talk.

Mickey knew about Marilyn's addiction to Dr. Feelgood's metham-phetamine injections. He also knew that his old friend Peter Law-ford was minding Marilyn for the Kennedy brothers. Mickey knew how dangerous Marilyn's making threatening phone calls to Bobby Kennedy would have been. Joe also knew how dangerous it was for Marilyn to have carried on a very open and scandalous affair with the president. Joe knew it would come to no good.

In their conversation on the set of *The First of May*, Mickey and Joe shared their memories of Marilyn and swapped theories about her death. They both believed she had been deliberately overdosed, and Mickey revealed to Joe that he believed Marilyn was in too deep with the Kennedys and that she was talking too much. On the day before her death, Tommy Jacobson dropped off a set of needles and syringes and vials of methamphetamine-laced special elixir from his father for Marilyn to self-inject, as Peter Lawford was urging her to do. Mickey must have known that his old friend and tale teller Peter Lawford, member of the Kennedy clan, Ava Gardner's modern-day Iago, was in attendance at her house on the day she died.

But these were just theories. The Los Angles County Coroner ruled Marilyn's death a suicide, an overdose of barbiturates, and that was the end of that. But maybe, just maybe, for an aged Mickey looking at his past glory days, Joe had a tidbit about Marilyn that Mickey could hang on to, a piece of the puzzle that tantalized Mickey. But Joe had nothing, only nodded, and time was short, shorter for Joe than for Mickey. In three months Joltin' Joe would be dead.

And the film *The First of May* would become a cult sweetheart.

Mickey continued to work in films wherever and whenever he could, even if a role was not high-paying. He needed to work. At the same time, he was still playing out his duet with his wife, Jan, seeking to get her into every film and television show offered to him, voice-overs, and even television commercials. (He even appeared with her in a commercial for Garden State Life Insurance.) But the film roles for both were small and very character based.

If we look at his body of work from his last decade, we see a hodge-podge of mostly small bit parts and cameos in mainly low-budget film projects, television programs, and even music videos, where the filmmaker wanted to have the experience of working with a film legend. (The complete list, including his final decade of work, is in the appendix.)

In addition to his acting and cabaret work, Mickey published a novel at Carroll Publishing in 1994 called *The Search for Sonny Skies*. The plot features a fictionalized Mickey Rooney, an MGM child star called Sonny Skies. (Remember that Mickey was called Sonny by his mother and father.) Sonny is used and abused by the studio system to the point where, despite his success, he loses himself and his child-hood in the maelstrom of assembly-line performances and publicity. He claimed to the authors that writing this book was a type of cathar-sis, without making his life at MGM too "real."

Mickey and Jan were on the go for much of his last decade, includ-ing their tour of Canadian dinner theaters in 1994 and 1995, playing in *The Mind with the Naughty Man*.

FOR TWO YEARS, ALONG with a month-long stand at Madison Square Garden in May 1998, and another turn in May 1999, Mickey head-lined New Jersey's Paper Mill Playhouse version of *The Wizard of Oz*, which toured nationwide. It was directed by Robert Johanson and starred Mickey as the Wizard and Eartha Kitt as the Wicked Witch, who was played later by Joanne Worley. The 1998 *Oz* tour began in March in Rosemont, Illinois, and returned to Madison Square Garden in May 1998. It was such a hit that it spawned a tie-in TV special when it touched down at the Pantages Theatre in Los Angeles.

The special, *Rainbows, Witches and Ruby Red Slippers*, an hour-long promotional spot, featured *Oz* celebs and "Oz on Tour" cast members looking back on the 1939 film.

Mickey and Jan followed the tour, again with their own show, this one called *The One Man, One Wife Show*, which took them throughout the country. As in their later version of this cabaret act, *Let's Put on a Show!* (so named by Jan's friend Ellen Easton), Mickey told stories, sang songs, and then sang with Jan in the second half. Chris Aber was the roadie, Kevin Pawley was Mickey's manager, and Robert Malcolm booked the venues. Mickey's team had a coordinated plan of attack in which Mickey and Jan did local newspaper, radio, and television interviews prior to their appearances in venues similar to the dinner theaters of the 1970s. They even recorded a CD of their songs, which they sold and autographed for buyers at the end of the show.

"It was a fun show. Jan has a wonderful voice," Ellen Easton recalled. Easton had remained a close friend of Jan's over the years.

Jan and Mickey also attempted an extravaganza called *Mickey Rooney's Christmas Memories*, at the Tropicana in Atlantic City, for nearly three weeks in December 2003. However, Mickey was eighty-three years old, and it was becoming apparent that his days as a song-and-dance man on the big stage were coming to an end, his acrobatic skills diminishing. The critic for the *Press of Atlantic City* was blunt: "Some will say I don't understand how great Mickey Rooney is because I'm too young. Untrue. I admire Rooney and even own a few of his movies. But it is disheartening to see Rooney still at it on the Tropicana stage when he clearly doesn't have the energy or the singing ability to anchor a Christmas show at 83 years old." After this last, large production, Mickey and Jan stuck to their cabaret act.

Mickey would pick up needed cash in the strange ways that are offered to a celebrity of his stature. Recent notables such as Lindsay

Lohan or Paris Hilton were asked merely to show up at clubs such as the Palms in Las Vegas, and received considerable fees just for doing so. Mickey, likewise, was offered money by wealthy film and culture aficionados just to visit their homes or attend their parties, where he would meet and reminisce with their friends, particularly if they were showing some of his older films.

Autograph czar Nelson Deedle told us, "Mickey had all kind of requests. In one visit, he was flown to the Chicago area when a wealthy old film buff decided to throw a 'Mickey' party. He would show a Mickey Rooney film in his screening room at his house and when the lights came up after the film, there was Mickey, who would answer questions and sign autographs. He would be paid five thousand to ten thousand dollars just for appearing, and he would get the dinner of his choice, which was [from Chinese restaurant] P. F. Chang's."

Deedle also recalled that his client and friend Michael Jackson worshiped Mickey and would pay to meet him. Deedle recalled, "Michael was a huge fan of classic child stars, maybe because he was one. He sought out these stars, and Mickey was at the top of his list."

Deedle also worked with Mickey and stepson Chris in selling his memorabilia, autographs, and other items at shows or on eBay. "Mickey did not trust his kids with his Oscars and other awards that he sought to sell. While he could sell his 'Juvenile' Oscar, the Academy prevented him, due to their rules, from selling his 1983 honorary Oscar. He would also get lots of cash when he would appear at autograph shows, where I would help him out," said Deedle.

Mickey was also still highly regarded worldwide. For three years, between 2007 and 2009, Mickey took part in a panto, a British musical comedy based on classic fairy tales, in which he played Baron Hardup in *Cinderella*. Jan was invited in 2007 and 2008 to play the Fairy Godmother. She was not invited back in 2009. "The first two years, Mickey demanded that Jan get a part; the third year, they invited Mickey but did not want Jan," Robert Malcolm recalled. According to the director, they wanted Mickey alone because the actor had appeared to be performing for Jan's approval, and not for the audience.

Throughout these appearances onstage in these last years, it was becoming apparent that Mickey was struggling. He had become almost farcical, and it was no longer "charming" to see him try to re-create his past triumphs; it was becoming almost painful, even creepy, to watch.

Dominic Cavendish of the *London Telegraph* described this in his December 13, 2007, review:

> There can be no stranger sight in panto this year than that of octogenarian Hollywood legend Mickey Rooney warbling "Let's Call the Whole Thing Off' with his wife of more than 25 years, Jan, on stage at the Sunderland Empire.
>
> He's dressed as Baron Hardup, she as the Fairy Godmother. They're in Cinderella but they've introduced a touch of Vegas to proceedings, taking the audience back to the era of Fred and Ginger when Rooney enjoyed his heyday.
>
> Is this an apt in-joke? Should they have called it all off? The answer is: probably yes. Not because Rooney's panto debut is a fiasco but because the little he achieves (which is still quite a lot for a man of 87) is bound to go under-appreciated by the audience—half of whom, let's face it, are children.
>
> Bald, diminutive and frail—looking not so much like the eternal kid as a very tired baby—Rooney makes his entrance with a buxom young maiden on either arm; a touch of Benny Hill that underlines the off-putting fact that he's old enough to be Cinders' great-grandfather.

Confronted with the inevitable allusion to his namesake Wayne Rooney, the former child prodigy jokes, "I have a history of scoring!" The quip lands with a thud because there's a few seconds' delay before every line he utters, as though his contribution is being telegraphed across the Atlantic.

Director Fenton Gray has seen to it that there's some compensating comedy at the expense of his advanced years: "I'm at the age when I kind of forget things, and I'm at the age when I kind of forget things" being one of the better gags.

And Rooney wins some sympathy when he ambles through the classic Smile (though your heart is aching) and acts as if he's having a ball.[3]

His Revels Are Now Ended

Mickey Jr. and his dad.
PHOTO COURTESY OF PAM MCCLENATHAN.

Everyone has their younger side inside of them, but Mickey's
was more apparent and palpable than most people.

SHAWN LEVY, DIRECTOR OF *NIGHT AT THE MUSEUM*

As Mickey entered his final year, the fissures separating his family
members finally erupted into cross accusations, allegations, and
legal controversies. All this broke around him and, again, wound up
in newspapers, gossip magazines, television news broadcasts, and on

various Internet gossip sites. Mickey had lived to enter a new era no longer dominated by newspaper gossip columnists such as Hedda Hoppers and Louella Parsons, but by entertainment TV shows, ragtag bloggers, and anonymous commenters on social media. He became an international topic of conversation, a victim whose claims of abuse, and whose congressional testimony thereof, spawned a documentary. The face of a battered Mickey Rooney flashed across television and computer screens, making him the poster boy for elder abuse.

The warring parties squared off on all sides: Jan and her son Chris; versus Jan's younger son, Mark; versus Mickey's biological children. He was an icon who had earned millions but who had been reduced, according to reports, to near poverty. When he was invited to testify before the U.S. Senate Special Committee on Aging to discuss elder abuse, Mickey, the master thespian, inhabited his part perfectly, playing for the camera before senators who sympathized with his every word.

Meanwhile, he continued to work, appearing in two films, and hawked his photographs for fans who still remembered the old days. Also, in a documentary about financial fraud and elder abuse, Mickey described in his own words how he was bilked out of money by those he'd trusted, complaining that his managers, agents, and even his own family simply drained money he made and used it for their own purposes.[1]

THE CAST OF CHARACTERS surrounding Mickey in his final year included his living children and stepchildren, Jan, and his obligees, including the federal government and the lawyers, managers, and business associates. All became part of a soap opera as they jockeyed for position. Still lingering, however, was a single question: where's the money?

Those paying him, including *Sugar Babies* producer Terry Allen

Kramer, have no idea, insisting only that Mickey had absolutely no ability to control his spending. Attorney Michel Augustine blamed Jan and Chris for draining Mickey's fortune, while Jan claims that she is the victim of false accusations. Left out in the cold are Mickey's biological children, whom attorney and court-appointed estate conservator Michael Augustine says were deliberately excluded from Mickey's last will and testament, whose legitimacy was upheld by the court. Augustine, who represents the designated heirs to Rooney's estate, Mark Aber "Rooney" and his wife, Charlene, told us that at the time Mickey's will was drawn and filed, he (Augustine) had Mickey examined by a mental health professional, who declared him competent to devise the will—this despite Chris Aber's assertion that Mickey was bipolar, on prescription medications such as Valium and lithium, and had suffered at least one nervous breakdown. According to forensic neuropsychiatrist and author John Liebert, MD, who has conducted examinations for mental competency with respect to last wills and testaments, the mere fact that a subject was diagnosed with bipolar disorder, was prescribed lithium as a mood stabilizer by a doctor, and had drawn up a new will within months of his death, would be enough to constitute a competency challenge.[2]

In looking for answers, we reviewed material from Bruce Ross of the law firm Holland and Knight, who represents Mickey's estate; spoke with Mickey's daughters with Barbara Ann Thomason, Kelly and Kerry; with son Teddy Rooney, with Martha Vickers; with publicist Roger Neal; manager Robert Malcolm; Jan's sister Ronna Riley; Mickey's daughter-in-law Carol Rooney; Mrs. Smith; and several others, to flesh out the mystery of Mickey's final days and his disappearing estate.

Michael Augustine told us that Mickey was fleeced, pure and simple, and that he, Augustine, was a witness to it. "I've been involved with Mickey for years," he said. "People will tell you that Mickey was abused. We have photos. Mickey was far from a perfect human, he had tons of faults, which is what you could expect when he had parents who sucked. Mickey was [Nell's] meal ticket, and she rode him like a pack mule." Augustine's objective, he said, was to get Mickey away from Chris Aber, whom he believed, he told us, was not working toward Mickey's best interests, "and get him working and safe." [3]

Augustine also said that he worked for Mickey as a representative:

> I used Robert Malcolm in New York to get parts, but I got some stuff directly for Mickey. I did some merchandising with CMG Worldwide, [a company that licenses images of dead stars]. *Night of the Museum* was great for Mickey, and he did so well and everyone was thrilled that Jan and [Chris] Aber weren't there with him. My job was to keep Mickey safe. We got a judgment of $2.8 [million] against Aber, which we know we will never collect. We now have this will contest, which is ludicrous. We have $15,000 left from Mickey. What is to contest? There is no money. He gets very little residuals. He had tax liens. Poor management and stealing over the years. I've got tax returns to support this . . . [from] '04, '05, '06, '07, '08. Mickey had earned $804,000 in 2004, $690,000 in 2005, and $500,000 or more in the other years.

But, Augustine maintained, that money was simply pilfered away while Mickey lived in a rat-infested house with an air conditioner that didn't work—this for an elderly person who still had to go to work to make a living. As for the money, Augustine said that in addition to the salary from performing, Mickey had pensions. His union pension was set up as a joint and survivor pension that lasted for the life of Mickey and Jan, and Jan now receives their Social Security. But Mickey's other pensions were his sole annuity, which meant that when he died, the pension payments ended. Augustine told us:

The reason I was appointed was because they knew that everybody was tainted. Mickey became my main concern. Mickey had no dementia. His conservatorship was self-appointed. Mickey requested the help. Prior to the conservatorship, Mickey went to the leading gerontologist in Los Angeles, Dr. David Spaar, who did a thorough evaluation that said he was perfectly fine. Prior to *Museum Three*, he had to be insured for the film, and he had no problem. He was the Energizer Bunny. After he finishes the film in March, he signed his new will in March. He was not demented. Not even close. His kids filed a contest to the will and said he was demented. He was not at all demented. He was very lucid. He had no relationship with his kids. He wasn't mad, he just didn't know them. Mickey's last will leaves everything to Mark and Charlene. His kids are contesting that.[4]

According to Augustine, Jan was kept away from Mickey due to a written agreement that Augustine orchestrated, and she signed, following a series of incidents that led Augustine to believe she was being physically abusive toward her diminutive husband. Although Jan, in our conversations with her, strenuously disputed this. While living with her, Augustine asserted, "Mickey had a tooth knocked out, he had a black eye, he ostensibly fell down the stairs. So Mickey, I felt, was physically in peril. In July 2012, I moved Mickey away. All of a sudden, Mickey's appearance and everything about Mickey improved. He started working again and he was doing much better."

Litigation ensued, and ultimately, court documents show, Jan agreed to live elsewhere in return for three thousand dollars a month in support from Rooney. In February 2011, after a complaint was filed by Rooney's attorneys on his behalf, a Superior Court judge granted LA-based lawyer Augustine temporary conservatorship over the actor and his estate and ordered Chris Aber and his wife, Christina, to stay at least one hundred yards from his client, according to the pleadings from Holland and Knight and our conversation with Michael Augustine. Rooney's attorneys alleged that Chris Aber "threatens, intimidates, bullies and harasses Mickey," and they refused to reveal Rooney's finances to him, "other than to tell him that [Mickey] is broke." He and his wife were also alleged to have withheld medications and food from Rooney, leaving him "extremely fearful that Chris will become physically threatening against Mickey and may even attempt to kidnap Mickey from his home." The paperwork and subsequent filings suggested that Aber gained access to Rooney's finances through his work as a "producer" at Densmore Productions Inc., a company Rooney formed in 1998—whereupon Aber issued himself majority stock, named himself treasurer, and began withdrawing substantial amounts of money.

Jan argued that "Mickey could not get any credit due to the bankruptcy. Chris mortgaged his house and used his credit to get loans for us. We owed Chris money that he risked to get for us."[5] Chris told us that because he had put his own credit on the line in order to secure credit for Mickey, to cover his travel costs, "I ended up without funds as I could not afford to pay the legal costs." And after he agreed to settle the controversy over Mickey's estate with Mickey's conservator attorneys for $2.6 million, on October 13, 2013, Chris and his wife declared bankruptcy, to avoid the debts he'd incurred from the legal and other costs from the Mickey Rooney dispute. The couple claim they do not have the money to pay the $2.8 million judgment.

Chris's résumé read in part:

> For the past years I have managed an Academy Award winning actor and was a partner of the production company Densmore Productions. In this position I functioned

in numerous roles, including, traveling Tour Manager for a major show, which toured both nationally and internationally. Responsibilities included coordination of all travel arrangements, public appearances, publicity, bookings and press releases as well as forecasting and overseeing budgetary matters. I also facilitated and developed multiple incoming leads for new business partnerships and future performances. Other responsibilities included assisting in all aspects of the actor's personal life, living arrangements, as well as supervising estate employees and managing three rental properties. As required, I accompanied this actor and his wife in their extensive travels as well as numerous social events.[6]

Aber said that the personal costs he incurred to keep Mickey on the road resulted in the draining of his own finances, which Jan confirmed to us.

Chris told us, "We worked for several months a year. Otherwise, my job, day after day, right up until he stopped cold turkey around 2000, I went day after day to the races with him. All over the world. Wherever we were."

It was Mark, with his wife, Charlene, who took guardianship of Mickey in his last two and a half years, after Mickey's conservator moved him from Jan and Chris's house and filed the separation agreement.

BEFORE SHE WAS ORDERED to stay away from him, Jan continued to appear with Mickey in their road show *Let's Put on a Show!* Even after Mick's ninetieth birthday, they continued to perform, taking the show to Chicago and other, smaller venues. They had to keep it going because, after Mickey's bankruptcy, with his inability to get credit in his or Jan's name and his ongoing expenses and tax liens, the money was drying up and they had very little savings left.

Jan's friend Ellen Easton told us, "Jan would cry to me, as they could not even afford to fix their air-conditioning. I gave them the idea for the *Let's Put on a Show!*, and for a long while it worked well. However, he was now in his nineties, and it became tougher for both of them to travel." In fact, toward the end of the show's run, Mickey had become so feeble that he could not effectively perform the numbers, and the show suffered to the point where some reviewers panned it and referred to Mickey as a "curiosity."

Mickey was still earning from the movies he was making and from some residuals, and he would get lots of cash when he appeared at autograph shows, according to Nelson Deedle, who worked to set up autograph sessions for Mickey during the latter part of his life. Mickey also appeared in television commercials. In 2005, Rooney filmed a commercial for a cold remedy, in which Rooney's towel slips off in a sauna, exposing his eighty-four-year-old buttocks for about two seconds. The ad, scheduled to premiere during the Super Bowl, was rejected by network censors. Rooney angrily described the commercial as "a fun spot," and said, "[T]he public deserves to see it." [7]

Mickey's anger issues started becoming more pronounced as he advanced into his nineties. His temper flared up at inappropriate moments in public, and he had less and less tolerance for any perceived setback. As he became more and more physically challenged, the athletic Mickey Rooney became angrier at himself, at his limitations. And as he confronted the final Ericksonian crises, reconciling himself with old age and the limitations thereof, he fought against them desperately, lashing out in frustration at the world around him. Cashing in on his fame, which propelled him for the last forty years of his life, had become an ongoing business, and when the reality television craze began to dominate cable, Mickey was there. In an attempt to cash in on the reality market, Chris Aber set up a deal to shoot a "sizzle" reel for a proposed reality series tentatively called *The Rooneys*, which is available on YouTube.[8] In it, you can see Mickey warts and all, his outbursts of anger and his tantrums on full display.

Another cogent example of the dynamics among the Rooneys was witnessed by the *Hollywood Reporter*'s Scott Feinberg, who said, "I'd met Mickey on many occasions at events and interviewed him when many of his friends passed away. However, I wanted to talk with him about his career at MGM. It was, by far, one of the strangest and most difficult interviews I've attempted. I have done literally hundreds of interviews with older actors, but it never approached the strangeness of this one."

Feinberg said that the interview was punctuated by Mickey's emotional outbursts, more like a toddler's tantrums. "Although there were [instigating] incidents, such as Jan kicking Mickey so hard under the table [that] Mickey let out a blood-curdling scream . . . Mickey had outbursts of rage and tantrum-like episodes in which we had to stop the camera. Mickey retold some of the fables he created from his career, along with some interesting stories."[9]

Feinberg also said—as did Jan and her sister Ronna—that Mickey had very little concept of the past. He could tell stories from his youth, but as he got older, the past seemed less and less relevant to him, and he seemed to disregard it. He would actually concoct stories, which could be contradicted by facts (for example, bragging about giving Marilyn Monroe her name, when this was patently untrue). He told different stories at different times about his final conversations with Judy Garland.

DESPITE THE ONGOING PERSONAL drama, Mickey forged ahead in his work as he had throughout all the other times of crisis in his life, now working with young filmmakers.

It may seem contradictory (after looking at Mickey's interview with Scott Feinberg) to state that Mickey could be difficult to deal with off-camera, beyond irascible and downright mean, but completely charming on a movie set. It is not really a paradox. There was only one reality to Mickey's existence, and that was performing. Whether onstage or on-camera, performing was the reality he lived in and longed for. Everything else was just a distraction. Worse, it was almost hateful. Nothing illustrates this better than the way he dealt with young Brooklyn filmmaker Keith Black in 2007.

That year, Mickey became intrigued with a communication from a Brooklyn inner-city teacher, Black, who for the previous twenty years had been spending his summer breaks, and his own money, financing his own low-budget movies. Black decided in 2007 to take a long shot and approach Mickey with an offer to appear in his debut feature film, a romantic comedy called *Driving Me Crazy*. Impressed by Black's charming script and relentless chutzpah, Rooney not only agreed, but said he would work for just a nominal hundred dollars. Mickey and Jan flew to New York and shot numerous scenes with Black, all the while entertaining his cast and crew with amazing tales of old Hollywood. Black recalled:

> Mr. Rooney loved the script and said it reminded him of the heartwarming romantic comedies Hollywood was famed for, stories that cared more about character and story than special effects. I didn't feel like I could be in the same room with him. He made me feel like an equal. He made me feel without saying it that I deserved to be sharing a set with him. We were instantly best friends. He listened to everything I said with such intense focus. He enjoyed talking to me and helping me. I felt like I was the new Judy Garland; he gave me the same consideration and respect he gave to her. There is no substitute for Rooney's close to eighty years

of acting experience. His kind words will last me a lifetime. I learned so much. It was like a crash course from a Hollywood legend.[10]

Black told us that working with Rooney was inspirational and propelled his career:

Mickey's total vote of confidence meant the world to me. I've won festival awards, received glowing reviews from critics, been on Showtime, but this meant nothing compared to him listening to me with respect. This man had worked side by side with some of the greatest stars. He came to the set early, stayed late. This was a guy in his late eighties working like a dog. A couple times I got worried because he got out of breath and requested a chair to rest in. On the set, he was like a mentor. It was remarkable. Besides having to know his own lines, he memorized mine and [those of] other actors, including Oscar winner Celeste Holm and Dick Cavett. Mickey didn't just drop by the set; he had clearly spent many hours with the script before he even got on the plane from LA. Even though mine was a small indie feature, he treated it like a big Hollywood blockbuster. Mickey was so humble and kind. The only time he sounded like a Hollywood leading man was when he requested ice cream and strawberries. What struck me about Mickey was that he was so focused on simply helping me make the best movie possible.[11]

Film producer and director Shawn Levy, who directed and produced the three *Night of the Museum* movies starring Ben Stiller, echoed Black's sentiments. Levy said:

Mickey certainly left us with a remarkable work and legacy. Mickey came in and auditioned for the first *Night at the Museum* in 2005. Both Ben and I were amazed . . . and despite being a legend with hundreds of films to his credit, this is a guy that so loved to work. He was willing and eager to work. This is an industry that now has performers with just a couple of performances in a TV show and they won't audition. It's called "offer only"—and Mickey, with four hundred films, coming in and laying it on the line to get the job. He auditioned on the backlot at Fox with myself [*sic*], the casting director, and Stiller. We created the role of Gus as a pugnacious little firecracker, and we so wanted Mickey to be the guy, and when he came in and auditioned, it was immediately clear that he was the guy. Comedy has evolved throughout the decades, and it has changed, and we live in a very improv type of comedy climate. He was prepared, knew his lines, did his lines, and he was prepared to ad-lib. So if Stiller or I threw him an idea in the middle of shooting a scene, he was great. So some of the insulting nicknames he said to Stiller in the course of the film were scripted, but many were created during filming. He was very light and fluid, and flexible enough to handle the changes even during the course of the shooting day. I suspect that his stage training was the case that allowed him to be that flexible.

Levy continued:

There were a couple things that were really impressive and central to his amazing talent. I saw clearly that the audition showed me that here was a guy that still burned with creative hunger, but he also had such respect and esteem for his fellow actors. He was thrilled to be working with Dick [Van Dyke], Bill [Cobbs], and Ben Stiller. Mickey just adored Ben Stiller. He had a big part in the first movie, and although he had a nice role in the second film, we ended up cutting much of the older guards' scenes. Coming into the third film, we knew it was going to be the last, the finish of the series, but I wanted it to mark the return of my senior citizen night guards. I'm told by his family that he went over the moon when he got the call for the film. So at ninety-three, he got on a plane, flew to Vancouver, and although he couldn't really stand up for long periods of time and his memory wasn't what it used to be, he came to work with a real fervor and gratitude. Real gratitude.[12]

Of Mickey's acting at such an advanced age, Levy said, "He was one hundred percent lucid. He was honest; he said he had a tough time standing up for long and 'I'm not great remembering the lines; could you feed them to me?' I said, 'No problem.' So I sat behind the camera, next to Ben Stiller, and I would feed him his dialogue. Not only was he completely lucid, but I would go as far as to say that he was *vital*."

"When Mickey finished shooting, I gave a small speech about him," Levy said. Because this was the last in the series of *Night at the Museum* pictures, it was a poignant moment and a chance to honor Mickey for his ninety-three years in show business. As the cast and crew stood up to applaud Mickey, no one realizing of course that this would be his final public appearance, Mickey gave one of the most heartfelt testimonials he ever had, about his years in the industry and how humbled he was to have been a part of it. It was an historic moment for everyone on the set. According to Levy:

They were applauding him, and he quieted the crew [and] then gave an impassioned speech that we were all lucky to

be able to do this wonderful work; he was really under-
lining this. I took pictures of this. . . . It was an honor to
direct him. I feel privileged to have been a part of making
his legacy.

At the premiere and after party for the first movie, my
grandmother-in-law, who is ninety-three, says it was the
night that she was charmed by Mickey Rooney. I'm grateful for the memories I have of Mickey, to this day, it was
a rare thrill for her to be charmed by Mickey Rooney. He
has fans, and will have fans, for all time. You can see his
soul.[13]

MICKEY WAS ABOUT TO turn ninety years old on September 23, 2010,
and there were no great honors or memorials planned for him. Other
entertainers before him had been honored for their body of work,
specifically by the American Film Institute. Yet there were to be no
honors from the AFI for Mickey, who had seemingly been forgotten,
despite his continued appearances in pictures. Author, publicist, film
lover, and one of Mickey's fans, Ellen Easton sought to remedy that.
She told us:

In the spring of 2010, when I learned that no one in the
entertainment industry had made any formal plans to
honor Mickey on his ninetieth birthday, I was appalled. I
thought that a man of his talents, who had contributed nine
consecutive decades of his life to his industry, deserved a
celebration. I approached John Iachetti, the director of entertainment at the Feinstein's Loews Regency's, New York,
to ask if he would host a birthday party for Mickey's ninetieth. He agreed immediately. Not only would it be a party,
John would hire Mickey and Jan to perform as well, in

Let's Put on a Show!. With Feinstein's on board, we were off and running.

My next step was to call Nathan Lane, a Broadway legend in his own right. Not only did he agree to attend, but he immediately bought two tables [and] said he would buy the entire room if needed, to ensure that Mickey had a full house. Donald Trump was my next call. At first Donald was scheduled to be overseas, but because of his friendship to Mickey, he changed his plans so he and his wife, Melania, could attend. Donald graciously gave me permission to use his name to help promote the event. I then called Regis Philbin. Regis and his wife, Joy, were also a yes. Soon thereafter, with more calls by myself [*sic*] and the Feinstein's team, many of the greatest luminaries in the industry followed, including Michael Feinstein, Tony Bennett, Rita Moreno, Matthew Broderick, Victor Garber, Jake "Raging Bull" LaMotta, Elaine Stritch, MGM's Arlene Dahl, and many others.

To make the evening extra special, I contacted President Barack Obama, New York City mayor Mike Bloomberg, and Brooklyn borough president Marty Markowitz to request birthday greeting letters in honor of Mickey's ninetieth. They all agreed. Brooklyn, the place of Mickey's birth, sent a beautiful proclamation. Richard Johnson of the *New York Post*'s Page Six wrote a generous lead piece that created a buzz, after which, the phones were ringing off the hook. The power of the press really came through for Mickey. Thus, due to the demand, what was to have been a one-night celebration turned into two.

We officially had two opening nights to accommodate the sold-out houses on September 19 and 20, 2010. And what a party it was! The program consisted of a four-course dinner, the show, the honor letters, and an after party to meet and greet Mickey. The room was literally filled to capacity, jam-packed to the walls, with everyone dressed in their finest evening clothes. There was an electric excitement in the air. It was a great big, fun party.

The show opened with a montage of Mickey's films, culminating with an old clip of Elizabeth Taylor presenting Mickey with the Hollywood Legend Award in 1996. By the time Mickey hit the stage with Jan for their entrance, the room was on its feet. The applause was long and thunderous. Mickey was truly amazing that night. The chronological years seem to have melted away as he came to life under the lights. He was in his prime, telling stories, singing songs, doing imitations of yesteryear stars Clark Gable, James Cagney, and the Barrymore brothers; bantering with his wife, Jan; and playing the piano. Jan, in her own right, sang a wonderful medley as Mickey looked on adoringly. After the performance, it was time to present the letters of honor.

As the emcee, I was trying my best to keep up with Mickey as Nathan Lane, Donald Trump, and [writer-director] Richard LaGravenese hosted the reading of the honors letters. Michael Feinstein and [Italian singer] Cristina Fontanelli, respectively, bringing a beautiful birthday cake onstage, led the entire audience in singing "Happy Birthday" to Mickey. Again, the audience was on its feet. And again, the applause was long and thunderous. The après show celebration continued, with the entire audience invited into the anteroom for champagne and birthday cake. Mickey greeted his guests until the wee hours of midnight. No one wanted to go home. On those two extraordinary celebratory nights, Mickey Rooney's star was the shiniest in the galaxy.

29

It's a Wrap

Mickey and young Timmy.

All I want to do is live a peaceful life, to regain my life and be happy.

MICKEY ROONEY, TO THE ASSOCIATED PRESS

Mickey died on Sunday, April 6, 2014, while living with his stepson Mark Rooney and Mark's wife, Charlene, in North Holly-wood. He died of congestive heart failure during a midafternoon nap, after Mark and Charlene discovered him struggling for breath. Rooney was pronounced dead by responding EMTs at about 4:00 p.m. and taken to the mortuary at Forest Lawn Cemetery. Jan—who apparently found out about Mickey's passing from a news story— and Chris Aber contacted Forest Lawn and tried to move Rooney's body to a joint plot in a Thousand Oaks cemetery that Mick and Jan had originally purchased, against his express wishes, according to Augustine, who also alleged this in court papers he filed the following day.

After Rooney's death, Michael Augustine informed us, there remained only eighteen thousand dollars in his estate. Our look at public records and legal documents revealed that prior to his death hundreds of thousand of dollars in fees and expenses by Augustine and Holland and Knight had eaten up much of Mickey's assets.

In the first part of 2011, over $300,000 had gone to these fees and expenses. After his death, draining expenses continued. Most of the funds that the estate collects from royalties, sale of images and memorabilia, and the like goes primarily toward legal fees and back taxes. Essentially, the fighting over the estate, which is being conducted mostly by Chris and Mark, is a modern-day replay of the neverending case of Jarndyce and Jarndyce in Dickens's *Bleak House*.

Mickey's last will, created approximately thirty days prior to his death, left the entire estate to Mark Aber (who uses the name Mark Rooney) and his wife, Charlene, who took care of Rooney in his last two and a half years. We asked Michael Augustine about Mickey's competency to redraft his will and how this competency was established by the court. Augustine explained that the geriatric specialist who examined Mickey on behalf of the court judged him capable of making his own decisions with regard to his living and custodial arrangements—his conservatorship petition, his prior diagnosis of bipolar disorder, and his prescription for lithium notwithstanding. We also raised the question about omitted parties from his will, and Augustine said that it was Mickey himself who made the determination to exclude all family members and leave the remains of his estate to Mark and Charlene. According to the Associated Press on August 20, 2015, the Los Angeles Superior Court formally accepted Mickey's redraft of his last will and testament after Mickey's biological children dropped their objections to the will and Judge David Cowan appointed attorney Michael Augustine to oversee the Andy Hardy star's estate.

When the time came for Rooney's burial, the attorneys intervened, saying that it was Mickey's last wish not to be buried next to Jan. Jan and Mickey had lived together for forty years, far longer than his previous seven marriages. However, the attorneys and Mark Aber said that the ninety-three-year-old Rooney's last wishes concerning his burial overrode the wishes of his wife.

Augustine told the authors that the burial dispute arose because Jan and Chris believed that Mickey should be buried at a Westlake Village cemetery where he had purchased plots years earlier, next to a future plot for Jan. The conservator and estate attorneys said that, nevertheless, Rooney wanted a Hollywood burial or a military one. In the end, Jan's attorney, Yevgeny Belous, said that while his client still wished to be buried next to Rooney, she decided that the Hollywood burial arrangement was appropriate. "After thinking about it and praying about it, she decided, for the sake of his fans and peers, that it was befitting of him as a Hollywood figure." Attorneys Belous and Augustine agreed, telling us in separate conversations in 2014 that "Mickey had enough lawsuits in life for ten people. The last thing he needs is for one over where he'll be buried." [1]

The settlement came just before a court hearing to resolve a claim, made by the conservator, alleging that Jan and Chris had attempted to move Rooney's body. Rooney would be buried at Hollywood Forever Cemetery, laid to rest among other Hollywood figures, including Cecil B. DeMille, Jayne Mansfield, and Rudolph Valentino. The funeral was a small, private family affair attended by Jan Rooney, but not by Chris Aber or his wife, Christina.

In *Life Is Too Short*, Mickey's own comments about dying reveal his wry, almost fatalistic sense of humor: "I've been short all my life," he wrote. "And if anyone wonders what my dying wish will be, they can stop wondering. That will be easy. I'll just tell them, 'I'll have a short bier.'"[2]

According to Jan and all the children, it was neither the family attorneys nor Augustine who ultimately arranged Mickey's funeral and burial. In a story confirmed by Mickey's biological children Kelly, Kerry, and Teddy, and by others, there were apparently no funds left for a proper burial. The entire estate went toward paying legal costs, and there were still taxes owed to the IRS and the State of California. When Kelly revealed this to noted publicist Roger Neal, he sprang into action, arranging (at his own cost) for a proper funeral service and burial in a beautiful crypt at Hollywood Forever, a fitting tribute to a Hollywood star who brought so much joy during the darkest days of the Great Depression.

Mickey's crypt is a beautiful marble memorial befitting Hollywood royalty. Topped by the U.S. Army insignia, with Mickey's picture below, it reads:

MICKEY ROONEY

SEPTEMBER 23, 1920–APRIL 6, 2014

ONE OF THE GREATEST ENTERTAINERS THE WORLD HAS EVER KNOWN

HOLLYWOOD WILL ALWAYS BE HIS HOME

According to various sources, there were two funeral services. The first was for Mark and Charlene, and was also attended by Mickey's granddaughter Dominique, Teddy's daughter. The visitation was on Saturday, April 19, 2014, from 9:30 to 11:30 a.m., with a service presided over by Rev. Gary Dickey at 12:30 p.m. at the Hollywood

Forever Cemetery Chapel that same Saturday. The second service, held on Saturday, April 19, was attended by Jan and her sister Ronna; Mickey's children Kelly, Kerry, Kimmy, Michael, Jonelle, Mickey Jr., and Teddy; their kids and spouses; and some friends. Jimmy Rooney did not attend. Also in attendance were Pam McClenathan and her husband, publicist Roger Neal, and grandchildren, including Dominique Rooney. Both services were held at the same chapel, with the first group cleared out before the second arrived.

EVEN WITH MICKEY GONE, his family remained in turmoil, awash in controversy, scandal, damaged lives, character assassinations, and accusations. Throughout our research for this book, we talked with much of the family and found each person to be charming and gracious. However, there was no final reconciliation of relationships on the various sides. The Rooney family members, extended as they have been across different marriages, wound up in factions looking at the detritus of Mickey's financial legacy, a sad outcome after the death of their patriarch.

The feud among family members prior to Mickey's death has been chronicled in the media throughout the world and continues in the tabloids even after his death. But few of the commentators truly understand the forces that propelled Mickey Rooney through the last part of life. Perhaps Jan was the most instructive, explaining that Mickey, who never really grew up in the first place, seemed to devolve into a toddler during his last decade, with tantrums, impossible demands, and reckless spending on self-gratification.

Jan revealed that she was shocked when Mickey petitioned the court for a conservatorship, leaving her squarely in the middle between her two sons and her husband. Jan's choice, and the legal fallout from it, has fueled a great deal of controversy. Add to this mix a legacy of eight marriages with children, in the throes of their own difficulties, and lurid stories of Mickey's many mistresses. Even today, there remains a morbid interest in Mickey's *affaires de cœur*, his off-spring, and his grieving spouse.

Mickey has left wreckage in his family spread across eight marriages and three generations, children and grandchildren, who have pursued their own careers, some in the entertainment industry, and must deal with their father's reputation and legacy, and one another, as they try to unravel the many mysteries of Mickey's life.

MICKEY'S CHILDREN

- Mickey Jr., the oldest son (with Betty Jane Rase), lives a reclusive life—"a hermit in Hemet," as child actor Paul Petersen has characterized him. According to his friend Pam McClenathan and his brother Teddy, he has found his own peace, but has suffered from years of addiction and alcohol abuse. He is a talented and respected musician. He recently suffered the passing of his spouse.
- Timmy—Timothy Hayes Rooney—was a musician and actor. His mother was Betty Jane. He costarred with his father in films and on the *Mickey* television show in 1964. He suffered from polio when he was ten years old. He toured for many years both with his brothers, in the Rooney Brothers band, and on his own. Timmy passed away in 2006 after suffering from dermatomyositis, a disease of the connective tissue. This degenerative disease was totally disabling, and Tim was relegated to a wheelchair and was living with Pam McClenathan and her husband in Hemet, California. During Tim's last days, in which he suffered greatly, his father was in rare contact with him. Tim passed away on his father's birthday, on September 23, 2006. According to Teddy, and Ronna Riley, Jan's sister, Mickey was angry that Timmy "wrecked up" his birthday by dying on that day. He did not attend Timmy's funeral.

- Teddy, whose mother was Martha Vickers, remained close to his half brothers. Teddy is married to Carol, but they have been separated for thirty years. They have two children, Dominique and Hunter, and grandchildren. Teddy, a great musician, played with talents such as Eric Clapton, but he suffered from heroin addiction and alcoholism. As of this writing, he lives in hospice care with Pam McClenathan and her husband in Hemet, suffering from cirrhosis of the liver. We have had several conversations with Teddy. He does not have many fond memories of his father, although he recalled enjoying working with him in films such as *Andy Hardy Comes Home*, where he had time alone with him.
- Kelly, Mickey's eldest daughter (with Barbara Ann Thomason), is now a cosmetologist and has made appearances as an actress. She has a daughter, Lucy.
- Kerry Rooney Mack (with Barbara Ann) is married and lives in Arizona with her husband, Jeffrey, and two children, Tauney and Kyle. She has also worked as an actress. Kerry told us about her father: "He had a lot of things go wrong in his life. A lot of marriages. He loved love. He didn't care what people had to say. He just lived his life the way he wanted to." She recalled the last time she spoke to him: "He said, 'I love you.' And I got to tell him, 'I love you.' And that's a blessing in itself." She said that when she was growing up she had no idea her father was a star. "He would just be standing there being Dad, and as soon as he heard some music or a song he would just break out."
- Michael (Kyle) Rooney (with Barbara Ann) is a world-renowned choreographer who has won the MTV Video Music Award for Best Choreography five times. He is currently the choreographer for the television series *Hit the Floor*. Kelly remembers when Michael was choreographer on *Dancing with the Stars*: "We wanted Dad to watch his number. . . . He was reluctant to go. But when showtime came, there was Dad. It was a special moment for Dad

and Michael. It was captured on-screen. My father was so proud of his son."

- Kimmy Sue (with Barbara Ann) has twin sons, Cameron and Conner.
- Jimmy is Carolyn Hockett's son from her first marriage, whom Mickey adopted.
- Jonelle, by Carolyn, is successful and lives in North Carolina.

JUST ABOUT EVERYONE WHO worked with Mickey said the same thing. Yes, he was always after his next female conquest. Yes, he worked like a dog in any medium in which he could find someone to hire him. Yes, he gambled and drank. But the good news was that Mickey was an earning machine, constantly generating revenue. And the better news was that he was an earning machine for those who hired him, those who produced him, those who managed and represented him, those who married him, and those with whom he gambled. The bad news was that Mickey got to keep none of it. He earned hundreds of millions of dollars over his lifetime, but died almost penniless.

He supported his parents from the moment he could walk onstage, even as his parents split in different directions as soon as he was born, like billiard balls on a break. He supported Larry Darmour, making him rich; and Joseph P. Kennedy, making him even richer. He sustained Louis B. Mayer and MGM during the Great Depression, keeping Mayer protected from Nick Schenck, and kept the studio alive and profitable. He brought Sam Stiefel and Maurice Duke into the motion picture business, floating their enterprises on his back; earned for Red Doff and Robert Malcolm; earned for all of them while he was alive. And when he died, he generated so many billable hours for his lawyers that whatever was left in his estate simply evaporated in a puff of smoke. And he will continue to earn revenues for the attorneys who handled his conservatorship and who will license his image and likeness for years to come. But throughout his ninety-three years, through his trail of broken marriages and the children he left behind whose lives were touched by the genetic tragedy he spawned, this walking ATM for all who knew him could not hold on to a single penny.

His profligate ways were the target of countless attempts to reform him. He abandoned a lucrative pension from MGM for the promise of establishing his own production company with Sam Stiefel. But he ran up such a tab through loans and advances to pay off wives, taxes, gambling debts, and parents that even Stiefel had to return to Philadelphia shaking his head at his inability to manage Mickey. Maurice Duke, perhaps one of his closest friends, had to dissociate himself professionally from Mickey because the actor put everyone around him in jeopardy from the mob. His wife Barbara Ann met a violent death at the hands of a suicidal killer whom Mickey had brought into their home and marriage, thus traumatizing his children.

Mickey's stepfather, Fred Pankey, tried to control him, rein in his spending, get him to sock money away for his old age. But Mickey never listened. A perpetual youth, he never dreamed of old age, until he was too old and weak to stand and had to be wheeled on and off the set. Investment banker Charles Allen set up a stock portfolio for Mickey, to provide him with interest and profits from capital growth of stock—until Mickey raided that portfolio, sucked money away to spend, and Allen threw up his hands and said no one could help the guy. Even his friend Donald Trump tried to give Mickey investment advice, or at least advice against bad real estate investments.

But, boy, could Mickey light up a stage, get an audience behind him, get folks leaving a theater humming the songs he'd performed. And dance—even at sixty—as if he were floating on air. He could do that. He could do that better than anyone in his generation. And at the end, his generation spanned over ninety years.

He knew every song, every gag, every pause before delivering the next line, every stutter step before the next pratfall the audience knew was coming.

Put him at a piano, and he played it with a ragtime honky-tonk beat as if he'd written the song himself.

He improvised, ad-libbed, cracked a joke out of nowhere, and when the time came for a dramatic performance, he could deliver a character that was as believable as if he were real.

While he was acting, he was also directing, because he knew the camera as if he were the camera.

He gave and gave and gave until, even as he staggered into his nineties, there was precious little to give. But he kept on giving because giving, entertaining, performing, was all that he knew, all that he would ever know.

He was born in a trunk, and breathed his last breath only weeks after his final performance.

Some may pity a guy who never really lived outside his own performance because he was always on, but they would be wrong to do so. In a world where people strive to understand themselves and the meaning of their lives, this guy, sometimes acting like the poor fool strutting and fretting his hour upon the stage, knew better than any of us the meaning of his life.

In that one precious moment, one following another and another, when he picked up his makeup bag, donned his latest wardrobe, walked out onto a set or a stage, Mickey was more alive than anyone could imagine. He knew, knew better than any of us, who he was, what he was, but most important, *why* he was.

How many of us experience that moment of pure, shining truth? Mickey did. But only in front of a camera or before an audience.

Even as he gambled, drank, and tossed away his life offstage, it mattered not, because his life was *on*stage. That was the real Mickey

Rooney. That was the only thing that counted. That's what he lived for: making an audience laugh, applaud, and leave a theater happy. What a mitzvah, making people happy.

Struggling for breath in his last moments of life, what visions might have penetrated his dreams?

The raucous laughter of an audience of men, as scantily clad women dance across a stage . . .

An end pony so delightfully cute that the men in the orchestra fall hopelessly in love . . .

A comic falling flat on his face after tripping over something that isn't there . . .

The snap of a slate before a director calls, "Action" . . .

The downbeat of the bandleader as a duet begins their song . . .

Look, there's Polly Benedict, smiling at you for the very first time . . .

The camera lens moves in for a close-up. It's big. It's enveloping. It embraces you.

It swallows you with its love into its fathomless maw.

It absorbs your very being.

You're free.

The tally light comes on.

It's all good.

Afterword by Paul Petersen

he Mick" came to my house unbidden in the spring of 1969. He didn't have to introduce himself. There he was, the prototypical child star, puffed up with self-importance, wearing a gold Nehru shirt complete with a peace medallion, pushing past me without my leave to take command of my flood-damaged living room.

Mickey Rooney was all that my mother had wished on me, aided by the fact that the Mick and I were born on the same day, twenty-five years apart. He could sing, he could dance, he could act, and so could I. My career was over, but I didn't know it. He understood. He'd been there.

He was a Hollywood Star of the First Order. As he took control of my ravaged home, I was speechless. He had a message to deliver to me, and I was stunned into silence even as a stream of motion picture images were awash in my mind. What was Mickey Rooney doing in the home I would shortly lose to foreclosure?

"I've been through this," he told me, taking up residency on a muddied couch. "Sit down and shut up," he ordered, clearly aware that I was friends with his sons Mickey Jr. and Timothy. It's hard for me to describe the indelible intensity of this undersize Film Giant. He was on a mission, former kid star to former kid star, although I didn't know I was already a has-been.

"Hollywood is done with you," he said, an earnest gaze locked on my eyes. "You have to get out of town, get your education, and maybe . . . maybe they'll let you work again in twenty-five years." And then he was gone, message delivered.

Do you have any idea what it feels like to be a bug trapped in amber? Look at your life at nineteen, and then freeze it. Nothing you do can diminish the impact and permanence of the images you unknowingly created in your youth. That's what the Mick had to deal with. He was a young man consigned to the scrap heap of history and he was only twenty-one, but his talent, experience, and value as a performing commodity were undiminished. This was universally important—except in Hollywood. Imagine your life when you're considered "old news" and discountable from age twenty-five to forty, most people's most productive epoch!

The Mickey Rooney I revere broke faith with his sons, both of whom I remained close to over the decades that followed. Timothy died of a muscular disease, unvisited by his father; Mickey Jr. is a hermit in Hemet. Mickey Rooney didn't visit them, support them emotionally or financially, and remained silent on his relationship with them. He is, without qualification, a failure as a father—and a human being. I continue to hold this view against his memory, without apology.

But as a former kid star, shielded from personal ruin by Mickey Rooney's advice, I want to testify on behalf of the Mick's legacy. He was always talented, man and boy. His artistic contributions to the history of film are beyond criticism.

So, why was he such an unpleasant man? As I told his long-suffering wife Jan, "Damaged goods."

Remember what he said when he received the Emmy for *Bill,* that wonderful television movie? "When I was nineteen and twenty," he said, "I was the most popular film star in the world, but when I was forty, you wouldn't give me a job."

Do you think that doesn't hurt? Do you think Mickey Rooney wasn't affected by this reality? Eight marriages, kids he didn't raise, a career that didn't continue smoothly—it all crafted the aging man.

I am grateful that I grew up without the need for continual industry attention and public reverence. And that's thanks to Mickey Rooney's intervention in my life. Oh, how I wish he'd listened to his own advice.

Paul Peterson was a Mouseketeer, along with Rooney's sons Mickey Jr. and Timmy, and then went on to costar in The Donna Reed Show. *He heads up the child star advocacy and support group* A Minor Consideration.

Acknowledgments

Telling this monumental story of Mickey's life, which is as much a part of American history as it is a biography, was a challenge, and it began over twenty years ago, when we were researching a story on Dr. Feelgood and Mickey Rooney was one of our ongoing sources for some of the most scurrilous goings-on in Hollywood. (He would know. He was the victim of some of them.) When we arranged for a series of lunches with Mickey Rooney in 2007–8 and a few phone conversations in 2009 and 2010, it sparked the idea of writing a historically correct biography of him, one not tainted by gossip column hype.

Each of our meetings with him followed a similar pattern. He would tell us stories and answer some of our questions. However, each time we asked similar questions, we received dissimilar answers. The lunches were interesting. One was at the Santa Anita Racetrack clubhouse, in between Mickey's trips to the stables to pick up tips on the horses and jockeys. He was the only guy who would measure the size of the jockey. If he was smaller than Mickey, then Mick would bet the horse. Our interviews there kept getting interrupted, however, because every time the starter's trumpet sounded, Mickey would get up and salute. Another memorable lunch was at Vitello's Restaurant in Studio City. We would mostly listen as Rooney told of his unparalleled life and career. As we discovered, many of his stories were apocryphal, but fun. It was at Vitello's that we discussed the possibility of writing the story of this icon, empirically, dispelling much of the myth (some of which he created) that surrounded his life.

In our research, we were lucky to have the help of family members, friends, associates, film historians, psychiatrists, attorneys, and others whose help we gratefully acknowledge. This book would have been incomplete without the invaluable assistance of, first of all, the Mick himself; the wonderful members of the Rooney family, especially Jan Rooney and Mickey's oldest daughter, Kelly Rooney; her younger sister Kerry Rooney Mack; son Teddy Rooney, who, despite his critical illness, was a valuable resource as he communicated with us through his respirator. Teddy's wife, Carol, was a huge help, as was Mickey's oldest stepson, Christopher Aber. Dan Kessel, a stepbrother to the Rooney brothers, looked up to Mickey Jr., Timmy, and Teddy and was an important asset to this book in every way. Jan Rooney's sister Ronna Riley was a great help as well. Grandson Hunter Rooney was also very helpful, as was Pam McClenathan, the patron saint to many in the Rooney family. She played an important role in the care of Mickey's late son, Timmy, during his fatal illness, and to Mickey's second wife, Betty Jane Rase, and to third wife Martha Vickers. She now provides hospice care at her own home for son Teddy Rooney. We are indebted to Pam for her kindness, her memory, and the countless records and photographs she provided that helped complete this book.

Our list of thank-yous continues with the Hollywood legends themselves, whose interviews became the background for this story. These include directors and producers George Cukor, Billy Wilder, William Asher, Dick Cavett, Jules White, Hal Roach, and Edward Bernds; writers, performers, and producers such as Sam Marx, Sheldon Leonard, Leonard Stern, Art Linkletter, Lois Linkletter, Bob Denver, Tony Curtis, Wallace Seawell, Roscoe Lee Browne, Roddy McDowall, Patty Andrews, Eddie Fisher, Milton Berle, Phil Silvers,

Eddie Carroll, Frank Bank, Ann B. Davis, Joey Bishop, Larry Gelbart, Del Reisman, Paul Henning, Dick Wesson, Robert Finkel, Irving Brecher, Hal Kanter, Morey Amsterdam, Ben Starr, Gary Owens, Sid Caesar, Richard L. Bare, Frank Faylen, Carol Hughes Faylen, Alice Ghostley, Bud Abbott, Grady Sutton, Moe Howard, Larry Fine, Joe Besser, Emil Sitka, Babe London, and Jean Hagen; talk show legend Joe Franklin; actress Carla Laemmle (niece of Universal founder Carl Laemmle); film editor Stanley Frazen; comic Billy Gilbert; and comedy duo George Burns and Gracie Allen. Using our combined notes dating back to the late 1960s, we were able to cull memories not only of Rooney but also of the era of burlesque and vaudeville, the structure and background of the film studios, and of the films specifically—all of which allowed us to paint a historical picture of the entertainment industry that Mickey thrived in for more than nine decades. We appreciate the assistance of Aaron P. McGarvey and Stephanie Reynolds.

Many others helped us with their memories of Mickey, a veritable "Who's Who" of Hollywood legends. We need to thank film legend Jerry Lewis, Julie Newmar, Academy Award–winning screenwriter Barry Morrow, artist and writer Stephen Carnegie, Scott Michaels, autograph expert Nelson Deedle, book editor and Sirius Radio host Judith Regan, film director Paul Sirmons, Mickey publicist Dick Guttman, filmmaker Fredrica "Fredde" Duke, our friend Melody Doff, film historian Lou Sabini, comic Rip Taylor, director William Friedkin, actress Quinn O'Hara, actress June Wilkinson, actress Jane Withers, MGM actress Margaret O'Brien, John Iachetti and Michael Feinstein, TV historian and friend Stuart Shostak, *The Hollywood Reporter*'s Scott Feinberg, Hollywood autograph impresario Ray Courts, the talented comic legend Shecky Greene, actor Walter Willison, *Los Angeles Times* reporter Susan King, film director Brian Barsuglia, and actor David Beatty. Also to my great friend, the talented and brilliant Austin "Rocky" Kalish and his wife, the pioneering writer Irma Kalish; musician Richard Kates; historian and attorney Jay Stiefel;

professor Adrienne Stiefel Callander, granddaughter of Mickey's partner and manager Sam Stiefel; author Steve Cox; author and film historian James Robert Parish; actor and producer Tim Dorian, television legend Norman Lear; TV writer and producer Bernie Orenstein; Saul Turteltaub; director Caroll Ballard; director Shawn Levy of the *Night at the Museum* films; film producer Kiel Servideo; actor Jerry Perna; writer Kliph Nesteroff; Hawaiian columnist and writer Pomai Souza; performer Nalani Kele; producer Karen Kramer and her daughter, actress Katherine "Kat" Kramer; actress Eileen Wesson; author and television columnist for the Cleveland *Plain Dealer* Mark Dawidziak; writer Monika Henreid; writer Meredith Ponedel; writer and celebrity columnist Richard Skipper; comic Sandy Hackett; Leatrice Gilbert Fountain; photo maven Howard Mandelbaum; author Ted Schwarz; Rooney estate executor and attorney Michael Augustine; Rooney attorney Bruce Ross; actor Ron Masak, publicist Roger Neal; comedy writer and historian Geoffrey Mark; Scott Gorenstein; actress Cathy Silvers; author E. J. Fleming; author Scott Eyman; Mickey's longtime manager and agent Robert Malcolm; writer Jean Rouverol; actress Shirley Jean Rickert; film director Keith Black; Mike D'Uva; classic film actress Marcy McGuire Cassell; film actor Wally Cassell; influential film historian and Penn State professor Dr. Kevin Hagopian; Max "Jethro" Baer Jr., of *The Beverly Hillbillies*; Rick Donat; producer Chris Lewis; Page Six columnist Cindy Adams; actor Martin Milner; syndicated columnist Liz Smith; Jennie Sevano; television historian Joel B. Gibson; Bud Abbott's nephew, TV and film director Norman Abbott; TV producer Michael Stern; film historian and author Jordan R. Young; TV director Peter Baldwin; actress/singer/dancer Ann Jillian and her husband, Andy Murcia; Jason, Sonja, Andrew, and Alyssa McGarvey; author Chris Costello, Lou Costello's daughter; Valentina Quinn; actor Dwayne Hickman; actress and former California state senator Sheila James Kuehl; actor William

Schallert, television legend Alan Young of *Mr. Ed*; television historian Barry Grauman; actor Ed Asner; Joan Howard Maurer, Moe Howard's daughter; Bill Berle, Milton's son; author Gerald Clarke; Edward "Ned" Comstock of the USC Film and Television Archives; journalist Sam Maronie; Norman Brokaw of William Morris Group; actor Jamie Farr; radio host Doug McDuff; actress Vicki Lawrence; character actor Jason Wingreen; writer Monty Aidem; legendary MCA agent and VP Jay Kanter; actress Melinda Cummings Cameron, Robert Cummings's daughter; actress Linda Henning, of *Petticoat Junction*; Rose Marie, of *The Dick Van Dyke Show*; actor Robert Easton; singer Phyllis McGuire, of the McGuire Sisters; Susan Oka from the Margaret Herrick Library, of the Academy of Motion Picture Arts and Sciences; publisher Larry Flynt; and countless others. If we left off your name, please forgive us.

We also thank Donald Trump for his advice and insights into Mickey's life. We thank the theatrical producer of *Sugar Babies*, Terry Allen Kramer; Roger Kahn and Jeanine Basinger, for the foreword and introduction, respectively; and the talented actor Paul Petersen (a former Mouseketeer, Jeff on *The Donna Reed Show*, and founder of A Minor Consideration) for his perceptive piece, which touches upon the pitfalls of being a child star. We are also thankful to the talented author Ellen Easton for her help and her contribution to this book.

We are indebted to our editors, Mitchell Ivers and Natasha Simons, at Gallery Books, for their guidance and direction. They helped us through the publishing process, enabling us to shape and create what we hope will be an enduring chronicle of the historic career and life of Mickey Rooney.

Rick and I are thankful for the background help we received from our family members, who were, in their different capacities, part of Hollywood history, ranging from performers and entertainment lawyers to agents and managers.

From Rick Lertzman: I'd like to send my unconditional love and my heart to my wife, Diana. Without my Lady Di and her unflinching support, I could never have attempted to undertake this project, which took my full focus. It was Mickey 24/7 during the research and writing, and throughout that process, she was my rock and sounding board. My love to my son, Matthew, for his great support as well.

From Bill Birnes: Thanks to my wife, Nancy Hayfield, for her love, her patience, and her support; to my children and grandchildren, who will now get the attention they deserve; and to my son David, who was there whenever necessary. Finally, to the great vaudeville team of Burns and Kaye, whose Broadway patter, songs, and taps on the bottoms of their dance shoes still echo in the rafters of the Palace Theatre.

Appendix
Mickey Rooney Filmography and Credits (in Chronological Order)

Sources listed here are from http://www.encyclopedia.com/topic/Mickey_Rooney
.aspx and FilmReference.com.

FILM WORK

Mickey McGuire Short Film Series
In this series, he played Mickey
McGuire, but was billed variously as
Mickey Yule or Mickey McGuire.
Mickey's Circus, 1927
Mickey's Pals, 1927
Mickey's Eleven, 1927
Mickey's Battle, 1927
Mickey's Parade, 1928
Mickey in School, 1928
Mickey's Nine, 1928
Mickey's Little Eva, 1928
Mickey's Wild West, 1928
Mickey in Love, 1928
Mickey's Triumph, 1928
Mickey's Babies, 1928
Mickey's Movies, 1928
Mickey's Rivals, 1928
Mickey the Detective, 1928
Mickey's Athletes, 1928

Mickey's Big Game Hunt, 1928
Mickey's Great Idea, 1929
Mickey's Menagerie, 1929
Mickey's Last Chance, 1929
Mickey's Brown Derby, 1929
Mickey's Northwest Mounted, 1929
Mickey's Initiation, 1929
Mickey's Midnite Follies, 1929
Mickey's Surprise, 1929
Mickey's Mix-Up, 1929
Mickey's Big Moment, 1929
Mickey's Strategy, 1929
Mickey's Champs, 1930
Mickey's Explorers, 1930
Mickey's Master Mind, 1930
Mickey's Luck, 1930
Mickey's Whirlwinds, 1930
Mickey's Warriors, 1930
Mickey the Romeo, 1930
Mickey's Merry Men, 1930
Mickey's Winners (also known as
    Mickey Wins the Day), 1930

Mickey's Musketeers, 1930
Mickey's Bargain, 1930
Mickey's Stampede, 1931
Mickey's Crusaders, 1931
Mickey's Rebellion, 1931
Mickey's Diplomacy, 1931
Mickey's Wildcats, 1931
Mickey's Thrill Hunters, 1931
Mickey's Helping Hand, 1931
Mickey's Sideline, 1931
Mickey's Busy Day, 1932
Mickey's Travels, 1932
Mickey's Holiday, 1932
Mickey's Big Business, 1932
Mickey's Golden Rule, 1932
Mickey's Charity, 1932
Orchids and Ermine, 1927
Mickey's Ape Man, 1933
Mickey's Race, 1933
Mickey's Big Broadcast, 1933
Mickey's Disguises, 1933
Mickey's Touchdown, 1933
Mickey's Tent Show, 1933
Mickey's Covered Wagon, 1933
Mickey's Minstrels, 1934
The Lost Jungle, 1934
Mickey's Rescue, 1934
Mickey's Medicine Man, 1934

Andy Hardy Series
(Metro-Goldwyn-Mayer)
Mickey Rooney played the title role of
Andy Hardy.
A Family Affair (also known as
 Skidding and Stand Accused),
 1937
You're Only Young Once, 1937
Judge Hardy's Children, 1938
Love Finds Andy Hardy, 1938

Out West with the Hardys, 1938
*Loews Christmas Greeting (The
 Hardy Family),* 1938
The Hardys Ride High, 1939
Andy Hardy Gets Spring Fever,
 1939
Judge Hardy and Son, 1939
Andy Hardy's Dilemma (short
 film; also known as *Andy
 Hardy's Dilemma: A Lesson
 in Mathematics . . . and Other
 Things*), 1940
Andy Hardy Meets Debutante, 1940
Andy Hardy's Private Secretary,
 1941
Life Begins for Andy Hardy, 1941
The Courtship of Andy Hardy, 1942
Andy Hardy's Double Life, 1942
Andy Hardy's Blonde Trouble, 1944
Love Laughs at Andy Hardy (also
 known as *Uncle Andy Hardy*),
 1946
Andy Hardy Comes Home, 1958
Alone: Life Wastes Andy Hardy
 (short film), Canyon Cinema,
 1998 (in archive footage)

Motion Pictures
Some sources cite an appearance in a
version of *Heidi.*
Not to Be Trusted, 1926 (short)
 Midget, the Nephew
The Beast of the City, Metro-
 Goldwyn-Mayer, 1932
 Mickey Fitzpatrick
Sin's Pay Day, 1932
 Chubby Dennis
High Speed, Columbia, 1932
 Buddy Whipple

Fast Companions (also known as
   *Caliente and the Information
   Kid*), Universal, 1932
Midge
My Pal the King, Universal, 1932
King Charles V
Officer Thirteen
Buddy Malone (billed as Mickey
   McGuire)
Emma, 1932
Sonny (unbilled bit part)
The Big Cage, 1933
Jimmy O'Hara
The Life of Jimmy Dolan (also known
   as *The Kid's Last Fight*), 1933
Freckles
The Big Chance, 1933
Arthur Wilson
Broadway to Hollywood (also
   known as *March of Time*, *Ring
   up the Curtain*, and *Show
   World*), 1933
Young Ted Hackett III
The Chief (also known as *My Old
   Man's a Fireman*), 1933
Willie
The World Changes, 1933
Otto Peterson as a child
Beloved, 1934
Tommy
I Like It That Way, 1934
Messenger
Upperworld (also known as *Upper
   World*), 1934
Jerry (scenes deleted)
Manhattan Melodrama, 1934
Blackie at age twelve
Love Birds, 1934
Gladwyn Tootle

Half a Sinner, 1934
Willie Clark
Blind Date (also known as *Her
   Sacrifice*), 1934
Freddie
Hide-Out, 1934
William "Willie" Miller
Chained, 1934
Boy Shipboard Swimmer
   (uncredited)
Death on the Diamond, 1934
Mickey
The County Chairman, 1935
Freckles
Reckless, 1935
Eddie
The Healer (also known as *Little Pal*),
   1935
Jimmy
A Midsummer Night's Dream, 1935
Puck, or Robin Goodfellow
Rendezvous, 1935
Country Boy (uncredited)
Ah, Wilderness!, 1935
Tommy Miller
Riffraff, 1936
Jimmy Thurger
Pirate Party on Catalina Island, 1935
Himself
Little Lord Fauntleroy, 1936
Dick Tipton
The Devil Is a Sissy (also known as
   The Devil Takes the Count),
   1936
James "Gig" Stevens
Down the Stretch, 1936
Fred "Snappy" Sinclair
The Lost Jungle, 1934
Boy with Dog (uncredited)

Captains Courageous, 1937
  Dan Troop
Slave Ship, 1937
  Swifty
Hoosier Schoolboy (also known as
    Forgotten Hero and *Yesterday's
    Hero*), 1937
  Shockey Carter
Live, Love and Learn, 1937
  Jerry Crump
Cinema Circus, 1937
  Himself
Thoroughbreds Don't Cry, 1937
  Timmie "Tim" Donovan
Love Is a Headache, 1938
  Mike O'Toole
Hold That Kiss, 1938
  Chick Evans
Hollywood Handicap, 1938
  Himself
Lord Jeff (also known as *The Boy
    from Barnardo's*), 1938
  Terry O'Mulvaney
Boys Town, 1938
  Whitey Marsh
Stablemates, 1938
  Michael "Mickey"
The Adventures of Huckleberry Finn
    (also known as *Huckleberry
    Finn*) 1939
  Huckelberry Finn
Babes in Arms (musical), 1939
  Mickey Moran
Young Tom Edison, 1940
  Thomas Alva "Tom" Edison
Strike up the Band (musical), 1940
  James "Jimmy" Connors
Rodeo Dough, 1940
  Himself

Trifles of Importance, 1940 (in
    archive footage)
Babes on Broadway (musical),
    1941
  Tommy "Tom" Williams
Men of Boys Town, 1941
  Whitey Marsh
A Yank at Eton, 1942
  Timothy Dennis
Personalities, 1942 (in archive footage
    of screen test)
The Human Comedy, 1943
  Homer Macauley
Thousands Cheer (musical), 1943
  Master of Ceremonies at Show
Girl Crazy (musical; also known as
    When the Girls Meet the Boys),
    1943
  Danny Churchill Jr.
Show Business at War (also known as
    The March of Time, Volume IX,
    Issue 10), 1943
  Himself
National Velvet, 1944
  Mi Taylor
Mickey the Great (short film), 1946
*Screen Snapshots Series 27, No. 3:
    Out of This World Series*, 1947
  Himself
Killer McCoy, 1947
  Tommy McCoy
Summer Holiday (musical), 1948
  Richard Miller
Words and Music (musical), 1948
  Lorenz Hart
The Big Wheel, 1949
  Billy Coy
Quicksand, 1950
  Daniel "Dan" Brady

The Fireball (also known as *The Challenge*), 1950
Johnny Casar
He's a Cockeyed Wonder, 1950
Freddie Frisby
The Strip, 1951
Stanley Maxton
My Outlaw Brother (also known as *My Brother, the Outlaw*), 1951
J. Dennis "Denny" O'Moore
Sound Off, 1952
Mike Donnelly
All Ashore, 1953
Francis "Moby" Dickerson
Off Limits (also known as *Military Policeman*), 1953
Herbert Tuttle
A Slight Case of Larceny, 1953
Augustus "Geechy" Cheevers
Screen Snapshots: Mickey Rooney— Then and Now (also known as *Mickey Rooney, Then and Now*), 1953
Himself
Screen Snapshots: Spike Jones in Hollywood, 1953
Himself
Drive a Crooked Road, 1954
Eddie Shannon
The Bridges at Toko-Ri, 1954
Mike Forney
The Atomic Kid, 1954
Barnaby "Blix" Waterberry
The Twinkle in God's Eye, 1955
Rev. William Macklin II
The Bold and the Brave, 1956
Dooley
Francis in the Haunted House, 1956
David Prescott

Magnificent Roughnecks, 1956
Frank Sommers
Screen Snapshots: Playtime in Hollywood, 1956
Himself
Operation Mad Ball, 1957
Master Sergeant Yancy Skibo
Baby Face Nelson, 1957
Lester M. "Baby Face Nelson" Gillis (title role)
A Nice Little Bank That Should Be Robbed (also known as *How to Rob a Bank*), 1958
Gus Harris
The Last Mile, 1959
John "Killer" Mears
The Big Operator (also known as *Anatomy of the Syndicate*), 1959
"Little Joe" Braun
The Private Lives of Adam and Eve, 1960
Nick Lewis (the Devil)
Platinum High School (also known as *Rich, Young and Deadly* and *Trouble at Sixteen*), 1960
Steven Conway
King of the Roaring '20s: The Story of Arnold Rothstein (also known as *The Big Bankroll* and *King of the Roaring Twenties*), 1961
Johnny Burke
Breakfast at Tiffany's, 1961
Mr. Yunioshi
Everything's Ducky, 1961
Kermit "Beetle" McKay
Requiem for a Heavyweight (also known as *Blood Money*), 1962
Army

It's a Mad Mad Mad Mad World
  (also known as *It's a Mad, Mad,
  Mad, Mad World*), 1963
  Ding "Dingy" Bell
The Secret Invasion, 1964
  Terence Scanlon
24 Hours to Kill (also known as
  Twenty-Four Hours to Kill),
  1965
  Norman Jones
Hollywood: My Home Town,
  1965
  Himself (in archive footage)
Inside Daisy Clover, Warner Bros.,
  1965
  Himself (in archive footage)
How to Stuff a Wild Bikini, 1965
  Peachy Keane
Ambush Bay, 1966
  Gunnery Sergeant Ernest Wartell
L'Arcidiavolo (also known as *The
  Devil in Love* and *Il Diavolo
  Innamorato*), 1968
  Adramalek
Skidoo, 1968
  "Blue Chips" Packard
Vienna (short film), 1968
The Extraordinary Seaman, 1968
  W. W. J. Oglethorpe
The Comic (also known as *Billy
  Bright*), 1969
  Martin "Cockeye" Van Buren
80 Steps to Terror (also known as
  80 Steps to Jonah), 1969
  Wilfred Bashford
Cockeyed Cowboys of Calico County
  (also known as *A Woman for
  Charley*), 1970
  Indian Tom

Hollywood Blue, 1970
  Himself
The Manipulator (also known as *B. J.
  Lang Presents* and *B. J. Presents*),
  1971
  B. J. Lang
Mooch Goes to Hollywood (also
  known as *Mooch*), 1971
  Himself
Journey Back to Oz (animated),
  1971
  Voice of Scarecrow
Richard, 1972
  Guardian Angel
Pulp, 1972
  Preston Gilbert
The Godmothers, 1972
  Rocky Mastrasso
That's Entertainment!, 1974
  Cohost and narrator
Thunder County (also known as *Cell
  Block Girls*, *Convict Women*,
  Swamp Fever, and *Women's
  Prison Escape*), 1974
  Gas Station Attendant
Juego sucio en Panamá (also known
  as *Ace of Hearts* and *As de
  Corazon*), 1974
  Papa Joe
Rachel's Man (also known as *Ish
  Rachel*), 1974
  Laban
Just One More Time, 1974
  Himself (uncredited)
Bons Baisers de Hong Kong (or *Good
  Kisses from Hong Kong*, also
  known as *From Hong Kong with
  Love*), 1975
  Marty

Hooray for Hollywood (also known
as *Hollywood and the Stars* and
Hollywood on Parade), 1975
Himself
It's Showtime (also known as *Crazy
Animals*; *Jaws, Paws, Claws*;
*Wonderful World of Those
Cuckoo Animals*; and *World of
Those Cuckoo*), 1976
Himself (in archive footage)
That's Entertainment! Part II: Metro-
Goldwyn-Mayer, 1976
Himself
Find the Lady (also known as *Call the
Cops!* and *Kopek and Broom*),
1976
Trigger
The Domino Principle (also known
as *The Domino Killings* and
El Domino Principe), Avco-
Embassy, 1977
Spiventa
Pete's Dragon (live action and
animated), 1977
Lampie
The Magic of Lassie, 1978
Gus
Arabian Adventure, 1979
Daad El Shur
The Black Stallion, United Artists, 1979
Henry Dailey
The Emperor of Peru (also known as
Odyssey of the Pacific; *Treasure
Train*; *La Traversée de la Pacific*;
and *L'Empereur du Perou*),
1981
The Railway Engineer
Hollywood Outtakes, 1984
Himself (in archive footage)

That's Dancing!, 1985
Himself (in archive footage)
Lightning, the White Stallion (also
known as *The White Stallion*),
Cannon, 1986
Barney Ingram
Erik the Viking, 1989
Erik's Grandfather
*My Heroes Have Always Been
Cowboys*, 1991
Junior
Maximum Force, 1992
Chief of Police
The Milky Life (also known as *La
Vida Lactea*), 1992
Barry Reilly
*Silent Night, Deadly Night 5: The
Toy Maker*, 1992
Joe Petto
The Magic Voyage (animated; also
known as *Pico and Columbus*
and *Die Abenteuer von Pico und
Columbus*), 1992
Narrator
The Legend of Wolf Mountain, 1992
Pat Jensen
Sweet Justice (also known as *Killer
Instincts*), 1992
Zeke
Revenge of the Red Baron (also
known as *The Adventures of the
Red Baron* and *Plane Fear*), 1994
Grandpa James Spencer
Making Waves, 1994
Gabriel
That's Entertainment III, 1994
Host
A Century of Cinema, 1994
Himself

Radio Star—die AFN-Story, 1994
Himself
The Legend of O. B. Taggart (also
known as *The Outlaws: Legend
of O. B. Taggart*), 1994
O. B. Taggart
Killing Midnight, 1997
Professor Mort Sang
Kings of the Court, Tennis Classics,
1997
Host (scenes deleted)
The Face on the Barroom Floor, 1997
Derelict
Animals with the Tollkeeper (also
known as *Animals*), 1998
Tollkeeper
*Michael Kael contre la World News
Company* (also known as
Michael Kael in Katango and
*Michael Kael vs. the World News
Company*), 1998
Griffith
Babe: Pig in the City (also known as
Babe in Metropolis and *Babe 2*),
1998
Fugly Floom
Holy Hollywood, 1999
Internet Love, 2000
Topa Topa Bluffs, 2002
Prospector
*Hollywood's Magical Island:
Catalina* (documentary), 2003
Himself (uncredited; in archive
footage)
Paradise, 2003
Simon/Henry Sr.
A Christmas Too Many, Echelon
Entertainment, 2007
Grandpa

*Hedy Lamarr: Secrets of a Hollywood
Star* (documentary; also known
as *Hedy Lamarr: The Secret
Communication*), 2006
Himself
Strike the Tent, 2005
David McCord
To Kill a Mockumentary, 2004
Max
The Thirsting, 2007
Savy (some sources cite Senoi)
Night at the Museum, 2006
Gus
Bamboo Shark, 2011
Brooks
Driving Me Crazy, 2012
Mr. Cohen
The Voices from Beyond, 2012
Johnny O'Hara
The Woods, 2012
Lester
*Night at the Museum: Secret of the
Tomb*, 2014
Gus
Dr. Jekyll and Mr. Hyde, 2015
Mr. Louis

Voice Work
The Fox and the Hound (animated),
1981
Voice of Todd
The Care Bears Movie (animated), 1985
Voice of Mr. Cherrywood
*Little Nemo: Adventures in
Slumberland* (animated), 1992
Voice of Flip
*Lady and the Tramp II: Scamp's
Adventure* (animated), 2001
Voice of Sparky

As Film Director

My True Story, 1951
The Bold and the Brave, 1956
  (uncredited)
The Private Lives of Adam and Eve,
  1960

As Film Producer

The Atomic Kid, 1954
The Twinkle in God's Eye, 1955
Jaguar, Republic Pictures, 1956
  Associate producer

TELEVISION APPEARANCES

Series

The Mickey Rooney Show (also
  known as Hey, Mulligan), NBC,
  1954–55
  Mickey Mulligan
Mickey, ABC, 1964–65
  Mickey Grady
NBC Follies, NBC, 1973
  Host
One of the Boys, NBC, 1982
  Oliver Nugent
The Adventures of the Black
  Stallion, The New Adventures
  of the Black Stallion, and
  L'Étalon Noir), YTV (Canada)
  and the Family Channel,
  c. 1990–93
  Henry Daley
Kleo the Misfit Unicorn (animated),
  (Canada), c. 1997–98
  Voice of Talbut

Miniseries

Bluegrass, CBS, 1988
  John Paul Jones

Luck of the Draw: The Gambler
  Returns, NBC, 1991
  D. W. (the director),
MGM: When the Lion Roars (also
  known as The MGM Story),
  TNT, 1992
  Himself
Life with Judy Garland: Me and My
  Shadows (also known as Judy
  Garland: L'Ombre d'une Etoile),
  ABC, 2001
  (uncredited; in archive sound
  footage)
The 100 Greatest Family Films,
  Channel 4 (England),
  2005
  Himself

Made-for-TV Movies

Evil Roy Slade, NBC, 1972
  Nelson Stool
"Donovan's Kid," Disney's
  Wonderful World (also known as
  Disneyland, The Disney Sunday
  Movie, The Magical World
  of Disney, Walt Disney, Walt
  Disney Presents, Walt Disney's
  Wonderful World of Color,
  and The Wonderful World of
  Disney), NBC, 1979
  Old Bailey
My Kidnapper, My Love (also known
  as Dark Side of Love), NBC,
  1980
  The Maker
Bill, CBS, 1981
  Bill Sackter
Senior Trip, CBS, 1981
  Guest

Leave 'em Laughing, CBS, 1981
  Jack Thum
Bill: On His Own, CBS, 1983
  Bill Sackter
It Came upon the Midnight Clear,
  syndicated, 1984
  Mike Halligan
*The Return of Mickey Spillane's Mike
  Hammer*, CBS, 1986
  Jack Bergan
Little Spies, ABC, 1986
  James Turner (Jimmie the hermit)
There Must Be a Pony, ABC,
  1986
  Himself
Brothers' Destiny (also known as
  Long Road Home and *The Road
  Home*), 1995
  Father Flanagan
The First of May, Showtime, 1999
  Boss Ed
Boys Will Be Boys, 1999
  Wellington
*Sinbad: The Battle of the Dark
  Knights*, syndicated, 1998
  Sage
Phantom of the Megaplex, Disney
  Channel, 2000
  Movie Mason

Specials
Mr. Broadway (musical), NBC,
  1957
  George M. Cohan
Pinocchio (musical), NBC, 1957,
  simulcast on radio
  Pinocchio
Glamorous Hollywood, 1958
  Himself

Santa Claus Is Comin' to Town
  (animated), ABC, 1970
  Voice of Kris Kringle
Hollywood: The Dream Factory,
  1972
  Himself (in archive footage)
Fol-de-Rol, ABC, 1972
The Year without a Santa Claus
  (animated), ABC, 1974
  Voice of Santa Claus
Backlot USA (also known as *Dick
  Cavett's "Backlot"*), CBS, 1976
  Himself
Hollywood der Erinnerungen
  (Germany), 1976
  Himself
*Rudolph and Frosty's Christmas in
  July* (animated), 1979
  Voice of Santa Claus
From Raquel with Love, ABC, 1980
  Himself
*All-Star Comedy Birthday Party
  from West Point* (also known as
  *Bob Hope's All-Star Comedy
  Birthday Party from West Point*),
  NBC, 1981
  Himself
Night of 100 Stars (also known as
  Night of One Hundred Stars),
  ABC, 1982
  Himself
Circus of the Stars #7, CBS, 1982
  Ringmaster
*Bob Hope Special: Bob Hope in
  "Who Makes the World Laugh?"
  Part II*, NBC, 1984
  Himself
*The Spencer Tracy Legacy: A Tribute
  by Katharine Hepburn* (also

known as *The Spencer Tracy Legacy*), PBS, 1986
Himself
Stand-Up Comics Take a Stand, Family Channel, 1988
Himself
Miss Hollywood Talent Search, syndicated, 1988
Master of ceremonies
"The Disney-MGM Studios Theme Park Grand Opening," *The Magical World of Disney*, NBC, 1989
Himself
When We Were Young . . . Growing up on the Silver Screen, PBS, 1989
Himself
Home for Christmas, 1990
Elmer
The Wonderful Wizard of Oz: 50 Years of Magic, CBS, 1990
Himself
The Family Channel's Fall Sneak Preview, Family Channel, 1990
Himself
Benny Hill: The World's Favorite Clown, BBC, 1991
Himself
A Closer Look: Elizabeth Taylor, NBC, 1991
Himself
Something a Little Less Serious: A Tribute to "It's a Mad Mad Mad Mad World," 1991
Himself and Ding "Dingy" Bell
Burt Reynolds' Conversations with . . ., CBS, 1991
Himself

The Carol Burnett Show: A Reunion, CBS, 1993
Himself (in archive footage)
Remember When, PBS, 1995
Host
The First 100 Years: A Celebration of American Movies, HBO, 1995
Himself
Here Comes the Bride, There Goes the Groom, CBS, 1995
Rev. Henderson (Jan played Mrs. Henderson)
"Musicals Great Musicals: The Arthur Freed Unit at MGM," *Great Performances*, PBS, 1996
Himself
The 1997 Hollywood Christmas Parade, syndicated, 1997
Himself
67th Annual Hollywood Christmas Parade, UPN, 1998
Himself
AFI's 100 Years . . . 100 Laughs: America's Funniest Movies, CBS, 2000
Himself
Elizabeth Taylor: England's Other Elizabeth, PBS, 2000
Himself (in archive footage)
The Hollywood Christmas Parade, 2000
Himself
The Hollywood Christmas Parade, 2002
Himself as Grand Marshal
Cleavage, 2002
Himself (uncredited; in archive footage)

Gossip: Tabloid Tales, Arts and
Entertainment, 2002
Himself
*Joan Crawford: The Ultimate Movie
Star*, TCM, 2002
Himself (uncredited; in archive
footage)
Hollywood Legenden, (Germany) 2004
Himself
The Happy Elf (animated), NBC,
2005
Voice of Santa
*Silent Hollywood: Cult, Stars,
Scandals*, Bayerischer Rundfunk
(Germany), c. 2006

*Awards Presentations and
Special Events*
The 29th Annual Academy Awards,
NBC, 1957
Presenter
*The Kennedy Center Honors: A
Celebration of the Performing
Arts*, CBS, 1979
Himself
The 52nd Annual Academy Awards,
ABC, 1980
Presenter
The 34th Annual Tony Awards, CBS,
1980
The 55th Annual Academy Awards,
ABC, 1983
*America's All-Star Tribute to Elizabeth
Taylor* (also known as *America's
Hope Award*), ABC, 1989
Himself
*The 48th Annual Golden Globe
Awards*, PBS, 1991
Presenter

Family Film Awards, CBS, 1996
Presenter
American Veteran Awards, History
Channel, 2002
Presenter
The 75th Annual Academy Awards,
ABC, 2003
Himself
The 76th Annual Academy Awards,
ABC, 2004
Himself (uncredited)

Episodic Television Appearances
"Saturday's Children," *Celanese
Theatre*, ABC, 1952
Himself
The Milton Berle Show (also known
as *The Buick-Berle Show* and
Texaco Star Theater), NBC,
1956
Himself
Alcoa Theatre, NBC, 1957
Eddie
"The Miracle Worker," *Playhouse 90*,
CBS, 1956
Host
"The Lady Was a Flop," *Schlitz
Playhouse of Stars* (also
known as *Herald Playhouse,
The Playhouse*, and *Schlitz
Playhouse*), CBS, 1957
Red McGivney
"The Comedian," *Playhouse 90*,
CBS, 1957
Sammy Hogarth
The Ed Sullivan Show (also known as
Toast of the Town), CBS, 1957,
1958, 1960, 1962, 1965
Guest

What's My Line?, CBS, 1957, 1958, 1960, 1966
Himself
"The Mickey Rooney Show," *December Bride*, CBS, 1958
Himself
"The Dean Martin Variety Show I," *Startime* (also known as *Ford Startime* and *Lincoln-Mercury Startime*), NBC, 1959
Himself,
"The Greenhorn Story," *Wagon Train* (also known as *Major Adams, Trail Master*), ABC, 1959
Samuel T. Evans
"The Money Driver," *General Electric Theater* (also known as *G.E. Theater*), CBS, 1960
Al Roberts
"Billy Barty," *This Is Your Life*, NBC, 1960
Himself
"Wagons Ho!," *Wagon Train* (also known as *Major Adams, Trail Master*), ABC, 1960
Samuel T. Evans
The Revlon Revue (also known as *Revlon Presents* and *Revlon Spring Music Festival*), CBS, 1960
Himself
"Somebody's Waiting," *The Dick Powell Show* (also known as *The Dick Powell Theatre*), NBC, 1961
Augie Miller
"Ooftus Goofus," *Naked City*, ABC, 1961
George Bick

"I Thee Kill," *The Investigators*, CBS, 1961
Jack Daley
"USO—Wherever They Go!," *The DuPont Show of the Week*, NBC, 1961
Himself (in archive footage)
"Who Killed Julie Greer?," *The Dick Powell Show* (also known as *The Dick Powell Theatre*), NBC, 1961
Mike Zampini
"Shore Patrol Revisited," *Hennesey*, CBS, 1961
Richard Winslow
"The Paper Killer," *Checkmate*, CBS, 1961
Steve Margate
The Jackie Gleason Show (also known as *You're in the Picture*), CBS, 1961
Guest
"Calamity Circus," *Frontier Circus*, CBS, 1962
Arnold
"Modern Prison Sketch," *The Jack Benny Program* (also known as *The Jack Benny Show*), CBS, 1962
Himself
"The Top Banana," *Pete and Gladys*, CBS, 1962
Himself
"Special Assignment," *The Dick Powell Show* (also known as *The Dick Powell Theatre*), NBC, 1962
Putt-Putt Higgins
The Andy Williams Show, NBC, 1962
Guest

"Five, Six, Pick Up Sticks," *Alcoa Premiere*, ABC, 1963
Babe Simms
"The Last Night of a Jockey," *The Twilight Zone*, CBS, 1963
Grady
"The Hunt," *Kraft Suspense Theatre*, NBC, 1963
Sheriff Williams
"Everybody Loves Sweeney," *The Dick Powell Show* (also known as *The Dick Powell Theatre*), NBC, 1963
Sweeney Tomlin
The Judy Garland Show, CBS, 1963
Guest
Laughs for Sale, ABC, 1963
Panelist
"Who Killed His Royal Highness?," *Burke's Law* (also known as *Amos Burke, Secret Agent*), ABC, 1964
Archie Lido
"The Seven Little Foys," *Bob Hope Presents the Chrysler Theater* (also known as *The Chrysler Theater* and *Universal Star Time*), NBC, 1964
George M. Cohan
"Silver Service," *Combat!*, ABC, 1964
Harry White
"Funny Man with a Monkey," *Arrest and Trial*, ABC, 1964
Hoagy Blair
"Incident at the Odyssey," *Rawhide*, CBS, 1964
Pan Macropolus

The Jonathan Winters Show, NBC, 1964
Guest
The Hollywood Palace, ABC, 1964, 1965, 1966, multiple appearances in 1967
Himself
"Kicks," *Bob Hope Presents the Chrysler Theater* (also known as *The Chrysler Theater* and *Universal Star Time*), NBC, 1965
Lefty Duncan
"This'll Kill You," *The Fugitive*, ABC, 1966
Charlie Paris
"Lucy Meets Mickey Rooney," *The Lucy Show* (also known as *The Lucille Ball Show*), CBS, 1966
Himself
The Jean Arthur Show, CBS, 1966
Eddie Julian
Shindig, ABC, 1966
Guest
The Carol Burnett Show (also known as *Carol Burnett and Friends*), CBS, 1967, 1968
Guest
The Dean Martin Show (also known as *The Dean Martin Comedy Hour*), NBC, 1968
Guest
The Jackie Gleason Show (also known as *The Honeymooners*), CBS, 1969
Guest
"Cynthia Is Alive and Living in Avalon," *The Name of the Game*, NBC, 1970
Les

"Mickey Rooney Episode," *The Red Skelton Show* (also known as *The Red Skelton Hour*), CBS, 1970
Himself

The Mike Douglas Show, syndicated, multiple episodes in 1970
Guest

Rowan & Martin's Laugh-In (also known as *Laugh-In*), NBC, 1970
Guest

The Merv Griffin Show, CBS, 1970, syndicated, 1971
Guest

The Tonight Show Starring Johnny Carson (also known as *The Best of Carson*), NBC, multiple appearances beginning c. 1970
Guest

"The Manufactured Man," *Dan August*, ABC, 1971
Kenny O'Malley

"Rare Objects," *Night Gallery* (also known as *Rod Serling's Night Gallery*), NBC, 1972
August Kolodney

"Judy Garland," *The Hollywood Greats* (also known as *Hollywood Greats*), BBC, 1978
Himself

"A Christmas Presence," *The Love Boat*, ABC, 1982
Santa Claus

"Mickey Rooney," *This Is Your Life*, syndicated, 1984
Himself

True Confessions, syndicated, 1986

"Mickey Rooney," *This Is Your Life*, Independent Television (England), 1988
Himself

"Larceny and Old Lace," *The Golden Girls*, NBC, 1988
Rocco

Reflections on the Silver Screen with Professor Richard Brown, American Movie Classics, 1990
Guest

Jack's Place, ABC, 1992
Harry Burton

Hearts Are Wild, CBS, 1992

Family Edition, Family Channel, c. 1992

"Bloodlines," *Murder, She Wrote*, CBS, 1993
Matt Cleveland

"Arrest Ye Merry Gentlemen," *Full House*, ABC, 1994
Mr. Dreghorn

Gottschalk Late Night, RTL (Germany), 1994
Himself

"Mickey Rooney: Hollywood's Little Giant," *Biography* (also known as *A&E Biography: Mickey Rooney*), Arts and Entertainment, 1995
Himself

"Radioactive Man," *The Simpsons* (animated), Fox, 1995
Voice of himself

"A Shaolin Treasure," *Kung Fu: The Legend Continues*, syndicated, 1996
Harold Lang

"Carmen Miranda: The South
American Way," *Biography*
(also known as *A&E Biography:
Carmen Miranda*), Arts and
Entertainment, 1996
Himself
"The Heart of the Elephant: Parts
1 and 2," *Conan* (also known
as *Conan the Adventurer*),
syndicated, 1997
Gobe
"Mickey Rooney," *Private Screenings*,
TCM, 1997
Himself
"The Snow Queen," *Stories from
My Childhood* (animated; also
known as *Mikhail Baryshnikov's
"Stories from My Childhood"*),
PBS, 1998
Voice of Ole Lukoje
"Exodus," *ER* (also known as
Emergency Room), NBC, 1998
Dr. George Bikel
"Lucky in Love," *Mike Hammer,
Private Eye*, 1998
Lucius
"The Follies of WENN," *Remember
WENN*, American Movie
Classics, 1998
Mr. Hardy
*Elizabeth Taylor: The E! True
Hollywood Story*, E!
Entertainment, 1998
Himself
Intimate Portrait: Donna Reed,
Lifetime, 1998
Himself
"Life Insurance," *Safe Harbor*, 1999
Art Sumski

"Judy Garland: Beyond the
Rainbow," *Biography* (also
known as *A&E Biography:
Judy Garland*), Arts and
Entertainment, 1999
Himself
"Goodbye, My Friend," *Chicken
Soup for the Soul*, PAX TV, 1999
Old Man
"Retribution," *Norm* (also known as
The Norm Show), ABC, 2000
Himself
Intimate Portrait: Ava Gardner,
Lifetime, 2000
Himself
Larry King Live, Cable News
Network, 2001
Guest
Intimate Portrait: Judy Garland,
Lifetime, 2001
Himself
*Last Days of Judy Garland: The
E! True Hollywood Story*, E!
Entertainment Television, 2001
Himself
"Wetten, dass . . . ? aus Leipzig,"
Wetten, dass . . . ?, (Germany) 2002
Guest
*Liza Minnelli: The E! True
Hollywood Story*, E!
Entertainment Television, 2002
Himself
"The Hangman's Noose," *The
Contender*, NBC, 2005
Himself (uncredited)
"Hollywood Goes to War," *War
Stories with Oliver North*, Fox
News Channel, 2006
Himself

"Mickey Rooney" episode of
Celebrity Golf (also known
as The Golf Channel Presents
"Celebrity Golf with Sam
Snead"), NBC, later broadcast
on The Golf Channel)
Appearances in other programs,
including Hollywood Squares
and various news telecasts

Pilots
The Mickey Rooney Show, ABC,
1964
Mickey
Superhero, Return of the Original
Yellow Tornado, 1967
Yellow Tornado
Ready and Willing, NBC, 1967, later
broadcast on Three in One, CBS,
1973
Joe the Drunk (cameo)
"Hereafter," A Year at the Top, CBS,
1975
Uncle Mickey Durbin
O'Malley, NBC, 1983
Mike O'Malley (title role)

As Television Director
Directed episodes of the series Happy,
NBC, 1960

STAGE APPEARANCES
Toured in vaudeville as Joe Yule Jr.
and later as Mickey Rooney
with his family; toured in
vaudeville with Sid Gold,
1932
The Tunnel of Love, 1963
Augie Poole

See How They Run, Alhambra
Dinner Theatre, Jacksonville, FL,
1973, 1974
Sgt. Clyde Vinton
Three Goats and a Blanket, Little
Theatre on the Square, Sullivan,
IL, 1976
Howard Travis
Sugar Babies (musical revue), Mark
Hellinger Theatre, New York
City, 1979–82
Mickey
Night of 100 Stars (also known as
Night of One Hundred Stars),
Radio City Music Hall, New
York City, 1982
Himself
The Will Rogers Follies (musical),
Palace Theatre, New York City,
1991–93
Clem Rogers
Lend Me a Tenor (musical), Chicago
area production, 1993
Henry Saunders
Crazy for You (musical), Royal
Alexandra Theatre, Toronto,
Ontario, Canada, 1995
Everett
Hollywood Goes Classical (concert),
Los Angeles Music Center,
Dorothy Chandler Pavilion, Los
Angeles, 2000
Guest
Singular Sensations, Village Theatre,
New York City, 2003
Also appeared in other productions,
including Gifts from the Attic
(musical), Minneapolis, MN; and
in W.C.

Major Tours

George M! (musical), U.S. cities,
    c. 1970
    George M. Cohan
Sugar Babies (musical revue), U.S.
    cities, 1983–87
    Mickey
Two for the Show, U.S. cities, 1989
    Mickey and Jan
The Sunshine Boys, U.S. cities, 1990
    Willie Clark
The Mind with the Naughty Man,
    Canadian cities, 1994
The Wizard of Oz (musical), U.S. and
    Canadian cities, 1997–99
    The Wizard, Professor Marvel, and
    other roles
Let's Put on a Show! (musical revue;
    also known as *Mickey Rooney:*
    Let's Put On a Show!; some
    sources cite original title as *The*
    One Man, One Wife Show),
    various international cities,
    beginning around 1998
    Mickey and Jan

RADIO APPEARANCES

Specials

Pinocchio (musical), NBC, 1957,
    simulcast on television
    Pinocchio

Episodic

Strike up the Band (musical), Lux
    Radio Theatre, 1940
Babes in Arms (musical), Lux Radio
    Theatre, 1941
Babes in Arms (musical), Screen
    Guild Theatre, 1941

RECORDINGS

Documentaries

Hollywood's Children, 1982
    Himself
1930s: Music, Memories &
    Milestones, 1988
    Himself (in archive footage)
Oscar's Greatest Moments, 1992
    Himself (in archive footage)
That's Entertainment! III: Behind the
    Screen, Metro-Goldwyn-Mayer,
    1994
    Himself
Judy Garland's Hollywood, 1997
    (in archive footage)
Broadway's Lost Treasures, Acorn
    Media, 2003
    (in archive footage)
Judy Garland Duets, Kultur Films,
    2005
    (in archive footage)
Appeared in various recordings and
    collections of videos and DVDs.

Albums with Others

Girl Crazy (original soundtrack
    recording), Decca, 1943
Sugar Babies: The Burlesque Musical
    (original cast recording), c. 1983
Mickey and Judy, c. 1991
The Wizard of Oz (cast recording),
    TVT, 1998
Appeared in other recordings,
    including *Pinocchio* (original
    television cast recording),
    Columbia.

Singles with Judy Garland
"Could You Use Me" (B side of
"Embraceable You"), Decca,
1944
"Treat Me Rough" (B side of "But
Not for Me"), Decca, 1944

Audiobook Narration
Hanno Schilf, *Silent Night*, 1994

WRITING

Songs
"Oceans Apart," a song performed by
Judy Garland

Film Music
"Blow Your Own Horn," in *Sound
Off*, 1952
"The Twinkle in God's Eye," and
"I'm So Lonesome," in *The
Twinkle in God's Eye*, Republic
Pictures, 1955
"The Bold and the Brave," in *The
Bold and the Brave*, RKO Radio
Pictures, 1956
"I'm So in Love with You," in *Baby
Face Nelson*, United Artists,
1957
"Lazy Summer Night," "The
Octavians," "U Gotta Soda,"
and "Unkwinit," in *Andy Hardy
Comes Home*, Metro-Goldwyn-
Mayer, 1958

Television Music
Song "Love Is Being Loved," in
Kathie Lee Gifford's *Lullabies
for Little Ones*, PBS, 1996

Screenplays
The Godmothers, Michael Viola
Productions, 1972
The Legend of O. B. Taggart (also
known as *The Outlaws: Legend
of O. B. Taggart*), Northern Arts
Entertainment, 1994

Writings for the Stage
With Donald O'Connor, *Two for the
Show*, tour of U.S. cities, 1989
With Jan Chamberlin Rooney, *Let's
Put On a Show!* (musical revue;
also known as *Mickey Rooney:
Let's Put On a Show!*; some
sources cite original title as *The
One Man, One Wife Show*), tour
of various international cities,
c. 1998

Memoir/Journalism
i.e., An Autobiography, Putnam,
1965
Life Is Too Short, Villard Books,
1991
Contributor to periodicals, including
Newsweek

Fiction
The Search for Sonny Skies, Carol
Publishing, 1994

Notes

Prologue: The Last Movie

1. "Mickey Rooney's Emotional Testimony on Elder Abuse," video, YouTube, https://www.youtube.com/watch?v=W9ikKP5-s5A.
2. Mickey Rooney, interview by Scott Feinberg, YouTube, https://www.youtube.com/watch?v=abhgk8Avjwo.
3. "Mickey Rooney's Sad Last Days: Forced to Sell Autographs After Being Fleeced of Millions," RadarOnline, April 7, 2014, http://radaronline.com/exclusives/2014/04/mickey-rooney-last-days-sell-autographs/.
4. http://radaronline.com/exclusives/2014/04/mickey-rooney-last-days-sell-autographs/.
5. Mickey Rooney, *Life Is Too Short* (New York: Villard, 1991), p. 336.

Chapter 1: Born in a Trunk

1. Mickey Rooney, *i.e., An Autobiography* (New York: Putnam, 1965), p. 25.
2. *Schenectady Gazette*, January 22, 1921, http://news.google.com/newspapers?nid=1917&dat=19210122&id=mEwhAAAAIBAJ&sjid=BYIFAAAAIBAJ&pg=4011,191733.
3. *Variety*, August 19, 1923, p. 10, http://fultonhistory.com/Newspaper%2015/Variety/Variety%201920/Variety%201920%20-%201876.pdf.
4. Arthur Marx, *The Nine Lives of Mickey Rooney* (Briarcliff Manor, NY: Stein and Day, 1986), p. 18; and Marx, interview by authors, June 2007, March 2008, September 2008, October 2009; by phone September and October 2008, June 2009, November 2009.
5. Ibid.
6. "Conversations with Mickey Rooney," video, YouTube, https://www.youtube.com/watch?v=gUnxLwKmKLA.
7. *Coronet*, vol. 24, no. 6, October 1948.
8. Ibid.

9. Robert Clyde Allen, *Horrible Prettiness: Burlesque and American Culture* (Chapel Hill, NC: University of North Carolina Press, 1991).

10. Rooney, *Life Is Too Short*, p. 13.

11. Ibid.

12. Ibid., p. 14.

13. Ibid., p. 15.

14. Marx interview.

15. Rooney, *Life Is Too Short*, p. 19.

16. Ibid., p. 23.

17. Ana-Maria Mandiuc, "The Impact of a Prostitute Mother on the Child Life Circumstances," International Association of Social Science Research, *European Journal of Research on Education* 2, no. 2 (2014): 1–9, http://iassr .org/rs/020201.pdf.

18. Robert D. Keppel, PhD, and William J. Birnes, *The Riverman: Ted Bundy and I Hunt for the Green River Killer* (1997; repr., New York: Pocket, 2004).

19. Rooney, *Life Is Too Short*, p. 28.

20. Ibid., p. 30.

21. Ibid., p. 41.

Chapter 2: Mickey McGuire

1. "A Queer Way to Make a Living," *Saturday Evening Post*, February 11, 1928, p. 6; see also http://en.wikipedia.org/wiki/Mickey_McGuire_(film _series).

2. 334 US 131 (1948).

3. Leonard Maltin, *The Great Movie Shorts* (New York: Crown, 1972), pp. 64–65.

4. Marx, *Nine Lives of Mickey Rooney*, p. 32.

5. Ibid.; and Marx interview.

6. Marx, *Nine Lives of Mickey Rooney*, p. 33.

7. Ibid., pp. 33–34; and Marx interview.

8. Billy Barty, interview by authors, March 1995 and June 1997.

9. Alvin H. Marill, *Mickey Rooney* (Jefferson, NC: McFarland and Co., 2005), p. 139.

10. Lou Sabini, interview by authors, June 17, 2014; July 12, 2014; November 7, 2014; and January 12, 2015.

11. "Child Star Delia Bogard Interview," video by Barry Conrad, YouTube, https://www.youtube.com/watch?v=5UYWilZywWk.

12. Screen Actors Guild Foundation Conversations: Mickey Rooney, ActorSpeak .com, http://actorspeak.com/2015/02/24/video-conversations-with-mickey -rooney-sag-foundation/.

13. Ibid.

14. Marx interview.
15. "Child Star Delia Bogard Interview."
16. Sabini interview.
17. Sidney Miller, interview by authors, June 1999.
18. Marx, *Nine Lives of Mickey Rooney*, p. 38; and Marx interview.
19. Ibid.
20. Joe Crow, *Hollywood Citizen-News*, February 11, 1932.
21. Rooney, *Life Is Too Short*, p. 40.

Chapter 3: Ma Lawlor and Universal Studios

1. Jack Townley, Review of *Fast Companions*, *Hollywood Citizen-News*, June 23, 1932.
2. Ralph Wilk, *Film Daily*, May 1, 1933.
3. Marx, *Nine Lives of Mickey Rooney*, p. 36.
4. Ibid., p. 37; and Marx interview.
5. Miller interview.
6. Ibid.
7. Mickey Rooney interview. Rooney was interviewed both in person and on the phone. The first interview was in June 1999 (Santa Anita Racetrack). Second, in person, was at Vitello's Restaurant (Studio City, California) in 2007, March 2008, July 2009. Various phone conversations in 2002, 2004, 2006, 2009, 2010.
8. Gerald Clarke, *Get Happy: The Life of Judy Garland* (New York: Random House, 2000), p. 45.
9. Jackie Cooper, *Please Don't Shoot My Dog: The Autobiography of Jackie Cooper* (New York: Morrow, 1981), p. 124.
10. Sabini interview.
11. Rooney interview.
12. Miller interview.
13. Rooney, *Life Is Too Short*, p. 58.

Chapter 4: Selznick Rescues Mickey: The Start at MGM

1. Carl Laemmle Jr., interview by authors, 2007.
2. Rooney, *Life Is Too Short*, p. 53.
3. The authors could not locate the original agreement. However, we estimated the signing date based on the work logs stating that he began work on an MGM loan-out for *Down the Stretch* on August 1, 1934.
4. Rooney interview.
5. Ibid.
6. Ibid.
7. Ibid.
8. Barty interview.

9. David A. Fury, *Maureen O'Sullivan: No Average Jane* (White River, South Africa: Artists Press, 2007), p. 165.

Chapter 5: *A Midsummer Night's Dream*

1. Steve Vaught, "The Indestructable [*sic*] Mickey Rooney," *Paradise Leased* (blog), March 4, 2011, http://paradiseleased.wordpress.com/2011/03/04/the-indestructable-mickey-rooney.
2. David Wallace, *Exiles in Hollywood* (Hal Leonard, 2006), p. 266. Kevin Hagopian, at http://albany.edu/writers:inst/webpages4/filmnotes/fns98n5.html.
3. Gottfried Reinhardt, *The Genius: A Memoir of Max Reinhardt* (New York: Alfred A. Knopf, 1979), pp. 275–91; and http://www.worldcat.org/title/reminiscences-of-gottfried-reinhardt-oral-history-1959/oclc/122597301.
4. Marx, *Nine Lives of Mickey Rooney*, p. 46; and Marx interview.
5. *A Midsummer Night's Dream*, 2.1.385–87.
6. Rooney, *Life Is Too Short*, pp. 60–61.
7. Kevin Hagopian, at http://albany.edu/writers:inst/webpages4/filmnotes/fns98n5.html.
8. Marx interview.
9. Marx, *Nine Lives of Mickey Rooney*, p. 47.
10. Marx interview.
11. Gottfried Reinhardt, *The Genius*, p. 270.
12. *Los Angeles Illustrated Daily News*, September 5, 1934.
13. *Midsummer*, 5.1.2281–90.
14. Rooney, *Life Is Too Short*, pp. 64–65.
15. Kevin Hagopian, New York State Writers Institute, State University of New York, Film Notes, *A Midsummer Night's Dream*, http://www.albany.edu/writers-inst/webpages4/filmnotes/fns98n5.html.
16. Gottfried Reinhardt, interview by authors, March 1991; and Bob Thomas, *Clown Prince of Hollywood: The Antic Life and Times of Jack L. Warner* (New York: McGraw-Hill, 1990), p. 209.
17. Marx, interview by authors, June 1998.
18. In the end, Oberon was played by Victor Jory; Frank McHugh was cast as Quince, and Hugh Herbert as Snout. Yeaman of course meant Snug, not Snig; and Arthur Treacher recited the Epilogue.
19. Hagopian, Film Notes: *A Midsummer Night's Dream*.
20. Rooney, *Life Is Too Short*, p. 67.
21. Marx, *Nine Lives of Mickey Rooney*, p. 52.

Chapter 6: The Gates of Hell

1. p. 72.
2. Joe Eszterhas, *The Devil's Guide to Hollywood: The Screenwriter as God* (New York: St. Martin's Press, 2007), p. 22; and Scott Eyman, *The Lion of Hollywood: The Life and Legend of Louis B. Mayer* (New York: Simon and Schuster, 2005), p. 223-224.
3. Eyman, *Lion of Hollywood*, p. 7.
4. The financial and legal records of MGM, particularly its dealing with contract players such as Rooney, can be found at the Index to Periodical Articles, Margaret Herrick Library, Oscars.org, http://collections.oscars.org/perindex/results.aspx?QF15=Image&QB15=AND&QB2=AND&QF2=Title+%7c+Author+%7c+Film+description+%7c+Name+%7c+Subject+%7c+Journal&QI2=%22mickey+rooney%22&QB0=AND&QF0=Journal&QI0=&QB1=AND&QF1=Date+%7c+Datesort&QI1=&TN=Perindex&AC=QBE_QUERY&RF=WebHostedReport&DF=WebHostedFull&MR=20&BU=http%3a%2f%2fcollections.oscars.org%2fperindex%2f&.
5. Rooney interview.
6. Eyman, *Lion of Hollywood*, pp. 223–224 and personal interview, October 29, 2014.
7. E. J. Fleming, *The Fixers: Eddie Mannix, Howard Strickling, and the MGM Publicity Machine* (Jefferson, NC: McFarland, 2004).
8. Scott Eyman, interview by authors, October 9, 2009.
9. E. J. Fleming, interview by authors, and personal interview (phone), October 7, 2014.
10. Fleming, *The Fixers*, p. 193 and personal interview (phone), October 7, 2014.
11. Charles Higham, *Merchant of Dreams: Louis B. Mayer, M.G.M., and the Secret Hollywood* (New York: Dutton, 1993), p. 177.
12. Fleming interview.
13. Peter Evans and Ava Gardner, *Ava Gardner: The Secret Conversations* (New York: Simon and Schuster, 2013), p. 139.
14. Quoted by Rowdy McDowell in episode 2, "The Lion Reigns Supreme," of the documentary *MGM: When the Lion Roars*, hosted by Patrick Stewart, broadcast March 1992, TCM and TNT.
15. Esther Williams, *The Million Dollar Mermaid: An Autobiography* (New York: Harvest Books, 2000), p. 122.
16. Eyman, *Lion of Hollywood*, pp. 3–4.
17. Ibid., p. 4.
18. Ibid.
19. Evans and Gardner, *Ava Gardner: The Secret Conversations*, pp. 136–37.
20. Arthur Marx interview.
21. Chris Whiteley, "Louis B. Mayer (1884–1957)," *Hollywood's Golden Age* (blog), http://www.hollywoodsgoldenage.com/moguls/mayer.html.

22. Eyman, *Lion of Hollywood*, p. 5.
23. Evans and Gardner, *Ava Gardner: The Secret Conversations*, p. 137.
24. Ibid.
25. Rooney, *Life Is Too Short*, p. 70.
26. Ibid., p. 72.
27. Fleming, *The Fixers*, p. 190; and Fleming interview.
28. Murray Lertzman, interview by authors, 1974, 1976, 1982, 1983.
29. Ibid.
30. Rich Cohen, *Tough Jews: Fathers, Sons, and Gangster Dreams* (New York: Vintage, 1990), p. 197.
31. Lertzman interview.

Chapter 7: Mickey and the Lion
1. Mickey Rooney, personal interview in 2008 during which Mickey expounded on meeting the sports greats such as Babe Ruth, Max Baer Sr., and Red Grange.
2. Rooney, *Life Is Too Short*, p. 75.
3. Ibid.
4. Marx interview.
5. Rooney, *Life Is Too Short*, p. 76.
6. Rooney interview, 2008.
7. Rooney interview by authors.
8. Marill, *Mickey Rooney*, pp. 21–22.
9. Rooney, *Life Is Too Short*, p. 94.
10. Ibid.

Chapter 8: The Make-Believe World of Andy Hardy's America
1. President Bill Clinton as told to Janis F. Kearney, *Conversations: William Jefferson Clinton, from Hope to Harlem* (Little Rock, AR: Writing Our World Press, 2006), p. 28.
2. Marill, *Mickey Rooney*, p. 20.
3. Jean Rouverol, "The Writer Speaks: Jean Rouverol," oral interview, May 1, 2000, https://archive.org/details/calawgf_00004.
4. Ibid.
5. Ibid.
6. Jean Rouverol, *Refugees from Hollywood: A Journal of the Blacklist Years* (Albuquerque: University of New Mexico Press, 2000), p. 148.
7. Bob Thomas, *Thalberg: Life and Legend* (Beverly Hills: New Millennium Press, 1969), p. 277.
8. Peter Hay, *MGM: When the Lion Roars* (Nashville, TN: Turner Publications, 1991), p. 14.

9. Marx, *Nine Lives of Mickey Rooney*, p. 57.

10. Ibid., p. 57.

11. Marill, *Mickey Rooney*, p. 19.

12. Ibid.

13. Marx, *Nine Lives of Mickey Rooney*, p. 57.

14. Rooney, *Life Is Too Short*, p. 84.

15. Ibid.

16. Marx, *Nine Lives of Mickey Rooney*, p. 59.

17. Marx interview.

18. Marx, *Nine Lives of Mickey Rooney*, p. 60.

19. Hay, *MGM: When the Lion Roars*, p. 135.

20. Marill, *Mickey Rooney*, p. 19.

21. James Robert Parish, *The Great Movie Series* (Lancaster, UK: Gazelle Book Services Ltd., 1972), p. 53.

22. Frank Rose, *The Agency: William Morris and the Hidden History of Show Business* (New York: Harper Business, 1996), p. 276; and Marx, *Nine Lives of Mickey Rooney*, p. 62, and confirmed by MGM Archives, http://lantern.mediahist.org/?q=Mickey+Rooney.

23. Based on Harry Friedman Memo, Margaret Herrick Library, Academy of Motion Picture Arts and Sciences, at http://collections.oscars.org/msinvent/results.aspx?AC=NEXT_BLOCK&XC=/msinvent/results.aspx&BU=http%3A%2F%2Fcollections.oscars.org%2Fmsinvent%2F&TN=msinvent&SN=AUTO23718&SE=1674&RN=0&MR=20&TR=0&TX=1000&ES=0&CS=0&XP=&RF=WebHostedReport&EF=&DF=WebHostedFull&RL=0&EL=0&DL=0&NP=255&ID=&MF=oscarmsg.ini&MQ=&TI=0&DT=&ST=0&IR=0&NR=0&NB=0&SV=0&SS=0&BG=&FG=&QS=&OEX=ISO-8859-1&OEH=utf-8.

24. Marx, *Nine Lives of Mickey Rooney*, p. 62.

25. Ibid., p. 63; and Martin Gang memo, Margaret Herrick Library, Academy of Motion Picture Arts and Sciences, http://collections.oscars.org/msinvent/results.aspx?AC=NEXT_BLOCK&XC=/msinvent/results.aspx&BU=http%3A%2F%2Fcollections.oscars.org%2Fmsinvent%2F&TN=msinvent&SN=AUTO23718&SE=1674&RN=0&MR=20&TR=0&TX=1000&ES=0&CS=0&XP=&RF=WebHostedReport&EF=&DF=WebHostedFull&RL=0&EL=0&DL=0&NP=255&ID=&MF=oscarmsg.ini&MQ=&TI=0&DT=&ST=0&IR=0&NR=0&NB=0&SV=0&SS=0&BG=&FG=&QS=&OEX=ISO-8859-1&OEH=utf-8.

26. Marx interview.

Chapter 9: Mickey and Judy and the MGM Backyard Musicals

1. Rooney, *Life Is Too Short*, p. 140.
2. Sabini interview.
3. Margaret O'Brien, interview by authors, October 7, 2014.
4. Paul Donnelley, *Judy Garland* (London: Haus Publishing, 2007), p. 72.
5. Rooney, *Life Is Too Short*, pp. 290–91.
6. Miller interview.
7. Kelly Rooney, interview by authors, July 7, 2014; September 10, 2014; October 12, 2014; November 12, 2014; January 7, 2015; February 3, 2015; February 12, 2015; April 7, 2015.

Chapter 10: Mickey Goes Wild

1. Evans and Gardner, *Ava Gardner: The Secret Conversations*, p. 115.
2. Nick Sevano, interview by authors, June 2008; interview with wife Jean Sevano, December 7, 2014.
3. Marx and Miller interviews.
4. Richard Quine, interview by authors, March 6, 1985.
5. Evans and Gardner, *Ava Gardner: The Secret Conversations*, p. 121.
6. Murray "Sonny" Lertzman, interview by authors, September 10, 1982.
7. Katharine Brush, *This Is on Me* (New York: Farrar and Rinehart, 1940), p. 121.
8. Marx, *Nine Lives of Mickey Rooney*, p. 66; and Marx interview.
9. Miller, interview by authors, 1997.
10. Marx, *Nine Lives of Mickey Rooney*, p. 76; and Marx interview.
11. Rooney interview.
12. Miller interview.
13. Rooney, *Life Is Too Short*, p. 98.
14. Ibid.
15. Marx, *Nine Lives of Mickey Rooney*, pp. 77–78; Marx interview; and Rooney interview, 2008.
16. Fleming, *The Fixers*, p. 192; and Fleming interview.
17. Marx, *Nine Lives of Mickey Rooney*, p. 78.
18. Ibid., and Marx interview.
19. Rooney, *i.e., An Autobiography*, pp. 89–90.

Chapter 11: Ava

1. Evans and Gardner, *Ava Gardner: The Secret Conversations*, pp. 111–13.
2. Rooney, *Life Is Too Short*, p. 182.
3. Evans and Gardner, *Ava Gardner: The Secret Conversations*, pp. 115–16.
4. Miller interview.
5. Evans and Gardner, *Ava Gardner: The Secret Conversations*, p.116.

6. Ibid., pp. 116–17.
7. Miller interview.
8. Evans and Gardner, *Ava Gardner: The Secret Conversations*, pp. 119–20.
9. Ibid, p. 119.
10. Rooney, *Life Is Too Short*, p. 125.
11. Evans and Gardner, *Ava Gardner: The Secret Conversations*, pp. 114–15.
12. Miller interview.
13. Evans and Gardner, *Ava Gardner: The Secret Conversations*, p. 153.
14. Ibid., p. 123.
15. Evans and Gardner, *Ava Gardner: The Secret Conversations*, pp. 123–24.
16. Ibid., pp. 126–27.
17. Ibid.
18. Ibid., p. 134.
19. Ibid., pp. 134–35.
20. Marx, *Nine Lives of Mickey Rooney*, p. 95.
21. Ibid.
22. Evans and Gardner, *Ava Gardner: The Secret Conversations*, p. 135.
23. Marx, *Nine Lives of Mickey Rooney*, p. 96.
24. Rooney, *Life Is Too Short*, pp. 186–87.
25. Marx, *Nine Lives of Mickey Rooney*, p. 97.
26. C. David Heyman, interview by authors, January 2006, March 2006, June 2007, October 2009, March 2010, June 2001.
27. Marx, *Nine Lives of Mickey Rooney*, p. 97.
28. Ibid.
29. Ibid.
30. Evans and Gardner, *Ava Gardner: The Secret Conversations*, p. 136.
31. Ibid., p. 135.
32. Ibid., pp. 136–38.
33. Ibid., p. 140.
34. Ibid., p. 141.
35. Ibid.
36. Marx interview.
37. Marx, *Nine Lives of Mickey Rooney*, p. 101.
38. Evans and Gardner, *Ava Gardner: The Secret Conversations*, p. 142.
39. Marx, *Nine Lives of Mickey Rooney*, p. 103.
40. Evans and Gardner, *Ava Gardner: The Secret Conversations*, pp. 142–43.
41. Rooney, *Life Is Too Short*, p. 189.
42. Evans and Gardner, *Ava Gardner: The Secret Conversations*, p. 145.
43. Marx, *Nine Lives of Mickey Rooney*, p. 104.
44. Ibid., p. 105.
45. Ibid.

46. Eyman, *The Lion of Hollywood*, p. 127.
47. Evans and Gardner, *Ava Gardner: The Secret Conversations*, pp. 153–56.
48. Rooney, *Life Is Too Short*, p. 191.
49. Marx, *Nine Lives of Mickey Rooney*, p. 10.

Chapter 12: The First Divorce
1. Rooney, *Life Is Too Short*, pp. 190–91.
2. Evans and Gardner, *Ava Gardner: The Secret Conversations*, pp. 157–60.
3. Nick Sevano and Ted Schwartz, *Sinatra: His Story from an Insider* (Wellesley, MA: Branden Books, 2013), p. 277.
4. Ibid., pp. 166–67.
5. Ibid., p. 168.
6. Marx, *Nine Lives of Mickey Rooney*, p. 113.
7. Fleming interview.
8. Evans and Gardner, *Ava Gardner: The Secret Conversations*, p. 168.
9. Huntz Hall, interview by authors, June 14, 1992.
10. Evans and Gardner, *Ava Gardner: The Secret Conversations*, p. 168.
11. Leatrice Gilbert, interview by authors, March 12, 2013.
12. Marx, *Nine Lives of Mickey Rooney*, p. 118; and Marx interview.
13. Marx, *Nine Lives of Mickey Rooney*, pp. 119–20.
14. Ibid., p. 119.
15. Evans and Gardner, *Ava Gardner: The Secret Conversations*, pp. 169–71.
16. Marx, *Nine Lives of Mickey Rooney*, p. 122.

Chapter 13: Mickey and the Pit Bull
1. Frances Pottenger Jr., M. D., *Pottenger's Cats: A Study in Nutrition* (Lemon Grove, CA: Price Pottenger Nutrition, 1995), p. 277.
2. Evans and Gardner, *Ava Gardner: The Secret Conversations*, p. 121.
3. Rooney interview.
4. Ibid.
5. Rooney, *Life Is Too Short*, pp. 153–54.
6. Sabini interview.
7. Marx interview.
8. Rooney, *Life Is Too Short*, p. 203.
9. Rooney interview.
10. Ibid.
11. Marx, *Nine Lives of Mickey Rooney*, p. 128.
12. Miller interview.
13. Marx, *Nine Lives of Mickey Rooney*, p. 127.
14. Ibid., p. 128; and Marx interview.
15. Lertzman interview.
16. Marx interview.

17. Marx, *Nine Lives of Mickey Rooney*, pp. 128–29.
18. Chris Costello, interview by authors, April 2012, June 2013.
19. Jay Robert Stiefel, interview by authors, November 6, 2014; November 17, 2015; January 20, 2015.
20. Marx interview.
21. Rooney, *Life Is Too Short*, p. 206.
22. Adrienne Callander, interview by authors, November 10, 2014; November 12, 2014.
23. Ibid.
24. Ibid.
25. Marx, *Nine Lives of Mickey Rooney*, p. 130.
26. Bill Ludwig, interview by authors, January 19, 1997.
27. Ibid.
28. Marx, *Nine Lives of Mickey Rooney*, p. 132.

Chapter 14: Greetings
1. Roland Flamini, *Ava* (New York: Coward-McCann, 1983).
2. Rooney, *Life Is Too Short*, p. 211.
3. Jane Ellen Wayne, *The Leading Men of MGM* (New York: Carroll and Graf, 2005), p. 256.
4. Fleming interview, in which he cited Flamini, *Ava*.
5. Miller interview.
6. Ibid.
7. Marx, *Nine Lives of Mickey Rooney*, p. 137.
8. Miller interview.
9. Rooney interview.
10. Quoted in Marx, *Nine Lives of Mickey Rooney*, p. 138.
11. Rooney, *i.e., An Autobiography*, p. 127.
12. Marx, *Nine Lives of Mickey Rooney*, pp. 139–40.
13. Ibid., p. 140.
14. Mickey's and B.J.'s letters were provided to us by B.J.'s friend Pam Mc-Clenathan, who cared for the dying Barbara Jane, Timmy Rooney, and now Teddy Rooney, who is in hospice care in her home.
15. Rooney, *Life Is Too Short*, p. 220.
16. Ibid.

Chapter 15: Rooney Inc.
1. Rooney, *Life Is Too Short*, pp. 222–23.
2. Mort Briskin, interview by authors, June 7, 1998.
3. Callander interview.
4. Rooney, *Life Is Too Short*, p. 221.
5. Ibid.

6. Ibid., p. 222.
7. Ibid.
8. Marx *Nine Lives of Mickey Rooney*, p. 148.
9. Rooney, *Life Is Too Short*, p. 223.
10. Miller interview.
11. Rooney, *Life Is Too Short*, p. 226.
12. Ibid.
13. Darwin Porter and Danforth Prince, *Elizabeth Taylor: There Is Nothing Like a Dame* (New York: Blood Moon Productions, 2012).
14. Ibid., p. 322.
15. Richard A. Lertzman and William J. Birnes, *Dr. Feelgood: The Shocking Story of the Doctor Who May Have Changed History by Treating and Drugging JFK, Marilyn, Elvis, and Other Prominent Figures* (New York: Arcade, 2013).
16. Irv Brecher, interview by authors, June 2006, March 2007.
17. W. Ward Marsh, *Cleveland Plain Dealer*, December 9, 1946.
18. Marx, *Nine Lives of Mickey Rooney*, p. 151.
19. Rooney interview.
20. Murray Lertzman archive and Greg Bautzer Law records.
21. Marx, *Nine Lives of Mickey Rooney*, p. 154.

Chapter 16: The Lion Strikes Back
1. Rooney, *Life Is Too Short*, p. 227.
2. Eyman interview.
3. Private Screenings: Mickey Rooney, 1997, Turner Classic Movies website, http://www.tcm.com/tcmdb/title/309370/Private-Screenings-Mickey-Rooney/.
4. Robert Osborne, interview by authors, March 2006.
5. Marx, *Nine Lives of Mickey Rooney*, p. 156.
6. Ibid., p. 157.
7. Marx, *Nine Lives of Mickey Rooney*, pp. 157–58.
8. Marx interview.
9. Sevano interview.
10. Lertzman interview.
11. Marx, *Nine Lives of Mickey Rooney*, pp. 158–59; and the personal archives of Murray Lertzman and his law office, Bautzer Law.
12. Marx, *Nine Lives of Mickey Rooney*, p. 160.
13. A. C. Lyles, interview by authors, March 2006, April 2007, April 2008. The late A. C. Lyles was one of the most gracious and cordial individuals we ever spoke to and was a source of profound insight. He was the embodiment of the perfect studio exec.
14. Marx, *Nine Lives of Mickey Rooney*, p. 162.

15. Marcy Cassell, interview by authors, January 2, 2014.
16. Wally Cassell, interview by authors.
17. Marcy Cassell, interview by authors, January 2, 2014.
18. Ibid.
19. Miller interview.
20. Marx, *Nine Lives of Mickey Rooney*, p. 168; and quoted in Harrison Carroll's column in the *Evening Herald Express*, June 4, 1949.
21. Marx, *Nine Lives of Mickey Rooney*, p. 168.
22. Sevano interview.
23. Marx, *Nine Lives of Mickey Rooney*, p. 165.
24. Barty interview.
25. Rooney interview.
26. *Los Angeles Times*, March 22, 1950, but also reported by Marx, *Nine Lives of Mickey Rooney*, p. 171.
27. John Liebert, interview by authors, November 19, 2014. John Liebert and William J. Birnes, *Wounded Minds: Understanding and Solving the Growing Menace of Post-Traumatic Stress Disorder* (New York: Skyhorse, 2013); and John Liebert and William J. Birnes, *Hearts of Darkness: Why Kids Are Becoming Mass Murderers and How We Can Stop It* (New York: Skyhorse, 2013).

Chapter 17: The Mick, the Duke, and the Deuce in the Coconut

1. Sevano interview.
2. Marx, *Nine Lives of Mickey Rooney*, p. 170.
3. Marcy and Wally Cassell, interviews by authors, January 2, 2014.
4. Roger Kahn, interview by authors, May 6, 2014.
5. Marcy Cassell interview.
6. Rooney interview; and Marx, *Nine Lives of Mickey Rooney*, p. 172.
7. "He's a Cockeyed Wonder: Original Trailer," video, YouTube, https://www.youtube.com/watch?v=hZjKRNLlZT4.
8. Marcy Cassell interview.
9. Pam McClenathan, interview by authors, January 7, 2015.
10. Sevano interview.
11. Wally Cassell interview.
12. Marx, *Nine Lives of Mickey Rooney*, p. 176.
13. Rooney, *Life Is Too Short*.
14. Rooney, *Life Is Too Short*, p. 240.
15. Marx, *Nine Lives of Mickey Rooney*, pp. 180–81.
16. Ibid.
17. Mrs. Smith, interview by authors, January 4, 2015. Mickey's mistress for sixty years, unknown to any of his wives, agreed to talk to us and to share Rooney's love letters only in exchange for our keeping her real identity secret.

18. Rooney interview.
19. Marx, *Nine Lives of Mickey Rooney*, p. 185.
20. Rooney interview.
21. Ibid.
22. Marx interview.
23. As recounted to Ted Schwartz, interview by authors, December 23, 2014. Schwartz and Sevano cowrote *Sinatra: His Story as an Insider* (Wellesley, MA: Branden Books, 2013).
24. Fredrica Duke, interview by authors, December 23, 2014; January 7, 2015; February 1, 2015, quoting her father's boast.
25. Sandy Hackett, who is comedian Buddy Hackett's son, in personal interviews on August 8, 2014 and January 7, 2015, told us that Joe E. Lewis used that joke in his act.
26. Rooney, *Life Is Too Short*, p. 248.
27. Duke interview.
28. Ibid.
29. June Wilkinson, interview by authors, January 12, 2015 and March 7, 2015.
30. Marx, *Nine Lives of Mickey Rooney*, p. 194.
31. Maurice Duke, interview in documentary *Fuck 'Em*, directed by Fredrica Duke, released 2011.
32. Maurice Duke unpublished notes as told to us by Fredrica Duke, October 22, 2014.
33. Ibid.
34. Rooney, *Life Is Too Short*, p. 247.
35. Marx, *Nine Lives of Mickey Rooney*, p. 187.
36. Ibid., p. 188.
37. Ibid., p. 189.
38. Ibid., p. 195.
39. Mrs. Smith interview.
40. Norman Brokaw, interview by authors, March 7, 2007.
41. Maurice Duke, interviewed in *Fuck 'Em*.
42. Marx interview.
43. Austin "Rocky" Kalish, interview by authors, November 7, 2014; January 6, 2015; and February 12, 2015.
44. http://www.originalmmc.com/mickey.html(http://www.originalmmc.com/mickey.html.
45. Paul Petersen, interview by authors, August 13, 2014.
46. Marx, *Nine Lives of Mickey Rooney*, p. 217.
47. Patricia Breslin, personal interview, March 14, 2002.
48. Marx, *Nine Lives of Mickey Rooney*, p. 218.

49. Teddy Rooney, interview by authors, October 27, 2014; November 13, 2014; November 20, 2014.
50. Marx interview.
51. Marx, *Nine Lives of Mickey Rooney*, p. 215.
52. Chris Aber, interview by authors, December 16, 2014; January 2, 2015; January 22, 2015; and March 10, 2015.
53. Melody Doff, interview by authors, November 10, 2014; January 10, 2015; January 14, 2015; February 7, 2015; March 7, 2015.
54. Kalish interview.
55. Miller interview.
56. Marx, *Nine Lives of Mickey Rooney*, p. 220.
57. Dick Cavett, interview by authors, May 23, 2014.
58. Marx, *Nine Lives of Mickey Rooney*, p. 224.

Chapter 18: Bigamy and Barbara Ann
1. Larry Gelbart, interview by authors, May 23, 2014.
2. Kelly Rooney interview.
3. Marx, *Nine Lives of Mickey Rooney*, p. 206.
4. Story from Red Doff in the *Los Angeles Daily Times*, September 13, 1958.
5. Ibid.
6. Pam McClenathan interview, October 27, 2014; November 13, 2014; November 20, 2014; January 2, 2015; May 7, 2015.
7. Maurice Duke, in his interview with Fredrica Duke, who repeated the story to us in our interview with her.
8. Mrs. Smith interview.

Chapter 19: The Mickey Jinx and the Murder in Brentwood
1. Belgrade, Yugoslavia: Knjizevne Novine, 1987.
2. Kelly Rooney interview.
3. Rooney, *Life Is Too Short*, p. 273.
4. Kelly Rooney interview.
5. Emma Brockes, "Murder in Tinseltown," *The Guardian*, October 17, 2005, http://www.theguardian.com/stage/2005/oct/17/theatre.
6. Milos Milosevic, entry on Murderpedia, http://murderpedia.org/male.M/m/milosevic-milos.htm.
7. Kelly Rooney interview.
8. Ibid.
9. Marx, *Nine Lives of Mickey Rooney*, p. 258.
10. Ibid., p. 260.
11. As quoted in the *Los Angeles Times*, February 6, 1966.
12. Rooney, *Life Is Too Short*, p. 264.

Chapter 20: Career Swings

1. George Raft, interview by authors, March 1978.
2. Martin Milner, interview by authors, April 2007.
3. Kalish interview.
4. Stephen Magagnini, "Mickey Rooney Upset about Claims His 'Tiffany's' Role Is Racist," *Sacramento Bee*, September 28, 2008.
5. Rooney, *Life Is Too Short*, p. 264.
6. Jeff Yang, "The Mickey Rooney Role Nobody Wants to Talk About," *Speakeasy* blog, *Wall Street Journal*, April 8, 2014, http://blogs.wsj.com/speakeasy/2014/04/08/the-mickey-rooney-role-nobody-wants-to-talk-about.
7. Teddy Rooney in Pam McClenathan interview.
8. Hackett interview.
9. Kramer interview by Garland.
10. Rooney interview.
11. Karen Kramer interview in which she related her conversation to Jeff Garland, January 20, 2015; February 12, 2015; March 7, 2015.
12. Sid Caesar interview by authors, March 7, 2007; April 2, 2007.
13. *It's a Mad, Mad, Mad, Mad World* reunion, October 27, 2013.
14. Statement made at the fiftieth-anniversary celebration of the film, October 27, 2013.
15. Marx, *Nine Lives of Mickey Rooney*, pp. 226–27.
16. *Forever Dobie: The Many Lives of Dwayne Hickman* (Birch Lane, 1994).
17. Interview by Scott Tobias, *The Onion*, A.V. *Club*, February 16, 2000, http://www.avclub.com/article/john-frankenheimer-13639.
18. Stuart Shostak, interview by authors, October 8, 2015.
19. Ibid.
20. Rooney, *Life Is Too Short*, p. 292.
21. Miller interview.
22. Marx, *Nine Lives of Mickey Rooney*, p. 236; and Marx interview, for Mickey's comment about the show that Marx and his partner, Bob Fisher, created for him.
23. Also cited in Marx, *Nine Lives of Mickey Rooney*, pp. 233–34.
24. Marx, *Nine Lives of Mickey Rooney*, p. 245; and Marx interview.
25. Ibid.
26. Ibid., p. 249.
27. Ibid., p. 250.
28. William Schallert, interview by authors, March 21, 2008, and July 21, 2013.
29. Ellen Wesson interview by authors, February 6, 2015.
30. Ibid.
31. Dan Kessel interview, in which he told us the entire story of the Rooney

Brothers and Mickey's heretofore untold story of his late-night meeting with Howard Hughes.

Chapter 21: The Seventies: Aftermath of Tragedy
1. Marx, *Nine Lives of Mickey Rooney*, p. 264.
2. Transcript from *Larry King Live*, broadcast on June 27, 2001, CNN.
3. Rooney, *Life Is Too Short*, pp. 288–90.
4. Mickey Deans and Anne Pinchot, *Weep No More, My Lady: Judy Garland* (Boston: G. K. Hall, 1972).
5. Rooney, *Life Is Too Short*, pp. 289–90.
6. Marx, *Nine Lives of Mickey Rooney*, p. 264.
7. Robert Finkel, interview by authors, March 10, 2007, and April 12, 2008.
8. Marx, *Nine Lives of Mickey Rooney*, pp. 266–67.
9. Ibid., p. 268.
10. Lertzman and Birnes, *Dr. Feelgood*.
11. Rooney, *Life Is Too Short*, p. 292.

Chapter 22: Escape from Los Angeles
1. Rooney, *Life Is Too Short*, p. 292.
2. October 17, 2005.
3. Rooney, *Life Is Too Short*, pp. 306–7.
4. Donald Trump, interview by authors, December 10, 2014.
5. Ruth Webb, interview by authors, September 20, 1991, and Marx, *Nine Lives of Mickey Rooney*, p. 282.
6. Webb interview.
7. Rooney, *Life Is Too Short*, p. 303.
8. Jan Rooney, interview by authors, December 4, 2014; January 16, 2015; January 18, 2015; February 7, 2015; March 7, 2015; and Jan's appearance on Future Theater Radio (www.futuretheater.com) with the authors on January 26, 2015.
9. Rooney, *Life Is Too Short*, p. 308.
10. Jan Rooney interview.

Chapter 23: Sugar Babies
1. Norm Abbott, interview by authors, February 7, 2015.
2. Ibid.
3. Marx, *Nine Lives of Mickey Rooney*, p. 289.
4. New York: Doubleday, 1972.
5. Terry Allen Kramer, interview by authors, January 21, 2015.
6. Merv Griffin and Peter Barsocchini, *Merv Griffin: An Autobiography* (New York: Simon and Schuster, 1980).

7. T. Morris, "John Kenley: On with the Show," *Dayton Daily News*, July 14, 1995.

8. Marx, *Nine Lives of Mickey Rooney*, p. 224.

9. Kramer interview.

10. Ibid; and Robert Malcolm, interview by authors, January 26, 2015.

11. Kramer interview.

12. Ronna Riley, interview by authors, October 7, 2014.

13. Kramer interview.

14. Ibid.

15. Joey Bishop, interview by authors, March 7–8, 2005.

16. Marx, *Nine Lives of Mickey Rooney*, p. 308.

17. Dan Sullivan, " 'Sugar Babies' Makes Whoopee in London," *Los Angeles Times*, December 3, 1988.

18. Miller interview.

Chapter 24: Mickey's Back: The Oscars, and the Emmys, and *Bill*

1. Sabini interview.

2. Rooney, *Life Is Too Short*, p. 307.

3. Carroll Ballard, interview by authors, June 27, 2014, for all the commentary in this section.

4. Jan Rooney interview.

5. Rooney, *Life Is Too Short*, p. 323.

6. Saul Turteltaub, interview by authors, August 21, 2014.

7. Bernie Orenstein, interview by authors, August 20, 2014.

8. Nathan Lane, in a presentation at Feinstein's in New York City at Rooney's ninetieth birthday party.

9. Rooney, *Life Is Too Short*, p. 324.

10. Barry Morrow, interview by authors, September 4, 2014, and May 7, 2015. For a fuller and more professionally detailed discussion of this issue of mainstreaming the developmentally challenged and the mentally ill into society, see Liebert, and Birnes, *Wounded Minds*; Liebert and Birnes, *Hearts of Darkness*, and the forthcoming Liebert and Birnes, *Psychiatric Criminology: A Roadmap for Rapid Assessment* (London: CRC Press, 2016).

11. Morrow interview.

12. Ibid.

13. "The Best and Worst Oscar Moments of All Time," Oscar, Oscar, http://www.oscarworld.net/ow.asp?P=10.

Chapter 25: Going Ungently into That Good Night

1. Ballard interview.

2. Abbott interview.

3. Kalish interview.

4. Chris Aber interview.
5. Donald O'Connor, interview by authors, September 2001.
6. Donald Trump, interview by authors, February 2014.
7. Mark Dawidziak, interview by authors, January 10, 2014.
8. Doug McDuff, interview by authors, January 26, 2015.
9. Geoffrey Mark Fidelman, *The Lucy Book: A Complete Guide to Her Five Decades on Television* (Metairie, LA: Renaissance, 1999).
10. Geoffrey Fidelman, interview by authors, November 15, 2014.
11. Chris Aber interview.
12. Ellen Easton, interview by authors, September 20, 2014; October 21, 2014; December 7, 2014; and January 22, 2015.
13. Feinberg interview.
14. Fredrica Duke interview.
15. Courts interview.
16. Rip Taylor, interview by authors, November 7, 2014.
17. Michael Simkins, *The Rules of Acting* (London, UK: Ebury Press, 2013), p. 12.

Chapter 26: Time May Lie Heavy Between
1. Mrs. Smith interview. This, and all quotes, including from Mickey's love letters, were read to us by Mrs. Smith.

Chapter 27: The Last Years
1. "Rooney Feels 'Great' After Bypass Surgery," *Daily Journal*, December 22, 2000, http://archives.smdailyjournal.com/article_preview.php?id=1431.
2. Nelson Deedle, interview by authors, January 30, 2015.
3. Dominic Cavendish, "Cinderella: Mickey Rooney Takes the Mickey," *Telegraph*, December 13, 2007, http://www.telegraph.co.uk/culture/theatre/drama/3669889/Cinderella-Mickey-Rooney-takes-the-Mickey.html.

Chapter 28: His Revels Are Now Ended
1. "Last Will and Embezzlement: Official Trailer," video, YouTube, https://www.youtube.com/watch?v=WJCDQpqHPEQ.
2. Liebert and Birnes, *Wounded Minds*; Liebert and Birnes, *Skyhorse*; and Liebert and Birnes, *Psychiatric Criminology*.
3. Michael Augustine, interview by authors, October 7–8, 2014, and February 3, 2015.
4. Ibid.
5. Jan Rooney interview.
6. Chris Aber résumé, at http://www.indeed.com/me/chrisaber.
7. Mickey's comments appear in Ann Oldenburg, "Butt Out: Fox Nixes Super Bowl Backside Ad," *USA Today*, January 5, 2005.

8. "Mickey Rooney Sizzle Reel," video, YouTube, https://www.youtube.com /watch?v=MKmSs684hS0.

9. Feinstein interview.

10. Keith Black, interview by authors, January 17, 2015.

11. Ibid.

12. Shawn Levy, interview by authors, January 27, 2015.

13. Ibid.

Chapter 29: It's a Wrap

1. Augustine interview; Yevgeny Belous interviews by authors, October 8, 2014.

2. Rooney, *Life Is Too Short*, p. 337.

Index

Page references in italics indicate illustrations. Rooney's films are indexed under "Rooney, Mickey—FILMS"